W9-BJV-277

HAYDN:
CHRONICLE AND WORKS

HAYDN: CHRONICLE AND WORKS

in five volumes by

H. C. Robbins Landon

**Haydn: The Early Years 1732–1765*

**Haydn at Eszterháza 1766–1790*

†*Haydn in England 1791–1795*

Haydn: The Years of 'The Creation' 1796–1800

**Haydn: The Late Years 1801–1809*

(†previously published; *in preparation)

HAYDN: CHRONICLE AND WORKS

HAYDN: THE YEARS OF 'THE CREATION' 1796–1800

For
Frederica Rhinelander Landon
with much love

'Nevertheless, according to the few lights that remain to Us, We may say that the Eighteenth Century, notwithstanding all its Errors and Vices, has been, of all that are past, the most honorable to human Nature.'

John Adams to Thomas Jefferson,
13 November 1815

Haydn: Chronicle and Works

VOLUME IV

HAYDN
THE YEARS OF 'THE CREATION'
1796–1800

H. C. ROBBINS LANDON

INDIANA UNIVERSITY PRESS
BLOOMINGTON LONDON

First American edition 1977 by Indiana University Press

Library of Congress Cataloging in Publication Data
Landon, Howard Chandler Robbins, 1926–
Haydn: chronicle and works.

Includes bibliographies and indexes.
CONTENTS:
v. 4. Haydn: the Years of 'The Creation', 1796–1800
1. Haydn, Joseph, 1732–1809.

ML410.H4L26 780'.92'4[B] 76–14630
ISBN 0–253–37004–3 1 2 3 4 5 81 80 79 78 77

Printed in Great Britain

Contents

LIST OF ILLUSTRATIONS

ILLUSTRATIONS IN THE TEXT *Page*

ILLUSTRATIONS IN THE TEXT *Page*

Preface

THERE IS HARDLY ANY DOUBT in the mind of the average music-lover that Haydn's Oratorio *The Creation* is, *tutto sommato*, his greatest single accomplishment, and certainly ranks as one of the greatest products of any eighteenth-century mind. It occupies a central position in choral literature and its composition and first performances were the dominant features of Haydn's life in the late 1790s. This volume, therefore, tells the story of Haydn's life and works from September 1795 – when he arrived back in Vienna following his second stay in England – up to 1800, the year in which the composer himself published the score of *The Creation*.

In dealing with this volume, the most practical way of presenting such an enormous amount of information seemed to be a strict division, year by year, into chapters headed 'Chronicle' and 'Works'. In reproducing contemporary criticisms of *The Creation* we were forced to be selective; obviously it is more important for us to know *all* the available facts about the first public performance in Vienna, whereas critical opinion about a later performance, say, at Madrid in 1805 or St Petersburg in 1806 would be of marginal interest only.

It is sometimes difficult to know what to omit from a large-scale biography such as the present one. Naturally we are all sceptical of anecdotes, especially at second and third hand. What does one do, for example, with the following report, in *The Harmonicon* (V, 1827), from the pen of François-Joseph-Marie Fagolle (1774–1852), who in turn, had it from the composer Anton Reicha (1770–1836), who was a witness of it?

> At one of the parties of the Prince Esterhazy, a coxcomb turned to Haydn in presence of a numerous company, and asked him in a flippant tone, how he had found the famous passage about the birth of light: 'Why, in sounding my tuning-fork, to be sure', said the composer, turning upon his heel with conscious dignity, and leaving the enquirer to the laughter of the whole company.

In the event, we omitted it from the biography; charming though it is, the evidence is late (1827) and slender. It seemed wiser to concentrate on the many Viennese documents of the period (Rosenbaum and Zinzendorf Diaries, etc.), as well as the 'authentic biographies' (Dies, Griesinger, Carpani) and newspaper reports – not to speak of Haydn's own correspondence and the valuable Griesinger correspondence with the Leipzig publishers, Breitkopf & Härtel. As the reader will soon perceive, there is material enough, a great deal of it unpublished.

It is, of course, something of a risk to speculate on the origins of a great masterpiece like *The Creation*: why did Haydn write it? Why did he turn more and more to vocal music in the last years of his creative life? Perhaps only a minor contribution to his decision was the fact that his previous vocal music, and especially his operas, had never reached a wide public because they had been written and performed in the obscurity of Eszterháza Castle. Haydn always had a special affection for these stepchildren of his muse. Thus it must have been rather galling to read, in the *Jahrbuch der Tonkunst für Wien und Prag* (Schönfeldischer Verlag, 1796),[1] the following (pp. 20ff.):

> HAIDEN, Joseph. Who does not know him, the great master, famous in the whole of Europe for 20 years? And enormous as the number of his symphonies is, one thirsts with parched throat every day for new ones. But it is certainly true that his symphonies are – despite their many imitators – unrivalled and inimitable; and it is also true that he has excelled particularly in this field, and that his symphonies have contributed more to his immortality than all the rest of his works. There are, moreover, some men of taste who listen more happily to his early products of this *genre* rather than to his latest, and it may be that Haiden himself would be inclined secretly to agree with them. Perhaps he wanted to show that he too could wear the cape of the latest fashion. Who is so fortunate as he in devising lusty, humorous and charming subjects? And who is able to develop them so naturally and yet so unexpectedly, so simply and yet so artfully? That old proverb – *il facile è difficile* – if it still circulates, is totally wrong. His piano pieces are mostly pleasant, simple and easy of execution; and for this reason are much more useful, for nowadays composers tend to concentrate on difficulties and to require of the pupil a standard which is often difficult for the master. In his quartets there are enchanting harmonies, and in their construction they have the special quality that they grip one's attention initially, hold it and then lead us, as in a labyrinth, now across flowering fields, now to a bubbling brook, now by a rushing stream. Often his themes seem to fall into two self-contradictory parts, which in their very contradictions join to form a wonderful agreement and are woven unexpectedly into a design of perfect accord. This stamp of a great genius is to be found particularly in those recent quartets [Opp. 71 and 74 (1793)] which he has written for Count von Aponyi [*sic*].
>
> The treatment of the voice, on the other hand, seems not to be his strong point, except for some single arias, and one usually notices a kind of embarrassment in his vocal music. Beautiful though his Cantata *Ariadne* is, one misses most acutely therein that sublimity [*Erhabenheit*] which Benda understood how to create so well in his melodrama. Also, we have not yet had any opera from him which enjoyed a career. He is more fortunate in his finely wrought church music, and immortal in his *Seven Words*.

We would not go so far as to propose that *The Creation* was written to refute the statements of a writer in the *Jahrbuch der Tonkunst* in 1796, but it is certain that Haydn's reputation did not lie in vocal music and many people who grew up on his quartets, sonatas and symphonies had never heard an opera of his, or even a Mass. Haydn knew this, and wanted to create a Handelian oratorio in modern language, a large-scale work which would 'last a long time'. In that he succeeded.

This volume is one of the five planned to provide a complete biography of the composer. The chronological contents of each volume is as follows:

Haydn: the Early Years (1732–1765);
Haydn at Eszterháza (1766–1790);
Haydn in England (1791–1795) (already published);
Haydn: the Years of 'The Creation' (1796–1800);
Haydn: the Late Years (1801–1809).

1 Haydn himself owned a copy of the *Jahrbuch*; see *Katalog der Haydn-Gedächtnisausstellung*, Vienna 1932, p. 9 (section prepared by O. E. Deutsch).

Each volume provides a history of the years mentioned in the respective titles, and is therefore complete in itself; the five when taken together will cover Haydn's entire career and constitute a complete biography. The master Bibliography, however, listing all the relevant literature, appears in the fifth volume (*Haydn: the Late Years*).

ACKNOWLEDGMENTS

As in the case of the other volumes of this biography, there are many private individuals as well as institutions I have to thank for countless favours of all kinds: for acting as my hosts on numerous occasions; for answering letters, often of a tediously detailed kind; and for sending photographs of documentary sources and illustrations. I must single out one person and one institution without which the biography would be very much the poorer: Dr Johann Harich, formerly Chief Archivist to Prince Esterházy and now in retirement in Eisenstadt, always placed at my disposal his vast knowledge of Haydn *documenta* in the Archives (now partly in Hungary and partly in Austria), and sent me numerous lists and photographs; and the Országos Széchényi Könyvtár, Budapest, where the Esterházy Archives are in part located. My many friends and colleagues in Budapest at the National Library have over the years sent thousands of pages of film to me, and they have pursued seemingly hopeless lines of enquiry in search of information and have in every case found the document in question, often after laborious searching; they were also my hosts on the many occasions when I worked in Budapest. When reading this and the other volumes, only these colleagues will know how much they contributed.

Among private individuals I would like to thank: Mrs Eva Alberman, who – apart from many other kindnesses – examined the watermarks of the autograph of a Haydn piano Trio which she owns, as a result of which the work could for the first time be precisely dated (*vide infra*, p. 72); Mr Roger Hellyer, Oxford, who kindly drew my attention to an interesting document in the Haus-, Hof- und Staatsarchiv, Vienna; the late Frau Maria Hummel of Florence, who placed her archives at my disposal – she was a direct descendant of Johann Nepomuk Hummel – and became a dear friend, one of the most civilized ladies of my acquaintance; Mr Louis Krasner, Syracuse (New York) who generously sent me a photograph of the interesting Kunike portrait of Haydn; Count C.-G. Stellan Mörner, Stockholm, for many favours over the years; my old friend Mr Albi Rosenthal, London and Oxford, *inter alia* for copying out a whole (unpublished) letter written by Adalbert Gyrowetz; and Herr Karl Stümpfl, Vienna, for allowing me to photograph his fine portrait of the Empress Marie Therese which is reproduced in this volume. I am also greatly indebted to Her Majesty the Queen for allowing me to reproduce the beautiful portrait of Nelson by Hoppner in the Royal Collection. The sources of the illustrations are given in the list appearing on pp. 9–11.

The following institutions have kindly provided source material: Albertina (Vienna); Archiv der Stadt Wien (Dr Mitringer); Bayerische Staatsbibliothek, Munich (Dr Robert Münster); Beethovenhaus, Bonn (Dr Schmidt); British Museum, London (Mr O.W. Neighbour); Burgenländisches Landesmuseum, Eisenstadt (Hofrat Dr Ohrenberger); Esterházy-Archiv, Eisenstadt; Galerie Liechtenstein, Vaduz-Vienna; Gesellschaft der Musikfreunde, Vienna (Frau Dr Mitringer); Harrach-Archiv, Vienna; Haus-, Hof- und Staatsarchiv, Vienna (Dr Clemens Höslinger); Historisches Museum der Stadt Wien (Dr Schöny); Huntington Gallery, San Marino (California); Institut für Österreichische Kulturgeschichte, Eisenstadt (Frau Dr Mraz); Kunsthistorisches Museum, Vienna (Dr Wegerer); Niederösterreichisches Landesmuseum, Vienna (Professor Rupert Feuchtmüller); Österreichische

Galerie des 19. Jahrhunderts, Vienna; Österreichische Nationalbibliothek (Dr Franz Grasberger); Prague – Lobkowitz Archives, formerly in Schloß Raudnitz, now National Library; Preussische Staatsbibliothek, Berlin; Stiftung preuss. Kulturbesitz, Berlin; Sotheby & Co. (Mr Michael Morton-Smith); Stadtbibliothek, Leipzig; Stadtbibliothek, Vienna; Universitätsbibliothek und Universitätsarchiv, Vienna (Dr Gall).

Vienna 1976 H.C.R.L.

AUTHOR'S NOTE

Haydn's music

Vocal music is identified by title and, on the occasion of the first or major reference, by its number in Hoboken's *Haydn Verzeichnis* (vol. II, Vocal Works, Mainz, 1971).

Instrumental music is identified as follows.

Symphonies are referred to by their number in Mandyczewski's list for the publishers Breitkopf & Härtel, which numbering was taken over by Hoboken in his *Haydn Verzeichnis* (vol. I), Mainz, 1955. Symphony No. 95, for example, is I:95 in Hoboken's list.

String Quartets are identified by their opus number and, like all instrumental pieces, by the Hoboken number at the first and/or major reference.

Piano Sonatas are listed by their chronological numbering in the *Wiener Urtext Ausgabe*, edited by C. Landon.

Piano Trios are identified by the new chronological numbering in the *Complete Edition of Haydn's Piano Trios*, edited by H. C. Robbins Landon and published by Verlag Doblinger.

Other instrumental works are identified by their customary title (e.g. 'London Trios' and 'Overture to an English Opera') and by their Hoboken number.

The system of pitch notation used is based on middle C being represented by the symbol *c'*.

Instruments (in order of their customary appearance in the orchestral score) are abbreviated thus: Fl. – flute; Ob. – oboe; Cor ang. – cor anglais; Clar. – clarinet; Bsn. (Fag.) – bassoon; Contrafag. – double bassoon; Hr. (Cor.) – horn; Trbe. (Trpt.) – trumpet; Trbn. – trombone; Timp. – timpani (kettledrums); V. – violin; Va. – viola; Vc. – violoncello; Cb. (B.) – contrabasso (double bass); Cemb. – cembalo (harpsichord).

Documents

In all documents cited in the text the original orthography – whether in English, German, French or Italian – has been retained. Thus, accents have not been inserted where they were omitted in the original document, notably in passages from the Zinzendorf Diaries. The language of the original document is indicated only in those cases which require clarification. Bibliographical references will be found in an abbreviated form in the text, at the end of quotations and in the footnotes; the full titles of works cited are given on pp. 16–18.

The abbreviations 'k. k.' and 'I. R.' (meaning '*kaiserlich-königlich*'/'Imperial Royal') are used interchangeably. Austrian money (see note on p. 255) is abbreviated thus: Gulden (gulden) = 'f.' or 'fl.' (or 'F.', 'Fl.'); Kreuzer = 'k.' or 'kr.' or 'xr.' (K.', 'Kr.', 'Xr.').

ABBREVIATIONS OF BIBLIOGRAPHICAL SOURCES

AMZ	*Allgemeine Musikalische Zeitung*, Leipzig, 1798 *et seq.*
Bartha	*Joseph Haydn, Gesammelte Briefe und Aufzeichnungen*, herausgegeben und erläutert von Dénes Bartha, Budapest–Kassel, 1965.
Bartha-Somfai	Dénes Bartha and László Somfai, *Haydn als Opernkapellmeister*, Budapest, 1960.
Beethoven-Handbuch	Theodor von Frimmel, *Beethoven-Handbuch*, 2 vols. 1926 (since reprinted).
Brand *Messen*	Carl Maria Brand, *Die Messen von Joseph Haydn*, Würzburg, 1941 (since reprinted).
Carpani	Giuseppe Carpani, *Le Haydine*, Milan, 1812.
CCLN	*Collected Correspondence and London Notebooks of Joseph Haydn*, translated and edited by H. C. Robbins Landon, London, 1959.
Da Ponte	*Memoirs of Lorenzo da Ponte*, translated from the Italian by Elizabeth Abbott, edited and annotated by Arthur Livingston; new edition, New York, 1967.
Deutsch *Freihaustheater*	Otto Erich Deutsch, *Das Wiener Freihaustheater*, Vienna, 1937.
Deutsch *Mozart, Dokumente*	Otto Erich Deutsch, *W. A. Mozart – Die Dokumente seines Lebens*, Kassel-Basel, 1961.
Dies	A. C. Dies, *Biographische Nachrichten von Joseph Haydn*, Vienna, 1810; new edition by Horst Seeger, Berlin, n.d. [1959].
Enciclopedia dello spettacolo	*Enciclopedia dello spettacolo* (11 vols.), Rome, 1954 *et seq.*
Farington	*The Farington Diary*, edited by James Greig, London and New York, 1923.
Gerber *NTL*	Ludwig Gerber, *Neues historisch-biographisches Lexikon der Tonkünstler*, 4 vols, 1812–14; new edition by Othmar Wessely, Graz, 1966.
Geiringer 1932, 1947, 1959 and 1963	Karl Geiringer, *Joseph Haydn*: Potsdam, 1932; New York, 1947; Mainz, 1959; Garden City, N.Y., 1963.
Grasberger *Hymnen*	Franz Grasberger, *Die Hymnen Österreichs*, Tutzing, 1968.
Griesinger	G. A. Griesinger, *Biographische Notizen über Joseph Haydn*, Leipzig, 1810; new ed. Franz Grasberger, Vienna, 1954.
Grove I, II, III, IV, V	Grove's *Dictionary of Music and Musicians*, first, second, third, fourth and fifth editions.

Hadden	J. Cuthbert Hadden, *Haydn*, London, 1902.
Hadden *Thomson*	J. Cuthbert Hadden, *George Thomson, the Friend of Burns: His Life and Correspondence*, London, 1898.
Hase	H. von Hase, *Joseph Haydn und Breitkopf & Härtel*, Leipzig, 1909.
Horányi	Mátyás Horányi, *Das Esterházysche Feenreich*, Budapest, 1959; English edition, *The Magnificence of Esterháza*, London, 1962
Landon *Beethoven*	H. C. Robbins Landon, *Beethoven: a documentary study*, London and New York, 1970.
Landon *Essays*	H. C. Robbins Landon, *Essays on the Viennese Classical Style*, London, 1970.
Landon *Supplement*	H. C. Robbins Landon, *Supplement to 'The Symphonies of Joseph Haydn'*, London, 1961.
Landon *SYM*	H. C. Robbins Landon, *The Symphonies of Joseph Haydn*, London, 1955.
Larsen *HÜB*	J. P. Larsen, *Die Haydn-Überlieferung*, Copenhagen, 1939.
MGG	*Musik in Geschichte und Gegenwart* (Allgemeine Enzyklopädie der Musik), edited by Friedrich Blume, Kassel, 1947 *et seq.*
Mörner	C.-G. Stellan Mörner, *Johan Wikmanson und die Brüder Silverstolpe*, Stockholm, 1952.
Neukomm	Sigismund (von) Neukomm, *Bemerkungen zu den biogr. Nachrichten von Dies* (MS. in Pohl's hand, owned by Friedrich Matzenauer, Vienna; published 1959).
Olleson	E. Olleson, 'Haydn in the Diaries of Count Karl von Zinzendorf', in *Haydn Yearbook* II 1963–4).
Olleson *Griesinger*	E. Olleson, 'Georg August Griesinger's Correspondence with Breitkopf & Härtel' in *Haydn Yearbook* III (1965).
Parke	W. T. Parke, *Musical Memoirs*, 2 vols., London, 1830.
Plank	Plank's MS. Diary (Archives of Kremsmünster Abbey), printed in P. Altmann Kellner, *Musikgeschichte des Stiftes Kremsmünster*, Kassel, 1957.
Pohl *H in L*	C. F. Pohl, *Haydn in London*, Vienna, 1867; reprinted, New York, 1970.
Pohl *Denkschrift*	C. F. Pohl, *Denkschrift aus Anlass des 100-Jährigen Bestehens der Tonkünstler-Societät*, Vienna, 1871.
Pohl I, II, III	C. F. Pohl, *Joseph Haydn* (3 vols.): I, Berlin, 1875; II, Berlin, 1882; III (completed by Hugo Botstiber), Leipzig, 1927. All three vols. since reprinted.
Radant *Rosenbaum*	'The Diaries of Joseph Carl Rosenbaum 1770–1829', edited by Else Radant, *Haydn Yearbook* V (1968); also as a separate publication in the original German.
Rosenbaum	'The Diaries of Joseph Carl Rosenbaum 1770–1829' (MS. in Österreichische Nationalbibliothek, Vienna); see Radant above.
Schindler	A. F. Schindler, *Beethoven as I knew him* (ed. D. W. MacArdle), London and Chapel Hill, N.C., 1966.
Scholes	Percy Scholes, *The Great Dr. Burney* (2 vols.), London, 1948.

Smart	*Leaves from the Journals of Sir George Smart*, by H. Bertram Cox and C. L. E. Cox, London, 1907.
Somfai	László Somfai, *Joseph Haydn. Sein Leben in zeitgenössischen Bildern*, Budapest and Kassel, 1966; also published in English, London, 1967.
Spohr	*The Musical Journeys of Louis Spohr*, selected, translated and edited by Henry Pleasants, Norman, 1961.
Thayer I	A. W. Thayer, *Ludwig van Beethovens Leben*, second revised edition (Deiters), vol. I, Berlin, 1901.
Thayer-Forbes	Thayer's *Life of Beethoven*, revised and edited by Elliot Forbes (2 vols.), Princeton, N.J., 1967.
Zinzendorf	MS. Diaries of Count Carl von Zinzendorf, in the Haus-, Hof- und Staatsarchiv, Vienna.

CHAPTER ONE

Vienna and its Musical Life in 1795

THE CITY OF VIENNA was to be Haydn's principal place of residence from the autumn of 1795, when he returned from his second triumphal visit to England, until 1809, when he died. Unlike Prince Nicolaus I Esterházy, who disliked his capital city and much preferred the isolation of Eszterháza Castle in Hungary, Haydn's new patron, Nicolaus II, found Vienna attractive. Esterháza was now completely abandoned, and even the best furniture and pictures were removed to Vienna or to Eisenstadt, the old family Castle (then Hungary, now capital of the Austrian province of Burgenland) where Prince Nicolaus II spent the summers and from which the huge Esterházy estates were managed. Haydn followed the Esterházy court to Eisenstadt in the summers and in September conducted the annual Mass in celebration of Princess Marie Hermenegild's name-day, for which event he composed a new Mass each year from 1796 to 1802, except for 1800. Otherwise the composer lived in Vienna and became the doyen of musical life there.

The young Emperor, Franz (Francis), had succeeded to the throne upon the death of Leopold II in 1792. He was married to Marie Therese, the daughter of King Ferdinand of Naples and Maria Carolina (who was in turn the daughter of the Empress Maria Theresa, thus making the young Imperial couple first cousins). We have discussed the character of Franz and his wife in *Haydn in England 1791–1795*; suffice it to say here that both were musical and played instruments. Marie Therese had a pleasant if weak soprano voice and could sing at sight a new Mass by Johann Michael Haydn (Joseph's brother who lived in Salzburg). In the second half of the 1790s, Haydn was frequently a guest at the Hofburg and we have evidence that both Franz and Marie Therese were proud of Haydn's successes and appreciative of his music. In the forthcoming Chronicle, this evidence will be presented in chronological order, and it will be seen that Haydn even conducted *The Creation* and *The Seasons* in private performances at the Hofburg, in which the Empress participated as solo soprano.

Politically, the 1790s were to be a time of great stress for the young Emperor and his huge empire. Although the Napoleonic Wars were still in their infancy in 1795, the next year was to see the General's devastating conquest of northern Italy, then under Austrian domination. At home, the Imperial Court was nervous of 'Jacobin' influence and in the forthcoming decade, the government was to become increasingly more conservative. The change from the Josephinian reforms to the Metternichian 'iron-hand' conservatism happened gradually but nonetheless inexorably. Censorship gradually increased, to the point where many of Schiller's plays were banned and Beethoven had to use the Empress herself in order to get *Leonore* (later *Fidelio*) staged. One of the curious side-effects of this gradually increasing literary censorship was to stimulate music, the one art which, except when allied to words, was 'above censorship' and could and did flourish in the last fifteen years of Haydn's life. Indeed, the Vienna of 1795 was a delightful place for a musician: delightful but financially precarious. Only four years earlier Mozart had died in extreme poverty, and the circumstances of his death were to haunt musicians for years; in 1799, Dittersdorf – once a Viennese idol – was to die impoverished and almost forgotten in a remote Bohemian town, his desk drawer full of unpublished compositions. In the course of our Chronicle, we can follow the constantly rising prices in Vienna and the difficulties that many musicians experienced in keeping alive. The inflation was to render almost worthless the noble gesture of three Austrian aristocrats (Archduke Rudolph, Prince Lobkowitz, and Prince Kinsky) who in 1809 guaranteed Beethoven a lifetime pension of 4,000 gulden. But despite rising prices, a nervous government, and a badly managed war, Vienna at the turn of the century seemed almost a paradise to many musicians in retrospect. Schindler, Beethoven's biographer, summed up the situation admirably:[1]

> The concept of nobility among the German nobles in Austria consisted of a perfect balancing of education and breeding, training in both thought and action, and attention to the development of will, character, and all the aspects of intelligence, all of which made this society worthy to be called the standard-bearer of German culture and morality. A cultured and enlightened upper class that also possesses tremendous wealth will certainly be in a position to serve both science and the arts. This state of affairs prevailed among the Viennese nobility who had a special penchant for music. There was a preference for music without ostentation – music which, whether performed by four voices or a hundred, would work magic on the listener, cultivating his mind and his senses, ennobling his emotions. It was characteristic of the whole German people to respond to the unpretentious greatness, true feeling, and pure human emotions that were inherent in its music. This people also knew how to derive from the mystery of musical tones their inexpressible meaning and lofty spirit. And yet this was not a time of philosophical sophistication; it was rather a period of uninhibited enjoyment whose purity lasted well into the first decade of our century. 'Anyone who was not a part of the music in Vienna in those days cannot know what it is to truly hear and truly enjoy music' – thus the older musicians later expressed their nostalgia for that time. . . .
>
> As for the music-lovers of that time, we know that they were found almost exclusively among the educated classes, who by inclination and breeding assigned to music its place among the disciplines. No amateur, therefore, presumed to usurp the role properly taken by the professional musician. [Schindler speaks of the orchestral concerts that took place at the Hofburg and, in summer, at Laxenburg. They] were sometimes conducted by Salieri but more often by Weigl, a disciple of Mozart who had studied with the composer himself [and was Haydn's god-child]. The writer [Schindler] has heard both conductors speak nostalgically of the golden age of Viennese music, for Fate had allowed them to witness the full glory of the time.

Possibly Beethoven's nostalgia – and also Salieri's and Weigl's – is slightly exaggerated, but as far as the nobility in Vienna is concerned, and also the upper bourgeoisie, we have a confirmation of their abilities by an unprejudiced foreigner, the Swedish diplomat Fredrik Samuel Silverstolpe. Silverstolpe arrived in Vienna in May, 1797, as Chargé d'Affaires to the Imperial Court, and soon studied musical life in Vienna and became a personal friend of Haydn's. We shall often cite his trenchant

1 Schindler, 64–6. Reprinted by permission of Faber and Faber Ltd, London, and the University of North Carolina Press, Chapel Hill, N.C.

observations about the less romantic side of Austrian musical life. On 20 September 1797 he writes back to Stockholm:

> The middle class [*Mittelstand*] among the population has everywhere in Germany where I have been much culture. I think that among the so-called better classes one seldom meets complete idiots as with us [in Sweden]. The officers of this day and age are supposed, however, to be the exceptions to this rule. . . . The women are much better read than ours. As a result they are not always unpleasant [*sic*], but mostly useless. In Vienna it is rare to encounter domestic virtues among that sex. . . . [Mörner, 321]

In the next twenty years, most of the private orchestras maintained by the Austro-Hungarian nobility had to be disbanded as a result of inflation, but in 1795 several of the wealthiest Viennese houses still boasted a full orchestra. Apart from Prince Esterházy, the Princes Lobkowitz, Schwarzenberg, and Auersperg – all of them Haydn's and also Beethoven's patrons – kept an orchestra and gave regular concerts in their Viennese palaces.[1] Prince Grassalkovics[2] (Grassalkovitz, etc.), who had wanted to engage Haydn as *Capellmeister* in 1790 after Prince Nicolaus I Esterházy had died, supported what was called a 'Harmonie-Musique', a wind band, which consisted of two oboes, two clarinets, two bassoons, and two horns. This popular combination was sufficiently small to enable the patron to take them with him to the country in summer, where he and his guests could hear arrangements from the latest operas. Count Zinzendorf had twice heard a wind-band arrangement of Mozart's *Le nozze di Figaro* at various Bohemian castles while visiting in September 1787. Prince Nicolaus II Esterházy also liked a wind octet, and much of the music played in the 1790s and early 1800s is still preserved in the Eisenstadt Archives, including arrangements of Mozart's operas. If the family could not afford a whole orchestra or even a regular 'Harmonie-Musique', they could perhaps support a string quartet, as did Prince Carl Lichnowsky, Beethoven's patron; almost anyone could work up a piano trio at short notice. The famous 'Briefe eines Eipeldauers', written in the excruciating local Viennese dialect by Joseph Richter, includes the following characteristic statement for the year 1794:[3] 'There's not a noble maid, not even a *Bürger*'s daughter, who can't play the piano and sing as well.'

There was still a vast social gap between the upper and lower classes. A visiting Englishman might note that 'The Emperor appeared abroad without any ostentation; riding in His carriage or on Horseback, with a servant or two, like a private gentleman, & no guards or parade of any kind' (Farington II, 261), but in the next sentence he noted 'The Nobility are not as in England, "Peers" (pares or equals), but are divided into classes: the higher orders such as Prince Esterházy, – the Prince de Li[e]chtenstein, &c. only receiving other Classes as Inferiors.' A similar observation was made by the German *Capellmeister* and composer J. F. Reichardt[4] in 1808:

> The higher nobility here [in Vienna] entertains rather a high opinion, a very high opinion actually, of its own nobility, and it is even for foreign nobility of

1 Thayer I, 343ff. ('Die Musik in Wien im Jahre 1793'). Rosenbaum, Introduction (an excellent description of Vienna in the 1790s). Mörner *passim*. MS Diary of Count von Zinzendorf. Most of these private concerts were not reviewed in any of the local newspapers and almost no complete programmes survive.

2 For Grassalkovics see Dies, 76.

3 E. Hanslick, *Geschichte des Concertwesens in Wien*, Vienna 1869, p. 67.

4 *Vertraute Briefe geschrieben auf einer Reise nach Wien, etc.*, ed. Gustav Gugitz, 2 vols., Munich 1915, I, 318.

very good houses not at all easy to penetrate the inner circle and intimate family parties.

The same opinion is expressed by the Duchess Hedvig Elisabeth Charlotte of Södermanland who with her husband visited Vienna in 1798 and 1799 and wrote in her Diary:[1]

> Altogether here [in Vienna] there reigns an unbelievable haughtiness in the highest circles. They think of nothing else but their ancestors and are so precise about it that untold difficulties can occur when someone is presented at Court.

It certainly grated on Haydn, after he had chatted tête-à-tête with the King and Queen of England, to return to his former status as a glorified servant, and we shall see that in his dealings with Prince Nicolaus II Esterházy he was impelled to remind his Gracious Lord that he was a Doctor of Oxford and not to be treated like a lackey. Haydn's worldwide fame indeed enabled him, perhaps for the first time in Austrian musical history, to establish something at least faintly resembling a democratic give-and-take between himself and the members of the Viennese nobility. We note in documents of the period that Haydn was now addressed as 'Sie' (formal address) rather than the 'Er' (third person singular) previously reserved for servants and musicians. Beethoven had his (spuriously noble) 'van' which the nobility took as meaning that he was one of them. 'It may be stated,' says Schindler (220), 'with . . . certainty that, had the nobles not believed him to be one of them, neither his genius nor his works of art would have won for him the favoured position he had enjoyed in aristocratic circles. . . .' Haydn had no social pretensions of that kind, but he considered that his position in the European cultural scene entitled him to a new degree of respect – new, that is, for the Austrian nobility. Haydn was always a diplomat, and prided himself on getting his way by tact with princes and counts; in any event, the Austrian nobility thought highly of Haydn and were to have even greater respect for him after the performances of the late Oratorios.

Haydn had far more freedom as a composer to Prince Esterházy than he had ever enjoyed before; thus he had more time to write music, and to conduct it, for other members of the Austrian nobility. Since the names of such families as Lobkowitz, Schwarzenberg, and Swieten will occur frequently in this Chronicle, a few words about these leading houses (insofar as they had some connection with music in general and Haydn in particular) may prove useful.

At the time it would have been difficult for the average Viennese music-lover to see much difference between the concerts of the top nobility such as Auersperg, Schwarzenberg, Lichnowsky, or Lokbowitz. For us, in retrospect, it is clear that the concerts of the old Bohemian house of Lobkowitz were, as far as Haydn and Beethoven are concerned, among the most influential and important in late eighteenth- and early nineteenth-century Viennese musical history. Until the discovery of Beethoven's début at the house of Lobkowitz,[2] it was not generally realized that at the time there were two Princes Lobkowitz each of whom held fashionable musical soirées. The older Prince Joseph Maria Carl of the younger 'line of Melnick' was seventy years old in 1795; he is listed in the *Hof- und Staats-Schematismus* of the period as 'Sr. Fürstl. Gnaden der Hochgebohrne Fürst und Herr Herr Joseph des

1 *Hedvig Elisabeth Charlottas dagbok*, edited and translated by Cecilia af Klercker. 6 vols., Stockholm 1927, VI, 161.
2 See *Haydn in England 1791–1795*, p. 294.

h[eiligen] r[ömischen] R[eiches] Fürst von Lobkowitz, Ritter des goldenen Vließes, und des militärischen Maria Theresia Ordens, Sr. röm. k.k. apost. Maj. wirkl. Kämmerer und geheimer Rath, Generalfeldmarschall, und Oberster eines Dragoner Regiments, woh[nhaft] in der Ungargasse 309.' This distinguished old military man had, in March 1784, been one of the subscribers to Mozart's Trattnerhof subscription concerts and it was at his concerts that Haydn played in March 1793, and Beethoven made his début in March 1795; the Ungargasse, where he lived, was in the suburb of the Landstraße, about a quarter-of-an-hour's brisk walk from the centre of the city.

The other branch of the family, called by Zinzendorf in his Diary 'les jeunes Lobkowitz' to differentiate between them and the old Prince's household, and known as the 'line of Raudni[t]z', was now headed by Joseph Franz (or Franz Joseph) Maximilian, a young man of twenty-three newly married (in 1792) to Marie Caroline, *née* Princess Schwarzenberg. They resided in the famous old Palais Lobkowitz in what was then called the Spitalplatz (now Lobkowitzplatz), opposite the Augustine Church. The Prince's father, Ferdinand Philipp, had been Gluck's patron and had died in 1784. Although Joseph Franz was to go down in history as Beethoven's patron – at the Palace took place the first performance of the 'Eroica', for example – at this period Lobkowitz was better known as one of Haydn's patrons. The writer of the spurious *Secret Memoirs of Princess Lamballe*, who met Haydn in 1806, describes the Prince's father, married to one of the Princesses of Savoy, and continues, 'whose son was the great patron of the immortal Haydn, the celebrated composer'.

The young Lobkowitz formed his orchestra in 1796, including among the members Anton Kraft, the 'cellist for whom Haydn had composed the famous D major 'Cello Concerto in 1783. The Prince played the violin, and the *Vaterländische Blätter* says of him, 'In the reigning Prince of Lobkowitz we admire a bass voice of rare beauty, in tonal quality as well as range and delivery.' Haydn's later biographer, the Saxonian *Legationsrath* Georg August Griesinger met Beethoven at the Palais Lobkowitz. The witty and slightly malicious Countess Lulu von Thürheim writes about the Prince:

> From morning to night he was occupied with music and squandered a large fortune in order to maintain the most distinguished musicians and singers in the city and on his country estates. In his castle at Eisenberg the door was open to artists and the dinner table was laid uninterruptedly. There the Prince kept up a truly royal state and even today in the neighbourhood they still tell about his magnificent entertainments. He himself composed several operas and, although he walked with a crutch, he took an active part in the performances. Even though he was himself a spendthrift, his purse was open to all and sundry who called on him for help. He died quite young [in 1816] and left his seven small children nothing but a load of debts, the larger part of which it was not possible to pay off.

It was to this attractive if financially irresponsible young aristocrat that Haydn dedicated the last finished string quartets of his career, the so-called Op. 77, composed in 1799. It will be remembered that Lobkowitz was one of the three men who guaranteed Beethoven's pension in 1809.[1]

1 O. E. Deutsch: Mozart, *Die Dokumente seines Lebens*, Kassel 1961, p. 488; *Hof- und Staats-Schematismus der röm. kaiserl. auch kaiserl. königl. und erzherzoglichen Haupt- und Residenz-Stadt Wien* [&c.], Vienna 1795 *et seq.*, also *Verzeichniß aller nummerirten Häuser in der k. k. Haupt-und Residenzstadt Wien* [etc.]. Olleson, 48. Thayer I, 353. Thayer-Forbes I, 229. Landon, *Beethoven*, 155f. Theodor Frimmel: *Beethoven-Handbuch*, Leipzig 1925, I, 367ff. *Secret Memoirs of Princess Lamballe*, edited and annotated by Catherine Hyde, St. Dunstan Society, Akron, Ohio 1901, p. 63. Grove I, Vol. II, 154f. (article by Thayer). *Adels-Schematismus* (ed. Ignaz Ritter v. Schönfeld), Vienna 1825, pp. 25ff. (Lobkowitz).

Another of Haydn's patrons from the highest nobility was Johann Joseph Nepomuk, Prince von Schwarzenberg, since 1794 married to Pauline, Princess von Arenberg (who was burned to death at a ball which her husband gave at Paris on the occasion of the marriage of Marie Louise to Napoleon). His brother, Carl Philipp, was the Austrian Field Marshal and victor of the battle of Leipzig. Schwarzenberg, born in 1769, was considerably younger than Haydn but the family had cultivated Haydn's music for years: in the music archives of the huge family *Stammschloß* at Krumau (now Český Krumlov) – which, incidentally includes a completely intact eighteenth-century theatre, even to the old scenery, costumes, musicians' candle-holders and ancient music stands – there is a large collection of Haydn material, including the earliest known dated copy of a symphony (No. 37, 1758). In Vienna, the Schwarzenberg winter palace was in the Mehlmarkt (now Neuer Markt), and it was there that the first performances of *The Creation* and *The Seasons* took place; the building no longer exists.

It was there, too, that Beethoven's Septet in E flat (Op. 20) was first performed, on the occasion of which the composer said 'That is *my* Creation', referring of course to Haydn's Oratorio. Beethoven dedicated to the Prince the Quintet for piano and wind instruments Op. 16. Schwarzenberg obviously had two kinds of concerts as far as Haydn's music was concerned. The one was the lending of his rooms for van Swieten's Gesellschaft der Associirten (about which more *infra*); in this capacity as host, *The Creation, The Seasons*, and other works such as *The Seven Words* in its vocal arrangement took place at the Palace on the Mehlmarkt. On the other hand, the Prince also gave his own musical soirées, at which, for example, the Septet (and presumably also the Quintet) by Beethoven were given.

Count Zinzendorf tells us that there was excellent 'Harmonie-Musique' at the Schwarzenbergs. On 19 February 1793, we read, 'Diné[,] après midi un peu dormi, chez la Pce Schwarzenberg avec les furstenberg, le Jean Li[e]chtenstein, Caroline Furstenberg, nous etions 13. Charmante musique apres le diner de Mozart, die Zauberflöte'; and a year later, 16 February 1794, Zinzendorf noted, 'Diné chez la Pcesse Schwarzenberg a 13 [again!] . . . Jolie musique de la Zauberflöte'. Many of these wind-band arrangements of Mozart's operas, including a particularly felicitous one of *Entführung* (which the late E. F. Schmid considered Mozart's own), are in the Krumau Archives. Schwarzenberg seems to have made a good impression on the Duchess of Södermanland, who after describing Prince Liechtenstein in biting words (we will quote them *infra*), says of Prince Schwarzenberg that 'his annual income is about a million. He has quite a different nature [from Liechtenstein], is very charming, is very interested in the fine arts and is a great Maecenas'.

It is perhaps worth mentioning that Prince Schwarzenberg subscribed to four copies of Beethoven's Piano Trios, Op. 1, the Princess to three and the Dowager Princess to one. (Altogether, this subscription list, reproduced in facsimile in Landon, *Beethoven*, 64f., is another fascinating document, linking as it does Beethoven's first patrons and well-wishers with many of the names known to us from Haydn's biography. Prince Nicolaus II Esterházy, for example, subscribed to three copies, and Countess Joseph Esterházy to one. Count Joseph Erdödy, to whom Haydn dedicated his great Op. 76 Quartets, ordered three copies, as did the Baron van Swieten and Prince Grassalkovics. Count Apponyi, to whom Haydn dedicated his London Quartets [known as Opp. 71 & 74] in the Autumn of 1795, ordered half-a-dozen of the Trios, and so did Prince Lobkowitz [which one is not specified, but probably the young Joseph Franz]. We shall have frequent recourse to this authentic and primary source for Beethoven's and of course also Haydn's aristocratic patrons in and about the year 1795.)[1]

Although Carl, Prince Lichnowsky, married to Maria Christiane, one of the beautiful Countesses Thun (known in their youth as the 'three graces'), is more closely linked to Mozart, whose pupil he was, and Beethoven, whose principal patron he was fast becoming in 1795, we nevertheless find Haydn's name appearing in connection with that of Lichnowsky. Frau von Bernhard, then a young girl studying piano in Vienna, remembered:

> I was frequently invited to the Lichnowskys, in order to play there. He was a friendly and distinguished gentleman and she a very beautiful woman. Yet they did not seem happy together; she always had such a melancholy expression on her face, and I heard that he spent a great deal of money, far beyond his means. Her sister [Elisabeth, married to Count Razumovsky], who was even more beautiful, had a husband who was a patron of Beethoven. She was almost always present when music was performed. I still remember clearly both Haydn and Salieri sitting on a sofa on one side of the small music-room [in the Alserstrasse house where Lichnowsky, and at this period also Beethoven lived], both carefully dressed in the old-fashioned way with perruque, shoes and silk hose, whereas even here Beethoven would come dressed in the informal fashion of the other side of the Rhine, almost ill-dressed.

Lichnowsky in those days had a quartet consisting of brilliant young virtuosi: Ignaz Schuppanzigh, then nineteen years of age, was the leader and would become Beethoven's leading quartet interpreter; Louis Sina, also very young, a pupil of Förster; Franz Weiss, then sixteen, was viola; and either Anton Kraft, Haydn's ex-'cellist, or his son Nicolaus (born at Eszterháza in 1778) was the violoncello player. Lichnowsky gave his weekly concerts on Fridays, and it was at one of these that Haydn is reported to have heard the first performance of Beethoven's Op. 1 Trios, dedicated to the Prince. (We shall examine the evidence of this whole matter *infra*.) Thayer also reports that Beethoven played his new piano sonatas, Op. 2, to Haydn at a Friday morning concert in 1795; the sonatas were, when they were published early in 1796, dedicated to Haydn. We shall return to this problem *infra*.

That Prince Lichnowsky sometimes produced music on a very big scale can be seen from an entry in Zinzendorf's Diary for 15 April 1794: '. . . P^{cesse} Lichnowsky ou l'on executa Judas machabaeus von Händel', the Handelian Oratorio which may have been one of van Swieten's Gesellschaft der Associirten operations.

Lichnowsky's mother-in-law, Countess Maria Wilhelmine, *née* Uhlfeld, frequented the Friday morning musicales. Frau von Bernhard says of her: 'I myself have seen [her] going down on her knees to him [Beethoven] as he lolled on the sofa and begging him to play something. But Beethoven did not. Countess Thun was, however, a very eccentric woman,' concludes Frau Bernhard. In earlier years, the Countess had taken some piano lessons from Haydn and later she became one of Mozart's admirers early in his Viennese career: in a letter to his father of 24 March 1781, he writes: 'I have lunched twice with Countess Thun and go there almost every day.' As for Haydn's later relationship to her, we may note that he gave her a manuscript score of his Oratorio *Il ritorno di Tobia*. In a Swiss antiquarian dealer's catalogue of *c*. 1930, we note the

1 Frimmel, *Beethoven-Handbuch*, II, 168f.; Georg Feder, 'Manuscript sources of Haydn's works and their distribution' (German), in *Haydn-Studien* I/1, 1965, p. 25, also (English) in *Haydn Yearbook* IV, 1968, p. 120; Landon *Supplement*, 20f.; Landon, *Beethoven*, 95, 97f. Zinzendorf Diary (MS). Mörner, 337.

manuscript (372 pages) being offered for sale with the note 'Manuscrit intéressant avec la remarque manuscr. sur la couverture, "Donné par l'auteur à Mme Thun *née* Ulfeld"'. She also subscribed to *The Creation*.[1]

Another aristocrat whose name in our minds is more closely associated with Beethoven than with Haydn is Andreas Kyrillowitsch, Count (after 1815 Prince) Razumovsky (Rasumowsky, etc.); yet we have first-hand information from none other than Schindler that Haydn was of great influence on the quartet supported by the Count, for which Beethoven was to write the Op. 59 Quartets that bear Razumovsky's name.

> Count Razumovsky was also a practising musician and, to sum him up appropriately in a few words, the chief upholder of the Haydn tradition in instrumental music. Alternating with Prince Lichnowsky, he would also gather the . . . musicians in his palace to perform quartet music, in which he himself played second violin. Soon, however, he decided on another course, which was to give his circle a higher significance: he placed a permanent quartet under a life-long contract. This was the first and only example of its kind in Austria. Not that other rich art-lovers did not follow this example, establishing permanent quartets in their households; indeed, there were several. But none of them did what the Russian Maecenas did, namely to provide these artists with pensions for the rest of their lives. . . . We have just named Count Razumovsky as the upholder of the Haydn tradition of quartet music. How can this be explained? Very simply: Haydn had revealed to this art-lover [Razumovsky] that *fine* sensitivity necessary to the understanding of many of those particular qualities in his quartets and symphonies which are neither superficial nor conveyed through the usual [musical] symbols. Since these things had eluded other artists, he undertook to acquaint the Count with his hidden intentions so that he might then transmit them to the performing musicians. This fact is of *great* importance in understanding the true qualities of the Razumovsky Quartet . . . [italics original].

Count Razumovsky, born at St Petersburg in 1752, was a Russian diplomat who was first in Vienna from 1777–9, where he no doubt became acquainted with Haydn's music, and possibly with the composer himself. In 1794 he followed Count Demetrius Galitzin as Russian Ambassador to the Court of Vienna. Immensely wealthy, he amassed a huge collection of art treasures which, alas, were almost totally destroyed in a fire that broke out on 1 January 1815. In 1794 and 1795, however, he had not yet built the large and elegant palace (which was to bear his name) near the Danube Canal; in his early days he lived, according to the *Hof- und Staats-Schematismus* in the Kaunitz Palais in the Johannesgasse. His soirées were perhaps less fascinating for non-musicians; Count Zinzendorf remarks tartly in his Diary for 11 March 1796, 'Au Concert de Lobkowitz, Caroline [his young wife, *vide supra*] engraisse beaucoup [as she was pregnant]. Il y avoit grand monde . . . De la chez Rasumofski, un ennui terrible.' In the remaining years of Haydn's life, the Count often had to go abroad on official missions, especially to Italy. He returned to Vienna for good in 1801.

At the period here under discussion – the middle of the year 1795 – we have an interesting undated letter from Razumovsky (in Vienna) to Prince P. A. Subov in St Petersburg:

1 Katalog No. 421, Henning Oppermann, Basel, item 244: 'Il Ritorno di Tobia. Parte Seconda', offered for thirty francs. Thayer I, 354f. *The Letters of Mozart and his Family* (Anderson), London 2nd ed. 1966, II, 717 (and *passim*). Pohl I, 188f. *Beethoven-Handbuch* (Frimmel) I, 345ff., II, 322ff. Landon, *Beethoven* 64f. Zinzendorf Diary (MS).

En fait de musique je n'en ai pris que pour la valeur de 14 florins de différents bons auteurs de cette ville [Vienne], comme étant ce qu'il y a de plus nouveau pour le moment et sachant d'ailleurs, que les magasins de musique de Pétersbourg sont bien assortis en tout genre. La perte du fameux Mozart et l'absence de Haydn nous laissent ici dans la pénurie à cet égard, et les autres compositeurs, tous bien subalternes vis-à-vis de ces deux-là, osent a peine donner quelque chose au public dans la crainte de n'avoir point le débit de leurs faibles productions. J'ai bien du regret, que les six derniers quatuors de Haydn [Opp. 71 et 74, Vienne 1793] que j'ai entendus avec le plus grand plaisir, ne se trouvent pas à acheter. Ayant été composés, il y a deux ans, pour quelqu'un [le Comte d'Apponyi], qui en paya 100 ducats la jouissance exclusive pendant la premiere année, ils ne seront probablement gravés et mis en vente que quand Haydn, qui est très attentif à ses intérêts, aura épuisé la ressource de les débiter personnellement en Angleterre aussi chèrement que possible. Si donc V. E. était curieuse de les avoir avant ce temps, il faudrait que la commission en fût donnée à Londres pour qu'on s'y adresse à l'auteur lui-même.

It was at Razumovsky's that the famous party took place after the Viennese première of *Don Giovanni* in 1788, in the course of which Haydn vigorously defended the opera and its composer.[1]

A man who played an important role in Viennese musical life, and in the late career of Haydn and the early career of Beethoven, was Gottfried Freiherr van Swieten, son of the Empress Maria Theresa's personal physician. Baron van Swieten was a year younger than Haydn and had spent many years in Berlin in Austrian diplomatic service, where he became an ardent admirer of the works of J. S. Bach and Handel. While at Berlin he commissioned six new symphonies from C. P. E. Bach (1774). In 1778 he returned to Vienna and became Prefect of the National Library; in 1781 he became President of the Education Commission and in that capacity was an integral part of Emperor Joseph II's reform plans. At his Sunday morning musicales in the National Library, Mozart often participated and it was at Swieten's invitation that Mozart reorchestrated various Handel Oratorios, including *Messiah*. Swieten now dedicated himself to the resuscitation of Bach's and Handel's music in Vienna, and it was almost entirely through his efforts that this great north German tradition was made known to Viennese musicians. Mozart's style was greatly influenced by the works of Bach and Handel which he came to know at the Sunday concerts, and Schindler assures us that Beethoven was equally influenced by Swieten's taste. We have a letter from Swieten to Beethoven, undated but obviously written about 1795, asking the young composer to come 'next Wednesday with your nightcap in your bag'. Schindler notes that Beethoven 'generally had to stay long after the guests had departed, for his elderly host was musically insatiable and would not let the young pianist go until he had "blessed the evening" with several Bach fugues'. Swieten, as one of Beethoven's most enthusiastic patrons, was instrumental in introducing the young man into Viennese society. In return for these favours, Beethoven dedicated his First Symphony to Swieten in 1800.

1 Schindler in the translation of Landon, *Beethoven*, 207; another translation in *Beethoven as I knew him* (ed. MacArdle), London 1966, pp. 59f. *Beethoven-Handbuch* (Frimmel) II, 51ff. Zinzendorf Diary (MS). Razumovsky subscribed to two copies of the 1795 Beethoven Trios, Op. 1, his wife to one (it will be recalled that she was one of the daughters of Countess Thun). He also subscribed to two copies of *The Creation*. Zinzendorf heard Beethoven playing at Countess Razumovsky's as early as 23 April 1795. Boris Steinpress: 'Haydns Oratorien in Russland zu Lebzeiten des Komponisten' in *Haydn-Studien* II (1969), 2, p. 83. *Vide infra*, p. 338.

The *Jahrbuch der Tonkunst für Wien und Prag, 1796* (edited by Johann Ferdinand von Schönfeld, a Viennese publisher who had a bookshop at the Kärntnerthor) describes Swieten as being

> . . . practically a patriarch in music. His taste is only for the great and elevated. Many years ago he wrote twelve beautiful symphonies. When he is present at a concert, our half-connoisseurs do not take their eyes off him, so that they can read from his expression (which, however, may not be so easily understood) what opinion he might have about the work in question. Every year he gives some very large and magnificent concerts, in which only pieces by old masters are given. He especially loves the Handelian style, and mostly gives large choral works by him. Just this last Christmas Feast [1794] he gave such a concert at Prince von Paar's, where an Oratorio by this master was performed.

Swieten himself wrote in the *Allgemeine Musikalische Zeitung*:

> I belong, as far as music is concerned, to a generation that considered it necessary to study an art form thoroughly and systematically before attempting to practise it. I find in such a conviction food for the spirit and for the heart, and I return to it for strength every time I am oppressed by the new evidence of decadence in the arts. My principal comforters at such times are Handel and the Bachs and those few great men of our own day who, taking these as their masters, follow resolutely in the same quest for greatness and truth.

We have seen in *Haydn in England 1791–1795*, p. 231, that Swieten lent a travelling coach to Haydn for his second journey to England. The Baron now became a close collaborator with Haydn, furnishing the texts not only to *The Creation* and *The Seasons* but also to the choral version of *The Seven Words*. Griesinger tells us that Swieten had composed eight (not twelve as in the *Jahrbuch* report) symphonies which Haydn described, 'they were as stiff as he'. Curiously, many of these symphonies were circulated in manuscript under Haydn's name, a fact which will have delighted neither the original nor the supposed composers.

Swieten alone could not, of course, finance the production of huge Handelian Oratorios, and to assist him in his efforts he formed the famous 'Gesellschaft der Associirten' (Society of Associates), which also guaranteed the costs of Haydn's Oratorios. According to Griesinger the members were the Princes Liechtenstein, Esterházy, Schwarzenberg, Lobkowitz, Auersperg, Kinsky, Lichnowsky, Trautmannsdorf, and Sinsendorf (not to be confused with Zinzendorf, but in fact it was not Prince but Count Prosper von Sinsendorf) together with Counts Czernin, Harrach, Erdödy, Apponyi, and Fries. Dies gives a slightly different and probably less reliable list: Princes N. Esterházy, Trautmannsdorf, Lobkowitz, Schwarzenberg, Kinsky, Auersperg, L. Liechtenstein, Lichnowsky and Counts Marschall, Harrach, Fries, Freiherr von Spielmann, and Swieten himself.

Relations between Haydn and Swieten always remained rather stiff and as we shall see in the Chronicle (*Haydn: the Late Years 1801–1809*), they grew worse when the two men collaborated on *The Seasons*. There is no doubt that Swieten was a rather formal man. Sigismund Neukomm, Haydn's composition pupil from whom we have many first-hand reports of Vienna of this period, told Otto Jahn, the Mozart scholar, of Swieten's behaviour at concerts. If anyone was caught whispering, Swieten, who used to sit in one of the front rows, would slowly rise to his feet and with a long, penetrating look would transfix the offender, slowly sitting down again afterwards. 'That would do the trick.' In Neukomm's *Bemerkungen Neukomms zu den Biographischen Nachrichten von Dies*, which we shall be quoting frequently in the Chronicle, we read: 'I would like to add a more precise word of explanation [to what Dies wrote], that the former Ambassador to the Court of Frederick the Great was not so much a *friend* of Haydn's and Moz[art]'s but very much a patron (protecteur) with a very high opinion of himself. . . .'

Count Zinzendorf, who frequented Swieten's parties in his apartment in the Renngasse, house No. 146, has several interesting notes about the Baron and his concerts. On 5 April 1795, Prince von Paar was again host to a Swieten-*cum*-Gesellschaft der Associirten performance:

> Au Concert de Haendel der Messias dans la maison du P[ce] de Paar. La chambre est trop petite, je ne trouvois pas l'effet de tous les morceaux que Forster indique. Celle des bergers me plut beaucoup[,] c'est une charmante Pastorale. Le Choeur double en second acte. Wer ist der König der Ehre? Hallelujah! dann Gott der Herr regierend – Dans le 3me acte. Ich weiß[,] dass mein Erlöser lebt et le choeur Würdig ist das Lamm.

We see that Zinzendorf heard the German translation and of course the new Mozartian orchestration which, whatever its faults, would have made the work more palatable to late eighteenth-century Viennese ears, to whom the *Coronation-Mass*-like orchestration of 'Why do the Nations' will have produced what Ernst Krenek has brilliantly called 'das Aha-Erlebniß' (literally the 'aha-experience', i.e. the recognition of a well-known tune, etc.).

As to Swieten personally, Zinzendorf notes in his Diary for 6 March 1796, 'Il diner chez moi [Singerstrasse 933] le Cte O'donel [sic] le Baron de Swieten et de Margerlik [etc., etc.] Swieten fit un peu le dictateur a sa guise.' On 21 January 1799, the Diary informs us:

> Après 9[hes] chez le Baron Swieten. Il n'etoit pas encore au logis. Il reçoit dans sa chambre a coucher. Ils y rassembla 3. Czernins, Lisette Schoenborn, Cobenzl et Herb. Moltke. On a mise a table a 10[hr] ½ on se leva a minuit un quart. Bourgogne, Champagne, Punch et Vin du Cap de Mr Offize. Ces Dames buvent joliment. . . .

Another time the food and drink were not so opulent: 29 November 1800 (the second time that month) Zinzendorf was at the Baron's and describes the many birds which Swieten kept in cages; the Diary notes, 'Il feroit maigre, en mangeant un pluvier doré.'

What really appalled the Count, however, was to hear Baron van Swieten talking of 'his' *Creation*; on 28 February 1799, the Diary informs us '. . . Le soir chez la P[esse] Starhemberg. Encore Swieten qui y est a tout moment. Il parla de sa musique de la création. . . .'[1]

Another patron of both Haydn and Beethoven was Johann Moritz, Count von Fries, whose large income was, apart from the usual estates, based on the famous banking house of Fries & Co. In 1800, Johann Moritz married the beautiful Princess Maria Theresia von Hohenlohe-Waldenburg: a pretty portrait in oils of the young couple was painted by François Gérard and is now in the Kunsthistorisches Museum, Vienna (reproduced in *Ludwig van Beethoven*, ed. J. Schmidt-Görg and Hans Schmidt, London 1970, p. 43). The Palais Fries, still extant, is on the Josephplatz opposite the

1 *Hof- und Staats-Schematismus* (op. cit.); Griesinger, 37; Dies, 160; *Beethoven-Handbuch* (Frimmel) II, 281f.; Schindler (MacArdle), 48ff.; Thayer I, 355f.; Olleson, 55; Neukomm, 31; Zinzendorf Diary (MS.). Edward Olleson, 'Gottfried van Swieten, Patron of Haydn and Mozart', *Proceedings of the Royal Musical Association*, 23 April 1963.

National Library. The palace was a centre for artists, writers, and musicians. Fries was an avid collector, and for sheer opulence, the furnishings of his house and its huge collection of *objets d'art* astonished visitors. Later he lost all his money and was declared bankrupt in 1826, dying shortly thereafter. But at the turn of the century, the Fries fortunes were at their height. Zinzendorf heard a performance of *The Creation* at the Palais Fries on 4 April 1800, arranged for nine strings; he considered that 'jamais la musique de la Création ne m'a plû autant quoiqu'il n'y avoit que neuf instrumens, et surtout point d'instrumens a vent.' Prince Lobkowitz sang the bass solos on this occasion 'malgré son peu de timbre avec expression'.

The year before, two visiting Swedish musicians, Johan Fredrik Berwald and his father (relatives of the great Franz Berwald) went to one of the Fries Monday musical soirées. Young Berwald in his Diary notes:

> A short while afterwards we were at a big musical soirée given by Count Fries, where there was a great number of fine guests and artists assembled. Among the first category we noted the Duke of Södermanland (later Carl XIII) and his consort. I received a gold watch from the Duchess. Among the artists may be mentioned: Josef Haydn, Beethoven (who gave his excellent Quintet for piano and wind instruments for the first time [*recte*: it was first given in April, 1797]), Weigl, Süssmayer, both the Wranitzkys, Vanhall, Kozeluch, Gyrovetz, Salieri, Abbé Stadler, Seifrid [Seyfried], Cartel[l]ieri, Krommer and others, all more or less famous men. I played and was applauded, especially for my Adagio; also from the old Haydn. He asked my father if he might keep me with him, for he had no children, he added, sighing; but my father answered, he only had one son, though this son would certainly be better off under Doctor Haydn's direction than he is now. . . .

It is possible that Haydn assisted at the marriage of Count Fries, in 1800, for we shall see that there was a 'Concert instrumental et vocal' and that the whole was 'la réunion des artistes les plus famés de l'Allemagne et de l'Italie qui prodiguerent leurs plus amiables talens dans l'ordonnances de ces Fêtes . . .' (see *infra*, 17 October 1800). We know for certain, from Zinzendorf's Diary and from the Vienna correspondent of the *Allgemeine Musikalische Zeitung* (*AMZ*) – Griesinger? – that Haydn 'produced once again two new symphonies at Count F[ries]', one of which seems to have been Symphony No. 102, at a concert on 5 April 1799.[1]

It is not known under which circumstances Haydn met Nikolaus Zmeskall von Domanowecz (Domanovitz), *Hof-Koncipist* (Secretary) in the Hungarian *Hofkanzley* (Chancery), 'a somewhat dry man', says Carl Holz, Beethoven's friend. Zmeskall owned vineyards in Hungary and lived in the Bürgerspital, an apartment house near the Kärntnerthortheater. There he gave quartet parties, in which he frequently played the 'cello, on Sundays. Pohl-Botstiber suggest that Zmeskall was one of those who welcomed Haydn back from England in 1792, but the evidence for this statement, undoubtedly known to Pohl, has not been transmitted to us. Zmeskall soon became a great friend of Beethoven's, and many letters from the composer to his 'cellist friend exist; they often made music together at the Brunsviks and later at Countess Josephine Deym's, *née* Brunsvik. In the winter of 1801 Countess Josephine Deym, who was studying piano, writes to her sisters that Beethoven and Zmeskall were often guests.

1 Olleson, 55–8; C.-G. Stellan Mörner, 'Haydniana aus Schweden um 1800', in *Haydn-Studien* II/1, 1969, p. 7; *Beethoven-Handbuch* (Frimmel) I, 154ff.; MS. letter by Hofrat Heinrich Gabriel Freiherr von Collenbach to his niece, dated 'Vienne ce 17 octobre 1800' (author's collection); Landon, *Beethoven*, 134–6.

About the latter, she writes that 'he is just the same as ever with his *Casus* and his severity; recently he gave me a very difficult time with a Trio by Mozart, which you were kind enough to send me. I can't thank you enough for the beautiful music and books. Now I am learning the Sonata [piano Trio No. 27] in A flat by Haydn.'

Haydn dedicated to his young friend – he was born in 1759 – the revised and corrected edition of the String Quartets Op. 20, which Artaria published in May 1800; perhaps they were special favourites of the Zmeskall Sunday morning concerts. The title page of the Artaria edition specially notes that the dedication is by the composer, not the publisher: 'Édition revue[,] corrigée et dediée a Mr Nicolas Zmeskall de Domanovetz par l'auteur.' A pen-and-ink profile of Zmeskall has survived and is now in the Historisches Museum in Vienna: it shows the 'Musik-Graf' with a characteristically 'craggy' profile and a jutting lower jaw similar to that of his friend Haydn.[1] The portrait is reproduced in Landon, *Beethoven*, p. 82. Beethoven dedicated to Zmeskall the F minor Quartet, Op. 95.

Unfortunately we have no records of the musical parties that undoubtedly took place at the houses of such friends and patrons of Haydn as Count Anton Apponyi (to whom the composer dedicated his London Quartets of 1793: see *Haydn in England 1791–1795*) or Count Joseph Erdödy von Monyorókerék, the Vice Chancellor, Lord of Warasdin, to whom Haydn dedicated his great Quartets, Op. 76. Beethoven became great friends with Countess Anna Marie Erdödy, whose husband Peter was a relation of Joseph's.

It should perhaps be mentioned that of these less exalted aristocratic friends of Haydn's, Baron van Swieten subscribed to four copies of *The Creation*, Zmeskall one, Count Apponyi two, and Count Erdödy two. The unswerving loyalty that the Viennese nobility, greater and lesser, showed to Haydn and Beethoven is as heartwarming as was chilling their abandonment of Mozart.

Undoubtedly the most important musical activity after the nobility's semi-private concerts was the Court Opera, of which the *Hof-Kapellmeister* was the Italian composer, Antonio Salieri, with whom Haydn was on polite terms. Most of the operas were Italian, and occasionally a celebrated composer was fetched from abroad, as had been Paisiello in 1784 and Cimarosa with his *Il matrimonio segreto* in 1792. Salieri's functions included not only conducting the opera but also running the boys' choir school (in which Haydn had been trained half a century before) and planning the religious music for the Court Chapel. The Court Orchestra was large for its day, much larger than Haydn's at Eisenstadt. It contained, according to the *Hof- und Staats-Schematismus*, five or six each of solo tenors and solo basses, two organists, some fourteen violinists and violists (possibly divided up into six first violins, five seconds and three violas, or else 6–6–2 with the weak viola section one usually finds in those days), three 'cellists, three double bass (*violone*) players, two trombonists, and two each of oboes, clarinets (first clarinet was Johann Stadler, well known from the Mozart literature though not as celebrated as Anton), bassoons, horns, three trumpets, and a timpani player. Many of the individual players were very well known and good composers in their own right.

The opera had two houses at its disposal, the Burgtheater, which then stood on the Michaelerplatz, and the Kärntnerthortheater, near the Kärntner Gate. In each were

1 Pohl III, 63; *Beethoven-Handbuch* II, 474ff.; Thayer I, 358f.; *Hof- und Staats-Schematismus* (op. cit.); Hoboken I, 391; La Mara, *Beethoven und die Brunsviks, Nach Familienpapieren aus Therese Brunsviks Nachlass*, Leipzig 1920, p. 15; Schindler (MacArdle), 88f.

given not only operas but also ballets and plays, and the houses were rented for benefit concerts, though it was very difficult to get either, since there were very few days when the opera or theatre was not using them. Operas in German were also staged, of course, and increasingly so as time went on.

Haydn had very little to do with this official world of the Court Opera; nor did Beethoven, except for his Ballet *Die Geschöpfe des Prometheus* in 1801. Haydn was on polite, if not intimate, terms with Salieri, who in his turn gave lessons to Beethoven in the art of writing music to Italian words (elision, and so on). Both Haydn and Beethoven followed the activities of the Court Opera as outsiders, though both must have known most of the orchestral players.

Apart from the Court Opera, there was also what was called the 'Operas in the Suburbs' (*Vorstadt*). At the time (1795), the most popular was Schikaneder's Theater auf der Wieden (now the Fourth District), where Mozart's *Die Zauberflöte* was earning its librettist a fortune. Later, in 1801, he closed down the Wieden Theatre and opened the larger Theater an der Wien, which still exists. German operas and German plays, mostly comedies of a low intellectual level, dominated the suburban theatre. The aristocracy patronized the Italian opera, the lower classes the German opera in the suburbs, though of course everyone, and from all classes, came to see Mozart's *Zauberflöte* in the Wieden. Another popular suburban theatre was in the Leopoldstadt, where Wenzel Müller was writing very successful German operettas, all of which have passed into oblivion. We shall see in the Chronicle that Haydn strenuously, and successfully, resisted Baron van Swieten's attempts to introduce a Wenzel Müller tune into Haydn's *The Seasons*. Neukomm tells us of an amusing story about Müller and Haydn:

> Wenzel Müller, for years *Kapellmeister* at the doggerel [*Kasperl*-] theatre of the Leopoldstadt in Vienna and the composer of many operas for the theatre, introduced a stranger to Haydn. This stranger, an enthusiastic admirer of Haydn's muse, exhausted himself in praises which Haydn accepted with his usual modesty. Müller, however, who was possessed of a really Ko[t]zebue-like self-esteem, finally burst, having been annoyed at this flow of praise which was not directed at *him*, and came out with: 'Yes, it's true enough, Herr von Haydn, in quartets you have no equal', whereupon Haydn answered quite indifferently: 'too sad, my dear Müller, that I didn't learn anything else.' – I have this anecdote from Haydn's own lips.

The Theater auf der Wieden was also available for benefit concerts, and we shall see Michael (and probably Joseph) Haydn attending such a concert in 1798, at which Beethoven played. Haydn himself was probably involved in the performance of his *Armida*, with the symphony by Mozart as entr'acte, at the Theater auf der Wieden in 1797; and on the hand-bill of a concert given on 20 March 1796 by Music Director Joseph Suche, we read that a band of sixty musicians played a Haydn symphony in MS. provided by the composer himself.[1]

1 O. E. Deutsch: *Das Freihaustheater auf der Wieden 1787–1801*, Vienna-Leipzig 1937.

I Joseph Haydn, wax bust by Franz Christian Thaller (Thaler), *c.* 1799; for a view in profile see pl. 2 in black and white. This is one of three Haydn busts known to have been made by Thaller (cf. pl. 1), two of which are lost; it is said to show items of clothing worn by Haydn, as well as his wig made from his own hair. The bust, formerly owned by Prince Metternich, is now in the Kunsthistorisches Museum, Vienna (at present in the collection of old musical instruments).

II The south front of Esterházy Castle, Eisenstadt; coloured engraving after a drawing by Vincenz Reim, 8 June 1851. Under Prince Nicolaus II, who succeeded as the ruling prince in 1794, the castle became the centre of the Esterházy Court once more and was the focal point of Haydn's last years in the service of the Esterházys.

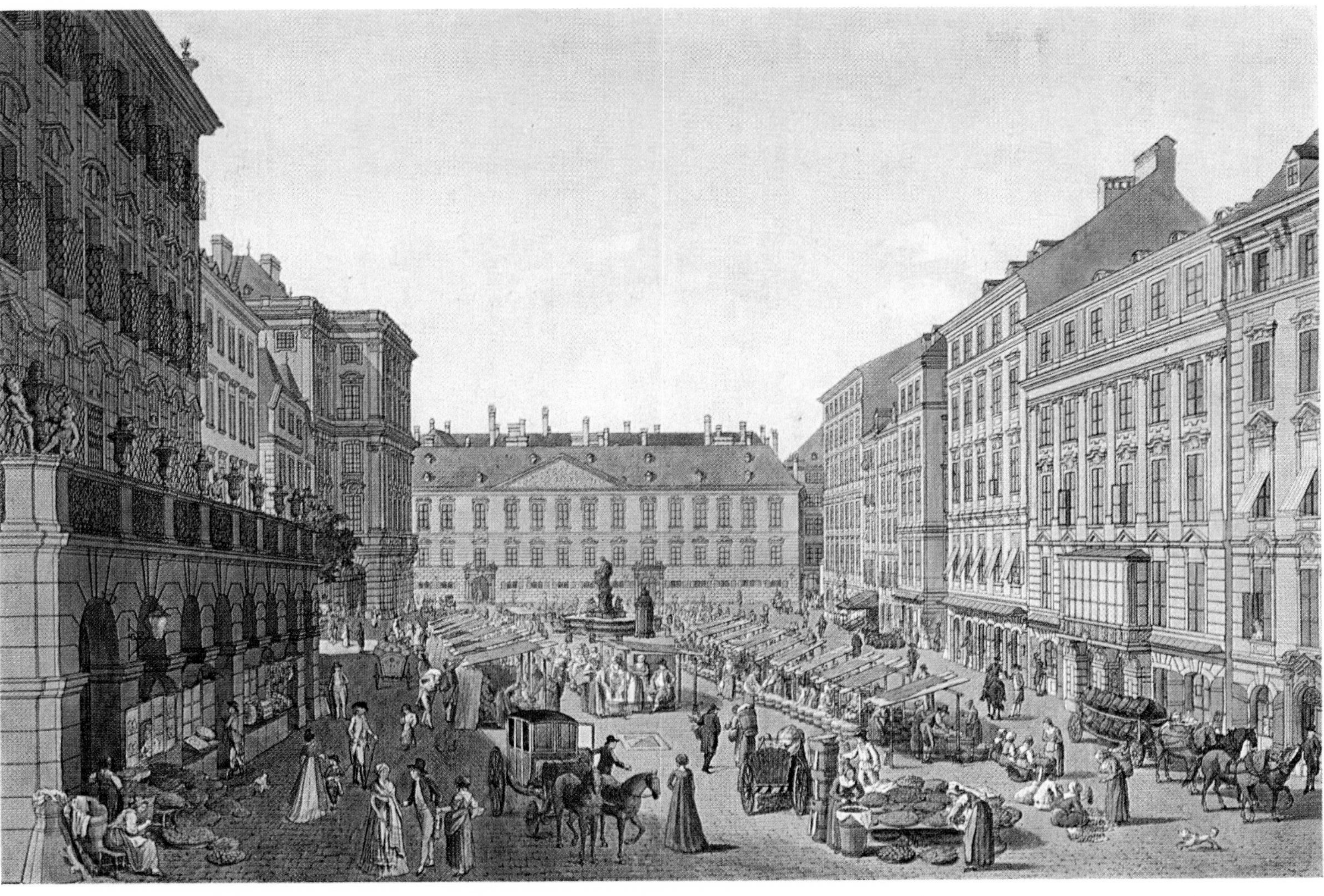

III The Neuer Markt (Mehlmarkt), Vienna; coloured engraving by Carl Schütz, published by Artaria & Co. in 1798. In the Schwarzenberg Palace (centre; since destroyed) the first performance of *The Creation* was given in April 1798 (cf. pp. 320f.).

IV Princess Marie Hermenegild Esterházy (*née* Princess Liechtenstein); portrait in oils by Elisabeth Vigée-Lebrun, 1798. The princess was the wife of Prince Nicolaus II, the fourth reigning Esterházy under whom Haydn served as Kapellmeister.

V Therese Saal, who sang the solo soprano part in the first public performance of *The Creation* in 1799; in this portrait by Friedrich Heinrich Füger she is shown holding music from *The Creation*.

Before proceeding to the public concerts, we should mention the masked balls at the Redoutensaal, which being Court functions, were under the jurisdiction of the Hofburg. It will be recalled that Mozart had written magnificent dance music for these functions, especially in the last years of his life, and that Haydn in 1792 had contributed Twelve German Dances and Twelve Minuets for the Pensionsgesellschaft bildender Künstler. For this same organization Beethoven was to compose brilliant dances in 1795 – his début as a composer of orchestral music in Vienna at which his old teacher, Haydn, was present. The Redoutensaal actually consisted of two rooms, a large one and a smaller; for the larger room an orchestra of forty-three (sometimes, as in Haydn's Dances of 1792, enlarged by four players) conducted by Johann Patatschny, for the smaller a band of twenty-seven conducted by Anton Höllmayr.[1]

The most important public concerts in Vienna were those of the so-called Tonkünstler-Societät, the Society of Musicians, whose biannual concerts, at Easter and Christmas, raised money for the Society's widows and orphans. Mozart had conducted for the Society, and Beethoven had made his first public appearance as pianist in Vienna at the Easter Concert of 1795. (Of course Beethoven had been presented to the *haut monde* at a Lobkowitz concert several weeks earlier.) Actually there were always two concerts at Easter and two at Christmas; the 'big' work was usually given twice but the entertainment offered in the intervals changed. Thus Beethoven appeared in his Concerto for piano and orchestra in B flat Op. 19 at the first Easter concert of 1795, at which the big work was Cartellieri's *Gioas, re di Giuda*, while at the second Easter concert there was a bassoon concerto by Cartellieri. The orchestra at these concerts was very large, often 180 or 200 musicians strong, and the Society rented the Burgtheater. Haydn became intimately connected with the organization; he had conducted the Christmas concerts in 1793, and, from 1798, he generally led one of his Oratorios. Beethoven continued to appear, and in 1798 he played at the second Easter concert (see 2 April 1798), between the 'acts' of Haydn's *The Seven Words*. In 1798 Haydn, who had been excluded from the Society, was made a member in a touching ceremony which made honourable amends for past offences. Naturally all the artists gave their services gratis for these concerts.[2]

In the summers, there were concerts at the Augarten, a handsome garden on the far side of the suburb called Leopoldstadt. For a time Mozart had participated in them, and the music had been furnished from the extensive library of Hofrat von Kees (who had died in January 1795). There were usually twelve concerts that took place at the extraordinary hour of seven o'clock on Saturday mornings. The *AMZ* of October 1800, devotes part of an article on music from Vienna to the Augarten concerts. The orchestra, wrote the correspondent:

> consisted mostly of amateurs, except for the wind instruments and the double basses. Even ladies of the highest nobility were to be heard. The auditorium was very brilliant, and everything went off with order and with decorum; everyone was glad to do their part in helping the organization. The income from the rather scanty number of subscribers [seven o'clock in the morning!] is entirely used to defray expenses. Later the direction was taken over by Herr Rudolph. It still went quite well, but no longer so brilliantly: the nobility retired, for the reason that most of them had attended was to please Emperor Joseph II – but the performances

1 The MS. files of the Pensionsgesellschaft are now in the Archives of the City of Vienna, which organization kindly provided photographs of the relevant years. Concerning the 1792 Dances, see *Haydn in England 1791–1795*. Concerning the Beethoven Dances, *vide infra*, 22 November 1795.

2 *Denkschrift aus Anlass des hundertjährigen Bestehens der Tonkünstler-Societät*, C. F. Pohl, Vienna 1871.

were still very pleasant. Now Herr Schupanzig [*sic*] runs it, and the merry auditorium has now quite disappeared. No amateur of any *real* stature wants to be heard; even the musicians themselves only rarely give benefit concerts. Altogether the fire of the undertaking is entirely spent. The concertos are seldom well accompanied: but the symphonies go better. Since the purpose of the undertaking is no longer love for the art or entertainment but a business proposition, in view of the small number of subscribers it is not at all possible to spend any proper sums on the music. The auditorium, as it now presents itself, is not very encouraging, nor very inviting; the room is very good, but the orchestra is badly placed (right in the middle, without being raised up), and there are other more or less important disadvantages, too. The greatest merit of Herr Schupanzig is probably his daring playing, which exerts a beneficial influence on his conducting. But despite all our acknowledgement of his merits, we cannot subscribe to the opinion, rather widely circulated, that he is what might be called a *great* director. . . . [He is], moreover, a good quartet player, plays well at sight; in concertos, however, he lacks the grand manner and its school. He goes out of tune quite frequently in double stops or in high positions – for which his large hand is mostly responsible.

Haydn often attended the Augarten concerts. In July 1796, a letter from the German composer Friedrich Witt, the composer of the 'Jena' Symphony (attributed to Beethoven until 1957), to a friend at Wallerstein informs us:

We are comfortably settled, and who wouldn't be happy here? For there are amusements of every conceivable kind in abundance; there is even a concert at the Augarten every Saturday at 7 in the morning. The day before yesterday I gave one of my symphonies there and Bär [Beer] played one of my [clarinet] concertos. Presumably the director trumpeted the news about, for Wranizci [Wranizky], Girowez [Gyrowetz] and our Papa Haydn were present. . . .

Beethoven played and conducted at the Augarten. On 24 May 1803, he accompanied the mulatto violinist George Polgreen Bridgetower at a noon Augarten concert, at which was heard the première of the 'Kreutzer' Sonata, Op. 47, originally composed for Bridgetower. And the next year Beethoven conducted a concert at the Augarten which included his Second Symphony and the Concerto in C minor for piano and orchestra, Op. 37, the solo part of which was played by the composer's pupil, Ferdinand Ries (who later wrote, 'probably no concerto was ever so beautifully accompanied'). No doubt Haydn was present at many of these occasions.[1]

Church music in Vienna was slowly recovering from the blow that it had been dealt during the Josephinian reforms. The Emperor's idea of reducing the orchestra except for special occasions and introducing music in which the congregation could participate was admirable, and indeed the Church itself periodically addressed itself to such reforms; but in Austria the result was primarily to dry up the inspiration for composers to write any large-scale music at all. Haydn composed his last Mass for the Styrian pilgrimage church of Mariazell in 1782; between 1781 and 1791 Mozart composed, apart from the specially commissioned *Requiem*, intended for a private chapel, only the unfinished Mass in C minor, the Kyrie and Gloria of which he conducted at Salzburg in 1783, and the *Ave verum corpus* of 1791 for Baden. Matters were better in the provinces, where in local churches, monasteries and private chapels, church music with orchestra flourished despite the Josephinian *Verbote*. In Vienna,

1 *AMZ* III, 46f.; Thayer I, 347f.; Landon, *Beethoven*, 131, 149; Landon, *Essays*, 155.

however, where the Emperor's stern eye could be turned on them, the churches strongly reduced the performance of, and thus the composition of, Masses with full orchestra.

Under Franz, conditions changed. There was no longer any *Verbot* on orchestral Masses, and music in the many Viennese churches began to improve again. The *AMZ*, in the report from Vienna of 1800 which we have quoted above in connection with the Augarten Concerts, tells us: 'In the Court Chapel of St Michael and at St Peter's there is good music by [Florian Leopold] Gassmann, Reuther [Georg Reutter Jr., Haydn's old teacher at St Stephen's Cathedral], Albrechtsberger and others; sometimes also by Mozart, and well performed. Herr [Joseph] Eybler at the Schotten Church shows signs of writing good church music; Herr Breindl [Joseph Preindl] and other young composers are frequently too gallant in their style.' St Stephen's Cathedral was now musically under the direction of Albrechtsberger, who succeeded the old Leopold Hofmann upon the latter's death in 1793. Joseph Eybler, formerly *Regens chori* at the Carmelite Church, was now in a better position at the Scottish Church. Haydn himself occasionally took over the conducting of one of his Masses at a Viennese church, for instance, at Christmas 1796, in the Piaristenkirche in the suburb of the Josephstadt. With his increasingly close connection to the royal household, it is not surprising to find authentic copies of many of the late Masses in the private library of the Hofkapelle (which was in the Burg). In 1799 or thereabouts, he composed his great Te Deum for the Empress Marie Therese.

Frederik Samuel Silverstolpe was not impressed with the quality of church music in Vienna. On 28 December 1796, he reported to Sweden that he had spent 'Christmas eve at home and without [the National Scandinavian dish of] rice soup. In the night I went from one church to another, till one in the morning, to see and hear the masses. They can be compared with the cries of the fire brigade. Compared to them, our peasants' masses are angels' music. The music in the churches was very mediocre.'[1]

It will have become apparent by now that there were in Vienna hardly any public concerts in the manner of those in London when Haydn was there (1791–5). The only Viennese equivalent was the benefit concert. The artist hired one of the buildings available for the purpose, engaged an orchestra and possibly other soloists, printed an announcement in the *Wiener Zeitung*, and hoped that the public would come. The larger halls were the Burgtheater, which was very hard to get, the Redoutensaal, the Theater auf der Wieden (after 1801 the Theater an der Wien, too) and occasionally the Kärntnerthortheater. A typical benefit concert, put on by the soprano Maria Bolla in January, 1796, took place in the small room at the Redoutensaal and was directed by Haydn, with Beethoven at the piano. And Beethoven himself hired the Burgtheater in April, 1800, for his first Viennese benefit. A few days before, at the Court trumpeter Anton Weidinger's benefit concert in the Burgtheater, Haydn's Trumpet Concerto had been presented for the first time in public.

There were also smaller rooms at the artist's disposal. The famous old rooms in the Mehlgrube, on the Mehlmarkt, where Mozart used to conduct, were for some reason out of fashion. Another of Mozart's concert halls, the room of the Restaurant Jahn in the Himmelpfortgasse, was still in use; Mozart had performed his last Piano Concerto (B flat, K. 595) there in March 1791. Jahn's house, the 'Römischer Kaiser' (the Roman Emperor), had the reputation of being the best restaurant in town; in an article of 1808

1 *AMZ* III, 51; Thayer I, 346f.; Mörner, 311f.; the date for the C minor Mass by Mozart in Deutsch, *Mozart, Dokumente*, p. 194.

we read, 'One eats most brilliantly in Vienna at Jahn's, and then comes Munier.' Beethoven performed his Quintet, Op. 16, at a concert given at Jahn's in 1797.[1] Naturally, the artist had to do most of his propaganda by word of mouth. Constanze Mozart, when she gave her benefit concert in 1795, went round soliciting tickets. On 30 March Zinzendorf's Diary reads: 'Me Mozart a passé a une porte pour me prier de venir demain a son Concert' and the day afterwards the old Count went: 'Le soir au Concert pour la veuve Mozart, on y donna en oratorie La clemenza di Tito. Le lustre fait un bon effet au theatre,' was Zinzendorf's comment on that particular event.

The musical strength of Vienna lay not only among the nobility and whatever public concerts there were but of course among its many private citizens. In this connection we must again cite the Vienna correspondent of the *AMZ* (III, 65ff.) who devotes considerable space to this aspect of musical life in the city:

> There are few cities where love of music is so widespread as it is here. Everyone plays, everyone learns music. Naturally among all this great mass there are very good amateurs, but not so many as elsewhere. Music is taken too casually, as if it could be learned *en passant*; they think they can learn everything at once, and in the final analysis they excuse themselves with the word *amateur*, and the whole thing becomes more a matter of gallantry and good tone. But nevertheless there are here connoisseurs and friends of music *as an art*, and more than people seem to think abroad. The reason why there is less noise about them is perhaps that they themselves make no noise, addressing themselves to their goddess and to their delight in stillness. So-called private 'academies', that is, music in the fine houses, are given here in numberless quantity throughout the winter. There's no name-day, no birthday, on which music is lacking. There is not much to be said about such occasions, and nothing at all if it is not to sound comical. Most of them resemble each other rather closely. This is the way they look: first a quartet or a symphony, which is seen as a necessary evil (you've got to start with *something*), and during which one chats. Then comes one Fräulein after another and rolls off her piano sonata – and probably not without charm and grace – as best she can. Then others appear and sing some arias from the newest operas, in the same kind of performance. People are pleased; well, why not? And who has the right to mix into it, so long as the thing remains in the family? . . . Every proper girl, whether she has talent or not, has to learn the piano or singing; first, it's the mode; secondly (and here business enters into it) it's the easiest way to produce oneself in society and thus, if one is lucky, to attract attention and perhaps make a good match. The sons also have to learn music; first, because again it's the mode; secondly, because it helps them in fine society, too, and experience shows not a few (here, at least) have by their music caught a rich wife or a very satisfactory position. Students without any fortune earn their existence by music, they get grants and positions; if he wants to become a lawyer, he wins by playing music everywhere to a mass of acquaintances and clients; the same applies to the would-be doctor. . . . The fortune of travelling artists lies in the hands of these amateurs, who really lack sufficient knowledge and are moreover often prejudiced. Unless the outsider appears at every invitation, and flatters, finds talent everywhere as he praises, and so forth, the man must have the *greatest* reputation to penetrate *everywhere* successfully. If it should occur to him to settle here, the whole *corpus musicum* becomes his enemy. Here one has a high standard in judging virtuosi, since one has got to know so many of the very finest; and not without reason; but one has no opinion at all of those who do not measure up to the greatest, and that is not

1 Deutsch, *Mozart, Dokumente*, 339; Frimmel, *Beethoven-Handbuch*, I, 237f.; Zinzendorf Diary (MS.).

exactly encouraging. And this should be even less the case when one considers that there is not a single one among the local practising musicians who would win a competition – at least none among the violinists; only a Beethoven or a Wölffl, and they as pianists.

The article concludes that the economic situation of a musician in Vienna is not all that rosy – the article was published in 1800. Musicians have a bad name which they have earned for themselves with their crude manners, lack of education, and so on; thus they are often treated *de haut en bas* in the great houses. Of course there are exceptions among the musicians and, adds the writer, among the great houses, too. Times had changed, naturally, from Haydn's youth, when musicians had often been treated like servants, but it was still possible, in the *Wiener Zeitung* for 23 June 1798, to find the following notice:

Musical valet-de-chambre *wanted*

A musician is wanted, who plays the piano well and can sing as well, and is able to give lessons in both. This musician must also perform the duties of a *valet-de-chambre*. Whoever decides to accept the post is to ask in the first floor of the small Colloredo house No. 982 in the Weihburggasse.

So long as advertisements such as this could be printed, and the position filled, as it presumably was, it was difficult for the professional musician to escape being treated as a servant. The continual mixing of professional and amateur status, as happened at the Augarten and also in many private salons, greatly helped to make the social status of the professional musician less lowly.

If the writer of the *AMZ* is less than wildly enthusiastic about the state of amateur music-making in Vienna, our Swedish diplomat Silverstolpe has some devastating comments concerning the first musical impressions he received in the city, and on 4 June 1796 he writes:

. . . I have seen several *spectacles* [operas, plays] here, but without pleasure, for here they act very indifferently, horribly recited for a Swedish ear, tasteless and often miserably sung, and moreover the orchestra does not fulfil its duties well. There is much talk about concerts, but they are not given in this season. After one has heard Naumann's orchestra in Dresden, one becomes quite *difficile* as far as virtuosi go.

On 30 July of the same year we learn:

Haydn and Salieri are here. Albrechtsberger is alive, but up to now I have not been able to meet any of them. That will happen in the winter. Gluck's operas are regarded as unmodern. Of his works there is only a booklet with odes for sale, and that I bought.

Silverstolpe soon noticed the vast gap between the *haut monde* and the dialect-speaking plebeian world that flocked to Schikaneder's theatre. On 24 August 1796, the Swedish diplomat informs us:

. . . now I have seen *The Magic Flute* on the stage and also the subjects for whom Mozart wrote this piece. The music is excellent. However, the whole opera is put together in such a way that it would certainly have no success in a Swedish theatre. I do not wish that any effort along these lines is expended. We're not yet German enough (*hoc est* for the theatre). . . .

On 26 October 1796, Silverstolpe tells us about his invitations to the weekly open houses in Vienna:

> . . . One is invited to so-called *assemblées*. They consist of eight or ten persons who drink almond milk and say nothing. To preserve the amenities I attend these every third or fourth invitation and during the others I sit at home in my room. [The great banking] house of Arnstein's is the most interesting of them all. There one finds all the *savants*, all the geniuses, and a lot of experienced people and foreigners, from whom one can get some idea of other countries. With this house I am on very familiar terms and now and then I hear good piano music with singing. . . .

In a long passage about musical taste in Vienna, we read (9 November 1796):

> . . . Haydn is not yet in Vienna, but is expected for the winter, when I shall meet him and describe him to you. . . . Salieri, too, is still unknown to me, but that shan't be the case for long. . . . In general, this is not the place where one can hear the best music. Haydn has certainly adapted himself to the Viennese taste, which fluctuates between the tragic and the comic. Among all those whom I have heard play the piano there is not one whom I would dare to entrust with an Adagio from [Joseph Martin] Kraus's piano sonatas. Gluck's operas are never played here, and many people answered my questions along this line by saying that they must surely be in the old-fashioned taste. The *spectacles* deserve little praise. The music is miserably executed. The machinery consists of the human hand. There is not one single male singer, not one female singer, who can be tolerated. There are a few excellent actors for the drama, but many for Arlequin roles. The dance enjoys a greater place of esteem than anything else I've seen up to now.
>
> Moreover there are here among famous *musici* Albrechtsberger, organist and fugal composer, who has written an excellent book about his science and from whom Kraus learned counterpoint. [Later remark by the writer, who reread these letters years afterwards: 'wrong. His thorough knowledge of this science was older than his acquaintance with Albr.'] [Johann Baptist] Vanhal and [Court Composer Leopold] Kozeluch, the latter is also a music publisher, and Beethoven, who passes for the greatest performer on the piano. Weigl is the leading opera composer apart from Salieri. His best works are music for pantomimes. Right after Weigl comes Süssmayer [Mozart's pupil, who had completed the *Requiem*]. But I don't think that any one of these has a feeling for the sublime. That's also not necessary to be a success in Vienna. . . .

The writer of the much-quoted essay on Vienna for the *AMZ* also has some hard things to say about operatic life in the city. Although the article was published in 1800, obviously much of what he writes will have applied to 1795 as well. After discussing the Italian soloists, he continues:

> . . . The other Italian singers, male and female, are less important. The orchestra is not lacking in good people, but it very much lacks good will, unity, and love for the Art. This unegoistic love seems to be quite unknown to them, and therefore the orchestra is often bad in its ensemble. . . . In the double basses one would wish that they didn't, all five of them, have five-stringers [with the Contra C as lowest] and that the gentlemen were a little less comfortable. In great fortes one tends to hear scratchings and gruntings rather than the clear, penetrating bass tone which would elevate the whole level of playing. The director, Herr Conti, is not up to his job; it often happens that half the orchestra are substitutes, sent by the gentlemen when they have other engagements or pleasures: the effect can be imagined. The choice of operas is certainly not good: the old ones which are known to be good are seldom played, while the new ones, which as is well known could not be called good *en bloc* by any connoisseur, are often given. They procure them from Italy, on the recommendation of this or that member of the company, often because of a pretty role or even because of one brilliant aria. There are many operas given of

which they are convinced during the first rehearsal that they can't succeed. Should Herr Weigel be of the opinion that his own works will thus succeed better? . . .

[The reviewer discusses the German opera in Vienna, includes a rather negative criticism of the soloists and objects to the poor translation, poor performance, and poor acting in Mozart's *Figaro* and *Don Giovanni*. He then continues:] The choice of operas for such a group is really difficult; and very few new ones are given, except for small works by Süssmajer [*sic*] or [P.] Wranizky. The ones which are far better, without any comparison, by Mozart, Winter, and so on are seldom heard: Gluck, Naumann, Reichardt, Kunzen, and other good modern masters are never heard. In every respect, therefore, the German opera does not fulfil the expectations that one rightly had of it (in Germany's greatest, royal and imperial capital city!). The orchestra includes many less proficient members than that of the Italian opera; the salaries are too poor. And yet one often hears symphonies by Haydn, or now and then an opera by Mozart, much better played than in the other [Italian opera], a circumstance for which the worthy director, Herr Paul Wranizky, is largely responsible. That much the worse, however, fare the overtures and *entr'actes*, mostly ancient symphonies, during the comedies, under the slow conducting of Herr Reinhard. . . . [III, 41ff.]

So on the one hand we have the enthusiastic description of musical life in *fin-de-siècle* Vienna as we have seen it in Schindler; on the other, the negative comments of Silverstolpe and *AMZ*. Probably the truth lies somewhere in between. No doubt a concert conducted and rehearsed by Haydn or Beethoven (which of course Silverstolpe at this juncture had not yet heard) was light years away from a miserable German *Singspiel* hacked out in the suburbs to a brawling audience of proletarians, or a stiff *opera seria* by an Italian nonentity, produced by a bored cast and orchestra in the Burgtheater.

Before we leave Vienna and proceed to Eisenstadt and the Esterházy family in 1795, we would add a few words about the rise of the fortepiano in Vienna during this period. In *Haydn in England 1791–1795*[1] we have noted that Haydn brought back to Vienna a handsome Longman & Broderip 'Grand Forte Piano' with the additional keys. The usual compass of Continental instruments was *F′* to *f‴*; by the 1790s, an extra note *g‴* was often added. In the *Wiener Zeitung* of 28 February 1798 we read, 'Two grand Forte pianos, one of which goes to the G and has a Fagottzug [a "bassoon stop"] . . . for sale', and in that same paper two other pianos are offered for sale. When Haydn's new British instrument arrived in Vienna, it must have been one of the first to include the enlarged treble compass up to *c⁗* but also the *sopra una corda* pedal. Soon these British innovations were adopted by Viennese manufacturers.

The leading piano maker in Vienna was Anton Walter (Walther), whose shop was on the Windmühl, Haus 27. He had made Mozart's piano and serviced the instruments at Eszterháza Castle and was to construct a new piano for Eisenstadt in 1801. Beethoven owned one of his instruments in his early Viennese years. Walter's instruments were so well known that his name was specially mentioned if someone wished to sell one through the columns of the *Wiener Zeitung*. On 16 May 1798, we read: 'Forte piano and double harpsichord./Next to the Hohen Markt in the Krebsengassel at the Blue Crab No. 483 first floor is a large Forte piano and a double [manual] harpsichord for sale at a cheap price. Also a Walter pedal [attachment to a

1 See pp. 413–5.

piano such as Mozart used] made in cherry wood may be examined there, and is for sale.'

Beethoven, as early as 1796 when he was giving a concert in Pressburg, preferred the pianos by Stein, who in 1798 moved out to the Landstrasse suburb. The *Wiener Zeitung* for 12 May 1798 notes:

> *To lovers of the Forte piano*
>
> The Stein Brother and Sister have the honour to inform the music-loving public, that they have changed their previous place of residence. They ask their friends abroad and here to use the following address in future: 'An die *Geschwister* Stein [brother and sister Stein], Clavier und Forte piano-Macher von Augsburg, wohnhaft auf der Landstraße zu Anfang der Ungargasse im Goldspinnerhaus Nr. 376.'

As the nineteenth century drew nearer, the pianists and the piano manufacturers exerted a beneficial influence on each other. We find Beethoven writing to Johann Andreas Streicher (who married Nanette Stein and took over her long-established factory) from Pressburg on 19 November 1796: 'I very much hope that the merits of your instruments will be recognized both here and everywhere.' In another letter to Streicher, he says: 'Undoubtedly, the manner of playing the piano is as yet the least developed form of instrumental playing. One often imagines one is listening to a harp, and I am happy, my dear friend, that you are one of the few who realize and feel that one can also sing on the piano, so long as one has feeling. I hope that the time will come when the harp and the piano will be regarded as two completely different instruments. . . .'

Later, in 1801, Haydn was to receive a beautiful piano from Erard in Paris, and we shall find Beethoven taking various Viennese piano builders to see the new Erard in Gumpendorf. Partly through the influence of Haydn's Longman & Broderip and Erard instruments, Viennese pianos began to change rapidly after the new century began. We soon find Beethoven specifying the entrancing new *sopra una corda* effect in his compositions; Haydn had required it in his English C major Sonata No. 60 (50) of 1795. And in 1802 we find Silverstolpe buying a Walter piano with the new *sopra una corda* device: 'the invention was made in England a long time ago, but it has only now been imitated here' (letter of 5 June 1802). Haydn was still composing piano trios – though no more piano sonatas – at this period and was thus taking an active part in the pianistic life of the city. In 1795 and 1796 he composed his last five Piano Trios (Nos. 41–5),[1] most of which he published abroad.

1 Mörner, 390; Landon, *Beethoven*, 92f., 95. Horst Walter, 'Haydns Klaviere', in *Haydn-Studien* II/4 (1970), pp. 256f.; H. C. Robbins Landon, 'Haydn's Pianos', in *The Listener*, 20 July 1972, pp. 90ff.

CHAPTER TWO

Eisenstadt and the Esterházys in 1795

THE FOURTH REIGNING PRINCE ESTERHÁZY under whom Haydn served was Nicolaus II, son of Prince (Paul) Anton[1] Esterházy, who had died in January 1794, and his first wife, Maria Theresia, Countess von Erdödy, a name frequently encountered in this volume of our biography. Nicolaus II was born on 12 December 1765 and, before his eighteenth birthday, married to Maria (Marie) Josepha Hermenegild, Princess von Liechtenstein (15 September 1783).

Prince Nicolaus was passionately interested in the theatre, and engaged troupes of players to perform at Eisenstadt in the summer and autumn of nearly every year in the 1790s; later he became connected with the Vienna Court Theatre as well. In his love for the theatre, then, he very much took after his grandfather, the great Nicolaus I 'The Magnificent'. Nicolaus II was well educated, spoke and wrote several languages, and one of the first things he did was to purchase Count Neuperg's library in 1795, thus greatly enriching the Esterházy family library; he was also interested in medals, snail shells and samples of minerals, all of which he collected for Eisenstadt. His particular attention, however, was devoted to the Esterházy picture gallery. Upon his accession, he found the gallery more or less in the same state in which it had been bequeathed to his father by Nicolaus I. Apart from the 'Esterházy Madonna', there were few really valuable masterpieces. First, Nicolaus II collected at Eisenstadt all the important pictures and engravings from his many remote castles; then he himself began to collect, using the services of Joseph Fischer as his collaborator; 'with his assistance,' writes the Hungarian scholar, Mátyás Horányi, 'he succeeded in creating one of the most beautiful and comprehensive collections of paintings and engravings in the entire Monarchy. This is the collection which was to serve as the basis of the Museum of Fine Arts in Budapest.'

The librarian and archivist of these collections was to be the poet and scholar, Georg von Gáal. Nicolaus was often very generous with visiting artists and entertained them handsomely in Eisenstadt, for instance, the famous sculptor Antonio Canova, the Austrian painter Johann Carl Rössler (who came to Eisenstadt in 1799 and painted Haydn's and Rosenbaum's portraits), and the young artist Isidor Neugass, who painted Haydn's portrait in 1805. Neugass delivered the painting to Prince Esterházy on 7 December 1806, was given 500 gulden by the Prince and promised a monthly stipendium of 50 gulden per month for the artist's further studies; in 1806

1 He is usually referred to as Anton, to distinguish him from Haydn's first Esterházy, Prince Paul Anton (died 1762), who was our Anton's uncle.

he painted the so-called Brunsvik portrait of Beethoven (reproduced for the first time in colour in Landon, *Beethoven*, 235).

Nicolaus's interest in music was principally in connection with the Church – a rather odd touch to his character, considering his broad humanistic education on the one hand, and his wildly licentious behaviour on the other (*vide infra*). Like his sovereign and lord the Emperor Franz, Nicolaus's taste in church music was decidedly conservative: he preferred Michael Haydn, the old Reutter (Haydn's teacher), Bonno, and Preindl; but he also engaged most of the leading composers to compose church music for Eisenstadt, such as Gyrowetz (at least three Masses and a large quantity of smaller church music, including 'Vespers Solemnes composées et dediées à son altesse serenissime le prince regnard d'Esterházi', mostly composed in the 1790s and all in MS., some autograph, in the Esterházy Archives at Eisenstadt), two Vespers and a Mass by Albrechtsberger (which Haydn rehearsed in 1802), several works by Michael Haydn and the Mass in C by Beethoven (1807). But if Nicolaus inherited his grandfather's love of the theatre, he did not inherit his understanding of music; all the earlier biographies are unanimous in asserting this. Actually we have one contemporary piece of evidence which is quite definitive: a private letter from Joseph to his brother Michael Haydn in Salzburg. Michael had been offered two positions: one as his brother's successor in Eisenstadt, and one with the Grand Duke of Tuscany. Finally, after much deliberation, Michael decided to remain in Salzburg. Joseph wrote to him on 22 January 1803:

> . . . Your decision, of which you wrote me, concerning his Royal Highness the Archduke [and Grand Duke of Tuscany] and my Prince, is well thought out and bold, but it must cause not only me but the whole world regret. Neither side can reproach you for having done anything wrong. Both are great, but the Archduke's love and understanding for music are greater than those of my Prince: your heart and your brain must make the decision here, to which of the two you give the preference. . . .

It would be happy to chronicle that Haydn's late years were spent in the employ of a prince whose instinct for music was of the kind shown by Nicolaus I; but alas, quite the opposite obtained. Not only was the new prince basically unmusical, but personal relations between Haydn and him were, at the beginning, strained. This was hardly a secret in Vienna or Eisenstadt, particularly since the whole Esterházy band knew it. But the earliest biographies – Dies, Griesinger, Carpani – do not breathe a word of this stiffness between *Capellmeister* and *Serenissima*. They could hardly do so: Dies was princely landscape painter, Griesinger was in diplomatic service in Vienna, and Carpani would have been very ill-advised to cross swords with the mighty Prince Esterházy (who lived on till 1833). It was indeed many years before anyone dared to reveal the truth. One of the first was Franz Lorenz, an Austrian doctor, who published interesting articles on Mozart and a study entitled 'Haydn, Mozart und Beethoven's Kirchenmusik' (Breslau 1866), for the research of which he interviewed former members of the Haydn orchestra who were living in retirement in Eisenstadt. Pohl never completed volume three of his biography, but he, too, interviewed such men as Michael Prinster (1783–1869), one of Haydn's horn players at Eisenstadt; and Botstiber's completion of the Pohl biography, with all its information on Nicolaus II and Haydn, is from Pohl's notes and thus based on some first-hand information.

The most revealing story concerns an orchestral rehearsal, probably *c.* 1795–6, which Haydn was conducting. The Prince came in and criticized something. Haydn said to him, in front of the whole orchestra, 'Your Highness, that is my business.' The Prince, white with fury, left the room. Another episode concerns the mode of address used by the Prince, in which Haydn was still referred to by the lackey's 'Er' (third person singular, e.g. 'He will conduct a symphony tomorrow'). The Doctor of Oxford University who had chatted *tête-à-tête* with the King and Queen of England protested, and it appears that he used the kind offices of Princess Marie, with whom he was always on the best of terms and to whom he had *in absentia* dedicated three piano trios while in England. As time went on, relations between the two men improved; but at best Nicolaus was a difficult and not very sympathetic man.[1]

As to his opinion of Haydn's music, we know very little. But we have a shocking example of his taste in a letter written to one of his countless mistresses, Countess Henriette von Zielinska, after the first performance of Beethoven's Mass in C, Op. 86 at Eisenstadt in September 1807: 'La messe de Beethoven est insupportablement ridicule et detestable, je ne suis pas convainçu qu'elle puisse même paroitre honêtement: j'en suis coleré et honteux. Gulistan [opera by Dalayrac] a été bien joué, viola nos raports. . . .'

The Duchess of Södermanland, Hedvig Charlotta, describes Nicolaus in her Diary as a 'gambler and dissolute *bon vivant*', the first hint of this lecherous side to his complicated nature. The Princess 'behaves in a ridiculously haughty fashion, but is nevertheless quite pleasant'. Her brother, the Prince von Liechtenstein, 'has the most curious taste. He is totally lacking in education, is never properly dressed and goes round like a coachman. . . .' Countess Lulu von Thürheim thought Princess Marie Hermenegild rather pathetic, clinging to her lovers long after they had lost interest. The Esterházy's daughter, Leopoldine, married to Moritz von Liechtenstein, was thought to be the most beautiful woman of her age.

Certainly the most interesting first-hand report on the Esterházy family and Eisenstadt is contained in the Diary of Frances, Lady Shelley, who visited the Castle in September 1816. She came to Eisenstadt from the Castle of Kittsee, where in the early 1760s Haydn and the orchestra had played for Prince Nicolaus I, who used this Castle, one of his many, when he had extended business to attend to in Pressburg, which lay on the other side of the Danube. Lady Shelley writes:

> Kitsie [*sic*]. The road passed fine avenues, until the château of Kitsie, standing on a bare plain without a tree near it, stared at us bleak and desolate.
>
> On this side of the plain herds of Hungarian horses were feeding; but on the other side lay land from which the corn had been carried, and which had been freshly ploughed. This looked as dismal as anything I ever saw in Norfolk.
>
> Never was a château so ill placed. It was built by the Prince's grandfather [Nicolaus I], merely to be inhabited for one week in the two years, during the time when the States of Hungary are assembled at Pressbourg. This immense house is so much surrounded by trees that it ought to be lighted by skylights. . . .
>
> September 16 [1816]. The Princess Esterházy, whom I did not know, and who does not live well with the Prince, sent to invite me to Eisenstadt. We set off one evening after dinner [from Kittsee], and arrived at eight o'clock. There were

1 We are fortunate in having Neukomm's authority for the 'Er' mode of address. In the *Bemerkungen*, we read p. 29) '. . . H. told me that after his return journey from his second sojourn in England, the then Prince Esterh[ázy] (husband of the Princess [about whom Dies has been talking]) addressed Haydn with the mode of address "Er" which at that time had not yet quite disappeared; about which Haydn in his rightful indignation objected to the high-minded Princess, and asked her to let the Prince understand that Haydn, now a Doctor of Music from the University of Oxford, should not be treated like a lackey. This plan worked, and the Prince always called his Kapellm. from then on '*Herr von Haydn*'.'

guards at the entrance of the courtyard, and the beating of drums marked a truly princely residence. The château was brilliantly lighted, and, after we had passed through twenty rooms, the Princess came to meet me in a corridor leading to a theatre, which had been fitted up in a large salon that was filled with people [the Great Hall, now known as the Haydnsaal]. On my inquiring if there was any town from whence this large society came, the Princess informed me that they were all *employés de la maison*. The Prince is, in fact, a sovereign Prince. The Princess has been very handsome, but is now near fifty, not in very good health, and has bad teeth. She told me that she was married to the Prince at fifteen, having seen him only once before, he being at that time seventeen years of age. On the day after they were married the Prince set off on his travels with his governor, while she remained under the tutelage of her governess! Can one be surprised at the misery which results from such marriages? Is it surprising that he should have a hundred mistresses, and she a lover? It seems that her lover has lately put her in despair by marrying at sixty-five. The late Empress [Marie Therese] was her great friend, and she talks of her with affection, while tears spring to her eyes. . . . She kissed me so often, and made me so many compliments, that I never was so sleepy in my life. . . . There were guards at every corner of the staircase and passages, presenting arms as we passed. . . . She talks incessantly, and hopes that you are not bored by her asking questions without waiting for an answer! It is evident that she wishes so much to please, and to be amiable, that it is impossible not to be interested and pleased by her.

. . . With all the magnificence of this château, I never slept in so bad a bed. Its curtains are of silk, and the whole furniture of my apartment is superb, but the bed is as hard as iron. . . . The moment I awoke, the Prince sent his compliments to me, and hoped that I would receive him as soon as I was dressed. . . . [She describes a hunting party, and there was a concert in the evening. As for the castle itself, she notes:] At present the antique Moslem-like towers clash unpleasantly with the simplicity of the new part, and disturb the repose which the architect [Moreau] has been particularly happy in seizing in his Grecian architecture.

The Prince is a perfect Sultan, and possesses ten or twelve houses, inhabited by different ladies, who share his favours and diminish his faculties.

I am struck by the change in his manners since I met him in England. Here he is ostentatious, haughty, sleepy, and dull. Not with us, however, for his adoration of the English makes him court us beyond measure. His haughtiness and dullness are reserved for the people who surround him. . . .

In the days of his glory he had a Court, like a sovereign Prince. The Princess had her Circle, where her subjects, from the different estates, assembled to kiss her hand. The Prince used to go to church [in the Bergkirche] surrounded by his guard. He rode on horseback through the church, to the door of his tribune, where he sat in solitary grandeur. The Princess also sat alone in her tribune opposite. The officers of the guard occupied another, and the visitors had another to themselves. All this was a good deal ridiculed by those who considered themselves his equals; and as the Prince has not been particularly fortunate either in a military or in a diplomatic career, having failed in both, he is not liked; and his low intrigues prevent his being respected. As a consequence, he hates Vienna, abuses his fellow country-men, and passes his time in rambling from one fine estate to another. He always winters in Italy. . . .

Vienna . . . The usual hour of dining is four o'clock. At about half-past five the company is increased by the arrival of evening visitors, who remain about an hour. Then they go to the theatre, or to a *soirée*.

[Description of the Esterházys at a ball:] Prince Esterházy's dress (for be it observed, the wearing of jewels is not confined to the women) was that of the

> captain of the Hungarian *Garde-noble*. It consisted of scarlet cloth, embroidered from head to foot in pearls. The tops of his yellow boots, and his spurs, were set with diamonds. His cloak, lined with the finest fur, was fastened with a magnificent cluster of diamonds, so also were the belt, sword-knot, the handle and scabbard of his sword. A heron's feather and aigrette of diamonds rose from his fur cap, whose loops, like his sabre-tache, were of pearls and diamonds. He and others told me that his dress that day [10 November 1816] was worth more than one million pounds sterling, and yet he had not on his person more than a quarter of the family diamonds, which have been collecting for centuries. . . . Princess Esterházy's [jewels] are considered the finest in Germany, and far superior to those belonging to the crown.[1]

An English woman, Martha Wilmot (Mrs Bradford), has left her impressions of a name-day celebration for Princess Marie Hermenegild in a letter from Vienna of 4 May 1820. The party was given by Princess Menchikoff.

> . . . It began with a concert, and verses for the occasion of her *Names day* [*sic*] were sung. All the party then repaired to another Saloon, the Princess Esterházy was seated in the midst of the Circle, when a curtain drew up, and three most elegant little girls came forward with wreathes of roses, and after dancing and twining their wreathes so as to form all the letters of her name they grouped themselves most gracefully, and dropping on one knee presented her with a Bouquet of roses, within which she found a copy of verses composed for the occasion. After this they danced some beautiful dances and then advanced a second time with an enormous basket of roses which was laid at her feet. I believe she did not know what in the name of fortune to do with all the *rosy gifts* when behold, up sprung from the base a little Cupid, and flinging the garlands aside, appeared before the *astonished* Princess with all the beauty and all the *danger* of his Profession, to do hommage to her (once) celebrated charms!!! Is not this very foreign? After this was over we returned to the concert room, where *showers* of ices, cakes, bon-bons and refreshments of all sorts, made the running base to a concert rather too much prolonged for pleasure. At last the supper was announced, and then you might have seen assembled Hungarians, Austrians, Moldavian and Georgian Princesses, Polish Princes, Italians – Princes and Princesses reignante – others who had not a Mouse to reign over – a Bourbon – a Chineese [*sic*] Consul – a Pope's Nuncio and an English Clergyman. . . . [*More Letters from Martha Wilmot: Impressions of Vienna 1819–1829*, ed. the Marchioness of Londonderry and H. M. Hyde; London 1935, p. 62]

Mutatis mutandis, Haydn must have witnessed, indeed participated in, many such festive name-day celebrations at Eisenstadt Castle.

We learn of one of Esterházy's seduction-houses from Zinzendorf's diary. On 7 August 1795, a week before Haydn left London for good, the Count relates: '. . . De la chez la P[csse] Auersberg [Auersperg] qui part demain pour Goldegg. Son pere nous

1 A Hungarian-language newspaper (*Magyar Hirmondó* 1802, No. 1, *para. XXI*; see Emile Haraszti in *La Revue Musicale* XIII 1932, p. 90) describes Prince Nicolaus's arriving at Court in 1802 as follows: 'Nicolas Eszterházy [*sic*] performed a dancing step on his marvellous dappled horse. On his riding-cap alone there gleamed about 100,000 gulden of diamonds in marvellous congregation. His hussar's pelisse, his doublet, his breeches are embellished with innumerable fine pearls aranged in large designs: the buttons are emeralds, diamonds or fine pearls. The pommel, sabre's sheath, are covered on two sides with diamonds to astonish the eye. The half-belt that holds the hussar's pelisse is made of large diamonds and pearls the whiteness of snow. The flaps of his boots, his brandebourgs, his spurs also gleam with jewels. The prince was followed by his noble guard, panther skins thrown over their shoulders. The cortège was closed by an empty carriage drawn by six horses.'

conta des details du jardin de P[ce] Esterhazy sur la Landstrasse dans le quel il y a un temple dedié a la debauche, des figures obscenes, des lits de repos qui survienent inopinément [?]; des echap[p]atoires, puis des canaux, des points, des trailles, le temple seul a couté 2500 florins. . . .' The next morning Zinzendorf strengthened himself with a cold bath in the Danube and then made off for the delights of Esterházy's 'maison' in the Landstrasse: 'Bain froid du Danube. Dela par Erdberg a la Landstrasse du P[ce] Esterházy.' The Count noted that the garden used to belong to Prince von Paar, then to a M. Zwereiz, and described in loving detail everything he saw in the temple: two Egyptian pillars which turn out to be, respectively, a gigantic penis and a female sex organ ('Quand on les côte, on voit d'un coté un grand priape, de l'autre les parties naturelles de la femme'), a bedroom that one reached through a revolving fireplace; the bedroom was decorated with frescoes and was made to look like a tent; and in the tent there was still another alcove with a day-bed in it and a curtain that could be drawn. One could leave by a secret door. Outside the temple, as we have seen, were canals, bridges, a trail-ferry and so forth.

As it happens, we have a fairly complete record of how a prince such as Esterházy managed to collect all the necessary girls for his various enterprises: the notorious case of Aloys Prince zu Kaunitz-Rietberg, who seduced numbers of girls in a systematic, business-like fashion by making contracts with the girl's parents. During his trial, Kaunitz plaintively said that there were others who did such seductions on the grand scale, such as Esterházy; but Nicolaus was perhaps more careful. Kaunitz used the children's ballet as a rich source, and Haydn must have seen – and at least in one case under his very nose – how the *Hochwohlgebohrner Reichsfürst und Herr Herr* bought a child from the Tomasini family. The late Gustav Gugitz published for private circulation a pamphlet on the Kaunitz trials and on Ferdinand Raimund's wife Louise, *née* Gleich; and in the Kaunitz trial files he discovered that the Prince also bought one of Johann Elssler's daughters. (Elssler, it will be recalled, was Haydn's faithful servant and copyist; the family lived at the house in Gumpendorf.) One of the daughters was Fanny, the world-famous dancer; another one, Theresia, born on 5 April 1808, was sold to Kaunitz. At first the Prince wanted to 'salary' (*salarieren*) her, as he explained to Johann Elssler, in his flat; but later he rented for the family – this was another form of his payments for deflowering the girls – an apartment of three rooms and three 'closets' (*Kammern*) in Bretfeldhaus in the inner city. In that flat, as Theresia later explained to the authorities, she gave herself to Kaunitz 'because she was attracted to him' (*aus Neigung*). Later she was married morganatically to Prince Adalbert of Prussia.

The other case began in Haydn's own house. The court records say that Kaunitz met Elisabeth Anna Tomasini (born 8 July 1788, at Eszterháza and the youngest daughter of Haydn's leader, Luigi Tomasini) at Haydn's house. Lisette, as she was called, was a member of the church choir at Eisenstadt, which she had joined in 1807. Haydn and the painter Basilius Grundmann had been her god-parents. Prince Nicolaus sent her to Vienna to learn singing and piano from good masters, but she proved difficult and, in October 1810, she was dismissed. When Prince Kaunitz tried to buy her, she also proved difficult (*störrig*), despite his strenuous efforts and financial promises; she married but became a widow, returned to Vienna in 1820 and finally succumbed to Kaunitz's charms.

If Kaunitz became infamous because his case was brought to trial and he was expelled from the country, Esterházy's was just as well known to the *cognoscenti* and of course to the Eisenstadt musicians including their old *Capellmeister* Haydn. And in all of this, what of the beautiful and vivacious Princess Marie Hermenegild?

Much of her husband's 'mistress operations' (*Maitressenwirtschaft*) went on with the full knowledge of the Court personnel. In the Esterházy Archives (Budapest), there is the following letter dated 26 May 1810, from Nicolaus to his son Paul:

> In haste! When Frau von Kemmitzer has her child, have it baptized in my name! Nicolaus Paulus, if it's a boy; Leopoldine Henriette, if it's a girl! I will write Frau v. Kemmitzer with the next courier. The expenses are to be handsomely paid! N. E.

The Princess, as we have seen, talked incessantly, had many lady friends among the aristocracy, took the occasional lover, and wrote large amounts of poetry in German, French, English, and Italian, with the titles such as 'Liebesschmerz', 'Glaube und Hoffnung', 'Pein der Sünde', 'Liebesqualen' – Höllenpein', 'Gebet (um inneren Frieden)' – shades of late Beethoven and the *Missa Solemnis!* – , 'La Piété', 'Joy', 'Mio primo amico'.

Die Träne

Im Winter, wo die Welt ringsher
So schauerlich erblichen,
Ist eine Träne trüb und schwer
Ins Auge mir geschlichen.
Die Welt erwacht aus ihrem Tod,
Der Winter ist vertrieben –
Ich rieb meine Augen feuerrot:
Die Tränen sind geblieben . . .
Vergebens wird sich Baum und Flur
Mit Frühlingsschimmer schmücken,
Ich kann die blühende Natur
Durch Tränen nur erblicken.
Ich dachte, was ich all'gestrebt
Und was mir alles mißlungen,
Und wie ich – ewig glutbelebt –
Doch nie ein Ziel errungen!
Ich fühlte, wie es schmerzt und brennt,
Dies ewig leere Streben –
Mein Denken war ein Monument
auf ein verfehltes Leben.
Mein Dasein ist so öd und leer,
Und alles Glück entwichen –
Da sind die Thränen trüb und schwer
Ins Auge mir geschlichen. . . .

In another document in the Esterházy Archives, she writes: 'Heil dem, dessen letzte Liebe alle Schulden der früheren bezahlt! Aber was bleibt der armen Verlassenen? Der Rest des Lebens ist zu kurz zu neuen Hoffnungen, und das Herz zu arm zum Vergessen und zu tief verwundet.' (Hail to him, whose last love has paid all the debts of the earlier ones! But what is left to the poor and abandoned one? The rest of life is too short for new hopes, and the heart too poor to forget and too deeply wounded.)

In 1804, Beethoven dedicated to Princess Marie Hermenegild his Three Marches for piano four hands, Op. 45 (Kunst- und Industrie-Comptoir, Vienna), which he had probably composed some years earlier. Beethoven undoubtedly came to the Princess's attention through Haydn.

Later, the Princess became the mistress of Baron Salomon Mayer von Rothschild

(1774–1855), to whom were entrusted the chaotic financial affairs of the Esterházy family; Prince Nicolaus's wild and dissolute life had brought to the edge of the abyss the fortune so carefully enlarged by his grandfather. Can the prose note quoted above ('paid all the debts') refer to Rothschild? This 'monument to a mistaken life' lived on until 1845; she, like Haydn, was seventy-seven when she died.[1]

Of the many other members of the mighty Esterházy family, we would mention two who played a significant role in Viennese musical society. The first is Johann Nepomuk, Count Esterházy 'of the middle line [branch] zu Frakno', born on 15 February 1754, and since 1778 married to Agnes, Countess von Banffy; he was Privy Councillor (*geheimer Hofrat*) and *Kämmerer* in the Royal Siebenbürgen Court Chancery, and formerly Master of the Masonic Lodge 'Zur gekrönten Hoffnung' in Vienna (the Masons were banned in Austria by an edict of 2 January 1795, part of the general trend against all French-inspired free-thinking). Count Johann had been a patron of Mozart's and was himself an oboe player.[1]

Count Franz Esterházy de Galantha, also a Privy Councillor and later Austrian Ambassador to the Court of Naples, was some ten years younger than Johann and also an ardent music lover, particularly of older music.[2]

No one could call the huge Esterházy Castle at Eisenstadt handsome: imposing might be the best word for it. Unlike many other Austrian castles, the rebuilding of

1 Pohl III, 106–9; Horányi, 159; a small collection of Prince Nicolaus's autograph letters in French and Italian (1792 *et seq.*) in the Campori Coll., Biblioteca Estense, Modena; on Neugass, Pohl III, 251 (Haydn painting reproduced in Somfai, 201); on Gyrowetz, MGG (Landon); on Albrechtsberger, CCLN 206; Radant, *Rosenbaum*, 17 *et passim*; Haydn's letter to his brother, CCLN 214; Haydn's rehearsal and Nicolaus leaving room in Pohl I, 225; Esterházy's letter to Zielinska in J. Harich, 'Beethoven in Eisenstadt', special supplement from the *Burgenländische Heimatblätter*, Eisenstadt 1959, 21. Jg., No. 2, pp. 173ff. Mörner, 337 (Duchess of Södermanland). *The Diary of Frances, Lady Shelley 1787–1817*, ed. Richard Edgcumbe, London 1912, pp. 289ff. On Kittsee in Haydn's earlier career: Landon, *Das kleine Haydnbuch*, Salzburg, 2nd ed. 1972, p. 40. Gustav Gugitz, *Die Ehetragödie Ferdinand Raimunds, nach den unveröffentlichen Akten des Wiener Stadtgerichtes im Archiv der Stadt Wien* (privately printed for the Wiener Bibliophilen-Gesellschaft), Vienna 1956, esp. pp. 26, 30. Zinzendorf Diary (MS.). J. Harich, 'Das Haydn-Orchester im Jahre 1780', *Haydn Yearbook* VIII (1971), pp. 12f. A. C. Kalischer, in *Beethovens Frauenkreis* (vols. II and III of *Beethoven und seine Zeitgenossen*, Berlin–Leipzig *c.* 1908–10), article on Princess Marie. Frau Gerda Gräser of Leipzig was kind enough to send us the MS. of her new (and unpublished) book on Beethoven which contains Prince Nicolaus' letter of 1810 and the Princess's poetry.

Another interesting and authentic view of Prince Nicolaus Esterházy's dubious musical education comes from Haydn's successor, the princely *Kapellmeister* Johann Nepomuk Hummel, former pupil of Mozart's who had played at one of the Haydn–Salomon concerts in 1792. Hummel was asked repeatedly to provide compositions as part of his salary as Esterházy *Kapellmeister*, i.e. without additional fee. Hummel answered this and other requests and objections which the Prince made in 1811. In October 1811, Hummel wrote 'Answer to nine questions'. Among other things he notes: 'Whether the Prince likes my compositions (as he pretends) or not is no proof that my works are valuable or not . . . Since the Prince is no connoisseur of music, he is not able to judge a work of art. . . .' In another document he suggests that the Prince ask an outside opinion from Salieri or 'Breindl' (Preindl, then Cathedral Chapel Master at St Stephen's), 'who as the most famous men at present resident in this capital city are each well known in their field and respected.' Hummel lists all the works he composed for the Prince, including five Masses, many smaller church works and three operas. Esterházy dismissed Hummel shortly after this exchange of letters. See *Johann Nepomuk Hummel – Komponist der Goethe-Zeit und sein Sohn Carl – Landschaftsmaler des späten Weimar*. Eine Austellung im Goethe-Museum-Düsseldorf, Aug.–Oct. 1971: Catalogue, pp. 15f.

2 Thayer I, 354; Deutsch, *Mozart Dokumente*, 197; *Hof- und Staats-Schematismus* 1795 *et seq. Genealogisches Taschenbuch der deutschen gräflichen Häuser auf das Jahr 1837*, Gotha, p. 172 (hereinafter 'Gotha' and the year, e.g. 'Gotha 1837, 172). 'Unsere Brüder im 18. Jahrhundert', section III: 'Das Ende der Oesterreichischen Freimauerei im 18. Jahrhundert', in *Fünf Jahre [der Loge] Libertas*, Vienna 1965, p. 51.

3 *Schematismus*; *Jahrbuch der Tonkunst für Wien und Prag 1796*, p. 703, says Esterházy gives 'larger and splendid concerts', mentioning as typical works performed Handel choruses, the C. P. E. Bach *Heilig* and the *Stabat Mater* by Pergolesi.

which from medieval fortress to Baroque castle to Rococo palace was accomplished with a certain amount of flair, the Esterházy Castle remained a compromise. In the seventeenth century, it had been given its Baroque appearance, with the characteristic onion towers and the new façade, containing eighteen busts of Hungarian military leaders which the sculptor Matthias Mayr delivered in 1667.

Prince Nicolaus 'The Magnificent' had hardly used Eisenstadt except as a central administrative headquarters; his attention had been devoted to Eszterháza Castle. But Prince Anton and Prince Nicolaus II lived many months of the year in Eisenstadt and they began to rebuild the Castle. In December, 1790, the construction of the balcony was begun, and in 1793 the handsome princely stables with their classical colonnades were designed by the Viennese architect, Henrizy, and built opposite the front of the Castle. The onion domes were demounted, the old medieval moat filled in, and the garden side was radically transformed, beginning in 1794, by the architect Charles de Moreau. His plans for the complete reconstruction survive, and if they had been put into effect, Eisenstadt would have had a beautiful Castle; as it is, the wings to the right and left of the main central building – they were to have housed the picture gallery and the theatre – were never finished. The garden was transformed into an English park, under the senior gardener, Matthias Pölt; classical temples, ponds and hidden groves sprang up, including the pretty Leopoldine Temple, decorated with a statue of Princess Leopoldine (Marie Hermenegild and Nicolaus's daughter) by none other than Canova. In the Grand Hall (now Haydnsaal), decorated with frescoes by the princely painter Friedrich Rohde, Nicolaus II was, on 24 June 1794, officially installed. 'The weather,' reports Rosenbaum, 'was most unfavourable: a terrible cloud-burst raged in the theatre, garden and moat, and about the triumphal arches that had been erected. . . .' Superstitious people will have wondered. . . .

The town of Eisenstadt, situated a comfortable half-day's carriage journey from Vienna (fifty-one kilometres away), was a 'free Reichstadt' and was then part of Hungary. The town was dominated by the Castle, of course, but had its own rather attractive market square, behind which was the large parish church (Stadtpfarrkirche) of St Martin in Gothic style, whose great, square tower recalled the days when the Turks had overrun Hungary. The Princes Esterházy had founded a ghetto directly behind the Castle and protected the Jews; further up the hill was the suburb of Oberberg, whose citizens were subjects of the Esterházys. Between the Castle and the Cavalry Church (Bergkirche) was the Hospital of the Brothers of Mercy (Barmherzige Brüder), for whose tiny chapel with its *positiv* organ Haydn is thought to have composed the *Missa brevis S. Joannis de Deo* (St John of God, Patron Saint of the Order). There was also a monastery below the Castle, run by Franciscan monks, in which were the Fürstengrüfte, or princely tombs. The Castle itself had a small chapel, with an organ and small organ loft, but contrary to the statement of the late German scholar, E. F. Schmid, there is no evidence that Haydn's large-scale Masses were first given in the private chapel, but rather in the Bergkirche.

The 'Mountain Church' was part of a double edifice on the hill of Oberberg (top of the hill or mountain), the corner stone of which was laid in 1701. Next to it was the hemispherical Mount of Cavalry, from which pilgrims could, at the top, obtain a striking view of the Hungarian plains stretching towards Oedenburg (Sopron). The Bergkirche is a typical Eisenstadt edifice – a curious and not very successful architectural conglomeration. But its organ loft is enormous and the interior, where the Prince sat on a dais on one side and the Princess on another, is not unimpressive. Here, as Rosenbaum's Diary notes, five of Haydn's last six Masses were first given.

The organ in the Bergkirche was made by J. G. Malleck of Vienna; it replaced the older 'Werner' (taking the name of Haydn's predecessor, Gregor Werner, who had died in 1766) organ. Malleck also designed the new organ for the Stadtpfarrkirche in 1778. Both instruments are restored and are in excellent working condition, though the two-manual keyboard of the 'Haydn organ' was replaced by a three-manual one; the original keyboard was piously preserved, however, and is shown to visitors.

Since the Castle housed a huge number of offices, half the town consisted of princely administration buildings and apartments for the officials and their families. At one time, Haydn had owned a house in the Klostergasse (today: Joseph-Haydn-Gasse) but it had been twice badly damaged by fire, in 1768 and 1776 (though rebuilt with assistance from Prince Nicolaus I), and in 1778 Haydn had sold it. When he came to Eisenstadt in the 1790s he could make use of a princely apartment in one of the buildings near the Castle.

Haydn was on friendly terms with the *Regens chori* of the parish church of St Martin, Carl Kraus, who died in 1802 and whose music collection, as we shall see, was incorporated in the Esterházy Archives upon Haydn's advice. The archives of the parish church show much interchange between the princely musicians, many of whom had been composers in Nicolaus I's reign, and the *Regens chori*. In the period under discussion, we note that Carl Kraus even managed to put on the new *Missa in tempore belli*, of which the parish church archives owns a copy he made (and one which is textually rather interesting, as we shall see when the time comes to examine the music itself). It is entirely possible that Haydn conducted the occasional performance at the Stadtpfarrkirche, as far as his time-consuming duties as Esterházy *Capellmeister* permitted.[1]

The Esterházy Castle at Eisenstadt was the scene of many fabulous celebrations in the years when Haydn was princely *Capellmeister*, and the ensuing Chronicle will provide us with many eye-witness reports of these long-forgotten *feste*. But not everyone saw the Castle and its proprietor in the rosy light of the *Wiener Zeitung*, *Pressburger Zeitung* or Rosenbaum. In 1828, at any rate, Eisenstadt made a very unfavourable impression on Martha Wilmot, one of whose letters from Vienna has been quoted, *supra*.

> 26th [September, 1828].
>
> . . . Eisenstadt, Prince Esterhazy's celebrated Chateau, surrounded by lands, woods, and every possible luxury, save that of good taste was our next station. The town is a very poor one, ill-paved and dirty. Even the Chateau stands in a square the pavement of which is enough to break the springs of a carriage, altogether it was very desolate looking, and grass grew (amidst the stones and large flags) before the door. . . . We quitted [the Convent of the Franciscan monks where they had spent the night] the next morning, 27th, to see Prince Esterházy's Chateau, which disappointed us most exceedingly. There are soldiers guarding

1 Radant, *Rosenbaum*, 15f.; E. F. Schmid, 'Joseph Haydn und das Burgenland', in *Oesterreichische Kunst*, Heft 3/4 1932, pp. 32ff., especially 35; J. Harich, 'Das fürstlich Esterházy'sche Fideikomiß', *Haydn Yearbook* IV 1968, pp. 13f. Recently, E. Power Biggs has made several records on the organ in the parish church, which although built by the same maker (George Malleck) as that in the Bergkirche, has been better restored, or let us say, more authentically preserved. Among other things, Mr Biggs has recorded the Three Organ Concertos by Haydn on MS. 6682 (Columbia Records, New York), with which project the author was associated; in our notes to the record, the disposition of the Stadtpfarrkirche organ is given. Philips plans to do a record, to be issued in 1973, including the Stadtpfarrkirche and Bergkirche organs, and also the *positiv* in the Hospital chapel of the Barmherzige Brüder. The Archives of the Parish Church, and also the Esterházy Archives in the Castle, were examined by us on many occasions from 1950 onwards.

the entrance, and a great deal of military parade and pride but a desolate appearance about the place, however, when his Chateau is thrown open during the hunting season, which sometimes happens, he can receive and accommodate with their attendants, 80 visitors. The bedrooms too, are in general, excellent, and some very handsome. The reception rooms are nothing remarkable considering the great scale of everything, except the grand banqueting room, and this is 180 feet long . . . here 300 guests dine sometimes, sometimes plays are acted by performers from Vienna, and in short it is a noble piece, the colonnade too, on the garden side, with its double row of pillars, is very handsome, from this, one descends into the garden, and there indeed one sees something worth looking at, for such a collection of plants scarcely exists in any public or private possession.

We walked up to a temple [still standing] to see a statue of the Princess Leopoldine, his daughter (now Pss. Maurice Li[e]chtenstein) done by Canova, and from thence we saw a most extensive view, all the possessions of Prince Esterházy who is about the richest subject existing, but who from vicious conduct, and self-indulgence, is overwhelmed in debt, and has scarcely any command of [his own] money. We quitted his greenhouses, his military guards, and his boundless domain, without hearing one good word about him. . . . [op. cit., pp. 323, 326]

Of course, this description is a generation after Haydn had presided over the *Missa in tempore belli* and the 'Nelson' Mass, but nevertheless in all the hectic and brilliant festivities of *fin-de-siècle* Eisenstadt there seems to hover something ephemeral, just as there did with Eszterháza. Apart from the buildings, it is only Haydn's music that survives.

The Esterházy orchestra that was put together in the autumn of 1795 was primarily a group for the church music at Eisenstadt, and therefore the musicians and their families lived in that town rather than in Vienna, to which city they were called only on special occasions (such as the performance in January 1796 of Antonio Draghi's *Penelope* at the Esterházy Palais in Vienna, for which the one or the other musician may have been recruited from Eisenstadt). The princely 'Conventionale' for the year 1796 lists (Pohl, III, 104f.) the Esterházy musicians as follows. The names are listed as they stand, with corrections and alternatives in brackets; for example, Barbara Pilhoferin's name was Pilhofer; the 'in' suffix denoted feminine gender; the same applies to Josefa Grießlerin (= Grießler). Many of the names will be familiar to those students of the Haydn orchestra before 1790.

Kammer und Chor-Musik (Chamber and Choir Musicians)

Joseph Haydn, *Capellmeister*.
Alois Tommasini [Aloysius Tomasini], *Konzertmeister* [leader].
Johann Georg Fuchs, organist and Castle Schoolmaster.
Barbara Pilhoferin [Pil(l)hofer] } Discant [Soprani].
Anna Rumfeld [or Rhumfeld] (1st chorus soprano) } Discant [Soprani].
Josefa Grießlerin [= Grießler] [engaged in 1797], Alto.
Josefa Hammer, Contralto [was first engaged in 1797 on probation, then regularly in 1798].
Johann Haydn, Tenor.
Christian Specht, Bass.
Franz Pauer } Violinists.
Luigi Tommasini [Tomasini] } Violinists.
Anton Tommasini, Violinist and Violist.
Ernst Michael [*recte*: Michael Ernst] } Violinists.
Josef Dietzl } Violinists.

Ignaz Manker, Violoncello.
Leopold Dichtler, Violone [Double Bass].
Casper Peczival [Kaspar Petzival], Bassoon [also played timpani; in *Exhibiten-Protocoll 1799* he calls himself, 'zugleich Bratschist und Pauker'; see *Haydn Yearbook* VIII 1971, p. 138].

Apart from this small string orchestra with organ and bassoon or timpani players, the *Conventionale* names the 'Feldharmonie bei der Hochfürstl. Grenadier-Compagnie, die aus 2 Oboisten, 2 Klarinettisten, 2 Fagottisten und 2 Waldhornisten bestand', that is to say, the customary 'Harmonie-Musique' mentioned several times *supra*. It was customary for the Haydn horn-players to be able to play trumpet, too; and in the two Masses composed in 1796, the scores are so laid out in their original form that the one pair of brass instruments was either horns or trumpets. Although Haydn will have had available the Eisenstadt *Thurnermeister* and his apprentices (the 'tower music' trumpet players with kettledrums), in fact he could have mounted both the *Missa Sancti Bernardi de Offida* and the *Missa in tempore belli* just using his own forces, to wit: two oboes, two clarinets, two bassoons, two horns or trumpets, kettledrums, strings, organ and S-A-T-B *soli* and choir. If anything, he may have called upon his colleague Carl Kraus of the parish church to help with some additional choir members. It should be stressed that the *Missa Sancti Bernardi de Offida* has no flute part, and that the flute part of the *Missa in tempore belli* is not found on the autograph and is patently a later addition: we shall discuss the authentic, larger orchestration of both works *infra*.

We have given the list of the 'Kammer und Chor-Musik' for 1796 as it appears in Pohl, but in the event Pohl has merged two 'Conventionale': 1796 and 1797, whereby he left out some essential musicians engaged in 1797. In Pohl's list, Anna Rhumfeld and Josefa Hammer may be found; but we know from authentic evidence that they were not engaged at all until 1797, first on probation, Josefa Hammer not being permanently hired until 1798. We therefore asked Dr Janos Harich, the former Archivist of Prince Esterházy in Eisenstadt, to clarify the situation. Dr Harich kindly supplied extensive notes as to the musicians engaged between 1795(6) and 1809, and we gratefully incorporate this vital information in the course of the Chronicle.[1]

The most interesting piece of information is that, in 1797, three trumpet players were engaged: Sebastian Binder, Michael Altmann and Johann Pfann; their names figure often in the Esterházy Archives. It seems, however, that they were not made permanent members of the band but were paid per performance (see CCLN and *infra*, pp. 476–7) until September, 1799. It would be interesting to know what the third trumpet played in Haydn's Masses.

Therefore, for the performance of the *Missa in tempore belli* at Eisenstadt on 29 September 1797, Haydn had available, in the event, not only the 'Feldharmonie bei der Hochfürstl. Grenadier-Compagnie' (oboes, clarinets, bassoon, horns) but also three trumpet players. The old tradition whereby in the *Missa in tempore belli* horns double the trumpets in the quick movements (the autograph specifying only trumpets) may have originated at the very first Eisenstadt performance: it is unlikely that the horn players, if they were not also the trumpets (as in 1796), remained silent except for their special parts in the 'Qui Tollis' and 'Et Incarnatus'.

Apart from the above-mentioned musicians, there is one more man who was part of the Esterházy establishment but probably followed the court to and from

1 Dr Harich's letter of 16 October 1972.

Vienna: we refer to Abbé Joseph Gelinek, the secular priest who became famous for his piano playing and, even more, for his variations on popular tunes, of which he published many dozens. Born in Selcz, Bohemia, on 3 December 1758, the son of a schoolmaster, Gelinek went to Prague where he studied philosophy and organ, becoming in 1783 a divinity student at the General Seminary. It is said that Mozart heard Gelinek in Prague and encouraged him. In 1786 Gelinek became a priest and thereafter was engaged by Prince Joseph Kinsky as domestic chaplain and piano teacher; Kinsky took the young man to Vienna, where he studied under Albrechtsberger. After a trip to Rome, in the entourage of Prince Poniatowsky, he returned to Vienna and in 1795 he entered Prince Nicolaus II Esterházy's household as chaplain and music master, in which position he remained until his death (Vienna, 13 April 1825). Students of Beethoven will recall that Gelinek had to compete with the young man from Bonn. Carl Czerny tells us:

> I still remember how one day Gelinek told my father that he had been asked that evening to compete with a foreign piano-player at a reception. 'We must make mincemeat out of him,' added Gelinek. The next day my father asked Gelinek for the outcome of the previous day's duel.
>
> 'Oh,' said Gelinek quite subdued, 'I'll never forget yesterday evening! Satan himself is hidden in that young man. I have never heard anyone play like that! He improvised on a theme which I gave him as I never heard even Mozart improvise. Then he played some of his own compositions which are in the highest degree remarkable and magnificent. He can overcome difficulties and draw effects from the piano such as we couldn't even allow ourselves to dream about. . . .

Gelinek's variations, of which André's thematic catalogue of them contains ninety-eight, became so famous that even Haydn's own piano arrangement of the variations on the 'Emperor's Hymn' (Quartet Op. 76, No. 3, slow movement) was marketed under the name of Gelinek! Carl Maria von Weber wrote the following epigram about Gelinek:

> An den berühmten Variationen-Schmidt-Gelinek.
> Kein Thema in der Welt verschonte dein Genie,
> Das simpleste allein – Dich selbst – variirst Du nie.

When he died, Gelinek left 42,000 gulden – the result of his nigh-incredible success as an arranger and 'light' composer. No doubt Prince Nicolaus Esterházy much preferred Gelinek to Haydn. There seems little doubt that it is the popular Abbé Gelinek whom Zinzendorf heard on 17 February 1796: 'Chez la P[csse] Auersberg [Auersperg] ou il y avoit le nôce de Lobkowitz, et l'epouse Sichy tres jolie. Un Abbé y toucha du clavesin. . . .'

Haydn's salary as princely Chapel Master remained that which it had been in the days of Prince Anton, the 1,000 gulden per annum which Prince Nicolaus 'The Magnificent' had willed him, the additional 400 gulden annually that Prince Anton had ordered, and his 'uniform according to princely discretion' ('Uniform nach herrschaftlichem Belieben'). Upon Haydn's return, Prince Nicolaus added the following 'improvement' to his *Capellmeister*'s *Naturalien* (for a part of Haydn's salary was in wood, candles, meat, and so on): an 'Assignation' reads 'according to which the Kapellmeister Josef Haydn is to receive, beginning on 1 October of this current year [1795], a daily allowance of one *Maaß* of officer's wine in Eisenstadt or Vienna.' (A *Maß*, as it is now spelled, is about a litre.)

This salary is not an exceptionally high one, either for the princely administration or for Court musicians. The bailiff of the Esterházy estates earned 6,000 gulden per annum; the *Wiener Zeitung* of 28 January 1792 notes the engagement of Haydn's god-child Joseph Weigl, then twenty-five years of age, as 'Kapellmeister und Kompositeur beim K. K. Nationalhoftheater, mit 1000 Gulden Gehalt' (precisely the size of Haydn's pension from Nicolaus I). Readers who may be interested in the purchasing power, and conversion rate of Austrian money into British currency, are referred to the following passage in Farington:

> The Ducat is abt. 9s 10d English abt. the value of a Roman 'Sequim' – a ducat is 5 Florins [florin = Gulden]. A Florin is considered to be abt. 2s. English. – a 'Florin', like a 'Livre', or a pound 'English', is only nominal. There is no Coin that answers to it, but the value may be made by smaller coins. [II, 261]

Thus ten gulden (florins) made, at any rate in 1804 when this part of the diary was written, one pound sterling; ten years before, if anything, the gulden will have been worth more. At this time (1804), James Boswell, son of Johnson's biographer 'called [on Farington]. He told me His salary as Professor at Oxford is £30 a year.'

Although Haydn's salary was not brilliant, there were two advantages to his retaining the position: (1) he was free to accept all sorts of other commissions of one kind or another, including concerts in Vienna and orders for music; (2) he would be guaranteed his salary, such as it was, for life, also when he was no longer able to compose (which in the event would occur in some seven or eight years).

To round off this brief introduction into Haydn's Austrian world *de anno* 1795, we should mention Haydn's living quarters. We have seen that he had an apartment at his disposal among the princely administration buildings near the Castle at Eisenstadt. In Vienna, Haydn had, of course, bought a house in Gumpendorf which was being rebuilt. Later it would be his principal place of residence. Haydn's wife, with whom he was on poor terms, lived sometimes at Gumpendorf and sometimes away, often in Baden (where in fact she was to die). Gumpendorf was not very practical for Haydn if he had regular concerts in the city itself, as he usually did in the winter months. Therefore he took what is called an 'Absteigquartier' (we might say, a *pied-à-terre*) in town. In December 1795, Haydn's 'Absteigquartier' was on the Mehlmarkt (Neuer Markt) in the house of the Court Fruitseller Pichler, third floor. Later Haydn lived at the Blue Sabre in the Krugerstrasse, No. 1046, where Constanze Mozart also lived for a time after Wolfgang's death.

Readers of *Haydn in England 1791–1795* will remember that Haydn's previous 'Absteigquartier' in Vienna was at Herr Johann Hamburger's house (No. 1275) on the Wasserkunstbastei; the composer seems to have given up this flat when he returned from England the second time; at any rate, the Neuer Markt address is known to us as early as 18 December 1795.[1]

We may now follow Haydn's activities in the ensuing Chronicle, based on documentary evidence of various kinds, and attempting to show his position in Viennese musical life at a period during which not only was Haydn at the zenith of his creative activities but the star of Beethoven was rising on the horizon.

1 Pohl III, 94f., 96, 104f.; Brand, 318; C. F. Pohl's article on Gelinek in Grove I, Vol. I, 587; Thayer I, 343f.; Radant, *Rosenbaum*, 15, 26; Landon, *Beethoven*, 110; Zinzendorf Diary (MS.); Deutsch, *Mozart Dokumente*, 413; Farington II, 248, 261. Franz Eibner, 'Die authentischen Klavierfassung von Haydns Variationen über "Gott erhalte"', in *Haydn Yearbook* VII (1970), 281ff.

CHAPTER THREE

Chronicle 1795

THE FOLLOWING ANNOUNCEMENT appeared in the *Pressburger Zeitung*[1] on 8 September 1795:

> According to letters from Hamburg, the princely Esterházy *Kapellmeister*, Herr Joseph Haydn, that universally esteemed and indeed very great composer whose excellent compositions are everywhere received with the greatest approbation, arrived there from London on the 20th of last month [August], continuing his journey to Vienna the next day.

We have seen in *Haydn in England 1791–1795* that Count Karl Leonhard von Harrach had erected a monument to Haydn in the Castle garden at Rohrau. The actual tablet was put up in 1794 (not in 1793 as Dies wrote) when Haydn was in England. Pohl (III, 97) informs us that 'in the Autumn of this year [1795] Haydn, in company with the Counts Franz, Karl and Ludwig Harrach and some other music lovers, went to Rohrau to see the monument which Count Karl Leonhard Harrach had arranged to erect in his garden two years [*recte*: one year] earlier.' Pohl then goes on to report that Haydn revisited his humble birth-place, kneeling down and kissing the threshold, and pointing out the bench round the oven on which his cousin from Hainburg, Johann Mathias Franck, had discovered the future musician. The company then went to the park to see the monument. We cannot now find any other evidence for this trip, which no doubt took place; the question is when. Count Harrach himself, when writing to Dies, said that when the monument was put up, Haydn 'was then in England and was but little known to me . . . and it was not until two or three years later that he happened to hear that this monument in Rohrau existed and without my knowing it went to see it.'

It would seem that on 21 September Haydn introduced to Vienna the 'Drum Roll' Symphony which he had composed early in the same year and first given in London on 2 March. Our evidence is Count Zinzendorf, who wrote in his Diary '. . . Au Spectacle. Der Jurist und Bauer. Symphonie de Haiden de Londres avec les tambours . . .' (Olleson, 49). The Burgtheater on that evening gave a one-act comedy by Beaunoir, *Die Freunde auf der Probe*, followed by the play Zinzendorf mentions, a comedy in two acts by Rautenstrauch. The symphony must have been played as an entr'acte. It is of course possible that the old 'Surprise' Symphony was the one given; it was known in German-speaking countries as 'mit dem Paukenschlag' (with the kettledrum stroke); but usually Zinzendorf refers to No. 94 as 'celle du coup de

1 *Haydn Yearbook* VIII (1971), p. 278. Pressburg (now Bratislava, ČSSR) is an attractive old town on the Danube sixty-three kilometres (by road) from Vienna. In his earlier years, Haydn had often visited the town. The *Pressburger Zeitung*, copies of which have become extremely rare, is full of useful information about Haydn, particularly during the Eszterháza years.

tonnere, destinée a reveiller les dormeurs au Concert anglois' (*vide infra*: 8 January 1796) or as 'la Symfonie de Haydn du coup de Canon'. It seems unlikely that Haydn himself conducted, for Zinzendorf would certainly have mentioned the fact; moreover, Haydn was almost certainly in Eisenstadt, where the season was at its height.

The year before, in June 1794, when Prince Nicolaus II was being officially installed at Eisenstadt Castle, there had been grand celebrations: the Leopoldstädter Theater was engaged *en bloc*, as were also the famous ballet dancers, Salvatore and Maria Viganò. The old theatre at Eszterháza Castle was plundered for costumes, and an orchestra of no less than thirty-six was engaged for the season. The festive illuminations required, according to a bill by Pietro Travaglia (well known to us from the Eszterháza years as a stage designer), 177 pounds of tallow.

The records for 1795 are less complete. Travaglia received 300 gulden from the princely *Generalcassa* on 17 September for fireworks on the feast day of Our Lady (the name-day of the Princess Marie Hermenegild). On 16 September a theatrical company, probably strolling players, gave the play, *Armuth und Edelsinn*; the next date we have is 8 October, when the play *Skizze der rauhen* [not *rauchen*] *Sitten unserer Vorältern* was performed. Travaglia's expense accounts, when submitted for payment, called forth objections as to the heavy expenses of the joiners and carpenters. The princely bursar admits that these extra expenses were justified by the haste with which the stage had to be constructed but admonishes that in future the regular princely *artigiani* ought to do the work.

There is some doubt as to where the theatre was. In the 1760s, when Prince Nicolaus I had wanted a stage, they had put it up in the conservatory. It is believed that this old theatre was refurbished for use in 1794 and 1795. Later, the manager of the Eisenstadt opera, Heinrich Schmidt, tells us that the stage was in the Great Hall (*Haydnsaal*). In 1794, we have an estimate for the costs of scenery representing a Gothic castle, a peasant's room and hall, from which we gather that the soffits had a length of 7·5 metres (the width of the stage). The perspective picture of the Gothic castle had a height of five metres. Thus, concludes the Hungarian theatrical historian Mátyás Horányi, '. . . the stage of [Eisenstadt] was smaller than that of Eszterháza.'[1]

It is doubtful if the Eisenstadt orchestra was functioning by the autumn of 1795; from the description in the archives, the 1794 orchestra seems to have been engaged from outside. And Haydn, barely returned from England, cannot have had time to organize anything much in the way of music at Eisenstadt by the middle of September. We cannot even determine when he was at Eisenstadt that year.

Readers of *Haydn in England 1791–1795* will recall that, in November 1792, Haydn had composed and presented at the Redoutensaal Masked Ball for the Gesellschaft bildender Künstler his Twelve German Dances and Twelve Minuets for orchestra, which had been eminently successful. Now, on 22 November (the feast of Saint Cecilia), the Gesellschaft gave its masked ball for the 1795 season, and Ludwig van Beethoven was invited to write Twelve Minuets (WoO7) and twelve German Dances (WoO8). Probably Haydn was instrumental in securing for his former pupil this introduction as an orchestral composer to Viennese society. The *Wiener Zeitung* of 14 and 18 November announces the music as follows:

> The music for the Minuets and German Dances for this ball is an entirely new arrangement. For the larger rooms they were written by the Royal Imperial

1 Horányi, 160.

Kapellmeister Süßmeyer; for the smaller room by the master hand [*die Meisterhand*] of Hr. Ludwig van Beethoven out of love for the artistic fraternity.

[Thayer I, 385; Thayer-Forbes I, 177]

Following close on Haydn's precedent, Beethoven also arranged his dances for the piano and published them with Artaria – just as we have seen with Haydn's Dances of 1792.[1] Haydn went to this masked ball and took another person with him. The Gesellschaft's Archives, now in the Archives of the City of Vienna, preserve the following note on free tickets for the year.

Freÿ = Billets sind ausgegeben worden. Anno 1795. [. . .]

Hr v.	Beethowen Music Compositor	12.
	Sussmaÿr Dto	16.
	Eÿbler hat Keine angenomen [did not take any]	
	Kozeluch	6.
	Capol	3.
	Richter	3.
	Haidn Music Compos.	2.
	Höllmaÿr Music Director	5.
	[. . .]	
	Hr v. Täuber Mus. Comp.	4.

The music that Beethoven wrote for the Redoutensaal was an astonishing achievement. Of course, he had composed orchestral music before he arrived in Vienna, for example, the Violin Concerto in C, the incomplete orchestral score of which is now in the Gesellschaft der Musikfreunde. If, up to 1792, Beethoven had been influenced primarily by Mozart, after 1792 it was Haydn who was to be the dominating force on the young man's musical style. In many cases, as in these very dances, we find a smooth juxtaposition of Haydnesque and Mozartian elements, e.g. (overleaf), in the Trio of Minuet No. 4 where, the clarinet runs remind us of Haydn's Symphony No. 99, Finale (1793), which Beethoven will have seen on Haydn's writing desk before he left for England, while the sinuous second violin part and the feminine ending in bar eight are more Mozartian, as are the long slurs found at bars 4 and 7 in the first violin part (and in bars 3–4 of the second 'posthorn' example, *infra.*) It will be noted that the dances are all scored for a string orchestra without viola part, but using, otherwise, the full classical orchestra including clarinets, trumpets, kettledrums and 'Turkish instruments'. In this, Beethoven was following the tradition of the period.

Both Haydn (in his 1792 Dances) and Mozart had often used 'Turkish' music in their minuets and German dances – that is, the piquant rhythms and harmonies of Eastern Europe, to which were often added, as also in Beethoven's case, 'triangolo, tamburino, gran tamburo' (whereby the tamburino was often replaced by cymbals). In No. 10 of Beethoven's 1795 German Dances we find 'Turkish' music:

1 *Wiener Zeitung* on 16 December 1795: 'Neue Music Artaria and Comp. on the Kohlmarkt. By Hrn. Ludwig van Beethoven 12 new Minuets and 12 German Dances arranged for piano, which were performed at the Royal Imperial Redoutensaal in a masked ball for the benefit of the Künstlergesellschaft on 22 November of this year, and which, as is well known [*bekanntermassen*] were received successfully. This piano arrangement was prepared by the composer himself. Of which the Minuets cost 45 kr [*Kreuzer*]; the German Dances 45 kr.' Copies of this authentic first edition have become rare: a particularly crisp one is in the Papafava Archives.

[Beethoven: Twelve Minuets (1795), No. 4: Trio.]

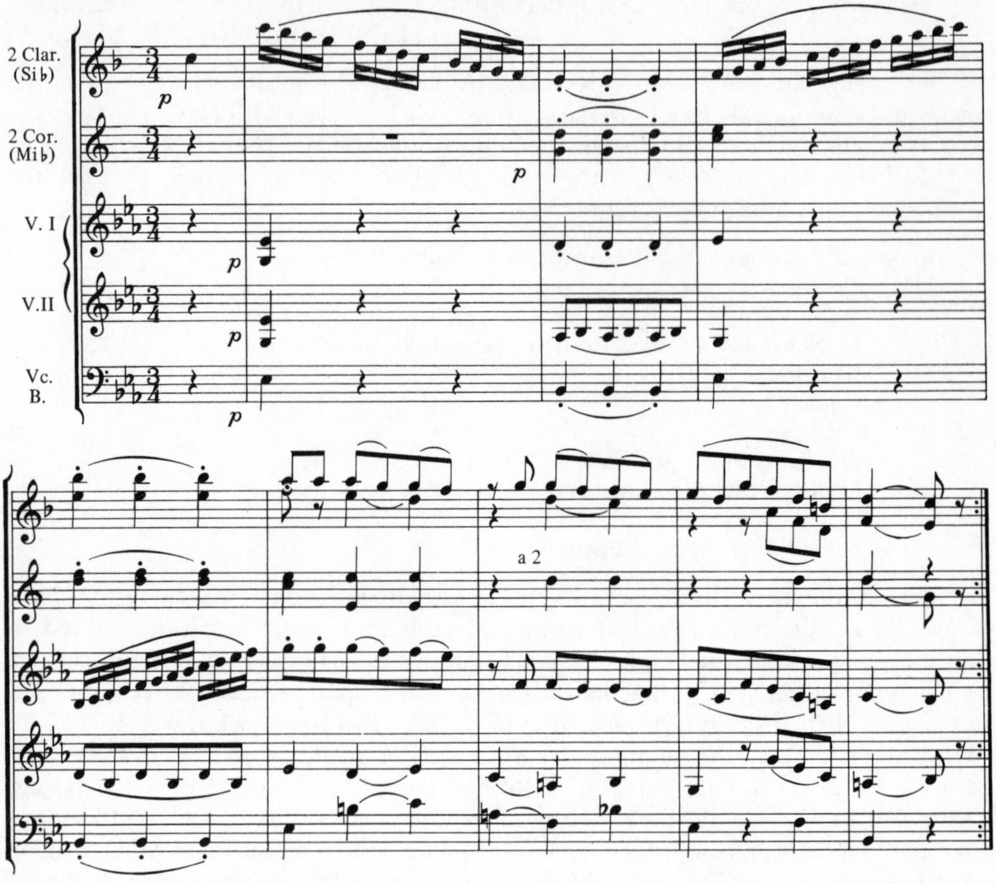

2 Clar. (Si♭)
2 Cor. (Mi♭)
V. I
V.II
Vc. B.
p
a 2

The Coda of the German Dances introduces a *Cornetto in C*, a posthorn, which instrument Mozart had used so enchantingly (together with tuned sleigh bells!) in the third of his *Drei Deutsche Tänze* (K. 605), composed four years earlier and no doubt well known to Beethoven. When the posthorn enters, it brings, somehow, the magic spell of the mail coach with the postillion, and perhaps a certain nostalgia:

Cornetto [Posthorn]
Str. (2 Clar. 2 Cor.)
p
etc.

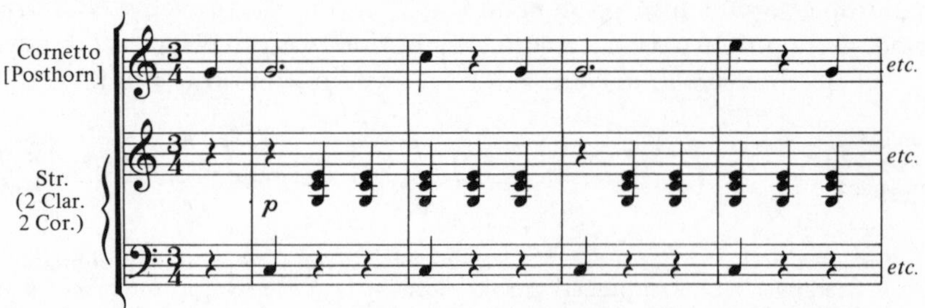

As this Coda develops, we can see the young composer flexing his muscles. There is a certain swashbuckling, brash feeling about the posthorn solo and the sweep of woodwind –

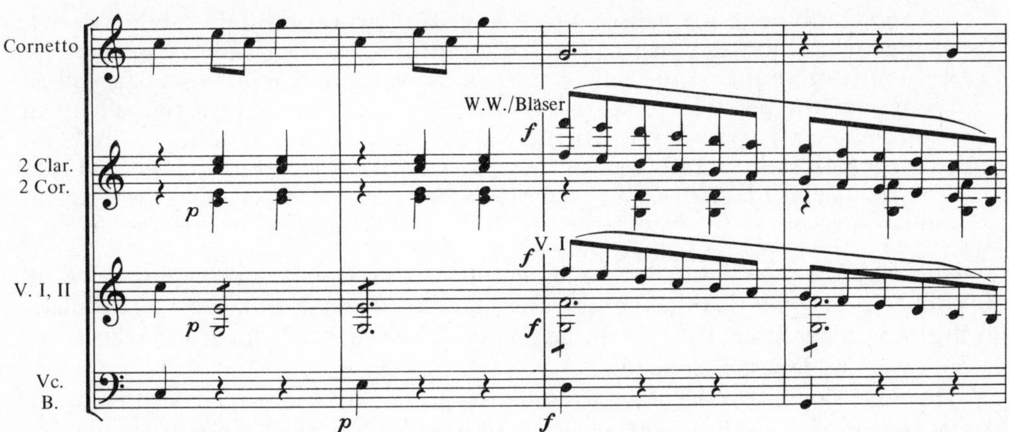

– which does *not* sound like Haydn, even at his loudest (in Symphony No. 97 in the same key as our example) and certainly not like the feline subtleties of Mozart. In fact, the musical connoisseur will have noticed, in this music, not only the amazingly self-assured accents of Bonn-on-the-Rhine but – dare we say it? – a certain vulgarity in such a passage as:

This was, *mutatis mutandis*, the authentic voice of Napoleon, the new age which was cocky, arrogant, and not without a touch of the vulgar. After Haydn's 1792 Dances, and the late Dances by Mozart, here was something really new under the Viennese sun. The voice of Ludwig van Beethoven was making itself heard, and very insistently, too, with *cornetto*, Turkish instruments and a great deal of panache.

It was natural that Haydn would wish to acquaint the Viennese with some of his newest works composed for the 1794 and 1795 seasons in London. Remembering his successful Redoutensaal Benefit in March 1793 (discussed in *Haydn in England 1791–1795*, pp. 215–6), Haydn again hired the small room there on 18 December 1795. Here is the announcement in the *Wiener Zeitung*:[1]

> On Friday next, the 18th instant, Herr Kapellmeister Haydn will give a grand musical concert in the small Redoutensaal, at which Mad. Tomeoni and Herr Monbelli [*recte*: Mombelli] will sing; Herr van Beethoven will play a Concerto of his own composition; and three grand Symphonies, not yet heard here, which Herr Kapellmeister composed during his last sojourn in London, will be performed. The entrance tickets are to be had of Herr Kapellmeister Haydn in his apartment on the Neuer Markt in the Court Fruitseller's House, third floor, at all hours.

Irene Dutillieu (*née* Tomeoni) was the leading soprano at the Vienna Court Opera. Bernhard Anselm Weber heard her at Vienna in 1793 and wrote of her:

1 16 December. Pohl III, 96; Thayer I, 386 (where, uncorrected, 'Monbelli') and Thayer-Forbes I, 178 (where erroneously 'Tomeni'); we have copied out all these *Wiener Zeitung* notes from the complete issue in the Stadtbibliothek, Vienna.

> She combines a marvellous voice with an equally admirable ability to act, with which she graces all her roles. Her beautiful figure, her walk and appearance are so attractive that if she sang only half as well, the public would be full of admiration for her. Her voice is full and strong, but also attractive and well trained; she employs but few ornaments, but those she does use are assured and certain. Coloraturas roll out of her voice with exceptional ease, and her performance in adagios is just as delicate as her performance in allegros is strong and Brilliant [*Berlinische Musikalische Zeitung*]

The *AMZ* in 1800 wrote that 'as *prima buffa* [she] is rightly much appreciated by the public; only a pity that she is often so exaggerated [*ausgelassen*]. Her voice is made for the theatre, her figure too.' At the beginning of the year 1801 she left the theatre to marry a wealthy Jewish merchant.

The other singer was the tenor, Domenico Mombelli, who was the year before in Naples (where *inter alia* he sang Gaetano Andreozzi's Oratorio *La morte di Saulle*); he was also a composer, publishing various Italian songs and duets with Artaria. Johann Friedrich Reichardt went in 1790 to Italy from Berlin to engage tenors and altos for the Royal Opera and reported in the *Berlinische Musikalische Monathschrift*; 'Mombelli pleased me very much. He has a very pleasant and ringing voice, especially in the low register, and sings with feeling and expression. Also his presence and action are pleasant and firm.'

Beethoven played his B flat piano Concerto, Op. 19, possibly with the revised Finale: it is thought that the Rondo in B flat (WoO6) represents an earlier Finale, and probably the one Beethoven had used earlier in the year at his concert with the Societät (March 29 and 30).

From the notice in Zinzendorf's Diary we know that Haydn conducted the 'Military' Symphony, but we have no hint as to the other two symphonies, nor do we know which vocal works were performed (possibly Haydn's *Scena di Berenice* which he had written for Banti and which we know he took back to Vienna, because we find him selling a full score in MS. to Mrs Peploe in December 1797). One offshoot of the concert would seem to have been that Haydn sold all twelve London Symphonies to Prince Karl von Fürstenberg, who was in Vienna at that time. The Donaueschingen *Wochenblatt* reports from Vienna that His Highness 'arrived here safely from Prague on the 12th of this month [November]' and reports of his being introduced to various ministers, etc. on 15 and 16 November. Probably Prince von Fürstenberg heard the concert of 18 December and asked the composer for copies of all his London Symphonies; anyway, the Fürstenberg Castle at Donaueschingen was the first German institution of its kind to receive authentic copies of all twelve Salomon Symphonies (they were discovered there in 1957).

Count Zinzendorf wrote in his Diary: '. . . Le soir a la petite Salle de redoute au Concert de Haydn. L'Adagio de la premiere Symphonie, l'air chanté par Mombelli et la Simphonie militaire me plûrent . . . Brouillard et boise.'[1]

It must have been a curious feeling for Haydn, that drizzly and foggy night, knowing that the next morning there would be no newspaper review of the concert, no official notice of it, indeed, of any kind whatever. Vienna was still a provincial city compared to London, at least as far as the daily press was concerned.

1 Pohl III, 96; Olleson 50; weather from Zinzendorf's Diary in MS.; Gerber, *NTL* III, 443f., IV, 370; *AMZ* III, 15 October 1800, p. 41; *Gazzetta Universale* 18 March 1794 (report from Naples, 11 March); Landon, *Supplement*, 34f.

The frequency with which Haydn's and Beethoven's names appear together in this Chronicle – especially in 1795 and 1796 – suggests that we may, at this point, begin our first analysis of a personal and artistic relationship far more complicated than was previously realized either by Haydn scholars or Beethoven experts. We hope, by presenting as much evidence as possible, to clarify the situation between the two men, though we cannot of course entirely clarify the ambiguity with which their intercourse was clouded almost from the beginning: and it will be seen, moreover, that their relationship changes constantly in the next decade.

In *Haydn in England 1791–1795*, we left Beethoven in Vienna when Haydn departed for England in January 1794. Originally Haydn had planned to take Beethoven with him in 1793 and also in 1794 (the original trip having been postponed for a year); but in the event Beethoven stayed in Vienna. Just before he left for London, Haydn turned Beethoven over to Albrechtsberger for further studies in counterpoint, and in December 1793 Haydn wrote a long letter on the subject of Beethoven to the Elector of Cologne, Maximilian Franz, the young man's patron at Bonn. The latter and its ramifications have been discussed in *Haydn in England 1791–1795* (pp. 222–3).

A week before Christmas, the two men collaborated at what must have been a brilliant concert at the Redoutensaal in Vienna; and this seems the place to discuss a particularly strange story that concerns the piano Trios, Op. 1, which Beethoven had published in 1795 while Haydn was still in England. The whole affair was published for the first time by Beethoven's pupil Ferdinand Ries; he writes:

> Of all composers Beethoven most appreciated Mozart and Händel, then S[ebastian] Bach. If I found him with music in his hand, it was certain to be compositions of one of those men. Haydn seldom escaped without several sideswipes [*Haydn kam selten ohne einige Seitenhiebe weg*], a grudge which Beethoven probably kept from earlier days. One reason for it may well have been the following: the three Trios by Beethoven (Opus 1) were to be presented for the first time to the artistic world at a soirée given by Prince Lichnowsky. Most artists and amateurs were invited, especially Haydn, about whose opinion everyone was curious. The Trios were played and immediately created an extraordinary effect. Haydn, too, said many complimentary things about them but he advised Beethoven not to publish the third in C minor. This struck Beethoven very much, for he thought it the best, just as today it is the favourite and the one that creates the most effect. Therefore this remark of Haydn's created a bad impression on Beethoven and left him with the idea: Haydn is jealous and envious [*neidisch, eifersüchtig*], and bears him no good will. I must admit that when Beethoven told me this, I didn't much believe it. Therefore I took the opportunity of asking Haydn himself about it. His answer confirmed Beethoven's statement, however, for he said he did not think that this Trio would be as quickly and easily understood, and as successfully accepted by the public.

Beethoven biographers have naturally relished this story for a century and a half. But it is pure fiction. Haydn left for London on 19 January 1794, and was away from Vienna until September 1795. Beethoven's Trios, Op. 1, were issued by subscription; the preliminary announcement in the *Wiener Zeitung* on 9 and 16 May tells us that the copies 'will appear within six weeks, engraved by Artaria', and on 29 August 1795 the *Wiener Zeitung* printed the notice: 'Since all the subscribers to Ludwig van Beethoven's Trios have received their copies, this notice serves to inform that the composer has available copies which will be offered at the subscription price of one ducat for one entire month more. He lives in the Kreuzgasse in the Ogilfisch House No. 35 on the first floor [behind the Minoritenkirche].' Haydn was, of course, nowhere near Vienna when the Trios were printed. Now if Haydn heard them at all, it can only have been before 19 January 1794. This presupposes (1) that Beethoven had finished the whole set in 1793 and, even more important, (2) that Lichnowsky would have been tactless enough to put on a concert at which Beethoven introduced his new Trios and to which Haydn, Beethoven's teacher, was invited to express an opinion as to the qualities of his pupil's new music. Even if such an improbable situation had arisen, it would be very curious for Beethoven to withhold the publication for one and a half years. But there is evidence of another kind which renders the whole story apocryphal. The great Beethoven expert, Gustav Nottebohm, discovered sketches to Beethoven's works of the period 1794–5 which enable us to date at least the Trio in G major, Op. 1, No. 2, as *post* January 1794. The sheet includes contrapuntal studies for the Albrechtsberger period (after Haydn had already left Vienna), two choral fugues, the beginning of an Italian song, the text from Metastasio's *Olimpiade*, a sketch to *Adelaide*, followed by a sketch to the beginning of the second movement of the Trio, Op. 1, No. 2; the sketches also include a fugue 'alla duodecima' and a sketch to the Finale of the First Symphony. Nottebohm concludes:

> Beethoven must therefore have occupied himself with these compositions during his studies. Evidence for determining the time when these studies were ended can only be provided approximately by the sketch pertaining to the Trio in G major. The sketch must have been written before 9 May 1795, because on that day the Trios were announced in the *Wiener Zeitung* as to 'appear within six weeks' on subscription, and were thus completed by then. Consequently the studies must have been already finished on that day, or very close to completion. It is incompatible with the evidence provided by the sketch that, according to a statement by Ries . . . the Trios were already completed by 19 January, 1794, on which day Haydn left Vienna; the existence of the sketch shows that the Trios were not yet completed by the *end* of 1794 [our italics].

In another place, Nottebohm has shown that the critical C minor Trio was also being sketched *during the year 1794*. Schindler, too, worried about the patent discrepancy of dates. He writes:

> We know that during most of 1794 and 1795 Haydn was in England. The fact of his absence from Vienna does not tally with the publication date of these trios nor with the remark attributed to him. If, in answer to a question from young Ries about the statement, he explained that he believed the public would neither understand nor respond favourably to the trio, the remark that Beethoven misunderstood may be dismissed from our minds. Anyone who knows Haydn's own trios, however, will be astonished at this reaction. For my own part, I can only think that this was merely one of the many unfortunate misunderstandings that marked the course of Beethoven's life.

What Haydn can very well have said when he returned from England and heard, let us say, all three trios at a Friday concert given by Prince Lichnowsky, was perhaps: 'You should not have published that third Trio ex C minore, it will be too difficult for the ladies to understand', or something similar. Or, alternatively, Ries may have confused the Trios, Op. 1, with the piano Sonatas, Op. 2. Thayer states that Beethoven played all three sonatas to Haydn at a Lichnowsky Friday morning concert soon after the old master had returned from England. That there was some friction between the two composers over the dedication of Op. 2 is attested once again by Wegeler-Ries (in this case, probably Ries).

> Haydn had wanted Beethoven to put on the title page of his first [?] published works the words, 'Pupil of Haydn'. Beethoven refused because, he said, that although he had taken a few lessons from Haydn, he had never learned anything from him. . . . Beethoven also studied counterpoint with Albrechtsberger and dramatic music with Salieri. I was well acquainted with all three teachers. All appreciated Beethoven highly but were of one opinion concerning his studies: all agreed that Beethoven was so headstrong and stubborn that it required bitter experience to teach him everything he had rejected in his formal lessons. Albrechtsberger and Salieri were especially of this opinion.

To clarify the whole question of Beethoven and Haydn at this relatively early period in their relationship we would quote from an interesting document which for some reason has for the most part escaped the biographers of both composers. It is a rather journalistically conceived but none the less characteristic report from the French flautist, Louis François Philippe Drouet (1792–1873) who knew Beethoven in Vienna; Drouet made an extended European tour in the year 1816, which took him as far as Naples, and it was probably on this tour that he stopped in Vienna, made Beethoven's acquaintance and became an enthusiastic admirer of his music. Drouet describes his relationship to Beethoven in a series of conversations with 'a highly educated, musical lady, the wife of an Englishman', which were published for the first time in 1858 in a Hamburg paper entitled *Zeitung für Gesangvereine und Liedertafeln*.

> 'Haydn,' said Drouet, 'was certainly a great *Musikus*, one of the greatest who ever lived, and yet he made a mistake about Beethoven, whom you love so much. When he saw his first trios, about which one had asked his opinion, he said: "Nothing will ever come of that young man".'
>
> 'Not true at all,' answered the lady. 'These words are attributed to Haydn, but he never said them and you know it, too, because you said so yourself in front of the Duchess of Belgiojoso. . . . When Beethoven, still very young [continued the lady], showed his first compositions to Haydn and asked him for his opinion, Haydn said to him: "You have a great deal of talent, and you will have still more, enormously [*ungeheuer*] more, talent. Your powers of imagination are an inexhaustible source of ideas, but . . . do you really want my frank opinion?" "Certainly," said Beethoven, "I came here to have your opinion." – "Well, then," said Haydn, "you will accomplish more than has ever been accomplished hitherto; you will have thoughts that no one has yet had; you will never (and you're quite right about this) sacrifice a beautiful thought to a tyrannical rule; but the rules will be sacrificed to your moods, for you make the impression on me of a man with several heads, several hearts and several souls, and . . . but I fear I annoy you". "You will annoy me," said Beethoven, "if you don't continue." – "Well," continued Haydn, "because you want me to do so, I will continue and will tell you that in my opinion there will always be something – if not eccentric [*Verschrobenes*], then at any rate unusual in your works: one will find beautiful things in them, even admirable passages, but here and there something peculiar, dark, because you yourself are a little sinister and peculiar, and the style of the musician is always that of the person himself. Look at my compositions. You will often find something jovial about them, because that's the way I am; next to a serious thought you will find a cheerful one, as in Shakespeare's tragedies." . . . By the way, at the time when Haydn saw the first works of Beethoven, the latter was very young, the tree was too heavily covered with foliage and needed pruning; in the first compositions by Beethoven, everything was in superabundance. . . .'

The Lady: 'You find the first compositions by Beethoven very good, because you know them as they are printed, but not in the form in which he showed them to Haydn.'

Drouet: 'This remark is quite correct, I didn't think of that, but now I remember very well that Beethoven told me, when he was speaking about his first efforts, "They are not printed as I first wrote them; when, after some years, I examined my first manuscripts once again, I asked myself if I had not been insane to cram into one single piece that which was sufficient for twenty. I burned these manuscripts, so that no one could see them, and I would have committed many foolish mistakes in my first appearance as a composer if it had not been for the good advice of Papa Haydn and Albrechtsberger."'[1]

Hans Gál was one of the first (1916) to discuss the stylistic elements that to make up Beethoven's so-called first period; in his brilliant article, Gál goes considerably further than even Jalowetz (1910), and in particular Gál shows a sensitive appreciation of the way Beethoven assimilated Haydn's and Mozart's styles. Gál is undoubtedly quite correct when he says that Beethoven's works composed in Bonn 'hardly show anything at all of this Haydnesque influence and we may therefore infer that Beethoven in those days will have known very little of Haydn's music.'[2] There is no doubt that the primary influence on Beethoven up to 1792 was Mozart's music, which was particularly popular in Bonn. What Beethoven was to combine in masterly fashion was a subjective Mozartian cantabile with Haydn's 'absolute melody' (based on an old tradition of folk music). Gál continues along these lines:

> Haydn was for two years Beethoven's teacher. That the latter knew the works of his master very thoroughly and appreciated them highly can *inter alia* be seen in the compositions of the first period. Even if Beethoven did not find in Haydn the teacher best fitted for the study of counterpoint and was forced to seek outside help when continuing his studies, nevertheless the great master, who passed uncon-

1 Ries came to study with Beethoven in Vienna in 1801. Dr F. G. Wegeler and Ferdinand Ries, *Biographische Notizen über Ludwig van Beethoven*, Coblenz 1838, pp. 84f. (quoted *in extenso* in Kalischer, *vide infra*). Gustav Nottebohm, *Beethoven-Studien*, Leipzig-Winterthur 1873, pp. 202f.; also *Beethoveniana* (II), Leipzig 1887, p. 27. Schindler (ed. MacArdle), 70. Wegeler-Ries, op. cit., p. 86 (about Beethoven's Sonatas, Op. 2). Thayer I, 380. Kalischer, *Beethoven und Wien* (part of *Beethoven und seine Zeitgenossen*), chapter 'Beethoven und "Papa" Haydn', pp. 8ff. Hans Gál, 'Die Stileigentümlichkeiten des jungen Beethoven', in *Studien zur Musikwissenschaft* IV (1916), pp. 58ff. Heinrich Jalowetz, 'Beethovens Jugendwerke und ihre melodischen Beziehungen zu Mozart, Haydn und Ph. E. Bach', in *Sammelbände der internationalen Musik-Gesellschaft* XII (1910).

2 We must, however, in fairness point out that if, as seems to be the case, Beethoven knew very few of Haydn's works before 1792, there were nevertheless many works by Haydn in Bonn. In an article dated Bonn, 2 March 1783, and published on 30 March 1783, in Cramer's *Magazin der Musik* (I, 377ff.), we read a report of Herr Hofkammerrath von Mastiaux, a musically inclined man born in 1726 who was one of the many cultivated amateurs in Bonn during Beethoven's youth. (A few pages later, the report deals also with 'Louis van Beethoven . . . a boy of eleven [*sic*] and possessed of a most promising talent.') On p. 393 of this report, we read of the music and instruments owned by the Hofrath, which included a harpsichord of 1646 by Andreas Rückers (the Elder), a 'large harpsichord' [two-manual?] by Johann Rückers of 1659, and '80 Sinfonien, von Joseph Haiden [*sic*: interesting to note that Beethoven always misspelled Haydn's name as 'Haidn'], 30 Quatuor, und 40 Trio, von ebendemselben [by the same author]'. It seems incredible that Beethoven would have wanted to ignore a Bonn collection with that amount of Haydn. Hofrath Mastiaux also owned some superb string instruments, *inter alia* a viola by Antonio and Hieronymus Amati (1642), a violin by Antonio Amati (1673), a violin by Nic. Amati (1682), a Stradivari violin (1670) and one by Andrea Guarneri (1693). It is true that Beethoven's *pre*-Vienna music shows surprisingly few elements of Haydn's style; grotesque though it may have seemed, Ludwig Schiedermair was quite right, in his standard book, *Der junge Beethoven* (Leipzig-Bonn 1925; reprinted, but in shortened form, in 1970), to devote a whole chapter to Mozart's influence on the young Beethoven but none at all on Haydn's – because in fact it was practically negligible. Can Beethoven have ignored deliberately all this amount of Haydn's music? Knowing his later character, it is entirely possible.

tradicted in the whole of Germany as the leading composer of his period, must have exerted a mighty attraction for the young composer. . . . Quite certainly there will have been a regular exchange of ideas between them. . . . Can it not be that we owe the enormous, unprecedented advance from the Cantatas of the year 1790 to the Trios Op. 1 . . . not only to the thorough contrapuntal studies with Albrechtsberger but just as much to the personal acquaintance with Haydn, and with his music? Especially since this acquaintance seems to have been quite new: Thayer gives in his lists of music performed at Bonn all sorts of contemporary composers but not a single piece by Haydn. . . . I will not go so far as to see in Beethoven's 'absolute melody' only [*durchaus*] Haydn's influence but only see a 'selected relationship' [*Wahlverwandschaft*] between both. . . .

Of ccurse there are strong elements of Haydn in the Op. 1 Trios. In some cases, it sounds so like the older composer as to be practically identical, for example, the Finale of the G major Trio (Op. 1, No. 2):

(Note how cleverly Beethoven adapts the unpianistic repeated *g*'s when the theme comes in the piano.) But Beethoven has also adopted many less obvious traits of the Haydn style, for example the poetic way in which the violin entry in the slow introduction (Adagio)

becomes the principal theme of the ensuing Allegro vivace

This is the kind of interthematic relationship Beethoven could have observed in Haydn's Symphony No. 90 (1788), of which there were manuscript copies circulating round Vienna in 1792 and 1793, or in Symphony No. 97, which Haydn will have often conducted in Vienna in 1793. The use of a third-related key, E major, as the slow movement of this same Trio in G carried on a long tradition in Haydn's music, for example in the A flat piano Trio No. 27 (slow movement E major), printed by Artaria and one of the works studied by Josephine Deym (*née* Brunsvik) at the time when Beethoven was intimate with the family.

Another Haydnesque device that Beethoven adopted wholeheartedly is the use of a turn. In *Haydn in England 1791–1795* (p. 509) we noted that this particular kind of turn had two distinguishing characteristics: (1) it is accompanied by a phrase progressing a third upwards; and (2) it occurs in slow tempo. Now we find Beethoven using it in many of his compositions, for example, the Andante of the C minor Sonata from Op. 10 (published in 1798), the Adagio from the Septet (played in April 1800) or the Largo from the piano Concerto in C, Op. 15 (*c.* 1798?):

In the first two Trios of Op. 1 there are two features that are distinctly Beethovenian: the first is the use of the Scherzo in both works. In itself, these scherzi are perhaps the most original pieces of both Trios, not only melodically but also formally. The second feature is the length of the works, not only the overall length (four movements, something we never find in Haydn's late piano Trios) but especially as regards the slow movements. Here we notice a luxuriant growth, and a very special kind of emotional intensity, which become hallmarks of Beethoven's slow movements. These are long and intellectually tough adagios (actually Op. 1, No. 2 is a Largo con espressione) of great melodic beauty and great emotional *density*. This quality will become even more apparent in the String Quartets Op. 18 (*c.* 1799–1800). Considering that, except for Haydn's late piano Trios (which Beethoven cannot have heard since they were all composed during or after Haydn's second London journey), the average late eighteenth-century piano trio was a light form, a *divertimento*, these Trios by Beethoven will have made an exceptional impression. Especially, of course, the third, which is unquestionably the greatest, the most personal and the most intense of them all. It is in the great Mozartian C minor tradition, of course, but nevertheless full of individual touches, such as the gruff *sf* (which Beethoven uses in the sense that Haydn used *fz*) *p* … *sf* … *sf* etc. It is a direct descendant of the Austrian *Sturm und Drang* but in its Mozartian rather than its earlier Haydnesque vein. Another mark of individuality is the way in which Beethoven treats the strings. In most eighteenth-century piano trios, the strings served as accompanying instruments, just as the old titles used to indicate: 'Sonata for the Piano-Forte, with Accompaniments for the Violin and Violoncello'. All this is changed in Op. 1. Although the violin had enjoyed a certain amount of freedom in Haydn's later trios, and even more in Mozart's, the 'cello had always been treated as a *basso seguente*. It must have created great astonishment, and a delight mixed with slight panic, when the amateur 'cellists opened their music and saw that they were playing difficult solo passages throughout these Trios, sometimes unsupported entirely as at the beginning of the Scherzo from Op. 1, No. 2.

If the connoisseurs found many details to appreciate in Op. 1, they will have found even more in the three Piano Sonatas Op. 2 dedicated to Haydn,[1] which Beethoven played to his old master at Lichnowsky's and which, since they seem to have been known to the musical world for some time before publication, we may mention briefly here. We say that they were known prior to March 1796, for the *Jahrbuch der Tonkunst von Wien und Prag* of 1796, which was written the previous year, says in an

1 The title page of the authentic Artaria edition reads: 'Trois Sonatas pour le Clavecin ou Pianoforte composées et dediées A Mr. Joseph Haydn Docteur en musique par Louis van Beethoven. Oeuvre II. à Vienna chez Artaria et Comp.' Artaria announced them on 9 March 1796; *vide infra*. Landon, *Beethoven*, 59.

appreciative article on the composer, 'There have already been several beautiful Sonatas by him, among which his latest is regarded as particularly outstanding,' presumably referring to Op. 2.

The *Sturm und Drang* manner of Op. 1, No. 3, is continued and refined in the great F minor Sonata with which the set opens. The same atmosphere of intellectual density that we noted with regard to the slow movements of Op. 1 prevails to an even greater extent in the new set: if the Adagio of Op. 1, No. 1, is a magnificent threnody, the Largo Appassionato in the A major (Op. 2, No. 2) is of a quiet grandeur and depth that must have particularly impressed Haydn, whose genuinely slow adagios (such as the great Largo in the 'Rider' Quartet, Op. 74, No. 3, which came out in Artaria's authentic edition about six weeks after Beethoven's Op. 2) were one of the features that set him apart from Mozart, whose troubled slow movements are usually in an andante tempo. Haydn will also have been impressed by the technical level of the piano part, for which the composer occasionally provided the fingering: the semiquaver octaves in triplets in Op. 2, No. 1, set a new standard in piano technique, and there are other passages equally startling to the amateur. 'One day,' reports Frau von Bernhard (whose eye-witness account of the Lichnowsky circle we have quoted *supra*), 'Streicher put some things by Beethoven in front of her; they were the Piano Sonatas, Op. 2, which had just appeared at Artaria's. He told her that there are new things in them which the ladies do not wish to play, because they are incomprehensible and too difficult; would she like to learn them?' Frau von Bernhard did learn them, was brought to the salons of Lichnowsky and Razumovsky, and finally introduced to Beethoven, who appreciated her talent. Not every Viennese *Fräulein* will have been so persistent.[1]

Beethoven did not publish his *bravura*, or 'encore' improvisation, the 'Alla ingarese [*sic*], quasi un capriccio' which we know as the 'Wuth über den verlorenen Groschen', Op. 129. Its inspiration is the Finale of Haydn's piano (or harpsichord) Concerto in D, known as Op. 21 (XVIII: 11), which Artaria published in 1784; Beethoven may even have known it from his Bonn years, because there were German editions of the period by Hummel and Schott. Erich Hertzmann discovered the autograph shortly after the Second World War in American private possession, from which source it may be demonstrated that the work was composed between 1795 and 1798, though in the light of what we know now, it would seem that 1795 is the more realistic date. It is amusing to think that this popular, folk-tune-dominated piece of Gypsy music appeared almost simultaneously with Haydn's 'Gypsy Rondo' Trio (discussed in *Haydn in England 1791–1795*, pp. 432–4).

A work that had a profound influence on Beethoven was Haydn's great *Scena di Berenice*, composed in London in 1795 for *la* Banti and which, as we have noted above, Haydn brought back with him to Vienna. We have analyzed the form – with its succession of accompanied recitatives, slow aria (broken off) and quick aria – and the content in the previous volume of this biography. Beethoven seems to have written his 'Ah! perfido' at Prague in 1796 (see Kinsky-Halm Catalogue for a description of the lost authentic manuscript copy with this date) for Countess Josephine von Clary. No doubt Beethoven revised it before its (much later) publication. The progressive tonality of both Haydn's (D major to F minor) and Beethoven's (C major to E flat) is also matched by the identical interval upwards of a minor third, and the formal organization is similar, too; except that Beethoven breaks up the pattern still more by

1 Friedrich Kerst, *Die Erinnerungen an Beethoven*, Stuttgart 1913, I, 23. Erich Hertzmann, 'The newly discovered autograph of Beethoven's *Rondo à Capriccio*', in *Musical Quarterly*. Vol. 32 (1946), pp. 171ff.

dividing up the final aria into alternating slow and fast sections, whereas Haydn, once he has started the concluding F minor Aria, pursues it to the end. An interesting feature of the Beethoven which no one seems to have noticed is the fact that all the vocal appoggiature are written out. Here Beethoven was abolishing a difficult and vexing custom, whereby the singer inserted such appoggiature as she thought necessary, since the composer did not put them into the score. Drops of a third, ,

were to be performed by singing a *d''* at the note marked with a cross; but it was an imprecise way of notation and gave rise to all sorts of uncertainties. Even today the notation causes untold difficulties when performing old vocal music of this style. By writing out all the appoggiature, Beethoven was inaugurating an entirely new way of vocal notation which, alas, was not adopted by other composers. The first few bars will show what is meant:

The two works are scored for almost the same orchestra: one flute, two oboes, two clarinets, two bassoons, two horns and strings in the Haydn (who had originally wanted trumpets and drums but immediately cancelled them) and the same without the oboes for 'Ah! perfido'. Once more we would point to a strong characteristic of Beethoven's music at this period, and in particular of the slow movements; and that is a yearning quality which fills the music, often nearly to the emotional bursting point. The beauty of Haydn's *Scena di Berenice* lies in the almost objective quality of the emotion, whether the quiet grandeur of the E major slow aria or the impetuous F minor conclusion. With Beethoven the whole text assumes a highly personal drama, and the astute listener will immediately see the yearning nature of such a theme as the Adagio given to the first clarinet and first bassoon:

The main subject of the final slow section (which is broken off several times but always returns) is likewise filled with this yearning; this section is also orchestrated in a particularly beautiful way, with for example an almost Mozartian wind-band solo that follows:

But Mozartian though some of the details are, it is surprising to note that Beethoven's clarinet writing is much more like Haydn's than Mozart's and this despite the fact that at least one of the Stadlers was first clarinet in the Vienna Court Orchestra (Johann; see *Schematismus* of the period). We miss the *chalumeau* register and the 'walking' clarinet figures that often come in the lowest register for the second clarinet (a kind of Alberti bass). In the development of Beethoven as a symphonic composer, it will be noted that his clarinet writing never really reverts to the Mozartian models but rather to Haydn's, where the instrument is generally written in a tessitura higher than Mozart's. It is a marvel how both Haydn and Beethoven were able to turn their Metastasian high drama into works of such real poignancy, elevating the fashionable Italian cantata into a fine Viennese work of art.[1]

Haydn used to term Beethoven *Großmogul* ('Grand Mogul') and would ask 'Was treibt denn unser Großmogul?' ('What's our Grand Mogul up to?'). Haydn may have been amused by his erstwhile pupil's delusions of grandeur but he was certainly very much aware of his artistic stature as revealed even in these early products of his muse.[2]

To conclude our Chronicle of the year 1795, we would like here to survey briefly the relative positions of Haydn and Mozart in the German-speaking world. In order to do so we shall have, in the case of Haydn, to discuss events that chronologically speaking have not yet occurred; yet it seems wise to disturb the strict order of events in the interests of clarity.

Haydn's English works appeared (insofar as they were printed at all) several years after they had been composed and first performed in London. Thus the Continental reaction was a delayed one, and it was not until after *The Creation* had appeared that France, Germany, and Austria finished their respective publications of the last Salomon Symphonies. The principal German publisher of Haydn's works was André, who seems to have had some kind of an arrangement with Salomon about publication rights of the 'London' Symphonies. It is not known how a Parisian publisher such as Imbault got hold of Haydn's London Symphonies. It is now known that Artaria in Vienna simply reprinted André's editions; thus Haydn was in no way responsible for the Artaria editions of the Salomon Symphonies.

In February 1795, André of Offenbach-on-the-Main printed the first two London Symphonies, Nos. 96 and 95 (which as we now know were also the first Haydn composed in 1791); six weeks afterwards, Artaria reprinted them. In August, André brought out no less than six Piano Trios composed by Haydn during the second London visit: Nos. 32–7 (XV: 18–23); he also printed the 'Surprise' Symphony (No. 94), another of the 1791 symphonic works. The Apponyi Quartets, Opp. 71 and 74, came out more or less simultaneously in London (Corri & Dussek), Offenbach (André) and Vienna (Artaria), the first three at the end of 1795, the second three in 1796. In January 1796, the last Piano Trios of the second London visit – those dedicated to Mistress Schroeter, Nos. 38–40 (XVI: 24–6) – were published by André; as with all these Piano Trios, Artaria immediately reprinted them in Vienna. In the first six months of 1796, André brought out the first editions of Symphonies 98, 97, 93, and the *Concertante* (I:

1 In a concert devised by us at Llandaff Cathedral (Cardiff) in the Autumn of 1971, the experiment was attempted whereby Haydn's *Scena di Berenice* was immediately followed by Beethoven's 'Ah! perfido'. The audience and the performers were struck by the basic similarity and also by the fascinating differences.

2 Kalischer, p. 6. The 'Great Mogul' or 'Grand Mogul' epithet also in Sir George Grove's article on Beethoven in Grove I, 168. We cannot find the original source for 'Großmogul' in the Haydn literature, but it appears in the Beethoven literature regularly; there seems to us no particular reason to doubt its authenticity.

105). It was not before 1799 that Germany saw printed editions of Haydn's second set of Salomon Symphonies: No. 100 ('Military') came out in two editions (Gombart of Augsburg, André of Offenbach) in February and March respectively, Nos. 101 ('Clock') and 103 ('Drum Roll'), also in two editions, during the summer. Nos. 99, 102, and 104 did not appear on the Continent until 1801, a year after *The Creation* had been published by Haydn himself in Vienna. Arrangements of the London Symphonies for piano trio, made by Salomon, appeared in London in 1796 and 1797; Simrock of Bonn also brought out his edition of the second set in the autumn of 1797. It was not until 1799 that any of the solo piano music appeared (Sonata No. 62[52]; *Andante con variazioni* [XVII: 6]).

All these publications gave Haydn a new lease of artistic life on the Continent. The great Salomon Symphonies, the Apponyi Quartets, the Piano Trios, and the piano solo music were on a much larger scale than almost any of Haydn's previous works in those forms; they immediately created a new image of their composer. Even the English *Canzonettas* are far greater than the earlier *Lieder*. We have read, in *Haydn in England 1791–1795*, that Englishmen were sure that Haydn must have 'written himself out', and we have followed their astonishment at the new works that the old composer poured out. The astonishment cannot have been any the less in Paris or Berlin.

The interesting thing, for us in retrospect, is that as Germany was exploring this last phase of Haydn's creative activity, it was also discovering Mozart, whose widow Constanze had made an agreement with André of Offenbach, whereby that German firm issued a large number of Mozart's works *for the first time*; later Constanze sold some other works to Breitkopf & Härtel, but it was André that got the lion's share. The operas were also appearing, one after the other. When they were performed, they were from manuscript parts; the printed editions were, as yet, only piano scores. In 1794 *Die Zauberflöte* came out in Leipzig and elsewhere. The next year Siegfried Schmiedt published, also in Leipzig, piano scores of *Così fan tutte* and *La clemenza di Tito*; the other great operas, *Le nozze di Figaro* and *Don Giovanni*, were already printed in many editions by the middle of the 1790s, but it is pleasant to record that *Idomeneo*, that brilliant first-fruit of Mozart's maturity, was published 'aggiustata per il Cembalo di G. Wenzel' at Prague in 1797. By 1802, André of Offenbach had engraved 109 works by Mozart with opus numbers and many others without.

Of Mozart's Viennese piano Concertos, only one early work (K.175, but with the new Finale, K.382, Paris, 1784), three relatively early ones (K. 414, 413, 415, issued by Artaria in January 1785), two works of 1784 (K. 451, Paris 1785; K. 453, Speyer 1787) and the last (K. 595, issued by Artaria in August 1791) were published in Mozart's lifetime. Constanze herself published posthumously one of the greatest in a private print (Vienna): K. 503, possibly on Haydn's recommendation (it would have been typical of him to choose the most intellectual of all Mozart's concertos, also the one with the most profound 'motivic' development in the Haydn tradition); later she sold the plates to Breitkopf & Härtel. Not only were the German publishers busily printing and pirating editions, but a brisk business in manuscript copies of Mozart's music flourished: in 1795 there were still many works available only in manuscript copies. Johann Traeg in Vienna, who sold manuscripts and was also a publisher, could offer by the middle of 1792 a large quantity of Mozart's music in MS., including six Masses, two horn concertos, fifteen symphonies, wind-band *Parthien*, and so on. A crucial development in the dissemination of Mozart's music was the long concert tour that Constanze Mozart made to Germany in 1796. Audiences in Dresden, Leipzig and Berlin had a chance to hear authentic interpretations of many unpublished works by

Mozart. Constanze hired an orchestra in each case; she gave no less than three concerts at the Gewandhaus in Leipzig; at one, Mozart's friend Anton Eberl played one of the dead master's piano concertos; at another, the *Requiem* was given its first German performance. (Beethoven was also touring Germany at that time; no doubt they met at Leipzig at the beginning of May.) But even in 1794 and 1795 Mozart's music was creating an enormous impact on the German-speaking world. In an article from *Teutschlands Annalen des Jahres 1794*, published at Chemnitz in 1795, we read:

> In this year, 1794, nothing is or can be sung or played, nothing listened to with applause, except that which the all-powerful magic name of Mozart can conjure up. Operas, symphonies, quartets, trios, duets, piano music, even dances – it all has to be by Mozart, if it has pretensions to win general approbation. The music publishers, too, have left no stone unturned in satisfying the hungry amateurs. By means of the fine art of *arrangement*, we already have *Die Zauberflöte* by this composer engraved and printed in all the forms listed above. Heaven knows how fantastically some of these attempts have turned out, and considering the nature of this piece, must turn out. Enough, one plays or sings Mozart, and what is more, from his *Zauberflöte*.
>
> That Mozart has in large measure deserved this success, no one will deny. But he was still sowing his wild oats and his ideas were still fermenting, and you can find far too much proof of this in his works. Just to remain with his *symphonies* for a moment: with all their fire, all their pomp and brilliance, they lack the unity, clarity and distinction of presentation that we rightly admire in *Jos. Haydn's* symphonies. Whoever has had the chance to undertake similar comparisons in Mozart's works *for the voice*, as against the works of other good masters, will find still more defects. When listening to Mozart's music one often would like to call out, as did that chamber maid [*Kammerjungfer*] in the comedy, 'Thank God, there's nothing natural about me!' It's almost all over-spiced food which, if eaten too frequently, ruins the stomach, and because of the countless imitators, who think that all they must do in order to be successful is to write Mozartian music, all noble simplicity is being banned from music. This could easily be the end result of this general deification.
>
> *Mozart's Zauberflöte*, piano score, [was published] in Maynz [Mainz], Mannheim, Offenbach, Leipzig, Berlin, and Braunschweig: that is to say, six times in one and the same year; an example hitherto unexcelled in the history of musical literature, and which more than vindicates that which was said above concerning the general enthusiasm for Mozart's works.

Within a few years, when a large part of Mozart's mature music became known in Germany – it would be another half-century and more before the youthful (or, say, pre-1780) works appeared, mostly for the first time, in the Breitkopf & Härtel *Gesamtausgabe* – the spectacular nature of his genius began to be appreciated by all classes, and not at the expense of Haydn or anyone else. It is interesting that this great discovery of Mozart should coincide, (1) with the dissemination of Haydn's late works, and even his London compositions, in the German- and French-speaking world, and (2) with the growing awareness of Beethoven as a new force in music. We should point out that while late Haydn was very much appreciated at the end of the eighteenth century and the first decade or two of the nineteenth, it took Mozart much longer to penetrate the French musical world, and Beethoven the longest of all.[1]

1 Wolfgang Matthäus, 'Das Werk Haydns im Spiegel der Geschichte des Verlages Jean André' in *Haydn Yearbook* III (1965), pp. 54ff. Gerber, *NTL* III, 491. Deutsch, *Mozart Dokumente*, 207, 350, 406f. Mozart: Köchel Catalogue, 5th (Einstein), 6th and 7th editions. Thayer-Forbes I, 184 (Beethoven's dates in Leipzig, 1796).

CHAPTER FOUR

Works of 1795

IN THE THREE AND A HALF MONTHS of the year 1795 that remained after Haydn returned to Vienna, we know with certainty of only a single new composition, the

Piano Trio No. 41

in E flat minor (XV: 31)

This Trio is dated on the autograph 'di me giuseppe Haydn [mpria] $\overline{795}$'. Unlike the autographs of works composed by Haydn in London, there is here no mention of 'Londra' or 'London' next to the date, nor is the Trio listed in the *Catalogue of Works Composed in England* (reproduced in *Haydn in England 1791–1795*, pp. 316ff.). We have in the autograph proof that this work was composed after Haydn had left England.[1]

There is, however, an aura of mystery about this small but potent work. It was not published until 1803. Why did Haydn withhold such an easily saleable work for so long? Perhaps he wrote it for someone in England such as Mrs Bartolozzi, who insisted on having all the rights to it. Perhaps, too, he did send it to an English publisher and no copy has survived, a situation which on the face of it sounds incredible but actually occurred with the next Trio, No. 42, of 1796.

Griesinger informs us that Haydn gave the *Sonata* (as Trio No. 41's autograph is entitled) to Johann Traeg. We shall be quoting the whole story *verbatim* when the time comes, and here we need mention only as much of the report as concerns our work. In the summer of 1803, Haydn got into an argument with Traeg. The composer was working on a new revision of *L'isola disabitata*, which he hoped to sell to Breitkopf & Härtel, and he learned that Traeg owned the autograph. It seems that Traeg had purchased that autograph and those of three other Haydn operas in 1788 from among the papers of the late Count Erdödy. Haydn asked Traeg for the autograph and Traeg sent it. 'After a certain time,' continues Griesinger, 'Traeg asked to have it sent back or that he be given 12 ducats instead. Haydn, enraged by this demand, sent for Traeg and, in the presence of other persons, thoroughly dressed him down. To avoid all further arguments, however, he finally handed over the Sonata *quaestionis* which he had composed in London' (Pohl III, 214). We have seen, however, that the Trio was not composed *in* England but certainly *for* England.

Traeg made haste with his new work and on 27 August 1803 he announced his new acquisition in the *Wiener Zeitung* as 'written especially for him [Traeg]'. This long-delayed first edition was dedicated to Madelaine von Kurzbeck (Kurzböck), to whom Haydn had also dedicated the Artaria edition of the Sonata No. 62 in E flat (see

1 The present owner of the autograph, Mrs Eva Alberman, kindly sent us a photographic copy. She was also good enough to inform us that the autograph's watermark is the usual three half-moons of decreasing size found in the Italian paper which Haydn used for all his compositions from 1795 onwards. Had it been composed in England, the Trio would have been written on paper with a distinctive British watermark.

Haydn in England 1791–1795). We shall see that in the same year, Haydn sent it to Paris with a covering letter to 'Mme le Genéralé Moreau' dated 1 November 1803. Traeg put on his edition 'Edition faite d'aprês le manuscrit original' – probably it was an Elssler copy, but perhaps it really was the autograph itself – and Nadermann, who brought out the work as a violin sonata, Haydn having dropped the 'cello part *en route* to Paris, boasted of the work as 'Dernière Sonate pour le piano avec accompagnement de violon composée expressement pour Madame La Maréchale Moreau. . . .' The French edition, by Nadermann, appeared only in 1820 or thereabouts.

Several things about this E flat minor Piano Trio are immediately striking. One point is the greatly increased role of the violin, which has many solos, including a particularly glorious solo in the slow movement; the violoncello is still part of the basso continuo and fulfils a largely colouristic function. Another point is the astonishing way in which Haydn treats his keys in this work. The very fact of E flat minor should lead us to expect something out of the ordinary, and Haydn does not disappoint us. We find him once again treating the third-related keys *enharmonically*: the great violin solo is in B major, related to E flat minor by treating E flat as D sharp, and this occurs in the middle of the first movement. In the wiry, tough, and very intellectual second movement, we are faced with a key signature of four sharps (in a movement in E flat) as early as bar 54. The arabesques of the piano part in this same second movement are free almost to the point of eccentricity. The formal scheme of Trio No. 41 is as follows:

I *Andante cantabile*. II *Allegro* (= autograph; the prints have instead 'Allegro ben moderato', possibly a change made or authorized by Haydn).

The opening slow movement is a variation movement but built on a rondo scheme. The opening phrase is used in inversion to begin the next section, in E flat major:

In rondo scheme, the movement would look as follows: A (a–b–a′), E flat minor – B (a″ inverted–b″–a″), E flat major – A (a–b–a′), E flat minor, a straight repetition of the earlier section but without repeats – C (new melody) in B major, followed by lead-back to A′ (a‴–b‴–a‴), that is, a variation of the original material in E flat minor.

It is a restless movement, in sombre autumnal colouring, except for the brilliant shaft of colour that is introduced by the big violin solo in B major:

The Finale, says Charles Rosen (p. 362), 'is . . . a German dance in elaborate and sophisticated style, where the accompaniment is so important it becomes a countertheme. The whole movement appears to be built out of fragments, almost without melody of any kind, yet the continuity and the lilt of the dance are always there. This is the kind of work that can only come at the end of a long career.'

The cautionary 'ben moderato' of the printed work is for sight-readers who might tend to take the tempo too quickly, not knowing the wild flights of fancy that Haydn has in store for the pianist:

We notice how naturally Haydn has now assimilated all the new pianistic devices: fast alternation of left and right hand on the same notes (bars 23/4), crossing the hands (bars 27ff.); and notice the independence of the violin's line:

The excursion into B major, though only four sharps are used, links this passage to the big B major solo in the slow movement: the way in which Haydn manages to pinpoint his two excursions into an enharmonic third-related key (the submediant of D sharp major/minor) is brilliant. When the opening material comes in again, there are fantastic eccentricities in the piano part; first, two bars of cadenza-like interludes:

and later a chromatic run that sounds as if it has escaped from a piano concerto (bars 101ff.).

All this is totally unlike Beethoven's piano trios of the mid-1790s, which are as charming, winning, and smoothly flowing as this music is thorny, dry, totally

[Piano Trio No. 41: Finale – Allegro].

intellectual, and almost devoid of normal emotions. There is, indeed, a curious avoidance of emotion in this Trio and a concentration on intellectual values which clearly point the way to much of Haydn's late chamber music (e.g. the Finale of the Quartet Op. 76, No. 6), which gradually comes to exist in an abstract world of its own.

Yet it would be wrong to underestimate the brilliance and panache with which the old Haydn infuses this last movement. He even thinks it necessary to write the fingering for the piano triplets just before the end of the work, no doubt to show that he did not disapprove of the old rule against using the thumb on the black keys. The fingering marked with an asterisk is thus Haydn's own, from the autograph:

We have no evidence that Haydn ever performed this Trio in Vienna, but we may suppose he did so, at least in his own circle of friends.[1]

Other Works

Although we are able to date the major works of the period 1795–1803 (the latter date marking the year when Haydn stopped composing almost entirely), there are some apparently late-period works which defy attempts to date them precisely. This is particularly true of two important works which we propose to discuss at this point.

1 Frits Noske, 'Le principe structural génétique dans l'œuvre instrumental de Joseph Haydn', a paper read at the Mozart Congress in Vienna 1956; Dr Noske kindly sent me a typewritten copy of it. Charles Rosen, *The Classical Style (Haydn, Mozart, Beethoven)*, London 1971, pp. 362f.

OFFERTORIUM: 'NON NOBIS, DOMINE' (XXIIIa:1)

This is a work which, in its whole conception, is difficult to date: it is described by Haydn in the *Entwurf-Katalog* – a running draft catalogue, mostly with *incipits*, which Haydn and his copyists maintained from *c.* 1765 to the early years of the nineteenth century – as 'Offertorio in Stillo a Capella'. It is a work scored for four-part choir (S-A-T-B) and basso continuo (organ and violoncello-basso) and is deliberately in the archaic, so-called 'Palestrina' style. Being in an old-fashioned manner, and since neither autograph nor contemporary dated manuscript copies of the work exist, Haydn scholars have, rather wildly, dated it variously from the beginning of the 1770s (Geiringer), during the 1770s (Pohl, Larsen), before 1790 (Brand) and *c.* 1799 (Pohl-Botstiber). Recently, Irmgard Becker-Glauch subjected the work to intensive study, and has come to several conclusions. (1) Haydn's autograph entry in the *Entwurf-Katalog* was made in great haste, as a result of which those typical, distinguishing characteristics of Haydn's handwriting in various periods of his life (compare his handwriting in the 1770s with that of *c.* 1795) are blurred. (2) Haydn made two versions of the work. The one which Becker-Glauch, undoubtedly rightly, decides is the later version is *not* the one printed in Pohl's authoritative score (1871) and *not* the one in modern editions by Müller (1958) and Geiringer (1960). Both versions are given in our edition for Verlag Doblinger (which was delivered many years ago but has had to be held up in favour of other works). (3) For neither the first nor the second version is there any copy which we can date with certainty before *c.* 1790. Becker-Glauch then points out the fact that the text (Psalm 115, v. 1),[1] 'Not unto us, O Lord, not unto us, but unto thy name give glory, for thy mercy, *and* for thy truth's sake', was very popular in England but hardly known (in the musical sense) in Austria. Becker-Glauch could locate only one other Austrian setting of the text: by Albrechtsberger's pupil Joseph Preindl, whose name has been mentioned several times in the course of the introduction to this year; Preindl's setting is also difficult to date, but the earliest known source is from the year 1804. In England, it was Byrd's famous Canon that circulated the text to every musician in that country; Mozart made a copy (leaving out the words) and the publishers Breitkopf & Härtel put this into the *Oeuvres complètes de Mozart*, Cahier 16, as a genuine piece. Haydn himself owned two copies of Byrd's music, one in his edition of the *Vollkommener Kapellmeister* by Mattheson and one which is listed in the catalogue, drawn up by Elssler, of MSS. and printed music in Haydn's library. In the *Verzeichnis gestochener Musikalien* is listed 'The Celebrated Canon. Non nobis Domine, adapted as a Fugue for the Organ, London, groß fol:' which turns out to be an arrangement by Haydn's friend, Joseph Diettenhofer, known to us from *Haydn in England 1791–1795*.

It would seem, then, that the inspiration for Haydn's 'Non nobis, Domine' came from England. He may have composed it for the church choir at Eisenstadt, but if that be the case, it is curious that the Esterházy Archives do not own a copy of the *first* version. As for the revised version, its authenticity is vouchsafed for us in a copy in the Esterházy Archives at Eisenstadt. It is a very late copy, perhaps even as late as *c.* 1801–2. Becker-Glauch is very careful and describes the Eisenstadt copy as 'wohl nicht vor den 1790er Jahren'. But in fact the watermarks of the copy (Italian paper with the letters 'FA' and a single half-moon with a profile) suggest the period immediately following

1 Becker-Glauch takes Geiringer to task for citing this Psalm; she says the correct reference is Psalm 113, v. 9, which, of course, it certainly is not in any St James version, some copies of which may possibly have reached Cologne by that time.

1800. In this connection we may mention Brand's suggestion that 'Non nobis, Domine' was one of the works that Prince Nicolaus II Esterházy delivered to the Parisian Concert des Amateurs; the package 'contenant une messe, une offertoire et un Te Deum' was acknowledged by the administrators in a letter to Haydn dated 11 January 1803. It is thought that the three works were the autographs of the *Schöpfungsmesse* of 1801 (now in the Bayerische Staatsbibliothek, Munich), the *Te Deum* of 1799 or 1800 (autograph lost) and 'Non nobis Domine'. It is the only work of its kind that Haydn himself entitled 'Offertorium'. Nor is there any other late-period piece of smaller church music which would be of a kind to match the splendours of the late Mass and late *Te Deum*. It is even possible that Haydn undertook the revision of the work when he sent it to the Concert des Amateurs; that would have been 1802, when he was still capable of writing the great *Harmoniemesse*.

Hesitant as one is to date a work in this peculiarly limited style, we see no alternative at the moment but to assign it to the period *c.* 1795, revised *c.* 1802. Perhaps one day new evidence will turn up which will enable us to date the elusive piece more precisely.[1]

The return to the 'stillo a Capella', however, is by no means peculiar to Haydn or the Austrian school. We find an equally surprising example in the works of the Italian composer Antonio di Donato,[2] a 'Graduale per la festività del Glorioso, e Protettor di Napoli S. Giacomo della Marca', of which the autograph is dated 1796. The difference between this severe *Graduale* and Donato's usual Neapolitan style is extraordinary. The contrast may be illustrated by comparing the extract from his *Salve Regina* in B flat with the choral entrance of the *Graduale*, opposite. (Cf. also 'Laudate pueri' from Mozart's *Vesperae solennes de confessore*, K. 339, of 1780.)

But in the case of the Haydn *Offertorium*, if the date is elusive, the work itself is a magnificent contribution to the 'Palestrina' style. The theme itself –

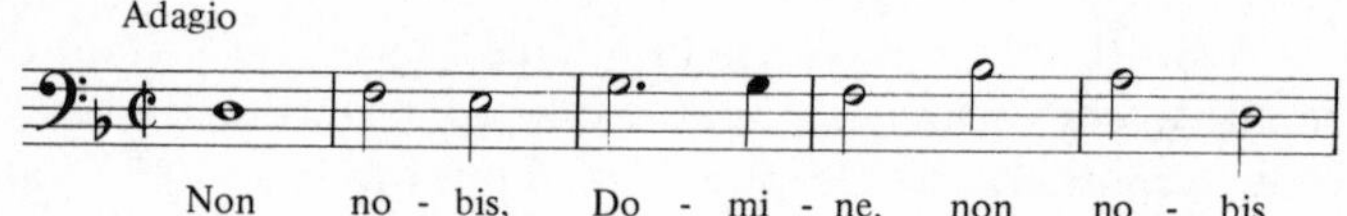

– is of the same kind as the *incipit* to the lost *Missa Sunt bona mixta malis* (*c.* 1768), which Aloys Fuchs in his thematic catalogue entitled 'a 4 Voci senza Strom[enti]' and 'Alla Capella'. Haydn associates this kind of 'stilo antico' with D minor, for another work in a similar 'antique' manner, and also in D minor, is the beautiful *Libera* setting of *c.* 1790 (published in *Haydn Yearbook* IV). Although the *Libera* is Gregorian chant alternating with homophonic settings, while the *Offertorium* is a huge polyphonic structure, there are similarities between the works, for example, the much disputed passage that Haydn revised (bars 60–9); which in the revised version overleaf –

1 C. F. Pohl's edition published by Rieter-Biedermann, Leipzig and Winterthur, 1871; Alois Maria Müller's edition published by Anton Böhm & Sohn, Augsburg, 1958; Karl Geiringer's edition published by Concordia, St Louis, Mo., 1960. Irmgard Becker-Glauch, 'Neue Forschungen zu Haydns Kirchenmusik', in *Haydn-Studien* II/3 (1970), pp. 167ff. and especially 224–8. Larsen, *HÜB*, 235; Pohl III, 149 (obviously Botstiber here, because Pohl himself dated the work in the 1770s in his Foreword to the Rieter-Biedermann edition). Karl Geiringer, 'The Small Sacred Works by Haydn in the Esterházy Archives at Eisenstadt', in *Musical Quarterly* XLV (1959), pp. 460ff., especially 466f. Brand, *Messen*, 414. CCLN, 213. *Thematisches Verzeichnis der sämtlichen Kompositionen von Joseph Haydn*, zusammengestellet von Alois Fuchs 1839 (Schaal), 1968, p. 177.

2 Autograph manuscripts of Antonio di Donato and other members of his family (one of whom was *Capellmeister* in Braunschweig) are preserved in the Bavarian State Library, Munich. The *Graduale* and *Salve Regina* are owned by the present writer.

[Antonio di Donato: *Salve Regina*]

Vivace
Sop. Solo
Ad Te cla - ma - - - - - - - - mus

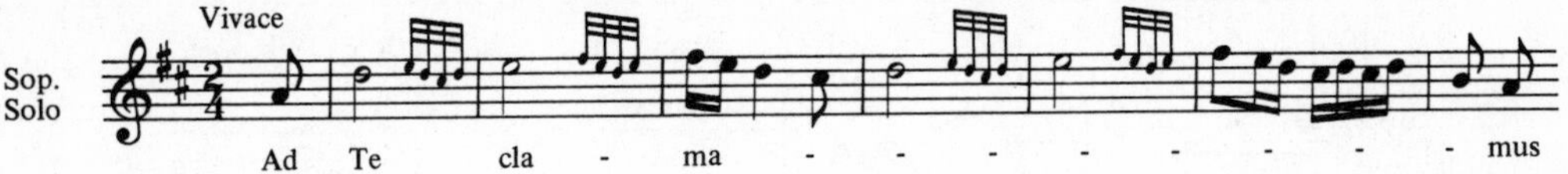

[*Graduale*]

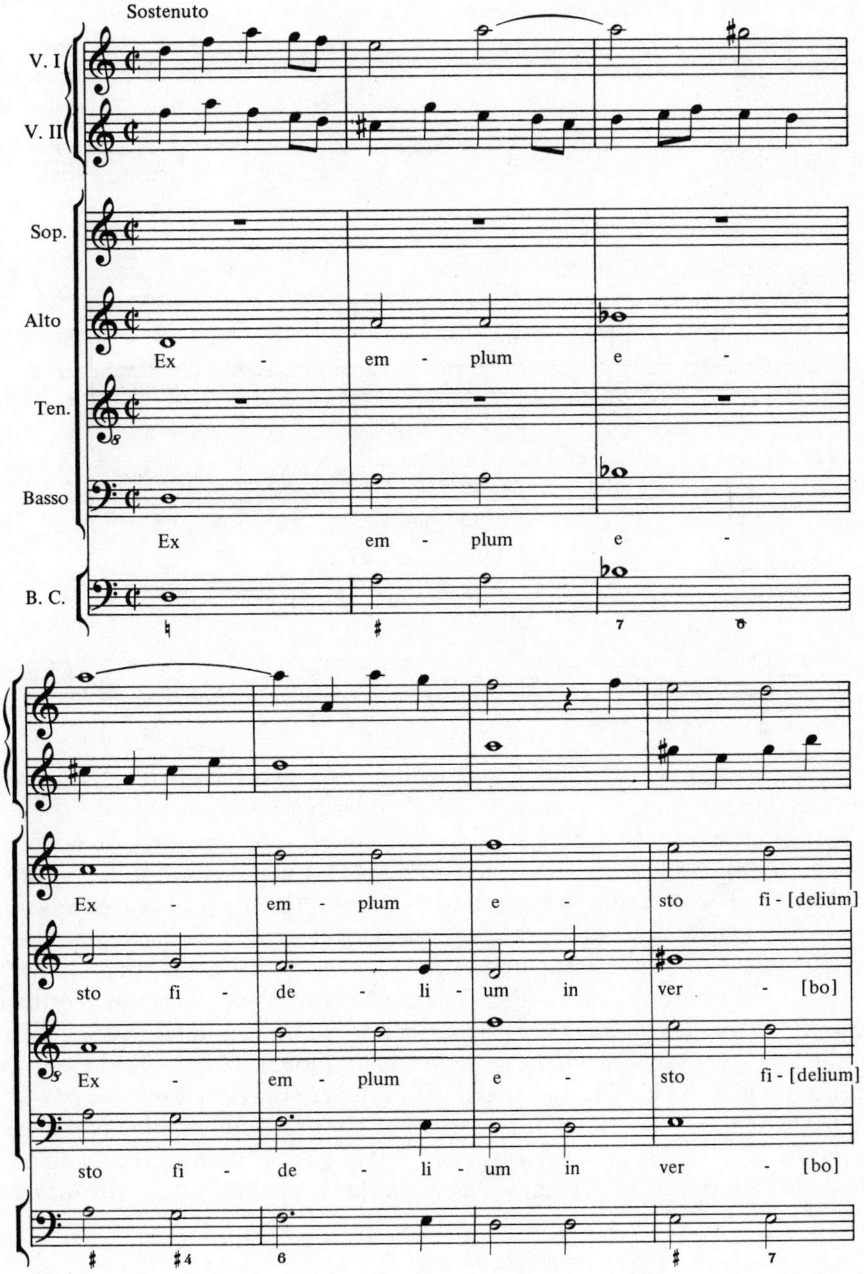

Sostenuto
V. I
V. II
Sop.
Alto
Ex - em - plum e -
Ten.
Basso
Ex em - plum e -
B. C.
Ex - em - plum e - sto fi - [delium]
sto fi - de - li - um in ver - [bo]
Ex - em - plum e - sto fi - [delium]
sto fi - de - li - um in ver - [bo]

– has what Becker-Glauch calls 'a surprising agreement' with the 'Dum veneris judicare saeculum per ignem' sections from the *Libera* (opposite).

It will interest Haydn scholars to see the simpler version of bars 60–9 in the *Offertorium* (see example overleaf). The work ends with a gigantic pedal point in the great old tradition followed by a stern, uncompromising cadence (see example, p. 83).

We would like to conclude this section on the *Offertorium* with a theory about the first performance of perhaps the first version; we advance this theory with the reservation that there is no additional information whatever to confirm it. Rosenbaum's Diary for Sunday, 10 September 1797, notes the following:[1] 'For the Feast of St Mary we had a new Mass, the music by [Johann Nepomuk] Fuchs, also a new chorus by Joseph Haydn. . . .' Rosenbaum does not make clear if the new chorus was part of the church ceremony or was given at a concert, for the next entry suggests that a concert of secular music also took place: 'Baroness Walterskirchen sang an aria.' Else Radant thought that Haydn's piece might have been the 'Storm Chorus'

1 Radant, *Rosenbaum*, 25; Becker-Glauch, op. cit., 234.

Sop.
Alto
Ten.
Basso
Dum ve - ne - ris ju - di - ca -
♭7
6
7
[Fine]
-re sae - cu - lum per i - gnem.
-re sae - cu - lum per - - gnem.
[+Pedale]
4
[Fine]

[*Offertorium*]

(Madrigal, London 1792) which by 1797 also existed in a German version. If on the other hand the new work was part of the religious ceremony, it cannot have been the 'Storm Chorus'. Becker-Glauch considers and rejects the Motet, 'Insanae et vanae curae', which Haydn himself arranged and reorchestrated (adding a kettledrum part) from a chorus in *Il ritorno di Tobia*, 'Svanisce in un momento', added to the Oratorio for a performance in 1784. Becker-Glauch thinks the orchestration was perhaps too large, especially the wind section, for the available Eisenstadt forces; but on the other hand, the *Missa in tempore belli*, which was given on 29 September 1797 at Eisenstadt, has almost as large a wind section. We wonder if the 'new chorus' for this occasion might not have been the *Offertorium* 'Non nobis, Domine'. Even if it was the work

performed on 10 September, it is a question, of course, how 'new' it was: new to Rosenbaum, certainly; perhaps also new to Eisenstadt.

The striking Motet, 'Insanae et vanae curae' is of course not a new work at all; but in Haydn's reorchestration it deserves brief mention here. Built like the 1792 Madrigal 'The Storm' in several sections, a stormy one in D minor and a more peaceful one in the major, which latter is also in a slower tempo, the Motet became one of Haydn's most popular religious works; it was later (1809) printed by Breitkopf & Härtel. The original scoring is for flute, two oboes, two bassoons, two horns in F, two horns in D, two trombones, strings, and four-part (S-A-T-B) chorus. Haydn gave the D-horn parts to 'clarini' (trumpets) and added a kettledrum part which gives an added dramatic touch to the work. In the Eisenstadt Archives there are two sets of parts. one by Johann Elssler (with later duplicate parts) on paper with the watermarks: three half-moons of decreasing size; 'REAL', 'GF' [Galvani Fratelli] under an ornament;

star-fish. And there are parts for the voices, strings, and the wind instruments, including the horns, trumpets and trombones. A second set of parts, of a later date, lacks the horn parts. In 1798, Silverstolpe acquired a set of parts of the work from Haydn; it was copied by a man whom we know only as 'Anonymous 63', who used to be confused with Elssler but who was obviously another man who often made authentic copies for Haydn in the period 1780–1800.[1]

TWENTY-FOUR MINUETS FOR ORCHESTRA
(IX: 6)

The second large work which is undated but which we have placed here is the collection of Twenty-four Minuets for orchestra (IX: 6). Its precise position in Haydn's *œuvre* presents the same kind of difficulty as the *Offertorium*, but for different, though basically not unsimilar, stylistic reasons. Dance music was, as far as the formal organization went, a stereotyped matter; and from the strictly formal standpoint, there is hardly any difference between the pre-1760 'Seitenstetten' Minuets (IX: 1) and the works under present consideration. What is enormously different is the melodic richness and the orchestration. No one familiar with Haydn would fail to recognize that the 'Seitenstetten' are very early, while the Twenty-four Minuets are very late works. But just how late? It would be a brave man who would – if he did not know the Köchel numbers and the music concerned – dare to guess the internal chronology of Mozart's dances of the years 1785–91. The only source for our Twenty-four Minuets is a set of MS. parts in the Berlin Staatsbibliothek from the Artaria Collection (a series of autographs and authentic copies sold to the Berlin Library in 1897). The manuscripts came from Haydn's legacy, for in a catalogue that August Artaria printed in 1893, the material is described as 'Verzeichnis von Musikalischen Autographen, Revidirten Abschriften und einigen seltenen gedruckten Original-Ausgaben, vornehmlich der reichen Bestände aus dem Nachlasse Joseph Haydn's und Ludwig van Beethovens' (Catalogue of musical autographs, revised copies and some rare original editions, mostly from the rich material of the estates of Joseph Haydn and Ludwig van Beethoven). Some of these manuscripts were no doubt part of the 'twelve pieces of music' that Haydn sent to Artaria with a letter on 17 August 1805. Others came, according to Pohl (who had access to the Artaria files), from Haydn's copyist Johann Elssler.

The title page of this unique source reads:

24 Menuetti
a
2 Violini
2 Oboe e Flauto piccolo
2 Flauti
2 Clarinetti
2 Fagotti
2 Corni
2 Clarini
Timpani e Violoncello
col
Basso
Del Sig^{re} Giuseppe Haydn

1 Becker-Glauch, 233, where there is some doubt registered about the handwriting (note 204).

and the rather accurate manuscript parts, by an anonymous (apparently Viennese) professional copyist, are on Italian paper in quarto format of ten staves per page.

The general style of the music is what would be called 'late Haydn'. If the Minuets were composed for local (Esterházy family) consumption, they can only have been composed after September 1795. From 1761 to 1791, Haydn had trumpets only for about a year in 1780, and clarinets only for a couple of years, in 1776 and 1777. Before 1790, Haydn used to employ the horns in C *alto* to act as substitutes for the missing trumpets; here in the Minuets, the opening No. 1 in C is marked for the horns 'in C Basso'. The clarinet writing shows the influence of Mozart and the Stadlers; Haydn *never* wrote for the instrument in this fashion, and using the *chalumeau* register, in the 1760 works using clarinets (for example, *Divertimento* in C for clarinets and horns [II: 14], 1761; *Divertimento* or *Cassatio* in C for two clarinets, two horns, two violins, two violas and *basso* [II: 17], *c.* 1761).

[No. 9: Trio]

The novel use of the *basso* horns in writing completely separately from the trumpets, such as in No. 8, is also a detail of very late-period Haydn. Altogether the orchestration is on a level with the Salomon Symphonies, both in brilliance of effect and refinement of detail. It is difficult to know what to quote in a work so full of genius, but for orchestral and technical reasons we shall first quote the Minuet No. 8 followed by another delightful detail: the 'Turkish' Trio, in the characteristic key of A minor, of No. 19, with *flauto piccolo* and the note in the violin part (which acted, patently, as the leader), 'Questo Trio deve essere accompagnato col Tamburo, Triangolo ed altri stromenti della musica turca, ma tutti pianissimo'; the parts for the 'Turkish' instruments no longer exist, and we have reconstructed them for our critical edition of the full score (Verlag Doblinger). It is a delicious and original trio.

The C *basso* horn parts, rising to high *b* and then to high *d* (sounding *b′* and *d″*) in the first horn at bars 17–9, cuts through the orchestral sound in a startling way; it will be noticed how cleverly the trumpets are devised at this point, remaining in a low *tessitura* until the horns' effect has been made (second crotchet of bar 19).

The Trio of No. 19 of the Twenty-four Minuets (Doblinger edition, page 55) is shown on pp. 88–9. If this particular Trio is exotic and piquant, there is another side to these incredibly diverse Minuets, and that is the sheer, naked power of No. 22, in D minor, to the establishment of which Haydn uses *ff* and *f assai* (see pp. 90–1).

We know that Haydn wrote Twelve Minuets for the Prince of Oettingen-Wallerstein, for he writes to the Prince's Viennese agent sometime in October (probably the 17th): 'At last I can deliver to you, Sir, the 3 Symphonies [Nos. 90–2]. . . . A week from today, at the latest, I shall take the liberty of sending 12 brand new Dance Minuets with 12 Trios for this wonderful celebration' (which was Prince Krafft Ernst's second marriage). The Wallerstein copy of these Minuets has disappeared. A few months later, we find Haydn trying to persuade a reluctant Artaria to print them: 'But in order to cancel my debt to you, you must also accept the 12 new

[Minuet No. 8]

Twenty-four Minuets for Orchestra: No. 19. Page from the first violin part, taken from the only extant source – an authentic set of parts formerly owned by Artaria & Co., Vienna. This page includes the 'Turkish' Trio in which a 'Flauto Piccolo Solo' is featured; it also includes the note 'Questo Trio deve esser accompagnato col Tamburo Triangolo, ed altri stromenti della musica turca, ma tutti pianissimo'.

[Minuet No. 19: Trio]

*) Note in original MS. 'Questo Trio deve esser accompagnato col Tamburo, Triangolo, ed altri stromenti della musica turca, ma tutti pianissimo.'

**) MS. [notated rhythm] (cf. Violino I)

---

and most splendid Minuets with 12 Trios, for 12 ducats.' Artaria did not take these but, as we saw, he accepted with alacrity the 1792 Redoutensaal Dances from Haydn. Now if Vienna had never heard these twelve 'splendid Minuets', it is conceivable that Haydn used them *en bloc* for the 1792 Minuets.

These Oettingen-Wallerstein Minuets are not the only insoluble problem, however, for in 1947, the Spanish scholar Solar-Quintes drew our attention to a series of works Haydn sent to the Countess-Duchess of Benavente and Osuna (María Josefa Alonso Pimentel, First Lady of the Court of Madrid), including twenty-four minuets and twenty-four country dances. This music was sent from 1783 to about 1789. Alas, none of these works has been uncovered in the Spanish archives. But it is improbable that the Countess-Duchess can have asked for works with a huge orchestra like that of the Twenty-four Minuets under discussion, and even more unlikely that Haydn thought Spanish clarinets (if there were any) can have negotiated *chalumeau* passages which were a speciality of the Stadler brothers in Vienna and hardly known outside Austria or Bohemia. But on the other hand, Haydn may have saved the music that he sent to Spain and it is possible that some of this dance music has survived in other collections of Haydn's minuets and country dances.

We will see, in the Chronicles of 1795 *et seq.*, that there were often grand balls at Eisenstadt. Haydn was probably too busy to conduct all the music for these occasions, but it is entirely likely that he found the time to conduct such a series of twenty-four

[Minuet No. 22]

---

minuets. The Esterházy's also gave elaborate parties in their Palace in the Wallnerstrasse, and Haydn may have conducted the dance music for such glittering occasions; in Vienna, moreover, there were many noble houses with which Haydn was intimately connected, and for whom he can have furnished dance music; engaging such a large orchestra would also be no problem in Vienna.

We have therefore placed these great minuets at the beginning of the last period of Haydn's creative life. Together with the famous Redoutensaal Music of 1792 (Twelve Minuets and Twelve German Dances), these minuets are Haydn's legacy to the Austrian dance tradition, a tradition to which Mozart had contributed some of the greatest dance music ever composed, to which Beethoven had offered his Redoutensaal Dances of 1795 and would compose many more such dances during his career, and with which, as time went on, Schubert, Lanner and the Strauss dynasty would be intimately associated. We have seen in *Haydn in England 1791–1795* that there is now evidence that the people of Vienna waltzed to Haydn's German Dances; but the

minuets are for more formal occasions, for the graceful Austrian nobility. They mark almost the end of an era, for within Haydn's own lifetime the minuet was to become old-fashioned and would be replaced by other, newer and more 'democratic' dance forms.

The first modern performance of any of the Twenty-four Minuets took place in connection with a conference at Eisenstadt in the autumn of 1971, organized by the Institut für österreichische Kulturgeschichte.[1] The first recording was in 1975 for Decca (released 1976), conducted by Antal Dorati.

1 Larsen, *HÜB* 31f.; CCLN 89, 94, 238; Nicolás A. Solar-Quintes, 'Las relaciones de Haydn con la Casa de Benavente', in *Annuario Musical* II, Barcelona 1947, pp. 81–88; Georg Feder gives a summary of this article in 'Manuscript sources of Haydn's works and their distribution', *Haydn Yearbook* IV 1968, pp. 133f. (German in *Haydn-Studien* I/1, 1965). Haydn: *24 Menuetti*, score; edited by H. C. Robbins Landon; Verlag Doblinger, Vienna–Munich, 1972. We are most grateful to the Duchess of Alba in Madrid for attempting to find the Haydn sources in the Alba Archives – alas to no avail (correspondence 1972–3).

CHAPTER FIVE

Chronicle 1796

ON 2 JANUARY, 1796, Schikaneder's *Freyhaus* (Freehold House) Theater auf der Wieden gave Gluck's epoch-making ballet *Don Juan* (now entitled in Italian *Don Giovanni ossia Il convitato di pietra*). As Silverstolpe observed, hardly any Gluck was given in Vienna during this period, and it must have been with a real sense of nostalgia that Haydn and the older generation of musicians saw the revival of a work which, in 1761, had caused such a profound impact on Austrian music.[1]

On 4 January 1796, Prince Nicolaus II Esterházy gave a huge *festa* at his Palace in the Wallnerstrasse. The choice of the opera given is so extraordinary for the period that one hardly knows whether to think that the Prince had a taste for Baroque opera, or that Haydn – who, as we shall see, was interested in old music and helped to form the first *Denkmäler* – talked his patron into a work which could only have had historical interest for most of the audience – *Penelope (o La Casta Penelope)*, with music by Antonio Draghi (1635–1700), the Hoftheater *Intendant* to Emperor Leopold I. The libretto is by Nicola Monato and the ballet music had been by J. H. Schmelzer when the opera was first performed at Vienna on 18 November 1670. Most of Draghi's music then existed in the Court Library, of which Gottfried van Swieten was the director: can Swieten, with his passion for old music, have had a hand in the choice?

Towards the end of 1795, the theatre designer Pietro Travaglia received an *à conto* payment of 300 gulden towards 'fireworks to be organized, illumination and theatrical bills'. The singers were engaged from the Court Theatre, as was the orchestra; which means that the Eisenstadt band was not considered up to this kind of thing; it will have been far too small, moreover, especially in the string section. Two copyists had to be engaged to prepare all the parts. For all this part of the operation, Haydn signed for the costs, which amounted to 1,100 fl. [the usual abbreviation] 51 x. [the usual abbreviation for Kreuzer] – more than the amount of the *Capellmeister*'s annual pension from Prince Nicolaus 'The Magnificent'.

Not everyone could be invited to this magnificent spectacle, of course. That evening Count Zinzendorf was a guest of Prince F. X. W. Rosenberg-Orsini, who was in charge of the Court Theatres. The old Count noted in his diary: '. . . Le soir chez le P^ce^ Rosenberg avec le P^ce^ Colleredo et la P^sse^ Kinsky, ni l'un ni l'autre n'etant invités au grand Concert du P^ce^ Eszterhasy [*sic*], qui tient la Wallner Straße assiegé de Cavalerie.' We shall often read, in the forthcoming Chronicle, that for large receptions of this kind, mounted cavalry was kept on hand to line the streets leading to the house and, generally, to keep the curious population in their proper places at the road side.[1]

1 Deutsch, *Freihaustheater*, 38.

2 Pohl III, 100; Olleson, 50; Grove I, Vol. I, 461 (article on Draghi by C. F. Pohl), article on 'Draghi' in *MGG*; article on 'Draghi' in *Enciclopedia dello Spettacolo*, IV 935–41.

On 8 January, Haydn and Beethoven again collaborated in a public concert in the small room of the Redoutensaal. It was a benefit concert for the alto singer, Maria Bolla. The programme, which has survived only in the form of a single copy of the hand-bill (Gesellschaft der Musikfreunde; here reproduced in facsimile in plate 13), reads as follows:

AVVISO

Oggi Venerdi 8. del corrente Gennajo la Sigra. Maria Bolla, virtuosa di Musica, darà una Accademia nella piccola Sala del Ridotto. La Musica sarà di nuova composizione del Sigre. Haydn, il quale ne sarà alla direzione.

Vi canteranno la Sigra. Bolla, la Sigra. Tomeoni, e il Sigre. Mombelli.

Il Sigre. Bethofen suonerà un Concerto sul Pianoforte.

Il prezzo dei biglietti d'ingresso sarà di uno zecchino. Questi potranno aversi o alla Cassa del Teatro Nazionale, o in casa della Sigra. Bolla, alla Parisergasse Nro. 444 al secondo piano.

Il principio sarà alle ore sei e mezza.

It is assumed, and probably correctly, that Beethoven will have once again played the B flat piano Concerto, Op. 19. The only piece we can identify with certainty is Haydn's Symphony No. 94, which Zinzendorf describes as 'celle du coup de tonnere':

> . . . Le soir au Concert a la petite Salle de Redoute. Haydn nous interessa avec ses Sinfonies, entr'autres celle du coup de tonnere, destinée a reveiller les dormeurs au Concert anglois. Mombelli nous toucha par son chant. La belle Me Bolla chanta d'une manière très insignificante et la Willmann fit des tours de force . . . Beau tems. Un peu plus froid.

Maria Bolla travelled all over Europe. In 1800 she made her English début, and Parke tells us that 'Madame Bolla, who was an excellent actress as well as singer, possessed a voice which combined strength and sweetness; and in her airs she displayed both grace and animation'. Two years later, George (later Sir George) Smart heard her in Paris, and in his Diary for 15 July 1802 we read: '. . . My father and our two new lodgers went to the Opera Buffa and heard Madame Bolla, who sang very well. . . .' The *AMZ* reviewed Bolla's operatic début in Vienna in 1805:

> Mad. Bolla, who appeared therein [Fioravanti's opera *Die gebesserte Eigensinnige*] for the first time, has a free and professional stage manner, and a handsome, effective, alto voice that somewhat resembles the tone of our Crescentini. Some of the ornamentation with which she richly provided her vocal pieces, as in the Italian manner, is highly successful; she only occasionally misses a passage. She was successful and took a curtsey.

It would appear that Magdalena Willmann, soprano, took the place of Tomeoni, who was perhaps indisposed. About Willmann, the *AMZ* writes: 'Madame Willmann Galvani, first lady singer [at the German Opera in Vienna], has a great deal of skill and through it, she attempts to improve her unequal voice; but she overlabours it with trills, *appoggiature*, and so forth. She is a good actress, and makes a pretty appearance on stage.' About Mombelli, who participated in Haydn's benefit in December 1795, *vide supra*.

The news of Haydn's second set of 'London' Symphonies was beginning to circulate among the German princes, many of whom had been, and were, avid patrons of Haydn's. We have seen that Prince Fürstenberg ordered all twelve London Symphonies for his Castle at Donaueschingen. Now we hear of another German Prince, Krafft-Ernst of Oettingen-Wallerstein, an old patron of Haydn's, who had, in 1793, received several of the first Salomon Symphonies. In January 1796, Prince Krafft-Ernst writes to his court agent in Vienna:

> P. P. As I understand, there are supposed to be 6 new symphonies by Haydn which have come out and are to be had in Vienna. My etc. [court agent] will not only send them here at my expense and inform of the price required but will also ask Haydn, if he should happen to be in Vienna, in my name if he is willing to compose some new symphonies and send them here . . .

The Prince thought, of course, that these '6 new symphonies' were ones that he did not yet own; in fact, they were not the *second* set of London Symphonies but the printed parts of the first which, as we have seen, appeared in installments in Vienna during 1795 and 1796. Haydn did not send Prince Krafft-Ernst any of the second Salomon Symphonies.[1]

On 31 January, Count Zinzendorf was, at last, invited to a 'grand souper' at Prince Esterházy's:

> 'Le P[ce] Eszterhazy me fit inviter a son grand souper de ce soir, et fesant des excuses de ce que je n'avois pas eté invité de meilleure heure, par une bevüe des m. d'hotel. . . . Au grand souper de P[ce] Eszterhazy. On m'y renouvella des excuses. Je saurois avec Saurau . . . Je vis les apartements ou reçevoit la P[csse] Veuve . . . Sont encore les memes portraits. La salle a manager est mauve de l'invention de Charles Eszterhazy qui a l' air du maitre d'hotel. . . . La P[cesse] Douainière [Marie Therese, *née* Comtesse Hohenfeld] resemble beaucoup a sa mere . . . Beaucoup de vent.'

Exactly how the rights for performance and publication of the London Symphonies were divided between Haydn and Salomon is not entirely clear. No doubt Haydn's rights consisted in selling MS. parts (for instance, to Prince Fürstenberg) and in performing the works at such concerts as his own benefit (1795) and the Bolla concert in Vienna. It is curious that while Haydn and Salomon signed an agreement for the first six English Symphonies on 13 August 1795, two days before Haydn left London, that for the second set was not made until 27 February 1796:

> [Agreement with Johann Peter Salomon, London. *German*.]
>
> Vienna, 27 February, 1796.
>
> I, the undersigned, testify and declare that Herr Salomon shall be in perpetuity the sole owner and proprietor of my last six Symphonies, of which 3 are of the

1 Olleson, 50, the weather from Zinzendorf's Diary (MS.); Parke I, 279; Smart, 29; *AMZ* VII, No. 43 (24 July 1805), 689 (English from Landon, *Beethoven*, 89); *AMZ* III, No. 3 (15 October 1800), 43; A. Diemand, 'Joseph Haydn und der Wallersteinsche Hof', in *Zeitschrift des Histor. Vereins für Schwaben und Neuburg*, Band 45 (1920–2), Document 21.

year 1794, and the last 3 of the year 1795, and promise on my honour to make no other but personal use of them.

Josephus Haydn [m. p]ria. [CCLN, 146]

Haydn lumps the works into the two years in which they were first performed in London, though of course the dates of composition were often earlier: No. 99 (Vienna, 1793), 100 (London, 1794, but begun in Vienna), 101 (London, 1794, but begun in Vienna), 102 (London, 1794), 103 (London, 1795) and 104 (London, 1795).

Beethoven was, meanwhile, passing the proofs of his Op. 2 Sonatas dedicated to Haydn, which appeared early in March. By that time, however, Beethoven was already in Prague, enjoying a great success both as a performer and as a composer (the magnificent 'Ah! perfido' dates from this journey). On 9 March 1796, the *Wiener Zeitung* carried this announcement:

> Artaria and Comp. 2 Sonatas for the fortepiano by Herr Ludwig van Beethoven Opera 2.
>
> Since the previous work of the composer, the 3 piano Trios Opera 1 which are already in the hands of the public, was received with so much success, one promises the same for the present works, the more so since, apart from the value of the composition, in them may be seen not only the strength which Herr v. Beethoven manifests as a piano player but also the delicacy with which he knows how to treat that instrument. Therefore, the greatest possible attention was given as well to the beauty and accuracy of this edition. The price is 3 gulden.

Some idea of the 'personal use' of Haydn's last six London Symphonies can be learned from a hand-bill of the *Freyhaus* Theater auf der Wieden for 20 March. It was the *Akademie*, or benefit concert, of Music Director Joseph Suche. Süssmayer's *Moses* was the principal work, but between the two acts a large orchestra ('60 Personen') performed 'eine neue Symphonie' by Haydn, 'who himself let me have the use of it'. We cannot identify the symphony.[1]

The spring concerts of the Tonkünstler-Societät in 1796 took place without Haydn's participation: he was busily at work on the vocal version of his Oratorio, *The Seven Words*, the first production of which witnessed his next major public appearance less than a week after the Tonkünstler-Societät's second concert. The principal works for the Societät's concerts were a Salieri Cantata *La Riconoscenza*, composed to honour the Society's twenty-fifth year of existence, followed by *Die Gewalt der Musik*, a Cantata by Peter von Winter, *Capellmeister* to the Palatine Elector. One of the soprano soloists was Therese Gassmann, the daughter of the composer Florian Leopold Gassmann and later the wife of Rosenbaum; she was to sing many of the solo parts in Haydn's late works. In the interval of the first concert, on 20 March, young Antonio Tomasini played a violin concerto by his father, Haydn's old leader Luigi; in the interval of the second concert, on 21 March, there was a harp concerto played by Demoiselle Müllner.[2]

1 Deutsch, *Freihaustheater*, 38.

2 Pohl, *Denkschrift*, 65. Pugnani concert: Pohl III, 101f. The autograph score of the Salieri Cantata has, at the end, the note: 'Greetings and peace offers the author of this Cantata from the realms of eternity to that composer who will compose the Cantata of Thanks to celebrate the half-century [of the Society], and to all those who will perform it.' Salieri never expected to live until 1821, but he did, and witnessed the celebrations in honour of Florian Leopold Gassmann, the Society's founder; Salieri wrote a March & Chorus for the occasion. Pohl, *Denkschrift* 50, 71.

The day after the second Tonkünstler concert saw a production of Gaetano Pugnani's music to Goethe's *Werther*. Pugnani, a fine violinist in the Corelli tradition, was Viotti's teacher and a well-known composer; he was not quite two years older than Haydn. At this concert on 22 March, a Haydn symphony introduced the programme.[3]

Haydn had dealings with several banking houses and merchants, *inter alia* Fries & Company, Mozart's friend and brother Mason Michael Puchberg, but especially with Friedrich Jakob van der Nüll, a wholesale merchant and partner in the firm of Ignaz von Schwab. Van der Nüll, a passionate admirer of Haydn and 'amateur' of music, had a house on the Michaelerplatz. Haydn had used his kind offices to help cash a cheque for one of his students in June 1790 (CCLN, 103). Now we read:

> [To Friedrich Jakob van der Nüll, Vienna. *German*]
> Pl. T.
> My good Herr von der Nüll!
>
> I herewith take the liberty of asking you respectfully if you would be good enough to lend me, just on the strength of my pock-marked face, one hundred Gulden in bank notes, to be repaid after 6 weeks. My signature below is your guarantee, so help me God, in whose Presence I have the honour to be, my dear Herr v. der Nüll, most respectfully,
>
> Your most sincere and obedient servant,
> Jos. Haydn.
>
> [Vienna] 25th March 1796.
>
> [Address:] Monsieur
> Monsieur Von der Nüll. [CCLN, 147]

Although it is not our custom to dwell on the provenance of many Haydn letters quoted in this biography (a description of the sources can be found in CCLN), nevertheless the history of this letter, first published in CCLN, is so extraordinary that it warrants brief comment. On a concert tour of the United States in the 1950s, Paul Badura-Skoda, the distinguished Austrian pianist, gave a concert at Louisville, Kentucky. There, he was invited to a music-loving house, the owner of which produced the above-cited letter. Mr Badura-Skoda had the presence of mind to photograph the letter on the spot, as a result of which we are in possession of this small but none the less interesting piece of biographica. One wonders how many other unknown Haydn letters are slumbering in private houses in the United States, their biographical value unknown to the owners. . . .

1 Pugnani was in Vienna at this time. Possibly the music to Goethe's *Werther* is the work referred to in a newly discovered autograph letter by Pugnani to an official at the Sardinian Court, for which institution Pugnani was in service at Turin, dated 'Vienna 17th November 1794'. The part that concerns us reads: '. . . Essendo stato richiesto qui, della direzione imperiale con consenso di S. M. l'imperatore di comporre un Opera con l'onorario di duecento zecchini, paga al doppio di quella que si dà ordinariamente agli altri Maestri di Capella. . . .' Pugnani asks for an extension of his leave-of-absence, which according to a short note on the letter, was granted to him by the King of Sardinia, Victoire Amadeus III. Katalog Nr. 172, Musikantiquariat Hans Schneider, Tutzing 1972, item 62.

It was a great mark of courtesy for the old Italian virtuoso to open his programme with a Haydn symphony, and there is every reason to believe that Haydn was present at the programme. Probably neither realized that a Pugnani String Quartet in E flat (Hoboken I: Es9) circulated also under Haydn's name – a popular work that was much admired by the anonymous author of the violently anti-Haydn brochure, *Portfeuille für Musikliebhaber* (Leipzig, Ostermesse 1792), who quotes the beginning of the Quartet in question and describes it as by 'my favourite composer' (p. 63). For Pugnani, see E. M. Zschinsky-Troxler's fine book, *Gaetano Pugnani (1731–1798). Ein Beitrag zur Stilerfassung italienischer Vorklassik*, Berlin 1939.

At the end of the Chronicle in the volume *Haydn in England 1791–1795* we saw Haydn travelling through Passau and hearing a performance of his Oratorio, *The Seven Words*, with vocal parts added by the local Chapel Master of the Cathedral, Joseph Friebert. Haydn, at that time, considered he could have done the vocal parts better himself.[1]

When he returned to Vienna in 1795, he probably related the story of the Passau performance to Gottfried van Swieten. Neukomm tells us:

> Immediately after his arrival in Vienna, H. began and completed this explanatory addition [*erklärende Zugabe*] in the way of vocal parts, to which Baron van Svieten [*sic*] furnished the German text and Carpani the Italian (a free translation).

Being a composer – even if his symphonies 'were as stiff as himself' – and knowing the instrumental version of the Oratorio, van Swieten was able to adapt Friebert's text to fit the available music. It is the kind of libretto fashionable in German-speaking religious music of the period: rather heavy but undoubtedly not without effect. Fortunately, we have Haydn's autograph: or rather, a fair copy of the score of the old version in Johann Elssler's beautiful hand. Haydn had *a priori* decided to add certain instruments, for example, flutes, clarinets and trombones, and Elssler, knowing this, wrote the necessary *instrumentarium* including the new instruments at the beginning of each section. Haydn himself then filled in the missing instrumental and the vocal parts (S-A-T-B *soli* and choir), as well as indicating the 'intonations' at the beginning of each 'Word'.

On a blustery evening (Zinzendorf: 'Vent impetueux et froid'), the first of the historic evenings at the Schwarzenberg Palais on the Mehlmarkt (Neuer Markt) took place. The concert on 26 March was probably financed by the Gesellschaft der Associirten and organized by Swieten, Prince Schwarzenberg acting as the host. The textbook for the occasion was printed by Matthias Andreas Schmidt in Vienna and is dated 1796. Count Zinzendorf writes: '. . . Au grand Concert de Haydn chez le P^ce^ Schwarzenberg aur les 7. dernières paroles de notre Seigneur. Le second et le septième me plurent devantage. Il fesoit bon effet dans ce salon. Je me trouvois devant Me de Hoyos entre Mes de Star[emberg] et d'Huerta. . . .' The work in its new guise evidently made such an impression on the old Count that he went the next day to the repeat concert: '. . . De nouveau au Concert. Toujours la 7me parole. Vater ich befehle – me plait le plus davantage que Es ist vollbracht. La P^cesse^ de Schwarz[enberg] me fit des reproches de ne pas y etre venu hier. . . . Jour gris. Pluye. Vent. Le soir neige.' (Olleson 51 and Zinzendorf Diary [MS.]).

1 Neukomm, *Bemerkungen*, 29, says clearly 'Auf seiner 2^t^. Rückreise aus Egld [England]'. We see no reason, as in Somfai (142), to place the incident in January 1794. In this, Somfai was following Pohl III, 102, and Adolf Sandberger, 'Zur Entstehungsgeschichte von Haydn's Sieben Worten des Erlösers am Kreuze', in *Peters-Jahrbuch*, 1903, reprinted in *Gesammelte Aufsätze zur Musikgeschichte*, Munich, 1921. Dénes Bartha has published a long and interesting article on the Friebert version in *Zenetudományi Tanulmányok* VIII (Budapest 1960). It is now believed that the original version dates from 1786, not 1785: a sketch to part of the original version is found together with a sketch to the Minuet of Symphony No. 86, the autograph of which is dated 1786. (The autograph of the original *Seven Words* has disappeared.) See Hoboken I, 562 for a brief description of the sketch. Olleson, 51. Pohl III, 102f. Facsimile of the first page of music of the Elssler score, with autograph additions, of the new vocal version (from the Esterházy Archives, Budapest) in Somfai, 162.

Haydn did pass through Schärding and presumably Passau on his way to England with Elssler: see Griesinger, 28, and *Haydn in England*, 231.

There was no doubt that Swieten and Haydn had calculated quite correctly. If the original (orchestral) version of *The Seven Words* had been appreciated by connoisseurs, it could not have been called a popular success; but Haydn always had a special place in his heart for this sincere, difficult, and at times deeply moving, series of seven slow movements, prefaced by an Introduction (Adagio) and concluding wih 'Il Terremoto', a hair-raising description of the Earthquake which uses, perhaps for the first time in music, the dynamic mark *fff*. In its new vocal guise, the work took on a new lease of life. The only entirely new music which Haydn added to the 1796 version is a stupendous wind-band solo piece, with contra-bassoon, which precedes the Fifth Word ('I thirst') and which will be discussed in connection with the actual music *infra*.

A contemporary discusses the differences between the instrumental and the choral versions, apropos a performance in Bückeburg in 1802 which, although it does not belong here chronologically, we take the liberty of inserting at this point because it clearly mirrors most contemporary thought on the subject:

> Saturday, 12 June, 1802. Haydn's *Seven Words* in Bückeburg.
>
> I shall tell you, my Dear Countess, that Haydn's *Seven Words* was given here on Good Friday, and with the new inserted choral parts, I shall tell you so as to make your musical heart doubly heavy not to have been present. If you knew what an effect this beautiful music produced when it was only instrumental music, you must believe me if I tell you that through the words which have been suitably added to it, the music gained much by a certain reinforcement of expression. Of course it remains a work that is not really suited to the general public: to appreciate six [*recte*: seven] adagios one after another [is at best difficult], and the satisfaction of our audience derived perhaps from the special emotion that fills all of us on Good Friday, thus linking the idea of a worthy composition with the feeling of boredom. The dynamic gradations with which the choruses were performed certainly pleased the connoisseurs doubly because they happen so rarely. The opening words, or rather the Seven Words themselves, created the most solemn impression before each chorus through their being only for human voices alone, without accompaniment, and in pure chanting. It was rather difficult to find the right pitch, with a long pause after the chorus, and with no instruments to give the pitch. Our concert was given only out of love for music; none of the usual reasons were necessary for the performance; it was not even for the benefit of the poor; sacred music ought to be free for every man who wishes to listen quietly.
>
> Do not laugh if I add that this music was performed here for the first time; if there is another town which can claim precedence, I will most willingly cede pride of position to it.
>
> S. H.

By now the 'Surprise' Symphony – in Germany 'mit dem Paukenschlag' – was as popular as it ever had been in England. Count Zinzendorf heard it at a concert given on 30 March 1796, at the house of his friend, Count Joseph Niclas Windischgrätz, in the Hauptstrasse, in the suburb of Gumpendorf, not far from Haydn's own house: '. . . Diné a Gumpendorf . . . Apresmidi un joli Concert la Symfonie de Haydn du coup de Canon. . . .'

When Haydn had lived in England, he had appeared frequently at concerts given by the Prince of Wales at Carlton House. Naturally the composer 'assisted' at such events in a strictly professional capacity, and although he was fond of the Prince of Wales, he considered quite rightly that the matter should have been treated in a different way than it was: to wit, that the Prince of Wales owed him quite a considerable fee for his many appearances as conductor. He obviously had British friends to advise him on this matter, for in the middle of April we find him sending a substantial bill to the Commissioners of Parliament, which was promptly paid.[1]

[To the Commissioners of Parliament. *English*]

Vienna, ye 15th Aprill 1796.

I empower herwith M^r^. Squire to receive for me from the H^ble^ Commissioners One hundred Pounds due to me by His Royal Highness the Prince of Walis and acknowledge hereby the receipt of that Sum in full of all demands.

Doctor Haydn [mp] ria.

[CCLN, 147]

Haydn had some years previously, in April 1789 [CCLN, 83f.], ordered some English engravings from Breitkopf & Härtel but apparently had not paid for them. Some of the correspondence between 1789 and 1796 has disappeared but apparently Haydn and the senior chief of the great Leipzig firm, Christoph Gottlob Breitkopf (son of Johann Gottlob Immanuel, who had visited Haydn in 1786), had come to an agreement whereby Haydn would pay the firm fifteen gulden in cash and deliver to them a new 'Sonata' – which was in the event a new Piano Trio (see *infra*, 9 November 1796).

[To Christoph Gottlob Breitkopf, Leipzig. *German*]

Vienna, 16th April, 1796.
[Breitkopf's clerk notes: 'rec'd the 21st'.]

Nobly born,
Most highly respected Sir!

I must apologize a thousand times for not having answered all your letters. Please do not be angry at a man who will never be ungrateful. If you will be patient a little longer, I shall send you the money and the music, and this as surely as I am, Sir, most respectfully,

Your devoted and indebted servant,
Jos: Haydn.

[Address:] Dem Wohl Edl gebohrnen Herrn
Breitkopf Music Verleger zu
zustellen.
Leipzig.

[Breitkopf's clerk notes above the address: '1796/16 Ap/21/(blank space for date of answer)' and to the right 'Wien/Haydn.'] [CCLN, 147f.]

We find Haydn's name on an interesting document concerning the replacement of the second horn-player in the Vienna Court Orchestra, Jakob Eisen, who died on 10 April.

To the Oberst Hofmeister Amt. Concerning the replacement of the vacant position of hunting horn arising through the death of the k. k. chamber wind-band horn-player Jakob Eisen.

Exp. 22 Junius 796 Debfitz [?]

Your Princely Grace,

The following candidates have presented themselves for the position made vacant by the death of the k. k. chamber horn-player Jakob Eisen on 10 April:

1 Griesinger (33f.) informs us: 'At the Prince of Wales, [Haydn] conducted six and twenty musicians, and the orchestra often had to wait for several hours before the Prince left table. Since these efforts were quite unremunerated, upon the advice of his friends Haydn sent from Germany [Austria] a bill for one hundred guineas, at the time when Parliament was paying the bills of the Prince; and he received this sum without delay.'

(1) Johann Hörmann, 2nd hunting-horn-player in the Imperial Royal National Theatre; he submits two recommendations of his ability, by *Kappelmeister* Haiden [*sic*] and Salieri in which his efficiency is praised, and in the second of these it is confirmed that he has already substituted for Jakob Eisen when the latter was unable to play.

(2) Franz Eisen, the late Jakob Eisen's younger brother. He refers to his experience and is ready to hold a rehearsal, and according to written references he has served in the *Feldmusik* of Count Colloredo's Regent and latterly was in Milan with Prince v Khevenhüller Metsch, whom he left in good standing to return to his fatherland to find a position. He requests this position the more since he would then be in a position to help his brother's children and widow.

(3) Joseph Hradezky, substitute in the Imperial Royal Court Theatre; and

(4) Mathias Nikl, former chamber musician with the Prince v Esterhazi. Both refer to their efficiency with the additional points that the former substituted for the late Eisen in the Court Theatre when the latter was sick, while the latter served as chamber musician for ten full years according to the reference by *Kappelmeister* Haiden and always behaved in an exemplary fashion.

[Another hand:] In order that the wind band may find a suitable replacement for the excellent late hunting-horn-player Eisen, I have suggested to *Hofkappellmeister* [*sic*] Salieri that he ask the above-listed applicants to give proof of their art in the presence of the whole wind band; and that he thereupon submit his opinion together with the sealed written votes of all the members of the wind band. Salieri followed this suggestion, only that Nickl[1] [*sic*], though informed of the forthcoming examination, did not appear and could not be considered.

The advice of the *Hofkappellmeister* and also the unanimous opinion of the members of the wind band would be that among those individuals that were examined, Johann Hörmann be given the preference. Suggestion From my standpoint I am the more in agreement with the above-mentioned proposal since on the one hand the artistic judgment and his colleagues give Hörmann the preference, while on the other there is no evidence known to me to reflect adversely on his morals and good conduct; and therefore I would not hesitate to advise H. Majest. that Johann Hörmann be awarded the vacant position of chamber wind-band hunting-horn-player with the full salary.

In July, Haydn was still in Vienna. We do not know if he attended the new opera at the Court Theatre, Domenico Cimarosa's *I nemici generosi*; Zinzendorf thought 'La musique de Cimarosa jolie, au fin beaucoup repeter la Bussani', referring to Dorotea Bussani, Mozart's first Cherubino – she had then just been engaged – and first Dorabella in, respectively, *Le nozze di Figaro* and *Così fan tutte*.[2]

We have seen above that in July Haydn attended an Augarten concert at which J. F. Witt introduced his newest orchestral works to Vienna (*vide supra*, p. 34). On 2 August, Paisiello's *Il barbiere di Siviglia* was given in German translation (G. F. W. Grossmann) at Schikaneder's Theater auf der Wieden and repeated twice. On the 17th, the Court Theatre gave Peter von Winter's new opera, *I fratelli rivali*, which had been first performed at the Teatro S. Bernadino in Venice in 1793. Count Zinzendorf

1 Mathias Nickl (*recte*) actually served at Eszterháza from July 1786 till the band's dissolution in 1790. Hörmann received the position. The document, to which our attention was kindly directed by Roger Hellyer, is in the Haus-, Hof- und Staatsarchiv, Vienna (Hofmusikkapelle Akten 1796, 75r, v & 76r); we have to thank our colleague Clemens Höslinger for providing a photograph of the pages in question.

2 Deutsch, *Mozart Dokumente*, 238, 240, 318. Zinzendorf's Diary (MS.) Cimarosa's new opera, which had been first heard during the previous Carnival at the Teatro Valle, Rome, was also known as *I rivali generosi* and today is usually referred to by its third title, *Il duello per complimento*. See *Enciclopedia dello Spettacolo* III, 771.

wrote in his Diary, 'La musique et le chant de la Willmann ne me plûrent pas, et il ne feroit point trop chaud.'[1]

By an extraordinary coincidence, the contract concluded in August 1796 between Haydn and Frederick Augustus Hyde in London turned up just before this volume was delivered to the printers. The contract was sold at Sotheby's on 8 February 1976, and was purchased by Mr Richard Macnutt of Tunbridge Wells for some £2,800. Thanks to the unfailing courtesy of Sotheby & Co., and in this particular case Mr Morton-Smith, we are able to supply details of the document.

> [Summary from Sotheby's Catalogue:]
> HAYDN (JOSEPH) SIGNED MS CONTRACT in the form of an Indenture, 3 *pages, folio, drawn up in London on* 30 *July* 1796 *and finalised in Vienna on* 10 *August* 1796, between Haydn and Frederick Augustus Hyde, 'Musick seller', agreeing that the former should write fifty-five compositions totalling £911, as specified, over a period of five years for a 'binding' fee of £300 and £150 per annum thereafter, that should Haydn take up residence in London during the period he would be able to compose certain Quartets and 'Simphonies' to be performed prior to publication; and it is [quotation from the actual document] 'mutually agreed by and between the said parties to these presents/that if the said Frederick Augustus Hyde shall be minded or desirous/to dissolve make void or disannul this Agreement at the end or expiration/of the first three Years of the said Term of Five Years it shall and may/be Lawful for the said Frederick Augustus Hyde so to do on giving/to the said Joseph Haydn three Months previous Notice in Writing of/such his intention IN WITNESS whereof the said parties to these presents/have hereunto [word added with carrot: "interchangeably"] set their hands and seals the day and year first above written. –
>
> Fredk Augustus Hyde [seal]
> [seal] Joseph Haydn mpria Doctor of Music.
>
> SEALED and DELIVERED
> in the presence of
>
> R: Schroeter
>
> Edwd. Medley St Margaret St Westm^r^
> Three Sonatas for the Piano Forte or Harpsichord with an accompaniment for a Violin and Violoncello £75
> Three Sonatas for the Piano Forte without accompaniment . . . [£]60
> Three Quartetts for two Violins Tenor and Violoncello . . . . [£]75
>
> [etc., etc.]

It is touching that Haydn's friend Rebecca Schroeter was still acting as a go-between for him in England. The contract itself is perhaps not, strictly speaking, an agreement for these fifty-five works but rather a price table to be used against whatever Haydn could and would deliver. Perhaps he intended to give Hyde the last three piano Sonatas (which however belonged to Mrs Bartolozzi), but certainly the first works listed, the 'Three Sonatas for the Piano Forte or Harpsichord with an accompaniment of a Violin and Violoncello' turned out to be the Op. 75 piano Trios (Nos. 43–5; XV: 27–9), which Longman & Broderip published in 1797, while the 'Three Quartetts' turned out to be the first 'sett' of the Op. 76, which Longman, Clementi & Co. issued in 1799.

1 Deutsch, *Mozart Dokumente*, 24, 39; Zinzendorf Diary (MS.); *Enciclopedia dello Spettacolo* IX, 1985.

The contract seems to be the written result of a verbal agreement made about 1794, because in 1799 Haydn told Griesinger, as we shall see, that the contract had been made five years earlier.

Haydn had been composing at high speed all the year. There are even major works – such as the Concerto for trumpet and the Duets for soprano, tenor, and piano – which are dated 1796 on the autograph manuscripts but the first performances of which cannot be determined. In the early part of the year he was finishing the revision of *The Seven Words*; from Easter to September he was completing the first of the six Masses to celebrate the name-day of Princess Marie Hermenegild; after September, he completed his last four Piano Trios, one of which he sent to Leipzig in November, and three of which he sent to England, where they were announced by the publisher Longman & Broderip in the *Oracle* on 20 April, 1797.

There has been considerable controversy among Haydn scholars, since the 1940s, as to the exact chronology of the first two 'Hermenegild' Masses. Up to and including the appearance of Pohl III in 1927, where (p. 111) we read 'The first great work which Haydn composed after his return from London was for Eisenstadt . . . the Mass in B flat composed in the Summer of 1796 . . .', it was always assumed that this B flat Mass, known in German-speaking countries as the 'Heiligmesse', was the work performed in 1796 on the Feast of Our Lady (Mariä Geburt). Then, in 1935, the Austrian scholar Alfred Schnerich, in an article[1] in the *Zeitschrift für Musikwissenschaft*, suggested that the order of the first two Masses should be reversed. At the same time the young German scholar Carl Maria Brand, whose thesis *Die Messen von Joseph Haydn* was not published until 1941, came to similar conclusions.[2] We may sum up their theories as follows:

(1) In the nineteenth century, the *Missa Sancti Bernardi de Offida* ('Heiligmesse') used to be dated 1792, an error which Schnerich corrected in 1913. But it led people to imagine that it was the first of the series; subconsciously, too, they were perhaps influenced by the fact that Breitkopf & Härtel issued this work as the first of their series of Haydn's late Masses, for example, No. 1 *Missa Sancti Bernardi*; No. 2 *Missa in tempore belli*; No. 3 *Missa in angustiis* ('Nelson Mass').

(2) Both the *Missa Sancti Bernardi* and the *Missa in tempore belli* (known in Germany and Austria as the 'Paukenmesse') are dated 1796 on their respective autograph manuscripts, but the latter is dated 'Eisenstadt' as well. Therefore Schnerich and Brand assume that the *Missa Sancti Bernardi* was composed in Vienna, which is undoubtedly true.

(3) The Credo of the *Missa in tempore belli* shows mistakes in the text, omissions, etc. The two scholars suggest that Haydn was writing the text from memory and since he had not written a Mass for fourteen years – the previous work having been the second Mass for Mariazell ('Mariazellermesse') of 1782 – he was out of practice. The Credo of the *Missa Sancti Bernardi* shows no such omissions and mistakes.

(4) The course of the war in Italy – about which more will be said *infra* – was such that Brand believed Griesinger's remark (p. 62) 'In the year 1796 he wrote a Mass which he entitled "In tempore belli", at the time when the French occupied Styria' should be altered to 'at the time when the French were approaching Styria'. Brand

1 'Zur Chronologie der Messen Haydns', November 1935, pp. 472ff.
2 Brand, *Messen*, 217ff.

assumes that by the time Napoleon occupied Graz, on 10 April 1797, Haydn had completed the 'Mass in Time of War', and that the Agnus Dei, wherein the kettledrums give the music a most ominous cast, was composed as 'a visionary view of a threatening future'.

(5) Rosenbaum's Diary tells us that on 29 September 1797 'a new Mass in C' by Haydn was performed at the Bergkirche in Eisenstadt. Brand and Schnerich quote another entry in Rosenbaum's Diary which says the same thing for 9 November 1797: examination of the original manuscript of the Diary, in the Handschriftensammlung of the Österreichische Nationalbibliothek, shows that there is no such entry for 9 November, only the one on 29 September. But in any case, Brand dismissed this evidence as simply meaning that 'new' meant different from Haydn's earlier Masses in this key (there are two: both for Mariazell).

(6) It is reported that Haydn wrote a new Mass for the *Primitae* ceremonies of Joseph Hofmann, which took place on 26 December 1796 in the Piaristenkirche in the Viennese suburb of the Josephstadt. Brand doubts that Haydn wrote a new work for the occasion and suggests that the *Missa in tempore belli*, which was the work performed, was in any case 'new' to Vienna, since the Eisenstadt performance was for the family and whatever members of the Eisenstadt population chose to attend.

(7) The ceremonies in Vienna to celebrate the beatification of Saint Bernard of Offida, to whom the *Missa Sancti Bernardi* is dedicated, occurred primarily in 1797, according to Brand. Thus he assumes that that Mass was begun in the autumn of 1796 in Vienna and completed the next year.

Brand and Schnerich have further arguments, but they are peripheral and need not be introduced here. If we sum up all the evidence for the chronology at this point, it would read as follows:

(1) The two Masses are dated 1796. The *Missa Sancti Bernardi* was presumably begun in Vienna, and the autograph of the *Missa in tempore belli* assures us that it was begun at Eisenstadt.

(2) We now have additional information that Brand and Schnerich did not have, the original performance material of both works in the Esterházy Archives at Eisenstadt. Elssler, the principal copyist of all the last six Masses, dates each of them 'Anno 1796', 'Anno 1798', and so forth. The original material of the *Missa Sancti Bernardi* is dated 'Anno 1796' and contains many corrections and additions by Haydn. The original material of the *Missa in tempore belli* was missing when we originally examined the Eisenstadt Archives in 1956 and 1957, but in 1959 it was discovered in a chimney, where it and the Bach Mass in B minor had been stuffed for safe-keeping when the Russians occupied Eisenstadt in 1945. Subsequently we examined this new material. It, too, is dated 'Anno 1796' and is the original version of the work – about which more anon; but it does *not* give the appearance of being the original performance material to the extent that was the case with the St Bernard Mass.

(3) Haydn certainly did conduct the *Primitae* ceremonies on 26 December 1796, because we have a printed report on it (*vide infra*). There is no reason to doubt that the *Mass in Time of War* was performed. We have examined the Archives of the Piaristenkirche and found an old set of MS. parts of the *Mass in Time of War*; but it is obviously not the original performance material.

(4) Rosenbaum tells us that on 29 September 1797, 'a new Mass in C by Haydn was performed' (Radant, *Rosenbaum*, 26). There is no reason to imagine that Haydn played the same mass two years consecutively at Eisenstadt and, indeed, every reason

to suppose that he conducted the *Missa in tempore belli*, which was 'new' to everyone at Eisenstadt, even if it had been performed at Vienna in a suburban church on the previous Feast of St Stephen.

For these reasons we are inclined to doubt Brand's and Schnerich's arguments, and to return to the traditional dating put forward by the older Haydn scholars. We would say that it is almost certain that the 1796 work for Eisenstadt was the St Bernard Mass and wholly certain that the 1797 work for Eisenstadt was the *Missa in tempore belli*. We would say, therefore, that the former was written during the summer of 1796 in Vienna, the latter begun in the early autumn of 1796 at Eisenstadt and completed in Vienna. The autograph of the *Missa in tempore belli* (Esterházy Archives, Budapest) was not known to Brand and only superficially known to Schnerich. It shows clearly that Haydn wrote the work *at different times*. The end of the Credo is marked 'Laus Deo', a prayer of thanks that Haydn otherwise puts only at the end of a work. The exceptions (for instance, at the end of the first movement of Symphony No. 97, and at the end of the second of Symphony No. 102) show some break in chronology. And another factor suggests that the *Missa Sancti Bernardi* is the first work. Schnerich worries about the inexact textual setting of the Credo in the other Mass; but what should have struck him more forcefully was the fact that the Gloria beginning in the St Bernard Mass contains vast changes, and unlike most of Haydn's changes, these lengthen the movement. (We refer to the opening 'Vivace', as far as the next section, 'Gratias agimus tibi'.) No less then three such insertions, comprising respectively bars 13–16, 27–34, and 55–62, may be found on the autograph, inserted by 'vi-de' and signs. Similarly, bars 145–9 of the Kyrie were added later. All this suggests that Haydn was unsure of the length of the Mass movements in the summer of 1796; there are no such doubts in the *Missa in tempore belli*.

We will therefore proceed on the assumption that Haydn brought to Eisenstadt the autograph manuscript and Elssler parts (Johann Elssler was now part of the Viennese Haydn household) of the *Missa Sancti Bernardi de Offida*, for performance on the Princess Marie Hermenegild's name-day (also the Feast of Our Lady).

Pope Pius VI had beatified St Bernard of Offida on 19 May 1795. Haydn scholars think that the composer must have become aware of the Saint because of the fact that he lived in the same square (Neuer Markt or Mehlmarkt) as the Capuchin Monastery, which Brotherhood even today faithfully guards the earthly remains of the Habsburg emperors, buried in its precincts. St Bernard was born near Offida in the Italian province of The Marche in 1604; he was baptized Domenicus, and his parents were pious peasants. He joined the Capuchin Monastery at Clorinaldo and was ordained on 15 February 1627, at Camerino. Later he was a member of Fermo Monastery (Province of Ancona) and at the age of sixty was transferred back to Offida, where he cared for the poor and sick. He died on 22 August 1694. His name comes in the *Martyrologium Romanum* for the Capuchins on 11 September.[1]

Haydn would have been attracted to just such a man – his goodness and simplicity may even be felt in this Mass, one of the composer's most beautiful, most earnest, and most fervent. In the Archives of the Capuchin Monastery in Vienna, Schnerich found a note which tells us an interesting fact, namely that Vienna was seized in 1796 by a

1 Dom. Baudot: *Dictionnaire d'Hagiographie mis à jour à l'aide des traveaux les plus récents par Dom. Baudot O.S.B.*, Paris, 1925; *Vollständige Heiligenlexikon*, Augsburg, 1858. Brand *Messen*, 263, also 223. The latest book on St Bernard is P. Francesco Maria da San Marino, *Il Beato Bernardo da Offida*, Offida 1974, with the delightful pen-and-ink sketch of St Bernard by Dr Ferdinando Fabiani.

wave of religious feeling: 'hoc anno concessae fuerunt a Pio VI. indulgentiae plenariae per modum Jubilaei ad impetrandam Austriacis armis divinam benedictionem. Durabat hoc Jubilaeum per septimanas.' It is quite true that the general celebration of St Bernard in Vienna did not take place until 1797. The Capuchin Annals read: '1797 . . . Hoc anno celebrata fuit in omnibus ecclesiis Capucinorum beatificatio Bernardi ab Offida, quem Pius VI. in Beatorum Album retulit.' But we know that Haydn began the Mass in 1796.

Before leaving the work's date and dedication, we would mention an interesting set of sketches to the Mass, which are in the Musiksammlung of the Österreichische Nationalbibliothek (Codex 16835). These sketches contain the concluding fugues of the Gloria and Credo and have been reproduced in Brand, *Messen* (285–7, 294f.), and, with corrections of Brand's text, in the Appendix of the volume concerned in the new Henle edition of *Haydn Werke*.[1] Apart from their intrinsic value – very few sketches of Haydn's have survived – they are also of interest in that they are bound with, and presumably belong to, the earliest sketches of *The Creation*, which (as we shall see) was in a sufficiently advanced state by December 1796 to enable Haydn to play parts of it to Albrechtsberger.

Haydn's new Mass was one part of the elaborate celebrations in Eisenstadt in September 1796. Preparations began in June. The theatre was repaired and Pietro Travaglia designed new scenery, while poor old Eszterháza was again plundered of its theatrical costumes (there was still a wardrobe attendant there). This year, the theatrical troupe of Johann Karl Stadler, himself a well-known young actor, was engaged and a contract made on 1 July. Although an actor who had begun his career playing *amoroso* parts in Laibach (modern Ljubljana) and Trieste, Stadler also had a good voice and could sing in operas.

On 4 March 1796, Stadler wrote to the Prince, asking to be engaged and explaining that the war had placed him (Stadler) in a difficult position; at that time Stadler, who had enjoyed a career in many German towns, was the manager of a company in Wiener Neustadt. With his letter he enclosed a list of sixty-three plays and twenty-three operas which were in the incredibly prolific repertoire of his company; among the operas were three by Haydn: *Armida*, *Orlando Paladino* and *La fedeltà premiata*, none of which the Prince, who seems not to have liked Haydn's music much anyway, accepted. Stadler then persuaded the City Council of Wiener Neustadt to send a letter of recommendation to the Prince, in which they say that Stadler's company had given complete satisfaction both in plays and operas and that the members of the company had behaved themselves properly.

The contract of 1 July required the troupe to give performances in German every Tuesday, Thursday, Saturday, and Sunday between 1 September and 15 October. Stadler agreed to extend his repertoire by additional popular plays, to provide all the costumes except those of the supers, and to engage carefully chosen singers. The company earned 110 gulden weekly. Finally, a MS. list of the players and the programmes was arranged. From it we learn that the personnel was:

> Actors: Peterka: first lovers, heroes; comic parts in operas. Schmidtmann: first lovers in operas, lovers in dramas and plays. Normann: basso; character parts in dramas and plays. [Cancelled: Schwartz, basso; secondary roles in plays.] Horst: intriguants, pedants. [Cancelled: Schletter.] Stadler: tender fathers,

1 Serie XXIII, Band 2. Also Bärenreiter miniature score (No. 93), which includes the sketches.

quarrelsome old people, decorous parts. Berke: baritone; dignified parts. Harrald: second tenor; subordinate parts in plays. Koch: secondary parts; prompter.

Actresses: [Cancelled: Eiersperg: comic parts in operas, heroines; decorous parts in plays.] Horst: mature lovers, young women, decorous parts. Normann: coquettish women, termagants. Stadler: young lovers, *ingénue* parts. Rumfeld: first singer. Willmers: comic parts, *soubrettes*. Kreutzer: dilettantes, first lovers, heroines, decorous parts.

The programme was as follows:[1]

Thursday, September	1	*Das rothe Käppchen*. Opera [by Ditters]
	3	*Johanna von Neapel*. Drama
	4	*Impressar in der Klemme;* *Der Dorfbarbier*. Two comedies [Cimarosa; Schenk?]
	6	*Die unmögliche Sache*. Comedy
	8	*Die Waldmänner*. Opera [by Schikaneder with music by Henneberg]
	9	*Haldane, König der Dänen*. Drama [*Alfred oder der patriotische König* from the English of Bicknell]
	10	An occasional play
	11	*Der Neffe*. Play
	13	*Rings 1ter Theil*. Comedy
	15	*Rings 2ter Theil*. Comedy
	17	*Graf Benyovszky*. Drama
	18	*Hieronymus Knüker* [Knikner]. Opera [by Ditters]
	20	*Bettelstudent; Schadenfreude*. Two comedies
	22	*Die drillings Brüder*. Comedy
	24	*Klara von Hoheneichen*. Drama
	25	*Die Zauber Zither*. Opera [*Der Fagottist, oder Die Zauberzither*, also known as *Kaspar der Fagottist*, by Wenzel Müller]
	27	*Die Fiaker 1ter Theil*. Comedy
	29	*Der Hochzeit-Tag*. Comedy
Saturday, October	1	*Kasper der Thoringer*. Drama
	2	*Der Gutsherr*. Opera [*Der Schiffspatron, oder Der neue Gutsherr*, by Ditters]
	4	*Die verschloßene Thür*. Comedy
	6	*Der Taubstumme*. Comedy
	8	*Otto von Wittelsbach*. Drama
	9	*Die Zauberflötte* [*sic*]. Opera [by Mozart]
	11	*Der Fremde*. Comedy
	13	*Das Ehrenwort*. Comedy
	15	An occasional play at the termination of the spectacles given

The documents do not tell us whether the troupe came with their own orchestra or not; presumably the Eisenstadt forces will have been supplemented with outside musicians if they in fact accompanied the operas, because Mozart's *Zauberflöte* requires, apart from a glockenspiel (which the troupe will have taken along), two flutes, two trumpets, three trombones, and more strings than were available from the local forces. (There were two horn players who also played trumpets, but Mozart's

1 Horányi 164–6. Corrected from MS., Esterházy Archives, Fasc. V/g. Fol. 127–8, Magyar Országos Levétár, Budapest, which contains the submitted programme.

score requires, simultaneously, pairs of horns and trumpets.) We are not told if Haydn conducted or if the whole *Gatspiel* was a 'package job' including the conductor.

Whether he conducted or not, Haydn had an enormous amount of work on his hands preparing for the first performance of the *Missa Sancti Bernardi* on the Sunday – or one of the Sundays – following the Feast of Our Lady. Tradition says that the ecclesiastical ceremony was always postponed to the Sunday after. But we doubt this, for the Feast of St Mary in 1798 was on Saturday, 8 September, and we know from Rosenbaum's Diary that the *Nelson Mass* was not performed until 23 September (Radant, *Rosenbaum*, 50f.), not on 9 September as Schnerich and Brand suppose. The same applies to 1797; the Feast of Our Lady was on a Sunday, as it happens (the 10th); but the new Mass was by Fuchs and Haydn's Mass was not performed until Friday, 29 September.[1]

In 1796, the Feast of Our Lady fell on Friday, 9 September. The day was celebrated with the usual pomp and ceremony, but there is unfortunately no contemporary chronicle to furnish us with details. However, the play *Alfred* proved to contain a name-day surprise for the princess; this will be discussed, *infra*. We have no way of knowing if Haydn's new Mass was given on the 11th or on one of the later Sundays. He obviously had a much larger group available than the meagre forces of his own *Capelle*, but he cannot have known, when he began the Mass, how many voices and instruments (if any) the Stadler group had at their disposal; so Haydn wisely scored the new Mass for the wind players he knew he had at his disposal: by making the two horn players of the *Harmonie* play trumpets, he had, as wind players, two clarinets, two bassoons, two trumpets, and otherwise a timpani player who was also a bassoonist. The wind band and percussion layout of the St Bernard Mass is precisely for this scoring. The strings will have been augmented by the theatrical orchestra, and everyone who could sing will have helped in the choir: the theatrical group boasted many trained singers who will have been proud to contribute their bit towards the first performance of what everyone soon realized was a major, large-scale work by *Capellmeister* Haydn. Later authentic sources indicate horns doubling the trumpets; Haydn may have done so, using the theatrical brass players, even at this first performance.

In the list of plays and operas quoted by Horányi there are several misreadings of the original German which we have corrected according to the original document from the National Széchényi Library in Budapest. Most of the misreadings are trivial, but one, the work performed on 9 September, is vitally important. It was a drama which in Horányi reads 'Huldana, König der Düren'. In fact the work is none other than *Alfred, oder der patriotische König*, the subtitle (or alternative title) of which is *Haldane, König der Dänen*. The drama was played on the evening of Princess Marie Hermenegild's name-day and Haydn planned a charming surprise for her. On the 9th, at least, he must have conducted the incidental music to this play, for it was all brand new and of his composition. Previously Haydn's music to *Alfred* was always thought to be connected with a performance at Schikaneders *Freyhaus* Theater auf der Wieden. On 11 July, 1795, when Haydn was still in England, they gave: 'Alfred [König der Angelsachsen] oder Der patriotische König, Tragödie in 5 Akten nach dem Englischen des J. Bichnell [*recte*: Alexander Bicknell] frey bearbeitet von Johann Wilhelm Cowmeadow.' But there is no evidence that the piece was still on the boards at Schikaneder's theatre in 1796 – on the contrary, according to the accurate Deutsch list

1 Brand, 264f., confused matters completely by getting the days of 1797 all wrong: he has the 29th a Wednesday. He also confuses all the dates of 1796 on p. 218, saying Our Lady was on 8 September.

(*Freihaustheater*, 37), it was taken off the repertoire in 1795.[1] The play was first printed in Berlin in 1795, and reprinted a year later in Graz.

Haydn wrote three substantial pieces for the Eisenstadt performance of *Alfred*: (1) The entrance chorus of the Danes, *Chor der Dänen*, 'Triumph dir, Haldane! die Schlacht ist gekämpft', from Act I, Scene i, of which the autograph manuscript is in the Esterházy Archives in Budapest, MS. mus. I 18 A, and which was printed in 1814 as 'Kriegerischer Chor' in Vol. XVI of the *AMZ*. (2) *Arie des Schutzgeistes* from Act I, Scene iv, 'Ausgesandt vom Strahlenthrone'. (3) Duet between King Alfred and Odun, Count of Devon, which in the textbook reads 'Horch, horch, schon hör' ich Hahnenruf' but which in Haydn's autograph reads 'Der Morgen graut, es ruft der Hahn', from Act V, Scene iv. The autographs of Nos. 2 and 3 are in the Preussische Staatsbibliothek, Berlin, Mus. MS. autogr. Jos. Haydn 31.

Haydn once again took care to score for the forces he knew would be available. The chorus uses the orchestra of the *Missa Sancti Bernardi*, with trumpets and kettledrums but with no clarinets or flutes. The Aria is, incredibly, scored for wind-band sextet – clarinets, bassoons, and horns – and also has, even more incredibly, 'Sprechgesang' (vaudeville is the old theatrical term), that is to say, the soprano voice speaks across the music in places (we shall show examples of this *infra*). In the noble Duet, Haydn uses only strings with 'Violino Princip: in die 8va' (a solo violin doubling the melody of the other violins but an octave higher) and a part for harp. Obviously Haydn, in Vienna, was not sure if the theatrical troupe was going to bring a harp with them, and so he left the part blank in the autograph. The original parts to the *Alfred* music no longer exist, and so we cannot tell if Haydn reconstructed the missing harp part *in situ*. Later we hear of Elssler lending the Aria to Rosenbaum, who copied it himself for Therese Gassmann in November, 1798 (Radant, *Rosenbaum*, 53).

The singers (players) of the Stadler Company probably had their own 'version' of *Alfred*, for as we have seen, there are sometimes small differences between the Graz textbook and the words Haydn used when composing the pieces. This was standard practice with these strolling players, who not only had their own 'performing versions' of plays but also of operas. There was, indeed, a wide flexibility in these matters not only in the eighteenth century but also during most of the nineteenth as well.[2] Anna R(h)umfeld, the 'Schutzgeist', was later engaged at Eisenstadt (p. 261).

The fact that Haydn provided (and obviously conducted) extensive incidental music to *Alfred* for Eisenstadt in the autumn of 1796 leads us to wonder whether, after

1 Pohl III, 103f. Also in our first edition of the *Arie des Schutzgeistes* (Haydn-Mozart Presse, Salzburg, 1961) and in the pamphlet *Joseph Haydn Arien/Sopran, Tenor, Bass/Revisionsberichte* (Haydn-Mozart Presse, 192, Salzburg, 1963, p. 18) the work was said to have been composed for Schikaneder's theatre. Haydn probably knew the Graz textbook, of which a copy is in the Theatersammlung der Österreichischen Nationalbibliothek, Th-Sl. 698427-A. Bicknell's drama, *The Patriotic King; or Alfred and Elvida. An historical tragedy*, was printed in London in 1788.

2 The cast, as listed in the Graz textbook of 1796, is as follows:

Personen

Alfred, König der Angelsachsen	Elvida, König Alfreds Gemahlinn
Ethelred, Graf der Sachsen, Elvida's Vater	Emma, des Grafen von Devon Tochter, Elvida's erste Hofdame
Odun, Graf von Devon	
Edwin, ein junger sächsischer Ritter	Gunhilde, Königin von Dänemark
Haldane, König der Dänen	Hofdamen
Gothrun, erster Herrführer der Dänen	Elvida's Schutzgeist
Harald, dänischer Hauptmann	En Geisterbeschwörer
Ritter, Soldaten, Gefangene, Wache, Gefolge	Ein Hexe

The play's popularity reflects the interest that even the waning eighteenth century had in historical subjects of this kind, an interest that would, of course, grow to huge proportions in the nineteenth century. British and Scottish subjects were particularly popular.

all, he did not conduct some of the operas as well. It is not likely, somehow, that he will have allowed some second-rate *Capellmeister* to conduct Mozart's *Die Zauberflöte* for the first time at Eisenstadt.

While on the subject of incidental music, we would like to bring up a delightful and totally forgotten piece that Haydn composed in the French language. The autograph of this incidental music, which begins with the words 'Fatal amour, cruel vainqueur!', is in the Preussische Staatsbibliothek, Berlin, and follows in the bundle of music containing *Alfred* Nos. 2 and 3 of our list. Someone has numbered each of the three items in the parcel: *Arie des Schutzgeistes* (1), Duet (2) and 'Fatal amour' (3); moreover the pages of all three (or rather the sheets) have been numbered consecutively. Fortunately we also possess Elssler's immaculate orchestral parts, undoubtedly the original performance material, which is also in Staatsbibliothek at Berlin (Mus. MS. 9944) and came from the Artaria collection; we have noted the importance of this collection in connection with the Twenty-four Minuets *supra* (p. 87).

There are remains of some kind of fanfare on the trumpet parts of the original performance material of the *Missa Sancti Bernardi*. The fanfare is marked 'furioso'. Can it be the remains of the *intrade* which were used in church performances? George Smart went to hear the Beethoven Mass in C at the Karlskirche in Vienna on 18 September 1825. He writes: 'The orchestra went well together. There seemed to be twelve violins, four viole, three 'celli, and three bassi, with the wind instruments including trumpets. I find the flourish of drums and trumpets with the organ extempore, to introduce each movement, is the usual mode in the church service . . .' (Smart, 126). No doubt the entrance of the Prince and Princess into the Bergkirche at Eisenstadt was greeted with fanfares of this 'furioso' kind.

The theatrical performances finished at Eisenstadt in the middle of October. We have no evidence to show how long Haydn remained in the town; certainly long enough to begin the *Missa in tempore belli*, the autograph of which, as we have observed, is dated 'Eisenstadt $\overline{796}$ Haydn [mpria]'. And with the beginning of Haydn's next great Mass, we must pause an instant in our musical chronicle and examine the military and political situation in Italy, where the Austrians were being soundly beaten by General Bonaparte.

The progress of the war, after a turn for the better in 1795 – when Mainz, Heidelberg, and Mannheim had been won back from the French – suddenly accelerated in a new and unprecedented way. The new system of war was inaugurated by General Bonaparte who, on 2 March 1796, was appointed commander-in-chief of the French army in Italy. Arriving at Savona, his Italian headquarters, he found a ragged and badly equipped army. On 28 March he had reviewed his troops on the Place de la République in Nice. On this or another occasion he had said: 'Soldats! Vous étes nus, mal nourris . . . Vôtre patience, le courage que vous montrez au milieu de ces rochers, sont admirables, mais ils ne vous procurent aucune gloire. Je viens vous conduire dans les plus fertiles plaines du monde. De riches provinces, de grandes villes seront en votre pouvoir, et là vous aurez richesse, honneurs et gloire. Soldats d'Italie, manqueriez-vous de courage!'

His troops inspired, Napoleon started his campaign on 12 April and won one smashing victory after another: Montenotte, Dego, Millesimo, and Mondovi. He defeated the Austrian army, separated it from its allies, the Sardinian army, and started to March on Turin. The King of Sardinia, Victoire Amadeus III, sued for an armistice;

it was signed on 28 April and became a peace treaty in Paris on 15 May. According to its terms, Nice and Savoy were ceded to France. Napoleon now resumed his campaign against the Austrians. He seized a bridgehead over the River Po at Piacenza and after the battle at Lodi, on 10 May, the Austrians began to evacuate Lombardy. On 15 May, the day of the treaty with the King of Sardinia, General Bonaparte occupied the city of Milan. Following the Austrian armies across the (neutral) territories of the *Serenissima* – after having requested the Venetians for permission to do so – Napoleon crossed the River Mincio at Borghetto on 30 May. The Austrians took refuge in their heavily fortified city of Mantua, to which the French began to lay siege. On 23 June, the papal states concluded an armistice with the French and Livorno (Leghorn), a strong British naval base, was occupied, much to the annoyance of Nelson and his fellow officers.

The Austrians had meanwhile gathered together another army under Wurmser, who marched from the north with the object of relieving the beleaguered city of Mantua. By a series of brilliant manœuvres, which involved abandoning the siege of Mantua, Napoleon fought off this new army. He won a decisive victory at Castiglione on 3 August and another at Bassano on 8 September.

At this juncture in the Italian campaign we must pause for a moment to recount the other battlefront in Germany. There Archduke Carl had assumed command of the Allies. When Jourdan at the head of a French army crossed the Rhine at Düsseldorf in late May, 1796, he advanced as far as Wetzlar-on-Lahn. Archduke Charles counter-attacked successfully and pushed the French back across the Rhine. General Moreau now traversed the Rhine at Strasbourg to find an Austrian army weakened by having been forced to dispatch Wurmser with a considerable body of men to relieve the fortress of Mantua. The Austrians withdrew from the Palatinate, whereupon Jourdan advanced across the Rhine and drove all the way into Bavaria. The Archduke, however, successfully counter-attacked and again forced the French back to the other side of the Rhine, while Moreau withdrew his forces to Strasbourg. This situation thus enabled the German armies to be in large part released for duty in Italy. Napoleon's position was now precarious, and his army was exhausted after the long series of battles. As we shall see, Napoleon soon recovered his initiative and in 1797 was to sweep up through northern Italy into Graz itself.[1]

While Haydn was at Eisenstadt, war fever gripped Vienna. It would be an exaggeration to say that Austria had not felt the effects of a major war since the disastrous Seven Years War at the time of the old Empress Maria Theresa (it had raged from 1756 to 1763 and had laid waste much of Bohemia); meanwhile there had been the long and costly war against the Turks. But the Turkish front had long since moved out of Austrian territory, and Belgrade (the place of the famous siege, successfully mounted by General Field Marshal Loudon [Laudon] in 1789) was a long way from Vienna.

The Viennese Volunteer Corps (Wiener Freywilligen-Korps) was now mobilized, and money for it raised by concerts which included a new patriotic Cantata by Rautenstrauch entitled *Der Retter in Gefahr* [The Saviour in Distress], music by

1 *Taschenbuch für die neueste Geschichte* (Fünfter Jahrgang 1799; herausgegeben von Ernst Ludwig Posselt. Feldzug 1796), Nuremberg 1799. Viktor Bibl, *Erzherzog Karl*, Vienna-Leipzig 1942; for a useful book on the Austrian leadership, particularly Archduke Carl, see Manfried Rauchensteiner, *Kaiser Franz und Erzherzog Carl, Dynastie und Heerwesen in Österreich 1796–1809*, Vienna 1972. On the vast literature concerning Napoleon, we have been greatly assisted by Professor Lamberto Scalabrino, an expert on the subject, who most kindly placed his extensive library of Napoleonica at our disposal. The address to the troops at Nice was not a proclamation. Louis Garros, *Quel roman que ma vie. Itinéraire de Napoléon Bonaparte 1769–1821*, Paris 1947, pp. 88f. Comte de las Cases, *Mémorial de Sainte-Hélène*, Paris 1842, p. 322.

Mozart's pupil Franz Xaver Süssmayer, and Haydn's 'Surprise' Symphony ('Symphonie mit dem Paukenschlag'). The *Wiener Zeitung* of 24 September informs us:

> On Wednesday the 21st inst., was repeated, at the general request, the well-known Cantata, *Der Retter in Gefahr*, in the Imperial-Royal large Redoutensaal, for the benefit of the Viennese Volunteers, and once again received with the unanimous and most fervent satisfaction. The Symphony by Hr. Joseph Haiden [*sic*], with which this Academy was opened on the 19th inst., also served to begin this time. . . .

The Cantata was repeated on 4 October and 15 November, and in the *Wiener Zeitung* on 12 October we read:

> The desire to follow the laudable example of the *Kaiserstadt* [Vienna] has moved the citizens of Wiener Neustadt to wish to perform in their own city the Cantata by *Herr Agent* [the Agent] Rautenstrauch, which has been performed in Vienna with such signal success. . . . The performance will take place in the Stadttheater on Saturday, 15th inst., [and] before the Cantata will be performed the popular *Symphonie mit dem Paukenschlag* by the celebrated *Herr Kapellmeister* Hayden [*sic*]. . . .

On 29 October the *Wiener Zeitung* reports of a repeat performance of the whole concert at Wiener Neustadt to celebrate the Empress's name-day:

> . . . at 6 o'clock the concert began. First they performed the well-known and everywhere popular *Symphonie mit dem Paukenschlage* by the celebrated *Hrn. Kapellmeister* Hayden. . . .[1]

The 'Surprise' Symphony was becoming as sensationally successful in Vienna (and indeed throughout Germany) as it had been, four years earlier, in London – one more proof, if any were needed, of Haydn's uncanny ability to sense the popular taste of Europe, whatever nationality, and to write music which instantly transcended ethnic barriers, national borders and differences of class.[2]

Beethoven had now returned from his successful concert tour through Germany, and in the autumn he participated in a concert given at Vienna by the two Rombergs. Andreas Romberg, the violinist, and his cousin Bernhard Romberg, the 'cellist, arrived from Italy, where they had spent the summer. Beethoven had known them from Bonn, where from 1790 to 1793 they had been engaged in the electoral orchestra. Johann Friedrich Rochlitz, in his famous memoirs, *Für Freunde der Tonkunst* (I, 122), which started to appear in 1824 but were not completed until 1830, relates that the two Rombergs often visited Haydn; both young men were talented composers, but in the event it was Bernhard who became the more celebrated of the two.

> Haydn received them, according to his simple and affectionate character, in the most friendly fashion and helped them to gain a most satisfactory entry to the

1 The *Wiener Zeitung* (No. 87, 29 October 1796, p. 3097) further reports that there was 'ein Konzert auf dem Fortepiano' played by 'Frl. v. Heißenstamm', and that the Cantata 'was sung by male and female singers especially down from the I. R. Court Theatre in Vienna', that twenty-three members of the orchestra were also imported from Vienna and added to the local musicians of Wiener Neustadt and the boys' choir (*Famular-Knaben*) from the I. R. Cadet School; the Cantata was performed by a total of seventy-four persons, and Süssmayer conducted.

2 *Wiener Zeitung*; Pohl III, 111f. Haydn had returned to Vienna at least by 9 November (*vide infra*) and could have witnessed the Cantata and his Symphony being performed to a full house at the Redoutensaal on 15 November. Count Zinzendorf notes in his Diary (Olleson, 51), '. . . Le soir au grand Concert dans la grande Sale de Redoute. Il n'y avoit pas moyen d'y entrer, tant grande etoit l'affluence du monde. . . .'

leading houses of the city; he was also glad to call Andreas his son, especially after his [Andreas's] Quartet had been performed; and as a composer he [Andreas] was just that. Father Haydn, for all the simplicity of his character, was not without knowledge of the world and without the means by which it could be treated, and bearing in mind his and the world's idiosyncrasies, he acted as he always did – namely, for others rather than for himself. For example, he introduced the young men as excellent performers into one of the leading musical salons of Vienna, and there he himself put out parts to a quartet. 'Father Haydn's got something new!' was whispered round the delighted company. The quartet was presented in the most beautiful perfection, was listened to with the deepest attention, and when it was finished, everyone hastened to Haydn to show their appreciation and thanks. He stood silently in their midst, with friendly nods of his head and with that peculiarly engaging, innocently arch expression which one was used to in him, and which anyone who ever knew him will certainly remember. 'Did you really like it?' he asked at last. 'That's very nice; because it is by that young man there – by our Andreas.'[1]

Andreas Romberg dedicated three quartets to Haydn which were reviewed very successfully in the *AMZ* (IV, 1802, 535–9). It is likely that one of them was the work presented to Viennese society in the manner above enumerated.

Trois Quatuors pour deux Violins, Alto et Basse, composés et dediée à Jos. Haydn par Andreas Romberg. Oeuvre II. Livre II. à Paris, aux Addresses ordinaires. à Bonn, chés l'Editeur, N. Simrock. Proprieté de l'Editeur et enregistré à la Bibliothèque Nationale. (Pr. 9 Francs.)

The short dedication is as follows:

A Joseph Haydn.

C'est à l'homme de génie, à l'immortel Haydn, dont l'approbation seul est l'éloge le plus flatteur, que je dédie un oeuvre de Musique auquel j'ai donné tous mes soins. J'ose le lui présenter comme un hommage que je dois à ses talens sublimes.

A. Romberg.

The *AMZ* notes that, if anything, the quartets go beyond the high expectations raised by the foreword. The reviewer praises the clean part-writing (*Reinheit des Satzes*), draws attention to a typically Haydn-inspired seven-bar phrase in the Minuet from the E major No. 1, and gives a liberal quotation from the brilliant counterpoint of the Minuet in No. 2, with its *al roverscio*. The reviewer also notices that Romberg uses the so-called Haydn ornament (a crossed turn: ∻ or ∻) more than a trill or turn: here, Romberg was following a very personal 'fingerprint' of the older composer. He also recommends Romberg and the younger composers not to be parsimonious with accidentals, particularly in those before notes at a different octave (e.g.

1 To one of the Rombergs, who had asked Haydn why he had never composed a quintet and was expecting a learned explanation, the composer gave an answer which astonished the young composer and was much quoted as a *bon mot* afterwards: 'Es ist halt keines bei mir bestellt worden' ('Well, no one ever ordered one from me'). Haydn is also quoted as having said that, after Mozart's quintets, it never occurred to the older man to compose a quintet. See *Haydn in England 1791–1795*, p. 505. Pohl III, 314. It is often difficult to know when Haydn was being sarcastic, when he was being serious, and when he was possibly able to be both simultaneously, as may be the case with the string quintets.

our invention to show the reviewer's point as quickly as possible) 'but to follow as a model the almost exaggerated caution of the unattainable Mozart in this respect'. We see, in this example, one more side of Haydn that Andreas Romberg was, no doubt to his detriment, slavishly following: namely, the imprecise notation which Haydn had come to use in orchestral (and operatic) works for the Esterházy band over some thirty years, or from 1761 to 1790. We shall bring up this point in connection with the notation of *The Creation* (*vide infra*, p. 393). Mozart, writing for 'pick-up' orchestras, was forced, early in his career, to be more precise. By 1790, many of Haydn's orchestral directions, and his training with the singers, had become exclusively oral: a practice which was no doubt highly beneficial to Haydn's group at Eszterháza but of no use whatever when the works in question were printed and circulated in Madrid or Rome or St Petersburg.

We have seen earlier, in the Chronicle for 1796, that Haydn had promised some new music to Breitkopf & Härtel in Leipzig. At the beginning of November he found a useful go-between, his godson Joseph Weigl, Jr, the composer, who was travelling to Leipzig and took with him Haydn's debt and the new piano Trio in E flat No. 42 (XV: 30) which he delivered to Christoph Gottlob Breitkopf.

[To Christoph Gottlob Breitkopf, Leipzig. *German*]

Vienna, 9th November 1796.
[Breitkopf's clerk notes: 'rec'd 10th Dec.']

Nobly born,
Most highly respected Sir!

The bearer of this letter, Herr Wägl from Vienna, will at last give you the promised pianoforte Sonata together with 15 f. in bank notes: meanwhile I thank you once again and am, Sir, most respectfully,

Your obliging and obedient servant,
Jos: Haydn
Fürstl. Esterhazyscher Capell Meister.

[Address:]

von Vienne
Monsieur
Monsieur de Breitkopf
Leipzig

[Breitkopf's clerk notes: '1796/9 Nov./(rec'd) 10 Dec./(ans'd) 2 Jan 97.' To the right: 'Wien/Haÿdn'.]

[CCLN, 148]

We have, in Hermann von Hase's book, *Joseph Haydn und Breitkopf & Härtel*,[1] a summary of the answer to this letter, taken from the firm's books which were destroyed in an air raid on Leipzig in 1944: 'On 2 January [1797], Breitkopf thanked [Haydn] for the excellent [*vortreffliche*] composition and assures the composer that he will make it his duty to see that the new work is presented to the public in the proper outer guise, that is, as far as the engraving is concerned. He asks Haydn for some of his vocal compositions, for which the *Notensatz* (a new kind of music typewriter on which all the late Haydn Masses were issued in score) is more fitted [than instrumental compositions, presumably].' It was not until October 1798, however, that Breitkopf &

1 Leipzig, 1909, pp. 6ff., hereinafter abbreviated 'Hase'. The dates of the letter and of Breitkopf's answer were misread by Hase as '9 November 1795' and '2 January 1796' respectively.

Härtel were able to announce their new edition (which was, actually, very handsomely printed) in the *AMZ*. Meanwhile Haydn had also sold the work to Corri & Dussek in London, of which the only known copy, seen[1] briefly some years ago at Blackwell's Music Shop in Oxford, then disappeared. Haydn also retained a fine MS. copy, by Johann Elssler, which is now in the Esterházy Archives at Budapest; of the autograph, only one sheet of the Finale survives (Pierpont Morgan Library, New York. *ex. coll.* Heineman Foundation).

In November 1796, Haydn began to make a series of MS. copies of his vocal music for a British singer, Mrs Peploe, who later subscribed to *The Creation* (in Haydn's list she is 'M[ris] Peploe. Curzon Street m[a]yfair'). Mrs Peploe was in Vienna in the autumn of 1796 and in 1797, and Haydn gave (or sold to) her Elssler copies of: the *Scena di Berenice* (London, 1795, with an important textual clarification in the Peploe copy: see *Haydn in England 1791–1795*, p. 373); an Aria from *L'anima del filosofo*; and two new Duets for soprano, tenor, and piano entitled 'Saper vorrei se m'ami' and 'Guarda qui che lo vedrai'. Haydn entered them in his *Entwurf-Katalog* as '2 Duette bloß mit Clavier v[on] Poet Badini aus England', i.e. from Carlo Francesco Badini, the author of the libretto to Haydn's English opera, *L'anima del filosofo*. The autograph for one of these duets, 'Guarda qui', exists (British Museum, Add. 32173, fol. 3–6) and is dated 1796. The copies for Mrs Peploe are signed by her as follows: 'Saper vorrei' is 'Vienna Nov[br] 1796' and 'Guarda qui' is 'Vienna Dec[br] 1796', and Haydn made small corrections, especially in the text of 'Saper vorrei'.[2]

In November in Vienna the annual masked ball of the Pensionsgesellschaft bildender Künstler was held, for which occasion Haydn had contributed dances in 1792 and Beethoven in 1795. This year, 1796, the Emperor and Empress were away attending the *Landtag* (legislature) in Pressburg ('sind auf dem Land = /tag in Pressburg/gewesen') but loyally purchased a dozen tickets each. Apart from various Archduchesses and Archdukes, we notice fewer of the usual names from the nobility, possibly because the music was considerably less interesting than Haydn's or Beethoven's, being composed by *Hofcompositor* Anton Teyber. Maria Christina von Braunschweig, Baron von Waldstädten and Countess von Kinsky, among others, ordered twelve tickets each. Among further subscribers was 'H[r] v. Grassi', the sculptor, who later executed famous busts of Haydn. The musicians received their usual free tickets, as did Haydn:

			Stük
Dem	H[r]	v. Capoll	6
–	–	Teÿber Mus. Compositor	14
–	–	Eybler D[to]	6
–	–	Beethoven/: ist nicht hier –	
–	–	Kozeluch	4
–	–	Süssmayr	4
–	–	Haÿdn	2

[etc. etc.]

[From the MS. Archives of the Pensionsgesellschaft, now in the Vienna City Archives]

On 14 December, the eldest son of Luigia Polzelli died: Pietro (known to Haydn and the family as 'Pietruccio'), born at Bologna in 1777. Haydn had particularly loved

1 By Dr Alan Tyson, who kindly wrote to us about it in 1962.

2 The Peploe manuscripts, *ex. coll.* Landon, are now in the Burgenländisches Landesmuseum, Eisenstadt.

this delicate boy, who had been a second violinist at Schikaneder's Theater auf der Wieden, and had been a composition pupil of Haydn and a violin pupil of Luigi Tomasini. He died in the 'Ringelschmidschen Hause' in the Schleifmühlgasse 'am Lungenbrand' (lung fever or, probably, pneumonia), aged nineteen. It was a bitter loss for Haydn, who seems to have thought Pietruccio more than ordinarily gifted. In *Haydn in England 1791–1795*, p. 199, we have printed a letter by him to his mother, dated 22 October 1792, in which he notes that he is living at Haydn's house.[1]

On 15 December Johann Georg Albrechtsberger wrote a letter to his and Haydn's erstwhile pupil, Ludwig van Beethoven. It is an historic document because in it we have the first written reference to Haydn's new Oratorio, *The Creation*. The letter reads as follows:

Vienna, 15 December 1796.

My dear Beethoven!

For your name-day [*recte*: birthday] tomorrow, I wish you all the best. God give you health and happiness and grant you much luck. If you, my dear Beethoven, should have a free hour, your old teacher invites you to spend it with him. It would give me great pleasure if you would bring the Trio with you, we could rehearse it straight away, and since I now have more time I will start directly making the scores.

Yesterday Haydn came to me, he is carrying round in his head the idea of a big oratorio which he intends to call 'The Creation' and hopes to finish it soon. He improvised some of it for me and I think it will be very good.

Don't forget to look in tomorrow and meanwhile hearty greetings from

Your Johann Georg Albrechtsberger.[2]

Beethoven, incidentally, had recently returned from a visit to Pressburg (Bratislava, ČSSR), where on 23 November he had given a concert, using a new piano by Streicher.[3]

The sketches to *The Creation* are contained, apart from some single pages (such as the first orchestral score in draft of 'Chaos', New York Public Library) in two books in the National Library at Vienna (Musiksammlung der österreichischen Nationalbibliothek), Cod. 16835 and 18987; the first of these is bound with, and apparently belongs to, sketches to the *Missa Sancti Bernardi de Offida*, the autograph of which is (as

1 Pohl III, 114; CCLN 137f. *Haydn Yearbook* VII (1970), p. 15.

2 Autograph owned formerly by Dr Guido Adler. It and two other letters from Albrechtsberger to Beethoven were first published by A. Weissenbäck in 'Drei noch unveröffentliche Briefe Albrechtsbergers an Beethoven', in *Musica Divina* (Monatsschrift für Kirchenmusik), IX. Jahrgang, Vienna–Leipzig 1921, pp. 10f. Apart from its containing the first dated reference to *The Creation*, the letter is interesting because it shows a warm relationship between Albrechtsberger and Beethoven such as no longer existed between Beethoven and Haydn. The Trio mentioned would seem to be either the Serenade, Op. 8 (published in October 1797), or, more likely, one of the Three Trios, Op. 9 – both *opera* being for violin, viola and 'cello. The second letter is dated 20 Feb. 1797, and in it Albrechtsberger relates that the old Baron Joseph Gleichenstein has sent his *Kammerdiener* to ask if Beethoven will play tomorrow evening at the Baron's in a piano concert and also if Beethoven were willing to give lessons to the Baron's son Ignaz; Albrechtsberger told the servant that he thought Beethoven was probably too busy to give lessons. The third letter, 8 June 1797 reads: '. . . I have just received your letter and am astounded that you withdraw the Trio, which is so successful and where I've already finished scoring it. It will also, surely, not be pleasant for the Count to cancel, now that he's already sent his guests an invitation. The orchestra is small but good and they will do it justice. So please send me news, for I must send over the music this afternoon. Many greetings. . . .' Beethoven, already being temperamental, seems to have had Op. 8 or 9 in mind for a performance with *orchestra*(!). Significantly, no more letters survive.

3 Landon, *Beethoven*, 92f.

we have seen) dated 1796. The second book contains later sketches to 'Chaos' and also sketches to Symphonies Nos. 99 and 101, the latter discussed in *Haydn in England 1791–1795*, pp. 492–4. If we would hazard a dating of these sketches, we would be inclined to place Chaos I (New York) and Cod. 16835 together with the Mass sketches in the year 1796, and perhaps Cod. 18937 in the year 1797. In any case, the fact that Haydn was well advanced in sketching *The Creation* during 1796 suggests that he must have had the word-book in front of him. The question now arises, which word-book? The original English or Swieten's German adaptation? To answer this question is of course now impossible, but a few words on the background of the libretto, and how Haydn came by it, may be welcome.

We are fortunate in having a letter from Baron van Swieten himself on the subject; it was first printed in the *AMZ* in January 1799 and was dated 'Vienna, End of December 1798'.

> . . . and now a few words on the poem which you choose to call *my* Creation. My part in the work, which was originally in English, was certainly rather more than mere translation; but it was far from being such that I could regard [the libretto] as *my own*. Neither is it by *Dryden*, as is erroneously stated in a letter from Vienna which appeared in the 6th number of the *Deutscher Merkur* for the current year, but by an unnamed author who had compiled it largely from *Milton's* Paradise Lost, and had intended it for *Handel*. What prevented the great man from making use of it is unknown; but when *Haydn* was in London it was looked out, and handed over to the latter with the request that he should set it to music. At first sight the material seemed to him indeed well chosen, and well suited to musical effects, but he nevertheless did not accept the proposal immediately; he was just on the point of leaving for Vienna, and he reserved the right to announce his decision from there, where he wanted to take a closer look at the poem. [On his return] he then showed it to me, and I found myself in agreement with the verdict he had given. But I recognized at once that such an exalted subject would give *Haydn* the opportunity I had long desired, to show the whole compass of his profound accomplishments and to express the full power of his inexhaustible genius; I therefore encouraged him to take the work in hand, and in order that our Fatherland might be the first to enjoy it, I resolved to clothe the English poem in German garb. In this way my translation came about. It is true that I followed the plan of the original faithfully as a whole, but I diverged from it in details as often as musical progress and expression, of which I already had an ideal conception in my mind, seemed to demand. Guided by these sentiments, I often judged it necessary that much should be shortened or even omitted, on the one hand, and on the other that much should be made more prominent or brought into greater relief, and much placed more in the shade. . . .

Griesinger's version of the work's origin was as follows:

> The first idea of the oratorio: The Creation, belongs to an Englishman by the name of Lidley [*sic*; see *infra*], and Haydn was to compose Lidley's text for Salomon. He soon saw, however, that he did not have sufficient understanding of the English language for this undertaking; in addition, the text was so long that the oratorio would have lasted close on four hours. In the meantime Haydn took the text with him back to Germany; he showed it to Baron van Swieten, the Imperial Librarian in Vienna, and the latter put it into its present shape. Salomon wanted to take Haydn to law for this, but Haydn put it to him that he had only used Lidley's idea and not his actual words; besides, Lidley was already dead – and thus the matter was suppressed. . . . [Griesinger, 37]

Haydn's other authentic biographer, Dies – for the third biography by an eye-witness, Giuseppe Carpani's *Le Haydine*, is not so accurate and can be used only with great caution as a source – informs us:

> The talk turned to *The Creation*. The first suggestion for this work was made by Salomon in London. Since he had been successful in so many musical enterprises to date – a success to which Haydn had contributed in no small measure – he became ever more venturesome for new undertakings. Salomon resolved to have Haydn write a large-scale oratorio, and for this purpose handed over to him an already old libretto in English. Haydn had doubts about his familiarity with the English language; he would not undertake anything, and finally left London on 15 August 1795. . . .
>
> Haydn only remembered the English text when Baron van Swieten said to him, shortly after his arrival in Vienna: 'Haydn, we're still waiting to hear another oratorio from you!' He told the Baron how things stood and showed him the English text. Swieten offered to prepare an abridged free translation of it in German, and once this was finished he so sang its praises that Haydn was no longer left any choice, and firmly made up his mind to set the German text. From this it can be seen that everyone was in error whose opinion on the origin of Haydn's work was that it had been written for London. [Dies, 158f.]

A further contemporary source gives us a slightly different slant to the way in which the libretto materialized; it is an extract from a series of letters from Princess Eleonore Liechtenstein to her daughter (Countess Harrach) which will be quoted more fully *infra*. In a letter dated 1 May 1798, she writes:

> . . . Je me trouvais à coté du Cte. Marchal [Marschall, who was one of the oratorio society's backers] . . . C'est le Baron [van Swieten] qui a fait [les] paroles, toutes tirées de la génèse et des psaumes et il a communiqué ses idées à Haydn pour la musique, il est sur que cela leur fait honneur à l'un et à l'autre. Marchal m'a dit que Haydn est venu d'Angleterre avec le projet de composer sur ce sujet, qu'on lui avait donné là un poëme anglais et c'est la . . . que le Baron a travaillé et sans lui rien oter je crois à-peu-près traduit . . . [Pohl III, 130f.]

The final source is an anecdote told by the 'veteran vocalist and composer', C. H. Purday (1799–1885) to Grove in 1878, who in turn gave the information to Pohl in a letter which is used in Pohl III (355f.):

> I have just seen old . . . Purday, born 1799, whose father was a Music seller, and who has been connected with Music all his life. He has told me one or two stories which may be useful to you. . . . Barthelemon told Purday's father that Haydn while here said to him, 'I wish to write something which will make my name last in the world. What would you advise me to do?' Barthelemon took up a Bible which was lying near and said, 'There is the book; begin at the beginning' – and this was the first suggestion of *The Creation*.

Purday's own words, in an English devotional magazine, appeared in 1880:

> . . . My father, who was a music publisher . . . during the years 1806–7 was very intimate with Barthelemon, the leader of the concerts of Saloman [*sic*], who engaged Haydn to come over to England. . . . During Haydn's stay in England he was so much struck with the performance of Handel's *Messiah* that he intimated to his friend Barthelemon his great desire to compose a work of a similar kind. He asked Barthelemon what subject he would advise for such a purpose. Barthelemon took up his Bible and said, 'There, take that, and begin at the beginning!'

Barthelemon assured my father that this was the origin of the idea of the composition of *The Creation*.[1]

Edward Olleson, commenting on this quotation, says: 'Neither is this account completely incompatible with those of van Swieten, Griesinger and Dies; though Purday's story differs from the others, it does little to actually contradict them, and there seems no reason why they should not continue to live together in peaceful coexistence.'

If we combine all these various sources, especially noting the statement by Princess Liechtenstein about Baron van Swieten, that the latter 'sans lui [un poëme anglais] rien oter je crois à-peu-près traduit', it would seem logical for Haydn to have begun the one major section *without any text*, to wit 'Chaos'. As for the text itself, modern scholarship believes that 'Lidley' is really Linley, and in particular Thomas Linley senior (1733–95), Sheridan's father-in-law and, during Haydn's visits to England, co-director with Samuel Arnold of the Drury Lane oratorio concerts. Note especially that 'Lidley [Linley] was already dead' by the time Salomon wanted to sue Haydn. It is now believed, however, that Linley did not actually write the libretto but 'passed [it] on to Haydn . . . from the library (or from the lumber room) of the Drury Lane oratorios. . . .' If this is what really happened, then there is no need to question any further van Swieten's claim that the text had been in the first place intended for Handel. The oratorio concerts that Linley directed were part of an unbroken tradition stretching back to Handel himself. Linley's predecessor was J. C. Smith the younger, who has assisted at the composer's own oratorio performances, and had taken over their direction after Handel's death. Smith, moreover, inherited from his father in 1763 an unspecified quantity of Handel's manuscripts. J. C. Smith senior, who had known Handel well, bequeathed to his son 'All my Musick Books and Pieces of Musick whether Manuscript or otherwise which were left to me in & by the last Will & Testament of my Friend George Frederick Handel deceased'. There was thus ample opportunity for a libretto to be handed down from Handel to the younger Smith, and thence to his successor Thomas Linley.'[2]

Who in fact can have written the original English libretto? Charles Jennens has been suggested, as has another Handelian author, Newburgh Hamilton, who wrote *Samson* – the Handel Oratorio closest, thinks Dr Olleson, to the spirit of *The Creation* and which, it is now believed, is not the work of Thomas Morell but rather of Hamilton. An even more ingenious idea attributes the libretto to Handel's old friend Mary Delany (Griesinger having misinterpreted Haydn's no-doubt curious pronunciation of 'Delany' as 'Lidley'). On 10 March 1743–4, writing from Clarges Street to Mrs Dewes, Mrs Delany informs her correspondent:

> The oratorios fill very well, not withstanding the spite of the opera party: nine of the twelve are over. Joseph is to be performed (I hope) once more, then Saul, and the Messiah finishes; as they have taken very well, I fancy Handel will have a second subscription; and how do you think *I have lately been employed?* [italics original] Why, I have made a drama for an oratorio, out of Milton's Paradise Lost, to give Mr. Handel to compose to; it has cost me a great deal of thought and

1 *The Leisure Hour*, London 1880, p. 528. We have used the extract in the most comprehensive article on this material, Edward Olleson's 'The Origin and Libretto of Haydn's *Creation*' in *Haydn Yearbook* IV (1968), pp. 148ff. We have also gratefully used Mr Olleson's excellent translations of the Swieten letter, etc., and followed his conclusions.
2 Olleson 'Origin', p. 163.

contrivance; D. D. [Mrs. Delany's husband] approves of my performance, and that gives me some reason to think it not bad, though all I have had to do has been collecting and making the connection between the fine parts. I begin with Satan's threatening to seduce the woman, her being seduced follows, and it ends with the man's yielding to the temptation. . . .

Although on the face of it, the contents would appear different, the late Edward J. Dent thought that Mrs Delany might in the end have written the word-book of Haydn's *The Creation*. Whatever her project turned out to be, Handel refused to set it. Dent thought that 'Linley was the nearest that German scholarship could approximate to Delany', a statement that is rather hard on Griesinger who, as O. E. Deutsch drily insisted, was no scholar. The actual spelling of 'Lidley' is also subjected to variation within the various articles on the subject. Deutsch, who deals *in extenso* with the Delany attribution, says categorically that in Griesinger's serialized version of his book as it appeared in the *AMZ* (XI[1809], 705), the name is spelled 'Linley (not Lidley, nor Lindley)'. In fact, *AMZ* only uses the word 'Lidley', and no less than three times.[1]

It is unlikely that we shall uncover the original English libretto, which has disappeared in the confusion of van Swieten's legacy along with the original manuscript scores of *The Creation* and *The Seasons*; it is in fact entirely possible that the actual MS. of the libretto listed no author's name (as van Swieten asserted in his letter) and that 'Lidley' is really an oral tradition from Haydn to Griesinger. With this inconclusive and contradictory evidence we close our brief summary dealing with the authorship of the word-book to Haydn's Oratorio.

In the course of this biography, we have often pointed to numerous pieces of evidence showing Haydn's uncanny ability to guess the truly international taste of the times in which he lived: perhaps the most dramatic evidence of all is the enormous change of style that took place in his music between *c.* 1750 and 1800 – a half century in which taste in music changed not only perhaps more rapidly than ever before in a similar span (except possibly during the lifetime of Claudio Monteverdi), but also changed in large measure through the efforts of Haydn and his most talented contemporaries, such as Vanhal and C. P. E. Bach. (The reader will by now have realized why Mozart's name is omitted from this list: his influence was definitely a delayed one, and was effective on a European scale only in the last few years of the eighteenth century.)

To write an Oratorio on the subject of the Creation would have seemed arrogant madness to many composers, and also to many librettists; but Haydn set about his task with a magisterial certainty which is reflected in almost every page of the finished product. Once again, he had written a work the subject of which was on every educated tongue throughout the civilized world: the enormous strides made by science had changed man's attitude towards the origin of the world. We need hardly cite chapter and verse for this statement, but we would quote from the diary of a man whose words, often superficial but often a brilliant mirror of the world in which he moved, have figured many times in this biography: Count von Zinzendorf, whose intensely moving farewell to the eighteenth century will be found *infra* in the Chronicle, p. 500 (31 December 1799). Probably during the very time, and the very

1 See O. E. Deutsch's interesting comments to the Delany letter in *Handel, A Documentary Biography*, London 1954, pp. 587f.

month, when Haydn was beginning to sketch 'Chaos'[1] of the new Oratorio, the old Count wrote, under the date 4 April 1796, on the 'probability of a central solar system', which fact he gathered by reading 'L'almanach de Berlin'. Zinzendorf ends with the words: '. . . grandeur de Dieu, petitesse infinie de l'homme!' As we shall see, on really important subjects (such as the one just quoted), Zinzendorf and Haydn absolutely saw eye to eye.

The Christmas concert of the Tonkünstler-Societät put on the now inevitable *Retter in Gefahr* by Süssmayer; there were, as always, two presentations. During the first concert Joseph Wölffl of Salzburg, a pupil of Leopold Mozart and Michael Haydn, played a piano concerto (probably his own). Wölffl was much esteemed as a pianist in those days. The *AMZ*, in a long comparison of the relative merits of Beethoven and Wölffl,[2] notes that 'W. has advantages in that he, sound in musical learning and dignified in his compositions, plays passages which seem impossible with an ease, precision and clearness that cause amazement. . . . That Wölffl likewise enjoys an advantage because of his amiable bearing, contrasted with the somewhat haughty pose of Beethoven, is very natural' (*AMZ*, 22 April 1799). During the second evening, Philipp Schindlöcker played a violoncello concerto: he was an excellent musician with whom Beethoven gave concerts.[3] In both concerts there were works by Haydn – an unidentified chorus (probably the *Madrigal* 'The Storm') and 'Das beliebte Andante' ('Surprise' Symphony, second movement) – and a 'Neue Sinfonie von Paul Wranizky, erster Violindirector im k. k. Hoftheater'. Zinzendorf went on the first evening and notes 'Des Symphonies et des Choeurs de Hayden' – not an entirely accurate description; possibly the Wranizky Symphony sounded very much like a work by Haydn . . .[4]

On the Feast of St Stephen, 26 December, Haydn conducted a new Mass in the beautiful Baroque church of the Piarists in the Viennese suburb of Josephstadt. As we have mentioned above, the occasion was the *Primitae* ceremonies of Joseph von Hofmann, whose father, the Imperial Royal *Kriegszahlmeister* (head of the Financial Department of the War Ministry) Johann Franz von Hofmann (who lived in Haus 250, Strauchgasse), had received permission for his son to be admitted to the priesthood before he finished his theological studies: this ceremony took place on 18 December, and the family had requested from Haydn a new Mass to celebrate the *Primitae* eight days later. The *Annalen* of the *Ordensprovinz* inform us:

> On 26 December, that is the Feast of Saint Stephen, our *Professkleriker* Joseph Hofmann, who was ordained on the 18th of this month, celebrated his *Primitae* in our Parish Church in the Josephstadt, to which a colossal crowd of people came from all over, also many of the nobility, the more so since the most respected and world-famous *Herr* von Heydn [*sic*], whom the parents of the new priest ['des Primizianten'] had invited and asked, performed his [Haydn's] new and certainly majestic ['feierliche'] Mass (*The War Mass* [*die Kriegsmesse*]), which he conducted.

1 We would remind our readers that an early sketch for 'Chaos' is contained in the Österreichische Nationalbibliothek, Codex 16835 fol. XIX, v., a manuscript that includes sketches for the *Missa Sancti Bernardi de Offida*. See Karl Geiringer: 'Haydn's Sketches for "The Creation"' in *Musical Quarterly* XVIII (1932), No. 2, pp. 299ff. The early sketch for 'Chaos' is reproduced on p. 306. Useful though the article is, the musical examples have a translated English text, while Haydn of course wrote in German. It is to be hoped that someone will publish all the sketches to *The Creation*, for it is the only large-scale work by Haydn for which very complete sketches have been preserved.

2 A good translation in Thayer–Forbes I, 205.

3 Emily Anderson: *The Letters of Beethoven*, London 1961, I, 56; also in Landon *Beethoven*, 101. Beethoven spells his name 'Schindleker'.

4 Pohl *Denkschrift*, 65; Olleson, 52.

The *Annalen* of the Collegium also reported that 'everything which was ecclesiastical magnificence was in evidence. *Herr* Natler, formerly a priest in the Hungarian province, preached and the new Mass by H. Joseph Heyden [*sic*] was given.'

It is clear from the various annals of the Piarist Order that the performers were not of the local church but appear to have been imported from outside. The records tell us that the large expenses incurred by Hofmann's parents included '7 *Plutzer* [Austrian measure] of beer for the musicians, 42 xr.' The 'Eipeldauer Letters' (actually written by a clever Viennese journalist, Joseph Richter) report on the event, not without a slight touch of malice, and in excruciating Viennese dialect which cannot, of course, be reproduced in English:

> . . . The famous Haidn [*sic*] wrote the music for it, and by a special favour I received an entrance ticket up in the choir balcony [at the back of the church, with the organ and room for a large group of musicians]; otherwise I'd have been squeezed to death down in the church itself. Dear Cousin, there hasn't ever been a sermon to pack 'em in like that, but it was well worth while, Dear Cousin, 'cause I never heard such beautiful music even in the theatre.[1]

We have saved to the last an interesting letter by Haydn which is not dated, and which can be placed only in approximate chronological order, as will be seen. The letter is a significant document both for Haydn scholars and for students of manners at the time, for it is couched in quite strong language for a 'house officer' of the Esterházy administration. The original letter has not been uncovered in the archives of the princely house, either in Austria (Eisenstadt, Forchtenstein) or in Budapest; until recently, it existed in one contemporary copy in the Nationalbibliothek, Vienna. But some years ago, through the kind offices of the pianist Mr Hans Kann, we received photographs of another source in Viennese private possession: a copy of the letter by Johann Elssler. The textual differences have been listed elsewhere.[2]

> [To Prince Esterházy's Administrator]
>
> [End of 1796 or beginning of 1797[3]]
>
> Nobly born,
> Highly respected Administrator!
>
> From the letter addressed to me and the enclosure of the worthy Privy Economic Administration of His Serene Highness Prince Esterházy, I saw that I am more or less CONDEMNED to pay the debt of Luegmayer,[4] who because of INSOLVENCY is not able to do so. Why? Because I am thought to possess the necessary MEANS: I wish to God it were so! But I SWEAR by the Kyrie eleison which I am at this moment supposed to compose for my FOURTH Prince, that since the

1 Archives of the Piaristenkirche: AMT *Hausannalen* V, 322; *Annales Provinciae* IV, 139. Brand, *Messen*, 221; Pohl III, 112f.; *Hof- und Staats-Schematismus* 1796. Otto Biba, 'Die Pflege der Kirchenmusik in der Piaristenkirche' in: *Festschrift 250 Jahre Piaristenkirche Maria Treu*, Vienna 1969, pp. 45ff.

2 *Haydn Yearbook* IV, 202.

3 The passage, '36 years in the Princely service', would place the date in the year 1797. Two Masses were written (or rather begun) in 1796, the *Missa in tempore belli* (dated 'Eisenstadt 1796') and the *Missa Sti. Bernardi de Offida* (1796, probably begun in Vienna), and no mass was composed in 1797. It seems probable, therefore, that the letter was written at the end of 1796, in which year the 'Kyrie eleison' of both Masses were begun.

4 Joseph Alois Luegmayer was married to Haydn's niece, Anna Katharina (daughter of Haydn's sister, Anna Maria Fröhlich of Rohrau). Luegmayer was often a source of embarrassment and frustration to Haydn, who gave him large sums of money over a long period of time: see also letter of 10 June 1798 and Haydn's Will.

death of my SECOND Prince – God rest his soul! – I have fallen into the SAME STATE OF INSOLVENCY as that of Luegmayer, but with the difference that he has fallen from his horse to the back of an ass, whilst I have managed to remain on the horse, but without saddle or harness.[1]

I therefore beg the worthy Privy Economic Administration of His Highness to wait at LEAST till I have finished the Dona nobis pacem, and until the Prince's house-master Luegmayer shall begin to receive the salary rightly due to him from his most gracious Prince, instead of drawing it, as he has hitherto done, from the SMALL salary of *Capellmeister* Haydn (who has been 36 years in the Princely service). For nothing is sadder or more dissonant than when one SERVANT pays another SERVANT, in this case the *Capellmeister* having to pay the house-master. If I should, perhaps today or tomorrow, be placed in a BETTER position, either as a result of my own merits or by the voluntary impulse of my most gracious Prince (FOR FLATTER AND BEG I WILL NOT), of course I shall not fail to comply with the above demand.

I am, Sir, with every respect,

Your most obliging servant,
Fran[z) J: Haydn [2]
Doctor of Oxford and Princely Esterházy
Capellmeister.

[CCLN, 149f.]

Luegmayer's financial problems seem to have become particularly acute at this time. Possibly Haydn's letter is to be considered in the light of a document recently discovered in the Esterházy Archives, Budapest.[3] It is a request by Joseph Lugmayr (*sic*) to Prince Esterházy, dated 17 February 1797, in which he requests the Prince for an increase in his salary as housemaster at Oedenburg (now Sopron, Hungary), saying that although Haydn has given him a pension of 68 fl. 42 xr. since 1793 and the Prince his 'Naturalien' (wine, corn, candles, etc.), Luegmayer cannot live, with a wife and three small children, on this small income in such an expensive place (Oedenburg was apparently more expensive than elsewhere in the provinces). We have broken the strict chronological order of our Chronicle to complete this small chapter of Haydn's poor relative in Oedenburg.

Two Haydn portraits, one very well known and one, alas, lost, may be placed in the Chronicle at this point. The lost one is by the Irish painter, Martin Archer Shee. It was exhibited at London in 1885, at which time it is described as follows: [Loaned by:] 'Barnard, Mr. J. T. – 107. Portrait of Haydn, by Sir M. Shee, P.R.A. 1796'. In the Joseph Müller Catalogue of 1932, the original painting is listed as being owned by the Royal Society of Musicians; but enquiry from that institution has revealed that the supposed Shee portrait is nothing but a (possibly contemporary) copy of the famous Hoppner painting (*Haydn in England 1791–1795*, pl. I); it, too, was exhibited in the 1885 'Loan Collection' where, however, it is described only as 'No. 43. Portrait of Haydn, the gift of Dr Selle' and as belonging to the Royal Society. The spurious Shee portrait

1 This robust simile has its basis in the difference in horsemanship between Don Quixote and Sancho Panza.

2 On the Elssler copy: 'J: Haydn.'

3 Arisztid Valkó, 'Haydn Magyarországi Müködése a Levétári Akták Tükrében,' in *Haydn Emlékére* (Zenetudományi Tanulmányok VIII, Budapest 1960, p. 610).

(i.e. the copy after Hoppner) is reproduced in Henri Marcel's 'L'iconographie d'Haydn'.[1] About this time, Haydn presumably sat for his portrait to a mediocre artist named Johann Zitterer. The gouache picture, in oval format, shows Haydn sitting at a keyboard with the music of the second movement of the 'Surprise' Symphony open on the music stand. The portrait, which is not dated, is now owned by the Historisches Museum der Stadt Wien and is exhibited in the Haydn Museum; its size is 24 × 18 cm. It was used as the basis for an engraving by J. H. Neidl which Artaria brought out in 1800; it also figures in Carpani's book *Le Haydine* (1812). The drawing of the face resembles strongly – perhaps suspiciously strongly – the Ludwig Guttenbrunn portrait (*c.* 1791?), which may be seen in one version (Mrs Eva Alberman, London) in Somfai (p. X) and in another (formerly Wolfgang von Karajan, Salzburg; now Eisenstadt Museum) in Landon, *Essays* (frontispiece – in colour). Various dates have been advanced for the Zitterer portrait (which is, by the way, an attribution: in Pohl III, 403, there is a question mark after the attribution; but since the Artaria engraving clearly names Zitterer as the painter, there is no reason to retain the question mark, and Somfai quietly drops it): Muller gives *c.* 1793; Somfai suggests, very cautiously, 'vielleicht 1795 in Wien(?) gemalt'. Since Haydn arrived in Vienna late in the year, and since 1796 marked, as we have seen, a veritable orgy of 'Surprise' Symphony performances in the k. k. Residenzstadt, we have tentatively placed the portrait – which is as mediocre as the artist who painted it – in the year 1796.

1 *Guide to the Loan Collection and List of Musical Instruments, Manuscripts, Books, Paintings, and Engravings, exhibited in the Gallery and Lower Rooms of the Albert Hall.* London 1885. [Joseph Muller] 'Catalogue of Haydn Portraits', *Musical Quarterly* XVIII (1932), No. 2, pp. 295ff. Henri Marcel: 'L'iconographie d'Haydn' *S. I. M. Revue musicale mensuelle*, Paris, Janvier 1910. In Pohl III, 404 the Shee painting is listed as 1795. In Thieme-Becker's *Lexikon* (article 'Shee') it is dated 1796. The question of interest to Haydn scholars is only whether Haydn can have sat for the portrait before he left London in August 1795, Shee finishing it in the course of the next six or eight months and then dating the finished product 1796. We have to thank Mr. Robin Gibson of the National Portrait Gallery for his kind assistance in trying to trace the Shee portrait. The Shee is missing in Somfai, but in that book there is a reproduction of the Zitterer portrait in several places: pp. X, 215, 225.

CHAPTER SIX

Works of 1796

THE TWO PRINCIPAL WORKS composed in 1796 are, of course, the *Missa Sancti Bernardi de Offida* and the *Missa in tempore belli*; and a discussion of these two Masses, the opening of a series of six which occupied the composer from 1796 to 1802, inevitably raises the whole question of Haydn's church music; for, apart from the operas, no single category of Haydn's vast *œuvre* has raised, and still in many quarters raises, such a storm of controversy.

Since a judgement of Haydn's late church music must begin with the composer's attitude towards religion, we allow the two earliest authentic biographers to speak for themselves. The more reliable of the two men, George August Griesinger tells us:

> Haydn was very religiously inclined, and a devoted follower of the religion in which he grew up. In his heart he was most firmly convinced that all human destiny lies under God's guiding hand; that God is the rewarder of good and evil; that all talents came from above. All his larger scores begin with the words 'In nomine Domini' and close with 'Laus Deo' or 'Soli Deo gloria'. 'If, when I am composing, things don't go quite right,' I heard him say, 'I walk up and down the room with my rosary in my hand, say several *Aves*, and then the ideas come again.' In religion, he also found the strongest consolation for his physical debility; in the final years of his life, he was quite reconciled to the idea of death, and prepared himself for it daily. Without speculating on the principles of faith, he accepted the 'what' and 'how' that his Catholic Church taught. . . .
>
> . . . Haydn left every man to his own conviction, and he recognized them all as his brothers. Altogether his devotion was not of a sort which is gloomy and forever in penance but rather cheerful, reconciled, trusting – and in this mould his church music, too, is composed. . . .
>
> A natural consequence of Haydn's religiosity was his *modesty*; for his talent was not of his own doing but a gracious gift of Heaven, to whom he considered he must show himself grateful. [Griesinger, 53–5]

Dies, the second of Haydn's two earliest authentic biographers, writes of the *Schöpfungsmesse* and a laudatory review of it in the *AMZ*. The passage to which Haydn alludes seems to be the 'Qui tollis' in which the music of *The Creation* is quoted (hence the name 'Creation-Mass').

> Now let us hear [Dies continues] how Haydn in his own particular fashion arrived at all these perfections. While composing he spoke to himself. 'I prayed to the Almighty not like a rejected sinner and in despair but calmly and slowly. In doing so I considered that an infinite God would certainly have mercy on his finite creatures, forgiving us as ashes to ashes, dust to dust. I was cheered by these thoughts. I experienced a certain joy that was so confident that I, supposed to express the words of the prayer, could not suppress my joy, but gave vent to my happy feelings and wrote *miserere* [*recte*: 'Qui tollis'] in *tempo allegro*. [Dies, 108]

Haydn's pupil, Sigismund Neukomm, adds the following note to this passage:

> The newer Masses by Haydn, against which the critics have been ruthlessly opposed because of their more elegant and less ecclesiastical style, were composed in Haydn's last and glorious period and each year for the birth- or rather the name-day of his deeply respected patroness the Princess Esterházy, for whom a mass in an attractive, elegant style would have more value than a learned or more serious work. [Neukomm, *Bemerkungen*, 30]

Speaking of church music (in Italy and in Haydn's hands) Dies, a few pages earlier, has this to say:

> Among the letters and papers that Haydn gave me, there was not one in which one could not find the esteem that rightly pertains to a noble genius. [Haydn was encouraged by Zelter to oppose the decline of church music.] If Haydn were really considered the man able to meet that challenge with success, the accusation of an anonymous critic falls to pieces: an accusation which, upon more careful investigation, is not the result of Haydn's creative spirit but rather of the lively tempi in three-four and three-eight time, because one is reminded in these tempi rather of minuets and waltzes. [The unnamed critic had found that Haydn's church music was not merely theatrical but better fitted to the dance hall; he discovered in them country dances (*Contretänze*), minuets and so on, but nothing worthy of the dignity that properly informs that species of music.] Nowhere, however, as in Italy have I heard in the churches not so much operatic but really dance music. During my twenty-one years of residence in Rome, I frequently had the opportunity in churches to consider the decline of music, and I always observed that the purpose of many local *maestri* must have been to tickle the ear, in which they seem to have been successful, for the people (in churches where the organ loft was situated opposite the high altar) turned round when the music began, turned their back to the high altar, and behaved almost as if they were in the theatre. [From Duparty's *Letters on Italy*, Dies quotes a passage written from Naples: 'People only go to the churches when they are illuminated or when there is music: in a word, when there is opera in church.' Dies adds: 'I was long a witness of it and I can assure you that this description is without exaggeration and literally true.']
>
> Theatrical arias with accompaniment of an obbligato instrument and to conclude a *concerto a solo* are everyday occurrences in Roman churches, and with their exaggeratedly sensual and superficial performances they can very easily banish devotion but can never awaken it.

In connection with the problem of lively tempi in Haydn's church music, and in particular those in triple time, we have a statement by Haydn's pupil, Sigismund von Neukomm, who lived long enough to be a rival of Mendelssohn's in England (Neukomm died in 1858):

> The criticism about the lively tempi in three-four and three-eight time may be attributed less to the composer than to the performances, especially in our restless railway age, in which the word 'Allegro' or 'con moto' placed at the beginning of a piece of music is the excuse for a crack of the whip, to drive the poor piece breathless over hill and dale. How often has one heard a *gemütliche* melody in three-eight time disfigured as a waltz caricature, and this is a result of the *Zappel-Wuth* [fidgety fury] which is supposed to make the music fiery. All Haydn's music, however, is full of evidence that whenever the circumstances require it, the inimitable composer of *The Seven Last Words of Christ on the Cross* can be just as full of pathos as Handel in his *Messiah* or *Israel in Egypt*.

By now the reader will have realized that Haydn's church music, even the last six Masses, produced very mixed emotions in many hearers – and even during Haydn's lifetime. To the words of Griesinger, Dies and Neukomm, we should now like to add a fourth authentic voice: less authentic than these, but of a certain interest none the less. Giuseppe Carpani (1752–1825), a poet and writer on music; as editor of the strongly anti-French *Gazetta di Milano* (1792–6), he was forced to flee Milan when it was taken by Napoleon, and came to Vienna where he soon became acquainted with Haydn. After a sojourn in Venice, following the peace of Campo Formio in 1797, Carpani returned to Vienna where he remained for most of his life. From a series of autograph letters of Carpani to his friend in Padua, the Abbé Francesconi,[1] we may see that Carpani was still in Venice in July 1804, so that his friendship with Haydn can only have lasted about a year (1796–7) when the composer's spirits were still high,[2] and from the middle of 1804, when Haydn was semi-retired, till his death in 1809. Thus Carpani's evidence on Haydn is not nearly of the first-hand kind provided by Griesinger, Dies and Neukomm. Nevertheless, as Pohl says, Carpani's *Le Haydine* (Milan 1812, revised and enlarged edition Padua 1823) is 'written with enthusiasm'. It was ruthlessly pirated by Stendhal and published in French translation (Paris 1814); notwithstanding Carpani's spirited defence, Stendhal again published his pirated edition in 1817 (*Vies de Haydn, Mozart et Métastase*) and then capped his effrontery by pirating Carpani's biography of Rossini, *Le Rossiniane* (Padua 1824). Carpani's style is very much Italian *Biedermeier*, with vast excursions into Italian painting and music (especially Cimarosa and Paisiello) – and it was of decisive influence on Stendhal who, being the better writer, was able to tighten up Carpani's discursive style. It is indeed most enlightening to compare Carpani's original with Stendhal's adaptation – for 'translation' is not a sufficiently accurate word to describe what the French writer did with the Italian original. In the passage quoted below, the end of the paragraph beginning 'Haydn, who was early sensible' was rewritten by Stendhal as follows:

> On hearing a Mass of Haydn's performed in one of the immense gothic cathedrals, so frequent in Germany, where a solemn twilight scarcely penetrates through the coloured windows, you feel, at first, agitated, and afterwards elevated, by that mingled character of seriousness, antiquity, imagination, and piety, which distinguishes them.[3]

Carpani had obviously read both Griesinger and Dies – indeed, he knew them both personally – before he published his own biography of Haydn in 1812. Nevertheless, Carpani has many ideas entirely his own, and his courtroom scene of Haydn on trial for his Masses is a literary conceit worthy of his great plagiarist:

> Come, my friend. – The same Haydn who, in instrumental music, was sublime, who was respectable in opera, now invites you to follow him to the sanctuary, where
>
> La gloria di colui che tutto muove
>
> inspired and transported him, at times, to write solemn and fiery hymns full of the

1 Author's collection. See otherwise the useful article on Carpani by C. F. Pohl in Grove, I.

2 Carpani was also in Vienna sometime in 1799: *vide infra*.

3 The English translation by 'The Author of the Sacred Melodies' (= William Gardiner, a warm friend of Haydn's and one of England's earliest champions of Beethoven) is delightful, and has been used whenever it corresponded to the Carpani original. It was published as *The Life of Haydn, in a series of Letters written at Vienna, followed by The Life of Mozart with observations on Metastasio and on the present state of Music in France and Italy translated from the French of L. A. C. Bombet*, London 1817. The passage above occurs on p. 209. Carpani, pp. 135–57.

glory of God, all of them revealing their treasures of art to honour the Divine Giver. Nothing has been more justly admired, and at the same time more warmly censured, than his Masses. He, creator of the new style, filled them with such beauty [*vaghezza*], and generally with such magnificence that they are truly a marvel to apprehend. Their defects [*tacce*], from which charge they cannot be exonerated, are (as it were) accidental, and concern only small parts of them, while the beauty that distinguishes them is full, solid and fundamental. The former are like those musical excesses of Michelangiolo, those false lights in Rubens, or those Levantine and Venetian costumes in Paolo [Veronese], which the austere critic cannot admit into the story of Jesus Christ; but that does not remove from those stupendous paintings their marvellous effects nor detract from the magnificence that informs them. Many of these masses circulate throughout the churches of Germany and serve as models in that country for young composers in their thirties. Others are owned only by Prince Esterházy, and these are, moreover, masterpieces. Here, the Haydnesque fantasy is no longer enslaved to the dialogue, nor to the imperious demands of the words, as in his theatrical pieces, in which he was obliged to do battle (as it were) with one arm only; but his inspiration is free and animated only by motives of feeling; there is room for his fertile invention and a proper vessel for his riches.

[There follows a history of church music which modern scholarship would in large part reject. The final section, however, is of interest in that it reflects with considerable accuracy the opinions about church music in the middle of the eighteenth century which were current at the time Carpani was writing and are thus of interest to our subject.]

. . . At length, about the middle of the century, Durante as head of his school conceived the idea of marking the sense of the words, and sought for agreeable melodies, which might give additional effect to the sentiments they expressed, just as in music for the theatre. Most of the *maestri* who followed him, some to a greater and some to a lesser extent, devoted themselves to grace and sentiment in their masses, psalms and hymns; but all of them, and especially those in Germany, preserved that veneer of a graceful and pathetic *stile fugato*, the application of which they believed would deliniate the boundary between sacred and secular music. Not so in Italy. There, the *maestri* almost without exception adopted the theatrical style also in the songs for the sanctuary, in such a manner that one could no longer distinguish between the one and the other; and just as in earlier centuries the church had given the law to the theatre, in the eighteenth century the theatre gave the law to the church. Except for a fugue to the words 'cum Sancto Spiritu', one only heard, after 1750,

> 'Cantare in su la cetra il miserere
> E con stile da farsa e da commedia.'

The arias, the little duets [*duettini*], even the recitatives from the theatre, and the rondos echoed from the organ lofts to the real scandal of Christian ears. Benedict XIV hoped to remove this abuse by proscribing, in a papal bull, the wind instruments, retaining only the organ; the vice was not in the instruments, however, but in the melodies, and they continued just as before, sustained by the violins. . . .

Haydn, who was early sensible of the dryness [*tisichezza*] of the ancient sacred music, and of the profane luxury of the modern Italians, not to speak of the monotonous character and lack of expressive thought that characterized the sacred music of his compatriots, decided to create an entirely new style all his own, without accepting anything, or hardly anything, from the theatrical style; but he preserved, by the solidity of his harmony, a part of the dark and lofty style of the ancient school; he supported, with all the richness of his orchestra, airs solemn, tender, and dignified, yet full of brilliancy; and from time to time, adorned with flowers and graces. . . . The Masses that Haydn wrote in this manner delighted by that mixture of gravity, attractiveness, scholarship, imagination and devotion which characterizes them.

Their effect is such that I want to tell you of a case that happened to me personally. In 1799, I was confined at Vienna by a fever. The bells announced a Mass at a church not far from my room: my ennui got the better of my prudence, and I rose and went to console myself with a little music. I inquired as I entered, and found it was the festival of St. Ann[e], and that in a church dedicated to her they were going to perform a Mass of Haydn's in B flat major [*Missa Sancti Bernardi de Offida*] which I had never heard. Scarcely had it begun before I felt myself affected. Charmed by such beautiful music, I was consumed with an inner fire that very quickly made me break out in a perspiration. I felt as if my head had been liberated of a great weight. An extraordinary cheerfulness invaded my soul, and when the mass was finished, I left, safe and sound, and the fever, which had visited me twice before, disappeared, never to return. You know that music played a part in the hygiene of the ancients, and on this subject our own Salvator Rosa sings to us:

> 'So che di Creta discacciò Talete
> La peste colla musica e Peone
> Guarda le malattie gravi, e segrete.'

. . . But let us return to our Haydn. His Masses are inspired by a sweet sensibility: the ideal part is brilliant and in general dignified, the style noble, full of fire and finely developed; the 'Amens' and 'Alielujas' breathe all the reality of joy and are of a spirit unequalled. Occasionally, when the character of a passage would otherwise be too gay, would be of too profane a cast, Haydn sobers it by profound and sonorous chords, which moderate this worldly joy. Observe his Mass *a quattro* in B flat [*Missa brevis S. Joannis de Deo*?]. His Agnus Dei are mostly very tender. Hiller describes that of the Mass No. IV [in the Breitkopf edition = *Schöpfungsmesse*] as the *non plus ultra* of beauty. His fugues are very different from those of many other masters in which, as Pliny would have said, their composer produced 'Multa ex industria, pauca ex animo'; [Haydn's] are like a stream [*elleno sono di getto*], they breathe fire, majesty and exaltation all at once.

. . . But in the midst of the praises which they deserve and obtain wholeheartedly from the best connoisseurs in Germany and from the literary journals of that learned country, Haydn's masses did not escape criticism, and in part vehement criticisms which are, in fact, at least in part justified; though the majority of them for my taste is unfounded. But I pass to you: place them in the courtroom and preside over them as a judge; hear the accusation, hear the defence, and then decide.

They accuse Haydn of having destroyed the species of sacred music established and adopted by all the professors. This species, however, no longer existed in Italy, as we have said earlier, and in Germany they had introduced a different species which, without being *fugato*, devoted little to the art of melody and nothing to the expression of the words and the emotions; everything consisted in richness of chords and in an *ostinato* movement in the orchestra, which made every piece sound like a continual arpeggio. [Georg] Reutter [Jr.] invented this species out of necessity. If monotony be seriousness, certainly nothing could be more so . . . I defy anyone who has heard on Easter-day a Gloria by Haydn to leave the church without feeling his heart expand with sacred joy; and I defy all the Masses by Padre Martini and the austere German composers to produce the same effect with their harmonious and most learned monotony. I doubt not, my dear judge, that if you are a man of taste and reason, you will not absolve Haydn from the accusation of being an innovator in the bad sense, but on the contrary you will approve of the happy revolution which has occurred in music for the church.

But the trial is not over and if Haydn will (as I hope) win it in the principal point, he will not win it in the others. Even if they have managed to accept his style, they accuse Haydn of having betrayed now and then the word; of having mixed all the styles; of having employed phrases and rhythms not suited to the church, and in fact there is, in the Dona nobis pacem of one of his masses [*Missa in honorem B.V.M.* in E flat, *c.* 1768], a pleasantry which repeats itself six times in *tempo presto* – an example to start with:

In one of his Benedictus [*Theresienmesse*, 1799], after other pleasantries in the orchestra this particular thought appears in *allegro*:

[The musical example is so badly engraved that one can hardly make out the notes lying above the ledger-lines, but apparently what Carpani is trying to show is this passage from this Benedictus – marked 'Moderato' incidentally:

(bars 55ff.).] The very same thought occurs in an *aria buffa* by Anfossi, and there it produces a good effect, because it is in its proper place. One could add similar examples of this unfortunate kind, but these will suffice. . . . Add to this evidence that he has composed some Kyrie eleison in sextuple time, and also some fugues in that same time. As concerns the Kyrie, this merry and vivacious rhythm is not at all suited to the devotional and tragic situation which demands pity and pardon in a fervour of composition. As far as the fugues in sextuplets are concerned, they become absolutely comic if the tempo is too quick. The precise master Albrechtsberger is quite right in advising his pupils to abstain from such *bizarreries*. . . . One can also hear, in a Qui tollis by Haydn [from the *Schöpfungsmesse*] music that is affected and anacreontic, wherein the maestro, in describing the sins of love and intemperance – these being the most common and easily committed – by attractive music, pretends thereby to give, on the other hand, more weight to the 'miserere nobis', written in a lugubrious and very heavy style. Also the Dona nobis pacem of this same Mass is of an exaggerated happiness, and reminds one of a dance of a person who, having got what he wants, abandons himself to the wildest transport of joy. These criticisms are just, especially that in which he is accused of using rhythms, means and ornaments which are not properly fit for their subject. In vain do some attempt to excuse him, saying that it is not the ideas or the phrases in Haydn's Masses that are profane and inopportune but that everything depends on the fast beat of which he availed himself in his frequent use of three-four and three-eight, tempi which easily call to mind, in the listener, the waltz, the minuet and the country dance [*contraddanza*]. *Qui s'excuse s'accuse.* I would say that there are organic expressions in nature which are the same in all nations. Joy accelerates the flow of blood and requires a *presto* tempo. Sadness retards, it slows up the speed of our humours, and it requires the tempo of *largo*; just as happiness requires the major key and melancholy the minor.

If, then, Haydn erred in his uses of tempo, employing *allegri* in places where *lenti* would have been more appropriate, he was certainly in the wrong, and the only excuse that can be given is that such things happen infrequently to men of talent. . . . Haydn apologized for these errors, which his judgement could not fail to recognize, by saying that whenever he thought of God, he could only conceive of Him as a being infinitely great and infinitely good. He added that this last quality of the Divine Nature inspired him with such confidence and joy that he could have written even a 'miserere' in *tempo allegro*. [Original footnote:] Sig. Diez [*sic*] has also reported this ingenuous expression on Haydn's part. This reasoning justifies his heart, does honour to his noble spirit, but does not excuse his attitude. . . . Let us conclude. Haydn's masses are of a magnificent cast, new, pleasing [*vago*], and sensible [*sensato*]. They are original, they are most beautiful; but now and then they have mistakes in their details. . . . However, his church music has increased his glory by opening new paths of the art and spirit.

We suspect that Carpani, who was a complete musical amateur, may have had his opinions on this subject formed by those of his compatriot, Antonio Salieri. Griesinger, in a letter to Breitkopf & Härtel of 20 June 1810, informs his correspondent that 'recently Carpani read me a letter from Salieri, in which he praises highly Haydn in the field of instrumental music (which isn't [Salieri's] field) but bitterly criticized his vocal writing, and simply wrote off his abilities as an opera composer; the masses, too, are treated roughly, for in them is a 'mescolanza di tutti generi' and great sins against the church style'.[1]

Thus we close our brief preliminary sketch of Haydn Masses in the eyes of his contemporaries and biographers Griesinger, Dies, Neukomm, and Carpani. Haydn himself said to Griesinger in November 1799 'Auf meine Messen bin ich etwas stolz' (I'm rather proud of my Masses).[2] They are every bit as typical of his muse as the string quartets and symphonies. It is useless to pretend that there are not theatrical moments in them, as indeed there are in equal abundance in the Masses of Mozart and Beethoven; but the timpani in the Agnus Dei of the *Missa in tempore belli* dare not offend us if we are to set the Beethoven *Missa Solemnis* on a pedestal, for exactly the same kind of kettledrum solo occurs there. The same abrupt contrast between the deadly earnest and the almost comical occurs even in the Masses. Who, after the ominous and tense Kyrie of the *Missa in angustiis*, with its low trumpet parts that pound out the repeated 'd's in our ears like the tramp of Napoleon's infantry; who, after the glories of the canon in the Credo and the soaring beauties of the 'Et incarnatus est', could expect in the Agnus Dei the following violin figure:

1 Brand, *Messen*, 429f. Note that Salieri's words 'mescolanza di tutti generi' is repeated almost *verbatim* when Carpani quotes, among other criticisms, that 'of having mixed all the styles', which in his original Italian reads 'd'aver mescolati tutt'i generi'. The proximity to Salieri's comments is too close to be coincidence.

2 Olleson, 'Georg August Griesinger's Correspondence with Breitkopf & Härtel', *Haydn Yearbook* III (1965), p. 12.

Yet we have seen these contrasts often enough in secular music; they should hardly surprise us in an age in which the border-line between the temporal and the spiritual was so thin. Haydn's critics would have been, no doubt, profoundly shocked if they had known, as we do (at least since the publication of O. E. Deutsch's standard article[1] on Haydn's canons in 1932), that the other-worldly beauty of the 'Et incarnatus est' in the *Missa Sancti Bernardi de Offida* is simply a reworking of a secular canon with the words:

> Gott im Herzen, ein gut Weibchen im Arm,
> Jenes macht selig, dieses g'wiß warm.[2]
>
> (God in the heart and a good wife on the arm,
> The one makes us holy, the other one warm.)

In those days, the idea of a secular canon becoming music for the central mystery of the Catholic faith was no stranger than Bach turning 'Tönet, ihr Pauken' into the *Christmas Oratorio*; but the idea was thoroughly repellent to the Victorians. Nowadays we have entered another secular age, and it is interesting to observe, in the quarter-century following the Second World War, an enormous upsurge of interest not only in Haydn's but also in Mozart's religious music. The 'Nelson' Mass (= *Missa in angustiis*) and Mozart's *Coronation Mass* have become best-sellers in France, Germany, England, and America. After more than 150 years of controversy, the religious music of *settecento* Austria has suddenly become accepted. In a few places, such as Austrian churches during high feast-days, the Masses can be heard in the setting for which they were composed; apart from Austrian (and a few south German) churches however, this music has now entered the repertoire *via* the media, concert hall, and gramophone recording. In a sense, much of the scandal surrounding them has evaporated; we shall pursue the matter further in the chapter with which this biography ends – a survey of Haydn's music a century-and-a-half after his death – but for the moment we proceed directly to the music.

The last work in this form that Haydn had composed was the *Missa Cellensis* ('Mariazellermesse') of 1782, composed for Anton Liebe von Kreutzner who intended it for the great Baroque pilgrimage church of Mariazell in Styria. In that Mass, Haydn had created a work in the full Viennese classical style, adapting sonata form to the requirements of the liturgical needs. In the fusion of secular and sacred, he had been judged eminently successful by his contemporaries, for contemporary copies of the 'Mariazellermesse' may be found in almost every great Austrian monastery and in many of the larger parish churches – *Regens chori* Kraus of the Stadtpfarrkirche in Eisenstadt owned a copy which later became incorporated in the Esterházy collection of church music at the castle. The vocal basis of the Mass had been S-A-T-B solo voices and the customary S-A-T-B choir, while the orchestra, apart from the traditional strings and organ continuo, had included oboes, one bassoon obbligato, trumpets, kettledrums, and strings – a standard church orchestra in Austria before the Josephinian reforms. In the *Missa Cellensis* of 1782, popular melodies such as that of the Kyrie for soprano solo were contrasted with more severe choral sections, such as the Qui Tollis; returning to a rather old-fashioned style, there was even a whole aria, 'Gratias Agimus', which on the other hand was balanced by brilliant fugues – that of the 'Dona Nobis Pacem' being particularly outstanding. The work begins, like many a Haydn symphony (and also like the huge cantata-mass, *Missa Cellensis in honorem*

1 *Zeitschrift für Musikwissenschaft* XV, 1932, especially p. 122.
2 See *Haydn in England 1791–1795*, p. 185.

B.V.M. of 1766, its predecessor for Mariazell), with a slow introduction. The way in which the orchestra and choir is laid out is also characteristic of all Haydn's later Masses: the chorus intones the words and moves in the basic tempo of the movement (for instance, in minims and crotchets in *alla breve*); the wind instruments block out the harmony, together with the organ, and/or double the upper (oboes) and lower (bassoons) voices in fugal sections; while the trumpets and kettledrums provide a sharp rhythmic accent to the whole, often contributing fanfare-like motifs of their own (♫♬ ♫ ♩ ♩), and the strings provide a constant forward motion in quick movements by repeated notes in quavers and semiquavers, or in passage work; and the whole is held together by the bass line, which often moves in quavers under the upper strings' semiquavers (or in crotchets under quavers, as the case may be). A typical page – there are hundreds – to illustrate this layout is the concluding part of the Gloria in the *Missa Sancti Bernardi de Offida* (see example above and overleaf), in which most of the devices enumerated above may be observed.

In this example, another typically Haydnesque feature may be observed: the use of an accent, which is usually marked *fz* (*forzato*) and often occurs on the weak beat, as in bars 294–5 here. The insertion of the *fz* here provides still another rhythmic impetus to a music already bursting with vibrant energy: to the semiquavers plus quavers of the basic rhythm, the timpani contribute an air of excitement all their own in that three-bar slow roll (293–5), the trumpets break the bar in half and fill the second part of bars

294 and 295 with motion, while the *fz* adds a new dimension (1) by accentuating the off-beat, second crotchet and (2) by drawing attention to the legato bass phrase (doubled by legato bassoons and violas), which is the only legato music in all this explosion of energy in quavers and semiquavers. The whole is grounded not only in the timpani but also in the held notes of the tenor at 294–5. And a final Haydn 'finger-print' is the extreme brevity of the final cadence: something which will occur again and again in the concluding bars of late choral music. All these elements contribute to making such a page of a Haydn Mass a unique *musical* experience, whatever one may feel about the religious content.

With this example, we are in the midst of another feature of Haydn's late Masses: their enormously symphonic content – symphonic not just in the use of the orchestra, which is as obviously related to the London Symphonies as is the *Missa solemnis* to the Beethoven symphonies – but also in the basic thought. In the concluding chapter of an earlier book on Haydn's symphonies,[1] we have been at some pains to show how

1 *The Symphonies of Joseph Haydn*: Chapter XIV 'Epilogue: Haydn's Symphonic Legacy', pp. 594ff. (London 1955, now long out of print). The same idea was developed by Anne Tatnall in her thesis *The Use of Symphonic Forms in the Six Late Masses of Joseph Haydn*, Northampton (Mass.) 1963, and Martin Chusid, 'Some Observations in Liturgy, Text and Structure in Haydn's Late Masses', in *Studies in Eighteenth-Century Music (A Tribute to Karl Geiringer on his Seventieth Birthday)*, ed. H. C. Robbins Landon and Roger Chapman, London 1970, pp. 125ff. For a contrary opinion, see P. H. Lang's review of our book in *Musical Quarterly* XLII, 1956.

Haydn transformed the instrumental forms into liturgical works. The composer stubbornly resisted all attempts to persuade him to write symphonies after 1795, whether they came, temptingly, from Paris in 1802, or from Count Fries in 1805 (who actually offered the staggering sum of 300 or 400 ducats).[1] He obviously regarded his contribution to the symphony as having closed with the magnificent twelve he had composed for Salomon in London, and (as we have had occasion to say before), there is something very final indeed about the subtitle on Symphony No. 104's autograph, 'The 12:th which I have composed in England/Sinfonia in D'. It is obvious that it never occurred to Haydn (or Mozart) to enlarge the size and scope of the symphony as Beethoven was to do with the 'Eroica'; but by applying symphonic principles to the mass form, Haydn was able to create a new kind of symphony, written for the glory of God (and the name-day of Princess Esterházy) and greatly increasing the 'orchestra' of the work by having a choir as well. In a way, Haydn's problem was Beethoven's problem (and everyone's, moreover, after 1805): what could a symphonist do after having composed a 'Prague' or E flat (K. 543), a 'Jupiter' or G minor (K. 550)? A symphony in B flat (No. 102) or a 'Drum Roll', a 'Clock' or 'London'? Or indeed a First or Second Symphony by Beethoven? Beethoven wrote the 'Eroica', Haydn wrote the 'Nelson' Mass; and both wielded musical power in an unprecedented fashion.

1 CCLN 211, and Haydn Yearbook III (1956), p. 49.

Recently, Martin Chusid (op. cit., *supra*) proposed an interesting idea as to the structure of the late Haydn Masses.[1] The idea has its origin in the scheme of a typical sung Mass ('Missa Cantata' or 'Figuraliter') according to the Roman rite, which we reproduce for the benefit of non-Catholics.

	ACCENTUS (recited or chanted by the priest)	CONCENTUS (sung by the choir) PROPER	ORDINARY
1		Introit	
2			Kyrie
3			Gloria
4	Collect(s)		
5	Epistle[★]		
6		Gradual Alleluja	
7	Gospel		
8			Credo
9		Offertory [Motet]	
10	Preface		
11			Sanctus
12			Benedictus
	[Consecration and Elevation of the Blessed Sacrament]†		
13	Pater Noster		
14			Agnus Dei
15		Communio	
16	Postcommunio		
17	Ite Missa Est (or Benedicamus Domino)		

Author's notes

[★ in some places, e.g. at Salzburg under Archbishop Colloredo, an organ sonata coincided with the reading of the Epistle, hence the phrase 'Epistle Sonatas' (*Sonate alla Epistola*) used to describe these works; in Eisenstadt there is no record of the use of Epistle Sonatas either during the period 1796–1802 or before or after, except for one such sonata by Carl Schiringer (*Haydn Yearbook* IX, 329)].

[† Chusid places this, incorrectly, between the Sanctus and Benedictus.]

It will be noted that some portions of the setting are heard successively, without a break, such as the Kyrie and Gloria, the music of which is separated only by the short chant of the priest, 'Gloria in excelsis Deo'.[2] Other parts are divided from each other by rather lengthy sections of the Accentus and Concentus. This is especially true of the Credo, which is isolated from the rest of the music by such extensive parts of the Accentus and Concentus. According to Chusid's scheme, therefore, Haydn composed all his late Masses in three vocal symphonies, each with four movements, to wit: (1) Kyrie – Gloria; (2) Credo; (3) Sanctus – Benedictus – Agnus Dei.

The scheme for dividing the two Masses under consideration into three symphonies would thus be as shown in the tables overlead. Chusid continues:

> The first and last of these movements are in the same key, and with a single exception [Kyrie of the 'Harmoniemesse'] they are fast. The first movement may

1 Extracts from *Studies in Eighteenth-Century Music* reprinted by permission of Allen & Unwin Ltd.

2 Sometimes composers begin the Gloria with the words 'Et in terra pax', since the opening words have been chanted by the priest. The same applies to the Credo: the priest intones the words 'Credo in unum Deum', and the music then, strictly speaking, begins 'Patrem omnipotentem'. However, Haydn and most other Austrian composers of the eighteenth century set the opening words of the Gloria and Credo over again. An exception is the *Missa in honorem B.V.M.* (*c.* 1768).

[Analysis of Masses, after Chusid]

MISSA SANCTI BERNARDI DE OFFIDA

Vocal symphony No. 1

MVT	TEXT	TEMPO AND NO. OF BARS	METRE	KEY
I	Kyrie	*Adagio* (12 bars) –	3/4	B flat → V
		Allegro moderato (146 bars)	3/4	B flat
II	Gloria	*Vivace* (66 bars)	4/4	B flat
III	Gratias	*Allegretto–più allegro* (152 bars)	3/4	G minor → B flat → E flat → C minor
IV	Quoniam	*Vivace* (82 bars)	4/4	B flat

Vocal Symphony No. 2

MVT	TEXT	TEMPO AND NO. OF BARS	METRE	KEY
I	Credo	*Allegro* (59 bars)	*alla breve*	B flat
II	Et incarnatus est	*Adagio* (60 bars)	3/4	E flat
III	Et resurrexit	*Allegro* (102 bars)	3/4	C minor → G minor → V of G minor
IV	Et vitam venturi	*Vivace assai* (111 bars)	3/4	B flat

Vocal Symphony No. 3

MVT	TEXT	TEMPO AND NO. OF BARS	METRE	KEY
I	Sanctus	*Adagio* (10 bars) –	*alla breve*	B flat → C minor → V
	Pleni	*Allegro* (35 bars)		C minor → B flat
II	Benedictus	*Moderato* (116 bars)	2/4	E flat
III	Agnus Dei	*Adagio* (46 bars)	3/4	B flat minor → V
IV	Dona nobis	*Allegro* (106 bars)	3/4	B flat

MISSA IN TEMPORE BELLI

Vocal Symphony No. 1

MVT	TEXT	TEMPO AND NO. OF BARS	METRE	KEY
I	Kyrie	*Largo* (10 bars) –	4/4	C major-minor → V
		Allegro moderato (83 bars)	4/4	C major
II	Gloria	*Vivace* (124 bars)	3/4	C major
III	Qui tollis	*Adagio* (71 bars)	*alla breve*	A major-minor
IV	Quoniam	*Allegro–più stretto* (102 bars)	3/4	C major

Vocal Symphony No. 2

MVT	TEXT	TEMPO AND NO. OF BARS	METRE	KEY
I	Credo	*Allegro* (33 bars)	4/4	C major
II	Et incarnatus est	*Adagio* (60 bars)	3/4	C minor
III	Et resurrexit	*Allegro* (91 bars)	3/4	C major → A minor → V
IV	Et vitam venturi	*Vivace* (128 bars)	*alla breve*	C major

Vocal Symphony No. 3

MVT	TEXT	TEMPO AND NO. OF BARS	METRE	KEY
I	Sanctus	*Adagio* (13 bars) –	4/4	C major → V
	Pleni	*Allegro con spirito* (25 bars)	4/4	C minor → C major
II	Benedictus	*Andante* (111 bars)	6/8	C minor → C major
III	Agnus Dei	*Adagio* (39 bars) →	3/4	F major → C major → V
IV	Dona nobis	*Allegro con spirito–più presto* (125 bars)	3/4	C major

> have a slow introduction, and the last movement is usually in a quicker tempo than the first. Each of the vocal symphonies has at least one slow or moderate movement, and it is always in a contrasting key or mode. As is to be expected in sacred compositions, there is no counterpart to the minuets or scherzos of the instrumental symphony. However, one of their principal functions, that of providing a contrast with an earlier, more solemn movement, is assumed by the more consistently cheerful sections such as the openings of the Gloria or the Et resurrexit. . . . It may be observed that the longest of the three symphonies is usually the first, the Kyrie – Gloria, and the shortest is the second, the Credo. Furthermore, in deference to the continuity required by the texts, those movements within any complete item of the Ordinary (the Gloria, Credo, or Agnus Dei) are usually linked or related in some fashion.

In *Haydn in England 1791–1795*, we have seen that, along with the Salomon Symphonies, Haydn composed music in other and often smaller forms (piano trio, string quartet, sonata) in which he allowed his intellectual curiosity to roam much further abroad in many respects than he could do in the stricter form of the symphony; this was particularly the case with complicated enharmonic modulations – though in the very last Salomon Symphonies we also find them, especially in the slow movement of No. 102 – and excursions into keys of related thirds, a process known to German scholarship as *Terzverwandschaft*. In the late Masses, we find frequent examples of mediant and submediant relationships which will be discussed as they arise.

Another important and seemingly obvious feature of these late Masses is the frequent use of contrapuntal forms and especially fugues – as befits one of the oldest forms of music in Western civilization. Haydn was perhaps the last great composer to whom counterpoint was inborn, immediate and intrinsically part of his musical expression; but more than that, Haydn was not content to write archaic fugues and scholastic canons; he brought the fugue up to date (as far as one can bring up to date a form which relies on a language already, by the 1790s, several hundred years old). In fact he gave counterpoint and church music, in the German-speaking world, a new lease of life: Haydn and his style lived on exclusively through the Masses and late Oratorios in many parts of the Austro-Hungarian provinces where the only place where music was heard – apart from the tap room – was the church. The tracing of Haydn's influence must belong to a later chapter, but we would only say here that even today in Vienna, Haydn's Masses and Oratorios are far better known to the average Viennese – who heard one almost every Sunday in church until recently, and the others several times a year in concert hall – than even the London symphonies and the string quartets, with the obvious exceptions of the 'Surprise' Symphony and 'Emperor' Quartet. If we pursue the matter, we shall note with some astonishment that Anton Bruckner, living in provincial towns in Upper Austria (St Florian, where there is still a large collection of important Haydn sources, many of them authentic; and Linz), was far more influenced by Haydn's Masses than by his symphonies. Without the *Missa in angustiis* ('Nelson' Mass), Bruckner's Mass in D minor quite literally would not have existed, at least in its present guise.

Thus, controversial though they may have seemed to many a nineteenth-century critic and musician, Haydn's Masses to a certain extent always enjoyed a flourishing life of their own, almost as if they assured the world, like the emperor, that they were above grammar.

Missa Sancti Bernardi de Offida ('Heiligmesse')
in B flat major (XXII: 10)

Basic scoring: 2 oboes, 2 clarinets, 2 bassoons, 2 trumpets in B flat, timpani (B flat – F), strings, organ, soli (maximum: SSATBB; usually SATB) and choir (SATB).

I. Kyrie (*Adagio–Allegro moderato*): full scoring (no vocal soli). Clarinets added later.
II. Gloria (clarinets added later throughout this movement) –
 (a) Gloria in excelsis (*Vivace*): full scoring (no vocal soli).
 (b) Gratias (*Allegretto–più allegro*): full scoring (with soli).
 (c) Quoniam (*Vivace*): full scoring (no vocal soli).
III. Credo –
 (a) Credo in unum Deum (*Allegro*): full scoring, without clarinets and vocal soli.
 (b) Et incarnatus est (*Adagio*): 2 clarinets, 2 bassoons, strings, organ, soli (SSATBB) and choir.
 (c) Et resurrexit (*Allegro*): full scoring, without clarinets and vocal soli.
 (d) Et vitam venturi (*Vivace assai*): full scoring, without vocal soli.
IV. Sanctus (*Adagio–Allegro*): full scoring, without clarinets and vocal soli.
V. Benedictus (*Moderato*): full scoring. Clarinets added later.
VI. Agnus Dei (*Adagio*): strings, organ and choir.
 Dona nobis pacem (*Allegro*): full scoring. Clarinets added later.

We have seen in the Chronicle that both this Mass and the *Missa in tempore belli* used the available Eisenstadt forces: the princely *Feld-Harmonie* or wind band (2 oboes, 2 clarinets, 2 bassoons, 2 horns) plus vocal forces, strings, organ, and kettledrums (played by Caspar Peczival, a bassoon player). In the original score of the *Missa Sancti Bernardi* Haydn never uses horns but only trumpets; in those days, it was customary for horn players to be able to perform on trumpets as well.

As we have seen in our analysis of the 'Salomon' Symphonies in *Haydn in England 1791–1795*, Haydn was very careful with his clarinet players; either they were not very good players in London or Eisenstadt, or their instruments were rather primitive – perhaps both. It was not till Haydn had the really first-class clarinets of the Court Orchestra in Vienna – players such as Johann Stadler, trained in the great Mozartian tradition – that he dared entrust that instrument with passages of a technical complexity and musical subtlety. In the original score of the St Bernard Mass, the clarinets do not play throughout, as the scheme shows above; before their big solo in the Et Incarnatus Est, for example, he has them marked *tacent*. Actually, they probably doubled the oboes in such movements as the Kyrie, even if their actual parts did not include any music for that movement. That was the kind of *ad libitum* tradition that we have come to know from Haydn's bassoon parts in his earlier works: in the *Missa Cellensis* of 1782, for instance, there are obbligato bassoon(s) only in one movement, the Gratias, but it is certain that they were expected to double the bass in the other movements, too. A similar situation obviously obtained with the clarinets at the first performance in Eisenstadt of the St Bernard Mass.

Later, when Haydn enjoyed the full complement of wind players, he had his copyist write out horn parts to the St Bernard Mass; they double the trumpets and are patently in the new crook of B-flat *basso* (not *alto* as they were in most of Haydn's and Mozart's earlier music). These horn parts also exist in other early materials, some of them authentic (by Johann Elssler and obviously made under the composer's supervision). In the Archives of the Hofburgkapelle (Court Chapel) in the Vienna Burg, we find old and reliable MS. parts of the St Bernard Mass, of which the title page lists the first performance as 8 November 1800. These parts have the added horns. There also exist revised clarinet parts which are apparently authentic afterthoughts. Obviously 'foreign' bands could not know of Haydn's *ad libitum* practice whereby the clarinets doubled the oboes in some movements, and so he created 'new' parts for the clarinets, which are sometimes independent of the oboes: they have been indicated in the new critical edition (Henle = Bärenreiter) by brackets and by an Appendix.[1] The reasons why we are inclined to believe that they are genuine are as follows: (1) they appear in many old and reliable MSS.; (2) they are musically attractive and fit extremely well into the orchestral score; (3) Haydn himself is known to have approved the added clarinet parts to the *Missa in tempore belli*, about which *vide infra*, and thus we know that he did add supplementary clarinet parts for at least one of these works. Note that in the *Missa in tempore belli*, the original score also included clarinets, but only in the 'Et incarnatus est' movement; the situation is, therefore, very similar, as we shall see.

Conductors therefore have a choice of Haydn's original Eisenstadt score with the sparse clarinets and no horns, or the enlarged scoring (useful if the work is given in a large church or concert hall).

This is not the first Mass in B flat to come from Haydn's pen; he composed the *Missa brevis S. Joannis de Deo* in the middle 1770s, which is also in B flat; but that latter work is a 'short Mass' with a tiny orchestra and for an entirely different purpose. In using B flat with a large orchestra, Haydn had several things in mind: first, the use of trumpets and timpani in B flat. They did exist in Austria, and Michael Haydn wrote for them at Salzburg (in the 1760s in church music and in 1788 for a symphony); but they were rare, and it was not till he went to England that Haydn wrote for them. In that key, the trumpets have a curiously sonorous, almost silvery tone, quite different from the aggressive brilliance of their sound in D or the martial 'open' quality they have in C; similarly, the kettledrums are less prominent, for one thing because low *F* (the dominant) is one of the lowest effective notes for the instrument. On the other hand, the wind instruments sound particularly full and attractive in B flat, which was always a favourite key for late eighteenth-century wind-band *Parthien* and serenades. The strings sound less brilliant than in sharp keys such as D major (where more open strings can be brought into play). The voices lie particularly well in B flat: the top *b* flat″ for the sopranos is at the one end of the gamut, while low *F* in the basses (the dominant) is at the other. The subdued brilliance – a typically Haydnesque tautology – of a Mass in B flat was obviously so attractive to its composer that he wrote no less than four of his last six Masses in that key (the present work, the *Theresienmesse*, the *Schöpfungsmesse*, and the *Harmoniemesse*); and some of the most exalted choral movements of the last two oratorios are also in B flat, including the final chorus of *The Creation*.

The German name 'Heiligmesse' comes from Haydn's subtle use of an old German-language chorale, 'Heilig, heilig, heilig' (the translation of 'Sanctus', of course), which he puts into the inner parts of the Sanctus, and which will be analyzed below.

The application of sonata form principles to liturgical uses may be observed at its most brilliant and convincing in the Kyrie of the present Mass. Following a slow introduction, the main body of the movement follows a sonata scheme except that

1 They are also included in the Bärenreiter miniature score (No. 93, 1962), edited by H. C. Robbins Landon.

instead of normal exposition and development sections there is a fugue. We shall see another variation of this fugal insertion in the Kyrie of the *Theresienmesse*. Here, the scheme is:

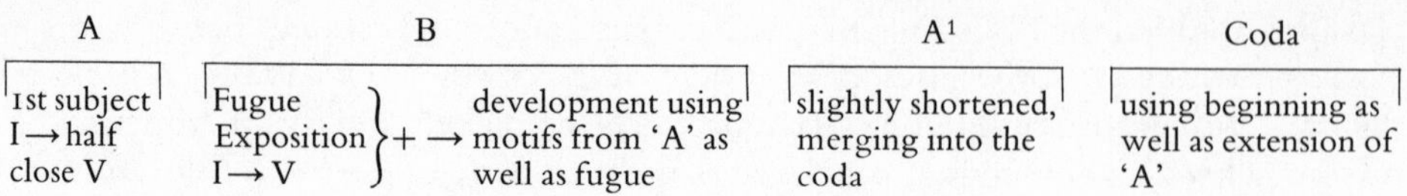

The whole movement, from the introduction, is in three-four time and the first subject of the *Allegro moderato* (A) has all the popular characteristics of a folk-song:

It is one of those melodies in late Haydn Masses which annoyed Victorian critics, being not only popular but of a serene and joyous luminosity considered at variance with the words 'Kyrie eleison'. The critic of the *Harmonicon*[1] noted:

> . . . We cannot help thinking that some of his movements are written in too theatrical a way for the Mass: in any other part of the service, such gaiety of manner might be tolerated, but when we hear the Kyrie eleison sung to a minuet tune, our feelings and judgement, – resulting, it may be said, from a cold, Protestant education – lead us to consider such a style as a breach of religious propriety, and a violation of good sense. . . . [The Kyrie of the *Missa Sancti Bernardi*] is the movement to which we have just alluded, the first sixteen bars whereof form as complete a minuet as ever ball-room or symphony claimed for its own.

It is curious to contemplate that this melody has undergone an almost complete transformation, or circle of the wheel, from 1796 to the present day: Princess Esterházy, and indeed most of the Austrian congregations of that day, found nothing incongruous in hearing a Kyrie sung to a melody of this sort; the Victorians were shocked, repelled and even enraged by it, as we shall see in our various quotations from their criticisms; and today, the 'ballroom' quality of the tune, if it ever existed except in the minds of the Victorians, has disappeared completely.

At the very beginning of the slow introduction, there was an unexpected *a* flat in the violins and oboes:

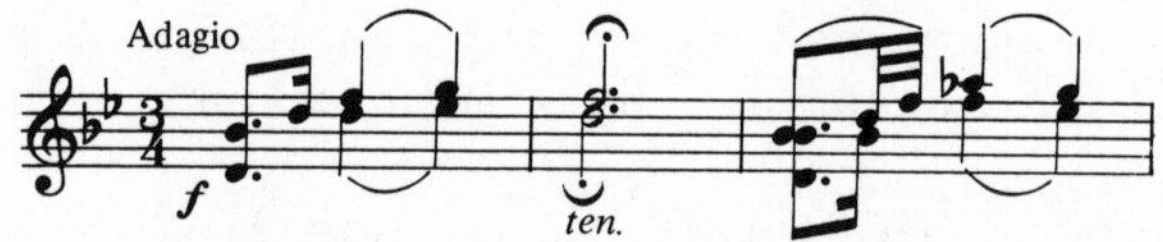

The minute we arrive at the fugue, which takes place after A (above) has been announced, we see that once again (as we have so often observed in *Haydn in England 1791–1795*) Haydn has prepared our ears for the unusual *a* flat in the fugue subject:

1 IV (1826), 165f.

The fugue breaks off after its 'exposition' in order to introduce the 'Christe Eleison', which consists of slow, blocked harmonies with the strings, as usual, providing the forward impetus in quavers and (when the *f* enters) semiquavers. The Kyrie fugue breaks in to carry the music back to the recapitulation ('A[1]'), which soon turns into a thrilling coda of the kind (if not the pattern) that we noted in the first movement of Symphony No. 100. In particular we would draw attention to the magnificent piling-up of tension which takes place at bars 134ff., to which we affix the preceding three bars to place the passage in context. This build-up is based on a motif deriving from the fugue tune quoted above: the increase in tension is effortlessly achieved by several factors which are worth analyzing: the slow rise in the violins' *tessitura*, moving from *b* flat′(bar 134) to *f*‴ (bar 143), which rise is also rhythmically accelerated by breaking up the first violins' pattern at 140ff. into stresses at every other quaver rather than the first crotchet of every *second* bar as happened before (arrows indicate stresses):

134 135 136 137 138 139 140 141 142 143 144

3/4 | / V V | V V V | / V V | V V V | / V V | V V V | /V/V/V | /V/V/V | /V/V/V | /V/V/V | /V/V/V |

↑ ↑ ↑ ↑↑↑ ↑↑↑ ↑↑↑ ↑↑↑ ↑↑↑

The increase in tension is also introduced by the figure of the bass and oboe line at bars 135, 137, and 139; in 135 and 137 only the oboes are *legato*, everyone else is *staccato*; in 139 everyone swerves into *legato* to introduce the climax of the passage. And in the actual climax notice how the timpani break into quavers and then semiquavers. We must not forget the slow harmonic pattern of the whole passage, which allows the rhythmic tension to increase without disturbing the harmonic paces – the music moves from tonic to one-six-four chord on V; nothing simpler could be imagined. Haydn's fantastic mastery lies in his being able to organize his material with such complete accuracy and efficiency – *Deo matematica* . . . Bars 145–9 were added after the movement had been completed; they were placed at the end of the Kyrie in the autograph and their insertion marked by a sign ⋕. This is the first of several times during this Mass when Haydn lengthened the music by short inserts – quite the contrary of what the composer tended to do otherwise – namely to shorten.[1] See example overleaf.

The first movement of the Gloria contained, in Haydn's original score, only forty-six bars: by three inserts (numbered by Haydn, for technical reasons, Nos. 1–5) the music was lengthened to sixty-six bars. These inserts were added between the end of the Gloria proper and the beginning of the next movement, which led Brand (*Messen*, 273) to suppose that it was wrong to imagine that in the first performance 'the Mass was sung *without* these added sections'. We have meanwhile examined the original Eisenstadt material, which was not available to Brand, and we can add that the addition to the Kyrie (*vide supra*) as well as the additions to the Gloria were, all of them, 'worked into' the performance material *a priori*. They were, in other words, corrections made *before* the work went into rehearsal. On the other hand, there are many added dynamic and phrasing marks which Haydn himself added to the performance material. The most important of these are not found at all in the autograph and thus must have been made after the parts had been copied, and presumably after the first orchestral rehearsal.

1 Typical instances of Haydn's shortening may be cited: in the first movement of the *Concertante* (1972) – discussed in *Haydn in England 1791–1795*; and in the orchestral interludes of *The Seasons* (1801) – discussed in *Haydn: the Late Years 1801–1809*.

131
[Allegro moderato]
a 2
2 Ob.
2 Fag.
2 Trbe.
Timp.
V. I/II
Va.
CORO
B. C.
-e e lei - son, e lei - son,
-lei - son, e lei - son,
-lei - son, e lei - son,
- - - son, e lei - son,
135
f
Ky - ri-e Ky - ri-e Ky - ri -
Ky - ri-e Ky - ri=e Ky - ri
Ky - ri-e Ky - ri-e Ky - ri -
Ky - ri-e Ky - ri -e Ky - ri

141
e e - lei - son, e - lei -
e e - lei - son, e - lei -
e e - lei - son, e - lei -
e e - lei - son, e - lei -
6 ♮6 6 4 7
145
son. e - lei - son, e - lei -
son, e - lei - son, e - lei -
son, e - lei - son, e - lei -
son, e - lei - son, e - lei -
5 3 6 4 4 2 6 6 4 (5) 3

From this point (beginning of the Gloria) we are fortunate enough to have Haydn's sketches, contained in Codex 16835 of the Musiksammlung der Österreichischen Nationalbibliothek (which, as we have seen, also contains early sketches to *The Creation*). Those who have studied the symphony sketches to Nos. 99 and 101[1] will remember that, except for complicated contrapuntal sections, they were mostly written on one line and were obviously not much more than devices to help Haydn in remembering the full score he had in his head; at the beginning of the *The Creation* sketches he noted 'So that I shall remember'. In the Gloria sketch Haydn notes the trumpets' opening, the vocal line, and very often the *basso continuo*. In the sketch to the 'In gloria Dei Patris' fugue we find Haydn using four lines (for the vocal parts) and numbering the sketches (which are not in chronological order), as he did for the sketches to the Finale of Symphony No. 99; for the sketch to the 'Et vitam venturi' fugue of the Credo, Haydn uses five lines, the four vocal parts and the *basso continuo*. The remaining sketch, for the Benedictus, is in one or two lines, as was that for the Gloria. This much is clear from looking at these sketches: the whole work was in Haydn's head, including the full orchestra; the sketches are just *pro memoria*, and as such they fulfil an entirely different function in Haydn's creative life than do similar sketches in Beethoven's. Whereas in Beethoven's sketch-books, we may very often follow the actual working-out of the material, from its often primitive beginning to its highly polished and sophisticated final state, in Haydn's case, the polishing had already happened before he started to 'sketch'. (One of the few exceptions to this rule is *The Creation*: there, the sketches show us Haydn experimenting, changing, trying out, in the Beethovenian manner.)

The rhythm of the Gloria beginning is matched to the words

Glori-a in excelsis | De - o |

and is known to us from some of the earlier Haydn masses, to wit: *Missa Sancti Nicolai*, *Missa Cellensis* of 1782. The opening words of the Gloria in fact often suggest to Haydn fanfare rhythms, just as he was very much rooted in the Baroque technique of word-painting ('coelum', 'ascendit', 'altissimus' = high tessitua or a rising line, 'descendit', 'sepultus est' = low tessitura or a falling line). The words 'glorificamus te' often call forth a burst of majesty on Haydn's part, and here we have massive chordal attacks, darting strings etc.) and a thunderingly independent timpani part ( ) which drive the music to its final cadence; it is interesting to note that Haydn's added bars included this particular fanfare section (bars 55–62) which was originally not nearly so prominent.

The 'Gratias agimus tibi' is combined with the 'Qui tollis' into one single movement, running (at allegretto tempo which is in the course of the music accelerated to più allegro) from bars 67–218. It is a stupendous intellectual achievement and one of the greatest of Haydn's choral inspirations. It begins quietly, almost old-fashioned in manner, in G minor (the relative minor of B flat), with a gradual approach to a solid, four-part texture. Using a kind of ritornello form, the individual sections are linked together with an extraordinarily subtle and beautiful motivic connection: out of the first announcement of the Gratias

1 Reproduced in Vol. XII of the Philharmonia edition of the Complete Symphonies of Haydn; also in *Haydn-Studien* II/3 (1970). The sketches for the *Missa Sancti Bernardi de Offida* are partially reproduced in Brand, *Messen*, pp. 285, 286, 294, 295; and completely in the Henle edition of *Haydn Werke* (Reihe XXIII, Band 2, 1958) as well as in the Appendix II of the Bärenreiter miniature score No. 93 (1962).

comes the accompaniment of the Qui tollis

while out of the basic shape of bar four in the tenor part quoted above comes

and other derivatives as well. The movement gradually gathers enormous momentum, and the actual tempo speeds up at 'Qui tollis' – as we shall see, this sudden shift in tempo (an afterthought in the autograph) worried Rochlitz in his first criticism of the work in *AMZ*. We soon realize that the whole movement is, like many others in this Mass, a vastly complex contrapuntal fabric in which, for example, the top and bottom of the orchestra are written in double counterpoint at the octave and may be reversed. We show the following excerpt, wherein bars 153ff. are *rectus* in motion and bars 161 *inversus* (later the direction of the motif is also reversed and becomes

and this version is presented in double counterpoint between top and bottom lines) – see overleaf, pp. 146–8.

Haydn, like Bach, is using every tool of his trade to praise the Almighty, much in the manner of a Medieval craftsman working on some tiny detail of a vast Gothic cathedral tower: the man far below in the street may not see the beauty of the tiny figure, but then it was made, not for him, but for the Great Architect.

The Quoniam Tu Solus Sanctus is in the nature of a fast (Vivace) introduction to another vast contrapuntal edifice – this time a double fugue of immaculate workmanship and soaring fantasy which culminates in a series of trumpet and kettledrum fanfares which match the soprano voices rising twice to high *b* flat″ (as will be recalled, their top range); after a short cadence the pattern is repeated but the parts reversed, the bass singing the *b* flat and the upper voices the counterpoint; the fanfares are different, too, in that only the trumpets now sound forth the ♫♬♫ | 𝅗𝅥 while the timpani subside into a semiquaver roll. (Incidentally, Haydn's notation of the timpani is such that 𝅗𝅥, particularly in slow movements, means *tr* 𝅗𝅥). We have quoted the final bars of this movement *supra* (pp. 132–3).

Eighteenth-century Austrian composers had a certain amount of difficulty in setting the words of the Creed up to the 'Et incarnatus est'; from that moment to the end, the words themselves were sufficiently evocative to stimulate the composers to great efforts of word-painting: the Incarnation, Crucifixion, and Resurrection are

---

infallibly the best parts of Haydn's (and many of Mozart's) Masses. But what was a composer to do with the doctrinal parts? We may find that Charles Rosen's words about the *Theresienmesse* are slightly exaggerated – the music 'has vigour and some power, but one would have to look far in Haydn's music to find another rhythmic structure equally turgid and unimaginative'[1] – but the problem was nevertheless an acute one. Haydn escapes this difficulty a couple of times by sheer contrapuntal virtuosity, in the *Missa in tempore belli* and even more magnificently in the straight canon in the 'Nelson' Mass. The Credo of the St Bernard Mass is straightforward and

1 *The Classical Style*, London and New York 1971, p. 370.

rhythmically somewhat square, though certainly not turgid; in a way it acts as a foil, and introduction, to the 'Et incarnatus est', whose delicate accents are set off by the 𝅗𝅥 𝅗𝅥 | ♩ ♩ ♩ ♩ | or 𝅗𝅥 ♩ ♩ patterns of the Credo proper. The words 'descendit de coelis' are, as we might expect, worked into a sequence that moves down the scale from *g''* to *g'* (bars 48ff.). The little movement is bound together musically by using derivatives of the opening motif (quoted above as the first of the two patterns), a technique closely related to that used in the so-called 'Credo' Masses (wherein the opening 'Credo' theme reappears throughout the whole Credo section) – the most famous being, of course, Mozart's 'Credo' Mass in C (K. 257) of 1776.

The 'Et incarnatus est' is based – if the reverse is not true – on the following canon, the autograph of which was formerly owned by Breitkopf & Härtel and was first printed from the manuscript by Carl Maria Brand in his book on Haydn's Masses (*Messen*, 291):

Adagio
Gott im Her - zen, ein gut Weib - chen im Arm, je - nes macht se - lig,
die ses g'wiß warm. Gott im Her - zen, ein gut Weib-chen im Arm,

je - nes macht se - lig, die - ses g'wiß warm. Gott im Her - zen, ein gut
Weib - chen im Arm, je - nes macht se - lig, die - ses g'wiß warm.

(We have translated the words *supra*, p. 131.) The text is an old German poem which exists, in somewhat different form, in a MS. *Sammelbuch* from the region near Danzig of the year 1629, and in Haydn's form in (for example) the *Stammbuch*, dated 1760, of a Helmstädt student named Jacob Schultz, where the text is 'Gott im Herzen, ein Mädgen [*sic*] im Arm, das erste macht selig, das andre macht warm'. It has been preserved in many other sources as well.[1]

In the Mass setting, Haydn allows the canon to proceed in song-form, like a strophic *Lied*, using as accompaniment clarinets, a solo bassoon, and strings *pizzicato* (the organ is silent); he breaks off the canon after the third voice has entered, turns the music into E flat minor and gives the words 'Crucifixus etiam pro nobis, sub Pontio Pilato' to tenor solo, two bass soli, obbligato 'Violoncello solo ma piano', the violas and the bass line (organo *tasto solo*, that is without adding any chords: just the bass line with the left hand). It is a very ominous sound, and we will encounter it in the famous passage in *The Creation* 'Seid fruchtbar' (Be fruitful). The chorus enters and moves to a beautiful cadence in G flat. We mention song-form, because when the 'Crucifixus' section is completed, we return to a four-part announcement of the canon. Thus we have: A (the canon) – B (the passage in E flat minor) – A[1] (the canon harmonized). Haydn seems to have intended the canon (in its worldly guise) for private use, for it was not included in the Forty-two Canons that Breitkopf published in 1810 and which are all secular (as opposed to the Ten Commandments, discussed in *Haydn in England 1791–1795*).

The 'Et resurrexit' begins rather austerely in C minor, without any wind instruments – the autograph manuscript instructs the 'Clarinetti tacent fin al vitam venturi' – for Haydn is saving his forces for the lightning stab that accompanies the words 'judicare vivos et mortuos': here the timpani, marked *ff*, announce the Day of Judgement. The remaining wind instruments also join the *tutti*. As is usual when setting the words 'et mortuos' Haydn drops the dynamic level and lowers the *tessitura*:

Timp.
ff
ju - di - ca - - - - - - - re vi - vos et mor - tu - os
ju - di - ca-
p
ju - di - ca - - - - re vi - vos et mor - tu - os

1 Fred Quellmalz, in an addition to Deutsch's above-mentioned article: *Zeitschrift für Musikwissenschaft*, January 1933, in which E. F. Schmid also drew Deutsch's attention to the fact that Haydn used the canon in this Mass. For a summary of the literature, see Deutsch's edition in the Henle Verlag's *Joseph Haydn Werke*, with critical report (Karl-Heinz Füssl), 1958.

Missa Sancti Bernardi de Offida: a page from the original performance material – the violoncello solo for the 'Et incarnatus est' – written out by Johann Elssler. Haydn himself added the words 'col'arco' (line 4), and 'Tutti ma piano' twice (lines 5 and 7) and 'Solo' (line 6).

The close of this particular section, which leads to the final fugue of the Credo section, is marked by a dozen bars that really do convey a waltz rhythm even though they are in V of G minor, especially when the chorus finishes and only the sustaining oboes cover the strings' ♩ ♩ ♩ | ♩ ♩ ♩. The fugue presents the subject almost simultaneously with the countersubject, and the progress of the words 'Et vitam venturi' is hastened by the almost never-ceasing movement of the violins in quavers. Haydn's sense of the orchestra is now infallible: remembering that the low *F* of the kettledrum tends to roar in almost indefinite pitch when played loudly, he cautions the player to accompany the (otherwise *forte*) pedal point at bars 287ff. in *piano*, bringing him up to *f* just before the end of the pedal point, at bar 292.[1]

Haydn had occasionally made use of Gregorian chants in his music – as early as *c.* 1760 in the wind-band Divertimento in F (II:23), where we find the *incipit lamentatio* theme, which recurs in 1772 (Symphony No. 45); in Symphony No. 26 (*c.* 1768) there is not only the *incipit lamentatio* theme but also an old Passion. As he grew older, Haydn tended to conceal the melody in subsidiary parts, as indeed he had done with all the melodies in Symphony No. 26.

It is therefore in the Haydnesque tradition that he should conceal an old German Sanctus melody ('Heilig, heilig, heilig') in the inner parts of the appropriate movement in the *Missa Sancti Bernardi*. Brand has traced several variants of the melody and also the text (*Messen*, 298f.). The *Gesangbuch Brixen* of the year 1767 gives the version which is the one best known in Germany today:

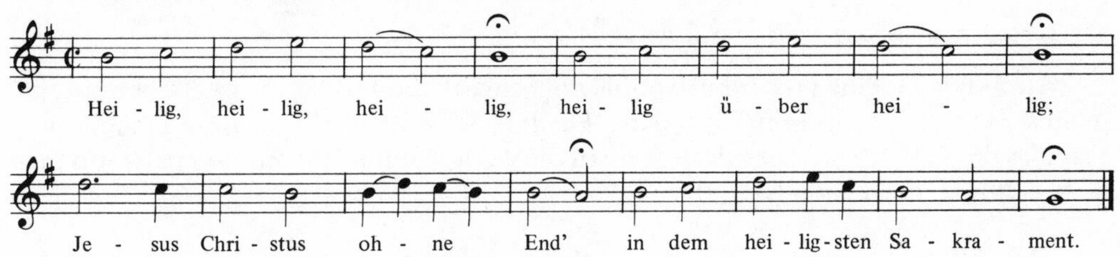

In the German Mass attributed to Michael Haydn we find the melody as follows:

1 Brand (*Messen*, 296f.) suggests a small correction at bars 252f. and 263f., where the original calls for ♩. | ♩. ♪♩ | ♩ ♩ ♩ | (Et vi - tam ventu-ri); he proposes the reading: ♩. | ♩. ♪♩ | ♩ ♩ | (Et vitam ven - tu - ri) which is undoubtedly better. Mozart often treats the word 'Osanna' in such fashion: see K. 257, Sanctus.

Another variant is found in *Domkapellmeister* Joseph Preindl's 'Melodien aller deutschen Kirchenlieder, welche im St. Stephansdom in Wien gesungen werden' (No. 2):

* 'The second part is sung in many churches as follows.'

Although Haydn takes the trouble to conceal the old song, in the autograph manuscript he notes, over the alto part, 'Heillig [*sic*] ⁓ ⁓' as a hint. Brand (300) notes that Haydn writes down the whole song in the second violin and bassoon part, and that he has chosen the version he preferred:

The Allegro begins at the words 'Pleni sunt coeli' and the use of keys is rather unusual: the Sanctus ends in a modulation to V of C minor; the Pleni begins in C minor and ends in B flat. The Osanna is fugal and curiously subdued, rather as if the composer was still under the influence of the German 'Heilig'.

The Benedictus has elicited much praise from the authorities. Brand (300) says it 'is one of the most remarkable . . . movements that Haydn ever wrote for the church', while Alfred Schnerich[1] calls it the 'most ideal' of Haydn's Benedictus movements. Rochlitz, writing in 1802, says it 'is a most excellent movement – so gentle, so moving and pious, so simple and easy to grasp and appreciate, yet so artistic!' The music is in E flat and, unlike many Austrian Benedictus movements of the period, the whole wind band and kettledrums are retained; but Haydn takes great care (1) to use the trumpets and drums sparingly – the former play in twenty-seven, the latter in only eighteen of the total 117 bars – and (2) to use them in B flat (the dominant) rather than in E flat, where the trumpets' *tessitura* would have been high and too strident in a subdued movement of this kind. Formally the movement is in three parts, the 'B' section being a kind of development. Another interesting factor is that, unlike most Austrian Benedictus, Haydn's has no sections whatever for the soloists: it is a choral movement from beginning to end. We quote the beginning of the choral entry to show the thematic material out of which Haydn creates this radiant movement, which shines with a quiet inner light:

1 *Messe und Requiem seit Haydn und Mozart*, Vienna–Leipzig 1909, p. 37. Rochlitz's review in the *AMZ* IV [1802], 715f. is quoted *in extenso* pp. 158ff.

Notice the extraordinary effect of the unsupported vocal basses in bars 16–18. Later, in the middle ('B') section, Haydn produces a hauntingly beautiful effect, whereby he uses a solo viola in an orchestral palette of Stravinskyan subtlety and the voices seem to be singing some ancient, mystical chant (see example opposite and overleaf). After all this music of delicate colours, even the Osanna – usually the excuse to repeat the music of the Sanctus's 'Osanna' with fanfares of trumpets and timpani – is mellow, quiet and in keeping with the inward beauty of the whole movement.

The Agnus Dei is scored only for the choir, strings and organ continuo. In fact the soloists have nothing to do in this whole Mass except for the 'Gratias' (where they sing, off and on, from bars 67–131) and 'Et incarnatus' (bars 60–106 of the Credo). Naturally in those days the soloists also sang the tutti parts throughout, as all the MS. solo parts in Haydn Masses (and all other Masses of the period) make abundantly clear; but the extraordinarily small portion of the work allotted to the vocal soloists lends support to our theory that this, rather than the *Missa in tempore belli* (which has many difficult and extended solo sections, as we shall see), was the first Mass for the Eisenstadt forces of 1796. Haydn did not know his soloists, who would have been members of the choir, or of the Stadler theatrical-operatic troupe, and was therefore careful to write no exposed parts for them, and not very much music.

63
[Moderato]
V.
Va.
CORO
S.
A.
T.
B.
B. C.
fz
fz
p
p
qui ve - nit in no - mi - ne Do - mi - ni,
qui ve - nit in no - mi - ne Do - mi - ni,
qui ve - nit in no - mi - ne Do - mi - ni,
qui ve - nit in no - mi - ne Do - mi - ni,
Tasto Solo
68
Solo
p
p
be - ne - di - ctus qui ve - nit
p
be - ne - di - ctus, qui
[Vc. e B.]

The wind instruments are omitted not only for aesthetic reasons – they had just enjoyed an exceptionally prominent part in the Benedictus – but also because they would have had almost insuperable intonation problems in the key in which the Agnus Dei is written: B flat minor, and equally in the keys through which Haydn passes, D flat major and E flat minor. As often in Agnus Dei movements, the thrice repeated text –

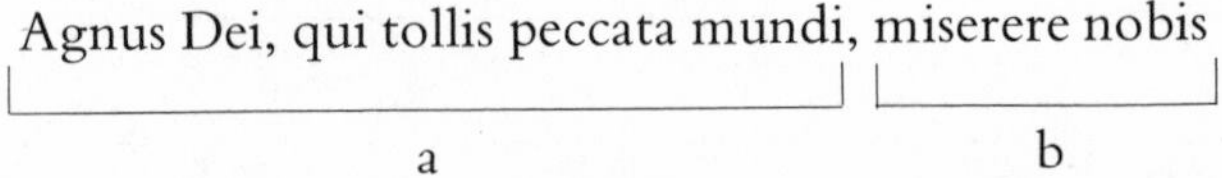

suggests a ritornello or rondo form, in the various uses of which Haydn proves to be brilliantly imaginative in the last six Masses. This is particularly true of the tonal relationships; Martin Chusid (op. cit., 129) notes, 'Because both text and thematic material furnish strong unifying elements, Haydn feels freer harmonically than in his instrumental music and the refrains to the text . . . recur less often in the tonic key.' In the St Bernard Mass, the division is:

(a) Agnus Dei etc. B flat minor – Miserere D flat major
(b) Agnus Dei etc. D flat major – Miserere E flat minor
(c) Agnus Dei etc. E flat minor – Miserere (modulation to the dominant of B flat).

After this very severe and wind- and timpani-less music, the 'Dona nobis' explodes with a real sense of theatrical brilliance. Haydn tends not to pray for, but to demand, peace in the finales of his Masses. The sense of drama is heightened by the use of piano sections for the choir, accompanied by pizzicato strings. In the middle, there is a fugato development section during which the main subject 𝅗𝅥 ♩ | ♫ ♩ (Do-na no-bis) is extended by the choir (with Haydn's typical 'rushing' semiquaver strings above) as we move slowly towards the recapitulation; the increase of tension that the music generates is mainly by decreasing the time between the entrance of the main motif: 𝅗𝅥 ♩ | ♫ ♩ becomes ♫ ♩ 𝄽 | ♫ ♩ 𝄽 | and then, in the bassoons and basso continuo ♫ ♩ ♫ | ♩ and finally ♩ ♫ ♫ | ♩ ♫ ♫ |. It is an impressive example of rhythmic acceleration used to increase tension, and its effect was not lost on future generations, including Beethoven (who knew Haydn's late Masses well). Just before the end there is a colossal deceptive cadence which must have stunned the first audience in the Bergkirche and of which Rochlitz spoke so highly (*vide infra*):

In a few swift cadential bars Haydn brings this powerful, impressive, and undoubtedly theatrical, Angus Dei to a close, signing the autograph manuscript 'Finis: Laus Deo'. With this great choral work, he had begun an entirely new phase in his late style and one which was to have a lasting, if not uncontroversial, effect on music for the next decades.

In the forthcoming Chronicle, we shall see that Haydn gave most of his late Masses – the *Theresienmesse* of 1799 is a curious exception – to Breitkopf & Härtel for publication, and asked no fee for them (we shall later examine this unhappy tradition in church music, for which composers were then so badly paid). He could have done so, of course, but it is unlikely that Breitkopf & Härtel would have paid it, since they already had the first two Masses by the time Haydn sent them authentic copies. From the correspondence between Griesinger and Breitkopf & Härtel, it is clear that Haydn furnished them with the authentic scores of both the *Missa Sancti Bernardi* as well as the *Missa in tempore belli*, but whether he had Elssler write out scores or whether he sent them the actual autograph manuscripts is not quite clear; that he did lend the Leipzig firm some of his autographs is to be inferred from a request in Griesinger's letter of 10 November 1802 in which he writes: 'Haydn asks to have the last sheets of his *Storm* [Madrigal] and the original scores which you have had from him and no longer need.' It is interesting to observe that Haydn sent the original (not the lengthened) clarinet parts of both works. If he sent the autographs or had Elssler copy them, these additional clarinet parts would have had to be entered on an extra line; probably Haydn did not think the matter worth bothering about, which is why Breitkopf received, and printed, the original versions.

Breitkopf decided to bring out the Masses in score, and used their new 'Typendruck' to produce them. The *Missa Sancti Bernardi* came out first, in an edition of a thousand copies (a large number in those days: Forster of London had brought out the first edition of Haydn's *Seven Words*, in the orchestral version, consisting of fifty copies, not so many years before, in 1787); it appeared in May 1802 and was soon afterwards (18 July) reviewed by the great German critic, Friedrich Rochlitz, in the *AMZ*:[1]

Review

Messe à 4 Voix avec accompagnement de 2 Violons, Viola et Basse, 2 Hautbois, 2 Clarinettes, 2 Bassoons, Trompettes, Timbales et Orgue, composée par Joseph Haydn. No. 1. Partition. Au Magazin de Musique de Breitkopf et Härtel, à Leipsic. (Pränumerationspreis 1 Thlr. 12 Gr. Ladenpreis 3 Thlr.)

The publisher continues in his efforts to lay before the public the best compositions of the greatest German musicians, entirely complete, in score, well printed, and at the most economical price. If an undertaking may be judged by the probable effect or damage it exercises on the whole, this one cannot be too highly praised. For all the signs indicate a wide dissemination of the very best that German music has to offer – and precisely at a time when culture shows interest not only in the better kind of music as opposed to its lighter by-products, and finds many friends in its swift progress; just there, such a dissemination *must* be of rich and beneficial influence on artists and amateurs; even on the art itself. If the support of this undertaking – this much may be stated here – brings honour to the publisher, it also brings still more honour to the friends of art among the public which so generously support him and enable him to execute his plan.

On another page of this publication [March 1801] it was said of Joseph Haydn's church music: 'If his other vocal works [his *Creation* and *Seasons*] have been misunderstood or misinterpreted – because they require a special understanding and thus allow of a faulty one – this is certainly not the case with those works in which the heart of a religious man flows and only expresses in its fashion that which every religious person feels and which must be mirrored in his works; where the artist is not distracted by a text that goes into details, and where, moreover, *certain outward forms* (the rough outline) *already exist*. Altogether in Haydn's masses there dominates not that dark devotion, that ever-present sense of atonement and piety, that we find in the masses of the great men of earlier times, especially in Italy; but rather a cheerful, reconciled devotion, a gentle melancholy [*Wehmuth*], and a happy confidence in heavenly goodness.'

I find that, as far as I know J. Haydn's Masses (only a few have become known), this statement is well grounded, and it is entirely confirmed by the present work. Confident devotion, pious joy, gentle melancholy and prayer succeed one another, as the words require, throughout the whole beautiful work. The cheerful movements are mostly very happy and enthusiastic, and some may appear too brilliant for the church and its liturgy; but this is more true in reading through the music than when one actually hears it. For the composer has understood how to achieve the most shining effects through a great deal of reflection and long experience; the nobility and pious attributes of the work are reached by devices not apparent at first glance – of which we would draw attention only to one feature, namely that in those movements of the Mass in B flat, the trumpets and drums (not used exactly sparingly) are, *because of their low pitch*, of the greatest strength, dignity and gravity. This work attests anew Haydn's inexhaustible invention, his admirable novelty of ideas and their development; almost everything is new, and especially several movements, in their accompani-

1 Brand, *Messen*, 130; Olleson, Griesinger, 39; *AMZ IV*, 705–18; William Sandys and S. A. Forster, *The History of the Violin*, London 1864, p. 312.

ment and orchestration, show that in the soul of this old man there blooms eternal youth; for I must be very mistaken and have followed badly H[aydn]'s spirit and the story of his development, if this Mass was not really composed in his late years and is not more than ten years old. I shall cite some details on the subject of this latter advantage.

After a few bars of Adagio – to elevate the tone and to prepare the spirit – the Kyrie moves into Allegro moderato: Kyrie, Christe, Kyrie. This movement contains many beauties, especially the thought [the review then includes, as a musical example, the theme of the fugue] – not a strict fugue but one that is pleasantly developed with no uncommon contrapuntal erudition and at the same time with much dexterity. However, this movement might be considered, for its words, perhaps too lively and brilliant. The Gloria is a joyful paean of voices and instruments: incidentally in free form and in an easy style. The Gratias, very simple, enters the more nobly and is composed more or less in the strict manner. One notes the beginning on which the whole is based and which reappears with ever increasing force and beauty [example of Gratias, bars 1–16, in short score].

To save space, I pass over the other notable thoughts which follow on this one, and would single out the ringing words 'Deus pater omnipotens' and 'Qui sedes ad dexteram patris' as well as the curious but forceful 'miserere nobis'. I would only add this: The Qui tollis peccata is included in this movement, and when it enters, there is the note più Allegro, which is very strange. The experienced composer felt that this simple continuation of the music, in the same flowing motion, might prove too long for the listener and thus had recourse to this emergency measure, forgetting the text for the music; at least everyone feels this at the first moment. But if one looks more closely, so closely that one hears clearly (or one really hears it in performances), one sees here, too, that a genius has no need of emergency measures, but that the spirit of the whole brings with it the necessary means; for by running together more closely ideas etc. which were partly scattered earlier on, the spirit from this point onwards is elevated to a plane more inward, more fearful, more important. We feel the truth, the rightness, the novelty, in the message of the words 'qui tollis peccata mundi, miserere nobis'. – The Quoniam tu solus etc., which begins in a very lively vein and continues swiftly, contains a well executed and also brilliant fugal movement on the words 'in gloria Dei patris &c.'. However I do not find it a good thing that here and in some other passages in other movements the alto lies high and even goes up to f^2. The effect of a real four-part choir, the strength of which rests largely on the inner parts in their middle registers, always loses if the alto part is treated like a second soprano. In operas the composer is sometimes forced to it because good alto voices are very seldom encountered in the theatre (especially in Germany and France); but in good church and concert choirs, one can reckon with them, and one ought to do them honour.

Up to this point, this Mass is the work of a quite good and talented artist, even worthy of a Haydn; but now, with the Credo, the spirit and our interest are raised higher, and assure the work of its place for all time among the select pieces in any musical library.

To save space for quotation and appreciation of details, I pass over many excellencies. The Credo begins with a strong unison in all parts:

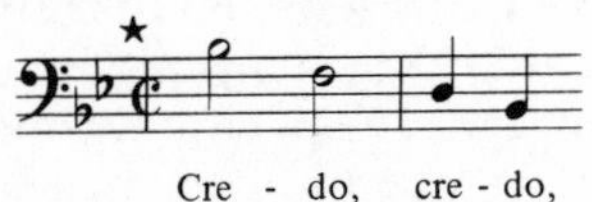

★ [*AMZ* has C rather than *alla breve*, a mistake of the Breitkopf score. We have silently corrected this and other small matters, and also transposed the old clefs. H.C.R.L.]

and this thought comes again in the vocal or instrumental parts whenever a new part of the dogma appears, for example:

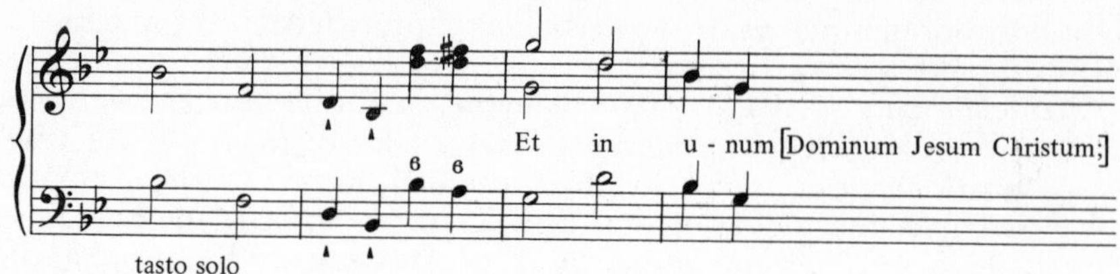

or with slight changes and new artistic animation:

This idea has been selected with great care and is of such good effect that one could wish that the composer had retained it during the whole of the Symbolum, especially since he would not have found it impossible to invest each new entry with novelty. After this Credo begins the very simple, inward, pious Et incarnatus est etc., which I give here complete in short score, since, apart from its moving loveliness, it can show the would-be artist eager for knowledge how through nobility of treatment he can make use even of an idea that might have been discarded if it were not so interesting. The music begins as a canon, and then the principal idea is treated differently – but one had better examine it oneself. The accompaniment is very simple, covers nothing but connects and supports; [There follows the whole Et incarnatus in short score.]

The following *Allegro*, Et resurrexit, is for me the most valuable of the quicker movements in the Mass. It is in free style until the words 'Et vitam venturi saeculi etc.' and so easily written that an unexperienced man might imagine that he could do it as easily; but apart from spirit and understanding, it requires a great deal of experience, and also a great deal of that which the painters call 'a sure hand' to be able to write just in this free style, and yet so well ordered, and just as lightly, and yet so significant. Not to overstep the bounds of a review I will not go into detail but will only mention that at the words 'Et vitam etc.', with increased tempo, the vocal parts, supported by the basses and wind instruments, begin a fugal movement and continue it very artistically and effectively; at the same time, moreover, the violins have their own, heterogeneous figure and they, too, continue with their pattern to the very end, lending to the whole the greatest vivacity and an enthusiastic fire, preserving however, through the great unity of this rich diversity, the movement's dignity and decorum. I repeat: I judge this movement to be a real masterpiece.

The Sanctus is short. The Benedictus, on the other hand, is once again a most excellent movement – so gentle, so moving and pious, so simple, so easy to grasp and appreciate, yet so artistic! It develops entirely out of the first few bars [musical example, bars 1–4] and, after its repetition, out of what follows. The bold, inward and deeply moving movement of the inner parts on page 87, and its repetition on page 92, and the often highly artistic development of the first thought, cited above (for example, page 89) – with difficulty do I refrain from quoting them. But I can refrain from doing so the more easily because it is certain that anyone with a heart, and to whom music means anything at all, must grasp the meaning of this Benedictus and the following Agnus Dei; and everyone who has even a modicum of musical knowledge will seek, and find, the means by which Haydn so wonderfully reaches his end. This Agnus Dei is again an uncommonly beautiful movement. It dispenses with all ornaments and is scored only for the four vocal parts and the usual strings. This is good, because it is placed between sections which are rich in wind instruments; moreover, it takes into consideration the difficulty of the wind players to perform in correct intonation when in B flat minor, in which key this movement is placed. The very key itself, so remote, from which the composer does not stray far, only to D flat major and E flat minor, assists in giving the whole something solemn and deeply felt. And in it, everything is prayerful entreaty and melancholy longing. Compare the beginning [musical example: bars 1–8]. Now the tenor appears with the following figure

which is continued in all the vocal parts. And from these two main ideas, the latter only slightly changed in the violins, is constructed the whole excellent movement, the value of which will be judged equally highly by every sensitive person and musician alike. To this is then added the Dona nobis pacem, a swift and intelligent *Allegro*, which for its words is perhaps somewhat too swift and brilliant; he who judges very severely and would go into detail, might find a touch of the theatrical in some passages (for example p. 102, bar 4 [the *pizzicato* passage of bars 79ff.] and others following it, as well as in the repetition on page 107 [bars 131ff.]); but other sections, such as page 103 bar 12 [bars 95ff.] up to the pause on page 105 [bar 114], he would find so lively and their accompaniment so shimmery, that he would make no objections. The deceptive cadence, when everything seems to be at an end [musical example: quoted in the analysis *supra*, p.157], is of excellent effect, not only because it is very surprising and impressive, but particularly because it is so fervent [*innig*].

Should I, in conclusion, excuse myself for having overreached the bounds of a normal review in this notice? No; I will close, rather, with the hope that the present composer will very often be the reason and provide the urge for my overreaching again.

The *Missa Sancti Bernardi de Offida* was recorded for the first time by the Haydn Society in 1952; that record was performed by the Copenhagen Boys Choir, the State Radio Orchestra, conducted by Mogens Wöldike.[1]

1 Obviously it is not within the scope of this book to list all the recordings of Haydn's music, a list which would, in any case, go out of date the day after it was published; but we have thought it useful to provide a list of the first recordings of these great late choral works, most of which were unrecorded until after the Second World War; this applies even to *The Creation* and 'Nelson' Mass. These first recordings, which brought the music for the first time to many thousands of people, have an historical significance which cannot be overlooked.

Missa in tempore belli ('Paukenmesse') in C major (XXII: 9)

Basic scoring (original version): 2 oboes, 2 clarinets in C and B flat, 2 bassoons, 2 trumpets alternating with 2 horns in C (concerning *alto*, *vide infra*) and A, timpani in C–G, strings, organ, soli (SATB) and choir (SATB).

I Kyrie (*Largo – Allegro moderato*): full scoring with soli, but the clarinets added later (*vide infra*).

II Gloria –

(a) Gloria in excelsis (*Vivace*): full scoring (no vocal soli, but the clarinets added later.

(b) Qui tollis (*Adagio*): 2 oboes, 2 bassoons, 2 horns in A, strings, violoncello solo, organ, bass solo, choir. Later Haydn added a flute part (*vide infra*).

(c) Quoniam (*Allegro*): full scoring (only soprano solo), but the clarinets added later.

III Credo –

(a) Credo in unum Deum (*Allegro*): full scoring (no vocal soli), but clarinets added later.

(b) Et incarnatus est (*Adagio*): 2 oboes, 2 clarinets in B flat, 2 bassoons, 2 horns in C (*alto*), strings, soli (SATB) and choir.

(c) Et resurrexit (*Allegro*): full scoring (no clarinets).

(d) Et vitam venturi (*Vivace*): full scoring, with clarinets.

IV Sanctus (*Adagio – Allegro con spirito*): full scoring; the clarinets added later.

V Benedictus (*Andante*): full scoring; 'Clarinetti tacent'.

VI Agnus Dei (*Adagio – Allegro con spirito*): full scoring; the clarinets added later.

As in the St Bernard Mass, Haydn's original scoring made use of the available forces at Eisenstadt: the princely *Feld-Harmonie* (2 oboes, 2 clarinets, 2 bassoons, 2 horns) plus vocal forces, strings, organ and kettledrums (Caspar Peczival, a bassoon player). We should add that Haydn himself conducted from the organ. The horn players, of course, also played the trumpet parts.

Irrespective of whether this was the Mass that Haydn conducted with such success at the Piaristenkirche in Vienna on St Stephen's Day, 1796, it is clear that he now knew that he would have first-rate soloists at his disposal, and thus we find that, unlike the St Bernard Mass (where there are hardly any soli at all), the Mass in Time of War has many difficult solo parts, especially for the soprano and bass. We shall see in the Chronicle for 1797 that two new female soloists from Pressburg, Anna Rhumfeld (soprano) and Josepha Hammer (alto) – later a protégé of Haydn's – were engaged and sang the soli (or at least some of the soli) in the new Mass in Time of War; the principal soprano soloist, however, was probably the great Therese Gassmann,[1] later a famous Queen of the Night at the Vienna Opera. It is very much an open question if Haydn

1 We know that Therese Gassmann sang in the Eisenstadt performance of *The Seven Words* on 27 October 1797. We do not know, however, when she arrived at Eisenstadt and if she was there to participate in the first (at least for Eisenstadt) performance of the Mass in Time of War on 29 September. Unfortunately there is a misprint in Radant, *Rosenbaum*, for the entry of Thursday 28 September. The whole paragraph (p. 25 in the English and, as it happens, also the German edition) beginning 'At 8 in the morning I visited the Gaßmanns . . .' belongs not to 28 September but to Saturday 28 *October*; in other words, Rosenbaum went to call on the ladies the day after the performance of the Oratorio.

The three trumpet players who were engaged in 1797 (*vide supra*, p. 52) obviously played in the Oratorio, where they have parts in the 'Earthquake' Finale. Haydn must also have ordered a flute player from Vienna, since there was none in the local orchestra.

knew, in 1796, which soloists he was going to have in Eisenstadt next year; but there is no reason that Therese Gassmann cannot have participated as soprano soloist in the Piaristenkirche performance. The great bass solo in the Qui tollis was probably sung by Christian Specht at Eisenstadt, unless they also imported a bass singer from Vienna for the occasion.

Haydn later enlarged the instrumentation of the Mass. Supplementary horns doubled the trumpets in the movements in which the latter instruments play. But the most interesting addition is the supplementary clarinet parts, which are found in several old and reliable manuscripts (such as the excellent old source in Klosterneuburg). In the MS. parts of the work at Eisenstadt, the clarinet parts include only the sections in which they are specified in the autograph, i.e. Credo; it is, of course, a moot point how much they doubled the oboes elsewhere. Similarly, Haydn added a flute part to the 'Qui tollis'; the flute and doubling horn parts are included in the Breitkopf score, but not the supplementary clarinets: presumably Elssler copied a score from the autograph (or Haydn sent the autograph itself), in which case he would have had to 'work' the supplementary parts into the score; apparently Haydn did not consider this worth while. The Breitkopf score's inclusion of the flute part – which is missing in the autograph – shows that Haydn considered it essential. As for the musical substance of these supplementary clarinet parts, they are beautifully worked out, including a passage of pure genius at the beginning of the Gloria (*vide infra*). In 1959, the present writer went through the Archives of the Hofburgkapelle (Court Chapel in the Burg), and found authentic parts of the *Missa in tempore belli*, containing corrections by Haydn. The flute part is there, and it is entirely in the hand of Johann Elssler; although it is included in the M. D. C. (*maestro di cappella*) part, nevertheless it has every appearance of being added after the rest of the parts had been copied. The Hofburgkapelle parts also include the supplementary horns parts and, best of all, the supplementary clarinet parts with autograph corrections by Haydn: in the Agnus Dei, the clarinets were corrected in the passage at bars 25ff. –  instead of 3. The Hofburgkapelle parts also include non-authentic trombone parts which are, however, marked 'in mancanza degli corni'. When Haydn made all these changes and additions is not clear: possibly for the Piaristenkirche performance where, having the whole *gros* of Viennese musicians at his disposal, he could have added the flute and horns, and increased the clarinets' role in the proceedings.

As in the St Bernard Mass, conductors thus have two choices with regard to the orchestral forces: the more restricted version of the autograph manuscript and the Eisenstadt performance material; or the enlarged version which has Haydn's seal of approval. In this particular case, we would prefer the latter: the additional flute part is a fine added orchestral colour; the horns (in C basso) give substance and body to the orchestral timbre; and no one would want to miss that wonderful clarinet sweep at the beginning of the Gloria. As for the horn parts of the 'Et incarnatus', they are clearly marked alto on the MS. set of parts by *Regens chori* Carl Kraus in Eisenstadt. The other sources contain no indication of alto or basso, and therefore the Carl Kraus source represents an oral tradition of the Eisenstadt performance of the Mass in 1797, at which Carl Kraus would undoubtedly have been present. The Carl Kraus source is part of the Archives of the Stadtpfarrkirche (now Cathedral), Eisenstadt.

Another collection, that of Prince Joseph von Lobkowitz, was formerly in two of his Bohemian castles, Eisenberg and Raudnitz (Roudnice), and is now in the National Library at Prague. It contains, among other authentic copies, the last six Masses, mostly copied by Johann Elssler. Of the *Missa in tempore belli*, there are also authentic copies in Ljubljana and in the Monastery of Heiligenkreuz in Lower Austria.[1] As we have suggested above, Haydn also supplied Breitkopf & Härtel with a source (either the autograph or an Elssler copy) of the Mass, and the Leipzig firm issued the score in *Typendruck* as No. 2 of their series of Haydn Masses in October 1802; the edition consisted of 1,000 copies. The German subtitle 'Paukenmesse' (Kettledrum Mass) refers, of course, to the famous solo for that instrument in the Agnus Dei.

It may also refer to the astonishing beginning of the Mass, a solemn slow introduction where the kettledrums thud softly behind the music (the trumpets are silent here), reinforcing the rhythm of each half-bar. The choral entry

contains in essence the *Urlinie* of the beautiful *cantabile* theme of the ensuing Allegro moderato. The introduction breaks into a *forte* hold in which the timpani, and only they, are marked *ff* – the first of many subtle markings for this instrument throughout the Mass. After this first pause (bar 6) there follows a striking modulation (in which the *g* flat of the sopranos and violins at bar 6 sounds astonishing). Thereupon the music moves into C minor, and in a final half-cadence the trumpets sound out in a military fanfare which sounds as ominous as the end of the introduction in the 'Military' Symphony – a work which also began in G and modulated to G minor. The *Allegro moderato* begins with an elaborate soprano solo, which seems to have caused considerable unhappiness among admirers of Haydn's music. Even Brand (*Messen*, 227ff.) seems forced to provide a lengthy *apologia*, and even in recent years not only the theme but, curiously enough, particularly the continuation in the violins

has upset people violently. Charles Rosen, who objects to Haydn's (and even Mozart's) church music in the strongest terms – he describes Haydn's Masses as 'uncomfortable compromises' – says of the latter part of this soprano solo that it 'has

1 Georg Feder, 'Manuscript sources of Haydn's works and their distribution' in *Haydn Yearbook* IV (1968), pp. 114f, 126. The Heiligenkreuz source was discovered by Dr Alexander Weinmann, who kindly informed us of it. Breitkopf edition: Brand, 130. In the autumn of 1974 the author was able to locate the authentic MS. parts in Ljubljana (Laibach) from the Philharmonische Gesellschaft, now in the National Library, Music Department, MS. 191. The parts, on 4to paper (watermarks: three half-moons of decreasing size, 'EGV' with a star, 'BA' under ornament) of Italian origin, are written by Johann Elssler and include clarinet parts only in the Credo (as in the autograph); but there are horn parts ('Corno I:mo in C', 'Corno II:do in C') doubling the trumpets as in Klosterneuburg and Hofburgkapelle. In the original horn parts, i.e. in the 'Et incarnatus', there is no indication of 'alto', as in Eisenstadt. There is no trace of the flute part. Local, duplicate parts include *inter alia* a first violin signed 'F. A. W./1800' on Italian paper ('AM' with bow and arrow, three half-moons); the Mass was performed at Laibach on 28 December 1800. The fact that Haydn sent, more-or-less, the original version (except for the doubling horn parts) to Laibach suggests that he was perhaps in physical possession only of it, in the form of his own autograph and the Eisenstadt parts. This would explain why he also sent the original version to Breitkopf & Härtel. The supplementary clarinet and flute parts possibly existed only in sources not immediately available to Haydn, e.g. the Hofburgkapelle; having given the Empress a set of parts, it might have been diplomatically a problem to ask for them to be returned.

passages that can only have sounded as trivial to Haydn's contemporaries as they do to us today.'[1] We beg leave to doubt that. Many people will have considered the Kyrie of the Mass in Time of War theatrical, symphonic, perhaps too brilliant and worldly, but surely not trivial. The ghosts of our Victorian ancestors are still with us, even in Charles Rosen. . . . On the contrary, this Mass and the 'Nelson' Mass of 1798 have always proved to be Haydn's most popular Masses, even today. We doubt that many people any longer object to the whole tone; nowadays we find that it is as brilliantly typical of the *settecento* Baroque in south German or Austrian lands as Vierzehnheiligen (which preceded it by some two and a half decades) or 'Kremser' Schmidt.

Haydn is now putting to subtle use the principles of sonata form. The symphonic introduction fulfils the same spiritual basis as in the 'Military' Symphony. The opening theme of the Allegro moderato

contains, as we have said, the *Urlinie*

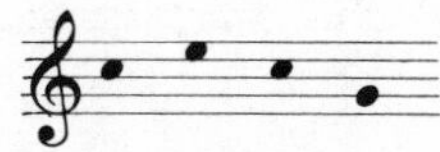

The movement is composed in monothematic sonata form. When the dominant is reached, the theme appears in G major and is given to the alto solo. The liturgical requirements do not necessitate a long development section, and Haydn contents himself with nine bars of modulation from the end of the alto solo (bar 57) back to the recapitulation; in these nine bars, the words 'Christe eleison' make their only brief appearance. Similarly the recapitulation is greatly shortened. The movement ends in a blaze of C major, the trumpets and timpani slashing through the orchestra with fanfares on Haydn's beloved rhythm ♪♬♫♩.

The Gloria once again uses the metre known to us from the *Missa Sancti Bernardi* and the earlier Haydn Masses, but here it is given a surprising twist by jumping into *f* sharp as early as bar 3:

Since most of the readers of this book will know only the 'original' version of the score, we would like to show the stroke of genius that is the solo clarinet passage from the revised version.[2]

1 *The Classical Style*, p. 369.
2 The first recording of this revised version was made by His Master's Voice in 1967 (ALP/ASD 2303), sung by Heather Harper, Pamela Bowden, Alexander Young, John Shirley-Quirk, the Choir of King's College, Cambridge, and played by the English Chamber Orchestra, conducted by David Willcocks. This record also contains the first recording of the Motet 'Insanae et vanae curae'.

It is also interesting to observe that the same *Urlinie* is found once again in the opening bars of the Gloria quoted above, namely *c''–e''–c''* and (this time) high *g* (*g''*), separated by the surprising *f*♯*''*. Possibly this kind of underlying motivic unity is entirely unconscious, but whatever its origin (conscious or unconscious) it lends a strong sense of coherence to the music and, incidentally, supports the idea of Kyrie and Gloria forming a symphony.

The first part of this Gloria is in free form, its content being in large part dictated by the words. This reliance on the text dictates the next formal section of the work, which is announced by the following orchestral interlude:

It is repeated two times to accompany the words 'benedicimus te' and 'adoramus te', each time with a more elaborate accompaniment. In the following extension of this new section, another orchestral tutti comes in three times at the words 'Domine Deus, Rex coelestis, Pater omnipotens', the third time (bar 76; see overleaf) with a slash of force from the kettledrums, which are marked *ff* against everyone else's *f*.

E. T. A. Hoffmann, that fascinating Renaissance man living in the Biedermeier, himself wrote a Mass in 1805, and in 1814 he published an article 'Alte und neue Kirchenmusik', wherein he deals with the violins' figurations in church music. The musical examples could almost come from Haydn's *Missa in tempore belli*. It is much better to break up the chordal passages in the violins in this way

rather than as follows, because 'this same passage, orchestrated as follows,

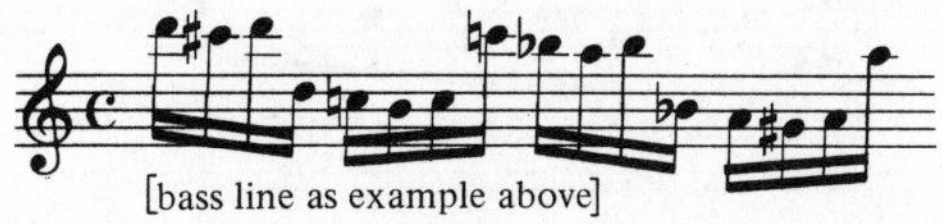

approaches the theatrical in its passing dissonant notes and sounds confused in the church. Altogether for use in the church such figures are the most fitted which without dissonances go through the basic chords, for in this way they disturb as little as possible the force and clarity of the vocal parts and, on the contrary, often do much to strengthen the effect.'[1] These wise words owe much of their practical force to the layout of Haydn's last six Masses. In this connection, one must bear in mind that the Bergkirche, for which these works were composed, has for Austrian churches exceptionally unreverberative acoustics. On the other hand, if the *Missa in tempore belli* was written for the Piaristenkirche in Vienna and not primarily for Eisenstadt, it might explain the orchestral score, which is much more like Haydn's earlier C major Masses, the *Missa Cellensis in honorem Beatissimae Virginis Mariae* (1766) and especially the other *Missa Cellensis* of 1782, both of which were composed for the huge baroque pilgrimage church of Mariazell, which Haydn knew personally – he had himself made the pilgrimage there in the 1750s – and which had very reverberant acoustics. The Piarist Church in Vienna, also a splendid and very large building with reverberant acoustics, is similar in this respect to Mariazell.[2]

The unity of this second section of the Gloria's Vivace is ensured by the repetition and development of the orchestral interlude quoted above; it binds together all the words by being constantly on our minds. It returns like a recapitulation at bar 101 to accompany the text 'Domine Deus, Agnus Dei, Filius Patris', and with this the opening section closes. One has noted that Haydn uses the orchestration of his Salomon Symphonies – such as No. 97 in C (1792) – and some of the instrumental techniques of

1 Brand, *Messen*, 231.

2 The present writer has studied the acoustics of all three churches under consideration and has heard Haydn Masses in all three. In 1947 he played the timpani part in an Easter Sunday performance of the *Missa Cellensis* in the Piaristenkirche, at which Anton Heiller was the organist and Hans Gillesberger (then *Regens chori* of the Piaristen) the conductor. The timpani used were eighteenth-century instruments with very hard leather sticks, also of Haydn's period.

[Gloria]

his earlier Masses; but formally, he has created an entirely new and free structure with this opening Vivace.

There follows a famous slow movement, the Qui Tollis (Adagio), with a long solo for the violoncello in its finest, upper tenor, register (finest, at least, for the kind of cantabile theme with which the composer entrusts it). Haydn had composed several concertos for this instrument which, though they are now famous almost to the point of nausea, were completely unknown in 1796 except perhaps to half-a-dozen people (the first Haydn 'Cello Concerto to appear in print was the famous D major of 1783 [VIIb: 2], which André issued 'après le manuscrit original de l'auteur' in 1804). Haydn's love for the 'cello and experience in writing concertos and solo passages for it are clear throughout this Adagio. Later a solo flute was added which sometimes doubles the 'cello at the octave and sometimes has an independent part. The melody is a long and rather intricate one which reminds many people of the solo and chorus 'Mit Staunen sieht dies Wunderwerk' ('The marv'lous work behold amaz'd') in *The*

Creation: and indeed the identical placing of the *fz* is rather revealing, and there is no doubt that precisely this first part of the Oratorio was in Haydn's mind, and in his sketch books, as he was writing down the Mass in Time of War:

We shall see that Rochlitz thought this was the most beautiful and pious movement that he had heard in a Mass for a long time. This was the eighteenth-century view, however, and the nineteenth century did not confirm it. Rosen, who is somewhat Victorian in this respect, writes:[1]

> . . . The incoherence of the late eighteenth-century's tradition of religious music and the lack of a stable and acceptable framework for liturgical settings can lead to effects of peculiar irrelevancy: the long sentimental [*sic*] cello solo of the Mass in Time of War has great sweetness, but to be accepted as an adequate setting of 'Qui tollis peccata mundi' it requires more tolerance than the most emotional religiosity of eighteenth-century painting, which had at least a coherent symbolic organization and a visual harmony with the architecture that surrounded it.

To express his large-scale musical thoughts, Haydn has chosen a kind of rondo form (or ritornello form, if the term be preferred). His formal choice was dictated by the text. The melody is announced by the solo 'cello, and the voice (bass solo) takes it up with the words 'Qui tollis peccata mundi'. The music continues but over it is then superimposed the choral entry, 'Miserere nobis' which, in the dominant, is then brought back to the tonic and a second statement of the main theme, the repetition of the words 'Qui tollis' for bass solo. The theme's progress is again interrupted by the choral entry, 'Suscipe deprecationem nostram', at which point Haydn also brought in

1 *The Classical Style*, pp. 369f.; reprinted by permission of Faber and Faber Ltd and The Viking Press, Inc.

the supplementary clarinets (i.e. parts not in the autograph's first version) and gradually brings the music round to the tonic minor, in which the movement surprisingly ends. The 'Qui tollis' theme, if we may call it that, is now introduced in A minor (bar 178), following a particularly dramatic build-up to the choral setting 'Suscipe', culminating in *ff* 'col Pleno Organo' (a reminder that the organ, contrary to some irresponsible statements by Paul Henry Lang[1] and others, is an integral part of the orchestral and choral apparatus in these late Masses). The bass solo and chorus are now in constant juxtaposition, and on the last page of this original and inventive movement, Haydn writes bold and forbidden octaves between the soprano and tenor parts of the choir (see below), and notes his famous 'cum licentia' above the tenor part (bars 188–9) of the autograph. We have discussed 'cum licentia' in *Haydn in England*

1 Particularly in his gramophone reviews of Mozart Masses in the 1971 and 1972 volumes of *High Fidelity*, to which readers are referred. In another unscholarly and unmusical statement, he would also have us ban the trombones from Mozart's religious music. Nowadays, it would seem, even such astonishing inanities are printed and accepted by the readers of the journal as musicological truth. See also Lang's article 'Musicology and Related Disciplines' in *Perspectives in Musicology*, New York 1972, p. 194, where it is actually asserted that Mozart did not write for trombones in the *Requiem*.

1791–1795 (pp. 470f.); and with the *Fantasia* of the String Quartet, Op. 76, No. 6, we shall encounter a particularly striking series of 'grammatical errors made on purpose' (if we may translate Haydn's design in writing 'cum licentia' on his scores).

The reader will have seen, even from this necessarily cursory examination of the 'Qui tollis', that the terms 'rondo' or 'ritornello' in describing the formal characteristics of such a movement in a Haydn Mass are of necessity not entirely accurate. The changes *vis-à-vis* the purely instrumental forms are so fundamental that the old terms have become outmoded; perhaps one day we shall have new ones.

The 'Quoniam' starts out, Allegro, in free form, held together by Haydn's impeccable sense of motivic structure. We notice, after a few bars, that Haydn is working towards some kind of cadence, and the music should give us the hint:

which is, of course, a clear derivative of the orchestral interlude in the first part of the Gloria. At bar 225, Haydn marks the music 'Più stretto' and we have a straight recapitulation of bars 28ff, but now Haydn smoothly leads us to a fugal conclusion on the word 'amen'; the music is by no means a strict fugue but more like a gigantic coda to the Kyrie-Gloria symphony, if one wishes to judge the Mass on these terms.

Haydn wrote down the words of the Mass by heart; and his memory was at fault in the Credo sections of the first four of the last six Masses. In the Mass in Time of War, Haydn omitted the words: 'Qui ex Patre Filioque procedit. Qui cum Patre, et Filio simul adoratur et conglorificatur'.[1] In the *Missa Sancti Bernardi*, curiously, the words 'Qui ex Patre Filioque procedit' are also omitted. In the *Missa in angustiis* are omitted 'Et in unum Dominum Jesum Christum Filium Dei unigenitum' from the first part of the Credo text, and from the second part once again 'Qui ex Patre Filioque procedit'. In the *Theresienmesse* of 1799, the 'Et in unum Dominum, etc.' is left out, but in the last two Masses (1801, 1802) the text is complete. Did someone gently point out the missing parts to the old man in 1800, when no Mass was composed? At any rate, the scholarly texts of the late Masses,[2] being what is known as a 'diplomatic rendering' of the autograph's text, present the Credo texts incomplete; but those who wish to perform the music in a church service are referred to the Böhm editions.

Haydn's solution of the difficult first part of the Credo text is particularly successful in the *Missa in tempore belli*: the music sits as firmly, even squarely, as the rock on which the Church was built, or at least the dogma proclaimed; but Haydn gives the text great musical interest by setting it in fugal form, and the complex contrapuntal writing flows with the apparent ease of a musical theorist like Albrechtsberger, to whose influence on Haydn's thinking Brand rightly draws attention (*Messen*, 242).

1 Alfred Schnerich, 'Die textlichen Versehen in den Messen Haydns und deren Korrektur', *Separatum* from the Vienna Congress of 1909 (Österreichische Nationalbibliothek seems to own one of the very few copies). See also Brand, *Messen*, 240.

2 They are all published by the Henle Verlag in the *Joseph Haydn Werke* (1958 *et seq.*) and reprinted in reduced size for the Bärenreiter Verlag's series of miniature scores. Other critical editions will be discussed in conjunction with an analysis of the works concerned. Schirmer in New York are in the process of publishing all the Haydn Masses, edited by the present writer and others. All these editions present Haydn's original texts, and for church services, the 'corrected' editions of Verlag Böhm in Augsburg may be used. Since apart from southern Germany and Austria, Haydn's Masses are hardly given as part of Catholic church services, it matters not at all that except for the Böhm editions, Haydn's Credo texts are either incomplete or, in some cases, in the telescoped 'missa brevis' form (only in the earlier Masses, e.g. the *Missa brevis S. Joannis de Deo*). That problem will be discussed in another place.

The mysteriously beautiful, very intense, 'Et incarnatus est' is close to the 'Chaos' beginning of *The Creation*, and not only because it is in the same key (C minor) but because of the use of small fragments to build up a vast structure which in the strict sense has no real melodies at all. The small motivic shapes develop themselves in the old preclassical *Fortspinnungstypus* method, 'spinning out' in a smooth progression of small mosaic-like fragments. It is the same basic idea as Chaos: out of nothing comes order; out of the Holy Spirit was the Incarnation. The ghostly orchestration includes *a priori* clarinet parts (also in the first version), and to continue the parallel to *The Creation*, these instruments emerge – as they did during 'Chaos' – in a solo of particular loveliness (bars 65ff.), the execution of which by Leopold Wlach on the old Haydn Society recording[1] was unforgettable. Among the many subtleties of this movement, we would draw attention to a sense of delicate vocal colour which Haydn's writing for the solo voices manifests: the alto soloist simply 'takes over' the line of the tenor, broken only by a crotchet rest. The colour of the tenor at a relatively high *tessitura* is seamlessly matched to the alto's entry in her middle *tessitura* so that, if the soloists take some care over the matter, one hardly knows where the male voice has left off and the female begun (bars 50ff.):

The passage which concludes this section, 'passus et sepultus est', is of extraordinary power, sinking away to *pp* in falling harmonies to which the wind instruments add layers of grey colour in slow, syncopated chords. Into this shadowy picture of death and burial, the Et Resurrexit bursts with C major trumpets[2] and kettledrums. In the course of this movement, there are orchestral touches of Mahlerian complexity: while holding the music together with a tight ostinato figure at bar 156, we find bassoons, timpani and viola playing a series of repeated '*g*'s, but while the bassoons go on with their 'normal' *forte*, the timpani are marked *p* and the violas *ff*. The pattern shifts slightly at bar 160, and the timpani are suddenly marked *ff*, which means that they explode into the general sound. The section is broken off by a long half-cadence and a bright fugue begins to the words 'Et vitam venturi saeculi amen'; the tempo changes to *alla breve* and vivace. It is not a strict fugue but is interspersed with long and rich sections for the four vocal soloists – a feature that Haydn took from his own, and of course Mozart's great operatic finales. Nowadays it does not seem so shocking to us to compare the great finales of (say) Haydn's *La fedeltà premiata* or Mozart's *Così fan tutte*, at the orchestral rehearsals of which Haydn had been present in 1790: *Così* is a highly moral work, and the conclusion of the Credo in Haydn's *Missa in tempore belli*, composed six years after *Così*, uses structural elements of an operatic finale to serve the glory of God and the Mother Church.

1 1950: It was the first recording, and included Jetti Toplitz, Georgina Milinkovic, Herbert Handt, Hans Braun, the Akademie Chorus, the Orchestra of the Vienna State Opera (Josef Nebois, organ), conducted by Hans Gillesberger. The recording is still available at the time of writing (1972) on Preiser Records in Austria.

2 The Eisenstadt horn players were expected to play a long pedal point in the bass clef, supporting the C minor tonic conclusion of the previous movement, change their instruments to trumpets and after one-and-a-half bars enter with their new instruments forte. The change is so swift that one wonders if Haydn did not imagine he could borrow a pair of trumpet players from the *Thurnermeister* so that the horn players would not have to change embrochure with such cruel rapidity. Haydn was otherwise very careful in such matters. We now know that he had three trumpet players as part of the orchestra in 1797.

The Sanctus starts with a slow (Adagio) orchestral introduction, into which the alto solo quietly introduces the first words, 'Sanctus, sanctus, sanctus, Dominus Deus Sabaoth', after which the choir dominates the proceedings of this introduction. The tempo change to *Allegro con spirito* accompanies the words 'Pleni sunt coeli et terra' and is, astonishingly, in C minor and with thundering timpani rhythms that once again bring this instrument into orchestral prominence. The tenor solo introduces the words 'Osanna in excelsis', and the choir (as it had done in the introduction) completes the movement, using the tenor's musical phrase. It is a very short but powerful movement, obviously designed by Haydn to balance the long C minor Benedictus which is one of the great movements in all these late Masses.

The music alternates between a quiet, melancholy phrase, *piano*,

(supported by staccato second violins, a curiously unsettling effect), and this stern, martial note:

The *f* is brought home by a single crotchet for all the wind instruments (clarinetti tacent), trumpets and kettledrums. This martial passage seems to be derived from a charming early symphony by Haydn, No. 12 in E (1763), in the Adagio slow movement of which there was the following:

[cf. also Notturno V (II: 29), Andante, for another quotation – this time in C minor, too.]

Here we find a whole movement for the four soloists; the choir does not enter until the very end, for the words 'osanna'. Among many other features of great attractiveness, we would draw attention to the sudden shift in the music from C minor to C major: the main theme (quoted above) is now supported by soft trumpets and timpani: it is a magical effect.

Haydn has carefully placed the whole weight of the last part of the Mass on the Agnus Dei. We have Griesinger's accurate description, including an actual quotation of Haydn's, about this famous and original idea:

> In the year 1796, he composed a Mass, at the time when the French were in Styria, and which he entitled 'in tempore belli'. In this Mass, the words 'Agnus Dei, qui tollis peccata mundi' are played in a curious fashion with the kettledrums, 'as if one

> heard the enemy approaching in the distance'. At the following words, 'dona nobis pacem' he has all the instruments enter in a very striking way.
>
> [Griesinger, 62]

Some scholars have considered the very rhythm of the timpani to be that of the French armies – 'the human heart thudding with anxiety' –

etc., the anapaestic rhythm of which creeps into Haydn's sinister drum-beats[1] of 'uncanny nervousness':

But even more terrifying are the trumpet calls (supported by the other wind instruments), which rage through the orchestra

at bars 25ff. Haydn in attempting to fuse the first part of the movement (slow introduction) with the second part ('Dona nobis pacem'), has the timpani carry over, entirely unsupported, from the anapaestic rhythm (*p*) to a sharp *f* crack with which the new tempo and words are announced (Allegro con spirito). With heavy fanfares, Haydn seems almost to have changed the words from 'Give us peace' to 'We demand peace' (see overleaf).

Its first performance will have left the audience shaken in a way that possibly no religious music had done since the days of Bach and Handel. Haydn had, with the whole *Missa in tempore belli*, but of course especially in the whispering doubt of the Agnus Dei and the rabble-rousing fanfares of the Dona nobis pacem, created a new church-music style as immediately influential as it was to become lastingly controversial. Rather surprisingly – because not even Haydn scholars expected it – the music has survived the critics to the point where even the distinguished Charles Rosen appears to be almost alone, nowadays, in persisting with his denunciation of the whole style.[2]

Formally this remarkable Agnus Dei has the same rondo (ritornello) feeling that we noted in the same movement of the St Bernard Mass: here, Haydn allows himself a particularly wide range of keys: F major → C minor → G minor → C major, as a result of which we are peculiarly satisfied with the 'grounding', tonic-oriented fanfares which announce the 'Dona' and (of course) Haydn's firm belief in the victory of the Allies over the atheist, Anti-Christ Napoleon. Haydn and Beethoven were, as we have pointed out in *Haydn in England 1791–1795*, on opposite sides of the political fence,

1 H. E. Jacob, *Joseph Haydn*, New York 1950, pp. 244f.

2 One of the few times that Jens Peter Larsen permitted himself the luxury of talking about the music, rather than the sources, in his epochal *Haydn-Überlieferung* (1939), was on the subject of the Haydn Masses, to the apology of which he devoted a huge footnote on p. 145. In those days, Professor Larsen could lament that in the Protestant parts of Germany and her neighbours 'a Haydn Mass is almost never heard'.

[Agnus Dei]

Beethoven[1] being (until Napoleon crowned himself Emperor) a fanatical believer in Republicanism, while Haydn was firmly allied to 'God, King and Country' (and, in 1797, was to prove it by the most beautiful of national anthems, 'Gott erhalte'). The *Missa in tempore belli* is the first proof, as it were, of Haydn's political convictions, which were to culminate, in his church music at least, in the 'Nelson' Mass of 1798.

1 As this Chronicle, and that of *Haydn in England 1791–1795*, attempts to show from contemporary documents, Beethoven obviously thought that Haydn had behaved incorrectly not only in his contrapuntal lessons but also in other matters. Gradually, however, Beethoven began to behave in a curiously jealous way about Haydn, making countless snide remarks about him and his music, most of which found their way back to the old man. Later, Beethoven became the greatest composer alive, and when Haydn was long dead, he seems to have regretted his occasionally outrageous remarks. The story of the engraving of Haydn's birthplace being given to Beethoven on his death-bed is well known. But another tribute, in fact a generous apology, is Beethoven's use of the timpani in the Agnus Dei of the *Missa solemnis*, based directly on Haydn's just discussed; it was Beethoven's public apology to his long dead master and the point will not have been lost on astute men.

It was, it seems, once again Friedrich Rochlitz who reviewed the Mass in Time of War and the 'Nelson' Mass in one long composite review for the *AMZ* on 5 October 1803 (VI, 1ff.).

Reviews

Messe à 4 Voix avec accompagnement de 2 Violons, Viola et Basse, une Flute, 2 Hautbois, 2 Clarinettes, 2 Bassons, Trompettes, Timbales et Orgue, composée par Joseph Haydn. No. 2. Partition. Au Magasin de Musique de Breitkopf et Härtel, à Leipsic. (Subscriptionspr. 1 Thlr. 12 Gr. Ladenpreis 3 Thlr.)
Messe – wie oben – No. 3.

It often happens to those who have lived for a time in Catholic countries, and heard a great deal of church music such as masses, litanies, vespers, etc., that they, long trained in the taste of music, gradually lose their interest in a *genre* which is usually so mediocre and witless. Only then, when a famous man undertakes anew to compose to these words – set to music so many, countless times – does one approach with curiosity and expectation; and even then, one finds oneself disappointed. – Haydn, too, the *inexhaustible*, has written masses and, as we are assured, many, and not only in his earlier but also later years; did he, who has given us masterpieces in so many different musical *genres*, provide us with models also in the so-called church style? Or does such a style no longer exist? And dare the opera and symphony composer approach such works without abandoning completely his usual style? Without new and special study? – The latter is hard to believe, and as for the first question: from a man such as Haydn, who is known by so many masterpieces in all Europe, it may be presumed that he would not place before the public anything that would be in the least inferior to his other works. The two Masses, which are presented to the public in handsome prints by the publishers Breitkopf & Härtel, show that our supposition may be called a certainty.

To introduce them herewith to the musical connoisseur; to show in some detail their beauties, and the way in which Haydn treats the text – is the purpose of this article. For these works are unquestionably products of the master's mature years; and where there is so much to learn, it seems ridiculous, and certainly petty, to point out small blemishes, or to give the impression of superiority by critical hypochondria or rude *sufficance*.

So now to the point. Haydn's Masses Nos. 2 and 3 are orchestrated with horns, oboes, bassoons, trumpets and drums, and thus they belong to the larger, or as they are called, solennis type of Mass.

The first in C major is different because its character is more gentle, more inward-looking – I would say, sweeter; that it speaks more to the heart than No. 3 ['Nelson' Mass], which is in a more lofty and fiery style.

The Kyrie begins with a ten-bar Largo of a quiet general song, has a pause at the eighth and tenth bars which is as unexpected as it is impressive. Then with a gentle cantabile, the 'Lord, have mercy on us' is continued, and one voice carries the principal thought, repeated by the whole choir, developed in the most varied manner and with harmonic differences, and brought to an end by cadences that are finely prepared. A correct style; a fine, interconnected series of inner parts; rhythmic order, not fearful or affected, but precisely calculated to grip the listener's attention – all these are predominant in this movement, and prepare the heart of the listener for even loftier things.

The Gloria, a fiery Allegro in 3/4 time, announces the words 'Gloria in excelsis' in an original way. They are put forth joyfully and immediately; then comes at once a gentle piano with the words 'et in terra pax'. The further development is exemplary and full of harmonic force. Especially remarkable, however, is the majestic way in which the words 'Pater omnipotens' are expressed, without in the least disturbing the progress of the whole. But we must hasten to the Qui Tollis, the second movement of this section. Such a touching Adagio, calculated for those whose hearts are receptive to the still and devotional, has surely not been heard in a church for a long time. It is in A major and with obbligato accompaniment of the violoncello.

Handel made use of this kind of violoncello writing in certain expressive parts of his oratorios – the Aria 'Oh wretched Israel' from *Judas Maccabaeus* and in 'Softly sweet in Lydian measures' from *Alexander's Feast*. This solo [in the Haydn Mass] is full of deep, intimate sentiment, and comes straight from the heart. The beautiful choral interludes, simple though the harmony is, make the words 'miserere nobis' exceptionally moving. Especially impressive, however, in performance (I have heard this Mass often, rather well performed, in a Catholic church) is the big interlude 'suscipe deprecationem nostram', where the growing strength of the harmony, and on p. 34 the thrice repeated harmonies rising to fortissimo – these express the inmost sensitivity; while the following pause, and the gentle moving tutti sections (in a deeply quiet context) reveal a soul really steeped in devotion and holy emotions. This is greatness, sublimity, and yet with but sparse use of new and studied harmonic effects. Here is real pathos! If we had more such pieces, if more young composers would distinguish themselves in this kind of work, what could not be expected from the art of music! How much would man be elevated by the excitement of the finest passions!

After this melting Adagio there follows a cheerful Allegro in C major, 3/4 time, which with various imitations and well prepared cadences close the section. We come now to the Credo. Whoever has read through the monkish Latin of the Creed must admit that there exists no drier text for music: periods of exaggerated length; words like 'et vivificantem – consubstantialem – sanctam catholicam apostolicam etc.' are really very hard to express in music! But a thoughtful brain always finds a way. Haydn chooses for the first movement a very simple theme

which leads through various keys for thirty-three bars, with fugal imitations; and he does this so rightly (as we say here 'fully' [*real*]) that the four voices and organ all by themselves make a complete entity and can be played without any of the instruments at all. We need hardly describe to anyone familiar with Haydn's services for instrumental music the art and understanding with which the violins and other instruments have been added.

The words 'Et incarnatus est' to 'et resurrexit' are treated Adagio by almost all composers. They want to express the feelings that we have when hearing the sufferings of Christ, Friend of man. Haydn, too, writes a sorrowful Adagio in C minor where one voice after another sings a short phrase with very simple accompaniment; and this is a beautiful change after the previous brilliant chorus. The two-part harmony of 'passus, passus' is very moving, and then comes a surprising, shocking tutti on p. 56 [bars 78ff.] that dies away to pianissimo; Haydn has at this point two triads in similar motion, the fifth and sixth bars of page 56 [bars 82–3], which have a fine effect. We remember a similar passage in [A. T. H.] Schweizer's *Alceste*, which is as follows:

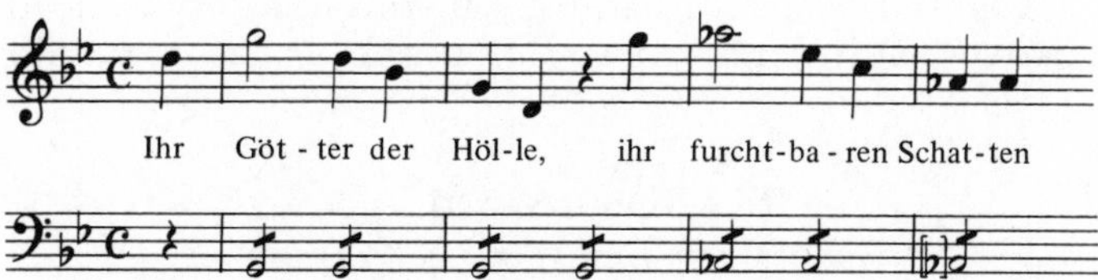
Ihr Göt - ter der Höl-le, ihr furcht-ba - ren Schat-ten

But Haydn has given the violins a small phrase which, without weakening the effect, robs the passage of a hardness that one might otherwise find in it. The Et Resurrexit is a large, fiery tutti with all the instruments. The unison at 'et expecto' and the two general pauses that follow, the half cadence in E at the words 'mortuorum' are when performed of a beautiful and sublime effect, which one would not expect just from looking at these simple harmonies. The Et Vitam starts as a fugue but is developed in a very original way. The theme comes in a beautiful solo passage with imitations, then we have large-scale harmonies, unexpected modulations . . . and a very curious closing cadence – everything in such admirable proportions that the teacher could extract infallible rules of composition just from this movement.

Dry as are the words of the Credo for musical composition, those of the Sanctus are rich and interesting. Here the composer has a free hand to show all the riches and greatness of his art, which our thoughtful master did *not* do this time, probably because after the great harmonic blocks of the Gloria and Credo choruses, a large tutti would now be of no particular effect. A beautiful song in the violins, without any of the wind instruments, begins the piece, in which first the alto voice, then the other vocal parts, enter in simple harmonies and continue to a pause on the dominant. The Pleni that follows has some great tuttis but soon closes, so as to prepare for the ensuing Benedictus, a kind of pastorale. This piece, an Andantino [sc.: Andante] 6/8 in C minor is composed in a most gentle and flowing style; it contains so many subtle modulations and the vocal parts are so well set one with another, and yet the whole is written quite naturally and limited to the proper range of each voice. The writing of the four parts is especially noteworthy when the key changes to C major . . . It has often been remarked that H. has the gift in large measure to make commonplace musical thoughts very interesting; and that he is especially clever in finding new and surprising ways to use the instruments to that purpose: we have an example in the Agnus Dei. How often have we heard the opening thought, and yet how new it sounds because of the two pauses that follow one another. But as for the kettledrum which enters at bar ten with a solo – who would have expected that in an Adagio cantabile written without trumpets and horns? Nevertheless, one's sensitivities are not in the least disturbed, and the piece continues, solemnly and in a spirit of devotion, to its conclusion, despite the repeated drum beats (which incidentally only occur in a piano context). The cadence in C minor [bars 17–18] . . . is particularly fine. But these are the marks of a genius and are not for everyone, and seldom to be copied. An Allegro spiritoso that now follows the Adagio concludes this work in a spirit of nobility.

These are the remarks that occurred to the writer on reading and hearing this Mass. It can serve as a model how to compose church music of this sort in the *new* taste: for not to speak of the beautiful and strict part-writing (which we know well enough from this master), the vocal writing, the still and quiet sensitivity throughout – all are adapted to the place and solemnity for which it is intended. Everything that is only playful, joking and affectation, and therefore unworthy of the holy service and otherwise out of place: all this has been omitted. For this reason let it come into the hands of all those who through duty or curiosity have to concern themselves with church music of this kind; let it be diligently and frequently studied by them.

The Seven Words

(choral version, 1796; XX:2)

In connection with the first performance of the new choral version of Haydn's Oratorio, *The Seven Words*, in 1796, we have mentioned the salient facts of this extensive rewriting. We repeat them briefly here: Haydn heard a choral version of his Oratorio when passing through Passau; it had been prepared by the local Cathedral Chapel Master Joseph Friebert. Haydn procured a copy of this choral version, the idea of which he approved but thought he might improve the choral writing. The Esterházy Archives owns the performance material of the Friebert version (MS. mus. I, 163 and 164/a), and it probably was the copy Haydn and Swieten used. The composer, in a letter to a Silesian Monastery in 1799, said, 'Three years ago I added a new four-part vocal music (without changing the instrumental parts). The text was written by a well-versed and musicianly canon at Passau Cathedral, and our great

Baron von [*sic*] Swieten corrected it; the effect of this work surpassed all expectation . . .' (CCLN 162). What Haydn says of the instruments, that there were not changed, is basically though not literally true: that is to say, theoretically you perform the Oratorio with the new choral parts and the old instrumentation. But Haydn, as we have mentioned above, not only added instruments (clarinets, trombones), he also merged the four horns of Sonata No. II 'Hodie mecum eris in Paradiso' into two and greatly enriched the original flute and bassoon parts; there are other retouchings, too. We refer the reader to the literature cited above (p. 97) and to the scores of both the instrumental and choral versions published in the new Collected Edition (*Joseph Haydn Werke*, Reihe IV and XXVIII/2).

A discussion of the music belongs to an earlier chapter of this biography. We have noted above that Swieten and Haydn judged correctly when they hoped that, with the addition of words, the piece would take on a new lease of life. The sentimental text, which utilizes C. W. Ramler's *Tod Jesu*, really did help people to come to grips with the intellectually difficult and uncompromising work. Whether the choral version is preferable aesthetically to the original orchestral score is to a great extent a matter of choice. For the next 150 years after its publication by Breitkopf & Härtel in 1801, it was the choral version (or, grotesquely, the arrangement for string quartet) that was known to the general musical world. This neglect of the original instrumental score may be laid entirely to one factor: the score had never been printed. It was all very well for orchestras in the eighteenth century to dare to play such a complicated work without a score, the leader trying as best he could to hold things together; but in the nineteenth century, no respectable orchestra was going to attempt the orchestral version of *The Seven Words* without a conductor and a full score; and there was no printed score and none had ever been printed. But when, in the 1950s, the Joseph Haydn Institut printed the orchestral version, and the Bärenreiter-Verlag the performance material and a miniature score (TP 92), the work suddenly blossomed into a popularity unrivalled since the eighteenth century. In 1972 there were no less than four[1] complete gramophone records of the original orchestral version as against only one – a Vienna performance conducted by the late Hermann Scherchen (Westminster) – of the choral version.[2] The discrepancy is partly the effect of novelty (the recent arrival of the orchestral version) but it may be symptomatic of a decisive and basic change in taste regarding the Oratorio. As to the choral version, we shall be hearing much more of it, especially in 1801, when Haydn was involved with the publication (see especially July 1801 in the Chronicle, for an interesting and lengthy announcement of the work's subscription edition by Breitkopf & Härtel in their *Intelligenz-Blatt*).

There are two really new compositions for the choral version: one is the series of choral chants, *a cappella*, that preface each Sonata and in which the Word is chanted; they are very beautiful and effective. The other is one of Haydn's most original and brilliant *tours de force*, the solo wind-band interlude (*Introductione*: *Largo e cantabile*) with which the second part of the work opens. It, too, is a slow movement, and is in the key of A minor, thus providing a tonal pivot between Sonata IV (F minor) and

1 By the Catalonian Chamber Orchestra, conducted by Antoní Ros-Marba (Schwann Verlag, two records); by Leslie Jones conducting the Little Orchestra of London (Nonesuch, one record); by the Solisti di Zagreb conducted by Antonio Janigro (Vanguard, one record); and most recently by the Prague Chamber Orchestra without conductor (Supraphon, one record).

2 The first recording of the choral version was made in the 1930s by Japanese Columbia in a performance by the Tokyo Academy of Music conducted by Charles Lautrop. The wind-band interlude was omitted, possibly because in those days the students of the Academy could not master the problems of intonation.

Sonata V in A major which it introduces. The wind band is a very large one, including trombones and contrabassoon, the first time that Haydn had ever written for the latter instrument.

It is very instructive to compare this austere, gaunt and cold piece of musical objectivity with Mozart's writing for wind band. In Mozart, there is always a reserve of sensuality, a desire to exploit the physical beauty of every voice and instrument; and this is particularly true of the music for solo wind band. There are so many examples of this that to single out one or two seems gratuitous, but the reader will recall the silken beauty of the serenade in Act II of *Così fan tutte* when the disguised lovers appear, or the charged sensuality of the third movement (Adagio) in the Serenade in B flat (K. 361). It may be objected that this worldly music cannot fairly stand comparison with a religious interlude; yet the point is that Mozart's music, and even his wind-band music in C minor (the famous Serenade, K. 388), almost always has a sense of warmth, colour and even eroticism that is totally different from Haydn and Beethoven. Haydn was a great orchestrator, but the principles on which he worked were entirely different from those of Mozart. In Haydn the structure is always the main point and the sheer sound and beauty of the instruments employed are of secondary concern. One only need remember the leaden-footed tread of Symphony No. 49 (*La Passione*) opening movement with its fastidious, grey-coloured orchestration to realize that basically, Haydn's wind writing has not changed *in substance* from 1768 – the date of the Symphony – to 1796. The Interlude from *The Seven Words* is 'cold as any stone', and it is fascinating to see how Haydn uses his large group of instruments to produce this effect of total objectivity: a sound, in fact, almost stripped of every sensual attribute whatever. The key of A minor is, incidentally, very rare for Haydn: he wrote no symphony, no quartet, no sonata, no piano trio in that key – which shows, at least negatively, that he must have entertained strong views as to the key's emotional significance; perhaps he felt that this key, often described as 'neutral', was of a cold objectivity suitable for a wind-band interlude in the middle of the Passion. At all events, Haydn succeeded in his portrayal, creating one of the few really chilling moments in his whole *œuvre*.

It is also instructive to compare it, for a moment, to Beethoven's wind-band music of this period, and in particular the *Sextetto* (as Beethoven himself entitled it)[1] in E flat, Op. 71, which was probably composed in the same year, 1796, as Haydn's Interlude. Beethoven used as his models the wind-band writing of Mozart and his contemporaries (since he would hardly have known any of Haydn's early wind-band *divertimenti* which, having been composed in 1760 or thereabouts, would have been considered hopelessly old-fashioned even by their composer). We notice that Beethoven has studied and assimilated the 'walking' second clarinet parts of Mozart's wind-band writing (Op. 71, 1st movt., bars 69ff.) and various other stylistic details of the Salzburg master; but despite that, there is distinct lack of sensuality in Beethoven's admirably concise and thoroughly professional *Sextetto*. For those who wish to pursue the matter further, we would suggest a comparison of Beethoven's Quintet in E flat, Op. 16, for piano and wind instruments (*c.* 1796) with its model, Mozart's work for precisely the same combination, K. 452; the similarities are obvious but the differences extraordinary, particularly the actual sound. The interesting fact that so much of Beethoven's best writing for wind instruments would seem to date from the year 1796

1 An authentic set of parts signed on the title page and corrected by Beethoven himself, in private possession in Florence; in this interesting and authentic manuscript, the 'Menuetto' was laid into the parts later.

suggests that the impact of Haydn's Interlude was felt by his erstwhile pupil, too; though as is always the case in Beethoven, the stimulation was direct but the application indirect.[1]

The Seven Words, despite the elaborate choral setting and the addition of the highly original Interlude, remains what it had been from the first: a beautiful but problematical work. It was, and indeed is, appreciated by connoisseurs, but it was never intended to win the larger public in its original state, and its temporary lease-of-life that it gained from the re-working of 1796 did not, in the final analysis, change its position in Haydn's *œuvre*.

We would sum up *The Seven Words* by quoting from an interesting criticism of the work which appeared in *Harmonicon* (VIII, 1830, p. 29). After citing a passage in which Abbé Stadler talked of the work to Vincent Novello ('the best judges in Germany . . . consider [it] the most profound effort of his genius, and the most lasting monument of his fame'), the reviewer added:

> Haydn, too, the Abbé told Mr. N., thought this 'the very finest of all his works'. Notwithstanding the weight of such opinions, we beg leave to differ from them. *Nullius addictus jurare in verba magistri* is our rule, and highly as we think of the learning and ingenuity of Haydn's work, yet we have never viewed it as one of the most striking evidences of his gigantic genius. It is exceedingly elaborate, exhibits a vast seal of vigorous thought, and portions of it are extremely effective; nevertheless it was written *to order* – if we may dare apply a mercantile phrase to a work of art – and is a study, a masterly one, but wants that 'fine frenzy', that unfettered play of the imagination, which is so much more apparent in his quartets and symphonies, in his canzonets, and in his chef-d'oeuvre, *The Creation*. The public, too, who *ultimately* are always right, have, after due deliberation, thus decided; and from such a judgement any appeal ought to be, and is, in vain.

Works for the stage

(1) INCIDENTAL MUSIC TO 'ALFRED' BY J. BICKNELL (GERMAN TRANSLATION BY JOHANN WILHELM COWMEADOW), A TRAGEDY IN FIVE ACTS PRODUCED AT EISENSTADT CASTLE BY THE STADLER TROUPE ON 9 SEPTEMBER 1796. (XXX: 5); (2) 'FATAL AMOUR', ARIA IN A PLAY (EISENSTADT, 1796?) (XXX: 4).

The three pieces that Haydn composed for *Alfred* have been listed earlier in the Chronicle; they are (1) *Chor der Dänen*; (2) *Arie des Schutzgeistes*; and (3) Duet Alfred-Odun.

The Chorus of the Danes, 'Triumph dir, Haldane! die Schlacht ist gekämpft', is clearly written in the shadow of the great *Missa in tempore belli*, the choruses of which it strongly resembles. Using the unusual time of 6/8, Haydn manages to write a stirring and really warlike chorus, to which the prominent part assigned to the trumpets and kettledrums contributes. One of the new features in the drum writing is the way it

1 The key of A minor for the Interlude and Haydn's use of it stayed in Beethoven's mind for years. Or rather Haydn's avoidance of it in his quartets; for when Beethoven started planning his last quartets, it occurred to him (as his Conversation Books show us) that Haydn had composed no quartet in A minor. Mozart, on the other hand, had composed a famous Sonata in that key (K. 310).

hammers out the quaver rhythm over two or three bars, and there is a burst of aggressive drumming as we approach the recapitulation:

There is an effective C minor section with tremolo-like semiquavers in the violins that reminds us of similar C minor parts of the *Missa in tempore belli*. But it is particularly the kettledrums and their insistent rhythm which place the Chorus of the Danes in the spiritual sphere of the 'Paukenmesse'.

Certainly the most beautiful and original piece in the *Alfred* music is the extraordinary *Arie des Schutzgeistes*, accompanied by a wind-band sextet of clarinets, bassoons and horns. If anything were needed to show that the Interlude from *The Seven Words* is not an isolated phenomenon, and that Haydn was becoming increasingly interested in the capabilities of wind instruments in general, this Aria is a perfect case in point. It opens with a long *ritornello*, which sets the scene for the guardian spirit's appearance; and the use of the solo wind-band lends a curiously disembodied spirituality which must have made the scene very effective on the stage at Eisenstadt. The Schutzgeist carries on a dialogue with Elvida, who has only spoken text (*Sprechstimme*). The spirit offers comforting words;

> Ausgesandt vom Strahlenthrone atm'ich Tröstung in dein Herz.
> Trau der Tugend hohem Lohne, trage standhaft deinen Schmerz.

Whereupon Elvida asks: 'Bote des Himmels! Lebt mein Alfred? Lebt Edgar?' The spirit answers: 'Hoff' Elvida!'

> Bange Sorgen machen oft das Leben schwer;
> doch der Zukunft heit'rer Morgen schwebt aus dunkler Ferne her.
> Wag' es nicht, sie durchzuschauen, bis der Vorsicht Vaterhand
> durch den Dornenpfad voll Grauen Wege deiner Rettung fand.

The end of this passage and the following *Sprechstimme* of Elvida may be cited as characteristic of Haydn's technique. The recapitulation follows the *fermata* at bar 60 (see example opposite). The Schutzgeist concludes her aria with the following words:

> Schützend will ich dich umschweben, wenn dir Wut und Rache droht;
> stärkend deinen Mut beleben: harr' auf Gott in deiner Not! –

Haydn's singer (Fräulein R(h)umfeld?) had a good range, from *e* flat′ to *b* flat″; she seems to have had a particularly good *g″*, which Haydn often writes for her as the top of a phrase. This *Arie* is *musique d'occasion* of the highest sort. It was first published in a series of Haydn Arias for Soprano, Tenor and Bass issued between 1959 and 1963 by the Haydn-Mozart Presse of the Universal Edition.[1]

1 Edited by the present writer. There were published full scores, the orchestral material and the piano scores (in volumes: two for soprano and one each for tenor and bass), with *Revisionsberichte* (HMP 192). The first performances of many of these arias, including the *Arie des Schutzgeistes*, took place in a series devised by the present writer for the British Broadcasting Corporation's Third Programme in 1959 and conducted by Maurits Sillem (Producer: Hans Keller).

[Arie des Schutzgeistes]

The Duet between Alfred and Odun (both tenors) 'Der Morgen graut, es ruft der Hahn' is an expressive Adagio of which, as we have noted above, the harp part on the autograph was not filled in. The opening bars will give an impression of this as yet unpublished work:

Violino Princip. nell' ottava
8va
Violino I
pizz.
pizz. 3
Violino II
pizz. 3
col Violino 2do
Viola
Alfred
Odun
pizz.
Violoncello e Basso
8
[col Violino 2do
8
loco
[pizz.]
etc.
[col Violino 2do
Der Mor - gen graut, es ruft

The sound of the *Violino Principale, arco*, against the whole string orchestra, *pizzicato*, is extremely effective. Unfortunately, the little piece cannot be used in concert form because it ends inconclusively on the dominant of B flat, the action broken off by King Alfred (Haydn's score has, on Alfred's line at the end of the work, 'haltet ein') with the words 'und dich verschlingt das Grab . . .' ('the grave swallows you up . . .'). Thus the Duet is doomed to oblivion along with Bicknell's play and the translation by Professor Cowmeadow. The incidental music to *Alfred* was, except for 'Fatal amour', Haydn's farewell to the theatre.

Aria: 'Fatal amour'

'Fatal amour', which we have discussed in connection with the 1796 theatrical season at Eisenstadt, is a 'vaudeville' in French and as far as we know, Haydn's only attempt to set the French language. It is a running accompanied recitative, interrupted by dialogue; for example, after a recitative ending 'pour me percer le cœur', there is the following spoken text: 'Baron Schloff! Altesse dite a ce Musicien, qu'il marche plus vite avec le chant. Oui, oui.' The recitative starts in F and modulates to a little 'arioso' in G.

It is quite unusual that Haydn writes the vocal part in the G clef, something he never did except occasionally when in England. Probably he was not sure who would sing the part. The autograph manuscript was apparently Haydn's conducting score, for we find his added notes 'NB' several times (a warning for cues, usually). The next larger section is in E flat and brings in the horns for the first time:

And this is the material with which this miniature *Maestro di cappella* (*à la* Cimarosa) ends, constantly broken off by spoken dialogue ('Oui, oui, brave compositeur'). Like the Duet from *Alfred*, the piece is doomed to the fate of the theatrical work with which

A page from the second violin part, taken from the original performance material copied by Johann Elssler, for Haydn's incidental music to a French play (with the opening words 'Fatal amour, cruel vainqueur' from the vocal line included for purposes of orientation). The play was performed at Eisenstadt, *c.* 1796–1800.

it was inseparably connected; but since it does have an 'end', the piece may be performed in concert form. As said above, Elssler's beautifully written performance material, probably the very one from which Haydn conducted in September 1796, has survived, and we are happy to show one page of it in facsimile. 'Fatal amour' remains unpublished.

Mehrstimmige Gesänge (part songs)
(XXVb: 1–4 and XXVc: 1–9)

In 1796, Haydn began a series of vocal pieces which later became known as 'Mehrstimmige Gesänge' (or 'Lieder'): two terzets and eleven quartets with harpsichord (or more likely pianoforte) accompaniment – the autograph specified 'Cembalo' which by 1796 had become a generic term for a keyboard instrument. The autograph is entitled

Aus des Ramlers Lyrischer Blumenlese
in die Music gesetzt
von Jos. Haydn 796.

C. W. Ramler (1725–98), a slightly older contemporary of Haydn's, published a collection of poems entitled *Lyrische Blumenlese* in which the names of the authors were not given, 'so that', explains Ramler not without a certain malice, 'those connoisseurs who are used to judging the excellence of a work only from the author's name may find it a little more difficult.' It was perhaps Haydn's intention at the beginning to rely exclusively on Ramler's *Blumenlese*, but in the course of composing the Songs he turned to other sources as well. In the first place Haydn used a *Sammlung der vorzüglichsten Werke deutscher Dichter und Prosaister*, a sort of poetry in instalments, published in a long series of pocket-size volumes by F. A. Schrämbl in Vienna (one of the volumes Haydn used was from the collected works of Friedrich von Hagedorn, which Schrämbl brought out in 1791); in the second place he turned to Christian Fürchtegott Gellert's *Geistliche Oden und Lieder* (1757). It is to be noted that the whole tone of the Songs changes, becoming increasingly more serious and in particular more religious. As to the chronology, the watermarks and paper of the autograph suggest that at least Nos. 1–9 of the Songs were composed more or less as one group (watermarks: Italian paper of ten staves with three half-moons and the letters 'AC') and may be dated 1796. The next fixed date is a letter from Haydn to the German lexicographer E. L. Gerber in Sondershausen of 23 September 1799, in which the composer talks of his *Mehrstimmige Gesänge* (Vocal Quartets, he now calls them), 'based on German texts of our greatest poets: I have already composed thirteen such pieces, but have not yet performed any of them . . .'; by which a public performance is meant. Haydn never finished more than thirteen, but originally he intended to make a collection of two dozen. On 14 June 1797, Silverstolpe writes from Vienna, 'Moreover he sang several Arias to me, which he intends to issue by subscription when their number has reached 24. His usual rhythm characterizes them and they reveal many strokes of genius and well-chosen thoughts.' (Previously it was considered that Silverstolpe was referring to some of Haydn's earlier 'insertion' arias in the Eszterháza productions of operas by other composers, of which Silverstolpe had some copied for him; but it is clear that Haydn regarded these earlier arias as real 'pièces d'occasion' and was certainly not disposed to issue them on subscription.) When Griesinger was negotiating for the publication of the Songs with Breitkopf & Härtel in 1801, we also learn that Haydn still intended to publish more than thirteen. At the beginning of December 1801, Griesinger writes to Leipzig: '. . . He has completed 13, which he showed to me. But now the work goes slowly and he wants for texts because, as he assured me, most poets do not write in a musical way.' A fortnight later, Griesinger writes 'Haydn won't go into the matter [of their publication] until there are a full 25 of them, for "if I'm going to print something nowadays, it has to be of a certain size" . . . You can do Haydn a great favour with texts, but nothing eccentric [*verstiegen*] and no involved periods.' Griesinger assured the Leipzig publishers that 'the Songs were written only *con amore* in happy hours, not to order'. We shall see that Breitkopf offered to publish them and after some procrastination – and a new dedication of the works to Count Johann Georg Browne, of Beethovenian fame, in 1802 – finally issued them in 1803.

Nos. 1–9 have a further feature in the autograph which differentiates them from the others: they have a figured bass only (which was 'realized' by Breitkopf & Härtel when they published the works), whereas Nos. 10–13 have a written out keyboard part (that is: both right and left hand) in the autograph – this pianoforte (as we judge it to be) part is on integral pillar of the composition and not merely, as they say, for rehearsal purposes. Nos. 1–9 may, as we suggest, be dated 1796 and Nos. 10–13 about 1796–99 (one of the watermarks – letters 'AM' and a bow-arrow – also appears in Haydn autographs of the years 1796 and 1799; another – a crowned eagle with the letters 'GFA' – also appears in a Haydn autograph of 1798; both papers come from Italian mills, the first from Andrea Mattizzoli's and the second from Galvani Fratelli's in Pordenone).

In the catalogue listed below, we have given the basic information about title, name of poet (according to the latest research), key, tempo, etc. Of the several practical editions, we would mention one by Fritz Jöde of 1932 and a later one by Bernhard Paumgartner of 1951.

MEHRSTIMMIGE GESÄNGE

(four-part unless otherwise stated)

No. 1. 'Der Augenblick'. A major, 3/4 *Poco adagio*. 'Inbrunst, Zärtlichkeit, Verstand' etc. Text by Johann Nikolaus Götz; Haydn's source: Ramler.

No. 2. 'Die Harmonie in der Ehe'. B flat major, 4/4 *Allegretto*. 'O wunderbare Harmonie' etc. Text by Johann Nikolaus Götz; Haydn's source: Ramler.

No. 3. 'Alles hat seine Zeit'. F major, 4/4 *Allegretto*. 'Lebe, liebe, trinke, lärme' etc. Haydn's autograph notes: 'from the Greek'. See J. Lunn in *Haydn Yearbook* IV (1968), pp. 197f. Haydn's source: probably Ramler.

No. 4. 'Die Beredsamkeit'. B flat major, 4/4 *Allegretto*. 'Freunde! Wasser machet stumm', etc. Text by G. E. Lessing. Haydn's source: Ramler.

No. 5. 'Der Greis'. A major, 4/4 *Molto adagio*. 'Hin ist alle meine Kraft' etc. Text by J. W. L. Gleim. Haydn's source: Ramler.

No. 6. 'An den Vetter'. Three-part (2 tenors and bass). G major, 2/3 *Allegro*. 'Ihr Vetter ja'. Text by Christian Felix Weisse. Haydn's source: Ramler.

No. 7. 'Daphnens einziger Fehler'. Three-part (2 tenors and bass). C major, 3/4 *Allegro*. 'Sie hat das Auge, die Hand' etc. Haydn's source: Ramler.

No. 8. 'Die Warnung'. B flat major, 4/4 *Andante*. 'Freund! Ich bitte, hüte dich' etc. Haydn's source: *Sammlung der vorzüglichsten Werke deutscher Dichter und Prosaister* (Hagedorn's translation of an anonymous Greek poem).

No. 9. 'Betrachtung des Todes'. Three parts (2 tenors and bass) A minor, 6/8 *Andante*. 'Der Jüngling hofft des Greises Ziel' etc. Text by C. F. Gellert. Haydn's source: Gellert's *Geistliche Oden und Lieder* (first ed. 1757, reprinted frequently).

No. 10. 'Wider den Übermut'. A major, 3/4 *Adagio*. 'Was ist mein Stand, mein Glück' etc. Text by Gellert (see No. 9).

No. 11. 'An die Frauen'. Three parts (2 tenors and bass). F major, 4/4 *Allegro moderato*. 'Natur gab Stimmen Hörner' etc. Text: Anacreon's Second Ode, translated from the Greek by Gottfried August Bürger. Haydn's source: Ramler.

No. 12. 'Aus dem Danklied zu Gott'. E flat major, *alla breve Poco adagio*. 'Du bist's, dem Ruhm und Ehre gebühret' etc. Text by Gellert (see No. 9).

No. 13. 'Abendlied zu Gott'. A major, 3/4 *Adagio*. 'Herr! der du mir das Leben' etc. Text by Gellert (see No. 9). In Gellert's original poems of Nos. 12 and 13 there were many more stanzas: in No. 12 Haydn set only the first of thirteen stanzas, and in No. 13 only the first of five.[1]

We may owe the existence of these part songs to Haydn's two sojourns in England; for the *Mehrstimmige Gesänge* may be viewed from one standpoint as being translations, as it were, of English catches, glees, etc., the performance and composition of which interested the composer highly. On the one hand, the experience of the Handel Oratorios in Westminster Abbey and the adjacent St Margaret's church was responsible for *The Creation*, *The Seasons* and indirectly the late Masses; while on the other, the smaller English vocal forms certainly intrigued Haydn and may have suggested his trying to produce a German-language equivalent.

Some of the part songs are as humorous – almost skittish – as a lusty English catch. 'Die Harmonie in der Ehe' has always been one of the most popular of this cycle:

> O wunderbare Harmonie.
> Was Er will, will auch Sie.
> Er zechet gern, Sie auch,
> Er spielet gern, Sie auch,
> Er zählt Dukaten gern, und macht den großen Herrn,
> Auch das ist Ihr Gebrauch!

Haydn, whose marriage was an example of horror to Mozart – 'He frequently compared his married fate with that of others, particularly the two Haydns, Joseph and Michael "But no one is happy as I am in a wife" he would explain'[2] – was capable of laughing at himself and marriage as an institution. The only touch of cynicism is the harmonic twist that Haydn gives each time to the word 'Harmonie'. 'Die Beredsamkeit' ('Freunde, Wasser machet stumm') ends with a mimic. Instead of finishing the cadence, the music hangs on a dominant chord and the singers are instructed to mime the last word 'Stumm' (silent) with their lips. For broadcast and recorded performances, the words are nowadays whispered: also an effective solution. One of the most admired settings is 'Die Warnung', of which *The Oxford Book of*

1 *Joseph Haydn Werke*, Reihe XXX, ed. Paul Mies (1958); *Kritischer Bericht* by Paul Mies (1958); Paul Mies, 'Textdichter zu J. Haydns "Mehrstimmigen Gesängen"', in *Haydn Yearbook* I (1962), p. 201. Jean Lunn, 'The Quest of the Missing Poet', in *Haydn Yearbook* IV (1968), pp. 195ff. Mörner, 318. Olleson, *Griesinger*, 29f. CCLN 167.

2 Michael Haydn's wife, the former soprano Lipp, was not a subject of admiration for the Mozarts. The quotation from *A Mozart Pilgrimage*, p. 98. Misquoted (line omitted) in Deutsch, *Dokumente*, 463. We mention the latter simply because the reference is significant in itself and Deutsch's condensation, 'He frequently compared the two Haydns, Joseph and Michael "But no one . . . [etc.]"', might lead to misunderstandings.

Greek Verse in Translation (T. F. Hingham; Oxford 1938, p. 205) has the following translation:

Beware the lurking scorpion, friend;
  There's one to every stone;
All dangers on the dark attend, –
  Leave mysteries alone.

Haydn seems to make us feel, with eerie realism, the myriad busy feet of scorpions, the sudden darkness, and the chattering background of 'Betrügerei' (deceit).

This is one side of the songs, while another side gradually becomes more and more insistent. In 'Der Augenblick', for example, we have an outwardly cynical description of seducing a fair one: it is not tenderness, understanding, tears etc., but a fortunate moment that brings luck to the lover. In Haydn's setting, the cynical idea gradually becomes nostalgic and so serious as to defeat the light-hearted original concept. Seriousness, in fact, comes to the fore increasingly. In No. 5, 'Der Greis', we find one of several texts which the composer sought out particularly because they express *in nuce* his philosophy. This song later became famous because Haydn made a visiting card out of the first two lines:

Hin ist alle meine Kraft,
Alt und schwach bin ich,
Wenig nur erquicket mich,
Scherz und Rebensaft.
Hin ist alle meine Zeit,
Meiner Wangen Roth ist hinweg geflohn,
Der Todt klopft an meiner Thür,
Unerschröckt mach ich ihm auf.
Himmel! Habe Danck,
Ein harmonischer Gesang
War mein Lebenslauf.[1]

Haydn expresses infinite weariness, almost a lack of breath, in the words 'Gone is all my strength,/Old and weak am I', by the use of rests in the melody:

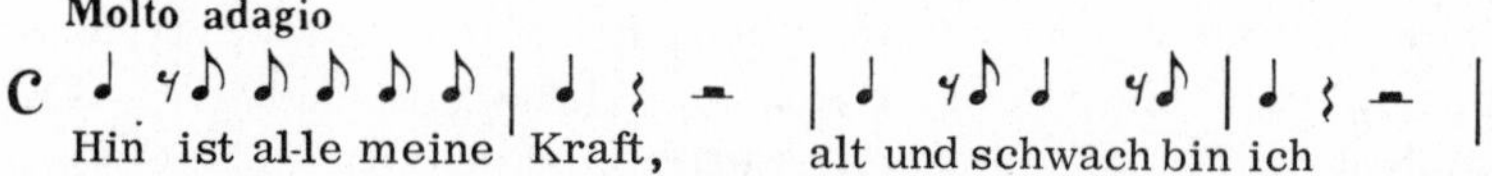

The three crotchets of rests after the word 'Kraft' are effective in a degree which reflects Haydn's old wizardry with silence. In the forthcoming Chronicle, we shall often read of the composer's preparedness for death, and the words here, 'Death is knocking at my door', are set with ominous precision; the impression is immediately erased by the proud words 'Unabashed, I open it'; while the last two lines 'A harmonious song/was my life's course' are set with a majestic calm and confidence.

In fact the shadows of the two Oratorios and the six last Masses fall even on the modest part songs. 'Alles hat seine Zeit', though a secular drinking song, seems to be an extract from a larger choral work like *The Seasons*. Of course, Haydn sought for and discovered texts that he found congenial. He used to say, 'The Heavenly Father preserve me from Pride', and in 'Wider den Übermut' (in which, incidentally, the

1 With the exception of some added commas, our version is that of a holograph sheet from Haydn's legacy now in the Esterházy Archives of the National Széchényi Library, Budapest (Ha. I. 8): the sheet contains the words of the poem with Haydn's autograph title 'Der Greis'.

piano has a rather long introduction) we find Haydn setting lines of an almost autobiographical cast,

Bewahre mich, O Gott!
Von dem ich alles habe,
Vor Stolz und Übermut.

(Preserve me, O God!
– To Whom I owe my all –
From pride and insolence.)

The last two of the *Mehrstimmige Gesänge* are pure religious music, overwhelmed by the language of *The Creation* and *The Seasons*. Fugal textures blend imperceptibly with the late harmonies of the 'Theresienmesse', the 'Schöpfungsmesse' and the other choral works of the turn of the century. There is a quiet assurance, a simplicity and a dignity about this music which somehow transform the whole series; what may have begun as a series of German glees ended as hymns. 'Lord, Thou hast always watched over my fate,/And Thy Hand was over me' ('Und deine Hand war über mir' . . .).

The general public heard of the *Mehrstimmige Gesänge* for the first time when the first edition – by Breitkopf & Härtel – was reviewed in the *AMZ* (V, 1803, pp. 799f.):

REVIEW

Drey- und vierstimmige Gesänge mit Begleitung des Fortepiano, von Joseph Haydn. Leipzig, bey Breitkopf–Härtel.

(They and many other songs may be also had in the eighth and ninth volume of the Oeuvr. complett. p. le Pianoforte, at Breitkopf–Härtel's.)

Through this pleasant and artistic collection of new terzets and quartets, a present lacuna is most richly and thankfully filled; and at the same time, there appears a new genre in the suite of our excellent master which deserves the greatest attention.

The collection itself consists of comic, serious and religious songs, which are not only beautifully and intelligently [*geistreich*] composed but are also especially satisfactory exercises for smaller singing groups. They are all in the fugal style and this requires each singer to pay attention. The use of the fugal style for the comical pieces, the simplicity of the accompaniment, the lovely and unfettered expression which abounds in each part: all this is as new as it is instructive for young composers in our times, when everything is calculated to the vast effect of instrumental accompaniment. One sees here how easy, natural and flowing is a good leadership of several simultaneous parts for one who was trained in the best school and is master of the tones. If only the noble Haydn would deign to present the world with more examples of this kind, in particular on religious, Latin or German Bible texts! The comic is certainly not to be spurned; yet we have a great deal of the comic nowadays and not nearly enough of the serious and religious.

The Canons
(XXVIIb: 1–47)

Apart from the *Ten Commandments* (*Zehn Gebote*) and some other canons which were clearly written in England (on the evidence of Haydn's *Catalogue of Works Composed in England*, CCLN, 309f., and *Haydn in England 1791–1795*, 316f.), it is very difficult, and in many cases downright impossible, to date Haydn's several dozen canons, except in a very broad and general way. Most of them are, one would guess, works written in the later years of the composer's life, when he was interested in German-language vocal music for several parts. Apart from the German canons, however, there are authentic Latin, Italian and English canons, but they form only a tiny minority. The late Otto Erich Deutsch was the first to bring some order into the authenticity and the literary sources of Haydn's canons, and he subsequently published them in the new Collected Edition,[1] to which publications the reader is referred. In many respects, Haydn's canons reflect the composer's attitudes in the same way as the part songs. 'Das böse Weib', with its nagging chromatics, is obvious, and so is the sarcastic 'Auf einen adeligen Dummkopf', which ridicules the aristocracy's ever-present preoccupation with lineage. Apart from the fantastic contrapuntal skill which these canons manifest (they extend from two to eight voices), and the composer's well-known irony and wit, they are also capable of enormous feeling. That they were intended for private entertainment is clear: no censor would have allowed some of the more earthy texts to be published; they are not quite so anally inclined as Mozart's more scurrilous words ('Leck mir den Arsch fein recht', etc.), but they reveal a healthy *settecento*-style lust for life.

One of the most extraordinary of these miniature masterpieces is a four-part work in F minor with the title *Tod und Schlaf* (the text begins, 'Tod ist ein langer Schlaf'). *Der Menschenfreund* reminds one of *Die Zauberflöte*; it is even in the crucial key of E flat major and breathes the same quiet radiance, but of course there is no certain dating for Haydn's canon and the influence may be in reverse.

Forty of these canons, in Elssler's copper-plate hand, were to be seen, framed, on the walls of Haydn's house in Gumpendorf. After the composer's death they were published, with some of the texts expurgated, by Breitkopf & Härtel, and reviewed in Vol. XII (December 1810, pp. 1006–10) of the *AMZ*:

REVIEW

1. *Die heiligen zehn Gebote als Canons.*
   (Pr. 8 Gr.) und
2. *42 Canons für drey (sollte heissen: zwey) und mehrere Singstimmen, von J. Haydn.*
   Aus der Original-Handschrift des Componisten.
   Leipzig, bey Breitkopf u. Härtel.
   (Pr. 1 Thlr. 8 Gr.)

> Every reader of the *AMZ* will remember from Griesinger's biography of Father Haydn how the latter decorated his best room not with paintings or engravings but with canons composed with much love and their delicate handwriting framed under glass; that when his miserly wife accused him of not leaving enough money behind to ensure his proper burial, he pointed to the canons and gave his word that any publisher would be glad, after he was dead, to pay whatever was needed for the purpose. Every friend of art wanted to have these canons, if only because of the anecdote, and also as a relic of the excellent man, the more so since it might be presumed that the great harmonist had composed something really excellent and of his own free will, out of special affection and even out of innocent pride. The 42 Canons are those left behind, and truly they disappoint not in the least, from

1 'Haydns Kanons' (in *Zeitschrift für Musikwissenschaft* XV, 1932). *Joseph Haydn Werke* (Henle Verlag), Reihe XXXI, 1959, and *Kritischer Bericht* (with Karl-Heinz Füssl), 1960.

whatever standpoint the educated amateur chooses to look at, judge and enjoy them. In great variety, partly because of their character – they range from the solemn to the merry – and partly because of their form – they range from the most severe and intricate to the most pleasant and easy –, they form a little garden of lovely and colourful flowers of the mind [*Geistesblüthen*]; every one is of value, every one is wholly that which it purports to be and produces the effect it should; and in the form and style of these canons, almost everything is employed that is possible in this restricted and difficult genre and which is (*nota bene*) compatible with an easy, flowing, unscholastic and unpedantic vocal line. If one classes them according to this standpoint, and in order to study the genre more attentively, one can have a rather complete course [*Cursus*] in the subject; and if one wants, as a non-professional, just to sing them through with a few friends for amusement, then (if lungs and voice allow) one can sing them straight through from beginning to end without any monotony. What both of these facets mean, anyone will know who understands even a modicum about composition in this genre; and that applies also to the reviewer: for how can he begin to analyze and describe the salient points of so many works? Or make a selection of works which are, each one, fine and beautiful in its own way? He prefers therefore to leave matters with this general notice and recommendation, and to add the following for those who might want to use both publications.

. . . No. 2, about which the anecdote told, all have good texts, appropriate to the words, of every kind: joking and serious, funny and solemn, words written by the composer, or sayings and proverbs, even good lines from German poetry of earlier and present times. Under most is the text that Haydn himself used; but since these were in some cases rougher or more obscure than could be presumed to meet the approval with our male and female singers, other and equally fitting words have been added; but since one did not want to do violence to the original manuscripts, the other versions with the next texts have been printed on separate sheets and laid in.

The canons are, by the way, *all* without accompaniment, and in two, three, up to eight parts – of which latter species the second publication contains several – and in them is joined to wonderful effect an admirable, mathematically refined art with the most beautiful inspiration and naturalness. The great artist, who more, perhaps, than anyone else of the modern age, understood not only with simple means but also *in a restricted genre* [original in italics: '*in enger Bahn*'] to express himself completely and easily, has made only very moderate demands in the *vocal parts*: any feminine, and masculine, voice, who is not just a high tenor or a low bass voice, can perform these canons. – And by way of conclusion, instead of anything further, we give Haydn's last request and word of farewell, as it reads here, and as it certainly, most certainly, will be faithfully observed by every friend of Art as he himself observed it in his own works. [There follows a score version of the Haydn's Canon, 'Denke mein, und liebe mich', reproduced in *Haydn in England 1791–1795*, p. 185 with the text 'Kenne Gott, die Welt, und dich, liebster Freund'; see also CCLN 268 for a reproduction.][1]

1 Of the many practical editions of Haydn's canons, we would draw attention to a good one by Wilhelm Weismann in Edition Peters (the original texts); the same publisher has also reissued Weismann's musical text with an English translation by Jean Lunn (New York 1966), for those to whom German represents an insuperable problem. A further edition, edited by Wilhelm Ehrmann, in Bärenreiter-Verlag, and others in Breitkopf & Härtel, etc.

Two Italian Duets for Soprano, Tenor and Pianoforte (Harpsichord)

(Carlo Francesco Badini)

(XXVa: 1, 2)

1. 'Saper vorrei se m'ami' ('Nisa' [Soprano] & 'Tirsi' [Tenor]). G major, *Adagio alla breve* → *Allegro* 2/4.
2. 'Guarda qui che lo vedrai' (same characters). F major, *Adagio alla breve* → *Allegretto* 6/8.

The autograph of 'Guarda qui' has survived in the British Museum; it is dated 1796. Johann Elssler made a copy of each duet for a visiting British lady, Mrs Peploe, who came to Vienna in 1796 and stayed for some months in the Austrian capital; she signed her copy of 'Saper vorrei' 'Vienna Nov^{br} 1796' and 'Guarda qui' 'Vienna Dec^{br} 1796'. She was an admired singer and later subscribed to *The Creation*, as we have pointed out above. There are some subsidiary manuscripts of the duets and later Haydn gave them to Breitkopf & Härtel, writing to Härtel on 1 July 1800 (CCLN, 171): 'Meanwhile I send you two little Duets, of which one is especially esteemed by the connoisseurs.' If we may hazard a guess as to which was the 'esteemed' Duet, we would suggest the G major 'Saper vorrei', with its canon (*vide infra*), a work that was separately published also by Artaria & Co. in June 1801 (Breitkopf did not issue the works until Cahier VIII of the *Oeuvres complettes*, June 1803). We know of the poet's name from Haydn's *Entwurf-Katalog*, where on the very last page he mentions Badini as the author (*vide supra*). The piano part of both Duets is beautifully written, with such typically 'English' details as the walking bass in bars 92ff. of the second Duet. Both works are full of delightful details. The texts are typically eighteenth-century pastoral. In Duet No. 1 Nisa asks 'Saper vorrei se m'ami' etc., 'Se per me sola vivi, se sai che vivo in te', to which the indignant Tirsi answers 'Questo saper vorresti? . . . oh quanto ingrata sei', causing the sorrowful Nisa to ask 'ingrata, oh Dio, perche?' This marks, very cleverly from an organizational standpoint, the end of the slow introduction; the Allegro section now begins in the dominant. Tirsi says that the plains, the mountains etc. all know it, 'e sola tu non sai l'anima mia qual'è?' Nisa says to this: 'lo so, ma bramo sentirlo replicar.' There now begins a very closely knit passage, in which both sing 'Se insiem lo replichiamo, qual armonia de' far', after which the soprano directs, 'Commincia tu che a cannone ti voglio seguitar', excuse for Haydn to write almost all the rest of the piece except the closing cadential bars 'a cannone'. We give a sample of this sophisticated treatment:

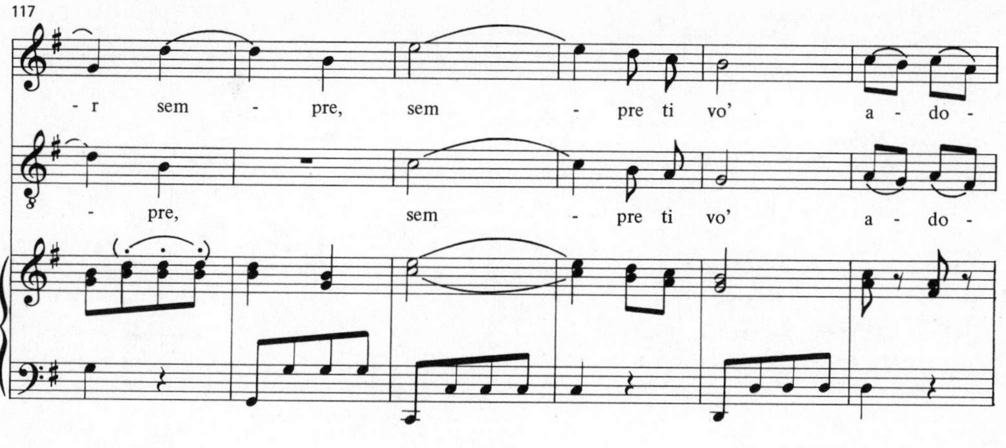

The opening introduction of 'Guarda qui' sounds as if it were a faint echo of Clarice's fast (Moderato) A major Aria, 'Son fanciulla', in Act I of Haydn's *Il mondo della luna* (1777). Nineteen years have transformed and transfigured this cheerful tune into the contemplative, gentle Adagio that opens the second Duet:

The text is at first an exchange: Tirsi finishes off, 'what see you in these eyes?' Nisa: 'What hear you in this breast?' In the quicker section we have a part of the text which reads, 'è il furbetto Cupido che dagli occhi al cor mi viene e per te, mio caro bene, mille scherzi in sen mi fa'. Haydn has many delightful ways to illustrate the 'mille scherzi', once with little grace notes, then with slithering chromatic lines, then with a series of rollicking semiquavers moving to the top of the Viennese piano (*f'''*), which part, when repeated, breaks into triplets:

65
sen mi fa in sen mi fà mil-le
scher-zi in sen in sen mi fà mil-le
69
scher-zi mil-le scher-zi in sen mi fà
scher-zi mil-le scher-zi in sen mi fà
73
mil-le scher-zi in sen mi fà e per
mil-le scher-zi in sen mi fà e per [etc.]
80

If the second Duet lacks the canonic brilliance of the first, it is the lighter and more 'open' of the two works; though the reader is, after studying them both, persuaded that the first, 'Saper vorrei', is definitely the one preferred by connoisseurs (and Artaria).[1]

The Piano Trios of the year 1796(?)

In the Chronicle for 1796, we have seen that Haydn entrusted his godson Weigl with a piano Trio to be delivered to Breitkopf & Härtel; Haydn's letter was dated 9 November. It must have been about this time or shortly afterwards that Haydn sent to Longman & Broderip, his British publishers, the three great piano Trios which may be considered the crowning effort of the series. They were dedicated to Therese Bartolozzi (*née* Jansen), the pianist for whom Haydn also wrote his last three piano Sonatas; we have examined her relationship to Haydn in *Haydn in England 1791–1795*.

Longman & Broderip brought out the three 'Sonatas', as they were still called by Haydn and his publishers, in April 1797. We give the list of these last four piano Trios:

Trio No. 42 in E flat (XV: 30), 1796(?). Published by Breitkopf & Härtel from a MS. sent by Haydn in November 1796. The Breitkopf edition (1798) was preceded by one issued by Artaria & Co. in 1797. An authentic Elssler MS., complete, survives in the Esterházy Archives of the National Széchényi Library of Budapest from Haydn's collection. One sheet (two pages) of the autograph, comprising bars 32–132 of the Finale, is in the Pierpont Morgan Library, New York (*ex. coll.* Heineman).

I *Allegro moderato*. II *Andante con moto*. III *Finale: Presto*.

Trios Nos. 43–45 (XV: 27–29), 1796(?). Published in 1797 by Longman & Broderip (entered at Stationers Hall on 27 April 1797; announced in the *Oracle* on 20 March 1797). Dedicated to Mrs Bartolozzi.

Trio No. 43 in C major. I *Allegro*. II *Andante*. III *Finale: Presto*.

Trio No. 44 in E major. I *Allegro moderato*. II *Allegretto*. III *Finale: Allegro*.

Trio No. 45 in E flat. I *Poco Allegretto*. II *Andantino ed innocentamente*. III *Finale in the German Style* [Continental editions: *Allemande*].

We have seen in the Chronicle that Haydn sent the E flat Trio No. 42 not only to Leipzig but also to Corri & Dussek in London; and presumably he sold the work to Artaria as well, for textually the Leipzig and Vienna prints, while similar, are independent. Each must have had an Elssler copy of the autograph similar to that which has survived in the Budapest library.

On these last four piano trios – and it must have been abundantly clear that very soon, works like *The Creation* would not allow Haydn to devote any more time to such smaller forms as piano trios – their composer lavished all his talents; it is almost as if he wished to show the world what possibilities in tonal relationships, harmonic

1 CCLN, 171; Hase, *Joseph Haydn und Breitkopf & Härtel*, op. cit., p. 20; Larsen, *HÜB*, 109. Critical new edition, Diletto Musicale No. 35 (edited by the present writer), Vienna-Munich 1960. The first modern performance of these Duets took place as part of a series for the British Broadcasting Corporation entitled 'The Unknown Haydn' (London 1958). The Duets were sung by April Cantelo and Wilfred Brown with Charles Spinks playing a fortepiano by William Stodart – at whose shop in Lad Lane Haydn had called when in London in 1795 – owned by Edward Croft-Murray, at whose beautiful house at Richmond this concert was recorded. The entire series was recorded for the B.B.C. Transcription Service and issued in 1958–59.

subtleties, instrumental combinations and sheer brilliance of form these trios could display in the hands of a master at the summit of his artistic career. Haydn in fact pursued several new avenues of thought in these trios, some of a purely technical (but nonetheless musical) nature; we shall examine these novelties in the course of our brief analysis.

The beginning harks back to the E flat Trio No. 36, one of the set dedicated to Princess Marie Hermenegild Esterházy:

The similarities are too obvious to stress, but it is only the very beginnings that are constructed out of the same rhythmic and harmonic material. The way in which the two movements are built is otherwise rather different: for an analysis of No. 36's first movement, see *Haydn in England 1791–1795*, pp. 426ff.

No. 42's Allegro moderato has been called 'one of the most massive of all Haydn's movements[; it is] expansive, almost leisurely, and has a Mozartean wealth of themes' (Rosen, op. cit., p. 363). In order to allow himself this 'Mozartean' luxury, however, Haydn has recourse to some intricate thematic and motivic relationships between his various new themes. Here is the opening:

Several things may be noted. The gravity of the first subject is, of course, greatly enhanced by that ambiguous *c* flat in bar 3. In a subject with as much disparity as this one, Haydn takes care to ensure unity by dwelling on the little figure with the turn (bars 4–5); even when it is altered, as in bar 10, the left hand of the piano remains constant. Although, after the first two bars, the music does not return to the root position of the tonic until bar 12, Haydn prepares this return to the tonic in a subtle way: the bass figure of bars 3–4 (♩) ♩ ♩ ♩ | ♩ ♩ ♩ 𝄽 (a, b) (which is broken down into two segments, *a* and *b*) is in bar 11 stretched into *four* crotchets and the return to E flat strengthened by removing the rest (as in bars 4, 5, 9, 10). Having strayed so far from the root position of the tonic, Haydn now remains in it comfortably, with a lyric violin subject (see example overleaf). The tonic is celebrated by a number of clear motivic and harmonic links with the beginning. The broken triad of bar one is found, in slightly changed layout, in the second half of bars 12–13 and, in diminution, in the accompaniment of the piano, r.h. in bar 16: 𝄽 ♩ ♩ ♩ = ♫♫.

As the exposition begins to unfold in long, majestic sections, we may observe that the leisureliness on the outside is matched with almost ferocious motivic concentration on the inside. At bars 33ff. we have:

The upward progression of a fourth in the piano part of bars 33f. (*g''–c'''*) is, naturally, the fourth progression of the piano r.h. in bar 1 (*e* flat–*a* flat); but this progression is now coupled with the figure of bar seven plus the rhythm of bar 2, second half: while the accompaniment in the left hand (bars 33ff.) is the figure of the left hand, upper part, in bars 1–2. By the time we arrive at the dominant, Haydn is using the little figure of bar 10:

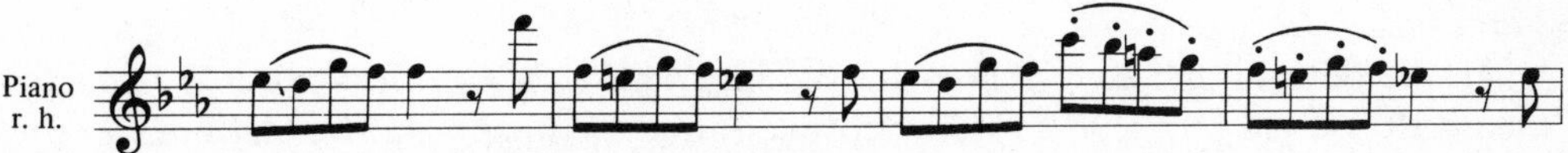

We have pointed out only the more obvious thematic and motivic interrelationships between the various parts of this exposition, but the student will, if he subjects the work to a thorough analysis, find many more, some of them of a Bachian complexity. On the other hand, this dominant minor subject looks forward to Schubert and the Austro-German *Biedermeier*:

The virtuoso piano writing reminds one, in its particular construction, of a similar passage, the opening of Sonata No. 62 (1794) for Therese Jansen (see *Haydn in England 1791–1795*, p. 450); it is perhaps no accident that the beginning of that Sonata has a very similar *Urlinie* to that of our Trio (and thus, of course, to Trio 36) and is in the same key. Obviously the key of E flat had definite associations for Haydn, and a certain similarity of mood in all three works will be noted: grandeur, a certain massive approach, and what Harry Halbreich calls 'une écriture somptueuse et riche, d'un souffle large'.

In the development we follow up the hint of another great work in E flat, the 'Drum Roll' Symphony of 1795, where we found excursions into C flat both in the Menuet and in the (later removed) original ending to the Finale. In our Trio, Haydn allows himself the tonal luxury of modulating from the dominant (B flat) to C flat as follows – the *Terzverwandschaft* of the jump from B flat to the dominant of G flat is obvious –

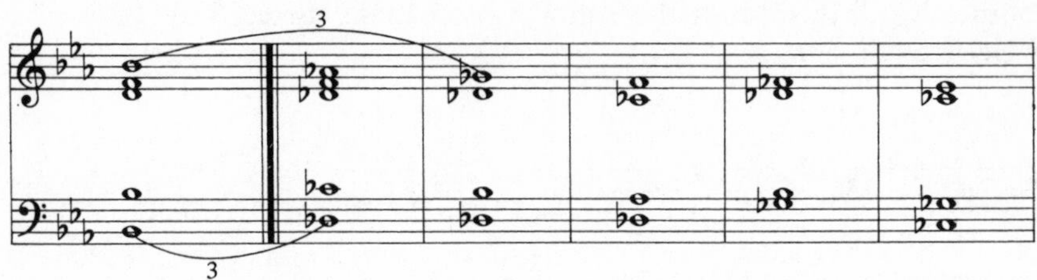

It is as bold a harmonic sequence as in any of the pages written in London. The rest of the development is, harmonically, as unexpected as this modulation, and even the recapitulation is reached in a surprising fashion – at the end of a long sequence that brings us from F minor to the dominant of C minor, we slide unobtrusively into E flat and the reprise. Although the piano part, and occasionally also the violin, are technically not easy, the movement as a whole is not nearly as virtuoso as those written for Therese Jansen (Mrs Bartolozzi) presumably in the same year.

The slow movement (Andante con moto) is in the submediant major, i.e. a third-related key. Its asymmetrical construction (4+6 bars) is marked by a breadth of dynamic range and a sense of harmonic *largesse* that shows (if we need to be reminded) that this is real *Spätstil* in Haydn:

It will not be thought exaggerated if we mention a subtle thematic connection between this theme and the beginning of the first movement, *viz.* the identical *Urlinie.* In I, E flat → A flat → E flat → D → E flat; while in II, E → A → E → D → E. If both 'lines' are placed together, the relationship will be clear (the bar numbers are placed in brackets above the notes):

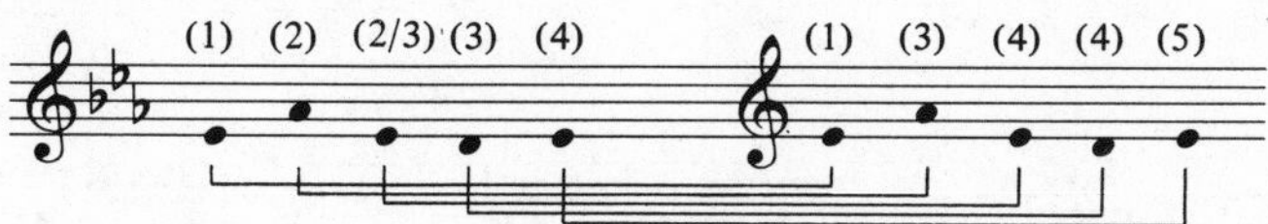

We consider that the succession, which is not a series of casual notes but the real 'high' and 'low' points of melodic and motivic stress, is too close between the movements to be considered fortuitous. Perhaps it happened at the unconscious level.

Formally this swiftly moving slow movement is tripartite, with a turbulent middle section in which demisemiquavers predominate, this more rapid motion carrying over to the varied repetition of the 'A' section. The chromatic variants with which Haydn now provides the main theme, e.g.

appear wilful almost to the point of eccentricity, but they are typical of the composer's last thoughts in this (for him) intensely personal medium, this display (as it were) of public privacy. The movement leads with a pause into the Finale. Here we have the 'German style' once more, a minuet tempo speeded up to scherzo speed and with a rhythmic freedom that is deceptive: there are two eight-bar phrases to the main theme, but rhythmically they are both highly assymetrical. Although the piano part breaks the crotchet pulse in bars 4–5 nevertheless the underlying rhythm is five bars of ♩ ♩ ♩ ♩ ♩ ♩ (notice the contradictory phrasing, the top line for piano r.h., the bottom line the violin and occasionally the 'cello) followed by three bars of ♩ ♩ ♩ ♩ ♩ ♩.

There is a gruff middle section in E flat minor in which the theme is with the violin, and even the 'cello has a rather independent part. The lead-back from E flat minor to the recapitulation (for the movement is in A–B–A–Coda form) is so bizarre, tonally, that Haydn removes all the accidentals from the key signature:

86
f
91
98
pizz.
[p]
pizz.
[p]
p

Actually, what Haydn has done is to modulate once again into C flat major (as in the first movement); but since the piano is alone here, he 'spells' the section in B major, moving enharmonically to flat keys at bar 96 *et seq.* so that the strings can come in 'normally' at bar 103. The whole passage is one further example of the tonal realms that Haydn explores with relish in these late chamber works, and of which we shall encounter equally daring examples in the last three 'Bartolozzi' Trios and, especially, in the string Quartets, Opp. 76 and 77.[1]

The *AMZ*, in its issue of 19 June 1799, devoted a long review to the Breitkopf edition of the Trio, which reads as follows:

> *Sonate pour le Clavecin ou Pianoforte avec un Violon et Violoncelle, composée par Joseph Haydn, Leipsic, chez Breitkopf et Härtel.* Op. 88 (Pr. 1 Rthlr.).
>
> The present Sonata is herewith engraved for the first time from the autograph manuscript which Haydn sent to the publisher. And his spirit reveals itself unmistakably in the work. The character of the first Allegro moderato in E flat is altogether gentle; it occasionally rises to a restrained vivacity. Out-of-the-way modulations, transitions and turns-of-phrase in all the three movements of which this Trio consists, reveal the hand of the master. The immediate succession of augmented triads, such as

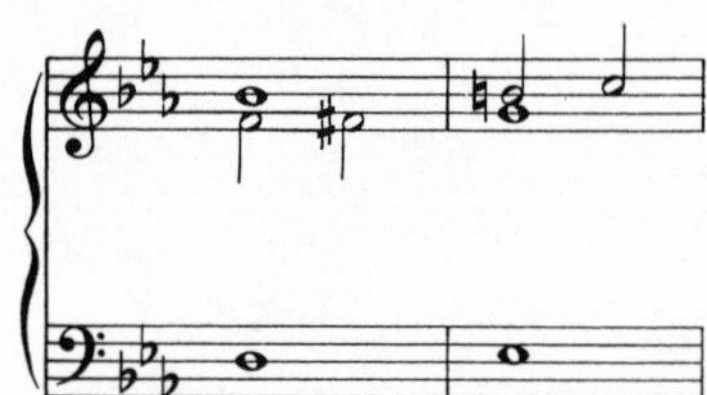

1 The first recording of this great work took place, incredibly, in 1971, as part of a complete recording of the last sixteen piano Trios played on instruments of Haydn's period and using our new critical edition by Doblinger. (*Les Seize Derniers Trios*, Valois Album GBM 15, four LPs, Paris 1971, played by Huguette Dreyfus on a Viennese pianoforte of Carl Schneider owned by Paul Badura-Skoda, Eduard Melkus, violin, and Elisabeth Vogt, violoncello; with notes by Harry Halbreich; the set won the Grand Prix du Disque for 1971; see the review by Marc Vignal in *Haydn Yearbook* IX [1973].) An earlier plan, to record a large selection of Haydn's trios, was begun under the supervision of Mr Walter Legge, that great gramophone pioneer, in 1940; it was called 'The Haydn Trio Society' and one volume, containing Trios 40, 43 and 45, played by Lili Kraus (piano), Szymon Goldberg (v.) and Anthony Pini (vc.) and containing admirable notes by Cecil Gray, was issued by subscription on Parlophone records. Unfortunately the beginning of the Japanese War found Miss Kraus in Asia; she was interned for the duration in a Japanese prison camp, and the whole project had to be discontinued. (From information received from Miss Kraus in 1952.)

of which the former is presented in the first inversion and the latter in root position (cf. bars 56 and 57 in the first part of the Allegro), is as striking as it is new. The lowering of the major ninth to the minor in [bar 214 of the same movement]

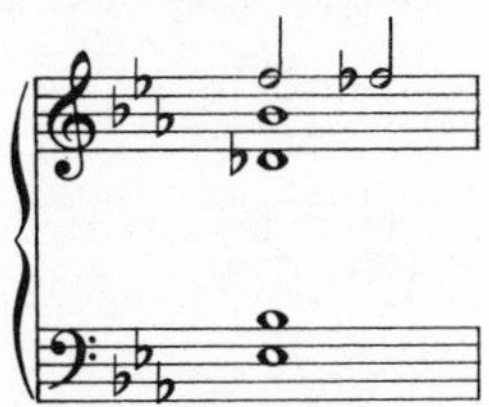

and no less the flowing transition from the diminished seventh to the augmented sixth in [bar 45] of the Andante

– we here cite the chord in root position but Haydn in fact uses the third inversion of it

– also deserve mention as harmonic rarities.

If the Andante con moto, the character of which is between gentle and happy, is played without a long pause after the Allegro, the key of C major (in which the movement is written) makes a pleasant contrast after the preceding key of E flat. The preparational transition between the Andante and the final Presto is surprisingly beautiful. In this Presto one notes Haydn's well-known learned manner; here the theme is sometimes set with a countersubject above it in counterpoint (dans le Contrepoint au dessus du Sujet), sometimes in retrograde motion (all'roverscio), sometimes with variations, and often in other keys.

It will perhaps be of value to some readers to illustrate with a few short examples in order to make more easily comprehensible to them things of this kind, the nature of which they perhaps understand only vaguely.

Thema und Subjekt [Theme and Subject]

Contrepoint au dessus du Sujet

Das Vorige mit Veränderung: [The same, varied:]

Das Subjekt umgekehrt: [The Subject inverted:]

Das Vorige auf andere Art: [The same in another fashion:]

Haydn, however, possesses the ability to give an attractive aspect to such movements, which some might wrongly hold to be empty pieces of scholastic virtuosity. Taking this into account, one ought to judge only the whole work of art, in all its aspects; then one will be satisfied.

From this and what we have said above it is clear that this Sonata is intended primarily for the fine connoisseurs and those who appreciate the learned manner. The technical difficulties that some will find in the work will be primarily the chromatic runs and modulations to very remote keys (usually in flats), in the ties that one occasionally encounters, and in the above mentioned learned manner.

The accompaniment of the violin is necessary because there are small solo passages for it in the first and last movements; but the violoncello can if necessary be omitted.

The Sonata's engraving is clean, clear and generally correct. To avoid incorrectness of execution with the violin we would, however, point out that in the piano part at the end of the second *reprise* in the Presto, the number 'I' ought to be one bar lower. [There follows the *incipit* of the work.]

Everyone is agreed that the last three piano Trios, dedicated to Therese Bartolozzi, *née* Jansen, are the most brilliant musically and the most difficult, technically, of all the works in this form. Undoubtedly the personality of the pianist to whom the set is dedicated influenced Haydn's texture, piano writing, and perhaps even the overall style: there must have been a real sense of panache about her playing, which we can sense dimly not only in these sparkling Trios but also in the final piano Sonatas, especially No. 62 in E flat. Perhaps the first of the Bartolozzi Trios, No. 43 in C major, is the most virtuoso of the three and the one apparently written for Therese's agile hand and quick brain. Formally we would note that the broad first-movement sonata form of Nos. 43 and 44 (that of No. 45 is in a different form) each contain as their highpoint, in the development section, a dramatic pause (or fermata) which leads to an intense statement of the theme in some third-related key: in our No. 43, at present under discussion, the main theme

is a series of segments which are, in the customary way, broken up and used separately. The section beginning with the upbeat of bar 5 is used for a very Baroque passage at the beginning of the development, which ends on the dominant of C and a pause; whereupon the main theme is brought in, but in A flat. It is the dramatic surprise in a movement full of drama and even fuller of surprises. The continuation of our musical examples leads to a passage in which the piano's right hand has a series of octaves. Rosen (op. cit., pp. 351f.) thinks they are intended glissando (as in various passages of this kind in Beethoven's works, notably in the 'Waldstein' Sonata, Op. 53), but in fact on a shallow-key fortepiano they can be played 'straight'. In the example below, we would draw attention to the breathtaking modulation in the second half of bar 16; Haydn draws our attention to it, too, by giving it a *sforzato* accent:

The thematic and motivic relationship between the various sections of this apparently disparate exposition is as tight as in the previous Trio in E flat. The techniques for increasing the overall tension are many and various in Haydn, but one sure of automatic success in his hands is the gradual speeding-up of metre which we noted in connection with the English piano Trios (*Haydn in England 1791–1795*). In No. 43, we begin with a crotchet and quaver metre, to which semiquavers are sometimes added; by bar 12 we have moved to a permanent base of semiquavers and in bar 14 to triplet semiquavers, which keep up until the end of the exposition, when for the 'closing material' (as the text books used to call it) it slides back to straight semiquavers. Out of the *Urlinie* of the main subject we now have a compressed statement in the dominant (opposite, top). The rolled chord in the piano's right hand is Haydn's hint to remember the rolled opening chords of the first subject. Similarly the grace note phrase of bar one now becomes

and the 'wrist-breaking' (Rosen) repetition in octaves for the piano's right-hand, and in turn

All of this is also in clear relationship to the octave passage in the piano at bars 12ff., quoted above.

We have hardly the space at our disposal to enter into the many technical problems that this movement posed for most pianists, but we would, *en passant*, draw attention to the rapid crossing of the hands that takes place at bars 32ff., etc. but particularly 33f. where the right hand swoops below the left at this tempo: *ff* .

We have the space only to illustrate one point. After a highly contrapuntal development, the music moves from *ff* (bar 70) to *p* and over a steady movement of semiquaver triplets in the piano's l.h., the music moves at first in slow lines and then in ever increasing tension towards the recapitulation; the whole organization is economical yet of a tremendous potency:

75

77
crescendo
[crescendo]
crescendo

[recapitulation]
79
f
p
f
p
f
[f]
f
p
f
f

The tripartite slow movement is in the submediant major, whose quiet principal theme is full of interesting accents (>) where one does not expect them. For example:  (bar 12). The middle section in A minor is of a restlessness and a temperamental angularity that set off admirably the more lyrical flanking sections. Two passages of a curious nature occur, and both seem to suggest the use of the *sopra una corda* pedal which Haydn, of course, had on his grand piano given him by Longman & Broderip which he took back to Vienna in 1795 (piano part only shown); the first is:

while the second is near the end, with its skittish cadenza:

This is almost like the extravagant cadenzas that a *primas* of a Hungarian (Gypsy) band introduces at the climax of his variations; it must have seemed exotic, if not downright eccentric, to the listeners of 1796 and 1797.

In the boisterous Finale, we are back on terra firma, and to the virtuoso rondo of which, by now, Haydn was a supreme master. 'Everything about the movement is unexpected', writes Rosen (358f.): 'the opening theme is an enchanting joke, with the harmony changing to make accents on off-beats, an angular melody that appears at times in the wrong register, and a scherzando rhythm that allows the melody to start when one is least ready for it. The style of writing for the piano in this movement is, at times, close to the Beethoven of Op. 31, No. 1.' We would draw attention to a new technical device which, in the later nineteenth and early twentieth centuries, was to become standard practice, to wit, writing the cross-beams of the notes *through the bar-line* if in that way clarity of line can be more easily obtained. A typical example is as follows (note that the violin and the 'cello do not yet follow this notation, which must have looked freakish in the extreme when it first appeared in the authentic Longman & Broderip print):

We find this notation in the Finale of Beethoven's Trio, Op. 1. The first edition (copy used: Gesellschaft der Musikfreunde) is written as follows (piano r.h. only is noted here):

We would put it forward tentatively as an excellent and novel way of notation that Haydn may have learned from looking at his former pupil's Op. 1. We will return to another point in that tremendously talented Op. 1 to which, we believe, Haydn had recourse in his Quartets, Op. 76. If Haydn was possibly indebted to Beethoven for the across-bar-line notation, we would close this brief analysis of Trio No. 43 with the following quotation, the end of a dashing *ff* passage where Haydn actually repeats the *ff* in bar 224; in listening to it, who does not think immediately of Beethoven?

218 [Presto]

V.

Vc.

[Presto]

Pf.

223

ff

p

It is certainly one of the most brilliant and, in its nature, symphonic movements of the whole series; it must have displayed Therese Bartolozzi's technique to perfection, just as it displays in full radiance the unbelievably youthful energy of its composer (who was nearly sixty-five years of age when he composed it and over that age when it first saw the light of day in London).

Trio No. 44

This, the second of the Bartolozzi set, is in E major, always a key for Haydn's special thoughts (a few examples: Sonata III, 'Mulier, ecce filius tuus, et tu, ecce mater tua!', from *The Seven Words*; the opening of Part III in *The Creation* with the three solo flutes; Vespina's Aria, 'Ho tesa la rete', in Act II of *L'infedeltà delusa*). Obviously all composers associate keys with special emotions, and C major for Haydn meant as definite an emotion as did E major: if the former might be summed up as martial, dynamic, brilliant, open, the latter might be said to have a peculiarly soft, radiant character. It is an accident that both Haydn's Symphonies in E major (No. 12 of 1763, No. 29 of 1765) open *piano*? The fantastic, fairy-tale world of Trio 44's opening is, then, in a key rare in Haydn but not so rare as in Mozart (whose use of the key is equally reserved for unusual thoughts: cf. the Chorus 'Placido è il mar' in *Idomeneo*). The strange, harp-like effect of the pizzicato strings, the 'staccato assai' bass of the piano, and the legato top line of the piano and the series of grace notes that set off that legato line – all is calculated for an eighteenth-century piano with its metallic bass and ringing alto register; but a careful pianist today can make the passage sound as eccentrically brilliant as its composer intended.

The repetition for unaccompanied piano has a chromaticism that is emotionally quite different from Mozart's chromaticism; the difference is so striking that one wonders how passing sharps can sound so different in the hands of two contemporaries; but they do. That which is emotional, anguished, nervous in Mozart sounds experimental, slightly bizarre but entirely unfrightened in Haydn.

We have noted that in the middle of the development sections of Trios 43 and 44, there is a large climax based on a third-related key. In No. 44, the climax is in A flat, and occurs shortly after the development section has begun. Actually A flat is really G sharp major, or the pivotal third between tonic and dominant, but Haydn prefers to 'spell' the passage in A flat, which he does by changing the whole signature before bar 44. The main theme, now in this third-related key, is played *f*, with *arco* strings and without the grace notes. The effect is enormous.

The Allegretto that follows has a curiously nightmarish quality about it. The strings and piano start an old-fashioned ritornello from which the piano breaks away, to continue alone in an eerie passage of mostly two-part writing, reminiscent stylistically of Haydn's early, C. P. E. Bach-influenced piano music (e.g. Sonata No. 30 [XVI: 19]), with a huge gap between top and bottom. But there is something very odd indeed about this music; it has the same spooky quality of the abandoned and empty dwarfs' quarters in the Gonzaga *Reggia* at Mantua or indeed of the dwarfish pictures in which Faustino Bocchi so sinisterly excelled. The strings suddenly join in the proceedings after Haydn has settled into the relative major. The insistence on long chains of dotted figures is equally unsettling, but the end, with its wildly eccentric cadenza, has to be heard (or seen) to be believed:

In a sensitive analysis of the curiously divergent stylistic elements that make up this Allegretto, Charles Rosen writes (op. cit., p. 360):[1]

> . . . The relationship of the classical style to the preceding Baroque and to the Romantic that was to come is posed by this piece; one of the most startling creations of Haydn, it is a passacaglia like no other. It is Baroque in formal character, in the unchanging, relentless rhythm of the bass maintained until the final cadence, in its 'terraced' dynamics, in its superimposition of one rhythm on another with each remaining absolutely distinct, and in its use of a sequential

1 Reprinted by permission of Faber and Faber Ltd and The Viking Press, Inc.

pattern as a generating force within the main theme itself and not only in its development. The music is classical, however, in its firmly established movement to the relative major, articulated by the introduction of new melodic material, and in its wealth of dynamic accents serving to vary the pulse. Finally, it is Romantic in its tension, keyed to a steadily higher pitch than most eighteenth-century works could bear, in its dynamics which give the impression not only of a step-by-step ascent but of a continuous *crescendo*, and, above all, in the fact that the final cadence after a fermata serves, not to resolve the excitement as a Baroque ending generally does, but to increase it through a series of Baroque but elaborate flourishes that offer a resolution only with the violent final chord. To the extent that Romantic style meant the reintroduction of Baroque procedures and textures modified by a classical sense of climax, the movement may be said to be already Romantic. This work is a warning against too unified and dogmatic a view of style, and reminds us how elements may remain dormant ready to reappear at any moment as an artist goes back to the day before yesterday to find something newer and more progressive.

The subtly irregular has by now become part of Haydn's normal musical procedure: the theme of the Finale is in twelve bars (4+8) and the upbeats are, as so often in these late trios, marked with an accent (>). In the usual three-part form (A–B–A–Coda), the 'B' section is once again an impassioned violin melody in the sonorous middle range of the instrument (mostly on the *d*-string), and in the tonic minor. In the middle of this section, we find ourselves in the unbelievable key of E flat minor (note: E minor *via* F sharp minor to E flat minor), which Haydn reaches by shifting the key signatures:

Note that the strings are silent during this escapade, leaving all the harmonic shifts to the 'well-tempered' piano.

In all this tonal intricacy, we should not lose sight of the fact that the whole movement is deliberately on a small scale, as indeed Haydn always treated the piano Trio as a miniature form – filled with delights and subtleties and containing some of his most adventurous thoughts, but all within the modest scope of the form as he knew it. That is why Haydn so often employs a kind of German dance, or minuet, for the final movements (as in the E-major Trio under discussion). We shall see that in the final work, the Finale actually bears the title 'In the German style'.

Trio No. 45

We presume the beautiful E-flat Trio No. 45 to be the last of the series; at any rate Haydn chose it to close this brilliant trilogy dedicated to Mrs Bartolozzi. In this Op. 75 (as Longman & Broderip numbered it), we have a microcosmic view of Haydn's art: if we study these last three Trios, it will be seen that their composer has managed to infuse into them an extraordinary amount of different emotions, a profound knowledge of harmony, form and counterpoint, and a finely developed sense of instrumental sound. What could be more different from the grotesque middle movement of the previous Trio than the Poco Allegretto with which Trio 45 begins? Here we seem to return to the old *sonata da chiesa* form, with its opening slow movement, something Haydn had long ago abandoned in the symphony (the last such 'church sonata' work was composed in 1768) but to which he occasionally has recourse in the piano trio: of the works in this form composed for London, Nos. 31, 33, 37 and 39 open with slow movements, as does the E flat minor Trio 41 discussed *supra*.

In this formally interesting movement, Haydn artfully combines song form with variation: basically in the customary A–B–A–Coda structure, it turns out that 'B' is a

variant of 'A', to wit the main theme given to the violin and in the tonic minor. The coda contains one of these whimsical passages in which these late trios abound; here, it is the lead-back to the very last statement of the theme, which even now is subjected to further exploitation and development (note the off-beat *fz* and the variant of the theme which accompanies itself at bars 171ff.) – see example opposite.

In the above example, it may be noted how finely Haydn has calculated that the *forte* chord of the piano left hand (which begins one bar before our example) will die out and so contribute to the general *decrescendo*.

In our brief analysis of the piano Trios composed in London, we established that in his older years Haydn regarded the third-related keys enharmonically: in Trio 45 we have a middle movement in B major, which is the submediant of D sharp major (in turn the enharmonic equivalent of E flat major). The movement is marked 'Andantino ed innocentemente'. Among its many other noteworthy features, it contains proof that Haydn wanted his appoggiature even in six–eight time to be executed as 'long' grace notes; the theme writes out the grace note the first time and then abbreviates it with a semiquaver appoggiatura:

The movement begins like a classic Italian serenade, first the accompaniment with the tune, then the voice (in this case the violin); but it soon develops into a much more ambiguous piece of music. Before we realize it the supposedly innocent theme is used with itself in canon (as at bars 21ff.), gradually shifts from five sharps to three flats and ends in E flat; or rather it stops on the dominant and leads directly into the Finale; as often in such a movement, there is an elaborate little 'Eingang' for the piano on the pause just before the end.

The Finale is a sturdy and rather bellicose German dance, marked 'Finale in the German Style' on the first edition. Yet although it is a bar-room tune of the heavier sort, we note that as in the slow movement the tune is used canonically with itself: *ars*, even *ars popularis* [or as the German scholar would have said *corpus musicae popularis Germanicae*] *sine scientia nihil est*:

We may point out a charming little conceit: Haydn changes the time from three–four to two–four, which (as in the Minuet of Symphony No. 65) he does without changing the bar-lines but by using *fz*. There is an original footnote here in the first edition. It says: 'It is necessary to observe that the Figures 1, 2, 3, 4, 5 in the 5th stave only allude to the Time which is Presto and the Performer will find great facility by reckoning the Numbers in mind while playing the passages thus mark'd'. The connoisseur will find many references, some ironic, some tenderly affectionate, to the *deutscher Tanz* of the period; such a passage as

must have sounded an echo in every heart in Germany and Austria; to us it brings back nostalgic memories of the ballroom scene in *Don Giovanni* (Orchestra III playing

)

and many other passages in the Viennese classical world. (Was the set of three appoggiature a kind of a cue to the dancers that the *deutscher Tanz* was about to begin?) and of course it looks forward to the famous wine scene in Autumn of *The Seasons*, 'Nun tönen die Pfeifen und wirbelt die Trommel, hier kreischet die Fiedel, da schnarret die Leier, und dudelt der Bock . . .'.

Thus we end our necessarily brief survey of the latest Haydn piano Trios. Although they did not contribute anything to the development of the piano trio as a *trio*, 'the musical contents', as Sir Donald Tovey asserted in 1928, 'are, with a few early exceptions, glorious; . . . [they] are far richer than the quartets in fine specimens of his smaller forms, such as alternating variations, sectional rondos, lyric "A, B, A" slow movements, and, above all, movements breaking off and leading into finales, a dramatic event that only twice happens in the quartets, but always coincides with Haydn's finest imagination in these smaller works. . . . The main thing to bear in mind is that Haydn takes the view that a quartet is a symphony, whereas a piano trio is an accompanied solo . . .'. 'They belong to an entirely different species,' wrote Cecil Gray in 1940, 'and this is probably the explanation of the neglect with which the trios have met in modern times, for they have been judged according to string quartet instead of sonata standards – from the standpoint of ensemble instead of solo texture – and have consequently been found wanting. But taken for what they are – the musical equivalent of drawings or etchings with a wash of colour – they hold their own with any other category of the master's work.'[1]

The Trumpet Concerto (1796)
(VIIe: 1)

Concerto for *Clarino* [in fact keyed trumpet] in E flat major. 2 flutes, 2 oboes, 2 bassoons, 2 horns, 2 *ripieno* trumpets, timpani and strings. I *Allegro*. II *Andante*. III *Finale: Allegro*.

The history of Haydn's famous Concerto for trumpet is as curious as any in that composer's career. From almost total obscurity it has now become his most popular recorded work and is, in fact, the only concerto by Haydn that rivals the concertos by Vivaldi, Bach, Mozart and Tchaikovsky (to name four whose names are constantly on the best-selling concerto lists). A similar situation obtains with regard to the two 'cello

1 The literature on Haydn's piano Trios is remarkably small; the essential works have been cited in *Haydn in England 1791–1795*. Here we quote from Tovey's great article on Haydn in *Cobbett's Cyclopedic Survey of Chamber Music*, London 1928, I, 542f., and from Gray, *A Limited Edition of Haydn's Trios*, London 1940, pp. 3f. Harry Halbreich, *Joseph Haydn, Les Seize Derniers Trios*, Paris (Vincennes) 1971. Rosen, *The Classical Style*, p. 360; Rosen's is the only serious, full-scale article on the Haydn trios to appear in many years.

concertos (in C and D), both of which were all but totally forgotten in, say, 1796, and both of which are nowadays best-sellers (though not reaching the incredible popularity of the Trumpet Concerto).

Haydn composed this work for a friend in the Viennese Court Orchestra: Anton Weidinger. The autograph manuscript, which is now in the Gesellschaft der Musikfreunde, is dated 1796, and it is supposed that it is Haydn's last concerto. This is, however, by no means established. The Elssler Catalogue of 1805 lists two concertos that are nowhere found in the earlier *Entwurf-Katalog* and thus may be presumed to have been written after the London visits: (1) the Trumpet Concerto; (2) *Concerto a due corni* in E flat, of which the *incipit* of this, alas, lost work is

The latter work existed as late as 1799. In Johann Traeg's printed *Verzeichnis* of that year we find, on p. 51, 'Concerti à Corno. Princip.', under which is this entry: '2 Haydn (Gius.) à 2 Corni di Caccia Con-/cert. 2 V. Viola e B[asso]. in Es. . . . 3 [fl.]'. If in fact this Double Concerto is *not* a late work – and the orchestration (strings alone) suggests that it is not – perhaps Haydn had forgotten it entirely, saw the entry in Traeg's *Verzeichnis*, sent Elssler for a copy of the Concerto, and thus could include it in the 1805 Catalogue. This lost Double Horn Concerto is also mentioned in an interesting MS. catalogue made by Elssler which seems, unbelievably, to have escaped everyone's attention up to now. We reproduce the little catalogue here, since it is not without a certain interest in that there is at least one work mentioned here which is not in the Elssler Catalogue of 1805: namely, a Bassoon Concerto. It is listed under the Double Concerto, as follows:

	[Stücke]
Waldhorn Concerten ein Duett	2
Flauten Concert	1
Fagott Concert	1

Moreover, we have autograph confirmation that Haydn really did write a (lost) concerto for bassoon. In the little catalogue in Haydn's hand – reproduced in facsimile at the beginning of Hoboken's Volume I (1957) – we note

[Concerten für]	
Waldhorn	2
Flaute	1
Fagott	1

Now this lost Bassoon Concerto is also missing in the *Entwurf-Katalog* (it is even missing in Hoboken, although he published the above-mentioned autograph catalogue in facsimile) and is possibly a post-London work. It is, unfortunately, improbable that we shall rediscover either the lost Double Horn Concerto or the lost Bassoon Concerto: if we consider on what a slender, slender thread the Trumpet Concerto has survived – namely, one single source, Haydn's autograph[1] (see pl. 8 and p. 240) – we may be thankful that we have at least that great and revolutionary work.

1 Haydn's concertos have survived almost by accident, and often in one single source: the Horn Concerto in D (VIId: 3) of 1762 has survived only in Haydn's autograph; the 'Cello Concerto in C (VIIb: 1) only in one contemporary MS. in Prague, the Lira Concertos (VIIh: 1–5) in one source each in the Esterházy Archives. They were all occasional works, and probably written for friends of Haydn's; only one 'cello concerto, and a few of the harpsichord (organ) concertos, were ever printed in Haydn's lifetime.

Weidinger seems to have invented a keyed trumpet in the year 1793. Geiringer (1947, p. 283) describes the instrument as having 'holes in the wall of the tube that are closed by keys. As a rule there are five such keys, which raise the pitch by successive semitones. They are so arranged that the performer can play them with his left hand while holding the trumpet in his right.' Many keyed trumpets have survived: they proved very popular with military bands, but of course once the valve trumpet became established in 1813, the keyed trumpet was doomed.

Naturally, instrument-makers and players had for long tried to find a way to increase the natural scale of the horn and trumpet. With the horn, they invented a tightly coiled instrument with crooks (*Inventionshorn*), the bell now being easily reached with the right hand; when the hand was inserted into the bell, the tone could be lowered by as much as a whole tone. This process was not practical for the trumpet, however, though German sources indicate that

> the tube of the trumpet was now turned into more coils, with this advantage, that by shortening the original length of the tube, a much greater number of notes could be produced in stopping than before, especially in the middle octave.[1]

But at the time Haydn wrote his Concerto, hardly anyone could play anything but the normal *clarino* or trumpet, which was used in B flat, C, D, E flat, E and (rarely) also in F and G – and very occasionally in other keys as well: a rare use of an A trumpet has been mentioned in *Haydn in England 1791–1795* (p. 357). In England, we hear (in Parke's *Memoirs*) of a small slide which could be used to raise or lower the tone slightly. 'The imperfect note on the fourth of the key [written *g''*] on the trumpet has since been rendered perfect by Mr. Hyde's ingenious invention of a slide.' And Haydn's own trumpeters must have had something of the kind, for we find him constantly writing *b* below middle *c* (written) – e.g. Symphonies 86 and 95, 'Nelson' Mass – which the players must have produced by just such a slide.

Although our Concerto dates from 1796, it was some years before Weidinger decided to produce it in public. The concert took place at the Burgtheater a few days before Beethoven's first benefit concert – Weidinger's was on 28 March 1800 and Beethoven's on 2 April – and the announcement in the *Wiener Zeitung* of 22 March 1800 reads as follows:

> Musical Academy. The undersigned has been permitted to give a grand musical academy in the Imperial Royal National Court Theatre on 28 March. His intention on this occasion is to present to the world for the first time, so that it may be judged, an organized trumpet which he has invented and brought – after seven years of hard and expensive labour – to what he believes may be described as

1 'On the trumpet, as at present employed in the orchestra, with a retrospective view of the earlier methods of using it' by Karl Bargans, first trumpeter to the King of Prussia. *Harmonicon*, VIII (1830), p. 23. The date of the valve trumpet from Curt Sachs, *Handbuch der Musikinstrumentenkunde*. Leipzig 1920, pp. 260, 287. Parke II, 41. Bellini's *Norma* even requires two keyed trumpets (*a chiave*).

Mary Rasmussen, in an article entitled 'A Concertino for Chromatic Trumpet by Johann Georg Albrechtsberger', in *Brass Quarterly* V/3, 1962, pp. 104ff., writes about a work dated 1771 on the autograph which is now in the Esterházy Archives, Budapest, having been acquired by Prince Nicolaus II as part of the Albrechtsberger legacy in 1812. Embarrassing as it is to relate, this whole article is based on a misreading of the autograph, the title of which reads: 'Concertino in E♭. a cinque Stromenti Tromb[ula], Cemb[alo] [ed Archi] Del Sig: G: A:'. There is a similar 'Concertino' by Albrechtsberger (autograph '1769') in which the instrument 'Trombola' is written out; in another work of 1771 the instrument is called 'Crembalum'. The instrument is not, of course, a trumpet (or keyed trumpet), but a Jew's harp; see L. Somfai, 'Albrechtsberger–Eigenschriften in der Nationalbibliothek Széchényi, Budapest', in *Studia Musicologia* I, 1961, pp. 175ff. We have examined the manuscript in Budapest (1960) and the instrument is without question a Jew's harp (for which see the article 'Maultrommel' in *MGG*).

> perfection: it contains several keys [*Klappen*] and will be displayed in a concerto specially written for this instrument by Herr Joseph Haydn, Doctor of Music, and then in an Aria by Herr Franz Xav. Süssmayer, Kapellmeister in the actual service of the Imperial Royal Court Theatre; which concert Anton Weidinger, Imperial Royal Court and Theatre trumpeter, has the honour herewith to announce.

Fortunately the hand-bill for Weidinger's concert has survived in the Theater-Sammlung of the Austrian National Library; we reproduce the text in facsimile. Therese Gassmann sang, and also Haydn's bass singer in *The Creation*, Herr Weinmüller. The works produced were:

> 1) A brand new [*ganz neue*] Symphony by Herr JOSEPH HAYDN, Doctor of Music and Kapellmeister to His Highness the Prince of Esterhazi.
>
> 2) Herr Weidinger will play a Concerto on the organized trumpet of his invention, composed by the above Master.
>
> 3) Mlle. Gassmann will sing an aria by the late Herr Mozart.
>
> 4) A Symphony by Herr Joseph Haydn.
>
> 5) A Duet by the late Herr Mozart, sung by Mlle. Gassmann and Herr Weinmüller.
>
> 6) An Aria with accompaniment of organized trumpet, sung by Mlle. Gassmann, the words of which are by Herr Lieutenant v. Gamerra, poet of the Imperial Royal Court Theatre, the music by Herr Franz Xaver Süssmayer, Kapellmeister of the I. R. Court Theatre.
>
> 7) A Symphony by Herr Joseph Haydn.
>
> 8) A Sextett, composed by Herr Ferdinand Kauer for the organized trumpet, with another trumpet played by Herr Joseph Weidinger, four kettledrums played by Herr Franz Weidinger, two clarinets played by Herrn Haberl and Mesch, and a bassoon played by Herr Sedlatschek.
>
> 9) To close, a Symphony will be given.

As the reader has by now realized, there were hardly any reviews of concerts in Vienna, but we have a note about Weidinger in the *Historisches Taschenbuch. Mit besonderer Hinsicht auf die Oesterreichischen Staaten. Zweyter Jahrgang. Geschichte des Jahres 1802* (Vienna 1806, pp. 220f.):

> The court trumpeter Weidinger invented a keyed trumpet, on which all the half notes can be produced very purely and with certainty over a range of two octaves. Really an important improvement; but it appears that through using the keys, the trumpet's tone loses something of its characteristic and prominent strength, and approaches more closely the tone of a strong oboe.

We have interrupted the chronological order of our narrative so as to present the documents – many of them unknown to the scholarly world – of our Concerto in one group, rather than split them up into three sections: 1796, 1800, and 1802 (1806). In the forthcoming Chronicle, we shall note Weidinger's appearance at the fashionable Tonkünstler concerts in 1798 (Christmas Concerts). We know almost nothing of Haydn's relationship to Weidinger except that it was a friendly one. Weidinger's biographer, Richard Heuberger, discovered that Haydn was a witness at the marriage of the trumpeter's daughter in Vienna on 6 February 1797.[1]

Vox populi = vox Dei: surely not always, yet there is no doubt that Haydn's most popular concerto (and probably his most popular work nowadays) is also his best. It is a heavily symphonic work on a large scale, and the only concerto that can compete, as

1 *Die Musik*, Jahrgang 7/2 (1908), pp. 164ff.

Heute Freytag den 28ten März 1800.
wird
Herr Anton Weidinger,
k. k. Hof- und Theater-Trompeter,
im kaiserl. königl. National-Hof-Theater nächst der Burg
eine große musikalische Akademie
mit Produzirung
seiner organisirten Trompete
zu geben die Ehre haben.

Die hierinn vorkommenden Stücke sind folgende:

1) Eine ganz neue Symphonie von Herrn Joseph Haydn, Doktor der Tonkunst, und Kapellmeister bey Sr. Durchlaucht des Hrn. Fürsten v. Esterhazi.
2) Wird Herr Anton Weidinger ein Konzert auf der von ihm erfundenen organisirten Trompete, von der Komposition des obigen Meisters spielen.
3) Singt Mlle. Gaßmann eine Arie von weiland Hrn. Mozart.
4) Eine Symphonie von Herrn Joseph Haydn.
5) Ein Duett von weiland Herrn Mozart, gesungen von Mlle. Gaßmann, und Hrn. Weinmüller.
6) Eine Arie mit Begleitung der organisirten Trompete, gesungen von Mlle. Gaßmann, die Worte davon sind von Hrn. Lieutenant v. Gamerra, Dichter der k. k. Hoftheater, die Musik ist von Hrn. Franz Xaver Sußmayer, Kapellmeister der k. k. Hoftheater.
7) Eine Symphonie von Hrn. Joseph Haydn.
8) Ein Sextett, von der Komposition des Hrn. Ferdinand Kauer auf die organisirte Trompete gesetzt, sammt noch einer Trompete, von Hrn. Joseph Weidinger, vier Paucken, von Hrn. Franz Weidinger, zwey Klarinetten, von Hrn. Haberl und Mesch, dann einem Fagot, von Hrn. Sedlatscheck gespielt.
9) Wird zum Beschluß eine Symphonie gegeben werden.

Die Logen und gesperrten Sitze werden wie gewöhnlich bey der Kasse vergeben.

Die Eintrittspreise sind wie gewöhnlich.

Der Anfang ist um 7 Uhr.

The text of the announcement of Anton Weidinger's benefit concert given at the Burgtheater, Vienna, on 28 March 1800; on this occasion Weidinger gave the first public performance of Haydn's Trumpet Concerto, written for him in 1796.

it were, with Mozart's and Beethoven's on their orchestral and stylistic level: all the other extant Haydn concertos, except that for 'Cello in D of 1783, are much earlier works, the majority composed in the first part of the 1760s and even before. With its heavy orchestration, the Concerto is a typical work of the 1790s. Actually, it is not so utterly isolated a phenomenon as might at first be believed; it is quite isolated as a trumpet concerto, of course, simply because Haydn has available all the chromatic notes of the scale between sounding *b* flat below middle *c* and *b* flat″ (*c‴* if we reinstate one cancelled reading: Finale bars 216–7: *vide infra*); and this fact alone places it in a category of its own. But as far as a heavily orchestrated concerto for a solo wind instrument is concerned, it is not entirely isolated: there are other such concertos, such as the brilliant Bassoon Concerto in C by J. A. Koželuch, cousin of the better known Leopold Anton; or the Oboe Concerto in C attributed to Haydn (VIIg: C 1) – certainly not by Haydn but an attractive and bright work by a good minor master: both these works are scored for an orchestra with trumpets and timpani.

Being a supremely professional composer, Haydn takes care to provide a few bars in the opening tutti for the solo trumpet to 'warm up' – a typical detail for which solo trumpeters playing this difficult work have been thankful ever since Weidinger, when he attempted the first orchestral rehearsal. Apart from a low (sounding) *e* flat, with which the solo trumpet propels the first tutti into action, Haydn even manages to make the 'warm up' passage thematic (or, if you will, motivic) – see example overleaf. We note the brilliant orchestration, which looks like a great Salomon symphony: the

horn and trumpet parts skilfully divided, the viola totally emancipated from the bass, even the bassoon no longer a slave of the basso continuo; even the kettledrums have their own rhythm to support, as it were, the solo trumpet. This is Haydn's last extant purely orchestral piece (if we except the introductions to the oratorios), and it closes his long symphonic career with a blaze of autumnal colour. The following passage in the ritornello plays a significant part in the course of the movement, and it is the first hint, perhaps, that Haydn will in this extraordinary Concerto treat the trumpet not only like the old military and martial instrument of its long history but also – and this is a new feature – as capable of great poetry and nostalgia. Actually, using the trumpet nostalgically was to become a great Austrian tradition (Johann Strauss, Bruckner, but above all Mahler): here, we believe, is its entrance into music history in that new and surprising function. We cite the first entrance of the passage without the trumpet (with the trumpet we first encounter it at bars 72ff.):

The development winds up in a burst of virtuosity for the soloist, culminating in a scale leading up to sounding *d* flat‴. The lead-back to the recapitulation is of particular beauty, and we note the strange harmonic excursion at bars 114ff., to which the trumpet then provides the bass line (115–6), showing off its ability even to play sounding *c* flat. The tension provided by the long pedal point is increased by the fact that the actual *b* flat is sounded only by the timpani and horns; the other bass instruments have *d* (including low *D* in the 'cellos and basses: of course Haydn had five-string basses capable of going down to contra C under the bass clef) – it is a very peculiar and effective orchestral concept.

109
Fl.
Ob.
Fag.
a2
Imo Solo
p
Cor. Mib
Trbe. Mib
Timp. Mib/Sib
Clarino Solo Mib (Trba.)
I
V.
II
Va.
B.

The recapitulation proper begins in the last bar of our example. Although it was usual for the first movement of concertos to be technically the most difficult part of the work – Mozart's K. 503 is a typical case in point – Haydn had a different idea for his Trumpet Concerto. He saved the real piece of virtuoso showmanship for the Finale; partly this was in accordance with Haydn's concept of sonata form (heavy and intellectual first movement, poetic slow movement, light-hearted and brilliant finale) but more especially he must have arrived at this idea because of the nature of the solo instrument. Tiring easily, Weidinger was given music that is, especially towards the end of the movement, difficult –

– but not such as to wear out his lip. By making the first movement weighty and symphonic, Haydn can shift the burden to the orchestra, making the whole an orchestral concerto with obbligato solo trumpet. There is room for a cadenza. In view of the wildly tasteless cadenzas for this concerto which have been perpetrated in recent years, we propose that used for the first LP recording of the work, made in 1950 under our supervision with Helmut Wobisch as solo trumpet; Wobisch wrote his own cadenza – as no doubt did Weidinger – and we offer it as an example of the very best in the Viennese instrumental tradition. (We shall elaborate on the recording *infra*.)

The second movement, in which the horns, ripieno trumpets and timpani are omitted, is a quietly poetic Andante in six-eight time that gives us a curiously intense *déjà vu* feeling until we realize that quite the opposite is the case: the main theme is like a foretaste of the Austrian National Anthem ('Volkslied'), composed a year later, while the cadence at bars 7–8 seems to come out of *The Creation* (soprano Aria 'Nun beut die Flur'; horn part at bar 16):

[*The Creation*, No. 8 (bar 16): horns]

We must remind our readers once again of the astonishment with which musicians in 1796 heard a trumpet playing in A flat major and in diatonic notes: the effect must have been so incredible as to suggest some kind of Satanic prestidigitation. It is hard to realize how deeply ingrained in men's subconscious minds must have been the harmonic scale of the trumpet –

– and the profound shock of hearing what had by 1796 become more or less a fanfare instrument (*clarino* playing having died out except in some isolated German towns and in London, where it prevailed because of the unbroken Handelian tradition) playing poetic and even very nostalgic music in its middle register.

It is a short movement – again because of the nature of the solo instrument – and in what may be simply described as A–B–A concerto form. In the middle part Haydn modulates to the submediant, C flat major, and the notational problems for the trumpet in the key caused Haydn to make one of the few mistakes of his career. He wrote (flute part omitted):

The trumpet part should, of course, read

Another curiously ominous passage is just before the return of the 'A' section, where just as in the first movement at structurally the same place, Haydn introduces the sequence dominant – half a note up – dominant (V–VI♭–V); in the first movement it was *b* flat – *c* flat – *b* flat; here it is *e* flat – *f* flat – *e* flat. It is a striking instance of Haydn's ability to make a stylistic entity out of two disparate movements, and one other proof (if any further be required by the doubting) that by this period, the Viennese classical masters were engaged constantly in linking the whole of the sonata form movements together by such means. The harmonic deviation which Haydn chooses is so striking that every musical person will immediately grasp the connection.

The third movement is without any question one of the most fascinating, scintillating and formally brilliant rondos that Haydn ever composed – and he wrote upwards of one hundred which could compete in such a contest.

12

Fl. a2 *f*

Ob.

Fag. a2 *f*

Cor. Mib *f*

Trbe. Mib *f*

Timp. Mib - Sib *f*

V. I/II *f*

Va. *f*

Vc. e B.

Actually we are dealing with a sonata rondo, in that the return to the tonic and the 'A' section at bar 125 marks the beginning of a kind of development section. The climax of the movement from the point of difficulty is the following extract, in which a series of fanfares lead to a fiercely involved series of octave jumps in the solo part (opposite). Here in the marvellous climax there arises a technical point which is of sufficient importance to bring to the reader's attention. We have seen that the top range of Weidinger's trumpet was the *b* flat above the staff. Actually, it may have been higher when Weidinger first invented his trumpet, because this is what Haydn wrote in the solo trumpet part at bars 216–7, and although we are always of the opinion that the composer's last wishes must be respected, in this particular case we believe strongly that the original version, with its stupendous high *c'''*, should be restored. Here is the original version:

202
Fl.
Ob.
Fag.
Cor. Mib
Trbe. Mib
Timp. Mib - Sib
Trba. solo
I
V.
II
Va.
Vc. e B.
fz
[Vc]
210
f
Solo
[p]
p
tr

In point of fact, the first recording of the work, with George Eskdale as soloist, used this version and so did our above-mentioned recording with Helmut Wobisch.[1] Shortly afterwards, the solo trumpet is asked to execute a series of trills (bars 249ff.) which lead into a huge *fortissimo* tutti; the end of that tutti is equally astonishing, the music striding down the violins to land in a *pianissimo* passage with the whole orchestra in semiquavers; and into this nervous, tremolo-like texture the next tutti bursts with a vengeance:

1 The first recording, on the Columbia label, included only the last two movements. The solo part was played by George Eskdale with an unnamed orchestra conducted by Walter Goehr. In those days, it was considered that Haydn's orchestration, like Handel's, could hardly hold its own, and Goehr was engaged to rewrite the orchestra part, enlarging the band with clarinets, and generally making the orchestral part sound like a combination of Mozart and Beethoven. The record proved to be an astonishing best-seller; it was first issued in the 1930s. The first LP of the work, and the first to use the autograph as the basis for the text, was the Haydn Society recording (HSLP 1038) with the Orchestra of the Vienna State Opera conducted by Anton Heiller, first issued in 1951.

It is almost the classic instance of the 'surprise' technique in which Haydn excelled, but which soon became an integral part of the Beethovenian technique as well. After this *tour-de-force*, the tutti ends in a six–four chord and two bars of rest (*not* the place, obviously, for a cadenza) which are the buffer to introduce the last, sentimental farewell – a sad little farewell – to this enormously successful Haydnesque rondo; and what do we find but that famous *c* flat again, this time in the upper part of the accompaniment. A *crescendo* brushes away the nostalgia and a final tutti of electrical force concludes this spectacular, popular and yet profound masterpiece. We present this last page of the autograph in facsimile, as its conclusion marks the end of Haydn the purely orchestral composer, and as such it is a milestone in musical (and concerto) history – see overleaf.

A brief epilogue: after its first public performance at the Burgtheater on 28 March 1800, Haydn's Concerto disappears from history for 129 years. In 1929, the first edition, for trumpet and piano, was issued by a Belgian publisher, followed two years

The final page of the autograph of the Trumpet Concerto, Haydn's last purely orchestral work. Cf. plate 8.

later by a German edition for trumpet and orchestra.[1] The great impetus in restoring the work to the permanent repertoire was not the printed edition, but the aforementioned incomplete gramophone record. We believe it is the first instance of a standard work being resuscitated permanently by means of a recording. Issued in the middle 1930s, the Eskdale–Goehr record brought the work to popular attention in England and America. In 1949, there appeared a pocket score by Boosey & Hawkes, and by that time there were several editions available, including one by Breitkopf & Härtel. The critical recording by Wobisch–Heiller followed (though between it and the Eskdale there had appeared, after the Second World War, the first complete recording, on the English Columbia label – two twelve-inch 78 r.p.m. records, with Harry Mortimer as soloist), and this too became a best-seller (30,000 copies within four years). In 1972 there were some fifteen gramophone recordings available. The first attempt at a critical score was the Eulenburg edition (No. 798), edited by Hans Redlich in 1951; but there are many mistakes in that score.

1 Hoboken I, 536.

1 Joseph Haydn, wax bust (lost), *c.* 1799, by Franz Christian Thaller; from an old photograph. Originally in the possession of the composer and kept by him under a glass dome, the bust later belonged to the music publisher Tobias Haslinger, and finally to the Museum der Stadt Wien; it was destroyed in 1945. This bust is one of three versions by Thaller; cf. pl. 2 and colour pl. I.

2 Joseph Haydn, wax bust by Thaller (cf. colour pl. I), *c.* 1799, seen in profile.

3 Joseph Haydn, lithograph by A. Kunike, published by the artist and by Steiner & Co., Vienna. This interesting portrait was published after the composer's death; it is a good likeness, showing him without his habitual wig (its source is uncertain—possibly the lost plaster bust by Anton Grassi, 1799).

4 Joseph Haydn, anonymous silhouette, *c.* 1798(?), presented by the composer to his copyist, Johann Elssler (cf. pl. 28).

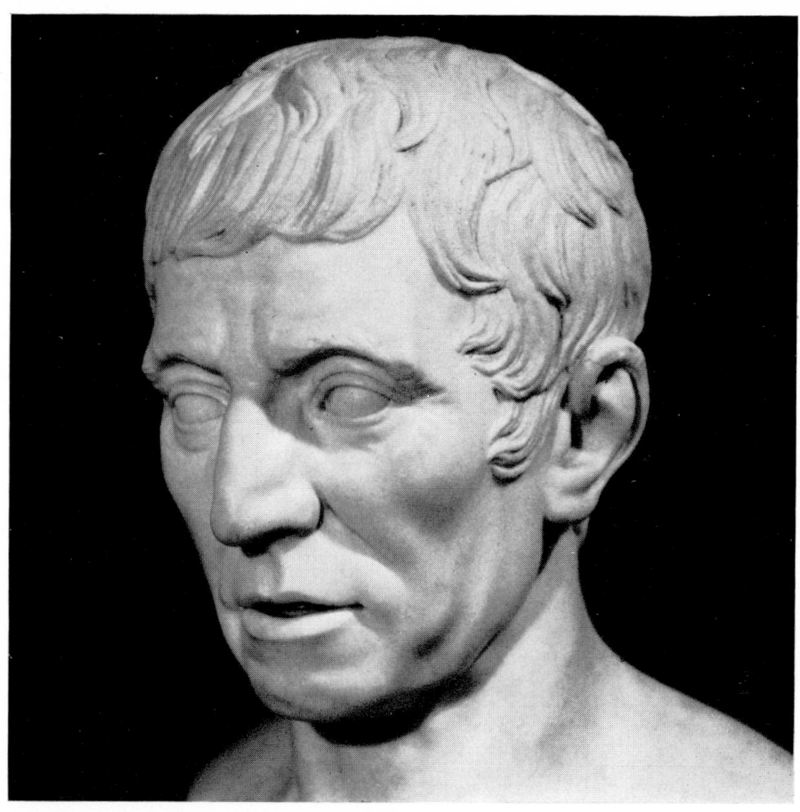

5 Joseph Haydn, life-size marble bust by August Robatz, *c.* 1799–1800, showing the composer without wig.

6 Joseph Haydn, engraving by Edmé Quenedey (1756–1830), inscribed (below) 'dess. au Physionotrace et Gravé par Quenedey, rue neuve des petits champs No. 1284 à Paris'.

7 The first page of the autograph of the *Missa in tempore belli* (1796) – the title-page is blank except for the title – inscribed by Haydn 'In Nomine Domini' and (right) 'Eisenstadt. 796. Haydn.'.

8 The first page of music from the autograph score of the Trumpet Concerto, inscribed 'In N[omine]. D[omini].' and (at right) 'Jos: Haydn mpria 796.'

9 The Bergkirche at Eisenstadt, lithograph by A. L. Jung, 1840; in this church the first performances of five of Haydn's late Masses were given.

10 The Piaristenkirche in the Josephstadt suburb of Vienna; coloured engraving by Carl Schütz, 1780. Here, on the Feast of St Stephen (26 December 1796), Haydn conducted the first Viennese performance of the *Missa in tempore belli*.

11 *The Creation:* the beginning of Baron Gottfried van Swieten's autograph of the libretto, with (on the left) his suggestions for its composition by Haydn. The manuscript was formerly in Haydn's own library.

12 *The Creation:* Haydn's sketch in full score for the beginning of the Introduction, 'Chaos'; this is transcribed on pp. 358ff. as 'Sketch II'.

13 Beethoven in 1800, engraving by Johann Neidl, from a drawing by Gandolph Ernst Stainhauser von Treuberg, published in Vienna by Cappi.

14 Announcement of a concert given by Maria Bolla at the small Redoutensaal in Vienna on 8 January 1796; both Haydn and Beethoven, who played a piano concerto, took part.

1796.

AVVISO.

Oggi Venerdì 8. del corrente Gennajo la Sigra. Maria Bolla, virtuoſa di Muſica, darà una Accademia nella piccola Sala del Ridotto. La Muſica ſarà di nuova compoſizione del Sigre. Haydn, il quale ne ſarà alla direzione.

Vi canteranno la Sigra. Bolla, la Sigra. Tomeoni, e il Sigre. Mombelli.

Il Sigre. Bethofen ſuonerà un Concerto ſul Pianoforte.

Il prezzo dei biglietti d'ingreſſo ſarà di uno zecchino. Queſti potranno averſi o alla Caſſa del Teatro Nazionale, o in caſa della Sigra. Bolla, nella Pariſergaſſe Nro. 444. al ſecondo piano.

Il principio ſarà alle ore ſei e mezza.

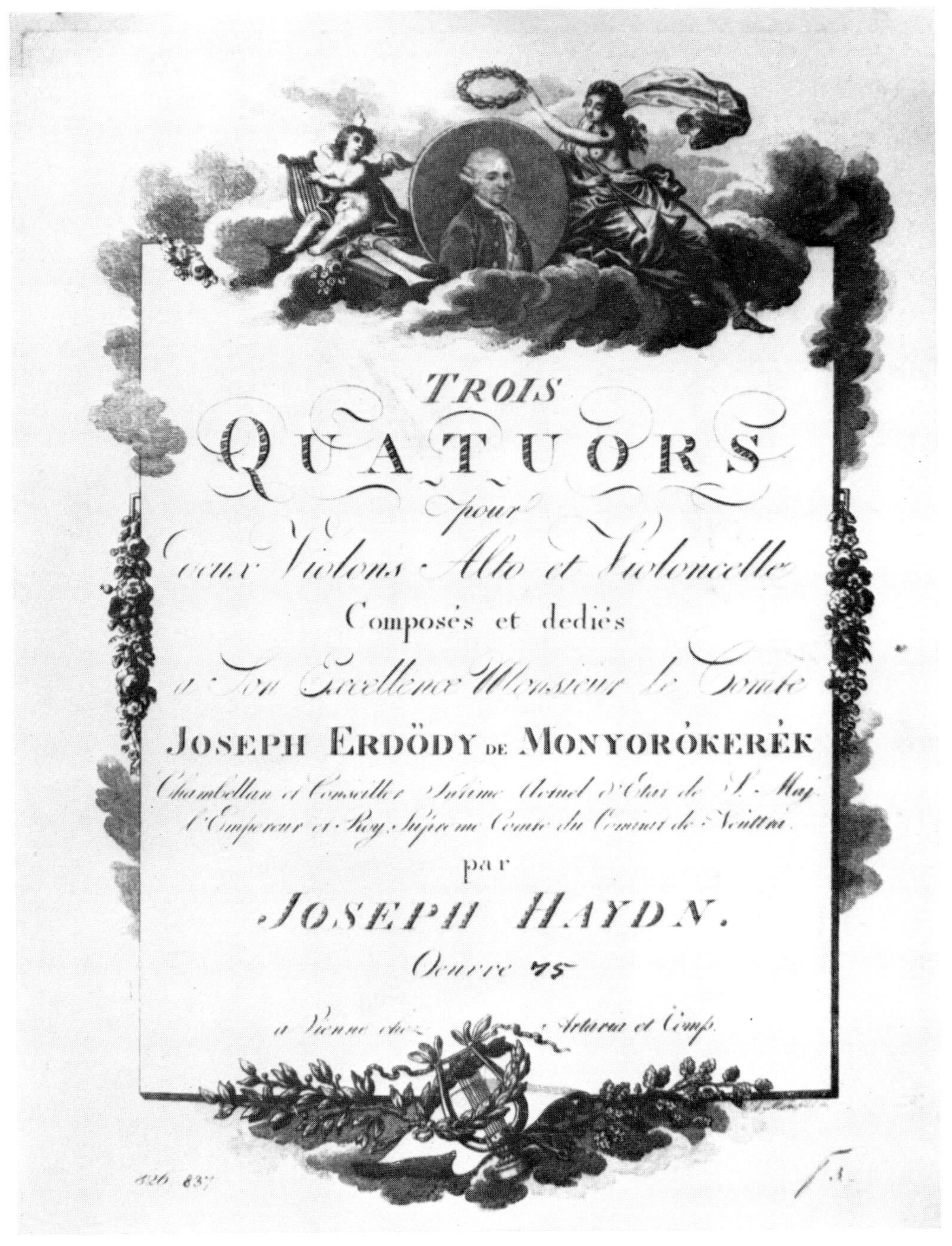
TROIS
QUATUORS
pour
deux Violons Alto et Violoncelle
Composés et dediés
a Son Excellence Monsieur le Comte
JOSEPH ERDÖDY DE MONYORÓKERÉK
Chambellan et Conseiller Intime Actuel d'Etat de S. Maj.
l'Empereur et Roy, Supreme Comte du Comitat de Neuttra.
par
JOSEPH HAYDN.
Oeuvre 75
a Vienne chez Artaria et Comp.
826. 837
f. 3.

15 Title-page of the authentic Artaria edition (1799) of Haydn's Quartets, Op. 76 (here listed as 'Op. 75'), Nos. 1–3, completed in 1797 and dedicated to Count Erdödy (cf. pl. 19).

16 Joseph Carl Rosenbaum who, after many requests to Prince Nicolaus II Esterházy, was finally permitted to marry the singer Therese Gassmann (11 June 1800); his writings are an important source of information about contemporary Austrian life and about Haydn's activities. Aquarelle by Charles Hummel, 1815 (lost).

Below
17 Therese Rosenbaum (*née* Gassmann) in the role of the Queen of the Night in Mozart's *Die Zauberflöte*; she sang the solo soprano parts in many of Haydn's works of the period 1795 *et seq*. Engraving by Carl Heinrich Rahl after Johann Friedrich Leybold, Vienna 1801.

18 Carl, Count von Zinzendorf, whose MS. diaries are an important documentary source for our knowledge of contemporary events in Vienna; portrait in oils by Friedrich Heinrich Füger.

19 Joseph, Count Erdödy, to whom Haydn dedicated the six Quartets, Op. 76 (cf. pl. 15), completed in 1797; engraving by Ehrenreich, *c.* 1824, after a painting owned by the Count's family.

20 Franz Joseph Maximilian, Prince Lobkowitz (1772–1816), to whom Haydn dedicated the two Quartets, Op. 77; engraving by C. H. Pfeiffer after a painting by F. A. Oelenhainz.

21 Joseph, Prince zu Schwarzenberg (1769–1833), at whose palace in Vienna Haydn's late oratorios were first performed; engraving by C. H. Pfeiffer after a painting by Oelenhainz.

22, 23 Prince Nicolaus II Esterházy (1765–1833), in whose service Haydn spent his last active years as Kapellmeister: (left) anonymous portrait in oils, lost in 1945(?); (right) pencil drawing by the Rev. William Bradford, Chaplain to the British Embassy in Vienna.

24 The Empress Marie Therese (wife of Francis I), portrait in oils by Joseph Kreutzinger.

25 Andreas Kyrillovich, Count (from 1815, Prince) Razumovsky (1732–1836); portrait in oils by J. B. Lampi. Cf. pp. 26f.

26 The Michaelerplatz, Vienna, showing the old Burgtheater (centre) in which the first public performance of Haydn's Trumpet Concerto – as well as that of *The Creation* – was given; coloured engraving by Carl Postl, 1810, published by Artaria & Co.

27 The interior of the old Burgtheater; from a coloured engraving, *c.* 1830.

28 Johann Michael Haydn in later years; pencil sketch by C. F. Stolze. In Vienna in 1798 the two brothers, Joseph and Michael, were reunited for the first time since 1771.

29 Johann Elssler (1769–1843), Haydn's faithful copyist and servant; anonymous chalk drawing after a miniature.

Opposite, above
30 Baron Gottfried van Swieten, silhouette by Gonord, 1786. Van Swieten, who was Imperial and Royal Librarian at the Kaiserliche Hofbibliothek, provided the libretto for *The Creation* (cf. pl. 11).

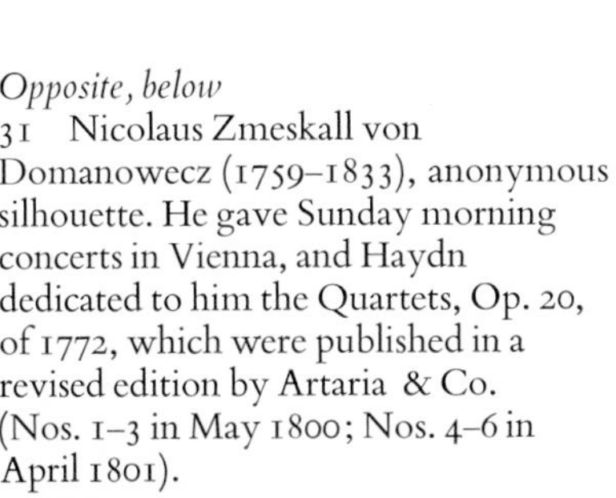

Opposite, below
31 Nicolaus Zmeskall von Domanowecz (1759–1833), anonymous silhouette. He gave Sunday morning concerts in Vienna, and Haydn dedicated to him the Quartets, Op. 20, of 1772, which were published in a revised edition by Artaria & Co. (Nos. 1–3 in May 1800; Nos. 4–6 in April 1801).

Above
32 Georg August Griesinger, the diplomat, who was in personal contact with Haydn from 1799 and who later wrote a biography of the composer; after a lost portrait.

33 Frederik Samuel Silverstolpe, the Swedish diplomat who arrived in Vienna in 1797 and soon became a friend of Haydn's; his writings are an important record of musical life in the Austrian capital. Portrait in oils by Hans Hansen, 1802.

34 Horatio, Lord Nelson, who was greeted as a hero by the Austrians when he and his party (en route from Naples to London) arrived in Vienna in August 1800, before visiting Eisenstadt as guests of Prince Nicolaus II Esterházy (6–9 September). Nelson's name has been associated with Haydn's Mass in D minor (*Missa in angustiis*, 1798), which was first performed at Eisenstadt on 23 September 1798 (shortly after Nelson's victory over the French fleet at Aboukir). Portrait in oils by John Hoppner, 1801(?). Royal Collection; reproduced by gracious permission of Her Majesty the Queen.

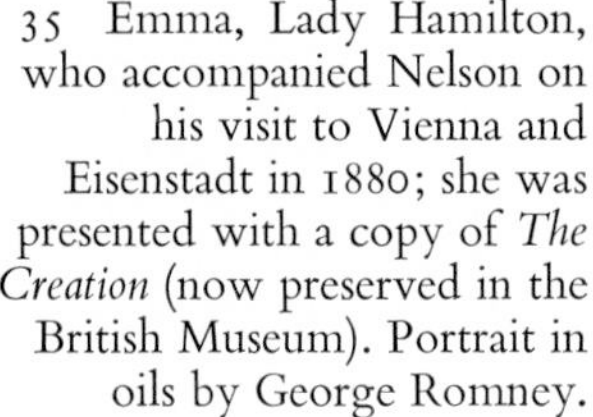

35 Emma, Lady Hamilton, who accompanied Nelson on his visit to Vienna and Eisenstadt in 1880; she was presented with a copy of *The Creation* (now preserved in the British Museum). Portrait in oils by George Romney.

CHAPTER SEVEN

Chronicle 1797

READERS OF THE *Wiener Zeitung* noticed on 14 January 1797 that

> His I. R. Majesty has graciously condescended to receive with every mark of approbation the very considerable financial contributions to the war effort made since the year 1793 by Prince Niklas [*sic*] Esterházy von Galantha, Councillor, Major-General, and First Lieutenant of the Noble Hungarian Bodyguard . . . and has now seen fit to confer on [Prince Esterházy] the Grand Cross of the Order of St. Stephen. . . .

Haydn, Chapel Master to his Serene Highness, was hardly in a position to make large financial gifts to defeat Napoleon; but he was able to make a contribution more lasting than any gift of money. For this is the period in which Haydn composed his gravely beautiful 'Volck's Lied' (People's Song), later known as the Austrian (and still later the German) National Anthem. To describe how Haydn came to write this 'Volck's Lied' we must return for a moment to the autumn of 1796, a period (as we have seen) of military defeat for Austria and its allies, Prussia and England.

There are two versions of the *Volkslied*'s origin. The first is that given by Franz Joseph, Count Saurau (President of the Lower Austrian Government, later Minister of the Interior), in a letter to Moritz, Count Dietrichstein (Director of Court Music) covering the transmission of Haydn's personal letter of 28(?) January 1797. Count Saurau wrote:

> I have often regretted that unlike the English we had no national anthem fitted to display in front of the whole world the devoted attachment of the people to its wise and good Father [*Landesvater*], and to awaken in the hearts of all good Austrians that noble pride of nation which is indispensable if they are to execute energetically each disciplinary measure considered necessary by the princes of the land. This appeared to me especially necessary at a time when the Revolution in France was raging at its strongest and the Jacobins were flattering themselves with the vain hope of finding among the good Viennese followers and participants in their criminal deeds.
>
> I had a text fashioned by the worthy poet Haschka, and to have it set to music, I turned to our immortal compatriot Haydn, who, I felt, was the only man capable of creating something which could be placed beside the English 'God save the King'.

The other version comes from Anton Schmid, Custodian of the Vienna National Library, who wrote it down in a pamphlet entitled *Joseph Haydn und Niccolò Zingarelli* (Vienna 1847):

> As far as the reasons for which the wonderful Haydn Song was composed, we may present to our readers the following plausible circumstances, which several of

the finest composers in Vienna, some of whom are dead and some still alive, remembered from those times and communicated to us.

In England, Haydn came to know the favourite British national anthem, 'God save the King', and he envied the British nation for a song through which it could, at festive occasions, show in full measure its respect, love and devotion to its ruler.

When the Father of Harmony returned to his beloved *Kaiserstadt*, he related these impressions to that real friend, connoisseur, supporter and encourager of many a great and good one of Art and Science, Freiherr van Swieten, Prefect of the I. R. Court Library, who at that time was at the head of the Concert Spirituel (supported by the high aristocracy) and likewise Haydn's particular patron. [Haydn] wished that Austria, too, could have a similar national anthem, wherein it could display a similar respect and love for its Father [*Landesvater*]. Also, such a song could be used in the fight then taking place with those forcing the Rhine; it could be used in a noble way to inflame the hearts of the Austrians to new heights of devotion to the princes and fatherland, and to incite to combat, and to increase, the mob of volunteer soldiers who had been collected by a general proclamation.

Freiherr van Swieten hastily took counsel with His Excellency, the then President of Lower Austria, Franz Count von Saurau, the author of that aforementioned proclamation; and so there came into being a song which, apart from being one of Haydn's greatest creations, has won the crown of immortality.

It is also true that this high-principled Count used the most opportune moment to introduce a *Volksgesang*, and thus he called to life those beautiful thoughts which will delight connoisseurs and amateurs here and abroad.

He ordered forthwith the poet Lorenz Haschka to draft the poetry and then requested our Haydn to set it to music.

In January 1797, this double task was resolved, and the first performance of the Song was ordered for the birthday of the Monarch.

No doubt Haydn's anthem was also supposed to be an answer to the *Marseillaise*, which was composed at Strasbourg in 1792 and on 7 July 1795 made the official national anthem of France. Franz Grasberger, from whose very useful book, *Die Hymnen Österreichs*,[1] this information is gratefully taken, discovered, in the Historisches Museum der Stadt Wien, a lacquered box, in which there is a German translation, together with the music, of 'God save the King', dated 'Vienna 797'. Grasberger rightly assumes that this box (which was one of several 'en manufacture') can hardly have been produced *after* the launching of Haydn's *Volkslied* on the Emperor's Birthday (12 February), and must therefore represent an attempt to harness the popular music of the British anthem to German words:

Heil Teutschlands Kaiser! Heil!
Heil unserm Kaiser! Heil!
Heil Kaiser Franz!
Segnend mit Vaterhand
Sieh, o Gott, unverwandt
Auf Franz, sein Volk und Land!
Heil Kaiser Franz!

[There follow four more verses.]

Saurau preserved in his archives not only the original text of 'Gott erhalte' (the *Volkslied*) but with it the original English words of 'God save the King' and a German

1 Tutzing 1968, pp. 11ff. with a large bibliography, to which the interested reader is referred.

translation. Obviously the English song was to serve as a model for the Austrian poet. Here is what Haschka delivered to Count Saurau together with a short poem to the Count, dated 11 October 1796 (all this material is from the Saurau Archives, now in the Styrian Landesarchiv, Graz):

Gott! erhalte Franz den Kaiser,
Unsern guten Kaiser Franz!
Lange lebe Franz der Kaiser
In des Glückes hellstem Glanz!
Ihm erblühen Lorbeer-Reiser
Wo er geht, zum Ehren-Kranz!
Gott! erhalte Franz den Kaiser,
Unsern guten Kaiser Franz!

Laß von seiner Fahnen Spitzen
Strahlen Sieg und Fruchtbarkeit!
Laß in Seinem Rathe sitzen,
Weisheit, Klugheit, Redlichkeit;
Und mit Seiner Hoheit Blitzen
Schalten nur Gerechtigkeit!
Gott! erhalte Franz den Kaiser,
Unsern guten Kaiser Franz!

Ströme Deiner Gaben Fülle
Über Ihn, Sein Haus und Reich!
Brich der Bösheit Macht; enthülle
Jeden Schelm- und Bubenstreich!
Dein Gesetz sey stets Sein Wille;
Dieser uns Gesetzen gleich!
Gott! erhalte Franz den Kaiser,
Unsern guten Kaiser Franz!

Froh erleb' Er Seiner Lande
Seiner Völker höchsten Flor!
Seh'sie, Eins durch Bruder-Bande,
Ragen allen andern vor;
Und vernehme noch am Rande
Später Gruft der Enkel Chor;
Gott! erhalte Franz den Kaiser,
Unsern guten Kaiser Franz!

It seems that Haschka really tried to copy the tone of 'God save the King', for his own poetry – Grasberger cites several extracts – is quite different. The 'Gott erhalte' *Volkslied* (Haschka's autograph is entitled 'Gott erhalte den Kaiser!') could not be described as great poetry but it was obviously just what Count Saurau wanted; and the tone of the poem was to mark the beginning of that great change in Austrian politics of which we have remarked in *Haydn in England 1791–1975*. From the liberal enlightenment of Joseph II to Metternich's rigid authoritarianism seems in retrospect a long road; a significant landmark along it is Haydn's and Haschka's hymn, wherein the Emperor is treated with that slightly mystical devotion, is looked up to, and is surrounded by that aura of stern yet gentle wisdom; he has become, in fact, a Sarastro-like father-figure (not that Franz would have been enchanted by the comparison, since Freemasonry had been forbidden in 1795 and was to remain outlawed until after the First World War), and Mozart at the end of *Die Zauberflöte* might have set to music the words of Haydn's hymn, 'Weisheit, Klugheit, Redlichkeit' (again almost word-for-word from a Masonic text).

Together with the autograph – which has only two small changes – Haschka enclosed the following poem ('in typical Haschka manner', says Grasberger, who describes this particular literary effort as 'mit einer untertänigen Anpreisung'):

An
Seine Excellenz
Franz Grafen von Saurau,

am 11. October, 1796.

Wie an dem Ölbaum hinauf ein schwaches Rebchen sich schlinget;
Schlinget an Deiner Gunst, Saurau! dieß Liedchen sich auf.
Trag es empor! Vielleicht, daß von Deinen Ansehn empfohlen
dennoch ein Beerchen davon unserm Augustus beliebt!

Lorenz Leopold Haschka has not won the sympathy of historians. Born in Vienna on 1 September 1749, he entered the Jesuit Order; influenced by the Josephinian ideas, he left the Order and became a Freemason, writing inflammatory pamphlets against Pope, Church and rulers. When Leopold II became Emperor and cancelled many of the Josephinian reforms, Haschka followed the trend and even became a police spy. Later he was made Professor of Aesthetics at the Theresianum and a Custodian of the National Library, in which positions he remained until his death in 1827. Haydn probably knew him as an admirer of Hofrat von Greiner, with whom the composer was on friendly terms; but there is, apart from their brief collaboration on the hymn, no record of any connection between the two men. His contemporaries took a jaundiced view of his poetry. Goethe writes:

> But now, I advise you, go! Lest there come the Gorgonic grimace, or a volume of Odes by Haschka.[1]

Whichever one chooses of the two versions concerning the origins of Haydn's *Volkslied*, the clear influence of 'God save the King' is well documented. In Schmid's version there is at least one mistake, in that the proclamation for the volunteers was not issued until 4 April 1797, i.e. well after the first performance of the *Volkslied*; but probably Haydn and Saurau had the same idea; possibly van Swieten brought them together and implemented the plan. Saurau, of course, was pursuing primarily a political aim, whereas Haydn's music shows that he wanted to compose a hymn-like national anthem of great beauty, simplicity and dignity; and in that, he succeeded perhaps even beyond his own expectations. It was now time to complete the orchestral score and to see that the first print was circulated throughout the monarchy.

Towards the end of January, the Austrian Government had made plans for the first performance of the new national anthem; it was to be played simultaneously in all the theatres on the Emperor's birthday, 12 February (*vide infra*). The authorities must have realized at a glance that Haydn's hymn was the greatest piece of propaganda ever devised to hold together a people made nervous and uncertain by the French Revolution and the ideas it had generated, by the bad progress of the war, and by a certain disenchantment with politics at home. Happily we are in possession of a letter from Haydn to Count Saurau, who in 1820 gave it, with an explanatory note, to Count Moritz Dietrichstein; since then, Haydn's letter has become part of the

1 'Aber jetzt rat' ich euch, geht! sonst kommt noch gar der Gorgona/Fratze oder ein Band Oden von Haschka hervor'. This sketch of Haschka is taken from Pohl III, 115f., and also details of the first performance (including the 'Eipeldauer' report).

Austrian National Library's *Handschriftensammlung*. The conjectured date may be explained as follows: on 28 January, Count Saurau gave his 'imprimatur' to the final proofs of the anthem. Thus, Haydn's letter must have been written *on* 28 January – or perhaps the day before – because he speaks of the 'Abdruck' (i.e. proof); if it had been printed, he would have referred to 'Exemplair' (copy). Presumably Haydn gave his 'imprimatur' for the musical part, 'deliver[ed] the proof by eleven o'clock to Saurau, who then gave the order to print' (see Pohl III, 115ff.). The 'mark of favour' was a snuff-box, containing the Emperor's portrait, and a substantial sum of money (Pohl III, 118).

[To Franz Joseph, Count Saurau, Vienna. *German*]

[Vienna, 28th January (?) 1797]

Excellence!

Such a surprise and such mark of favour, especially as regards the portrait of my dear monarch, I never before received in acknowledgement of my unworthy talents. I thank Your Excellency with all my heart, and am ready at all times to serve Your Excellency. I shall deliver the proof by 11 o'clock. I am, in profound respect,

Your Excellency's
Most humble and obedient servant,
Jos. Haydn. [CCLN, 151]

The first edition, as Grasberger suggests (op. cit., p. 27) 'must have been prepared in great haste and printed in a large quantity'. The news of the fall of Mantua – *vide infra* – on 14 January reached Vienna shortly before the Emperor's birthday, and large-scale celebrations to strengthen the great father figure's image were planned. On 3 February the Graz *Präsidialgeschäftenprotokoll* noted that

> G[raf] Saurau presented text and music for a song which is to be sung in public at Vienna on the birthday of H. M. on 12 *inst.* – It was explained to Ct. Saurau that here, too, one would have the song presented with the greatest possible ceremony, to the promulgation of which a circular has been sent to all interested departments [*Kreisämter*].

The music sent round to the provinces was a print in the form of a piano score (mostly in four parts); it is reproduced in facsimile in Grasberger, p. 29.

It is altogether astonishing to see with what almost Prussian efficiency the government pursued the distribution of the *Volkslied*. On 30 January 1797, Saurau wrote to the authorities in Prague as follows:

Nobly born Count!

Your Excellency will be aware of the effect on the populace caused by the well-known English song [*Volkslied*]: God save the King; and how for a long time it has admonished that people to a common defence against foreign foes.

The Song which is herewith enclosed, written by Haschka and set to music by the famous Haydn, will be sung by the people in all the theatres of Vienna on 12 February, and I take the liberty of sending one in confidence to Your Excellency, in order that the Song, if you judge it to be a good idea, may be sung that same day also in Prague; and may the wishes of the whole populace for the continued welfare of His Majesty resound on that day!

I remain with every respect,

Your Excellency's
obedient servant
Saurau.

Vienna, 30 January 1797

Before continuing with the chronicle of the Emperor's birthday on 12 February, and the many contemporary reports on it, we must interrupt our history of the *Volkslied* in order to introduce an important letter written to Haydn in the middle of preparations for the printing and distribution of 'Gott erhalte'.

On 20 January Haydn received a letter from the Tonkünstler-Societät; it was written primarily as an apology for the way in which the Society had treated the composer in 1779, at which time Haydn withdrew his application for membership because the Society had stipulated that he provide them with oratorios, cantatas, and so forth, as they needed them. Haydn naturally thought this demand excessive; the Society was happy to receive his withdrawal – and this despite the huge sums they had made as a result of the Oratorio, *Il ritorno di Tobia*, which Haydn had conducted for the Society's benefit in 1775. We have seen in *Haydn in England 1791–1795* that Haydn bore the organization no ill-will and gave concerts for them between his London visits.

[To Haydn from Antonio Salieri and Paul Wranizky, on behalf of the Tonkünstler-Societät, Vienna.[1] *German*]

To Herr Joseph Hayden, *Capellmeister* to His Serene Highness Prince Esterházy.

Most esteemed *Herr Capellmeister!*

You must and should rightly be accustomed to hearing the praises of your own unattainable services to music, and accustomed to being admired for your inexhaustible creative mind, for you have won the most fervent and justified approbation of entire nations.

The Society for the Promotion of Musicians' Widows and Orphans – for which you, worthy Sir, have so often earned considerable sums through your admirable compositions – will therefore forgo all eulogies; it now has the honour of thanking you for all the kindnesses you have shown it in the past, and assures you of its boundless admiration. As a small token of its gratitude, it sends you a free ticket of admission for all future concerts of the Society; you need only show this ticket when you enter, retaining it for further use. Please do not in any way consider this act to be a kind of small recompense,[2] but rather the wish to show you our kindest and best intentions, and to assure you of the gratitude, but also of the eternal obligation which will always be owed you by

The Society for the Promotion of Musicians' Widows and Orphans.

Ex concluso Sessionis
dat. 20 January 1797
Anton Salieri.

Paul Wranizky,
pro tempore Secretary.

[CCLN, 150]

As mentioned, the first edition of the *Volkslied* was a piano score; when it was transmitted to the theatres in the provinces, presumably every local *Capellmeister* made

1 The two brothers, Anton and Paul Wranizky (or Wranitzky), were among Vienna's leading musicians and composers. Anton (1761–1819) was a violinist and was *Kapellmeister* to Prince Lobkowitz; Paul (1756–1808), also a violinist, studied with Haydn, was one of the moving figures in the Tonkünstler-Societät, and was leader of the Court Theatre Orchestra in the Burgtheater. His opera *Oberon* (Vienna, 1789) is generally cited as his outstanding work.

2 For the appalling way in which they had treated Haydn in 1779. Wranizky was in large measure responsible, not only for this letter, but also for making the Society admit Haydn as a member without charging him any entrance fee. In the session of 20 January, Wranizky hoped that the Society's 'previous conduct would be forever erased from my memory, and from Haydn's too, if that is possible.' (Pohl, *Denkschrift*, p. 23). Haydn was elected in December 1797, and made *Assessor senior* for life (*vide infra*, pp. 266–7). His performances of *The Seven Words*, *The Creation* and *The Seasons* brought the Society a huge fortune.

his own orchestral arrangement. For the Emperor's birthday celebration held at the Burgtheater ('Nationaltheater') in Vienna, however, Haydn wrote his own orchestral score. The autograph is in the Österreichische Nationalbibliothek and is signed 'v. Jos: Haydn 797'; an authentic copy by Elssler is in the Esterházy Archives of the National Széchényi Library in Budapest. There is in this orchestral score a line for the 'Canto', and the orchestration is for one flute, pairs of oboes, bassoons, horns in G, trumpets in C, kettledrums and strings. The score is in G major and it begins with a full chord in G about which Haydn made a note in the score: 'NB: die allererste Note wird nur anfangs gespielt, um dem Volck den Ton zu geben' (the first note is only to be played at the beginning so that the people may find the right pitch). Incredibly this beautiful orchestral score is hardly known today: there is no modern edition and the first print occurred in a British magazine (*The Harmonicon*) of the year 1825. In this biography, the full score is printed *infra*, pp. 279ff., for the first time in the twentieth century.

On 12 February, the celebration took place in the Burgtheater. Grasberger suggests (*Hymnen*, p. 30) that the Emperor may have known nothing of all these preparations and that the celebration in the Burgtheater was a surprise to him: we beg leave to doubt that. It is quite in keeping with the fast-developing concept of the Emperor as a near monotheistic appearance that he not only knew about the event but pretended to be surprised when the *Volkshymne* first sounded that evening of 12 February.

At six-thirty in the evening, the Burgtheater opened with Act II of Dittersdorf's *Der Apotheker und der Doktor* (now known as *Doktor und Apotheker*). Grasberger believes that this particular selection was made because in it, there appears an invalid captain with a wooden leg and patch over his left eye who sings:

> So verfährt man mit Soldaten?
> Ha, pots Bomben und Granaten,
> Wart', du kriegst schon deinen Lohn! –
> Unter dichtem Kugelregen
> Half ich Tausende erlegen;
> Stürtzte wie ein Löw' ins Feuer,
> Fetzte, würgte wie ein Geier,
> Bis Appell den Garaus machte
> Und man Siegeszeichen brachte;
> Ich war auf dem Schlachtfeld da,
> Bis man schrie Viktoria! Viktoria! Viktoria!
> Bis man schrie Viktoria! –

Following this rabble-rousing piece was *Alonzo und Cora*, a 'heroisch-tragisch-pantomimische Ballett' in five acts by Joseph Trafieri with music by Haydn's godson, Joseph Weigl.

Count von Zinzendorf was present and wrote in his Diary:

> . . . Le soir au Théatre . . . J' assistois au chant des vers de Haschka Gott! erhalte Franz den Kaiser unsern guten Kaiser Franz! sans le Schelm und Bubenstreich les vers seroient bons parcequ'ils sont simples. La musique est tres simple. L'Empereur applaudi a son arrivée pour son jour de naissances, fit des reverences sans nombre, j'ai eté touché vivement de ce spectacle rendu plus interessant par la clarté que le lustre allumé repandoit sur tout le théatre. Sa Majesté l'objet de cette touchante Harmonie, a dû etre emüe bien davantage . . . .
>
> [Olleson, 52]

From this report is is not clear when the Haydn–Haschka song was performed, but presumably before the Ballet. The 'Eipeldauer sprung to new life' (Der wiederaufgelebte Eipeldauer), whom we noted as a witness to Haydn's Mass in the Piaristenkirche on 26 December 1796, writes as follows:

> Now, my dear Cousin, I should have a more clever pen to describe to you all the fine goings-on that have occurred here in the last few days.
>
> A worthy man wrote a song for the birthday of our gracious Emperor, and another worthy man – the one who wrote the church music for the *Primitiae* ceremony at the Piarists – set it to music; and the song was given in all the theatres. And you could see how precious to the faithful Austrians were their princes.
>
> The theatre was never so jammed, and since some people couldn't see enough to sing, they lighted up little lamps like at Johannis Service and they wanted to show that our Emperor Franz is really our patron saint. The song will now be sung as well in all societies and in public places and especially by Fräuleins at the piano. But if only they won't sing so much as to forget the money, 'cause we aren't to be helped just with singing in these days.
>
> Since our best Emperor is no friend of compliments and flattery, he came to the theatre late on purpose. But the Viennese were smart, too, and they waited with the song to the monarch, and he had to listen to it all the same; but then he showed how touched he was to see his subjects' devotion. [Heft 33]
>
> [Pohl III, 116f.]

The *Magazin der Kunst und Literatur* also carried a report:

> Gott erhalte den Kaiser
>
> The twelfth of February, the birthday of our exalted and much beloved Emperor, was celebrated this year in a fashion that was up to now unknown in Austria. A warm admirer of this monarch found a way – and in this he could not have approached closer to the general desire – for the loyal subjects in all places of the Austrian monarchy to display the sensitivity of their hearts for the well-being of their beloved Prince of the Land, and to show it openly and in consort. A *Volkslied* in the manner of that in which the loyal Englishmen sing for the preservation of their king, seemed to be the most efficacious means. Haschka wrote the song and Haydn set it to music: a choice that reflects credit on the highly placed men who made it. It was sung this year on 12 February in all the theatres. The enthusiasm of the public which was displayed on this occasion as on several others allows us to hope that we will have frequent occasion to hear the voices of the people joined together for the preservation of the Emperor . . . . [Jahrgang V]
>
> [Grasberger, *Hymnen*, 31f.]

The popular success seems not to have been the exclusive invention of the government-controlled newspapers; for we find the clever impresario Emanuel Schikaneder placing on the hand-bills of his programmes for 13 and 14 February, 'Der Laute und allgemeine Beyfall . . . gibt mir einen Wink, den Chor von Herrn Heyden heute noch einmal zu wiederholen' (the loud and general applause . . . gives me the hint to repeat once again today the chorus by Herr Heyden). On 22 February the official *Wiener Zeitung* informs us of the *Volkslied*'s reception not only in Vienna but also in the provinces:

> . . . From the various reports received [about 12 February], it was everywhere celebrated throughout the length and breadth of the I. R. states: a festive day of rejoicing and delight, full of the warmest blessings and wishes for their beloved Father. These feelings were expressed in particular when in all theatres was sung

the *Nazional-Lied* 'Gott erhalte den Kaiser', written by Herr Haschka and composed by the most celebrated composer of our day, Herr Hayden; and when it was announced by the orchestra [in the Burgtheater], every heart jumped for joy. They broke into loud applause when H. M. himself appeared in the box and condescended graciously to receive their marks of esteem [*ihre Rührung*].

At the same time this day was celebrated in all the cities of the monarchy . . . At Graz the public gathered in the theatre, where at the end, under specially constructed allegorical decorations, the above-mentioned National Song was produced by the opera singers, to the delighted applause of the public. The Land's Redouten-Sa[a]l was decorated in many ways, doubly illuminated, and improved with pictures of the monarch. Here, too, the National Song was again produced.

Other, similar festivities are reported from Judenburg and Leoben. . . . In the first of those towns . . . the words 'Gott erhalte den Kaiser' appeared as a transparence. . . . When the curtain rose, accompanied by music, shepherds and shepherdesses came forward and laid their gifts at the altar and then sang the National Song.

. . . Just this very Song, translated into Italian, was produced at Trieste in the magnificently illuminated opera house, and in the presence of H. R. H. the Archduke Ferdinand and his serene highness' consort.

At Innsbruck, where the theatre is at present closed, a large musical academy was given in the hall of the University Library, and at the beginning and also the end, the oft-mentioned National Song was produced.

At Prague the University organized special festivities . . . Afterwards all the academic gentlemen produced a National Song of Bohemia, entitled Franz the Second, written by Herr Meinert and set to music by Herr Weber . . . and finally Herr Haschka's National Song, 'Gott erhalte den Kaiser' was sung . . .

Similar reports have reached us from Brünn, Krakau, Ofen, Pest and other cities.

[Grasberger, *Hymnen*, 32f.]

The events of 12 February were celebrated in verse by the ubiquitous Haschka. The thirteen strophes concluded with an apotheosis on Count Saurau:

> Saurau! Saurau! dem Land' unter der Ens von Ihm
> Selbst vorgesetzt! du weih' Ihm den Tempel ein,
> Und entflamme den Altar!
> Reiner stieg noch kein Opfer auf!

and begins with a hymn of praise to Francisus secondus:

> Lasst uns feyern! Der Tag, welcher Franciscum uns
> Vor fünf Lustern und vier Wintern geboren hat,
> Kehrt, mit Strahlen umwunden,
> Heut' im Cyklus des Jahres zurück.

[Grasberger, *Hymnen*, 33]

Haydn's Hymn has remained one of the composer's most popular works; it survives in Protestant Anglo-Saxon countries as a church hymn, 'Glorious things of Thee are spoken', and of course it remains the German national anthem; but more than that, it is embedded in one of Haydn's most popular Quartets, 'The Emperor' (Op. 76, No. 3) – still popular by reasons of a *Volkslied*, the original *raison d'être* of which is nowadays unknown to many listeners. We shall examine Haydn's own variations, which also exist for piano, in the next chapter.

On 21 February Archduke Carl arrived, and Zinzendorf noted 'On illumine la ville pour l'arrive de l'archiduc Charles . . . Le graben tres beau illuminé, des lampions colorés . . .': it was the least that a thankful Vienna could offer to one of the few heros in the Austrian military establishment.

On 24 March Prince Joseph Schwarzenberg was host to van Swieten's Gesellschaft der Associirten in a performance of Handel's *Acis & Galatea*. Zinzendorf noted

> . . . Le Soir apres 6[h] chez Schwarzenberg, ou il y avait le Concert de Händel: Acis et Galathée. La musique chantante, les paroles de Dryden traduites par Alxinger, Mlle Gerhardi, Spangler . . . Grande monde.

Haydn was there and finally the Swedish diplomat Frederik Samuel Silverstolpe had a chance to meet the great composer. On 1 April Silverstolpe writes to Sweden:

> Last Monday there was a grand concert at Prince Schwarzenberg's which I attended. It was an Oratorio by the famous Händel called 'Acis and Galatea'. Certainly among the finest things that I ever heard. – There I made Haydn's acquaintance, and since then I have kept it going by paying him a visit. He is a modest man and does not receive compliments gladly. His looks are *speculativ* [Silverstolpe means, more or less, 'the man of a speculative mind'] but not so much as one might expect. On 7 April I will hear another concert at Prince Schwarzenberg's, which Haydn will conduct, and he made me promise to come, when I said to him what a pleasure it had been for me to hear his so-called 7 Words. 'I could never praise [*rühmen*] myself,' said he, 'but as far as that work goes, it is not without merit, et je me flatte que c'est le meilleur ouvrage que j'ai fait.' – He asked me if I had known [Joseph Martin] Kraus, who was supposed to have been in Sweden and died there. 'I own', he said, 'a symphony [in C minor] by him, which I preserve comme un souvenir d'un des plus grands genies que j'ai jamais connûe. Je n'ai que ce seul ouvrage de lui, et je sai[s] qu'il en a fait d'excellents.' He was very pleased when I promised him further works. – I am the more curious to hear Haydn's 7 Words, for meanwhile they have been changed in that they have received choruses. . . .
>
> [Vienna 3 May 1797] . . . The concert at Prince Schwarzenberg's, of which I spoke earlier, and in which they had the intention to giving Haydn's 7 Words with choruses, will not take place, and thus there won't be any of the promised description. I know this music, since Haydn changed it, only by hear-say, and that's an insufficient sign-post. – I have cultivated Haydn's acquaintance. After a more extended conversation with this remakable man I shall really have to try to give an idea of him. Also Kozeluch, Vanhall, Albrechtsberger and Salieri are men of merit, and they will play a certain role in the letters that I intend to write in the future to Secretary [Pehr] Frigel [a Stockholm friend] about music in Vienna. . . .
>
> [Mörner, 314–6]

Silverstolpe fulfilled his promise; no doubt he circulated his report to his friends in Sweden before he published it in 1838; it is a long, authentic and interesting report which we have for convenience's sake divided up into several parts. We shall call it Silverstolpe's 'Report I' (II, III, etc.).[1] Silverstolpe had a remarkable memory, for we can compare his 1838 report with the contemporary letters he wrote to Sweden and observe that he recalled accurately his conversations with Haydn almost word for

1 Published for the first time complete in German in C.-G. Stellan Mörner's 'Haydniana aus Schweden um 1800' (*Haydn-Studien* II/1, 1969, pp. 24ff.). A part of the report was published in Karl Friedrich Schreiber's *Biographie über den Odenwälder Komponisten Joseph Martin Kraus*, Buchen 1928, pp. 69ff.

word. They were, as we have seen *supra*, held in French, a language which Haydn spoke and wrote with tolerable fluency.

[*Silverstolpe's Report (I)*]
If one could acquire as much fame through the characteristics of the heart as through the intellect, and through that heavenly spark out of which artists are made, then Joseph Haydn should enjoy no less reputation for his virtues than for his spirit. The concept of his personality is for me dear in every respect, for I enjoyed the chance of appreciating in him much more than his talent, with which he delighted the world. It is a pleasant task for me to dedicate a few pages to our acquaintance of many years. – I had been ten months in Vienna without being able to lay eyes on this man, so excellent in his art, although I very much looked forward to it. But he had spent most of the time at his Prince in Eisenstadt, and moreover my affairs now permitted me more free time than hitherto. On 27 [24?[1]] March, at Prince Schwarzenberg's, to whose Lenten concerts I had received an invitation, I saw Haydn for the first time and arranged to be introduced to him. We had just heard Händel's *Acis & Galatea*. This work at first provided us with a topic of conversation. 'It was well performed,' said Haydn, 'but in Westminster [Abbey] with an orchestra of 500 or 600 persons, the way the works of this great master ought to be heard, there it moved me the most.' I said how glad I was soon to hear Haydn's great music to *The Seven Words of the Saviour on the Cross* with the text, which had been recently fitted to the work (itself known long before). 'I flatter myself', said he, 'that you will find the work changed for the better. That is the best that I ever wrote in my life. When I was on the trip back from London,[2] in Passau I was told that there was a monk who was at work to add words to my music. I visited him at once and asked to take part in the undertaking. On the whole, he had understood the particular character of each piece. We then worked together, and the result you will see on 7 April.' [Note by Silverstolpe: that concert was cancelled; the approach of the French army excited the horror of the whole of Vienna.] Thereupon he spoke to me about our late Kraus: 'What a loss', he said, 'is that man's death! I own a symphony [etc. as in the letter cited *supra*]. He was often in Vienna with me and visited me in Esterhaz, too, where I spent the summers; that must have been only 13 or 14 years ago [it was in October 1783].' – I promised Haydn to show him some other works by Kraus which I had with me. He seemed to be highly pleased about this promise and asked me to come and see him soon.

That occurred shortly thereafter. He then lived in the Krüger-Strasse [*sic*] No. 1075; the house was called *der blaue Säbel*. He only rented this lodging for a short period to be near Baron van Swieten, the librettist of that great musical work on which Haydn had been engaged for some weeks. It was *The Creation*. Baron van Swieten, at the head of 12 or 13 other music lovers, had ordered the piece so that it could be performed the next year at Prince Schwarzenberg's, who likewise belonged to the Society. 'I find it necessary', said Haydn, 'to confer often with the Baron, to make changes in the text and moreover it is a pleasure for me to show him various numbers in it, for he is a profound connoisseur, who has himself written good music, even symphonies of great value' [for Haydn's private opinion of Swieten's symphonies, *vide supra*, p. 28]. – Soon Haydn let me hear the introduction of his oratorio, describing Chaos. He asked me to come and sit beside him, so as to follow the score. When the piece was ended, he said: 'You have certainly noticed how I avoided the resolutions that you would most readily

1 Zinzendorf attended on the 24th. Perhaps the usual repeat concert was on the 27th.

2 Another authentic source that this event occurred in September 1795 and not January 1794. *Vide supra*, p. 97.

expect. The reason is, that there is no form in anything [in the universe] yet.' – During the conversation which followed, I discovered in Haydn as it were two physiognomies. The one was penetrating and serious, when he talked about anything exalted [*Erhabene*], and only the expression 'exalted' was enough to show him visibly moved. In the next moment this atmosphere of exaltation was chased away, quick as lightning, from his every-day expression, and he became jovial with a force that showed on his features and which then passed into waggishness. This was his usual physiognomy; the other one had to be induced. – As I left him, he said, 'Do you know that this house has something remarkable about it: here, and just in these very rooms, we lost Mozart; what a gap that has left for us!' – I felt that I stood on hallowed ground.[1]

We have been obliged to break the chronological order of this Chronicle in order to present an important piece of evidence from the pen of F. S. Silverstolpe without any more interruption than necessary. A nostalgic event for Haydn had meanwhile occurred: a concert performance of his opera *Armida* (1784), produced at the Freyhaus Theater auf der Wieden for the benefit of that orchestra on 25 March 1797. Between the acts they performed a Mozart symphony.[2]

On that same day the *Wiener Zeitung* carried an announcement of the charity activities for the benefit of the war, organized principally by Prince Nicolaus II Esterházy; in that same report, we learn that Haydn's patron had been in Italy:

Out of gratitude and respect for the great services of H.R.H. the Archduke Carl, and from the general satisfaction afforded by H.R.H.'s recent return to Vienna, as well as from the desire to show a proper feeling for his noble character, a society has been formed for the support of worthy wounded officers, and for widows and orphans of non-commissioned officers and soldiers fallen at the front; this society, with the support of Princes von Esterházy and von Paar, has raised the sum of 51,350 gulden. The money was delivered to H.R.H. on the occasion of a trip which Prince Esterházy made to the headquarters of the Italian army, with the request that H.R.H. distribute it as he sees fit among the most worthy of those in need.

. . . To the above-mentioned sum . . . the following persons contributed:
. . . Prince Esterházy 4000 gulden.
Maria Princess Esterházy, *née* Princess v. Li[e]chtenstein 500 gulden.
Maria Dowager Princess Esterházy, *née* Countess v. Hohenfeld 500 gulden.
Joseph Prince v. Schwarzenberg 2000 gulden.
Prince v. Lobkowitz 1000 gulden.
Dowager Princess Grassalkowitz, *née* Princess Esterházy 1000 gulden.
The Count Fries guardianship for their guardians, Moritz Count v. Fries 1000 gulden.
. . . Count Joseph v. Erdödy 500 gulden.
Count Broune, Russian Brigadier 300 gulden.
Prince v. Lobkowitz, Field Marshal 250 gulden.

The progress of the war in Italy went swiftly from bad to worse. To trace its progress we must return to the point, late in 1796, when we left Napoleon at a crucial

1 Mozart died not in the Krugerstrasse but in his apartment in the Rauensteingasse; Haydn has in fact confused the fact that the widow, Constanze, had rooms in the same house ('Zum blauen Säbel im zweyten Stock'), at least in December 1794. In Deutsch, *Mozart, Dokumente* (413) the house number is given as 1046 (not 1075). Haydn assumed that Mozart had died there.

2 The Gesellschaft der Musikfreunde owns a copy of the invitation to that concert as well as a hand-bill; Pohl III, 118. Deutsch *Freihaustheater*, p. 40.

juncture in his Italian campaign. The course of the war in Germany had, as we have seen, permitted the Allies to send extensive reinforcements to Baron Alvinczy (Joseph von Barbarek) at the head of the Italian armies. The French army was exhausted and now also outnumbered, and in the inconclusive battles fought near Arcole during November it appeared that Napoleon had overstretched his resources. But he recovered and, after a very costly battle, forced Alvinczy to retreat. The Austrians mounted a new counter-offensive, but were decisively defeated by the French at Rivoli on 14 January 1797. Napoleon then turned his attention to Mantua once more and an Allied force under Giovanni di Provera sent to relieve the garrison there (under a state of siege by the French for some time); Bonaparte defeated Provera on 16 January and Mantua was obliged to surrender on 2 February.

Next came the Papal States, which were defeated in a campaign lasting a fortnight: according to the terms of the peace treaty of Tolentino on 19 February 1797, Pope Pius VI ceded Romagna and the legations of Bologna and Ferrara, paid a large indemnity (which also included many priceless works of art) and renounced the Holy See's claims on Avignon. These territories – Avignon excepted, naturally – were joined to the Duchy of Modena and turned into the Cisalpine Republic, modelled after French Republican ideals and, of course, under French rule. Having settled the question of the Papal States to his satisfaction, Napoleon turned northwards once again and on 16 March crossed the strategic river Tagliamento and entered Austrian territory through its southern border (Isonzo). As the French poured into Styria on 4 April, Count Saurau published a war proclamation, asking for volunteers; and two days later he made a brilliant speech which finally aroused his countrymen to action; within eight days, 37,600 men were armed. On 10 April the French entered Graz and occupied the Schloßberg; after midnight Napoleon entered the city and took up quarters in the house of Count Stubenberg. Three days before, on 7 April, Bonaparte had signed armistice preliminaries at Judenburg, and on 18 April at Leoben – barely two days' march from Vienna – the armistice was ratified and peace preliminaries signed. The chaotic Allied armies were now in the charge of Archduke Carl, who replaced Baron Alvinczy after it had become manifest that the French were about to lay siege to the mother country. In May, Napoleon abolished the ancient republic of the Serenissima in Venice and put in a Republican-type government. The final peace treaty between France and Austria took place at Campo Formio on 17–18 October 1797, leaving England almost single-handed in the fight against France.[1]

We have seen that the big concert at Prince Schwarzenberg's (Haydn's *The Seven Words*), scheduled for 7 April, was cancelled because of the catastrophic war news. The average Viennese citizens were apparently more sanguine. On 9 and 10 April, the Tonkünstler-Societät gave their Easter concert as usual, the principal attraction being a Cantata, *Timotheus* 'or the Power of Music' (*die Gewalt der Musik*) by Peter Winter in which Maria Anna Willmann, Therese Gassmann, Joseph Simoni, and Ignaz Saal were the vocal soloists. On 9 April there was a double concerto for oboe and violin by Triebensee (played by him and 'Violindirector' Anton Breymann from the Liechtenstein orchestra), and on the 10th a concerto for two clarinets by Casimir Antonio

1 For the Napoleonic sources, *vide supra*, p. 110. To this add Franz Martin Mayer, 'Die Franzosen in Steiermark', in *Geschichte der Steiermark*, Graz 1913, pp. 475ff. In the sudden wave of patriotic enthusiasm, many composers – among them Beethoven with his *Kriegslied der Österreicher* – wrote music to awaken popular enthusiasm for the cause: 'with little success', notes Pohl-Botstiber drily (III, 118).

Cartellieri (played by the Stadler brothers). The day afterwards Constanze Mozart gave her 'benefit academy' in which she participated in a concert performance of *La clemenza di Tito*.[1] Silverstolpe tells us that Georg Nikolaus Nissen, Constanze's second husband, had rented rooms from her in 1797, apparently in the Judengäßchen House No. 535; she became his mistress shortly thereafter.

On 12 April, just before the armistice preliminaries were to be signed at Judenburg, the *Wiener Zeitung* carried the following notice:

> . . . And finally, a special corps of mounted cavalry, under the command of I. R. Major General Prince Johann v. Li[e]chtenstein, will be established. . . . The City of Vienna will in any event be completely defended, the fortifications organized, the walls to receive cannon, stores and provisions laid in, and preparations made for any eventuality. To implement the transportation of this material, all luxury horses are to be requisitioned . . . His I. R. Majesty will only leave Vienna at the last moment if the situation requires it, and will betake himself to the nearby provinces, there to inspire and to order, through his high presence, whatever organizations are necessary to, and have already been provided for, the salvation of the Austrian monarchy.

This was followed by further reports in the same paper:

> [15 April:] . . . The plans for defending the city are being implemented with all speed, and the necessary troops to occupy it are gradually arriving . . . H. M. [informs a proclamation of the Lower Austrian Government's President, Count Saurau] gives the assurance to all house-owners in the city and suburbs that they will be fully recompensed, as soon as peace is restored, from the I. R. privy purse, for any damaged caused to their houses as a result of the city's defence or through enemy activity.
>
> [19 April:] . . . The troops destined for here arrive steadily, to take up entrenched positions on the Vienna hills and in other parts outside the city. . . .
>
> [29 April:] . . . New music. Artaria and Comp. . . . Österreichs Kriegslied, by Friedelberg, set to music for the piano by Ludwig v. Beethoven. 20 kr. . . .
>
> [3 May:] . . . Among the countless indications of true love for Prince and Fatherland . . . [must not be forgotten] Count Prosper von Sinzendorf, who offered gratis 200 pails [*Eimer*] of wine in order to refresh and rally the exhausted . . . I. R. troops who have moved into field positions here . . . and this noble example was followed . . . by the Prince zu Schwarzenberg with 400 [*Eimer*] and the Prince v. Lobkowitz with 200. . . .
>
> [6 May:] . . . The same industry burst upon the capital city when the Government's President, Count v. Saurau, in the name of H. M., informed the public of the danger nearby. . . . The citizens of Vienna were called to defend their city. . . . Everyone left their peaceful occupations . . . in order to subscribe to the Volunteers. . . . And so great was the love for their monarch . . . that within a few days the capital city had raised in their midst an army of fearsome proportions – for their numbers and also for their courage. . . . The citizenry undertook the defence of the city, the University marched out in great numbers, the Merchants formed their own corps, the guilds of carpenters, silk-weavers and others set up their own special companies, the others were divided by city and suburban districts, and finally, through the efforts of the I. R. Major General

1 Pohl *Denkschrift*, 65. The Mozart concert, not in Deutsch, *Mozart, Dokumente*, was announced in the *Wiener Zeitung* on 1 April 1797 (issue No. 26). About Nissen, see Mörner 335, also Deutsch, op. cit., p. 422.

Prince Johann v. Li[e]chtenstein, our own cavalry was established. . . . The command of this noble army was given by H. M. to General of the Armies Prince von Würtemberg, who considered it a special honour to be its leader. . . . Meanwhile the Lower Austrian Government and the Academy of Fine Arts founded their own corps. . . . On the occasion of the worthy Vienna Volunteers entering the city, Freyherr v. Braun . . . gave free theatrical entertainment in both houses. . . .[1]

On 23 May 1797 Silverstolpe's mother (who died later that year, on 12 September) wrote a charming letter the contents of which her son will certainly have communicated to Haydn:

. . . My dearest Frederik, now you've seen and heard so much in the course of a year that I can never see or hear, but there is nothing I envy you more than seeing Haydn and hearing his concerts. I would gladly have been there. He was, is and in my opinion will remain the most distinguished [*den förnämsta*], for all his music defines [*marquerar*] the most delicate and gentlest of emotions, composed with clarity and combined with strength. If you meet him again, tell him that he has an adorer in me, and I thank him for every glad hour that I have had when listening to *The Seven Words*. . . . The Lord's Blessing be with you too. Pray to God for grace to fear and love Him above everything, and to place all belief and trust in Him. Then I know that you love me, and I remain till death takes me your dearest Mother

E. C. Leijonhufwud.

[Mörner, 317]

On 14 June Silverstolpe writes to Stockholm:

. . . A few days ago I went to see Haydn again, who now lives right next to me, since he gave up his customary winter and spring lodgings in one of the suburbs [Gumpendorf] and moved a whole quarter-of-a-mile away. On this occasion he played to me, on the piano, violin quartets which a certain Count Erdödi has ordered from him and which may be printed only after a certain number of years. These are more than masterly and full of new thoughts. While he played, he let me sit beside him and see how he divided the various parts in the score. Moreover, he sang some arias for me [*mehrstimmige Gesänge*?] which he intends to issue by subscription when their number reaches 24. His usual rhythm characterizes them, and they reveal many touches of genius and exceptional thoughts. He himself told me, how he proceeds when he intends to compose something, and I shall discuss this very thoroughly in my annotations.

A young man from Stralsund [the Prussian Province of Pommern] named [Paul] Struck has enjoyed Haydn's teaching for nearly two years, and has already come out with a volume of trios and a quartet which are rather good. He has much genius and promises to become a great composer in the field of instrumental

1 The first signs of what would be a frightful inflation – one that would bankrupt the country a few years after Haydn's death – may also be noted in the *Wiener Zeitung* at this time. On 31 May, we note: 'Furnished monthly rooms. In the Spiegelgasse, not far from the I. R. Burgbastey, Graben in the Casino [House] No. 1163 on the first floor, is an apartment with 7 rooms and a large kitchen for rent at 15 ducats monthly, then an apartment with 5 rooms at 10 ducats monthly, both apartments with a parquet floor . . .'. A double-ducat coin (= 2 ducats) was about nine Gulden, which meant that the seven-room flat cost some 67.50 Gulden monthly or 810 Gulden annually. One ducat, as Professor Eduard Holzmair, a Viennese expert on the subject kindly informs us (letter of 17 November 1967), would have had about the purchasing power of twenty-five U.S. dollars. Rental of a seven-room apartment at $375, or a five-room one at $250 per month, is obviously expensive even at today's standards. (Subsequently values have of course changed with variations of the dollar's rate of exchange.)

music. . . . Herr Struck's society is rather pleasant for me, since he has a good character and has much sympathy for the country which we both regard as our home. His industry and capacity for work exceed every description. . . .

[Mörner, 318]

[Vienna 21 June 1797] . . . My dear mother congratulates me, quite rightly, on my acquaintance with Haydn. I delight as often as I can in his society and he always offers me music. Once I too intend to offer him something along those lines, for I will ask four musicians and make up a quartet, for which, as he himself tells me, my rooms are well fitted. Since the walls are painted in the local fashion, the echo is good and I imagine that Haydn's music, well played, will give its master pleasure. – As far as symphonic music goes, I find he is the most distinguished, he excels even Mozart (though the latter excels him in pure genius). Kraus is more sublime than either of them, but not so imaginative. He is more delicate and never has such distractions as in Mozart. Haydn is more learned than Kraus, but Kraus could have been more learned if he had not pushed that attribute aside for the reason that the human heart approves of. – I have made Haydn a present of Kraus's Music for the Funeral of King Gustav III [*vide infra*] and I suppose he will regard it as a masterpiece of learnedness, depth and sublimity. – To the things I have dared to say here, I ought really, *au fin*, to say 'in my opinion', otherwise I will receive no pardon for the mistakes I might have made. Music and painting are now my pastimes during my free moments, that is not as *practicus* but as one who studies and observes. . . . [Mörner, 319]

[*Silverstolpe's Report (II)*]

When Summer began Haydn moved back to his own house in the suburb of Gumpendorf, Kleine Stein-Gasse No. 73. It lies on the edge of town, not far from the Mariahülf [Mariahilf] Line which one passes in order to get to Schönbrunn. When I entered the room I heard a parrot calling 'Papa Haydn!' In one of the rooms to the right one often saw the great man with his undistinguished features getting up from his work, but also sometimes remaining seated at it until the visitor was quite close. *There* it was that he showed me the [D minor and] D major Aria from *The Creation* ['Rollend in schäumenden Wellen'/'Rolling in foaming billows'] which describes the sea moving and the waves breaking on the shores. 'You see,' he said in a joking tone, 'you see how the notes run up and down like the waves: see there, too, the mountains that come from the depths of the sea? One has to have some amusement after one has been serious for so long.' – But when we arrived at the pure stream, which creeps down the valley in a small trickle, ah! I was quite enthusiastic to see how even the quiet surface flowed. I could not forbear putting an affectionate hand on the old and venerable shoulder and giving it a gentle squeeze, who sat at the piano and sang with a simplicity that went straight to the heart. – In the same room where the instrument stood, there was a bookcase with glass doors. There I specially noticed a collection of the best poets of Germany, and when we spoke of them, it seemed Gellert was his hero. – Left was a little room of which the walls were decorated with a collection of canons under glass, all by Haydn and on paper with red music lines.

On my third or fourth visit I took with me a copy of the Funeral Symphony [*sic*] in C minor that Kraus wrote for the funeral ceremony of King Gustav III.[1] Haydn, to whom it had not occurred that I intended to present him with the work, sat down at once to read it straight through. After the end of each part he said: 'That's excellent, that's most touching', and after the last movement, 'It is

1 Composed in 1792.

music of a quite astonishing perfection. It is worthy of him.' Shortly afterwards he added, 'I would like to read it through again.' But, I replied, the piece is yours. 'A thousand thanks,' answered Haydn, 'then I shall read it several times more.' Later I gave him the two Overtures, to *Aeneas in Karthago*, to *Proserpine*, a Symphony in E flat and also the one in D with the fugato. When Haydn returned these works to me, he said: 'Pity about that man,[1] as with Mozart! They were both still so young.' – The Quartets of our brilliant [Johan] Wikmanson, which his daughter (now Frau Präsidentin Westerstrand) arranged to have printed and dedicated to Haydn, also found the complete approval of the master [*vide infra*, p. 570]. . . .

. . . I kept up my connection with the great master, and his personality was so fixed on my memory that I certainly could not forget any of its smallest details. He never hesitated to play me his compositions or to sing them. Sometimes a little aria, sometimes a violin quartet; and I remember that one day he was just in the process of discarding and crossing out a Finale of such a work [quartet] in order to replace it with another final movement. 'The first one', he remarked, 'is just a piece of *work*, it doesn't flow freely from its source.'

[Mörner in *Haydn-Studien* II/1, 1969, pp. 26, 28]

It is fair to assume that Haydn completed most of the famous string Quartets, Op. 76, dedicated to Count Joseph von Erdödy, by the time the composer played them from the autograph (now, alas, lost) to Silverstolpe in the middle of June 1797. The arrangement, which by the time Beethoven was in full possession of his powers was standard practice, was to write such works on commission for some patron who had the exclusive rights of performance for a number of years. Then the composer was free to negotiate their sale to a publisher. Of course, Haydn was not in a position to take advantage of such offers until after his return from England; before 1790, he had been in the country most of the year and busy, from 1776 to 1790, with an exhausting opera season each year; besides which, he was supposed to compose exclusively for Prince Nicolaus I. Nicolaus II was much more lenient in such matters. Beethoven, as we learn from Ries, sold works in this manner to Lobkowitz. 'Afterwards Prince Lobkowitz bought [the *Sinfonia Eroica*] for several years' use, and it was performed several times in his palace.' A similar arrangement was made between the composer and Count Franz von Oppersdorf regarding the Fourth Symphony, for which Beethoven received 500 gulden in February 1807. Thayer by this period speaks of 'the customary six-month period' and quotes a letter from Beethoven to Breitkopf & Härtel of 18 November 1806: 'I cannot give you the promised symphony yet – because a gentleman of quality has taken it from me, but I have the privilege of publishing it in half a year.' It may well have been Haydn who invented this rather clever idea, whereby the patron had an important work or works as his exclusive property for some years and paid

1 Concerning Kraus, Silverstolpe wrote a letter in French to Kraus's sister, Marianne Lämmerhirt on 9 December 1801; the original letter no longer exists, only a German translation in the hand of Marianne's husband (Berlin Staatsbibliothek). We take the liberty of quoting it here out of chronological context. Haydn, says Silverstolpe, said about Kraus that he 'was the first man of genius that I met [in 1783 – *vide supra*, p. 250; at that date Haydn had probably not yet met Mozart]. Why did he have to die? It is an irreplaceable loss for music. The Symphony in C minor which he wrote in Vienna specially for me, is a work which will be considered a masterpiece in every century, and believe me: there are few who could write a similar work . . .'. Those who knew that magnificent Symphony – now available in a scholarly modern edition (for a review, see *Haydn Yearbook* III, 1965, p. 172) by Richard Engländer – will agree with Haydn: the Kraus Symphony is one of the late eighteenth-century's greatest instrumental works. If Mozart's name were attached to it, the work would rival the G minor Symphony (K. 550) in popularity. The *Funeral Music for King Gustav III* is also a stunning piece of music; Haydn's copy was catalogued in the Elssler *Verzeichnis geschriebener Musicalien* as No. 195 'in der Partitur gebunden.' K. F. Schreiber, *Biographie . . . Kraus*, p. 69, n. 2.

handsomely for that privilege; after which the composer could publish the work and collect a second honorarium. Spohr had a similar arrangement with Haydn's old patron, Johann Tost.[1]

It must have been about June 1797 that Haydn reached the half-way mark in composing his large Oratorio, *The Creation*. We learn from Griesinger (54f.) that

> His patriarchal, devout spirit found particular expression in *The Creation*, and therefore this composition must have been more successful than if it had been written by a hundred other masters. 'It was not till I reached the half of my composition that I noticed that it had turned out well; I was also never so devout as during that time when I was working on *The Creation*; every day I fell on my knees and asked God to give me strength to enable me to pursue the work to its successful conclusion.' Who is not transported back by such statements to the period of an Albrecht Dürer and other artists of the German *Vorwelt*? They, too, wrote in their simple and direct way that whatever they accomplished was not the result of their strength of genius but came from Him who gave them the necessary gifts. A natural result of Haydn's religiosity was his *modesty*; for his talent was not his own work but a gracious gift from Heaven, to whom he believed he must show himself grateful.

It was soon time for Haydn to go to Eisenstadt, where (as we shall hear from Silverstolpe) he completed *The Creation*; but no doubt he revised the work and made many changes between the late autumn, when he returned to Vienna, and April 1798, when the work was first performed. This year (1797) Prince Nicolaus II expected a very noble guest: none other than the Empress herself. On 19 August, Marie Therese visited not only Eisenstadt but also Eszterháza Castle. The *Wiener Zeitung* reports:

> . . . Yesterday on 18 [August] their Majesties left the camp of the Volunteers. Her Majesty the Empress went to Esterhaß, where Prince Esterházy went in haste as soon as manœuvres were over, and [she] examined the beautiful castle, the magnificent garden, the Bagatelle [Chinese Pavilion], the theatre, and all the other beauties and curiosities of the place. . . . Today in the morning at 6:00 a.m., once more the thunder of the cannon announced the joyous arrival of Her Majesty the Empress, who had spent the night in Esterhaß and had been given breakfast at Groß-Zinkendorf, where Frau Countess v. Széchényi had prepared everything under a tent which had been put up in the driveway [*Allee*]. . . . Accompanied by many good wishes and the thunder of cannon, Her Majesty the Empress left Oedenburg and went straight to Eisenstadt, where This Most Highest One was received by Prince Niklas Esterházy. After refreshments, Her Majesty, accompanied by the Prince, the Princess and the princely family, was shown the castle, the zoo, said farewell between 10 and 11 o'clock and left for Laxenburg . . .

Whether Haydn's presence was required for this brief official visit, we do not know; perhaps he did not need to be in Eisenstadt before the first week in September, to assist in the celebrations for Princess Marie Hermenegild's name-day on the 10th of that month. One reason for his presence in Vienna might have been the centenary celebrations at the Piaristenkirche. On 27 August the Annals inform us that 'at 9

1 Wegeler and Ries, *Notizen*, pp. 79f. Thayer (Forbes) I, 350, 432. See also Spohr, pp. 88f. Tost suggested that Spohr should turn over to Tost, for a fee, all the works he would compose in Vienna for a period of three years. Each time they were to be performed, the score and parts were to be borrowed from Tost and the work in question played in Tost's presence only. Tost 'would prefer works suitable for performance in private circles, such as quartets and quintets for stringed instruments, and sextets, octets, and nonets for strings and winds.' Haydn had dedicated to Tost the Quartets, Opp. 54, 55 and 64.

o'clock *Herr* Augustin Ortmann, a curate from the Metropolitan Church of St. Stephen, preached, and the sermon was printed. Then the Mass with music by H. Joseph Heyden [*sic*].'[1]

At this point our first-hand knowledge of life at Eisenstadt, and later at Vienna, is immensely enriched by the diary of an official at Prince Nicolaus's Court, Joseph Carl Rosenbaum, who had been controller of the stabling accounts since 1795. In 1800 he married Therese Gassmann, the well-known soprano, who participated in the performances of several Masses at Eisenstadt in the period at present under discussion. Large extracts from the diary have been published in the *Haydn Yearbook*.[2]

On Sunday, 10 September, Princess Marie Hermenegild celebrated her name-day. Rosenbaum tells us (p. 25):

> For the Feast of St. Mary we had a new Mass, the music by Fuchs, also a new chorus by Joseph Haydn; Baroness Walterskirchen sang an aria. At mid-day a banquet, vespers later in the afternoon, then Turkish music on the square. In the evening, fireworks by the princely Fireworks Master, Wiener, then illumination of the castle, garden and town; finally a ball in the grand hall, lasting until 4 a.m. The company numbered 800.

It has been suggested above that the new chorus was Haydn's Offertorium 'Non nobis, Domine' (*supra*, pp. 80, 82); but it may have been the Motet 'Insanae et vanae curae'. Baroness Walterskirchen, or Freiin von Schönfeld, was a well-known dilettante. Franz Wiener, the pyrotechnist, belonged to the armoury personnel of Forchtenstein Fortress, an old Esterházy family seat which had seen valiant service in the Turkish wars.

On 17 September, Rosenbaum tells us, officials of the princely Court and the guests collaborated in the first rehearsal of August Wilhelm Iffland's play *Die Aussteuer*. There were further rehearsals on the next two days, and the first performance took place on 20 September. The next day, Carl (later von) Marinelli's company arrived at the Castle; Marinelli was head of the Leopoldstädter Theater in Vienna and had been asked to Eisenstadt earlier, in 1794; he was now, 1797, in residence for some time to give plays, starting on the 21st.

On 26 September, most of the suite of Palatine Archduke Joseph, since 1796 Viceroy of Hungary, arrived at Eisenstadt; the Viceroy himself arrived a day afterwards. A shooting party in honour of the guests took place on 27 September. At night there was a ball and once again the castle was illuminated for the 1,200 guests. Of this occasion Rosenbaum noted: 'The illumination was the most beautiful ever seen in Eisenstadt.'[3]

We have a report about the festivities in the *Wiener Zeitung* of 7 October:

> On 30 Sept. a letter from Eisenstadt was addressed to us as follows: H.R.H. the Archduke Palatine had lunch on the 26th inst. at Zinkendorf with Count von

1 This and the previous documentary accounts of Haydn's relationship with the Piaristenkirche come from Otto Biba, 'Die Pflege der Kirchenmusik in der Piaristenkirche', in *Festschrift 250 Jahre Piaristenkirche Maria Treu*, Vienna 1969, pp. 45ff.

2 *Haydn Yearbook* V (1968), two separate publications (German and English), ed. Else Radant. A few entries not in the *Yearbook* are included here as being of possible interest to the specialist, e.g. 9 Sept.: '. . . At 4 p.m. the first Vespers were given in the newly decorated Bergkirche . . .'. The new decorations also included a handsome new organ built by Johann Gottfried Malleck, who had earlier (1778) built the organ in the Stadtpfarrkirche. We are indebted to Dr Otto Biba for this important information.

3 Part of the Rosenbaum entries are not quoted in Radant, since they concern Haydn only peripherally. Horányi, 167f.

Széchényi, who had invited many guests to his table. Then they went to an amusement devised by the Count for H.R.H.'s pleasure which took place on the Neusiedler See and showed a naval battle, after which a fortress specially designed for the purpose was stormed. In the evening H.R.H. returned to Zinkendorf where there was a splendid ball. The next day, 27th inst., H.R.H. arrived at Eisenstadt to take part in this year's hunt. Already at 9 a.m. the local town militia company, the citizen corps and the princely subjects from the Berg, with large and side arms, flags and military band, drew up in rows before the castle, followed by the Jewish community and all the schoolchildren. In front of the throne were six princely cannon mounted on a high rise. One cannon gave the signal for the arrival of H.R.H., whose high person Prince Esterházy strode out to meet. At 11:30 a.m. the high person and Prince Esterházy, accompanied by the thunder of cannon and the sound of trumpets and kettledrums, rode into the princely castle, where all the princely officials were standing in ranks, and afterwards they went into the small hall accompanied by the town magistrates. The banquet, to which the staff- and other Insurrection Battalion-officers were invited, was provided by the surrounding cantons, and was for 100 [Rosenbaum: 800!]. In the afternoon and the next morning there was hunting on the preserves [*Lust-Remise*] and animal-farms, where H.R.H. shot some 560 venison, hare and pheasant. In the evening was a ball, opened by H.R.H. and the Princess. The princely castle, with the buildings opposite and the walled gardens, were magnificently illuminated. In the town a triumphal arch was erected and all the houses lighted up. At H.R.H.'s request, a new Quartet by Kapellmeister Joseph Haydn was played by the princely chamber musicians, and after that the young Luigi Tomassini [*sic*], in the service of His Highness, played on the violin artistic variations written by his father, the princely concert master Luigi Tomassini. Finally H.R.H. visited the local Bergkirche and after table on the 28th inst., to the tune of all the bells and with the thunder of the cannon and the people's endless shouts of 'Vivat', he left Eisenstadt.

[*Wiener Zeitung* No. 80 (1797), pp. 2983f.]

Rosenbaum also writes extensively about the Viceroy's arrival:

Wednesday, 27th: The Viceroy arrived in Eisenstadt at about 12 noon. His approach was announced by the thunder of cannon, which lasted until he arrived and was received in the castle. He was received on the steps by a cordon of princely officials, in the anteroom by the liveried servants, and in the small hall by the house officials. On the square were the princely grenadiers, then the free citizens of the town with their clergy and town council, then the princely subjects from Oberberg and the Jewish community. It was a most ceremonious reception, a brilliant demonstration of the greatness of Prince Esterházy. At mid-day there was a banquet in the grand hall; places were laid for 800 persons, on two tables. As toasts were drunk, trumpets and drums sounded from the balcony of the hall, and cannon were fired in the garden of the castle. . . .

Thursday, 28th: At about 10 a.m. the Viceroy, in the company of the Prince and several cavaliers . . . went hunting. . . . At mid-day a banquet was held in the small hall. In the afternoon the citizens of the town, then the princely citizens and the Jewish community, all with their superiors, and the musicians, gathered on the square and welcomed the Viceroy with a display of flags and with music. . . . The town parson, the magistrate and the town council then went into the small hall where they were received by the Viceroy who thanked them for the particular attentions which had been paid him. New quartets by Haydn were played, [one of them] based on the song *Gott erhalte Franz den Kaiser*, and a seven-year-old boy by the name of Böhm played the violin, earning unanimous applause. At the

Viceroy's departure, cannon were fired and trumpets and drums resounded from the balcony of the castle.

[Radant *Rosenbaum*, 25f.]

The new quartets were from Op. 76, and this is the first recorded performance of any of them. Franz Böhm was a child prodigy from Vienna who excited a great deal of attention at this period. The *Wiener Zeitung* (as we have seen) adds that Luigi Tomasini junior – son of the old leader – also played (variations for violin solo by Luigi senior). Rosenbaum tells us (p. 26) that

> On the 28th two choral singers arrived from Pressburg: Anna Rhumfeld, a soprano, and Frl. Hammer, an alto; the former is already in service, the latter will also be engaged.

These were reinforcements for the *Missa in tempore belli* which was being rehearsed by Haydn. Josepha Hammer was a protégée of Haydn's, as we shall see (CCLN, 203), and in 1802 he described her as possessing 'an alto voice of . . . rare beauty'. Anna Rhumfeld later married the princely accountant Siess. The next day, the new (*vide* pp. 106ff.) Mass was given at Eisenstadt, certainly the first time for the town. Rosenbaum (26) writes: 'Friday 29th [September] . . . a new Mass in C by Haydn was performed; both women sang and both were very successful.' On 2 October, Rosenbaum reports on a theatrical performance with the guests and members of the Court:

> Monday 2nd [October]: the comedy *Stadt und Land* by [Christian Heinrich] Spieß was performed. The cast:
> Countess von Albingen, a rich widow: Countess Charlotte Weißenwolf
> Baroness von Halben, her sister-in-law: Countess Charlotte Hohenfeld
> Miss Lottchen, daughter of the Baroness: Princess Graßalkovics
> Miss Beata: Countess Fanny Weißenwolf
> General v. Hilsenburg: Kühnel, an officer of the mounted cavalry
> Major, Count v. Wieden: Secretary v. Karner
> Baron v. Schildberg: First Lieutenant Seitz
> Herr v. Wattsdorf: Count Johann Weißenwolf
> Nanette, Maid-in-waiting to the Countess: Countess Julia Esterházy
> Michel, Servant to the Baroness: Rosenbaum the younger
> Servant: Rosenbaum
> Servant: Grundmann
> The comedy did not come off very well. . . .

[Radant, *Rosenbaum*, 26]

The princely family was related to the Weissenwolfs (Nicolaus I had married Elisabeth von Weissenwolf and his son, Nicolaus, married Anna Franziska von Weissenwolf) and to the Hohenfelds. Haydn's former Prince, Anton, had been married to Marie Therese von Hohenfeld. Princess Grassalkovics (Grassalkowitz, etc.) was the Prince's sister, Leopoldine, who had married Anton, Prince von Grassalkovics in 1793. Julia Esterházy came from the 'gräfliche Linie'. Rosenbaum and his brother Johann also participated, as did the princely Court painter, Basilius Grundmann, who had painted Haydn's portrait many years earlier. (Rosenbaum may also have meant Nicolaus Grundemann, who worked in the forestry office at Eisenstadt.)

Apparently Marinelli had returned to Vienna; Rosenbaum was shortly to engage him for a return visit. On 4 October we learn from the Diary that:

> Pölt gave an academy in Eisenstadt; his daughter played a [piano] concerto by Mozart, Elsler [*sic*] played an oboe concerto by Fuchs, and v. Székely performed

> his 12 new German Dances. Everyone who is anyone in Eisenstadt was at this academy, which lasted from 4 p.m. until 8 o'clock in the evening. [Radant, *Rosenbaum*, 27]

Johann Pölt was the engineer responsible for the renovation of the Castle. Joseph Elssler was the oboist in the princely orchestra. Franz Székely, Secretary, was in the Household Management. On Sunday 8 October, we learn:

> . . . In the evening . . . I went walking in Oberberg. Then I walked towards the shooting range and had supper at the Engel; Mlle Grießler, Lichtscheindl, Specht, Haydn, Grundemann and I were there. We had an excellent time together, and it was 10 o'clock before we toddled off home. [Radant, *Rosenbaum*, 27]

The inn 'Zum Engel' was located near the Bergkirche. Josepha Griessler was an alto singer; Mrs or Miss Lichtscheindl, either the wife or daughter of the princely book-keeper Anton Lichtscheindl, who had bought Haydn's house in Eisenstadt in 1778; Christian Specht was a bass singer; Nicolaus Grundemann (of the forestry office) or Basilius Grundmann (the painter).

Haydn had planned a performance of *The Seven Words*, to which end he imported outside help from Vienna, including Therese Gassmann, the soprano. Rosenbaum obviously took a liking to the girl immediately and went to call on her at the rather incredible hour of eight in the morning: 'At 8 in the morning I visited the Gaßmanns, who were staying at Svoboda's, the soap-maker's . . . mother and daughter invited me to visit them [in Vienna], and told me they lived in the Singerstrasse, $3\frac{1}{2}$ floors up on the 5th staircase of the Deutsches Haus' [of Mozartian fame].[1] Rosenbaum was also sent to Oedenburg (now Sopron) to look after the printing of the libretto at the widow of the printer Siess, who had printed almost all the librettos for the princely opera house under the reign of Nicolaus I: 'Thursday 19th [October]: I was in Oedenburg to look after the printing of the *7 Words* by Haydn . . .' (Radant, p. 27). A few days later he was sent to Vienna:

> Friday, 20th, and Saturday, 21st: . . . travelled to Vienna and stayed until about 9:30 on Saturday night. I had to look after the ball tickets, and then to make arrangements for the Marinelli Company to come to Eisenstadt to perform a piece on the occasion of the feast there. [Radant, 27]

The festive occasion was a double one: the return to Eisenstadt of the Viceroy and the celebration of the Peace of Campo Formio (17 October). We have several first-hand accounts. The Palatine Archduke, coming from Budapest (then Ofen and Pest), arrived on 26 October in time to participate in a hunt at Zillingsdorf, followed by a lunch for 200 in the great hall of the Castle. The newspaper *Magyar Hirmondó* (1797, II, 574–6) reports:

> The Palatine and, together with him, the illustrious guests were received and honoured here yesterday and the day before. His Royal Highness, arriving from Laxenburg, began hunting on Prince Esterházy's estates near the border. When the chase was over, he betook himself amidst the boom of cannon to Eisenstadt.

1 Radant, *Rosenbaum*, 25. By a printer's error the entry is misdated: it should read precisely one month later, viz. 28 October and not 28 September. The day before we read, '. . . After the theatre I went . . . home, then I looked for a while at the ball and then went to the oratorio, where the Viganòs and Mlle Gaßmann were dining, I laughed and joked with them until after 1 a.m. and then accompanied them home.' (not in Radant)

Soon after his arrival, almost a hundred [*sic*] guests took their seats at richly decorated tables. The palace, together with the building opposite and the park, were illuminated in the evening by green, red and gold-coloured lamps, and the illumination was so splendid that its like has seldom been seen anywhere in the world. Artificial fires conjured the picture of the King and Queen [Emperor and Empress] and also their names. Comedians brought from Vienna performed a merry play in the Prince's theatre; and a new ballet, with the title *Pygmalion*, was then presented by the famous Viganò, his wife and young daughter. This was followed by a fancy-dress ball and an opulent banquet in the great hall. . . .

[Horanyi, 169f.]

[Rosenbaum:] Thursday 26th: . . . In the evening at the theatre a farce by [Carl Friedrich] Hensler, *Der reisende Student*, played by the Marinelli Company. Afterwards, a ballet by Viganò to music by [Ignaz Wenzel] Raphael [*recte*: Raffael].

Friday, 27th: . . . a shoot for hare and pheasant . . . After the party returned, supper in the grand hall at 5:30, then illuminations; in the theatre the song *Gott erhalte den Kaiser* was sung by the whole audience, then the Words of the Redeemer [*The Seven Words*] by Haydn. There followed the ballet *Pygmalion* by Viganò. The theatre lasted until 11 o'clock. Before it started I chatted very pleasantly with the 2 Mlle Gaßmann. . . . In the theatre I passed out 1,000 copies of the text of the Words of the Redeemer, and 1,500 copies of song [*Gott erhalte*] texts, both by Haydn.

[Radant, 28]

[*Magyar Hirmondó*[1] continued:] The Palatine rose early the next morning, 27 October, in order to inspect the coal mines of Wandorf where he was received by

1 Horányi, 170. The report in the *Wiener Zeitung* is similar. In the issue of 4 November 1797 (No. 88, p. 3290) we read: 'Hungary. From Eisenstadt, 28 Oct. For the last fortnight preparations for a large festival have been in the making when on the 23rd the most welcome news of the peace treaty arrived here through Estafette. Thereupon Prince v. Esterházy ordered a hunt at Zillingsdorf for the 26th, in which H.R.H. the Archduke Joseph, Hungarian Palatine, participated. In the afternoon towards 3 o'clock there was a salvo of 10 cannon, and H.R.H. with his train arrived in the princely castle, where a table with 200 couverts was prepared in the great hall, during the course of which, under the noise of trumpets & kettledrums and the thunder of cannon, a toast was proposed many times to the all-highest person. In the evening, there was a comedy in the princely theatre performed by the Vienna Marinelli Troupe, then there was a beautiful ballet danced by the famous Mad. Viganò. The conclusion of this day was a masked ball in the great hall, attended by more than one thousand guests, all of whom were served refreshments. H.R.H., with the all-highest *Obersthofmeister* Count v. Zapary, and the whole general staff as well as many members of the nobility from Vienna, participated. The whole lower grounds of the garden (in which a temple preceded by two pyramids had been erected), the princely castle up to the second courtyard, and the steps in front, were illuminated with many thousand lamps. But the principal object of admiration were the large stable-houses, the columns of which were covered with green glass lamps and wound with garlands in the form of laurels, while the rest of the façade was decorated with red, yellow and white lamps, all of which presented a most attractive appearance. Between the two wings of the stables was a triumphal arch with two vases, in the middle of which was the Hungarian crown with the coats-of-arms of all the provinces, and on each side of the decorated names of their Imperial, Apostolic, Royal majesties there was a 'Vivat'. There was also a triumphal arch put up in front of the Rathaus, and all the houses were illuminated. The next day, in the morning of the 27th, was again a hunt on the nearby mountain of Fölling; altogether two thousand and ten of hares and pheasants were shot. In the evening, when H.R.H. entered the theatre, to the sound of endless 'Vivat' cries, there was sung the popular *Volkslied* 'Gott erhalte den Kaiser etc.', and after that *The Seven Words*, composed by the great *Kapellmeister* Joseph Hayden [*sic*], was performed, and the Ballet by Mad. Viganò repeated. In the morning of today H.R.H., after repeated assurances of the all-highest's pleasure in these doings, started the trip back under the thunder of the guns.' We would remind our readers that it can have been for such a masked ball that Haydn composed the Twenty-Four Minuets which have been discussed above in the list of works assigned – in this case hypothetically – to the year 1795. (*Vide supra*, p. 84.) Although the wind-band music at Eisenstadt Castle has been recovered, the dance music seems completely to have disappeared except for those pieces by Haydn which, with his estate, passed to the Esterházy Archives after the composer's death in 1809.

> Count Saurau, Councillor Ruprecht and other gentlemen. He returned to Eisenstadt at mid-day to consume a light meal, and then he participated in a shooting party at which a thousand hares and nearly as many pheasants were brought down. Dinner began at 6 o'clock followed by the performance of Haydn's splendid composition *The Seven Words* for which many musicians and singers had been engaged from Vienna. Before this, when the Palatine entered the theatre, Haydn's well-known composition 'Gott erhalte den Kaiser' was sung. After these delightful musical performances, Viganò and his family danced again. The same evening, the castle and the building opposite were illuminated, and a ball was held in the smaller dancing room of the palace.

Rosenbaum noted, ruefully, that 'on the 26th a great hole was torn in my frock coat as the audience entered the theatre.' 'On the 28th, about 9 a.m.,' continues the Diary, 'the Viceroy left Eisenstadt to the thunder of cannon, and travelled to Preßburg. . . . While the Viceroy was here, a total of 300 cannon shots were fired.' (p. 28). We learn that Therese Gassmann received a fee of fifty ducats for her performances in Eisenstadt (Pohl III, 120). She had, as Rosenbaum noted in 1801, a voice of 'purity, modulation and unusual range' (p. 94), and Haydn obviously appreciated her gifts. In November Rosenbaum went to Vienna and began to call on Madame Gassmann and her two pretty daughters: 'Thursday 30th [November] . . . In the evening I was at the Gaßmanns; there was singing, and we talked a great deal about the theatre, my favourite activity (29)'. We also learn that Marinelli's fee for his (second?) appearance at Eisenstadt was 100 gulden (Rosenbaum, 5 December 1797). On 'Tuesday 12 November . . . In the evening I visited the Gaßmanns . . . We talked of various things concerning the theatre, then about the Prince sending Therese 50 ducats for her singing in the *7 Words* by Haydn, and finally about the age of the two girls: it was established that Nanet is 28, and Therese 24' (p. 30).

To return to Eisenstadt, we must now record the visit of F. S. Silverstolpe to Haydn in September:

> [*Silverstolpe's Report (III)*]
> In September 1797 I gave myself the pleasure of seeing Haydn in peace and quiet in the country. I visited him in Eisenstadt in Hungary, almost a day's trip from Vienna. It is a so-called *Landstadt*, free of all noise, with a castle which is used at certain times by the owners, the Princes Esterházy. The view of the Neusiedlersee was most pleasant. In this place of refuge, Haydn completed his Oratorio, *The Creation*. [Mörner, in *Haydn-Studien* II/1, 1969, pp. 27f.]

Prince Esterházy, perhaps as a result of the spectacular success of 'Gott erhalte', and perhaps encouraged by his wife, now raised Haydn's salary – which, as we have observed above, was not princely. As from 1 October 1797, Haydn received 1,000 gulden as a pension from Nicolaus I and, as salary from Nicolaus II, 400 gulden plus an additional 300 gulden (total: 1,700 gulden annually), and 'die Uniform nach herrschaftlichem Belieben' (the uniform to be given as His Serene Highness sees fit): according to Pohl (III, 121) the uniforms were now a green frock coat with red trimmings, whereas at Eszterháza the musicians had worn a blue frock with gold or silver embroidery (at least for much of the period).

Haydn must have stayed in Eisenstadt until the beginning of November, perhaps even longer. About this time he will have received a parcel of music from the publisher Nicolaus Simrock in Bonn with the following note:

[Bonn] 20 Oct. 1797.

Kindly accept this copy, worthy man, which should persuade you of the complete sincerity with which I remain as always your

N. S. [Nicolaus Simrock]

[Not in CCLN; Bartha, 315]

It is thought that the complimentary copies were the second set of Salomon Symphonies arranged for piano trio, which Simrock issued at the beginning of October. It is, moreover, believed that Haydn later gave the prints to a Herr von Stam. (In the Elssler Catalogue of Haydn's library, this note, 'an Herr von Stam verschenkt', was placed next to Salomon's own editions of these works; but since these Salomon prints came into the Esterházy Archives with the rest of the music, it is assumed that the note about Herr Stam refers to these Simrock copies, which did *not* appear in Haydn's legacy.)

It is worth noting that between Haydn's letter to Count Saurau of January 1797 and his letter to Kürchner of 1 June 1798 we have no extant letters by the composer; and after 1 June, we must wait until about the end of April 1799 before another Haydn letter appears. It is, of course, unlikely that Haydn wrote only one letter from January 1797 to April 1799; but it is clear that he was saving all his energies for *The Creation* and his other compositions (and duties as *Capellmeister* to the Prince). It is not until the middle of 1799 (*vide* Chronicle *infra*) that Haydn letters begin to reappear with ever increasing frequency.

Haydn returned, then, to Vienna with all (or at least most) of the first draft of *The Creation* completed. We first hear of the composer[1] in the account books of F. S. Silverstolpe, where we read: 'Supé för Haydn den 4. dec. + 10 pers. och omkostnader för en konsert' [supper for Haydn the 4th Dec. plus 10 persons and the costs of a concert] '11 [gulden] 14 [kreutzer]'. In a letter home, the Swedish diplomat writes:

Vienna, 13 December 1797.

To give you some information about how I amuse myself, I shall tell you that some days ago I had a concert in my quarters, given by four good musicians. A transverse flautist, Turner, who has been to Sweden, also participated, so that we could give quintets as well. Haydn was one of the four listeners and amused himself well. We gave music by three masters who were present. Also we gave a Quintet by Kraus, which is one of his most beautiful.

[Mörner, 322f.]

1 Haydn did not attend the annual masked ball of the Pensionsgesellschaft bildender Künstler, given this year on 26 November at the Redoutensaal. Since he faithfully attended most of the other years, perhaps he was not yet in Vienna. The beautiful Dances by Beethoven ('die beliebten Menuette und Deutschen', said the *Wiener Zeitung* in its pre-announcement on 18 November), which he had first conducted for that organization in 1795, were now repeated in the small rooms. The free tickets included:

Herr v. Henneberg Mus. Compos.	12 [Stücke]
– Täuber D^to	12
– Beethowen [*sic*]	6
– Süssmayer	4
– Kozeluch	4
– Eybler	4
– Capoll	3
– Kuster	3

Anno 1797/haben Freÿ-Billets erhalten.

[Archives of the City of Vienna]

The Dances in the large room were by Music Director Henneberg (*Wiener Zeitung* No. 92, 18 November 1797, p. 3438).

To this we may add another section of Silverstolpe's Report:

> [*Silverstolpe (IV)*]
> In the winter months, I used generally to put on quartets for Haydn. Apart from these society evenings, I also tried to get him to come to lunch. Then he spoke gladly and his good heart poured out without reserve. His two trips to England gave him material of a special sort. Without the least trace of pride he told of his receiving the doctor's degree at Oxford, of the robes that he had to wear, and how, in his ceremonial robes, he had to sit at the organ. He told, too, of the courtesy which was shown him in London. An unknown person invited him to tea in the evening. He arrived there and found the whole numerous family sitting round the fire. It had almost burned itself out, and the room became darker and darker. After a long while, lights were brought in and the chandelier lighted. Haydn, sitting in the middle of the group, now realized that all the women were identically dressed. A white ribbon enclosed their hair, and on each ribbon glittered the name Haydn in steel buttons [*Stahl-Strauß*]. On another occasion with unknown people the host suggested exchanging snuff-boxes. That meant gold for a very ordinary material. Haydn, rather embarrassed, was finally persuaded to receive a present in exchange for something he considered worthless. – Everything that he related bore the stamp of his goodness and his trust. Never did I hear him criticize anyone out of ill-will. About mediocrity he was silent; he melted with inner joy, however, if he had the possibility of displaying a growing and good talent. Morality always had a value in his thinking, and his comportment radiated nothing but modesty, honour and benevolence.
>
> [Mörner, in *Haydn-Studien* II/1, 1969, 27, 32][1]

Silverstolpe also carried on an extensive correspondence *via* the diplomatic pouch. He was supposed to inform the Prince-Regent (later King) of the general political situation in Austria. His dispatches, some in code and some *en clair*, include Court gossip and matters of general interest. Mörner (325) informs us that on 23 October 1797, Silverstolpe reported to Gustav IV on the enthusiastic reception of 'Gott erhalte' at the theatre the night before.

Meanwhile Haydn's former pupil and friend, Paul Wranizky (*vide supra*, p. 246), was trying to get Haydn accepted gratis as a member of the Tonkünstler-Societät, which organization had behaved so shabbily towards the composer almost two decades earlier. Wranizky, according to the records of the Society,[2] stated that

> It is true that this is against the rules of the Statutes, but the Society must make an exception here and consider itself honoured to have as a member such an exceptional man, who has been responsible for such unexampled progress in music and has provided the Society already with so much profit as a result of his compositions.

This resolution was presented to Haydn in the house of Count von Kuefstein in the presence of the Vice-President (Antonio Salieri) and the other Directors, Friberth, Pable, Orsler and Wranizky; and Haydn was invited, in the most flattering way, to attend the next session of the Society *in pleno*. Johann Ferdinand, Count von Kuefstein, I. R. *Hofmusikgraf*, was patron of the Society until his death in 1818; and it was he who

1 The story of Mr and Mrs Shaw and the ladies with the name Haydn embroidered in their head-dresses is related in CCLN, 275; also in *Haydn in England 1791–1795*, p. 116.
2 In the Archives of the City of Vienna, but alas now very incomplete. Pohl's *Denkshrift* is thus invaluable (pp. 23f.). Radant, *Rosenbaum*, 30. *Wiener Zeitung*, 16 December 1797. Pohl III, 122f.

presided at the plenary session held on 11 December, accompanied by Count Johann Esterházy, *Hofrat* of the Transylvanian Court Chancellery. Rosenbaum informs us:

> Sunday 17th: . . . The Vienna newspaper of the 16th[1] also describes the ceremony of 11 December at which Joseph Haydn, my honoured friend, was received into the Society of the Institute of Musicians with all formalities waived, by virtue of his extraordinary merit as father and reformer of the noble art of composition. He was unanimously elected Senior Assessor [for life] by a committee under the chairmanship of Count Küfstein, the *Hofmusikgraf*. Count Johann Esterházy conducted him into the hall which is the large anteroom of the Redouten-Sall [*sic*]; at the entrance he was received by the Tonkünstler with cries of 'vivat' and with hand-clapping, and Paul Wranizky, the *Actuarius*, gave a speech in his honour.

The men who received Haydn at the house of Count Kuefstein were all 'brother composers': Carl Friberth had been at Eisenstadt when Haydn was first engaged in 1761 and the two men had collaborated on the opera *L'incontro improvviso*, Friberth (otherwise a tenor) writing the libretto; Salieri and Wranizky are well-known to us, while Joseph Pable was a composer of church music and Joseph Orsler a 'cellist and the composer of several symphonies, quartets, trios, etc. Most of Vienna's leading musicians were members of the Society, which was primarily an organization to assist widows and orphans of musicians who had been members (a kind of pension organization, in other words). It must have pleased Haydn to have that old 'debt' of 1779 so nobly cancelled. He attended six more sessions, the last on 14 November 1800. In the Society's records, he is referred to as 'our dear' or 'our worthy Assessor'. A facsimile of the protocol for such a session is reproduced on p. 315.

The Society's Christmas concerts took place on 22 and 23 December at the Burgtheater. This time it was 'a mixed programme', with many smaller numbers:

> Grand Symphony by Paul Wranizky.[2] – Chorus by Handel. – The favourite aria from the Cantata 'Der Retter in Gefahr', (by Süssmayer, sung by Schulz and

1 The *Wiener Zeitung* (No. 100, 16 December 1797, pp. 3706f.) writes: 'The Tonkünstler-Gesellschaft in Vienna has sent a deputation to wait on Herr Joseph Haydn, asking him to join the Society in view of his exceptional services for music. And to demonstrate how much they venerate the fruits of his art, they have waived all his entrance fees etc. On the 11th inst. he was received by all members of the organization under the chairmanship of Herr Hofrath, Count von Kuefstein, *Hofmusikgraf* and the chief director of that Society; and was led in accompanied by that well-known lover of art, Count Johann Esterházy von Galantha. Some of the older and several of the younger musicians went to meet [them], and when he entered the room, he was greeted with triumphal [*frohlockenden*] applause and cries of 'vivat'. Herr Paul Wranitzky [*sic*], at present *Actuarius* of the Society, made a fitting speech to Herr Haydn, and at the conclusion of it, Haydn was unanimously elected a Senior Assessor in perpetuity. It will always remain very fitting for the Society to have honoured in such an excellent – and for that Institute hitherto unusual – fashion the father and reformer of the noble art of music, by which they have assured for themselves the approval of all those who honour real genius and also the active participation of a great man who is recognized in his field.'

The Society had also behaved in an almost insane way about the score and parts of Haydn's Oratorio, *Il ritorno di Tobia*, which had been such a success at its première in 1775 and also at its repetition in 1784. In 1797 it happened that the Empress Marie Therese wanted to get hold of a copy of the Oratorio, and after (as it would seem) ascertaining from Haydn that he no longer owned a copy, she turned to the Society. It turned out that they, too, no longer owned a note; the work had been 'ausgemustert' (discarded). Wranizky said he considered this an act 'of disrespect *vis-à-vis* a composer who was still alive and who perhaps with reason deserved to be called a benefactor of the Society.' (Pohl, *Denkschrift*, 45f.)

2 This Symphony probably took the place of a 'Friedens-Sinfonie' (Peace Symphony), written to celebrate Campo Formio, which was ready for performance but then forbidden by a Court decree of 20 December – another sign of the times and the coming political repression. Why forbid a Peace Symphony? Pohl, *Denkschrift*, 50.

accompanied on the clarinet by Stadler), – Oboe Concerto by Krammer, played by Czerwenka [2nd evening: Anton Wranizky, Concerto for violin, 'cello and orch. played by A. Wranizky and Kraft], – Alleluja, Chorus by Albrechtsberger, – Aria by Cimarosa (Therese Gassmann), – Aria by Righini (Ignaz Saal), – Chorus by Sacchini. [2nd evening: *Terzett mit Variationen* from the Opera *Don Giovanni* for two oboes and cor anglais composed by Beethoven, played by Czerwenka, Reuter and Teimer.] – Quartet for solo voices and chorus by Righini.

Therese Gassmann 'sang . . . very beautifully', wrote Rosenbaum (31), who was by now very attracted to the girl. The *Wiener Zeitung* (6 January 1798) listed the programme, including the 'Trios von Herrn v. Bethofen' and concluded, 'All these artists received lively applause . . . Among those present were the Emperor, the Empress and the Archduchess Christina . . .'.

The new opera, in which Therese also sang, was Giovanni Simone Mayr's *Un pazzo ne fa cento*, which had been first performed the year before at Venice. Therese Gassmann 'sang very beautifully, and she alone made the hours pleasant for me,' writes Rosenbaum on 27 December (p. 31). On that same day, Silverstolpe wrote to Sweden:

> On the morning of the first Holiday (25 December) I heard at St Stephen's Cathedral one of the most beautiful masses by Albrechtsberger . . . In the afternoon I attended a large concert at Count Esterházy's, where symphonies by Wranitzky were performed.
>
> . . . As far as my great hobby, music, is concerned, I have had an idea which I would like to communicate to you. The Swedish Musical Academy would doubtless gain respect if, like our other similarly organized academies, it would nominate foreign members. That would entice composers to Sweden, for composers are mostly very vain. Haydn was made doctor of music in England, and despite his great natural modesty, that flatters him to such an extent that it makes him more inclined to undertake a third trip to that country. Naumann, who has been to Sweden, who wrote for the Swedish theatre, and Haydn, at present the Father of Music, would probably be the first ones to be considered, Salieri and Albrechtsberger, the greatest contrapuntist in Europe and recognized as such by Haydn, would certainly give a great lustre to our music; several others remained unnamed here. You could discuss the question with Secretary Frigel. The letter of nomination for such members should not be connected with any kind of expenses, considering the difficulty of collecting such unimportant sums, which the *musici*, however, with their usual avarice, would not regard as unimportant. It would be a particular pleasure for me to present the letter of nomination to the one or the other Viennese composer who would come into consideration. – In case the project is dropped, you should nevertheless credit me with the honour of having made the proposition.
>
> The [Swedish musical] Society 'Utile-Dulci' has been resurrected to new life? At least speeches are held there. Shouldn't there be given a speech in Kraus's memory? Couldn't Secretary Frigell [*sic*] hold it? Here he [Kraus] is more highly valued than in Sweden. Haydn, Albrechtsberger and others refer to him as one of the greatest geniuses who ever lived, and they cite certain pieces (certainly known to you) as classical works which cannot be excelled. I am *surprised* to find academicians, officials, educated persons of rank and educated ladies asking to hear about him. . . . [Mörner, 323f.]

The answer from Stockholm was positive.

> . . . I read to Secretary Frigel, who was with me in the afternoon, everything that you wrote for him. Recently he wrote to Naumann and thinks that he must have

> the letter by now. . . . Your idea about nominating foreign members of the Musical Academy and especially those you named finds his complete approval, and he intends to support them, which he can more easily do now than beforehand, because he has been for some months Secretary of the Academy . . .
> [Letter dated Stockholm, 6 February 1798: Mörner, 326]

Two operas by Salieri were now running in the Vienna Court Theatres. One of these was *Axur, Re d'Ormus*, originally written in 1787 for Paris with spoken dialogue (libretto by Caron de Beaumarchais) and revised by Lorenzo da Ponte in Italian. Rosenbaum went to the première and wrote on 8 December:

> . . . and around 5 o'clock I went to the opera *Aecur*, which was given for the first time with recitatives at the Kärntner Thor Theater. I enjoyed it immensely. The opera surpasses all expectations. [Radant, p. 29]

A little later, Silverstolpe writes to Sweden (21 February):

> . . . Two beautiful operas by Salieri are the works most often given, the one is called *Axur, King of Ormus* and the other *Palmira, Queen of Persia.* They are masterly, but now and then comical in the Italian manner . . . [Mörner, 327]

The first performance of the revised *Palmira* took place on 1 January 1798.

The Austrians returned to a life of peace; there were many who doubted if that peace would be permanent, but all were convinced that it was more than necessary. The war had never been popular. Ernst Wangermann[1] writes:

> The chief source of discontent [on the part of the Austrian people with their Emperor and government], of course, was the government's obstinate continuation of the war. No amount of pompous publicity for the [Jacobin Trials'] verdicts against 'black traitors' for their 'monstrous crimes' could persuade the public of the necessity or desirability of war. As in 1792 and 1793, public discontent would be loudest in expression and most formidable in extent whenever the fortune of war deserted Austrian arms and favoured the French. And after 1795 the French were winning nearly all the time. In Vienna the demand for peace was becoming so strong that the threat to the government from that source almost seemed to overshadow the blows inflicted by Bonaparte. Thugut wrote to Colloredo in July 1796,
>
> 'Je crains toujours plus Vienne que toute la fureur de l'ennemi, et c'est de là que viendra notre ruine. Je me propose d'avoir demain une conférence avec M. de Saurau sur cet objet, car après tout, c'est la police surtout qui devrait aviser aux expédients de diriger l'opinion, particulièrement dans les lieux publics.'

Since then Napoleon had advanced almost to the gates of Vienna and peace had been obtained, as it were, at the last minute. No doubt Haydn's 'Gott erhalte' had been a major stroke of propaganda, but there were many people who were secret Jacobins – in spirit if not in deed – and one of them was Ludwig van Beethoven, whose sympathy for the French was probably public knowledge (or at least well known to the efficient Austrian police and its Minister, Count Johann Anton von Pergen). Possibly one of the many sources of estrangement between Haydn and his former pupil was also purely

1 *From Joseph II to the Jacobin Trials: Government Policy and Public Opinion in the Habsburg Dominions in the Period of the French Revolution*, 2nd ed., Oxford University Press, 1969, pp. 189).

political: the inevitable clash between the Establishment composer *par excellence*, faithful to *Kaiser und Vaterland*, and a politically violent, pro-Republican, anti-Establishment young man. Beethoven's political views may have been momentarily altered by the Napoleonic invasion of Austria in 1797, but the composition of patriotic songs was patently an expediency, and in 1798 he was one of the French Ambassador Count Bernadotte's circle of friends. (According to Schindler, Bernadotte's 'salon was frequented by distinguished persons of all ranks among whom was Beethoven, who had already expressed great admiration for the First Consul of the Republic. The suggestion was made by the General [Bernadotte] that Beethoven should honour the greatest hero of the age in a musical composition [the *Sinfonia Eroica*].')[1] And at this period, we cannot but suspect Beethoven of entertaining a certain amount of anger and jealousy for the old Haydn, fêted by princes and kings at home and abroad and chosen to write the official *Volkslied.* After the series of concerts in which the two men appeared together with some frequency – the end of 1795 and the beginning of 1796 – personal contact between them seems to have lessened considerably in 1797; though we shall see that they appeared together at a Tonkünstler-Societät concert on 2 April 1798. Otherwise, however, their worlds were becoming more and more diverse.

1 Schindler (MacArdle), 111f.

CHAPTER EIGHT

Works of 1797

The Volkslied 'Gott erhalte'

(XXVIa: 43)

Haydn's *Volkslied* has long been recognized as a masterpiece of construction; for many years, moreover, a variety of sources for various components of its melody has been located. Haydn was clearly trying to create a classical melody of great simplicity which would sound like a synthesis of church and secular. Wilhelm Tappert, whose research more than a century ago (1868) brought much clarity into the melodic origins of the *Volkslied*, was followed by Frantisek Sandor Kuhač (1880 and 1886), who proclaimed that he had found Croatian folk-songs with a very similar melody. Jenö Garldy (1902) stated that in Haydn's tune there could be found 'the Hungarian folk-song, unadulterated by any foreign influences'. Further research was carried out once again by Tappert (1904), Botstiber (in Pohl III, 1927), E. Schmid (1934), etc. A summary of this research follows. It will be seen that the opening phrase of Haydn's melody

has many sources among earlier church music and is basically the Ionic tetrachord. Here are some instances:

(1) From the *Missale romanum* [edition consulted here: Venetiis, MDCCXIII Apud Nicolaum Pezzana: Canon Missae (p. 193)]:

(2) From a Processionale of the fourteenth century (Prague)

(3) From a Processionale of the fourteenth century (Province of Friule in Italy): The two Marys

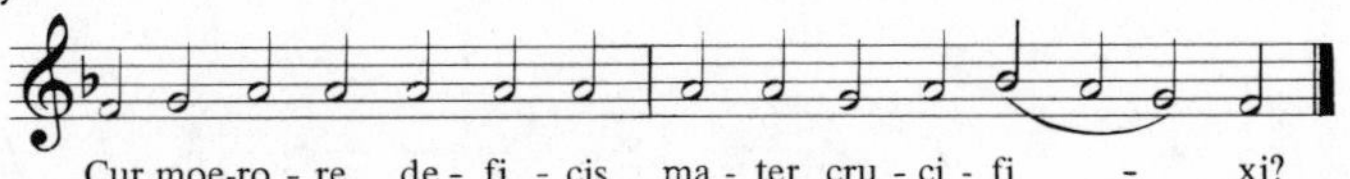

(4) Cantus Ecclesiasticus Sacrae Historiae Passionis Domini Nostri Jesu Christi [Rome, middle of thirteenth century] / Vienna 1761 [etc. etc.] [Christus]

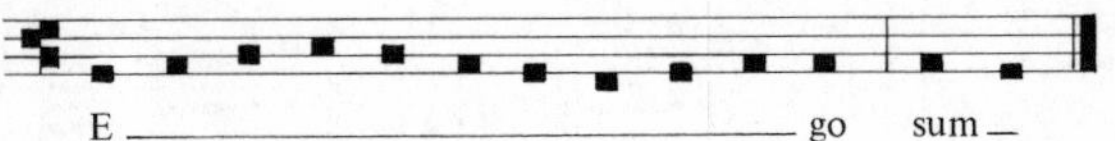

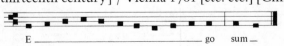

(5) Joseph Haydn: *Sinfonia Lamentatione* (*c.* 1768), Allegro assai con spirito (from MS. Herzogenburg)

(6) Old Latin church song translated into German

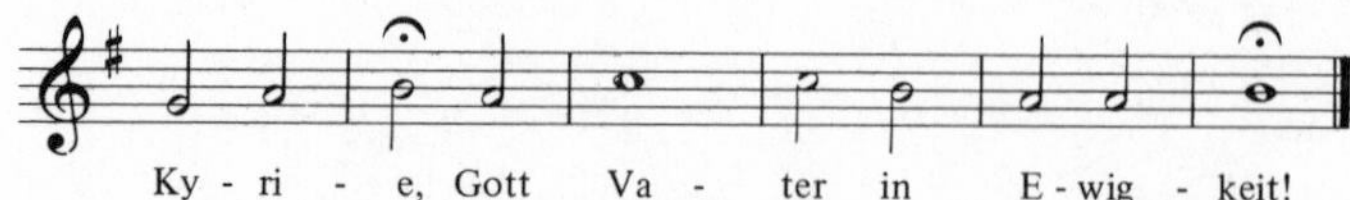

(7) Chorale from Zinkeisen's *Gesangbuch*, 1569

(8) Michael Praetorius, 1610 (see previous tune)

(9) Chorale, 1681

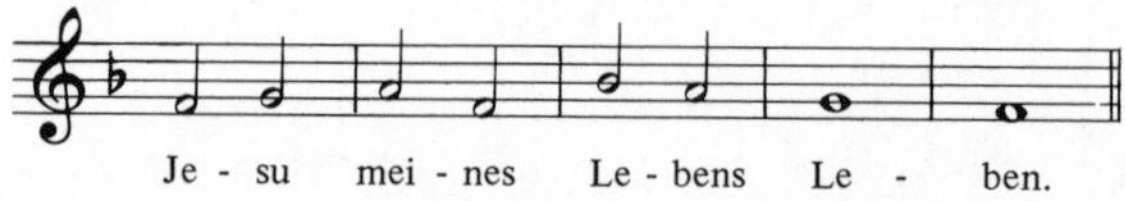

(10) Reinhard Keiser *Jodelet* (comic opera, 1726): Overture

(11) *Rondeau* from *Der getreue Musik-Meister* (Hamburg, 1728) by Georg Philipp Telemann – Cembalo Solo

(12) *Pièces de Clavecin ou Sonates avec accompagnement de Violon par Mr. [Jean Joseph Cassanea de] Mondonville*, Oeuvre 3, Sonata V, 2nd movement (Aria)

(13) Žalostna zaručnice (The sad bride). Croatian melody from the Eisenstadt region

(14) First Psalm Tone = W. A. Mozart, *Maurerische Trauermusik* (K. 477), 1785 (*cantus firmus* as noted at end of MS.)

Although there are also secular melodies among these interesting and heterogeneous sources, it is clear that the average man would feel an instinctive connection between church and the beginning of Haydn's 'Gott erhalte'. For the second part of the melody, or rather the glorious refrain, we have as many older sources, including some of Haydn's own. E. F. Schmid quotes a popular German canon which combines the melody of the beginning with the ♩ ♩ | ♫ ♩ of the second part:

Otherwise we may quote from Tappert and other sources (in the above examples, some have been added by the present writer):

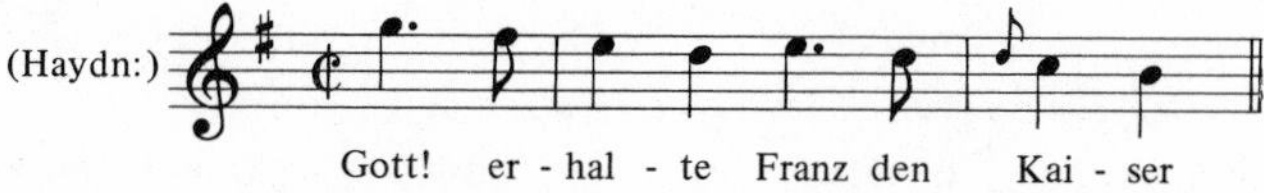

(1) '75 Lieder gedruckt zu Köln durch Arndt von Aich' (1525):

(2) Sperontes' *Singende Muse an der Pleiße* (Leipzig, 1736), No. 36 'Menuet'

(3) J. A. Hasse: *I Pellegrini al Sepolcro di N. S.* [Nostro Salvatore], Dresden 1742

(4) W. A. Mozart: Motet, 'Exsultate, jubilate', K. 165 (Milan, January 1773), 3rd movt., bars 134ff.

Al - le - lu - ja, al - le - lu - ja

(5) Joseph Haydn: *Il mondo della luna* (1777), Aria di Ernesto 'Qualche volta non fa male' [later: J. Haydn *Missa Cellensis* 1782, Benedictus]

Allegretto
Quan - do poi ces - sa lo sdeg - no

(6) W. A. Mozart: violin Sonata, K. 296 (Mannheim, 11 March 1778)

(7) 'Chur-Trier'sches Gesangbuch 1786'; Church Song for the Procession of Maundy Thursday

Das Ge - heim - nis sei - ner Lie - be

(8) Joseph Haydn: *Die sieben Worte* (Orchestral version of *c.*1786), No. 2 ('Amen dico tibi: hodie mecum eris in paradiso'), bars 37ff.

Grave e cantabile

(9) Christoph Gottlob Breitkopf: 'Terpsichore im Clavierauszuge, oder Sammlung von Anglaisen, Deutschen Tänzen, Françaisen, Quadrillen und Menuetten', Leipzig 1789: 'Gewitter – Anglaise': 'Die wieder hervorgekommene Sonne brennt aber heftig, es türmen sich neue Wetter auf' (The sun, reappeared, burns strongly, but new storms are in the making.)

The Croatian folk-song quoted above – one of several versions and that which is nearest the Haydn *Volkslied* – was sung at Kohlnhof (Kopház) near Eszterháza, also at Čembe. The Phonogrammarchiv of the Vienna Akademie der Wissenschaften recorded a man of eighty who sang this Croatian melody in Lazina in Croatia itself.[1] The words of the old song are very much like a German folk-song 'Ich stund an einem Morgen . . .' and are in English: 'Just after dawn I rose and left.' There are indubitably eastern European elements in the melody, particularly the little cadential figure , strongly reminiscent of a heart-broken little Roumanian melody used just before the close of Enesco's *Roumanian Rhapsody* No. 1 in A (Op. 11, No. 1)

But on the other hand, as we have observed in connection with the Croatian (Hungarian) tunes in Haydn's Symphony No. 103 (*Haydn in England, 1791–1795*, p. 598), it is very difficult to use Kuhač's material scientifically; hardly anyone alive today sings the melody, and one will never know how old it is, or if it were, perhaps, influenced by 'Gott erhalte' rather than the other way round. We would say, rather, that Haydn's ageless melody draws its strength from an immense well of old, traditional melodies, church, secular, and folk.

The Österreichische Nationalbibliothek in Vienna owns a whole series of sketches, manuscripts and the orchestral score of 'Gott erhalte' (as well as the first edition, of course). We here enumerate these MSS., following the list prepared by the present director of the Musiksammlung, Dr Franz Grasberger (*Hymnen*, 33), to which we take the liberty of adding some pertinent authentic material from the Esterházy Archives so as to give a complete picture of all the extant authentic manuscript sources. They are:

(1) The first draft of the melody. Twelve-stave Italian paper in oblong format (facsimile in Grasberger *Hymnen*, facing p. 16). The melody is written in the soprano clef with all four verses of the German text underneath. The second part was originally the following:

Near the bottom of the page, on the left-hand side, is a sketch for the beginning of this second section in the form as we know it today, viz.:

That is the first change, and it is a great one. The first part of the melody stayed, basically, in the tonic; and the climax of the minim *d''* presupposes a tonic orientation. So does the second part in the original; by introducing the *c* sharp, Haydn greatly

1 Record No. 3168; Schmid, *Vorfahren*, 292.

strengthened his harmonic scheme. The third-last bar of the original is also weak: the repeated *a′* – even if we presuppose a change of harmony, e.g.

– have a deadening effect on the basic melodic line.

(2) The first draft of the melody, harmonized in a kind of piano score, in the form as we now know it. Ten-stave Italian paper in oblong format. In the harmony we can see that Haydn erased some of the notes and made changes (facsimile in Grasberger, *Hymnen*, facing p. 17). Haydn wrote the work on two staves, between which is the first verse of the text. The last four bars already have the indications to repeat them.

(3) The final copy of the melody in piano score with the first verse of the text, signed to the right of the last bar of music by Haydn, and on the reverse side of the sheet 'Imprimatur den 28. Jänner 1797. Saurau.' Ten-stave Italian paper in oblong format (reproduced many times in facsimile, e.g. Geiringer 1932, p. 121).

(4) The orchestral score. Twelve-stave Italian paper in oblong format (four pages), signed on the top right-hand side 'v. Jos. Haydn [mpria] $\overline{797}$' (for further details, *vide supra*, p. 247). An authentic copy of the score by Elssler from Haydn's own library is in the Esterházy Archives of the National Széchényi Library in Budapest (Ms. mus. I. 172). Facsimile of page one of the autograph in Schmid, *Vorfahren* (facing p. 289). This orchestral score, in English translation (John Crosse), printed in *The Harmonicon* 1825, pp. 229ff., with a four-part vocal line. Haydn's original tempo here is 'poco Adagio'.

The first page of the autograph score (in the orchestral version) of the *Volcks Lied* ('Emperor's Hymn'). Cf. pp. 279ff.

The first edition was printed from source (3) above. A critical edition of that version in *Joseph Haydn Werke* (Breitkopf & Härtel), Serie 20, Band I (Friedländer), 1932, and also in *Joseph Haydn Werke* (Henle), Reihe XXIX, Band 1 (Mies), 1960.

Haydn's 'Gott erhalte' has been subjected to a stringent and elaborate analysis by Heinrich Schenker (1924), to which has been added a further analysis by the Schenker pupil Franz Eibner: these may be consulted conveniently in Grasberger, *Hymnen*, pp. 50ff., to which the reader is referred. Here we would point out only a few details. The subtlety with which Haydn has constructed the whole may be seen in the way the melody begins on the third beat of the bar: in this way the critical closes and half-closes – bars 4, 8, 12 and 16 – come on the strong beat; the central part of the structure, argues Schenker, is in bars 11–12, with its strong progression to the dominant; 'from this point Haydn may have decided the beginning and the end of the Song'. We may also note that the changes Haydn made from the sketch to the end are all calculated to make the vocal line easier to sing: in the finely constructed melodic pattern, the climactic *g''* that begins the last strophe is figuratively and also literally the high-point of the piece. In the orchestral score, the trumpets and timpani enter here for the first time. And finally, we would note the care with which Haydn marks the legato slurs: the whole piece is to be sung, then, in the great legato choral tradition; the orchestral players are similarly instructed in the full score.

This is not the place to trace the chequered history of Haydn's great *Volkslied*; we would, however, single out one fateful moment in the work's passage through the nineteenth century. After the good Kaiser Franz died all manner of men tried their hand at new words, even Franz Grillparzer in 1849. On 26 August 1841, a German poet, Hoffmann von Fallersleben, famous for his children's songs, wrote new words to Haydn's hymn, 'Deutschland, Deutschland über alles, über alles in der Welt'. From that time, Haydn's music existed as a national anthem for both countries. In 1945, the Allied Commission for Austria refused – mainly through stubborn resistance on the part of the French – to allow Haydn's hymn to be the national anthem of Austria, and in November 1946 a new *Bundeshymne* was chosen: an old Freemasons' song which is possibly (but not probably) by Mozart. By 1946, Haydn had ceased to mean much to the average Austrian, and there were few objections to letting 'Gott erhalte' disappear as the official *Bundeshymne*. As Franz Eibner sarcastically noted, if the music had been by Beethoven . . . or even better Bruckner. . . . Haydn's music is now the German national anthem.

In 1797, Haydn completed the String Quartet Op. 76, No. 3, in which the second movement is a set of variations on 'Gott erhalte'; we shall discuss this adaptation *infra*. As Franz Eibner has shown, Haydn also made a piano arrangement of this variation movement.[1]

1 The literature on Haydn's hymn is enormous. We confine ourselves here to the essential books and articles on the subject. Anton Schmid, *Joseph Haydn und N. Zingarelli*, Vienna 1847. F. S. Kuhač, *Južnoslovjenske narodne popievke* (Chansons nationales des Slaves du Sud), III, Zagreb, 1880, esp. pp. 89, 93, 95; 'Ursprung der österreichischen Volkshymne' in *Kroatische Revue*, Agram, May 1886. Wilhelm Tappert, *Wandernde Melodien*, Berlin 1868, 2nd ed. 1889; 'Die österreichische Nationalhymne', in *Die Musik* XV (1904), pp. 415ff. W. H. Hadow, *A Croatian Composer*, London 1897 (reprinted in Hadow's *Collected Essays*, London 1928). Alfred Heuss, 'Haydns Kaiserhymne', in *Zeitschrift für Musikwissenschaft* I (1918–9), pp. 5ff. Heinrich Schenker, 'Haydns Kaiserlied', in *Der Tonwille*, 1924 Heft 10. O. E. Deutsch, 'Haydn's Hymn and Burney's Translation', in *Music Review* VIII (1943), pp. 157ff. Pohl III, 318ff. Schmid, *Vorfahren*, 291ff. Franz Grasberger, *Die Hymnen Österreichs*, Tutzing 1968. A. van Hoboken, 'A rare contemporary edition of Haydn's 'Hymn for the Emperor"', in *Studies in Eighteenth-Century Music (A tribute to Karl Geiringer on his seventieth birthday)*, London 1970, pp. 292ff. Concerning the piano variations, see Franz Eibner, 'Die authentische Klavierfassung von Haydns Variationen über "Gott erhalte"', in *Haydn Yearbook* VII (1970), pp. 281ff. (with interesting facsimiles).

Note on the orchestral score and text of 'Gott erhalte'

It seems scarcely credible, but there is no modern edition of Haydn's authentic orchestral version; indeed, apart from its publication in *The Harmonicon* (1825), the score is as good as unknown. We take particular pleasure, therefore, in including it here. We have used the two authentic sources: (1) the autograph manuscript, now in the Österreichische Nationalbibliothek, and (2) the Elssler copy of the score (from Haydn's own library), now in the National Széchényi Library, Budapest; we are indebted to these institutions for kindly supplying photographs of the original scores.

The vocal line is to be sung by everyone, of course, in unison. We include the original text (1797) of the first verse in our musical example. The English translation by Haydn's friend, Dr Charles Burney, was printed with piano accompaniment by Broderip & Wilkinson and (with slight textual changes) by Monzani & Cimador in their respective editions of the 'Emperor's Hymn' (as it was then called). The first verse of Burney's translation (Broderip & Wilkinson edition) reads:

God preserve the Emp'ror Francis
  Sov'reign ever good and great;
Save, o save him from mischances
  In Prosperity and State!
May his Laurels ever blooming
  Be by Patriot Virtue fed;
May his worth the world illumine
  And bring back the Sheep misled!
God preserve our Emp'ror Francis!
  Sov'reign ever good and great.

Because each verse in Burney's rendering consists of ten lines (eight in Haschka's original, with the last two lines repeated in Haydn's setting), it became necessary to repeat in addition bars 5–8 of the melody to cater for lines 7 and 8 of the English version (corresponding to lines 5 and 6 in the German, sung once only). The final two lines are repeated as in the original. The *Volkslied* tune may also, of course, be used to accompany the words of the present German national anthem or as the English hymn-tune, 'Glorious things of thee are spoken, Zion, city of our God'. In large-scale performance the woodwind (especially the single flute) may be doubled.

NB: Die allererste Note wird nur Anfangs gespielt, um dem Volck den Ton zu geben.
('N.B. The very first note is to be played only at the beginning in order to give the pitch to the people.')

Franz! Lan - ge le - be Franz der Kai - ser in des Glück - es hell - sten

[p]
[f]
f
f
1mo Solo
p
f
[p]
ff
fz
fz
ff
Glanz! Ihm er - blü - hen Lor-beer Rei - ser wo er geht zum Ehr-en Kranz. Gott er-
fz

*Autograph *ff* only for the trumpets; *ff* given here as in Elssler's copy of the score.

fz
p
hal - te Franz den Kai - ser, un - seren gu - ten Kai - ser Franz.
da capo

String Quartets (Op. 76)
dedicated to Count Joseph Erdödy
(III: 75–80)

Six string Quartets, each entitled on the surviving Elssler MSS. 'Quartetto' – the autographs have disappeared entirely – for two violins, viola and violoncello, composed in 1796(?)–1797 for Count Joseph Erdödy. Published in 1799 by Artaria & Company (announced in the *Wiener Zeitung* on 17 July 1799) as Op. 75 (first three works) and Op. 76 (second three). Also published in authentic prints by Longman, Clementi & Co.: they issued them in two instalments: I–III announced in *The Times* on 19 April 1799, IV–VI in *The Times* of 7 January 1800 ('shortly will be published'). Haydn had sent the manuscripts in two parcels, one on 27 March 1799 and the other on 15 June, but the second parcel seems to have taken a very long time to get to London. Longman, Clementi & Co. entitled their edition Op. 76, the last three works being subtitled 'Book 2[d.]'. We shall see that Haydn may have sold them to Sieber in Paris: *vide infra*, pp. 538f.

Quartetto I in G ('Op. 76, No. 1'). I *Allegro con spirito*. II *Adagio sostenuto*. III *Menuet Presto & Trio*. IV *Finale. Allegro ma non troppo*.

Quartetto II in D minor ('Op. 76, No. 2'). I *Allegro*. II *Andante o più tosto Allegretto*. III *Menuet Allegro & Trio*. IV *Finale. Presto*. Known in Germany as the 'Quinten' ('Fifths') Quartet.

Quartetto III in C (Op. 76, No. 3') ('Kaiser / Emperor'). I *Allegro*. II *Poco Adagio Cantabile*. III *Menuet Allegro & Trio*. IV *Finale. Presto*.

Quartetto IV in B flat ('Op. 76, No. 4'). I *Allegro con spirito*. II *Adagio*. III *Menuet Allegro ma non troppo & Trio*. IV *Finale. Allegro ma non troppo*. Known in England as 'The Sunrise'.

Quartetto V in D ('Op. 76, No. 5'). I *Allegretto*. II *Largo ma non troppo. Cantabile e mesto*. III *Menuet Allegro ma non troppo*. IV *Finale, Presto*.

Quartetto VI in E flat ('Op. 76, No. 6'). I *Allegretto*. II *Fantasia Adagio*. III *Menuet Presto & Alternativo*. IV *Finale, Allegro spiritoso*.

Critical edition: part of the Complete String Quartets published by Doblinger: Op. 76 edited by the present writer (1973).

When Charles Burney first heard these Quartets in 1799, he wrote to their composer (CCLN, 164) that he 'never received more pleasure from instrumental music; they are full of invention, fire, good taste, and new effects, and seem the production, not of a sublime genius who has written so much and so well already, but of one of highly-cultivated talents, who had expended none of his fire before'. In those days, people were always astonished that Haydn's 'genius-box' seemed to be bottomless; and even from our twentieth-century vantage, it seems scarcely believable that Haydn could have bettered the great 'Salomon' Quartets of 1793 (Opp. 71 & 74). Yet Op. 76 is even more perfect than the previous set. In a sense, the experience of writing quartets for the public concert room effected a fundamental change in Haydn's quartet style. We have come a long way from the slow moving, intellectual, almost discursive style of even such a late work as Op. 64, No. 1 (1790). The tightness, economy and the explosive 'symphonic' style of the 'Salomon' Quartets are all elements that remain with Haydn's latest quartets. Such a passage as the close of the exposition in Op. 76, No. 4 –

– is a heritage from the 1793 quartets for the London concert hall. Altogether there is a boldness in Haydn's quartet style which no doubt reflects his new position in musical life: for in 1796 and 1797 he realized that the entire civilized Western world considered him the greatest living composer. *Noblesse oblige*, and Haydn was aware that every note he composed was being judged in the light of his position as doyen of music. The self-confidence of this music is as enormous as was Haydn's personal modesty. Years of experience had given him a technique such as hardly any other composer except J. S. Bach and Mozart had possessed, and this mechanical virtuosity is now put to work in tonal experiments which gave a new and – for the professional musician – immensely stimulating dimension to the art. Such a movement as the Fantasia from Op. 76, No. 6, with its subtle marriage between highly involved tonal experiments and a practical way to notate the music, is one of Haydn's intellectual conceptions on a giant scale. The slow movements of these works have not only a profundity that is a step further than anything in Op. 71/74 except for the 'Rider's' (Op. 74, No. 3) slow movement, but they are also bathed in a curiously impersonal and remote melancholy for which the German language has an excellent word, *Wehmut*. Another general feature of these slow movements is the very slow tempo of them: by that we do not mean the tempo *marking* but the way in which the movement is constructed: long and sustained lines in a very slow-moving context. It is one of the aspects of Haydn's style which he transmitted directly to Beethoven, whose Op. 18 Quartets have slow movements of this same density and sustained musical thought.

The Finales have also changed considerably. No longer do we have those racy, sophisticated sonata-rondos on a popular melody such as the closing movements of Op. 74, No. 1, and in particular Op. 74, No. 2. Two Finales from major-key Quartets of Op. 76 actually begin in the minor: Nos. 1 and 3. And not only do they begin in the minor but they remain in the minor until the final pages and are of such a turbulent nature – especially No. 3's – as to give an entirely new shape to the Quartet as a whole. Throughout these works we notice that Haydn was becoming more and more intellectual. The Finale of Op. 76, No. 6, is almost abstruse in its cerebration, toying with the shape, and number of notes, in the upbeat to the principal theme; while the opening movement of Op. 76, No. 2, with its austere nature and contrapuntal virtuosity, shows Haydn in anything but a smiling guise. The meltingly, even hauntingly beautiful final variation to 'Gott erhalte' (Op. 76, No. 3), of such a profound emotion, almost seems to belong to the Romantic era. Op. 76 is full of long looks into the future. The most obvious innovation, but one that certainly struck contemporaries, was the speeding-up of the minuet into the scherzo. Here we may permit ourselves a brief digression. Where did Haydn get the idea of writing a one-in-the-bar scherzo (though he still called it 'Menuet') as in Op. 76, No. 1? Years before, in the Op. 33 Quartets of 1781, he had actually used the word 'Scherzo' instead of 'Menuet', but in those works, there was little difference in tempo between a Haydn 'Scherzo' and a Haydn 'Menuet'. In one Symphony of 1765 (No. 28) we find a fast minuet, 'Allegro molto'. During the London visits, we have noted that the symphonic minuets, as well as those of the string quartets, speeded up considerably: many are marked 'Allegro' and one (Symphony No. 94) 'Allegro molto'. Still, all these are movements in a basic three-four time, and Op. 76, No. 1, is clearly one-in-the-bar, or very close to it. We believe that Haydn was directly influenced by the Beethoven compositions he had heard after returning from England in 1795: the Op. 1 Trios contain just such movements, marked 'Scherzo', in the first two works (not, interestingly enough, in the fine C-minor Trio, which has a 'Menuetto' marked 'Quasi allegro'). Haydn always retained his agile and youthful mind: he was open to any new impressions if he considered them a useful addition to his vocabulary. His dynamic marks over the years changed from Baroque to Romantic, from the old 'terraced' dynamics to the crescendos, diminuendos, and so on, of the nineteenth century. He must have found the quick scherzo an interesting innovation and promptly adopted it, and the impetus really seems to have come from Beethoven and his extraordinary Op. 1 Trios.

What is new in the most profound sense about these Quartets is the scope of Haydn's language and the range of his vision. We notice all kinds of small technical innovations (such as the string figure in Op. 76, No. 2's opening movement, where a crescendo is combined with lifting the bow off the string after the phrase  which is also found in 'Chaos' of *The Creation*). All these devices are invented to serve some new musical aspect. The range of Haydn's vision is apparent in movement after movement. It is particularly striking in the opening bars of Op. 76, No. 4 (*vide infra*), and it will put these works in the proper historical perspective if we play that beginning and contrast it with the beginning of any quartet from Haydn's so-called Opp. 1 and 2 (*c.* 1757–60?). No other great musician had ever made a progress so profound, a metamorphosis so great.

The Opp. 71/74 Quartets required a virtuoso string quartet and, of course, a leader of spirit and great technical abilities. The Op. 76 Quartets require a quartet of equal skill, but even more a body of players capable of doing justice to the interpretive difficulties with which these works abound. The slow movements, in particular, require a high degree of concentration from the players if they are to hold together at the slow tempo Haydn requires. No other string quartets by Haydn, except for the great Op. 20, pose such formidable (and in our day, alas, usually quite unresolved) problems of interpretation.

In C. F. Pohl's article on Haydn for Grove's *Dictionary* (this part was first published in 1879), we find 'the Erdödy family' listed among Haydn's pupils. One of Haydn's patrons at the time of Nicolaus I had been Count Ladislaus Erdödy, who had sent Ignaz Pleyel to study with Haydn and had, in March 1776, given the composer two horses and a carriage 'because of his satisfaction with the pupil entrusted to me' (CCLN, 18). Count Ladislaus supported a famous opera company in Pressburg which staged several of Haydn's operas in the 1780s; the Count also owned the autographs of four Haydn operas including the only two marionette operas that have survived,[1] which were acquired (much to Haydn's later annoyance) by the Viennese music-seller and publisher, Johann Traeg, when the Count withdrew from the operatic undertaking in 1788. We suppose that Haydn must have known many of the numerous Erdödy family – there were three branches, an older, a middle and a younger, according to Schönfeld's *Adels-Schematismus* (1824) and to the *Genealogisches Taschenbuch der deutschen gräflichen Häuser* (Gotha) – and perhaps even the attractive Anna Marie, *née* Countess Nickzy (Nisky), who married Count Peter Erdödy on 6 June 1796 and later became Beethoven's friend. Peter belonged to the older line, while Joseph, the patron of Op. 76, was head of the younger line. Born in 1751, he was first married to a daughter of Prince Batthyan-Strattmann (who died in 1794) and later to Elisabeth von Mayer; he lived in the Teinfaltstrasse (house No. 74). One of Joseph's daughters, Theresia (born in 1748), married Count Johann Nepomuk Esterházy. Apart from these biographical details,[2] we knew nothing of the family's relationship to Haydn, nor how Count Joseph came to order the Quartets Op. 76 from Haydn.

Experience should have taught us to be careful when trying to establish the inner chronology of a set of works for which there is an authentic print but no autograph. Haydn wrote the Paris Symphonies in 1785 and 1786, and sent the autographs to Paris, where they were published by Imbault. He also sent them to Artaria of Vienna, specifying a different order, and when he sold them to Forster of London, he put them in a third order. Part of this rather mysterious manipulation may be explained by Haydn's desire not to make it too obvious that he was selling the works to different persons (or rather publishers) at the same time, i.e. Artaria could not tell from a publisher's catalogue of Imbault or Forster that they were also selling the same six symphonies. But in the case of the Op. 71 and Op. 74 Quartets, the autographs are numbered and theirs is the order of the authentic publication by Corri & Dussek, and also the presumably authentic second publication by Artaria. For the Op. 76 Quartets we have no autographs and the three authentic MS. scores by Johann Elssler, obviously copies of the autographs (they came from Haydn's own library and are now in the Esterházy Archives of the National Széchényi Library in Budapest), carry no numbers. However, the two authentic editions, by Artaria and Longman, Clementi & Co., are both in the same order and it is likely that it is the order in which they were composed, or put down, by Haydn.

Op. 76, No. 1.

Even if it was not actually the first of the six to be composed, this quartet is certainly the most closely allied in spirit to the preceding Quartets of Opp. 71 and 74. It is an extraordinary mixture of the gay, the serious, the flippant and the highly original. The opening flourish of three chords reminds us of similar devices used in almost all the Opp. 71 and 74 works, but the idea of introducing the main theme entirely unaccompanied (first by the 'cello, then by the viola), as if it were the beginning of a fugue, is very comic and at the same time most original. Note that, like every great comedian, Haydn never repeats a good joke, and like the kettledrum solo in the final movement of the 'Military' Symphony, the joke of the main theme unaccompanied is not

1 H. C. Robbins Landon: 'Haydn's Marionette Operas and the Repertoire of the Marionette Theatre at Esterház Castle' in *Haydn Yearbook I* (1962), pp. 133ff.

2 Ignaz Ritter v. Schönfeld's *Adels-Schematismus*, Erster Jahrgang (1824), pp. 67ff., esp. p. 72. Address from *Hof- und Staats-Schematismus*.

repeated. In the recapitulation, the theme is given to the 'cello but with the countermelody (in the first violin) that we have come to know in the development section. The way in which Haydn keeps developing the theme in the recapitulation – even introducing a little canon on the first subject (bars 143ff.) – suggests a fusion of the development and recapitulation, and also serves to do away with the formal repetition of the main subject as it first appeared. What preserves the symmetry is the regular appearance, in exposition and recapitulation, of the second subject. 'It should be noted,' writes the perceptive Charles Rosen, 'that when the opening theme has a markedly regular character, the closing theme is generally made even more decisively popular in style. The first theme of . . . Op. 76, No. 1 is, on the surface, as jolly and square as one could wish . . . but the end of the exposition outdoes it with ease'.[1] The parallel with the 'Military' Symphony, written some three years earlier, is striking; both second subjects begin with the same kind of bustling lower-string accompaniment. The very last time it appears in the Quartet, Haydn provides the second subject with a new bass, viz.

– which gives a droll, village-band feeling to the music, making a popular tune also 'of the people', as it were.

The central part of this Quartet, like the final work of Op. 74 (the 'Rider'), is its solemn slow movement, a fine example of that sustained adagio writing which is so much a part of Haydn's late style. With a main subject in such a slow tempo, Haydn takes care to have all the rest of the material in this movement except the main subject (whenever it returns) move in a pattern of semiquavers and demisemiquavers. There is a famous passage which appears three times and during which the first violin moves in perpetual syncopation after the rest of the strings, and which is a test for the performer's rhythmic stamina (bars 25ff., 61ff., 83ff.). At the end of this passage, in exposition and recapitulation (the movement is in compressed sonata form), there is a written-out cadenza for the first violin; the first time it ascends to *b'''*, but the second time to what were then the dizzy heights of *e''''*.

Haydn calls his scherzo a Menuet, but it is (as we have observed above) the first real scherzo in Haydn's music, possibly inspired by Beethoven, certainly in close proximity to the style of Haydn's erstwhile pupil. As if to reassert himself, the Trio, on the other hand, is very popular in the old Haydn tradition and was obviously performed at a much slower tempo:

What is perhaps most Beethovenian of all is the *ff* explosion (in the middle of *p*) that comes at the end of the Minuet's 'A' section:

1 *The Classical Style*, p. 336.

The Finale suddenly changes the mood of the whole Quartet. We move to the tonic minor and a restless, even turbulent mood seized the music. The mood becomes considerably darker as the music proceeds. Being in G minor, the exposition ends in the relative major, B flat. There then follows one of Haydn's enormous harmonic plans which includes a fascinating enharmonic deception to avoid landing in a series of double-flat keys. Somfai's brilliant analysis (1970, pp. 374f.) informs us that the

> enharmonically spelled deception appears . . . in a passage of third-related keys (−4 fifths), thus turning from D flat minor to A major (= D flat minor – B♭♭ major, bars 100–102):

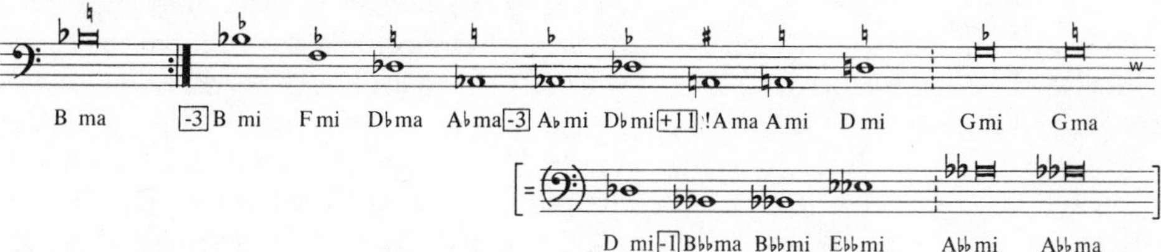

> To achieve 'pure' intonation here means solving an extremely delicate problem. Though the melodically broken chords are entrusted at the critical moment to the first violin (and he may turn for support to the objective security of the open A string), the viola is forced four bars earlier (starting at bar 98) to fit the note E as the third in a chord of D flat minor; the second violin plays the chromatic progression A flat–A, while the 'cello even performs the enharmonic exchange of D flat to C sharp. . . .

This is surely the most ingenious and astonishingly original Haydn finale since the 'Farewell' Symphony or that of Symphony No. 67 (with its built-in slow movement starting off with a solo string trio). At the upbeat to bar 139, the music shifts into G major: the formerly turbulent and rough opening theme is marked 'dolce' in the first violin and 'mezza voce' in the middle strings. Once again, we are witnessing one of Haydn's transformations of darkness into light, the most spectacular example of which comes at the end of 'Chaos' in *The Creation*. The coda of this movement effects another fantastic transformation of the main theme. From its radiant guise when the music changed from minor to major, it is now made to sound positively flippant, even trivial, as if Haydn were attempting with every means at his disposal to wipe away the serious tone that had prevailed not only at the beginning and middle of the Finale but also elsewhere in the Quartet. This 'flippant' section is played twice: first *p* and then *f*; the second time (which we quote here) with more exaggerated dynamic markings, *pp* and then *ff*. It is really a passage from the sublime to the ridiculous and one more example of that famous change of physiognomy in Haydn's features which Silverstolpe has so accurately recorded for us, and which is here, once again, documented in a striking fashion by Haydn himself. The change was certainly not, even *de anno* 1797, to everyone's comprehension or sympathy . . .

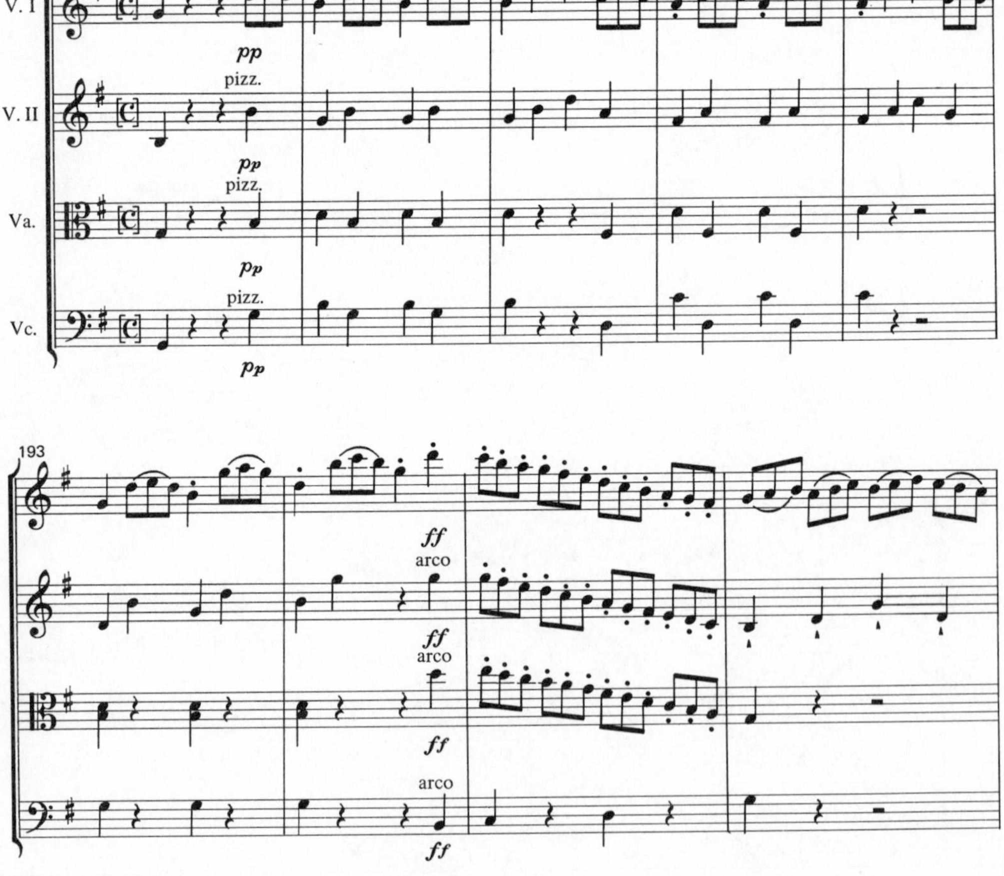

Op. 76, No. 2

This D minor Quartet is the third in a line of D minor masterpieces by Haydn and Mozart, beginning with the work that may be considered Haydn's first great string quartet (Op. 9, No. 4), and continuing with two such works by Mozart, the strongly Haydnesque K. 173 (1773) and the strongly Mozartian K. 421 in the set dedicated to Haydn. Hans Keller calls K. 421 'one of the greatest tragedies in human creation – one, moreover, which stands above itself with an uncanny inconsistency and a smile, both confidential and confident, that was not to be renewed until Kafka. Usually the tragedy is behind the humour; here the humour is behind the tragedy.'[1] A study of these D minor works by both composers reveals *in nuce* the spectacular way in which Haydn influenced Mozart and then the more oblique fashion in which Mozart influenced Haydn. The younger man in fact assimilated the Haydn style more slowly than many scholars realized, for in K. 173 it is largely undigested. Haydn, on the other hand, never attempted the shattering Mozartian tragedy; the older composer was not insensitive to it but the methods of presentation which Mozart used were entirely different. The kaleidoscopic nature of the Mozartian style, its multi-level emotional content, were fundamentally at variance with Haydn's unified intellectualism. Haydn's Op. 76, No. 2, is definitely not in the tragic style, but it is one of the most serious, learned and intellectually formidable works he ever wrote.

In Germany the work is called 'Die Quinten' ('The Fifths') because of the series of fifths which comprise the main theme of the first movement and, as matters turn out, of much of the whole work. We shall illustrate this latter point very briefly: at a deeper level, the matter may be pursued much further.

1 'The Chamber Music' (p. 116) in *The Mozart Companion* (ed. H. C. Robbins Landon and Donald Mitchell), London 1956.

This latter section (bars 57ff. of the foregoing example) is then followed by a stretto on the main subject preceded by a short canon on the 'fifths' at the interval of a fifth (in the middle voices):

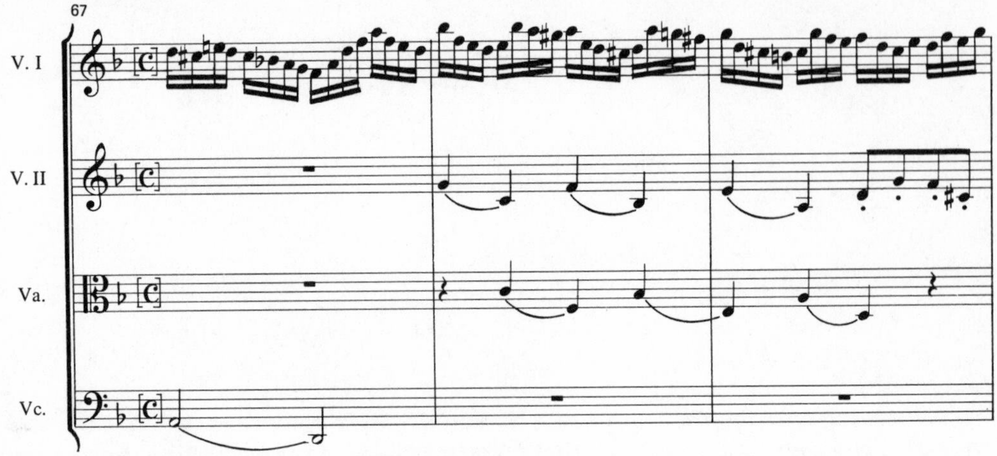

In the second movement, *Andante o più tosto allegretto*, we may note a whole series of falling fifths, viz.

In the 'Witches' Minuet' ('Hexenmenuett'), as it is called in Germany, there are as many examples of rising and fallings fifths, e.g.

while in the Trio the whole trend is from *d* to *a* and back again, but the return to *d* is emphasized as follows:

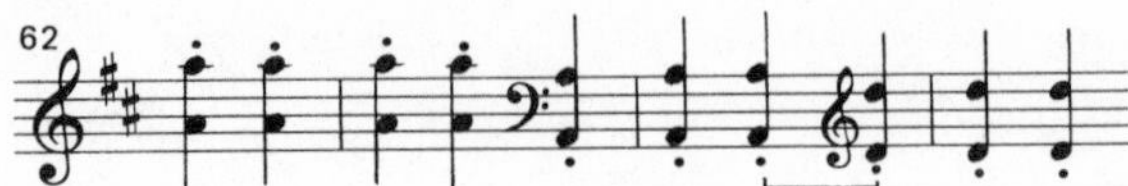

In the Finale there is a strong upwards fifth in the theme:

but once again it is in another context (bars 21 ff.) where, perhaps, the fifths are made especially apparent:

Here the fifths are vertical and horizontal at once. It will be noted with increasing frequency that Haydn is now marking the violin parts more carefully than ever before ('2' occurs no less than three times within the first eight bars: *vide supra*): sometimes this is for the sound wanted, at other times (as we shall see in a famous passage in the first movement of Op. 77, No. 2) it is to help a problem in group intonation.

The 'fifthy' quality of much of this music is, of course, a technical device to assist in the unification of a work with many diverse stylistic elements. After the contrapuntal severity of the D minor opening movement, we have a theme and variations in a fairly quick slow tempo, in *siciliano* six-eight rhythm. The first variation (none of them is entitled as such) cancels the two sharps, begins in D minor but only uses the key as a spring board to modulate to B flat – another interest of the constant fascination Haydn now felt for third-related keys (bars 16ff.). By the time we arrive at the canonic Minuet we realize what a well-constructed foil the (not-so-)slow movement was. This two part canon returns to the language of about 1772, when Haydn was writing gaunt canonic minuets such as that in Symphony No. 44 in E minor. The Trio has been much quoted, and its progress from unharmonized octaves in D, to D minor, then to D major, all with a mighty *crescendo*, must have struck the first listeners as brilliantly original. The Finale, in sonata form, is in D minor but in the middle of the recapitulation (*after* the main subject has returned in D minor), the music shifts to D major, and the theme appears in that key, *pianissimo*, with most of the motion taken out of the inner parts: the ethereal effect is surprising and effective. Thus, the piece ends in the major, as do most of Haydn's minor-key works of his later years (e.g. Symphony No. 95 and the 'Rider' Quartet, Op. 74, No. 3). In the language of this late style, the darkness always ends in light: or almost always, for we have seen two great exceptions to the rule (the so-called 'Andante con variazioni' in F minor [1793] and the great F sharp minor Trio No. 40 [1794–5?], discussed in *Haydn in England 1791–1795*.

Op. 76, No. 3

This No. 3 is probably Haydn's most famous Quartet, thanks to the presence of the Emperor's Hymn as the subject for the slow movement's variations. Since that slow movement is clearly the central point of the work, some critics have misunderstood the first movement (which is artfully designed to provide a majestic and spirited opening to 'Gott erhalte') and even the Quartet as a whole.[1] The second movement is on such a high level of emotionalism that what could precede it must be, as Haydn imagined it, a broad allegro of almost symphonic proportions, whereas what followed

1 Geiringer (1947) writes that it 'is a surprisingly uninspired quartet and would hardly deserve its place among Haydn's last works of this type were it not for its [slow movement].'

it directly must be a rather bland minuet. In the Finale, as we shall see, Haydn once more has recourse to planning the whole movement except the very end in the tonic minor.

The *intrada* quality of the opening movement is underlined by the dotted rhythm of the old French Overture, which first makes its appearance as a countersubject to the main theme but gradually assumes a great importance. Once again, too, we are given passages with heavy 'concert hall' treatment, such as the closing part of the exposition (and recapitulation) where the following massively 'orchestrated' subject (a derivative of the first theme) appears:

This is, of course, the heritage of the Quartets for Salomon and the Hanover Square Rooms in London.

The central portion of the development section is an incredible transformation of the main theme into a wild country dance, as rough and 'unbuttoned' as Beethoven's. It is in E major, the mediant, and is thus the pivotal third-related key between tonic and dominant. The *danza tedesca* foreshadows Beethoven in a most uncanny way, not only in the aggressive spirit but in the heavy accents (*fz*) with which the music abounds:

In the end of the recapitulation, at bar 105, when the coda begins, the music is marked 'la seconda volta più presto' – an entirely new idea which increases the brilliance (and also shows that Haydn expected all his repeat signs to be faithfully observed). There is some brilliant and difficult writing for the first violin, which rises to *c''''* and makes one wonder which quartet Haydn had in mind for the first performance. Altogether, this Allegro is a perfect introduction on a grand scale to the central part of the work.

The variations on 'Gott erhalte' are as simple, unaffected and beautiful as the theme itself. Haydn's plan, realized with great perceptivity, is to create a grand arch between the full harmony of the theme (bars 1–20) and the final variation (Var. IV), where the harmony is exquisitely rich. Thus Var. I (*sempre piano*) is just for the two violins, violin II having the melody; Var. II gives the melody to the 'cello. Var. III to the viola. Var. IV is perhaps the first time in music that a composer set out to write this kind of apotheosis. Some critics have singled out the *Missa in tempore belli* as an example of Haydn's patriotism; but surely this movement is a much clearer case for showing where Haydn's sympathies lay. Never has a reigning monarch been the recipient of such heartfelt and beautiful music except King Ludwig of Bavaria. Cecil Gray, speaking of the melody, relates the many uses to which later generations put it (including the 'Brotherhood' anthem of Freemasony, and 'Praise the Lord! ye heavens adore Him' in the *Hymns Ancient & Modern of the Church of England*) and adds; 'One cannot imagine the Marseillaise or any other anthem serving as the thematic basis of a movement of a string quartet, as here. It inhabits all three worlds; the world of religion, the world of national politics, and the world of pure art. It is perhaps true to say that it is the greatest tune ever written, from whatever point of view one chooses to look at it. . . . With the fourth variation the melody returns to the first violin, and the movement ends with some of the loveliest polyphonic writing for strings which has ever been penned by any composer.'[1]

The fast (Allegro) Minuet is another well considered buffer between the high emotions of the slow movement and the intensity of the Finale. The Trio is a particularly fine example of Haydn's successful quest for new tonal relations: here we have the same mediant relationship as in the first movement. The Minuet is in C major and the Trio, beginning and ending in A minor, has a long middle section in A major (the mediant of C, of course), marked *pp*. It stands out just as strongly as the *danza tedesca* in its context in the opening movement.

A strong Finale is now needed to balance this special architectural edifice that Haydn has created. As in Op. 76, No. 1, it begins in the tonic minor and does not turn to the major until just before the end. It is a highly unsettled movement, making great use of triplets, which appear soon after the movement begins (bar 12), and composed not in some kind of rondo but in sonata form. The ending in C major is a defiant gesture and has none of the humour of the similarly devised Finale in Op. 76, No. 1. If we study the structure of the 'Emperor' Quartet we can see that it has two clearly established summits, the slow movement and the Finale, to which the first movement and Minuet respectively lead. The Quartet's perennial popularity is not exclusively because of the 'Gott erhalte' variations. Many Haydn scholars have used the word symphonic in connection with the fast movements. Cecil Gray writes: '. . . At moments the richness and volume of sound produced by the four instruments is almost orchestral, and the structure seems at times almost symphonic' (op. cit., p. 14); while Rosemary Hughes (*Haydn*, London 1950, p. 165) notes that 'The work as a whole has a symphonic massiveness. . . .' Yet the sound that Haydn gets from his four strings is *always* within the realms of pure chamber music. Everyone knows that not only Schuppanzigh and the Razumovsky Quartet could sound like an orchestra when they attacked a *fortissimo* passage. It is one side of the string quartet's many capabilities, and

1 The *Haydn String Quartet Society*, Vol. IV (1935), London, p. 15.

Haydn, in exploiting it as he does here in many parts of the quick movements, is not only displaying his virtuosity but also setting up a proper recipient for the quiet, ethereal beauties of 'Gott erhalte' and its variations.

Haydn arranged the movement for piano solo. Franz Eibner, who first brought clarity into the authentic arrangement,[1] notes the rather incredible fact that Artaria published the piano arrangement first anonymously but then 'arrangés pour le Clavecin par M^r^ L'abbé Gelinek' (whom we have met earlier in these pages: p. 53). Gelinek's variations were both famous and excellent business, and Eibner suggests that Artaria 'might have hoped for better sales by offering the piece as one of Gelinek's extremely popular sets of variations'. Perhaps after Haydn's death, Gelinek was a better drawing-card than Haydn. . . .

Op. 76, No. 4

With No. 4 of the set of six, we enter that which Longman, Clementi & Co. entitled 'Book 2^d^'; without knowing for certain if Haydn thought of this great opus as two sets of three works, one cannot but notice that the second half is intellectually tougher and musically perhaps more perfect, certainly more difficult to assess rapidly, than the first half. Here, then, we have the opposite of that which obtained in the six Mozart Quartets dedicated to Haydn, where, as Leopold Mozart observed, the second set is 'somewhat easier, but at the same time excellent compositions'.[2] In Haydn's Op. 76, the most intellectual and emotionally the most reserved is the final work of the set (E flat).

Op. 76, No. 4, is in B flat. Without wishing to enter into a discussion of Haydn's use of keys – an interesting but precarious subject with any composer – we would nevertheless observe that B flat major occupies a very special position in Haydn's late style. Arguably the most profound of the first six Salomon Symphonies is No. 98, and No. 102 has long been admired as one of the composer's giant creations. In the Salomon Quartets, the B flat major work (Op. 71, No. 1) has always been a favourite, and it is well known that four of the last six Masses are in that key. (It seems clear that Haydn's last, unfinished Quartet Op. 103 would have been in D minor, not in B flat, the key of its slow movement.) And No. 4 is perhaps the greatest of Op. 76. It is not written round a single movement – as Nos. 1, 3, 5 and possibly 6 seem to be – and is not only of flawless construction in all its movements but is filled with a magical spirituality and possessed of a depth at the same time profound and radiant.

The work's English sobriquet, 'The Sunrise', is a rather simple-minded description of the opening. 'Out of sustained harmonies', writes Karl Geiringer (1953, p. 3), 'played by the three lower instruments the poignant song of the first violin rises like the sun slowly emerging from a bank of clouds, and a feeling of growth and expansion permeates the whole movement.' (See example overleaf, top.)

It is one of the greatest openings in chamber music. We have given 'in diplomatic fidelity' the slurs of the Elssler MS. in Budapest because it is undoubtedly a faithful copy of the lost autograph: it shows the difference between the heat of inspiration and realities of performance, for the interlocking slurs over violin I in bars 1–4 are, if we

1 *Haydn Yearbook* VII (*vide supra*), p. 303.

2 Letter to his daughter of 16 February 1785; Anderson, *The Letters of Mozart and his Family*, 2nd ed. (A. Hyatt King and Monica Carolan) London 1966, II, 885. Despite the astonishing beginning of the 'Dissonant' Quartet, K. 465, the other two, in A major and B flat (K. 464 and 458), are indeed slightly less complex than the first three. 'Easier' in Leopold Mozart's sense obviously meant not merely technically.

Allegro con spirito

* = Elssler MS.

may coin a phrase, 'thought slurs', and when the composer came to deliver the works to the publisher, he wrote –

– at least such is the phrasing of Longman, Clementi & Co. (The two long slurs of Elssler's copy – top – are combined by Artaria into one, shown above in square brackets.) What is so admirable about this long subject is the poise with which Haydn has constructed the dissonant half steps. Beginning with the *e* natural, we find its complement in the *b* natural; but we also note that Haydn has carried on this idea in non-dissonant form with the second notes of violin I, bars 2 and 3/4, viz.

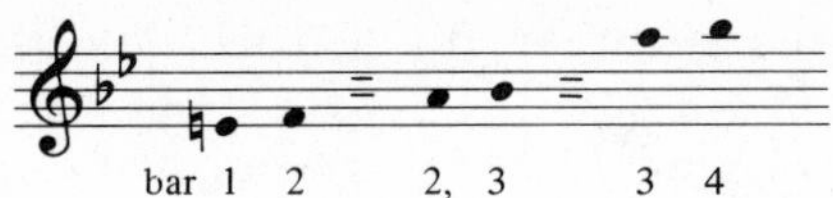

When the second part of the theme begins, we note that the continuation is more involved: the *b* natural is repeated, turned into *d–e* flat (bar 8) and into *f* sharp″–*g*″ (across 9–10), but the pattern is subtly broken by introducing an appoggiatura before the *g*″. In the third section of the theme, the half-step is extended in various ways, in augmentation in the violin I and 'cello (bars 13–15) and in diminution in the viola and later in the first violin, where the appoggiature have also proliferated. In its steadily darkening harmonic contours at bars 18–21, the pattern of the slow-moving accompaniment is given a tremendous gush of colour with the *d* flat in bar 20, after which the nervous rhythm of the tutti (we show only the beginning) in a long section in B flat grounds the harmony and returns to earth after that aerial progress of the first subject. When the first subject returns in the recapitulation, Haydn does not repeat the feathery atmosphere of the beginning but marks the first four bars of each section (corresponding to bars 1–4 and 7–10) *crescendo* leading to sharp staccato chords (*forte*) in what were originally bars 5–6 and 11–12. Earlier in the analysis of these Quartets, we have quoted a virile *ff* passage which graces the end of exposition and development. Just before it appears for the last time, we have a farewell to the first subject with a viola part in its darkest register that Haydn wrote for himself (he was a viola player, like his colleagues Mozart and Beethoven, and judging from the technical standard of the viola part in this Quartet, he must have been a very good one).

Haydn, the great architect, has even constructed the *fortissimo* passage quoted (p. 285) from the bracketed portion of bar 2, i.e. becomes . In its combination of poetic inspiration and masculine drive, this first movement achieves a perfect synthesis, at the same time being a work of astounding modernity: consider the fantastic clash of *f* sharp (V. I) against *f* natural ('cello) in the course of this *fortissimo* passage, which is repeated in the recapitulation (*b* flat–*b* natural). Formally we note that development and recapitulation have by now become merged, and that Haydn takes more and more pains to do away with the dividing lines in the second part of his first movements. But this outer formal freedom is always matched by a motivic concentration which becomes ever more distilled as Haydn's long and active life draws slowly to its close.

The Adagio, one of Haydn's slowest, is haunted by that sense of impersonal mourning of which we have spoken earlier. It is monumental in its sense of 'grief from without' and uses sonata form in a telescoped fashion, sheared of all inessentials. We note, in the Elssler score at Budapest and in the other authentic sources, that the fingering and the choice of string are occasionally indicated, for instance in the section just before the end:

There are two passages which must be quoted. The one is a stretto based on the main subject, approached by a kind of cadenza:

The very end is of immense, boundless sadness – the November greyness of All Souls – and the sextuplets in the second violin (then in the 'cello) sound like the last ghostly stirring of dead autumn leaves. Here is a slow movement that, like 'Chaos' in *The*

Creation, gives music a new depth, a new dimension. It is the direct link between late Haydn and late Beethoven quartets. Sir Hubert Parry was wrong: it is not Mozart who was The Great Precursor but the Haydn of Op. 76.

The fast Menuet (marked allegro) is full of energy and drive; the music is developed as if the piece were in sonata form. From the opening

the whole piece develops. The very long section after the first double bar (9–50) begins thus:

and shortly thereafter we have the theme in the 'cello:

entering in a dissonant way that again looks into the Beethovenian future. In the following passage we are reminded of the

of the Menuet in Symphony No. 102, its work of kindred spirit:

But what are we to say of the Trio, with its violence and its wave of grief in that unison descent to the fifth? The acute Cecil Gray thought[1] that the 'broad, impassioned strain [was] . . . suggestive of southern, and especially Neapolitan, folk-song'; but the folk-song here is strongly Balkan in feeling. It is one of the last times that we have an exotic excursion (as Bence Szabolcsi terms it) into the lonely world of eastern European folk-song: a last impression of the bleak and icy marshes surrounding Eszterháza and the Croatian, Hungarian and Gypsy peoples that lived their solitary life there. Haydn had been the first to import this fascinating lore and to present it to the concert halls and chambers of western Europe; this was his farewell to it:

1 *The Haydn String Quartet Society*, Vol. VIII, London 1939, p. 18.

The concluding rondo pursues one of the new ideas of Op. 76 first promulgated in the first movement of No. 3: a speeding-up of the tempo. In this Finale to No. 4 the tempo is accelerated twice. The basic structure is as follows:

A (B flat major) → B (minor) → A (major) → Coda.
a–b–a a–b–a a–b–a

The theme is as follows:

Allegro ma non troppo
mezza voce
fz

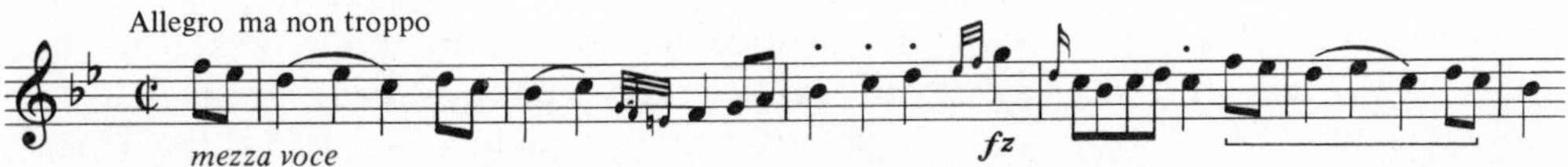

In the second statement of the big 'A', the theme is slightly transformed; from the bracketed portion of the above example, the music now goes as follows:

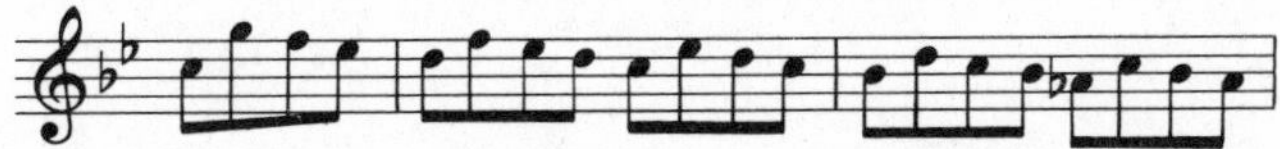

The huge coda, which comprises no less than 65 bars (total length of the Finale; 175 bars), starts with the first change of speed, using a variant of the above transformation:

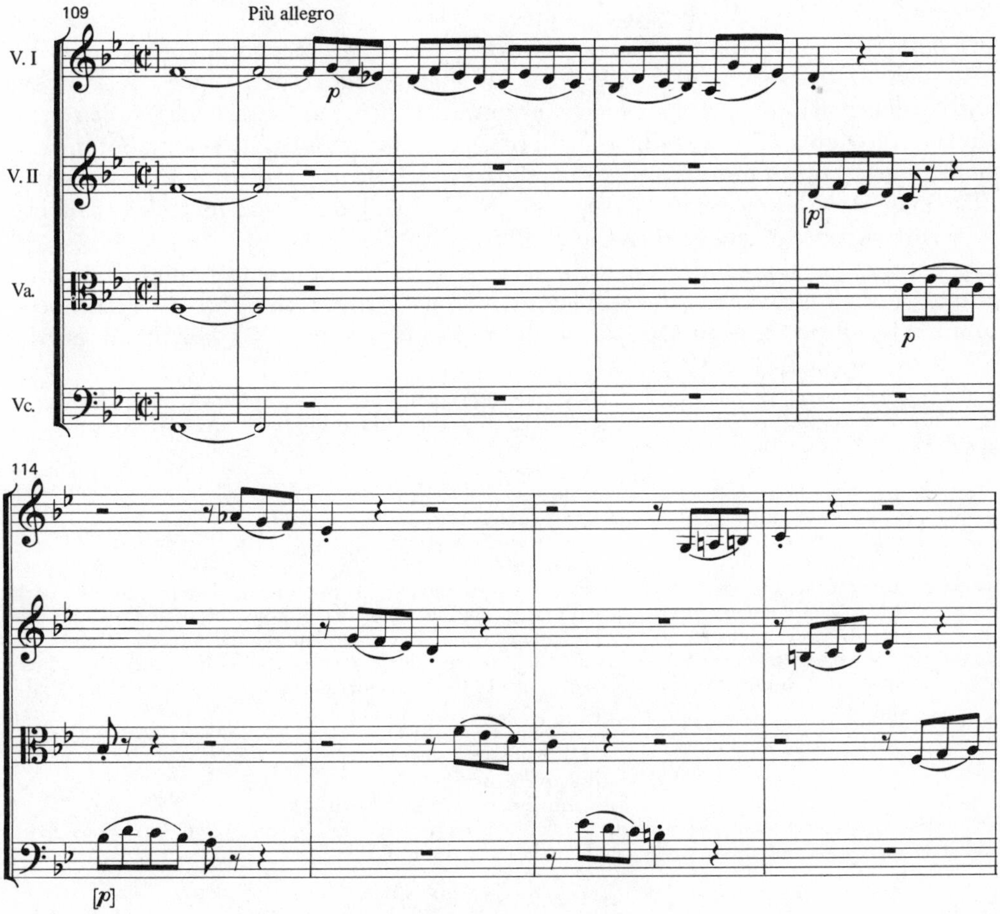

109
Più allegro
V. I
V. II
Va.
Vc.
p
[p]
p
114
[p]

All this is buffoonery on the Falstaffian scale, and carries a Haydnesque trend a step further, making the fun at the same time a great virtuoso trick. A few bars later the tempo speeds up once again (più presto); the Quartet ends in a *fortissimo* unison and a cadence with triple stops for most of the instruments. In this Finale we have one of Haydn's famous rondos in a new guise. The theme is less immediately fetching than the kind of popular rondo conclusions of the previous decade (e.g. Symphonies Nos. 88, 92, 94, etc.) and there is less serious development in the sonata-rondo tradition, of which the Finales to the three Symphonies quoted above are celebrated examples, that could be continued indefinitely. But in Op. 76 No. 4 Haydn thought that there had been enough serious music in the first three movements and so we return to a much earlier kind of straight rondo, of the type of Symphony No. 42 (1771), but with a huge coda and a whole new series of technical devices to make the ending exhilarating, humorous, brilliant and of very considerable technical (ensemble) difficulty. In this, he succeeded in creating yet another type of rondo finale which would serve composers as a model for many years.

Op. 76, No. 5

Among quartet players, this work used to be known as 'the one with the Largo'. Considering that Haydn's quartets abound in Largo movements, this singling out of the F sharp major would appear to be a typically superficial procedure. In fact, however, this particular Largo is unique in Haydn's quartets: not only because it occupies the central position in the work – we have encountered several other examples of that – and is in the mediant major; but as it happens, it is of an extraordinary length, within some two minutes of being as long as the whole rest of the work together. The slow movement of Op. 76, No. 1, is nearly as long but the rest of the work is much more lengthy than the comparable movements in Op. 76, No. 5. The long slow movements of Op. 76, Nos. 4 and 6, are balanced by flanking movements more extended than those of No. 5.[1]

If it may be said that the rest of the work was, at least in Haydn's mind, composed round the slow movement, the problems which arise from such a procedure have been admirably solved, both in Op. 76, No. 5, and in No. 6. In No. 5 Haydn adopts the

1 Performances vary, of course, but we may take the Haydn Society's recordings with the Schneider Quartet as being typical as far as the average tempo is concerned. In Op. 76, No. 5, all Haydn's repeat signs are observed, with the following result:

Opus 76, No. 5
1st movement: 4′ 40″
2nd movement: 9′ 02″
3rd movement: 3′ 23″
4th movement: 3′ 39″

Their performance of Op. 76, No. 1, which has a slow movement of comparable length, omits both repeats in the first movement and the first repeat in the Finale; we have, however, added these to our timings. The Schneider Quartet, whose performances contain curious lapses in taste (particularly some unattractive scoopings from Mr Schneider himself), take the Finale too quickly; we have therefore added a more appropriate timing in brackets following that of the Schneider group.

Opus 76, No. 1
1st movement: 9′ 16″
2nd movement: 8′ 41″
3rd movement: 2′ 15″
4th movement: 5′ 38″ [7′ 30″]

For purposes of comparison, we also add the Schneider Quartet's timings of Op. 76, No. 6; we have added the missing second repeat in the Finale to the overall timing.

Opus 76, No. 6
1st movement: 6′ 56″
2nd movement: 7′ 27″
3rd movement: 4′ 00″
4th movement: 6′ 58″.

astonishing innovation of beginning with a variation movement in moderately slow tempo (Allegretto). It was many years since Haydn had composed an instrumental work in *sonata da chiesa* form, i.e. with an entire opening slow movement; but just as he returned to the old canonic minuet in No. 2, he now adopts and adapts a kind of *sonata da chiesa* scheme for No. 5. It is a movement without any double bars and there are no outward indications (as in No. 3's slow movement) that this is a set of variations, and we grasp the form only during the course of the music.[1] The first variation is in D minor and during it the first violin reaches the very high note *f‴* (bar 36). Var. IV is back in the tonic; it breaks off and the tempo changes to allegro, giving a brilliant ending to a movement excellently calculated to introduce the famous slow movement.

The Largo, with the additional description 'cantabile e mesto' ('mesto' means, simply, 'sad'), is another one of these late-period slow movements with a profound but *objective* sense of melancholy – as if its composer were mourning for some lost antique thing of beauty. It is the emotion that we feel gazing down over the ruins of Epidaurus or walking along the Via Appia antica. Formally it is in a kind of sonata form, but there is also a strong ritornello feeling to the movement; this latter is obtained not only by a heavy reliance on parts of the only subject, but in particular by that subject's appearing unexpectedly in the middle of the development section in E major. The freedom of writing the piece in the mediant major is matched by the modulatory freedom within the movement: the development, after stating the theme in E major, modulates from E minor to G major before preparing for the recapitulation. The ending is a model of dignity and restraint, quietly dying away to *pp*. It is one of its composer's greatest slow movements.

The rest of the Quartet is intended to round off the Largo. The fast Menuet is full of warmth, while the Trio (in D minor) has a faint touch of the exotic, particularly in the rather eerie effect of the repeated *gruppetti* which at the end clash strangely with the second violin's trill:

1 In a highly technical article entitled 'Haydn: string Quartet in D major, op. 76, no. 5' (*Music Review* XXI/2 [May 1960], pp. 94ff.), J. K. Randall asserts, and constructs the entire article round the supposition that 'The tonal organization of Haydn's . . . Quartet . . . derives from a progression of tonicizations stated in its opening section. Not only does each subsequent section derive tonally from the first by means of three basic operations; but, in addition, within each movement these operations appear in the same order. Furthermore, the special tonal characteristics of the individual movements form a progressive sequence, in which the final movement serves as a summation of the preceding three.'

In the Finale, Haydn makes fun of his old habit of ending a work with a particular cliché: prototypes may be found throughout his music of the 1780s, e.g. the Finales of Symphony No. 80 or 'La Reine' (No. 85). By starting the music with this ending, an indescribably comic effect obtains; and, being a born comedian, Haydn knows (a) not to repeat the effect at the beginning of the recapitulation but to vary the theme by a running second violin part, and (b) to be sure that the work ends with the cliché intact (which it does). For the rest, this zestful Presto makes brilliant use of repeated accompanying quavers and is altogether a model of formal compactness and unity.

Op. 76, No. 6

The sixth Quartet is certainly the most difficult of the set, and its slightly remote quality has puzzled critics. It is easy to take at face value Haydn's outer shell, the part he exposed to the public eye, as being the whole man. The Finale of No. 6 is dry, but the point that is being made is not one that admits of a Mozartian warmth, while the opening Allegretto fulfils exactly the same function as that in No. 5 – that of preparing for the slow movement. And like No. 5, this movement is also a set of (unnamed) variations in an 'easy' metre (No. 5 in six-eight, No. 6 in two-four). As for the Fantasia, it can only be described as one of the boldest and most original movements in the whole eighteenth century. Consequently one is rather aghast to read, in Sir Donald Tovey's analysis[1] of the Op. 76 Quartets, that 'the graceful ingenuities of . . . No. 6 . . . roll away like the process of peeling an onion; the fantasia . . . seems more arbitrary than free. . . .' This *ex cathedra* statement seems to have coloured everyone's opinion of the work. Karl Geiringer (1953, p. 4) writes that it 'is perhaps the only one of the splendid set in which the composer's age occasionally makes itself felt through a slight decrease of creative imagination.' It was not until November 1971 that the work was ever subjected to a serious and total analysis (Somfai's searching comments – *vide infra* – applying only to a significant detail in the Fantasia) in a fascinating public lecture by Hans Keller, broadcast by the British Broadcasting Corporation but which, having been improvised without a complete script, has not been published.[2]

The variations of the first movement are based on a curious theme which Haydn proceeds to use like a *cantus firmus*, sometimes in two-parts (as in the first variation), later even as a fugato. Var. II stresses the *intrada* nature, with its French Overture dotted rhythm (this had appeared in the theme's statement), of the movement, and after Var. III, the tempo is accelerated to allegro. Note that in Op. 76, no less than four of the six quartets have movements in which the tempo is speeded up; it is a new feature of this late style (we find it in the choral works, too). This acceleration is always towards the end of a movement, at least in the instrumental music, and is often connected with some structural division; here it is the occasion for the *cantus firmus* to form the basis of a little fugue which merges into the coda and finishes off this introduction to the great Fantasia.

If we hear the beginning of the Adagio without a score, it sounds as if the music were in C flat major (a submediant minus four fifths away from E flat). Actually the

1 The 'Haydn' article in *Cobbett's Cyclopedic Survey of Chamber Music*, London 1929, I. 545. The late Quartets are discussed in a rather summary fashion, partly because the article had, by the time Tovey reached Op. 64, reached vast proportions.

2 We heard the lecture while in England. The information on the lecture's nature (no script) was kindly furnished by Mr Keller.

score is written without any key signature (that will appear later) but is notated in B major. The harmonic plan of this incredibly advanced Fantasia has been analyzed by Somfai (1970, pp. 375f.) so well that it would be a pity not to quote from it. For the purposes of orientation, the first sixty bars are in free form, but constructed so that the main subject appears in various remote keys, to which it is guided by a unison passage in three cases. Before continuing with Somfai, we would point out an interesting fact that cannot be seen from modern editions, and that is Haydn's constant indication of 'cum licentia', the meaning of which has been discussed *supra* (p. 171). We have added these markings to the music examples below; they are Haydn's notes of '*sic*' to the enharmonic deceptions he was forced to employ in the interests of intonation, and to the wrong spelling of the chord in bar 47.[1]

Somfai's reduction of bars 1–60 is as follows:[2]

1 Theme 'scale' · 20 Theme 'scale' · 31 Theme 'modulation' · 49 Theme 'scale' ‖ 60 Theme ~

+10 · −9 · +9

B ma – C♯mi . . . . E ma, E mi – G ma..B♭ma, B♭mi – B ma G♯mi A♭ma . . . . . . ‖ B ma

−2 ↘ · +3 [=G♯ma!] −3 ↘ ‖ [C♭ma]

[=C♭ma A♭mi A♭ma ‖ C♭ma]

The modulation of −1 fifth to the relative major in bars 16–20 from C sharp minor to E major, both presented scalewise, is surprising but, however, still playable. In bars 27–31 something similar occurs with a modulation from G major to B flat major (−3 fifths), third-related keys. The first difficult moment occurs in bars 35–39 when the beginning of the theme appears after B flat major in B flat minor and with the help of a Neapolitan sixth = I^6 in C flat major, the modulation reaches – not C flat major but: B major. According to the spelling, the enharmonic change does not occur simultaneously in the four parts, but in three different steps.

1 Somfai says (p. 380): 'However, Haydn's mixed spelling in bars 46–49 cannot be called correct from the viewpoint of harmonic logic. Based on the relationship of G sharp minor to G sharp major or else on the relationship of A flat minor to A flat major it ought to read:

Although Somfai had at his disposal the Elssler copy of the autograph in Budapest, for some reason he omitted all the markings 'c:l:' (abbreviation for 'cum licentia' which is written out in full in Italian in the Longman, Clementi print), which in the case of bar 47 should have told him that Haydn was fully aware that his choice of spelling was theoretically wrong; thus the 'cum licentia'.

2 Reprinted by permission of George Allen & Unwin Ltd.

This passage, which is also quoted in Karl Geiringer's book, offers one of the critical problems of 'pure' intonation to the quartet player. The second enharmonic deception is to be found in bars 46–49 and is of special interest because Haydn (in order to avoid playing in G sharp major) 'returns' to the logical tonality of A flat major. As a correction was just made in two neighbouring diminished sevenths, the pure intonation is not threatened.

The 'last' trick of enharmonic spelling is the most obvious one: in bars 56–60, this time in the relationship A flat major to B major (= A flat major to C flat major) Haydn prescribes enharmonically the same modulation of keys a third apart of −3 fifths which he had employed in bars 27–31 where he was dealing with simple keys. This passage may, however, with a small correction of intonation by the 'cellist reconstitute the movement's basic key of B major.

[op. cit., 375f.]

Hans Keller, in the above-mentioned lecture, pointed out the spiritual proximity of this movement to 'Chaos' in *The Creation*, where the same nebulous harmonies establish an uncertain tonal system. There is another interesting aspect to this movement, and that is the curious appearance of a modal line towards the end of the music. The *a* natural in the second bar of our example has occurred three bars earlier in the same context:

This whole part of the movement, with its free part writing and antique harmonic aspect, reminds one of music which had been almost forgotten by 1797: Purcell's Fantasias for strings. Could Haydn perhaps have seen this music at the home of his friend Dr Burney in England (or indeed at Shield's or Dr Arnold's)? It is curious that Haydn's Fantasia really seems to have echoes of the great English composer.

The scherzo which is the Presto Menuet acts to reduce the emotional tension generated by the Fantasia; it is a fast three-in-a-bar movement. The second section is called not Trio but 'Alternativo' (another look-over-the-shoulder to historical[1] models) and is of great originality, consisting, as Tovey (p. 545) says, 'wholly of the scale of E flat in iambic rhythm, descending and ascending with counterpoints as multitudinous and heavenly as the angels on Jacob's ladder'. Haydn wrote the movement without any repeat signs and was obviously worried about its excessive length (four bars short of being 100 bars); in the Elssler copy there is a note at the end of the 'Alternativo' which reads 'NB: Allenfals dieses Alternativo jemanden solte zu lang seÿn, so kann man es entweder bey N[ro:] 1. oder N[ro:] 2 endingen, und alsdan den Menuet Da Capo' (N.B. In case this Alternativo should prove too long for anybody, it can be ended either at No. 1 or at No. 2, and then the Menuet repeated). The places

1 Dittersdorf in his autobiography (ed. Miller, Munich 1967, p. 147) speaks of one of his works ending with a *tempo di minuetto* which 'is varied by twelve *Alternativen* (entirely wrongly called Trio[s] nowadays)'.

marked Nos. 1 and 2 in the score are bars 92 and 124, respectively; apparently no one was bothered by its Schubertian heavenly length, and this remark was dropped when the work was sent to the press in 1799.

The Finale contains *inter alia* a witty play on rhythmic effects, most entertainingly illustrated by Hans Keller in his lecture (which included a live string quartet for his musical examples; afterwards it gave a complete performance of the Quartet). The theme itself, as Rosen (339) puts it, 'sounds clearly not like three upbeats, but like *five*', while the development pushes rhythmic displacement to the point where Haydn had to throw in a *forzato* (at bar 118) to show the players where the recapitulation begins – 'Haydn's charity,' writes Rosen (340), 'otherwise we should never recognize the first note of the theme at all.' This rhythmic displacement is only part of the Finale's bag of tricks, which ranges from short double canons (bars 111–14) to clownish trills (bars 25ff.:). The humour is all intellect, but 'the comic rhythmic complexity is a true display of virtuoso invention' (Rosen, 340).[1]

In the *Allgemeine Musikalische Zeitung* of 11 September 1799, the Artaria edition of Op. 75 (i.e. our Op. 76, Nos. 1–3) was reviewed as follows:

> *Trois Quatuors pour deux Violons Alto et Violoncelle composés et dédiés à Son Excellence Mr. le Comte Joseph Erdödy de Monyorörerëk etc. par Joseph Haydn. Oeuvre 75. à Vienne chez Artaria et Comp. (3 Fl)*
>
> These Quartets, the announcement and arrival of which have really delighted the reviewer, are again proof of the inexhaustible, never-ending source of mood and wit that come from their famous composer; they are wholly worthy of him. The reviewer could hardly single out any as being the best, for they are all beautiful and original, but perhaps the third and last, principally because of its *Andante* [*sic*] (already well known as a song but here a set of excellent variations on it) will be the most successful. Even in the first Allegro of this Quartet, the imitation of the drone or bagpipes will find its admirers and connoisseurs. It is regrettable that in the otherwise very clean engraving there are frequently missing dynamic marks, which are necessary, for example *piano*, *forte*, and so on. In the Finale presto of the last Quartet there is even a bar of rest missing in the viola part after bar 20, or else after bar 22 this is missing:

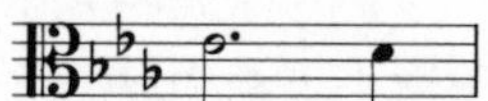

[There follow the *incipits* of the three Quartets.][2]

1 The basic literature on Op. 76 is that of Opp. 71 and 74, listed in *Haydn in England 1791–1795* (p. 459). Apart from the standard biographies of Pohl, Geiringer, Hughes, etc., we have specialized studies from Sondheimer in his strangely antagonistic book (Robert Sondheimer, *Haydn: A historical and psychological study based on his quartets*, London 1951), Somfai 1960 (A Klasszikus Quartetthangzás Kialakulása Haydn Vonósnégyeseiben', in *Zenetudományi Tanulmányok* VIII, Budapest 1960, pp. 295ff.), Somfai 1970 ('A bold enharmonic modulatory model in Joseph Haydn's String Quartets', in *Studies in Eighteenth-Century Music, A Tribute to Karl Geiringer . . .*, London 1970, pp. 370ff., wherein is also contained a useful article by Louise E. Cuyler, 'Tonal exploitation in the later quartets of Haydn), Karl Geiringer 1953 ('Opus 76' in the Haydn Society's *Complete String Quartets of Joseph Haydn*, Boston 1953), Charles Rosen (*The Classical Style*, London 1971) and Reginald Barrett-Ayres (London 1975). The analyses by Cecil Gray in the *Haydn Quartet Society* booklets (1932 *et seq.*) have been listed above as far as they apply to Op. 76. The theses are listed in the bibliography (see *Haydn: the Late Years 1801–1809*).

2 The drone or bagpipes effect in Op. 76, No. 3, has been discussed *supra*, including musical example. As for the printer's error in the Finale, viola part, bar 21 is missing (bar of rest); in later editions, this bar was added to the plate. Hoboken I, 431. The rest of the set, Artaria's Op. 76, was not reviewed in the *AMZ*, which (as in music journals of our own day) was forced to be selective.

CHAPTER NINE

Chronicle 1798

WE BEGIN THE YEAR 1798 with an authentic document written by Haydn's copyist and servant, Johann Elssler. It exists in at least two copies, one in the Mozarteum, Salzburg, and one in the Bibliothèque de l'Opéra, Paris, and we probably owe its existence to Dies, who (on pp. 209ff.) published it in his biography. We reproduce it here directly from the Elssler version, which is undated.[1]

Daily Schedule of the late Herr v. Haÿdn

In the summer time he rose at half past six. The first thing he did was to shave, which he did for himself up to his 73rd year. After shaving, he got dressed completely. If a pupil were present, he had to play the lesson he had been assigned on the piano [*Clavier*] to Hr. v. Haÿdn as he was dressing. The mistakes were at once corrected, the pupil instructed about the reasons thereof, and then a new task was assigned. For this one and a half hours were required. At the dot of 8 o'clock breakfast had to be on the table, and right after breakfast Haÿdn sat down at the piano and improvised [*fantasirte*], whereby at the same time he worked out the sketch of the composition; for this, a daily period from 8 to 11:30 in the morning was required. At 11:30 visits were paid or received; or he took a walk until 1:30. From 2 to 3 o'clock was the hour for lunch. After lunch Haÿdn always concerned himself with some small domestic task, or he went into his small library and read a book. At 4 o'clock Haÿdn returned to musical affairs. He took the sketch which had been prepared that morning and put it into score, for which task he took three to four hours. At 8 p.m. Haÿdn usually went out, but came home again at 9 and either sat down to write scores or took a book and read until 10 o'clock. The hour of 10 o'clock was supper time, which consisted of bread and wine. Haÿdn made it a rule not to have anything else except bread and wine in the evening, and he broke the rule now and then only when he was invited out for dinner. At table Haÿdn liked light conversation and altogether a merry entertainment. At half past eleven Haÿdn went to bed – in old age even later. – The wintertime made no appreciable difference in the daily schedule except that Haÿdn got up in the morning a half hour later, otherwise everything was as in the summer. In old age, mainly during the last 5 to 6 years of his life, physical weakness and illness disturbed the above schedule. The active man could, at last, find no occupation. In this latter period Haÿdn used to lie down for half an hour in the afternoon.

New Year's Day 1798 saw the revival of Salieri's *Palmira* (text by G. de Gamera). Rosenbaum's Diary also introduces some singers of whom one, Therese Saal, will occupy a significant portion of the Chronicle concerning *The Creation*.

1 The MS. in the Paris Opéra is entitled 'Tages-Ordnung des seel. Herrn H: Kapellmeisters Joseph Haÿdn', that in Salzburg 'Tages Ordnung des Selg: Herrn v. Haÿdn.' Perhaps the Salzburg MS. is earlier. We follow it here (the differences are minimal'. See Geiringer (1947), pp. 151f.

> Monday, 1st: . . . At mid-day I lunched at Frau v. Gaßman's, where I began the new year and brought the old one to a close. In the afternoon I was in the very pleasant company of the two young ladies – they are so sweet, and certainly deserve good husbands. In the evening I went to the theatre, where *Palmira* was performed for the first time in two years. [Irene] Tomeoni played Palmira, [Joseph] Simoni was the Arcidoro and Joseph[a] Umlauf sang for the first time, together with the young Fr[äu]l. Saal, the companions of Palmira, and sang quite well. I was entertained as well as could be desired. [Radant, *Rosenbaum*, 31]

Josepha Umlauf was the daughter of the well-known composer Ignaz and sister of the composer Michael. Therese Saal was soon to become Therese Gassmann's great rival, and it was the young Miss Saal (she was sixteen in 1798) who was to sing the first public performance of *The Creation* in 1799 and to start her short but meteoric career – she retired in 1805 to marry a wealthy merchant – as *The Creation*'s leading lady; her father, Ignaz Saal, was a well-known singer and he, too, participated in that historic first public performance.

On 10 January, Silverstolpe announces the forthcoming performance of *The Creation*; he writes to his father in Stockholm:

> . . . After the Carnival comes Lent, and the time for concerts. Two grand concerts will be given at Prince Schwarzenberg's, the music for them is being prepared. Haydn has played me a part of it and it promises to give me much pleasure. It is an oratorio called *The Creation* . . . [Mörner, 325]

That same day Rosenbaum learned a part of the widespread plans for transforming Eisenstadt Castle. 'We heard the distressing news that our pretty little theatre in Eisenstadt is to be razed for the sake of the grounds and view of the new English garden' (Radant, *Rosenbaum*, 32). Only a small part of the architect Moreau's plans was ever realized, but the theatre was destroyed. Rosenbaum's relationship with Prince Nicolaus started to deteriorate about this time. On Sunday the 14th, we read in the Diary: '. . . As I went home, my quite happy disposition was somewhat clouded by meeting the Prince on the Graben . . .' (p. 33), while on 28 January (p. 34) we read the rather sinister note, 'Today it happened that the Prince opened a letter from Therese to me in which she sent me a cut-up cartoon.' The Prince, then, felt free to intercept the correspondence of his employees. To continue with Haydn's friend Rosenbaum for a moment, at the end of February we read 'Therese spoke to Salieri [the girls' teacher and unofficial ward] about our relationship, then her mother spoke to him, and finally I was also called in. It was one of the most serious discussions I have ever had in all the years of my life; I found Salieri favourable and wise, and I was happy to have to do with such an important man, who is so much concerned for the well-being of his ward . . .', and the following day, 28 February, we read: 'I told v. Karner that I had spoken to Salieri and Therese's mother about our relationship, and that her mother wanted to see the Prince about it herself. V. Karner promised to arrange a meeting and was in agreement with everything; this made me so happy!' (p. 35) Little did Rosenbaum know . . .

In the Court Theatres they were giving *inter alia* Süssmayer's *Die edle Rache* and Paisiello's *La contadina di spirito*, both with Therese Gassmann (Radant, *Rosenbaum*, 33, 35).

Haydn was with Prince Esterházy in Eisenstadt, preparing some musical festivity or other. In the protocol of the Tonkünstler-Societät for 19 January 1798 (Pohl III, 123) we read: 'Herr Jos. Haydn excuses himself that he could not come to today's session, because he has to go to Eisenstadt with his Prince, but meanwhile he offers the Society for its Lenten Academy the *7 Words* in the vocal version. The Society accepts this offer with the greatest thanks and profound pleasure.'

During February there were private concerts at the composer's Adalbert Gyrowetz, one of Haydn's London acquaintances now returned to settle in Vienna and to work for the Court Opera, and at the famous portrait painter's, G.-B. Lampi Sen., director of the Vienna Academy 'where', writes Silverstolpe – our source for both concerts, 'I met at one stroke almost all the Viennese artists whom I had known before more or less intimately . . .'. (Mörner, 327f.)

On 10 March, Haydn attended his first business session of the Tonkünstler-Societät, and the records have him down as saying that 'arrangements must be made for the future academies whereby all the members without exception appear *in person* [italics original] and for both days [the concerts were always repeated, as we have seen, with a slight change of programme], staying to the very end and not, as experience has unfortunately taught us, coming late, leaving early, or not even appearing at all the second day' (Pohl III, 123).

That same Saturday, 10 March, Rosenbaum's marriage plans were put before Prince Nicolaus Esterházy by Rosenbaum's friend, von Karner. 'The Prince seemed to disapprove, and v. K— said no more about it' (Radant, *Rosenbaum*, 36). The next day Rosenbaum notes:

> As the Prince left to drive to Court, I asked him on his way down the stairs for his permission to marry. – The Prince was gracious but could not quite make up his mind to permit it, and instructed me to submit my request in writing. – Monday, 12th: I arose at about 5:30 a.m. and wrote a petition asking for permission to marry . . . I went to the Prince for signatures [on documents], handed him my petition and presented my case in the best possible light. I also made the same request of the Princess; since she is ill, I made the request through her maid. Since the Prince has such a repugnance to marrying, I have little hope of obtaining permission. The Prince treated me wisely and graciously. The Princess Dowager[*née* Countess Hohenfeld] promised to do everything possible for me. . . . Friday, 16th: This morning I worked from 6 until 8:30, then went to the Prince, . . . [then] to the Princess Dowager, where I heard most unfavourable news. I stayed at home until 4 o'clock, then I went . . . to see Therese, who was at the theatre with her mother. I took a walk, returned to their house and dined there. Her mother told me, after the most gloomy prologue imaginable, that she had received an anonymous letter describing me as a dissolute wretch and warning her against me. . . . Saturday, 17th: . . . I went to see Therese and learned that they had been at Haydn's; he had said many nice things about me, and they both were cheerful and reassured. I also visited Haydn and talked to his wife until he came home. I told him at great length of my love for Therese and my desire to marry her, and implored him to help us in any way he can; this he faithfully promised to do. [pp. 36f.]
>
> Tuesday 20th: . . . Therese and Ninna lunched with Countess Traun, which left me with their mother . . . At table she broached the same subject again; having heard that the Prince was dismissing so many of his staff and that sweeping changes were being made, I should not spend so much money on presents for her daughters. If nothing came of the marriage, everything would have to be given back. . . . Tuesday 27th: . . . After lunch I went to look for v. Karner at the Steindl . . . He also told me that the Princess spoke yesterday at table of my union with Therese, and used her influence on my behalf. – Later I went to see Haydn, stayed two hours and chatted a great deal about music, new arrangements in the house,

> the dissolution of the band [wind instruments], and about my Therese, whom I love so very deeply; I had a very cordial conversation with him. [pp. 37f., 39]

It is astonishing that Haydn, who was preparing for the first performance of *The Creation* at the end of April, and who must have been supervising the great task of having the parts copied (mostly by Johann Elssler), could find time to talk to Rosenbaum for two hours about his problems with Therese Gassmann and the Prince. The house of Esterházy was now practising economy: on the one hand, there were lavish entertainments such as we have witnessed in the summer of 1797, but on the other, drastic curtailments in personnel were being implemented. The princely *Feld-Harmonie* (the wind-band octet discussed *passim*) was now dismissed, leaving a small nucleus of string players and singers to perform the regular Sunday musical services at Eisenstadt. We shall see, later in the year, that Haydn took these reduced circumstances into account when composing the *Missa in angustiis* ('Nelson' Mass), and that the reduced wind band also affected the scoring of the Mass for 1799 ('Theresienmesse').

On the 24th, the forthcoming Lenten concert of the Tonkünstler-Societät for 1 and 2 April was announced in the *Wiener Zeitung*, with '*The Seven Words* in the vocal version by Herr Joseph Haydn, Doctor of Music and Kapellmeister in actual service of his Highness, the reigning Prince Esterházy, also member of the above Society . . . Not only the greatly respected master but also the work are too well known to require any further recommendation.' A few days later, on 28 March, the same paper notes that Prince Esterházy, upon dissolving his battalion (*Insurrection*), displayed his love for fatherland and *Landesfürst* by giving the 120 horses of that force to 'the all-highest service' (i.e. to the Emperor), 'and this example was followed by various other patriots'. That very day, Silverstolpe reports to Stockholm:

> . . . For the past few weeks the well-known music composer and violin virtuoso [Rodolphe] Kreu[t]zer has been here in Vienna [as a guest of the French Embassy], who . . . wrote the music to *Lodoiska*. I have heard him in private concerts.[1] He travelled in Italy for two years at the cost of the Fr[ench] Republic to collect old music for a National Institute, among the teachers of which is Kreuzer. He found over 2,000 scores of Léo, Corelli, Jomelli, Durante, Pergolesi, etc., and also some by Händel. He assures me that music in Italy has now fallen so low that the great masters such as Cimarosa and Paisiello are forced to fill their operas with chansonettes and vaudevilles, since the public immediately berates them as 'Capel-Meister' and forces the orchestra to stop the moment a piece appears in a higher vein or a more learned style. Also one works at the most a month for a whole opera. I imagined something like this, for here I have heard so much second-rate music by the most famous Italian composers . . . [Mörner, 328]

On 29 March, Josepha Duschek (Dussek), Mozart's old friend from Prague, gave a concert in the Jahn'sche Rooms, at which 'Acadamy' she sang a Mozart Rondo with obbligato basset horn, played by Anton Stadler; it was probably the famous Rondo from *La clemenza di Tito*. What makes the programme even more interesting is that Beethoven played one of his own violin sonatas with Ignaz Schuppanzigh (Deutsch, *Mozart, Dokumente*, 422). It is the kind of concert which, rather remarkably, Haydn seems to have attended even during these last-minute preparations for *The Creation*, for on the 30th he was seen at an 'Academy' at the Burgtheater for the benefit of his godchild, Joseph Weigl. Rosenbaum tells us that he 'went to hear Weigel's Cantata

1 Zinzendorf heard Kreutzer and Beethoven playing together at a Lobkowitz Soirée on 5 April.

A page from the protocol of the meeting of the Tonkünstler-Societät, held in Vienna on 13 March 1798; among those who signed it are 'Ant[onio] Salieri / Maestro di Cappella della / Corte Imp[le]', Haydn's old friend and collaborator Carl Friberth, Haydn himself ('Joseph Haydn mpria Assessor') and 'Paul Wranizky mpria / p. t. Soc: Act'.

Gefühle meines Herzens. Therese [Gaßmann], Tomeoni, [Calvani-]Willmann, [Johann Michael] Vogel [the later friend of Schubert] and Angrichani [*recte*: Angrisani] sang, Therese best of all. The Cantata was received the way it deserved to be; it is a great bore and was not a success. After the theatre I spoke to Haydn, later to v. Karner, then bade them both farewell and dined at Therese's; we were happy and cheerful' (Radant, *Rosenbaum*, 39).

The programmes for the Lenten concerts of the Tonkünstler-Societät were as follows (Pohl, *Denkschrift*, 66):

> 1 April 1798. Grosse Sinfonie von Eybler.
> *Die Worte des Heilands am Kreuze* (Haydn), Soli: Therese Gassmann, Antonie Flamm, Carl Weinmüller, Sigismund Hüller. Dirigent: Haydn. In the interval: Clarinett-Concert, played by Beer [Joseph Beer, first clarinet of the Liechtenstein Orchestra].
>
> 2 April 1798. Grosse Sinfonie von Eybler.
> *Die Worte des Heilands am Kreuze* (Haydn). Soli: Therese Gassmann, Antonie Flamm, Ignaz Saal, Sigismund Hüller. Dirigent: Haydn. In the interval: 'spielt Herr von Beethoven ein Quintett von seiner Erfindung auf dem Piano-Forte begleitet von' (. . . plays a Quintet of his composition for piano-forte accompanied by) Triebensee (oboe), Beer (clarinet), Matouschek (bassoon), Nickl (hunting horn).[1]

On 1 April it was Therese Gassmann's birthday, 'A stormy, raw December day marked by heavy snowfall', notes Rosenbaum (40), who 'laid a little poem and a couple of engravings on her table . . . When Therese came home and read my little present, she fell on my neck and kissed me warmly; this gave me great joy, was so dear to me, that I can only repay such devotion with all my love and affection. I remained until 5 o'clock, then went to the theatre where Haydn gave the words of the Redeemer to benefit the Society. Ninna and Agnes came along later, and we conversed together. Haydn was received with threefold applause, the same again at the end. Therese sang quite well despite her catarrh, and was deservedly applauded.' The 'threefold applause' – an old tradition also in Masonic circles – may perhaps be best shown by a graph: x–x–x, x–x–x, x–x–x. Count von Zinzendorf noted in his Diary for 1 April, '. . . au Spectacle Le grand Concert des Veuves des dernieres paroles de notre Seigneur. La dernière surtout superbe . . .' (Olleson, 53). Silverstolpe was present and reported back to Sweden:

> . . . On 1 and 2 April, on two successive days, was performed under Haydn's own direction the *7 Words* with the additional vocal music not only a quadro [soloists] but also with choruses. It is quite indescribable how much this music gains in effect by the change. There are many mistakes in declamation, however, but these couldn't be avoided since the words were added to the instrumental music later. For this reason one mustn't examine the words all too closely; but the effect of the whole is astonishing. Haydn was applauded several times, not only because of his music but also for his own person. [Mörner, 329]

1 Beethoven's Quintet, Op. 16. The wind players were all well known; the horn player, Matthias Nickl, had been in the Haydn orchestra at Eszterháza from 1786 until the orchestra's dissolution in 1790. The Quintet had been performed for the first time in public at a benefit concert by Schuppanzigh given at the Jahn'sche Rooms on 6 April 1797 (fascimile of the programme in Landon, *Beethoven,* 117); Beethoven later dedicated the work to Prince Schwarzenberg when it was published in March 1801.

The *Wiener Zeitung* reviewed the concert (No. 28, 7 April), but its note was more in the nature of a Press release, with a list of all the performers. Still, after listing the Beethoven work and its players, the paper noted, 'All received undivided and loud applause'. The Imperial Family was present, including the Archdukes and Archduchesses, and donated a gift of money to the Society. 'The income was also enlarged by a generous gift of H.I.H. The Archduchess Christine, which example was followed by several members of the nobility.' The chorus was 150 strong, the orchestra also very large; it was a performance in the Handelian tradition of Westminster Abbey and no doubt many people considered the work a foretaste of *The Creation*. The financial success was as great as the artistic. In the Society's protocol, Wranizky, commenting on the highest income ever received in a Tonkünstler concert, pointed out: 'This Academy, for which we have to thank only Haydn, brought in an income of 2,768 fl. [*recte*: 2,734 fl. 21 kr.] brutto and 2,367 fl. 48 kr. netto. Proof that Haydn's free admission to the Society is a great gain for it.' (Pohl, *Denkschrift*, 50).

On 6 April, Prince Joseph zu Schwarzenberg was informed that the new Haydn Oratorio was ready for performance (i.e. Elssler and his team had finished copying the parts), and a performance in the Palais Schwarzenberg on the Mehlmarkt (Neuer Markt) was planned 'as soon as the circumstances of the Princess allow it'. Princess Pauline Schwarzenberg had given birth to a daughter on 20 March and was still confined. It was some weeks before the general rehearsal (public, of course) was announced for 29 April and the official 'first' performance on 30 April 1798.[1]

The ten 'associates' were to pay 50 ducats (= 225 gulden) each to make a total of 500 ducats, and the document of 6 April puts this into effect; on 14 April the money was paid by Prince Schwarzenberg to van Swieten 'to whom the organization of the business has been entrusted' (Croll, 87).

The 'affair' of Bernadotte and the French Tricolore hanging from the Embassy window in Vienna may be summarized in a quotation from the *Wiener Zeitung*:

> Before [on Sunday, 8 April], the accredited Ambassador of the French Republic, Cit. Bernadotte, was received in first audience by H.M. the Empress and then by their R. H. the Archdukes and Archduchesses. [No. 29, 11 April]
>
> On the 13th of this month a large Tricolore was seen quite unexpectedly to be hanging from the house of the French Ambassador, and the populace, regarding its appearance as entirely out-of-the-ordinary, considered it a sign of alarm, became restless, and mishandled in various ways the house in which the Ambassador lived; but speedy action, and the obedience of the entire population, not only prevented more serious outbreaks but also rather soon allowed peace to be restored. The Ambassador, in the circumstances, found it advisable to leave on the following Sunday, together with his suite, for Rastadt. [No. 31, 18 April]

On the evening of the 13th, there was a benefit concert for the singer Luisa Caldarini in the Jahn'sche Rooms, at the outset of which there was a Symphony 'by the famous *Herr Kapellmeister* Hayden', of whose composition the evening ended with an

1 Pohl III, 126, based on Anton Morath, 'Die Pflege der Tonkunst durch das Haus Schwarzenberg', in *Das Vaterland*, 10 March 1901. On a trip to the Schwarzenberg Central Archives in Český Krumlov (Krumau) in 1959, we tried to locate the relevant documents; but to no avail. The relevant documents have since (1974) come to light again and have been published by Gerhard Croll in *Haydn-Studien* III (1974), Heft 2, pp. 85–92, hereinafter abbreviated 'Croll'. The Central Archives also house an important collection of Haydniana, including the earliest known dated MS. of a Haydn Symphony (No. 37, dated 1758) and a valuable set of MSS. of the rather rare *Scherzandi* (II: 33–38; see our critical edition for Verlag Doblinger, Vienna 1959–60).

'Allegro' – that which the contemporary programmes in London used to call a 'Full Piece'. It is perhaps symbolic that Haydn, representing, as it were, law and order, was performed at the same time that Bernadotte, and with him the Republican-thinking hotheads of Vienna, were – at least on Bernadotte's part, perhaps deliberately – inciting the population to riot. Silverstolpe, incidentally, had several conversations with the French Ambassador which he reported back to Sweden *via* the diplomatic pouch. As we have said, Beethoven was a regular attender of the soirées at the French Embassy, as was Johann Nepomuk Hummel. Silverstolpe, on 25 April, reports to Sweden that the famous singer Marchesi was in Vienna. 'The greatest *prima donna*, Madame Billington, was to be engaged, like Marchesi, for several months, but she isn't coming because she has a French lover and doesn't want to leave him. . . . Kreu[t]zer, who composed *Lodoiska*, left with Ambassador Bernadotte. Haydn's *Creation* . . . will be performed for the first time a week from now. I've heard the greater part of it played by the composer himself from the full score. . . .'

On 27 April, we read in Rosenbaum's Diary (41): '. . . In the evening I went to Mme Mozart's concert, which was quite well attended. She gave *Clemenzo* [*sic*] *di Tito* and sang herself with Therese [Gaßmann], Bescher, [Josepha] Umlauf, [Georg] Stengel and Rathenmayer [Mathias Rathmayer]. Clementi [Franz Clement]played a violin concerto, and played it beautifully.' We quote the extract (1) because Deutsch could find no evidence that the concert took place (*Mozart, Dokumente*, 422), and (2) because it is interesting to see that Rathmayer sang in the Mozart opera on the 27th, rehearsed *The Creation* all that week, and gave the performances on the 29th and 30th – a considerable feat at any time.

About *The Creation* rehearsals we are informed by Silverstolpe:

> [*Silverstolpe's Report (V)*]
> This work [*The Creation*] was first given on 30 April 1798. I was among the audience, and a few days beforehand I had attended the first rehearsal. At the latter Haydn was surprised afterwards by a present. Prince Schwarzenberg,[1] in whose rooms the work was prepared and later also performed, was so utterly enchanted by the many beauties of the work that he presented the composer with a roll containing one hundred ducats, over and above the 500 that were part of the agreement. – No one, not even Baron van Swieten, had seen the page of the score wherein the birth of light is described. That was the only passage of the work which Haydn had kept hidden. I think I see his face even now, as this part sounded in the orchestra. Haydn had the expression of someone who is thinking of biting his lips, either to hide his embarrassment [*Verlegenheit*] or to conceal a secret. And in that moment when light broke out for the first time, one would have said that rays darted from the composer's burning eyes. The enchantment of the electrified Viennese was so general that the orchestra could not proceed for some minutes.
>
> [Mörner in *Haydn-Studien* II/1, 1969, p. 28]

1 Schwarzenberg Archives, 30 April 1798. 'Kappellmeister [*sic*] Haydn to be paid by gracious order one hundred ducats, that is 450f., and to be debited properly to the cassa . . . L. Ploch v. Seinsberg'.

For the military guards which were placed outside the Palace on 7 and 10 May, Schwarzenberg paid another twenty-odd ducats, so that within one month the costs for *The Creation* performances amounted to 170 ducats (675 Gulden). *Vide* Croll, 88. Later, in 1799 and afterwards, there are constant bills for the cavalry and police guards necessary to keep order outside, and presumably within, the Palace during performances of the Oratorio. In 1800, Schwarzenberg bought six copies of the score from Artaria (Haydn's agents in the subscription). The same procedure obtained with *The Seasons*, for the first public performance of which in the Redoutensaal (29 May 1801) Schwarzenberg donated 885 Gulden, including a double honorarium (twice 50 ducats or 550 Gulden) for Haydn. It was a touchingly generous act on both occasions. Croll 91f.

Among the eye-witnesses of those historic days at the Palais in the Mehlmarkt was Princess Eleonore von Liechtenstein (*née* Princess von Oettingen-Spielberg), who kept up a steady correspondence with her daughter, Countess Josephine von Harrach; this correspondence, in so far as it concerns Haydn, was first printed by Botstiber in 1927, who copied it from the family archives in Bohemia (Czechoslovakia).

> Samedi ce 28 Avril 1798
>
> Maurice qui vous embrasse, vous et votre mari, prie, mais très fort à sa manière ce dernier, de ne pas oublier de lui donner un billet pour le concert de Schwartzenberg [*sic*] qui sera mardi, il dit, que ce sera la plus belle chose du monde, il prétend que la Lorel [Sorel ?] en voudrait bien aussi en avoir un.
>
> Le dimanche 29 Avril 1798.
>
> Cette musique de Heiden de la création du monde fait grand bruit, on dit, que jamais on n'a rien entendu de semblable; l'auteur convient que l'est son chef-d'œuvre, le poëme est fait dit-on par le Baron; il n'y a que 3 voix, Melle Gerard [*sic*] émigrée allemande qui a une voix superbe, Sale [*sic*] et un autre, je ne sais qui, ces sont tous des anges Raphaël, Gabriel et Uriel; on dit qu'on ne fait que pleurer d'attendrissement sur la grandeur, la majesté, la bonté de Dieu, l'âme s'élève, on ne peut se défendre d'aimer, d'admirer ce grand et admirable ouvrier. Il y a eu 2 répétitions hier et avant-hier [le jour alors du concert de Madame Mozart!] et hier la P^esse.^ Clary y a été à l'invitation de Mme Chotek qui l'en a conjure. . . .

The principal performers were Christine Gerardi (soprano), Mathias Rathmayer (tenor) and Ignaz Saal (bass); Antonio Salieri sat at the fortepiano; Haydn himself conducted. A few words about the principal vocal soloists may be welcome. Christine Gerardi (Gerhardi) was then a popular amateur (in the eighteenth-century sense) singer, only twenty-one years of age, who shortly (20 August 1798) was to marry Dr Joseph Frank, son of Hofrat Peter Frank, a celebrated physician and the director of the Allgemeine Krankenhaus (General Hospital) in Vienna. Peter Frank had among his many illustrious patients Ludwig van Beethoven, who 'corrected the un-correctable compositions [of Joseph, who was a dilettante musician], was often a guest in their home, sometimes played, and helped the son sorting out his music' (Schönauer to Sonnleithner; Pohl, III, 128). We shall see (in *Haydn: the Late Years 1801–1809*) that Haydn, Christine Gerardi-Frank, Beethoven and the horn virtuoso Punto all collaborated at a charity concert for wounded soldiers on 30 January 1801. Christine, described by Princess Eleonore von Liechtenstein as 'emigrée allemande' and as 'cette jeune fille d'un négociant qui a fait banqueroute', is listed in her marriage document as daughter of 'Christian Gerhardi, director of a cotton-factory in Moravia' and his wife, Sophie, *née* Monti. We read that, in the concerts given by the Gesellschaft der Associirten at the Palais Schwarzenberg and Palais Lobkowitz, she sang the soprano solo parts in Salieri's *Axur* (*Aecur*), Gluck's *Alceste* and Handel's *Acis and Galatea*. The Vienna correspondent of the *Neue teutsche Merkur* (3 May 1798) reports on *The Creation – vide infra* – and says *inter alia*, 'In the Society of Music Lovers [Gesellschaft der Associirten is meant], Miss Christine Gerardi has the first place among all female singers; an excellent voice, flexibility and a pleasing tone, a pretty appearance and attractive movements but especially a fiery eye, give strength to every word and grace to every tone that issues from her breast.' In 1804 the whole Frank family moved to Wilna (then Poland; now Vilnjus, U.S.S.R.), where father and son had secured appointments as professors; in 1809, Christine sang in a Polish-language performance of *The Creation* conducted by Daniel Steibelt.

The tenor solo was sung by another amateur singer who often participated in the Tonkünstler-Societät concerts: Mathias Rathmayer, who was Doctor of Law and Professor at the Theresianum. Ignaz Saal, a versatile bass singer who encompassed serious and comic roles as well as speaking parts in straight theatre, was the father of the soprano Therese, who would soon become the toast of musical Vienna.

On 29 April 1798 the day dawned beautifully but later the weather changed and it rained a great deal in the evening (Zinzendorf: 'Il y a beaucoup plû dans la soirée. La matinée belle'). Such a press of persons with tickets, but also idle spectators, was expected that Prince Schwarzenberg had the market-stalls (*Mehlstandsetzer*) in front of the Flour Market (Mehlmarkt) cleared away; they had to take away their sacks of flour and dried beans etc., for which the Disbursing Office (*Hauptcassa*) of the princely administration paid them 10 fl. 20 Kr. The entrance to the Palais Schwarzenberg was soon in such a state of chaos that eighteen mounted and twelve ordinary policemen had to be employed to keep the crowd in check.[1]

At least five contemporaries recorded their impressions. Griesinger (37f.) wrote:

> I had the fortune to be a witness of the deep emotion and the most lively enthusiasm which were felt by all the audience at several performances of this Oratorio under Haydn's own direction. Haydn admitted to me, moreover, that he could not describe the feelings with which he was filled when the performance went just the way he wished, and the audience listened to every note in total silence. 'Sometimes my whole body was ice-cold, sometimes a burning heat overcame me, and more than once I was afraid that I would suddenly have a stroke.'

Princess Eleonore Liechtenstein writes:

> Ce mardi 1. Mai à 10 h. et un $\frac{1}{4}$.
>
> A 11 h. part l'occasion et je loge à une lieu de chez vous ma chère Pepie, je n'ai donc pas beaucoup de temps, pour vous dire qu'en effet ce concert est une chose superbe, admirable et qui mérite très certainement; si votre santé le permet et que ce soit votre bon plaisir à l'un et à l'autre de revenir un peu de Brug pour l'entendre; je voudrais que quelqu'un de plus habillé que moi puisse vous en parler dignement de ma vie, je n'ai vu un tel enthousiasme, je me trouvais à coté du Cte. Marchal et tout près d'Op . . . qui surtout le premier était absolument hors de lui. Tout ce qui est outré, affaibli chez moi le sentiment, mais en me mettant tout seule et uniquement livrée à moi, mème, je puis vous assurer que je n'ai guère entendu quelque chose de plus beau qui enlève, qui tire des larmes, qui entre dans le sujet tout grande et relevé, qu'il n'y a pas d'athée [?] comme je l'ai dit au Mr. Marchal, car si une voix l'était élevée dans l'assemblée qui eut Ad . . . tout ce D[ieu]. créateur cet être si grand, dont les oeuvres sont si admirables, joignons nos voix pour le louer, je crois que tout le monde ce serait levé pour le faire et que chaqu'un l'a fait souvent dans son coeur. C'est le Baron qui a fait [les] paroles, toutes tirées de la génèse et des psaumes et il a communiqué ses idées à Haydn pour la musique, il est sur que cela leur fait honneur à l'un et à l'autre. Marchal m'a dit que Haydn est venu d'Angleterre avec le projet de composer sur ce sujet, qu'on lui avait donné là avec un poëme anglais et c'est là . . . que le Baron a travaillé et sans lui rien oter je crois à-peu-près traduit. La musique a été parfaitement executée, dirigée par Hayden [*sic*] qui donait la mesure des 2 mains. Gabriel est cette jeune fille d'un négociant qui a fait banqueroute, elle a une belle voix, jeune et facile. Raphael était Sale [Saal] et Uriel un Mr. qui est professeur au Thérèsien, belle voix de tenor qui

1 Pohl III, 126–31.

m'a beaucoup plu. Le chaud a été terrible; j'y ai vu mais de loin votre cher Guerin[?]; il y avait beaucoup de monde, nous 4 vieilles figures, le Françoise, Clary, Kinsky et moi, du reste toutes les élégantes Polonaises, Anglaises et Viennaises. Adieu ma très chére Pepie, je vous envois les livres, 2 sermons de Schneller et le restes de ces graines rouges, dont nous ne pouvons pas faire usage manquant des serres. Adieu, je vous embrasse, Nani a bien pleurée surtout à ce duo d'Adam et d'Éve; on ne sait pas, à quand la seconde représentation, cela dépend de Mr. Braun qui ne se montre pas facile, il y en aura une troisième, voilà tout ce que j'ai pu apprendre. [Pohl III, 130f.]

It is not clear if the Princess attended the first or the second performance, or perhaps even both.

Giuseppe Carpani (165f., 182) was also present:

Chi può descrivervi l'entusiasmo, il piacere, gli applausi di quella sera? Ben io che mi trovai presente, posso assicurarvi che non vidi mai cosa simile in vita mia. Il fiore degli uomini colti e de' signori tanto nazionali che forestieri, era colà radunato. La megliore orchestra possibile; *Haydn* stesso alla testa; il più perfetto silenzio e l'attenzione più scrupolosa; una sala favorevole; un'esattezza somma negli esecutori; un sentimento quasi di divozione e di rispetto in tutta l'assemblea: ecco le disposizioni con che partì il primo colpo d'orchestra, che dischiuse le porte alle non più intese armoniche bellezze. Estatiche le menti, sorprese, rapite, ebbre di piacere e d'ammirazione, provarono per due ore consecutive, ciò che provato non avevan mai prima; una esistenza beata prodotta da desiderj sempre maggiori, sempre rinascenti e sempre soddisfatti. . . .

Siccome, allorchè scrisse la *creazione*, aveva il maestro la sorte di far eseguire la parte del *soprano* alla egregia cantante madame *Franck*, in allora madamigella Gherard, così non lasciò di trarre il più gran partito della bellissima ed agilissima voce di quella rara *dilettante*, e non fu delusa la sua aspettazione. Questa musica va esiguita con semplicità, esaltezza, espressione e portamento, ma senza *fiorettare*. . . .

The *Neue teutsche Merkur* (part of the article from which we have quoted, *supra*) writes under date 3 May 1798: 'Already three days have passed since that happy evening, and it still sounds in my ears, in my heart, and my breast is constricted by many emotions even thinking of it' (Pohl III, 129), while Ignaz Edler von Mosel in his memoirs, *Die Tonkunst in Wien während der letzten fünf Dezennien* (Vienna 1840), writes, 'The evening in which *The Creation* was first performed under the composer's own direction before a brilliant audience at the Palace of the art-loving Prince Josef v. Schwarzenberg will remain unforgettable for those to whom, like myself, it was granted to be present.'

The big social event seems to have been the second evening, 30 April. Count von Zinzendorf was present and wrote:

. . . a 6[h] ½ au Concert de Haydn de la maison de Schwarzenberg intitulé die Schöpfung, tiré de la bible et de Milton, traduit par le B. Swieten, la musique faite expres pour les paroles pour 500 Ducats. L'Ouverture qui doit depeindre le Chaos, le Chant de Gabriel au second jour, les Airs de la troisième Scene. Le lever du Soleil, la marche de la Lune. Dans le II[d] Acte, L'Aigle, l'Alouette, le verd des prairies, les trois Archanges. L'air qui annonce la création de l'homme, e celui d'apres, celui de Raphael a la fin. 'in Staub zerfallen sie'. Tout la 3me acte l'Adoration et le Duo d'Adam et Eve. J'avois une place a coté de M[r] Giacomarzi. Je la sedois a La C[sse] Elisabeth Schoenborn, qui vient avec Mr de Croy. J'ai vû la M: et Me de Nostitz de Prague . . . Lu dans Gibbon, les victoires de Totila. . . . Journée plurieve. [Olleson 53 and Zinzendorf MS.]

It was one of the longest and most enthusiastic reports in his Diary to deal with music, and the old Count decided to get tickets – obviously very difficult to obtain – for a repeat series of performances at the Palais Schwarzenberg on 7 and 10 May. At the first set of performances on 29 and 30 April, the audience were given a libretto printed by Mathias Andreas Schmidt (copies in the Österreichische Nationalbibliothek, Gesellschaft der Musikfreunde, etc.) and a long printed poem by the orientalist Joseph, Freiherr von Hammer-Purgstall ('Wen lüstet die Triumphe noch zu schauen'), who was later Sir Sidney Smith's interpreter and secretary in the Egyptian campaign against Napoleon (1798–9).

The Creation was causing such a furore with the Viennese aristocracy (and anyone else who was fortunate enough to secure an entrance ticket to the Schwarzenberg performances) that a new Cantata for the benefit of a town in what is now Jugoslavia, called Cilli (which had been destroyed by fire), was played to an almost empty house. On Friday 4 May, Rosenbaum writes about the Cantata performed at the Redoutensaal. 'It was empty – scarcely 300 persons. The music is by Süßmayer, the words by Kotzebue. Therese [Gaßmann] sang very prettily.' (Radant, *Rosenbaum*, 42). The next day Rosenbaum went to Gumpendorf (*recte*):

> Sunday, 6th [May]: . . . After 11 o'clock we drove into town. I went to see Haydn, found that he was not in his quarters but in Guntendorf [*sic*] instead. Then I went to v. Karner. . . . Later I met by accident a drover, Prax, who went with me to see Haydn out in Guntendorf; we chatted along quite pleasantly. We did not find Haydn, so I told his wife v. K— wanted a ticket for the concert at Schwarzenberg's on the 7th, and about the prospects of engaging the wind players [for the Esterházy band: this was not done until late in 1799.] [*Rosenbaum*, 42]

Zinzendorf, that same day, reported that 'La P[esse] Auersb[erg] m'envoya un billet pour le Concert', and on 7 May we read in the Count's Diary:

> . . . Le soir *au Concert*, je me trouvois entre la P[esse] Ruspoli et Lise Reischach vis a vis la Chanteuse Melle Gebhard [Gerardi], qui et jolie. L'ouverture indique qu'il y avoient de grands vens [vents] dans le Chaos. 'Es ward Licht' est un bel effet. L'air 'Nun beut die Flur das frische Grün'. Le Choeur 'Stimmt an die Saiten', Le Trio 'dem kommenden Tage sagt es die Nacht.' – 'In alle Welt ergeht das Wort – keiner Zunge fremd.' – 'Wie viel sind deiner Werke! Gott!' L'air – 'dem Ganzen fehlte das Geschöpf' – – 'Mit Würd und Hoheit angethan' – – et toute la troisieme partie . . . Beau tems et chaud. [Olleson 54 and Zinzendorf MS.]

The Princess Auersberg who gave Zinzendorf the ticket was Maria Josepha, wife of Carl, one of Swieten's members of the Gesellschaft. On 7 May, the old Count's neighbours were Princess Marie Leopoldine Ruspoli, *née* Khevenhüller-Metsch; and Elisabeth Freiin Reischach, later Countess Marschall. On 30 April his neighbours were Countess Schönborn, an unmarried daughter ('Stiftsdame zu Thorn' in Schönfeld's *Adels-Schematismus* of 1824) of Eugen Franz Erwein, Count von Schönborn; the head of the Prague Nostitz branch was Count Joseph, *k. k. Kämmerer*, and his wife Johanne, *née* Countess von Bees; we have no information about Signor Giacomarzi.

On 10 May 1798, the fourth performance of *The Creation* took place at the Palais in the Mehlmarkt. Zinzendorf was once again present and wrote: '. . . A $6^h\frac{1}{4}$ passé au Concert de Haydn chez le P[ce] de Schwarzenberg. On distribuoit des vers imprimés a son honneur. J'eus une bonne place dans la première Sale a coté de Me Schaeften. La musique me parut marquer mieux et on souffroit moins de chaud en l'ecoutant . . .

Beau tems mais du vent.' (Olleson 54 and Zinzendorf MS.). The verses were probably another issue of the above-mentioned ones by Hammer-Purgstall.

Meanwhile the famous castrato Luigi Marchesi made his début in Zingarelli's *Pirhus* (*Pirro*), in the production of which – at the Kärntnerthortheater – Therese Gassmann also sang. Rosenbaum, who was there (9 May) wrote: 'Even before the performance I was bored by the Italians, and even more during it by their impetuous, extremely disagreeable behaviour. Therese had 2 terrible arias, but was applauded just the same.' (Radant, *Rosenbaum*, 43). The following day, when the fourth performance of *The Creation* took place, Rosenbaum wanted to take the Gassmann girls to the suburb of Hütteldorf,

> . . . but since the mother had tickets to *The Creation* by Haydn, nothing came of the lovely plan. We drove with the equerry's blacks through the Weisgärber, the Prater and the Brigitten Au to the Jäger Haus, strolled through the little forest, drank milk, slipped over . . . to the Danube, lay in the grass, joked and flirted, and stayed until after 5 o'clock. Then we drove the same way home, the girls got dressed for the [Haydn] concert and I wandered off to Marinelli's theatre. . . . The opera, *Wer den Schaden hat, darf für den Spott nicht sorgen*, is a terrible, extremely vulgar, boring farce; it was, however, received as it deserved. [*Rosenbaum*, 43]

On 20 May we learn from Rosenbaum that there was 'a mass by Haydn at St Michael's [Church]' (p. 44), conducted by Haydn's old friend and brother Mason, Georg Spangler, son of the tenor J. M. Spangler who had helped Haydn in the 1750s. We have no way of knowing which mass was given. Marchesi was now singing in Simone Mayr's *Lodoiska*; both Zinzendorf and Rosenbaum went to hear it on 31 May, and both liked it ('though', added Rosenbaum, 'opinion about it is divided'); later (23 June) Zinzendorf writes, 'La propre mort de Lodoiska est une bien belle musique . . .'.

One of the very few extant letters by Haydn of this period was written on 1 June:

> [To Herr Kürchner, Prince Esterházy's *Valet de chambre*, Oedenburg. *German*]
>
> Vienna, 1st June 1798.
>
> Dearest Friend!
>
> I would ask you to be good enough to advance my niece [Anna Katharina] Luegmayer 25 fl. (though she really doesn't deserve it); you shall be repaid this sum at the earliest possible moment by the Chief Cashier Stessel, whom I have already informed about the matter. For this kindness I shall wait on your dear daughter, when I arrive in Eisenstadt, with a new pianoforte Sonata. Meanwhile I am, with my kind regards to your wife, most respectfully,
>
> Your most obedient servant,
> Joseph Haydn.
>
> [Address:] Monsieur
> Monsieur de Kürchner Valet
> d Chambre de S: Alt. Monseig. le
> Prince Nicolaus Esterházy
> in fürst Esterhazisch[en] a OEDENBURG
> Hauss. en Hongern. [CCLN, 151f.]

We have seen Haydn almost at the summit of his career, with the first, semi-private performances of *The Creation*; we say 'almost' because the actual summit may be reckoned the first public performance in 1799. We may now turn for a moment to watch the rising fortunes of Beethoven, and to this end we will begin our brief survey with an interesting subscription appeal in the *Wiener Zeitung* No. 50 of 23 June 1798.

Notice

Joseph Eder, Art and Music-Publisher at the Golden Crown on the Graben, will publish within 3 weeks 3 very beautiful piano sonatas, without accompaniment, composed by Herr Ludwig v. Beethoven. Since I wish to cover, at least partially, my costs, and since the name of the composer is warranty enough for the quality of his work, I take the liberty of opening a subscription for the above-mentioned work and of fixing a termination date of 8 weeks. The subscription price is 3 fl., after expiration of the date, however, each copy will not be sold for other than 3 fl. 30 kr. Vienna, 18 June 1798.

It was becoming an honour – if also a very slight risk (note Eder's anxiety to cover his costs), which would however soon disappear entirely – to publish Beethoven's music. A month later, on 21 July 1798, the *Wiener Zeitung* carries an announcement of Johann Traeg, the Viennese professional music-copyist and publisher which reads as follows: 'Johann Träg: Beethoven 3 Trios pour un Violon, Alto & Violonc. Op. 9, 3 fl. 30 kr.' To this 'bare' announcement Traeg added the following note in the *Wiener Zeitung* No. 63 of 8 August: '. . . that he has spared neither work nor costs in order to approach even approximately, with the exterior, the inner value of this excellent [*vortrefflichen*] work.'

Beethoven's list of publications was growing apace. Apart from many works which he was still withholding (e.g. the *Scena* 'Ah! perfido', the *Alla ingarese quasi un capriccio* [later Op. 129], the first piano Concerto [in B flat, later published as No. 2, Op. 19] and at least one of the violin Romances – *vide infra*), a substantial quantity was now being released to the public. We noted that early in 1796, Beethoven issued the piano Sonatas, Op. 2, dedicated to Haydn. Between then and the end of 1798 the following *opera* appeared:

Op. 3 Trio for violin, viola and 'cello, Spring 1796
Op. 4 String Quintet in E flat (arrangement of the Octet for wind band, later Op. 103), Spring 1796
Op. 5 Two Sonatas for piano and 'cello, February 1797
Op. 6 Sonata for piano four-hands, October 1797
Op. 7 piano Sonata, October 1797
Op. 8 Serenade for violin, viola and 'cello, October 1797
Op. 9 Three Trios for violin, viola, 'cello, July 1798
Op. 10 Three piano Sonatas: publication in September 1798 (see notes above; the actual publication announced in the *Wiener Zeitung* on 26 September)
Op. 11 Trio for piano, clarinet and 'cello, October 1798

[From the Kinsky-Halm *Verzeichnis*]

For a young composer it was a very impressive achievement. Once more we would point out that all the genres of works listed above were ones no longer being practised by Haydn (or, as in the Quintet, never attempted by the older composer): Beethoven was still being very cautious and avoided any direct confrontation with Haydn's music, i.e. no symphonies, no string quartets, no Masses, no Oratorios, not even any more piano trios. (Haydn's latest trios had suddenly started to flood the local market: Artaria had issued Nos. 38–40 [XV: 24–26] in November 1796, Nos. 42 [XV: 30] and Nos. 43–45 [XV: 27–29] in October 1797 – the end of a long series of the Trios composed in London which Artaria started to bring out in July 1795, two months after Beethoven had contracted with Artaria to engrave his Op. 1 Trios; Beethoven had not reckoned on Haydn's having a sudden new lease-of-life in that form.) It is certainly significant that Beethoven did not renew his publishing activity on a large scale until the latter part of 1801 (Quartets, Op. 18) and 1802, after Haydn's *The Seasons* and when it was perfectly clear that the older composer's strength was finished for good: in fact, Haydn completed only two more major works after *The Seasons*: the *Schöpfungsmesse* (begun 28 July 1801) and the *Harmoniemesse* (Summer 1802). At the end of the Chronicle for 1802, we shall again take up Beethoven's publications, for that year will mark a significant advance in the younger composer's number of published *opera* and thus increase his music's dissemination throughout Europe. In 1798, however, Haydn was the idol of Viennese society, and within two or three years *The Creation* was to become the most popular large-scale work of its kind in the whole of the civilized world. In the shadow of this mighty Oratorio, Beethoven was contemplating a whole new series of works, and especially string quartets and a symphony, which would suffice to place him on the scene as a serious rival of the older man. As sharply as Haydn's compositional activity ceased, Beethoven's rose; the descending and ascending lines were to meet, as it were, about the time of *The Seasons*' first public performance at the end of May 1801, when the Redoutensaal would witness one of the first signs of Haydn's gradually waning popularity.

Emanuel Schikaneder had meanwhile launched what he called 'the second part of *Die Zauberflöte*', an Opera by Peter von Winter entitled *Das Labyrinth, oder der Kampf mit den Elementen* (text by Schikaneder). The première was on 12 June at the Freyhaustheater and Rosenbaum cautiously notes, 'The opera was generally successful throughout . . .' (Radant, *Rosenbaum*, 46); Schikaneder himself published the piano score (Henneberg), and the entrance prices were raised and kept at that level until 24 November 1798 (incl.); there were thirty-four performances in 1798, but the work did not really become a lasting success.[1]

On Thursday 28 June, Anna Ascher, second soloist of the Italian and German opera at the Kärntnerthortheater, sang Haydn's Cantata *Arianna a Naxos* at a morning Augarten concert, accompanied by the composer Wenzel Raffael (*recte*). Rosenbaum (46) writes: 'The early morning was cool and rainy . . . I drove to the Augarten for the concert, at which Ascher, with Raphael accompanying her on the Fortepiano, sang Ariadna in Italian, and rather indifferently.'

Pohl (III, 132) reports that Haydn suffered from exhaustion after the first performances of *The Creation*, he 'even had to be confined to his rooms because of illness'. Confirmation of an authentic kind comes in a roundabout way from G. A. Griesinger, who in his biography reports, 'For each of the twelve Symphonies that Haydn composed in England, he required – naturally beside other occupations – one month, for a Mass three months; but he remembered having written one in a month, because he was ill and thus could not go out' (pp. 61f.). If, as it seems, Haydn was overworked and the doctor ordered a rest, the result was one of the composer's most stupendous works: the *Missa in angustiis* ('Nelson' Mass), the autograph manuscript of which bears the dates 'di me giuseppe Haydn mp[ria] $\overline{798}$ 10ten Juli Eisenstadt' (beginning) and 'Fine. Laus Deo 31 August' (at the end) – rather more than a month, of course, but there seems no doubt that Haydn referred to this Mass in the Griesinger quotation.

We see, then, that Haydn was in Eisenstadt by 10 July, the date, incidentally, for the German-language première of Mozart's *Die Hochzeit des Figaro* at the Court

1 Deutsch, *Freihaustheater*, 41.

Theatre in Vienna, with Therese Gassmann as the Countess, Calvani-Willmann as Susanna and Nanette Gassmann as Marcellina (Rosenbaum [48] recorded that he 'was greatly gratified to note that the opera was highly successful; the entire cast was called out at the end. . . .'). Two days later Rosenbaum went off to Eisenstadt:

> . . . I talked with Therese, spoke of our love and our happiness. At about 4:30 I took my leave, kissed the girls and their mother . . . I then hurried home; it was after 5:30 when [my friend] Kupferfeld and I drove off from [the Esterházy's administrative centre in Vienna] the Red House, and about 9:30 when we arrived in Eisenstadt.
>
> I began to unpack and put everything in order, and worked until 12 o'clock at night. Saturday, 14th: . . . I received two letters at once from Therese, the dear girl. God! I love her so intensely and I am with heart and soul so confident that it would be a joy to possess her, and yet am so far from the goal of my happiness – Thursday, 19 July 1798: – At 5 in the afternoon I visited [various Esterházy officials] Zechelen, Parkh and Haydn, and chatted with them for more than an hour. . . . [p. 48]

A few days later Rosenbaum visited the old Esterházy painter Basilius Grundmann (or the Forestry Official Nicolaus Grundemann) and saw Haydn, taking the sulphur baths at what Rosenbaum calls Gscheiß, which is now Schützen am Gebirge, near Eisenstadt: 'Monday, 6 [August] . . . Today there is a hunt in Pottendorf. – Kupferfeld and I had lunch together; afterwards we and Walter drove out to Gscheiß, visited Grundemann and saw Haydn at the baths. The bath-house is very dirty and dilapidated . . .' (p. 49).

We have seen that Prince Nicolaus Esterházy dismissed his *Feld-Harmonie*, the wind band of oboes, clarinets, horns and bassoons, which had participated in the first performances of the *Missa in tempore belli* and *Missa Sancti Bernardi de Offida*. Haydn had at his disposal a body of strings and he hired the three trumpet players, Sebastian Binder, Michael Altmann and Johann Pfann, whenever they were required, e.g. in the new Mass of 1798 (*Missa in angustiis*), the scoring of which takes into account the now restricted forces at Eisenstadt: three trumpets, timpani, strings, choir and soloists, solo organ (= Haydn himself). But now we read in Rosenbaum the following entry for 12 August:

> Sunday 12th: Windy but warm. At 7 in the morning I went to the benefactor's [Count Carl Esterházy], took Parkh in, and paid him my respects as he came out; I was with him for more than an hour. At about 10 o'clock [the physician Anton] Röckl and I went to the Bergkirche where the Mass by Haydn was done that has the Donna [*sic*] nobis I like so much. Prince Dominic Kaunitz arrived and was also at church.

We cannot, of course, identify the Mass with the 'Donna nobis' that Rosenbaum especially liked, but we suppose it was the *Missa in tempore belli*, with its famous kettledrum solo in the Agnus, which Rosenbaum heard when it was given for the first time at Eisenstadt in 1797. But if we are correct in our identification of the Mass, how did Haydn conduct it without any of the woodwind? Did he fill in the missing parts on the organ? Or – and this is a new suggestion – was Rosenbaum's favourite 'Donna nobis' perhaps the beautiful *Missa brevis S. Joannis de Deo*, scored only for soprano solo, choir, strings and solo organ, which has a very moving Dona? That month, Rosenbaum and some friends went to Eszterháza Castle (Friday 24 August): 'We had great fun with the theatre-wardrobe mistress, Straier, and amused ourselves until long after 11 o'clock [at night].' The next day – the party had spent the night in Eszterháza – was 'cool, rainy', and 'we prowled about the theatre and the new English garden'. At the beginning of September there was a chamber music evening at Eisenstadt Castle: 'Monday 3rd: . . . In the evening I listened to the quartets in the castle, and was with Ku— [Kuperfeld] afterwards. . . .' (p. 49). It is not clear whether there was 'figuraliter' music in the Bergkirche on Sunday 16 September: 'A bright morning, but cool. Worked from 6 o'clock until 8; then Rubini and [Haydn's pupil Sigismund] Neukam [Neukomm] came and I went with them to see Haydn, then to the *Bergkirche*, the *Calvarien Berg* and into the castle, leaving them in the church . . . we dined at the [Gasthaus] "Engel" in the company of the two Haydns [brothers] and Tomasini. . . .' (p. 50).

On Sunday, 23 September, the new Haydn *Missa in angustiis* – the name 'Nelson Missa' was not widely known until afterwards, probably on the occasion of Nelson's visit to Eisenstadt in 1800 – was first performed, not in the Bergkirche but in the town parish church (Stadtpfarrkirche). Rosenbaum records (p. 51): 'At about 10 o'clock [a.m.] I went with Carl to the large church, where the new mass by Haydn was done . . . We returned about 7 o'clock and went to our renowned theatre, where the [Philip] Hafner comedy, *Die beschäftigten Hausregenten*, was played.' We do not know if the play was given by a professional theatrical troupe, such as had been engaged in years past, or was an amateur affair, played by the guests and local officials.

When Haydn, confined to his quarters (or to the local baths at 'Gscheiß'), was writing the 'Nelson' Mass at top speed, the Admiral for whom the work was later named was making history at a far away place in Egypt. Since our Mass is now inseparably connected with Nelson, we may break the local Chronicle to examine briefly the new European situation which had called forth such intense activity on the part of the British fleet.

On 19 May 1798, Napoleon sailed with a large fleet and some 40,000 men from Toulon, slipping through the otherwise effective British blockade and making for Egypt; *en route* he captured Malta, and on 30 June he landed near Alexandria. No one among the British fleet knew for certain of Napoleon's real destination; it could have been Ireland, where a fierce revolution had broken out. Nelson's flagship, the *Vanguard*, ran into a gale and nearly foundered ('I firmly believe it was the Almighty's goodness to check my consummate vanity', wrote Nelson to his wife). Nelson had received false information about the French departure from Malta, and on 23 June he missed attacking the main body of the French fleet with its troop transports because he was sure that the sails his lookouts had sighted on the horizon on 22 June did not belong to the main French fleet. A week later Bonaparte arrived in Egypt, and on 1 July he issued a proclamation calling on the Faithful to revolt against the Mamelukes. On 5 July he stormed Alexandria, a fortnight later he defeated the principal Egyptian army under the Pyramids, and on 22 July he entered Cairo.

Nelson tacked up and down the Mediterranean, looking for his enemy. He reached Alexandria on 28 June without finding a trace of the wily Corsican, and sadly turned back to Sicily. Then he gathered his fleet and sailed off again to find the French ships. As news filtered back, with great delay, to the capitals of Europe, time seemed to stand still; this was possibly the great crisis of the war, the first significant break-through of the iron British sea blockade round Europe, stretching from Denmark to Egypt. It appeared that Napoleon had once again outwitted his enemy and was about to conquer Egypt, perhaps then to continue towards India. The possibilities were infinite, and all to the great discomfort of the Allies in general and England in particular.

On 1 August, Nelson, then aged forty, sighted the French fleet at anchor in the Harbour of Aboukir and in a daring manoeuvre the British fleet sailed without a chart of the shoals into Aboukir Bay and blew the French fleet to bits. It was the most brilliant victory for the allies in a long and seemingly hopeless war.[1]

Fast couriers from Naples brought the news to London, to Berlin, to Vienna, as soon as an authentic report reached Italy. On 15 September Count von Zinzendorf notes: '. . . Thugut [the Chancellor] a fait assurer à Saurau que l'admiral Nelson a brulé la flotte de Buonap. dans le port d'Alexandrie'; the next day, the Count added laconically, '. . . la bataille a eté a Abukir. . . .' (Olleson, 54).

The news would have reached the Esterházy Court at Eisenstadt about a week before the first performance of the Mass on 23 September, and listeners would have felt an exultant thrill as they listened to the ominous D minor Kyrie and Benedictus with the menacing trumpets and timpani. It may even be that the listeners in the Eisenstadt Stadtpfarrkirche christened the work 'Nelson Missa' because they associated it with the great naval victory, and that when Nelson himself arrived at Eisenstadt the Mass was resuscitated in his honour. Within a few years, no one seemed to know quite how the title had been conferred: in 1829, Vincent Novello was at Munich, and in talking with the Cathedral organist we learn; '. . . No. 3 of Haydn (in D minor) he told me was known in Germany under the name of Nelson's Mass, but the reason why it had acquired this particular title he could not explain to me.'[2]

To complete our report about the Autumn season of 1798 at Eisenstadt, we would add that there is no information about the soloists for any of the performances of the Masses, and one wonders for whom Haydn can have written the taxing and poetic solo soprano part for the 'Nelson' Mass; for the young girl from Pressburg, Anna Rhumfeld? (see 28 September 1797, *supra*); it seems hard to believe; or did Haydn import a few soloists and the odd instrumentalist from Vienna, as he had done for *The Seven Words* in 1797? Princess Marie Hermenegild's name-day, in 1798, fell on Sunday, 9 September (Rosenbaum went 'to congratulate the Princess Marie' [not in Radant]), but we have no record of any special musical or theatrical entertainment; the Prince was now on a campaign to save money.

A further piece of non-local news, not so enthralling as the victory of Aboukir but more of personal interest to Haydn, was the news of his brother, Johann Michael's, arrival in Vienna.

In 1771, when Joseph Haydn had been seriously ill, his brother in Salzburg asked Archbishop Sigismund von Schrattenbach for (and received) permission to visit Joseph. After all these years – the brothers had last met in the early 1760s – Johann Michael finally decided to make a long trip to Vienna, to visit his brother, and see many friends and pupils. Thus, on 12 August 1798, Beda Plank of Kremsmünster Abbey reported to the Monastery's *Hofmeister* in Vienna: 'Tomorrow the famous Herr Michael Haydn leaves here to go to Vienna. He stayed with us for eight days, and now he thinks he will visit his brother in Vienna, Herr Joseph Haydn, whom he hasn't seen for 27 years.' On 18 August, Michael was in Linz and wrote to his wife in

1 Our account of the Battle of Aboukir and the preceding chase is based on that eminently readable, yet scholarly account in Sir Arthur Bryant's *The Years of Endurance (1793–1802)*, London 1942, pp. 239ff.
2 *A Mozart Pilgrimage*, p. 60.

Salzburg: 'Dearest Wife! It was not till yesterday evening that I arrived here from [the Monastery of] St Florian; my trip is proceeding rather comfortably, because I have been held up everywhere, especially in Kremsmünster, where they showed me every kind of honour . . .'. It is not known exactly when Michael reached Vienna – probably about 24 August – or where he stayed; but it seems possible that he put up at his cousin's, the composer Joseph Eybler, with whom he was in regular correspondence. Michael also kept a diary, which is lost.[1]

Rosenbaum left Eisenstadt on Saturday, 20 October, which means that the rest of the Esterházy court (insofar as they were not 'stationed' in Eisenstadt) will have left about the same time. We may assume that the two Haydns met in Vienna in time, perhaps, to attend Ludwig Fischer's come-back in Mozart's *Entführung*, in which opera the great bass singer had created the role of Osmin; of course Haydn will have remembered him, too, from London, where they appeared together in the Salomon concerts of 1794. On 24 October Rosenbaum notes: '. . . The famous Fischer sang in *Die Entführung aus dem Serail*, with unanimous applause, although I venture to say to myself, with my memory as a guide, that one notices his not insignificant number of years in his voice.' (p. 51). Apart from *Die Entführung*, the German version of *Figaros Hochzeit* was also on the boards (there was a performance on 3 November), and Michael Haydn can also have heard Guglielmi's *La bella pescatrice* (1 November: Burgtheater) and a new opera, *Il principe di Taranto*, by Ferdinando Paer (Burgtheater; première on 6 November).

Michael, accompanied no doubt by Joseph, attended (according to Hans Jancik) two concerts in the Theater auf der Wieden for the benefit of Ludwig Fischer (who, incidentally, like Joseph Lange, had been a member of the Viennese Freemasons' Lodge 'Zur Beständigkeit'). In the first concert, the famous singer performed four arias, among them 'Steffen-Romanze' from Umlauf's *Irrlicht* and 'In diesen heil'gen Hallen' from *Die Zauberflöte*. Beforehand there was that latter opera's popular Overture. The third item (group) is interesting: '3. Wird Herr von Beethoven ein Concert auf dem Fortepiano spielen von seiner eigenen Komposition', which we suggest may have been the Viennese première of the C major Piano Concerto, Op. 15. The concert ended with 'die beliebte Sinphonie' (the popular Symphony, probably the 'Surprise') by Haydn; there were no free tickets. At Fischer's second benefit concert, some of the arias sung by him remained the same (Umlauf, Mozart), and the 'beliebte Sinphonie' by Haydn concluded the evening as before; between them, however, there was another highly interesting event which seems to have escaped music historians. It is reported that Ignaz Schuppanzigh played a Viotti violin concerto but also 'ein Adagio von Herrn v. Böthoven' – this latter obviously being one of the famous Romances for violin and orchestra (Opp. 40 or 50), probably Op. 50, the autograph of which has been dated independently by Max Unger to *c.*1798–9 and

1 In Pohl III, 133, we read of a letter to Eybler from Salzburg dated 5 November 1799. 'Now consider what a wonderful time I have had recently! You know that during my last Vienna trip I used to write down every evening where and how I had spent the day. Since the anniversary of those days was approaching, nothing was more pleasant for me than to look into my pocket book every day so as to refresh my memory about everything.' About the trip see also Hans Jancik, *Michael Haydn, Ein vergessener Meister*, Vienna 1952, pp. 222ff., where we read 'Michael Haydn is supposed to have attended *inter alia* two musical academies at the Schikaneder Theater auf der Wieden, on 27 October and 5 November . . .'; this is our only evidence that Michael actually attended the concerts, but it seems very plausible anyway. P. Altman Kellner, O.S.B., *Musikgeschichte des Stiftes Kremsmünster*, Kassel-Basel 1956, p. 560. For details of concerts, see Pohl III, 134, and Deutsch, *Freihaustheater*, 41. About the dating of the Beethoven Romances, see Max Unger in *Neues Beethoven-Jahrbuch* VII, 158f., where Op. 50 (autograph in Library of Congress, Washington) is dated 1798 or 1799. See also Kinsky-Halm, *Verzeichnis*, p. 117.

which is marked *Adagio cantabile* (Op. 40 is without tempo). Unless we err, Michael and Joseph Haydn can have witnessed two historic Beethoven premières, the one being the popular Op. 15 Concerto (for it is highly unlikely that Beethoven would still be appearing with the B flat Concerto, Op. 19, more than three years after he had introduced it to Vienna) and the other possibly his most popular light music altogether, at least on the Continent and at the present day.

Rosenbaum had arranged to borrow the score (autograph, probably) and parts (in the Diary they are described as 'instruments') of Haydn's 'Arie des Schutzgeistes' from *Alfred*, which Therese Gassmann intended to sing. We read:

> Monday 12th November 1798: A foggy morning . . . Elsler [*sic*] brought me the Aria of the Schutzgeist from *Alfred*, which I wrote [copied] myself and took to Therese. Wednesday, 14th: At last a clear morning again. Elsler brought me the intruments for the Schutzgeist aria. . . . Saturday 17th: . . . After lunch I went with Elsler to see Haydn out in Gumpendorf; he was just going out, so I accompanied him. We drank coffee at a coffee-house in the neighbourhood, then drove into town; he went to Quarin, I to the princely house. We talked about the theatre, about Therese, about our music and about the anecdotes of the last hunt in Stinkenbrunn. . . . [Radant, *Rosenbaum*, 53f.]

An interesting personal detail about a lunch Joseph gave to Michael Haydn appears in an unpublished letter of Michael's recently sold by the Viennese antiquarian bookseller Ingo Nebehay (List 50, February 1974, item 145). The letter is to Sigismund (later von) Neukomm, Michael's ex-pupil, now studying with Joseph (*vide infra*, p. 335, for another such letter).

> Salzburg, 23rd November 1799.
>
> Dearest Cousin!
>
> You gave me the greatest pleasure with your *Hochgesang* [which was performed at a surprise party in honour of Michael's name-day]. . . . I thought at once of my dearest brother (please be good enough to pay him, and his wife, my respectful compliments). When I lunched with him he surprised me most pleasantly with wind-band music [*Harmonie-Musik*] quite unknown to me then, and even his parrot cried out when he heard it: *what's that*? . . .

The wind-band music may have been one of the British marches – Haydn himself owned the autograph of one of the Marches for the Derbyshire Cavalry Regiment (VIII: 1) and Elssler seems to have once owned the other (VIII: 2) – or even the Aria of the Schutzgeist.

The annual masked ball at the Redoutensaal for the Gesellschaft bildender Künstler was announced in the *Wiener Zeitung* No. 93 for 21 November 1798, the music for the large and small rooms being composed by Anton Teyber. The list[1] of free

1 MS. protocol 'Frey = Billets haben erhalten Im Jahr 1798.' from the Society's Archives in the Archiv der Stadt Wien (Rathaus). Since Haydn no longer appeared at the Society's annual balls, we sum up the free tickets for 1799 and 1800. In 1799 the music consisted of German Dances by Teyber in the large rooms and Minuets by Joseph Lipavsky in the small (*WZ* No. 93, 20 Nov. 1799): 'Frey-Billets haben erhalten Im Jahr 1799': 'Herrn v Teÿber/:Anton. . . . . 13. – – Teyber/:Franz. . . . . 6. Lipavsky . . . . 12. Beethowen der Altere . . . . . 4. Beethowen der jüngere . . . . . 4 [the first appearance of Carl, who was at this period helping Ludwig with his various projects]. Mascheck . . . . 4. Henneberg . . . 2. Eybler . . . . 3. Süssmayer. . . . . 2. Kozeluh . . . . 2.' In 1800, the music was by Wenzel Pichl in the large rooms and Ignaz von Seyfried in the small (*WZ* No. 92, 15 Nov. 1800). Pichl received 18 free tickets and v. Seyfried 12, 'Beethoven Compositor . . . 4' (no Carl this time), and the others: Anton Teyber 6; Franz Teyber 'Capellmeister' 2; Lipavsky 4; Henneberg 2; Eibler [*sic*] 3, Süssmayer and Kozeluch each 2, Capoll 3. In 1801, the music was by Anton Teyber (large rooms) and Joseph Lipavsky (small) (*WZ* No. 93, 21 Nov. 1801). Beethoven's rather regular appearance in these years shows that he was still going out in society.

tickets shows that Haydn did not attend this year; but 'van Beethowen' did, and received four tickets, as did (with three tickets each) Süssmayer, Kozelu[c]h, Eybler, Capoll, etc., while 'v Täuber/:Anton' received fourteen, and 'v Täuber/:Franz' (the violinist) a dozen tickets.

With the success of *Figaros Hochzeit* in German, the Court Opera decided to stage *Don Juan* with the German text by K. F. Lippert. The cast included Therese Gassmann as Elvira, and she also inserted an aria from Mozart's *La clemenza di Tito*, 'which met with general applause' (*Rosenbaum*, 55). But curiously enough, the reception by the Viennese was cool, just as it had been in Mozart's lifetime in the imperial capital. *Figaro* was a success in the 1790s, as it had been in 1786 and at its revival in 1789. The new *Don Juan* was first performed on 11 December 1798, and the next day we read: 'Wednesday, 12th, the Prince's Birthday: . . . In the evening I went to *Don Juan* [Kärntnerthor Theater]. It was empty, a sad evidence of its lack of success. Therese sang very well' (p. 55).

German publishers were finding that if they were to be kept *au courant* of music in Austria, they must have some kind of agent in Vienna. Breitkopf & Härtel would soon have an excellent man in the person of G. A. Griesinger. One of the most important publishers in Germany at that time was the firm of André in Offenbach, who had brought out the first editions of Haydn's 'Salomon' Symphonies and had acquired many unpublished works of Mozart from the widow. André later had no less a personality than J. P. Salomon as their unofficial agent in London. From a newly discovered letter, written by Paul Wranizky to André, we see that Haydn's pupil was now André's agent in Vienna. The letter is altogether valuable because it gives a survey of the musicians active in Vienna in 1798. We publish the letter here for the first time (see overleaf).[1]

1 Mary Flagler Cary Music Collection, now in the Pierpont Morgan Library, New York. The writer would like to thank the Library for many courtesies during several years, *inter alia* for permission to copy and/or photograph so many autograph letters in their possession. The André Archives in Offenbach own a 'Brief Copirbuch' from October 1805 to September 1807 in which many letters to Paul and Anton Wranizky are registered. Since some of these have to do with Haydn, a brief summary of their contents may be useful. On 9 June 1806 to Paul Wranizky (pp. 300–2) saying that Härtel owns HV ('Härtel sagt mir in Leipzig . . .'); on 19 July 1806 to Mr Salomon, N. 18 Suffolk St, Tottenham Court Road, from which we see that Salomon was André's London agent (pp. 354f.); on 9 December 1806 to Paul Wranizky about the 'Dernier Quatuòr de J. Haydn': 'An wem hat H das Quart. verkauft?' It is also worth mentioning that at this time André tried to find out if Mozart's Mass in C minor (K. 427) existed somewhere in a complete state; letters were written on this subject to Domorganist Klinger and Benedikt Hacker. On 13 February 1807, André wrote to both Anton and Paul Wranizky, asking the latter to go to Traeg and get the Finale of Symphony No. 45 ('Farewell') and also copies of Symphonies 6–8 ('Le Matin', 'Le Midi' and 'Le Soir') and 60 ('Il distratto') (p. 552). On 14 March 1807 there is a letter to Paul Wranizky about a Haydn canon (p. 557), and on 11 April there are again letters to both Anton and Paul, thanking the latter for 'Il distratto', which had arrived safely in Offenbach. There are further letters to Anton Wranizky on 4 May and 30 May 1807 (pp. 597, 615, 629). We were able to examine this 'Brief Copirbuch' in the offices of the Neue Mozart Ausgabe at Augsburg in the Autumn of 1957, when the late Dr E. F. Schmid kindly placed it at our, and at Mr Christopher Raeburn's, disposal.

In an earlier letter (20 October 1798), Wranizky replies to what was evidently an attempt on Andre's part to buy *The Creation*. 'Hayden wrote *The Creation*, it was produced under my direction, it is a complete work in itself which he wrote for a society of amateurs here, but now it can't be had in any circumstances and at any price.' Versteigerungs-Katalog 53 (8 March 1929), Leo Liepmannssohn, Berlin, item 227.

Vienna, 19 December 1798

[underneath in an unknown hand: 'Offenbach a[m]/m[ain] the 27th ditto; [answered:] 9 January 1799.]

Most excellent Friend!

You must put it down to my many affairs that I sent you without notice a package of music from [Zingarelli's opera]Pirro which cost 13f 16x, Hoffmeister's Catalogue of Flute Music (20x); the other catalogues aren't ready yet. Hum[m]el's op. 3 and 6 for 2fl. 30x, also the carriage charges of this 1.10.

F 17. 16x W[iener] C[onv.]: noted

Cagiati is not in Vienna. Förster, a worthy composer born in Prussian Galicia, gives piano lessons here. Fuchs is in the orchestra of the Italian opera and engaged as a violinist in the Court Orchestra, is a very good sight-reader, and although he is wounded in his right arm, has much flexibility with his bowing. Grill is a valet-de-chambre at Count Zeczini's [Széchényi]. Kromer – his main instrument is the violin, but he also plays oboe, fortepiano and cymballum [Hackbret] with great dexterity. Gives lessons and composes. Born at Trebitsch in Moravia. Possinger – pupil of Albrechtsberger. Member of the Court Orchestra. A Viennese. Raffael sings, plays the fortepiano well and all string instruments, is a Bohemian and works for the I. R. Exchequer. Went – oboist in the theatre orchestra and the I. R. wind band, a Bohemian, mostly arranges the operas for wind band and aquadro [*sic*]. Woelfl. One of the best piano players in Vienna. Gives lessons. A Salzburgian. Süssmaÿer – Kapellmeister at the German Opera. From Upper Austria. Pupil of Mozarth [*sic*] and Salieri, writes nicely for the voice but apart from that hasn't done much. Weigl Joseph. Kapellmeister at the Italian Opera, worthy in his job but even greater in intrigues. A Viennese. Writes mostly vocal pieces. Weigl Taddäus. His brother. A young man full of pride and insecurity. Composer in service with the Court Theatre Management. Director of the music publishing house of the Court Theatre. Everything through [? connections], nothing by his own efforts. Zingarelli, a Milan composer, is here. Schenk – piano correpetitor at Prince Auersperg's. Slow, hard-working man. Nature has dealt rather sparingly [*karg*] with him. Apart from these we have in Vienna: Albrechtsberger, Kapellmeister at the Cathedral Church of St Stephen. Great contrapuntist. Haÿden. Kapellmeister at Prince Esterhazi's. Kozeluch. I. R. Chamber Kapellmeister. Salieri. I. R. Court Kapellmeister. Conti conducts the orchestra of the Italian Opera, from Milan, has composed several violin sonatas and concertos. Plays the violin nicely. Composes badly. Kletzinsky. Conducts the orchestra for the ballets, has composed little, plays the violin well. Teyber Ant[on]: gives piano lessons to the Archduchesses. Plays his instrument right well. Has little imagination in composing. Gyrowetz, Hoffmeister, Petthoven [*sic*], Jos. PreindlRegens chori at St Peter's. Eybler ditto at the Scottish [Church]. Hauschka – virtuoso on the violoncello. A Bohemian, a dilettante. Has written some songs. Likel gives piano lessons. Kauer conducts the orchestra in the Leopoldstädter Theatre. Miller is Kapellmeister there. Hen[n]eberg. Kapellmeister at the [Freyhaus] Theatre auf der Wieden. Cartelieri: Lipowsky, Freystadler. Haüsler. Haensel. Struck. Pär. Cornetti. Kirzinger. Pogdanowitsch. Maschek. Ulbrich. – all these above-named are composers in Vienna, there is no more place or time to tell you more. I am very much pleased that your father has recovered. He should go on living to please me for a long, long time. Give me news and soon that he has recovered completely, and assure him of my regards and respect and I remain Your obt. Servt.

Wranitzky.[1]

1 We read 'Wranitzky', but in the autograph letter he wrote to Bland in London dated 12 December 1790 (see *Haydn in England 1791–1795*, pp. 27–8) the signature is clearly 'Wranizkÿ', as it is in most of the Tonkünstler-Societät documents. Many of the composers and performers are already familiar to us. We provide herewith brief notes on the others. *Giovanni Cagiati*, a pianist and composer, published works with Artaria in Vienna (1794) and André (1795). *Peter Fuchs*, member of the Court Orchestra. *Franz Grill*, who lived at Oedenburg for some years, was a composer who dedicated a set of string Quartets, Op. III, to Haydn. *Franz Krommer,* himself a prolific composer, was music director to Prince Grassalkovics (Grassalkowitz, etc.); he later succeeded Kozeluch as Court *Capellmeister* and Composer. *Franz Alexander Pössinger* (Pösinger, Pessinger), also a composer of various works for strings, including quartets (his Op. 1 had been published by André in 1792). *Wenzel Raffael*: *vide supra*, p. 325. *Johann Went (Wend)*, also a composer of at least one symphony and various chamber pieces, including three string Quartets, Op. 1, published by André in 1792; Wranizky means 'a quattro' by his 'und aquadro'. *Joseph Wölffl*: *vide supra*, p. 120. *Süssmayer* and the *Weigls* are well known to us, *passim*, as are *Zingarelli, Schenk, Koželuch* and *Salieri, Giacomo Conti*, who published largely in Vienna (Artaria and elsewhere). *Johann Kletzinsky (Klerzinsky)*, composer of various string music, including Trios published in 1798 by André. We have already encountered *Anton Teyber, Gyrowetz, Hoffmeister, Beethoven (note the spelling), Joseph Preindl* and *Eybler. Vincenz Hauschka*, formerly in the service of Count Thun in Prague, later (1803 *et seq.*) published some violoncello sonatas in Vienna. *Johann Georg Lickl*, a popular composer of operas (*Der Zauberpfeil* for Schikaneder, 1793) and various kinds of chamber music, including three string Quartets, Op. 1, published by André in 1797; André published some Variations by Lickl on 'Nel cor più non mi sento' from Paisiello's *La molinara. Ferdinand Kauer,* popular operatic composer (*Das Donauweibchen*). 'Miller' = the famous operetta composer, *Wenzel Müller*. *Johann Baptist Henneberg*, composer of the well-known opera *Die Waldmänner* for Schikaneder (1793) and known to us from the Redoutensaal masked balls for the Gesellschaft bildender Künstler. *Cartel[l]ieri* and *Lipavsky* ('Lipowsky') are known to us from the Tonkünstler concerts and the Redoutensaal balls. *Franz Jacob Freystädtler* published many pieces for piano, mostly with Artaria. 'Haüsler' is probably *Ernst Häusler*, a German 'cellist and composer formerly with the Princely Fürstenberg band in Donaueschingen who was living in Zürich in the early 1790s and published some songs with Mollo in Vienna. *Peter Hänsel, Capellmeister* to Princess Lubomirska 'about the year 1798' (Gerber, *NTL*), was a pupil of Haydn, whose first nine string Quartets, Opp. 1–3, were published by André in 1798, his Opp. 5 and 6, six Quartets, by the same publisher a year later. *Paul Struck*, also a Haydn pupil, has been mentioned above (pp. 255f.); André started to publish his works in 1797 (three piano Trios), and brought out several *opera*. 'Pär' = *Ferdinand Paer,* the well-known operatic composer who was at the time (1798) composing works for the Vienna Court Theatre; we have seen his name *passim. Cornetti* appears to be a pseudonym for *Alessandro Cornet*, who published 'VI Duettini per 2 Soprano con acc. di Cembalo' with Artaria in 1793 and also seems to have collaborated with Mozart and Salieri on a (unfortunately lost) Cantata 'Per la Ricuperata Salute di Ophelia' on a text by da Ponte (K. Anh. 11a): see Gerber, *NTL*, and Deutsch, *Mozart, Dokumente*, 222–4. *Paul Kürzinger* (*Kirzinger*), a German composer of operas, church music, etc., living in Vienna; he composed Redoutensaal Dances which were published in 1792. 'Pogdanowitsch' = *B. Bohdanowicz* (his own spelling on the announcement of a concert in 1802), who issued *Daphnis et Phillis avec un Adieu pour le Fortepiano à 4 mains* (Artaria 1798). *Paul Maschek*, composer and piano teacher, wrote *Das allgemeine Wiener Aufgebot, eine characteristische Sonata fürs Fortepiano mit Begleitung einer Violine und eines Violoncells* (Artaria, 1798) to celebrate the volunteer regiments of Vienna organized in 1797; he also composed other piano pieces (*Ländler, Petits Rondos*, etc.). *Maximilian Ulbrich* was a bookkeeper in the Lower Austrian Government (in the *Hof- und Staats-Schematismus* he is listed as 'Vice-Buchhalter' of the *Landschafts Buchhalterey*), a dilettante but apparently a rather successful composer of operas, operettas, oratorios and symphonies (six of the latter advertised by Johann Traeg in MS. in his Catalogue of 1799).

We have, of course, provided only skeleton biographies, and since most of these composers do not exist in the larger modern *lexica*, we have been obliged to rely on Gerber, *NTL*, and other material of the period. If one considers this long list of *Kleinmeister* (and a few *Grossmeister*), and bears in mind that there were as many other composers working in Vienna but not listed by Wranizky (especially in the churches), one can get some idea of the mammoth amount of music being composed, performed and often even printed in the Austrian capital.

The Christmas concerts of the Tonkünstler-Societät for the year 1798 included two works by Haydn:

22 and 23 December 1798:

Sinfonie von Eybler

Arie von Joseph Haydn 'gesungen aus Achtung für Witwen- und Waisen von Demoiselle Flamm' [sung by Dmlle. Flamm out of respect for the widows and orphans]. – Militär-Sinfonie, componirt und dirigirt von Haydn.

Concert von Kozeluck, k. k. Compositeur und Kammer-Capellmeister, ausgeführt von Anton Teyber (Piano-Forte), Zahradnizek (Mandoline), Weidinger (organisirte Trompete), Pischelberger (Contrabass).

[Part Second]

Cantate mit Chören, componirt von Capellmeister Romagnoli. Soli: Therese Gassmann, Antonie Flamm, Ignaz Saal, Sigismund Hüller.

(Concert und Cantate wurden von Ihrer Majestät für diese Akademie zugestellt) [the concerto and cantata were provided for this academy by Her Majesty].

[Pohl, *Denkschrift*, 66]

This is the first appearance of Anton Weidinger and his keyed trumpet (here entitled 'organized trumpet'); but the fact that the Concerto by Koželuch in which he appears was provided by the Empress Marie Therese shows that it was composed before and probably played in a private Court concert. Joseph Zahradnizek was officially a trumpet player but also an engraver of music (for Artaria and others); he engraved the authentic Torricella edition of Haydn's Symphonies Nos. 76–78, where he signs himself 'Jos: Zahradniczek'). We have met Anton Teyber frequently. Friedrich Pischelberger was the great double-bass player for whom Mozart wrote the Aria 'Per questa bella mano' (K. 612) together with Franz Gerl, the first Sarastro.

The most intriguing work is, of course, the Haydn Aria, which is specially mentioned in the brief review in the *Wiener Zeitung* (No. 3, 9 January 1799): 'Nachher sang die Demoiselle Flamm eine Arie von der Erfindung des Herrn Haydn, Doktors der Tonkunst, und Kapellmeister [etc, etc.]'. From all the programmes of the Tonkünstler-Societät, it is clear that Demoiselle Antonie Flamm was an alto. But we do have a new Haydn Aria composed in 1798: *Aria da 'Il Canzoniere' di Francesco Petrarca*' (XXIVb: 20), the Petrarch words (Sonetto XXVIII) of which were suggested to Haydn by some now unidentifiable Grand Prince of Russia (the autograph notes, in Haydn's hand, 'le parole del gran Prencipe di Russia'). The autograph is dated on the first page of music. The orchestration – with clarinets, bassoons and horns – suggests that it cannot have been composed for the Eisenstadt festivities of 1798 where, as we have seen, there were no wind instruments except for three trumpets. But if Antonie Flamm was really a pure contralto singer, she will have found this Aria rather high, for its range goes up (only once, it is true) to high *b* flat; perhaps she had delusions of soprano grandeur, because in the protocol of the Society (12 February 1799) concerning the concert, we read: 'Mlle Flamm was found very unsatisfactory by the public' (Pohl III, 135). Rosenbaum went on Saturday, the 22nd, and wrote: 'Cold and windy . . . then I went off to the Academy of the Society. Haydn's Military Symphony was the best, the Concertino with mandolin and organized trumpet was also well received; Teyber, at the pianoforte, was extremely wretched and confused, and the Empress's Cantata fell straight into the pit. No one [of the soloists] other than Therese was applauded.' (Radant, *Rosenbaum*, 55). Haydn conducted the 'Military Symphony' and probably the Aria and even the opening Eybler Symphony; it is unlikely that he conducted the Romagnoli Cantata (or the Koželuch piece, which was probably played without conductor, being chamber music).

The end of this eventful year may be traced in Rosenbaum's Diary.

Wednesday, 26th [December], St Stephen's Day: Such an extreme cold that one cannot recall another like it over a long span of years. The guard is changed every half hour because one man froze to death yesterday. – . . . Thursday, 27th . . . After lunch [the singer] Wiedman [Weidmann] came by with Wollaschek

> [the actor Wallaschek]; we chatted together and made a rendez-vous to visit Haydn tomorrow . . . Friday, 28th: [Grohmann] bought 2 tickets to academies at Jahn's and Tonerl and I received them . . . Therese [Gassmann] sang very beautifully, saving the reputation of German art, and was to the 2 Italians, Comorra and Ferlendis,[1] as the sun among comets. . . . Saturday, 29th, 1798: . . . After lunch I drove with Wollaschek, whom I visited, to see Haydn. He received us in a most friendly way, showed us his valuables and talked to us about his works; before we knew what had happened, an hour had passed.

In Rosenbaum's Diary, we have seen that Haydn's pupil, Sigismund (later Ritter von) Neukomm, was with his teacher at Eisenstadt on 16 September of this year. It is thought that not only Neukomm but also Franz Lessel became Haydn's pupil early in 1798, and both soon won the heart of the kind old master. Neukomm was born in Salzburg in 1778, the son of a teacher and through his mother a nephew of Michael Haydn's, with whom he began his first musical studies. After being correpetitor at the Salzburg Court Theatre, he went to Vienna and was received by Haydn, who accepted him as a pupil. Of all Haydn's numerous pupils, Neukomm seems to have been one of the most charming, educated and sophisticated, later becoming a successful composer and a man of the world. Haydn used him for some of the Scottish songs, as we shall see, and by 1799 we shall read, in a letter of Michael Haydn's to his nephew, that Neukomm was already making a success of his piano teaching. Later Neukomm went as conductor of the German Opera to St Petersburg in Russia, from where he kept in affectionate touch with his old teacher.

Franz Lessel was a Pole from the great estates of Prince Czartoryski; the young man was sent to Vienna in 1797 to study medicine but soon changed to music and was accepted by Haydn as a pupil. He returned to Poland in 1810 and became the representative of the Haydn school in his native country.[2]

F. S. Silverstolpe gives us an interesting eye-witness description of Haydn teaching one of his pupils during the year 1798 (or so it would appear in context):

> [*Silverstolpe's Report (VI)*]
> Once when I visited Haydn, he was just in the process of going through the work of a pupil. It was the first allegro of a symphony, in which form the young man was displaying his first essay. When Haydn cast his eye over the attempt, he found a long passage in which the wind intruments had rests, and he paid the pupil a compliment and said in a half-joking tone: 'rests are the most difficult thing of all to write; you were right to remember what a big effect longer piano passages can have.' The more he read, the darker became his mien. 'I haven't anything to find wrong about the part writing [*Satz*],' he said; 'it is correct. But the proportions are not as I would like them to be: look, here is a thought that is only half developed; it shouldn't be abandoned so quickly; and this phrase connects badly with the others. Try to give the whole a proper balance; that can't be so difficult because the main subject is good.' – This was all spoken with charm, and the young man, hungry for knowledge, was – far from being hurt – full of thankful recognition. I never knew his name; perhaps he later became one of the well-known ones.
> [Mörner in *Haydn-Studien* II/1, 1969, p. 27]

1 Antonio Camerra (violinist) gave a concert with Angelo Ferlendis, the oboe and cor anglais player (who had appeared together with Haydn at the Opera Concert in London, 1795: see *Haydn in England 1791–1795*, p. 311) at Jahn's Rooms; Grohmann was also an oboist. See Radant, *Rosenbaum*, 56f.

2 Pohl III, 134. Constantin Schneider: *Geschichte der Musik in Salzburg von der ältesten Zeit bis zur Gegenwart*, Salzburg 1935, pp. 145f. Artaria published two flute Duets and a flute Quartet by Lessel.

Of the (obviously incomplete) list of pupils listed in Dies (p. 197), the following, apart from Lessel and Neukomm, appeared to have studied with Haydn from 1795: Johann Spech (Dies: Specht), a Hungarian, for whom Haydn wrote a certificate in 1800 (*infra*, p. 557); Paul Struck, who is mentioned as Haydn's pupil (or *ex*-pupil) by Silverstolpe (*supra*, pp. 255f.) and possibly Peter Haensel, who was born the same year as Beethoven and may not have started lessons with Haydn until 1795. There are no doubt other, less illustrious pupils whose names have simply disappeared. From 'those who could afford it', writes Dies, 'Haydn was paid 100 ducats, half in advance and the other half at the end of the course.'

Two publications during the year 1798 were of immediate interest to Haydn. The one was the first attempt at a systematic biography of Mozart. It was written by Franz Xaver Niemetschek and published in Prague with a dedication to Haydn which read:

This little memorial to immortal Mozart
is dedicated by the author
with deepest homage to
Joseph Haydn
(Kapellmeister to Prince Esterházy)
Father of the noble art of music
and the favourite of the Muses.

The author went to considerable lengths to write his book 'nach Originalquellen' – Mozart's family and friends, papers from the widow, 'the witness of many trustworthy people whom Mozart knew at various periods of his life', and the *Nekrolog* by Schlichtegroll. In the Niemetschek biography, we find many touching tributes to the great friendship between Mozart and Haydn, including the story of Mozart who, after hearing a 'certain man' criticizing a new work by Haydn and ending his grumbles, 'I wouldn't have done that', answered, 'Neither would I, but do you know why? Because neither of us could have thought of anything so appropriate'.[1]

The other publishing undertaking was on a very large scale: the *Allgemeine Musikalische Zeitung* (*AMZ*), which began life on 3 October 1798. It was to become the most important, and the longest-lived, of all the German musical papers which we have hitherto noticed in this biography, such as the *Wöchentliche Nachrichten* of Hiller, the *Berlinische Musikalische Zeitung*, *Cramer's Magazin der Musik*, etc. It was published by Breitkopf & Härtel but from the beginning the editors tried to be impartial and took care not to turn the publication into a Breitkopf *Hausorgan*. Some handsome engravings were included: the first was a portrait of J. S. Bach. There were also interesting pieces of music attached, generally in a fold-out. The *AMZ* came out weekly, and some idea of its size may be gathered from the fact that in October 1798 the five numbers contained eighty columns (the printed page had two columns but the page itself was of a large size (25 × 21 cm.), while the first *Jahrgang*, from 3 October 1798 to 25 September 1799 contained 888 columns, twenty 'Intelligenzblätter' (information about Breitkopf's new publications and other matters of interest), four

1 F. X. Niemetschek (Němeček), *Leben des K. K. Kapellmeisters Wolfgang Gottlieb Mozart, nach Originalquellen beschrieben*, Prague 1798; 2nd edition, Prague 1808, with additions and changes. There is supposed to be a Leipzig edition of 1803 which we have not been able to locate. We used the Leipzig edition of 1942 in *Mozart-Almanach*. An English translation by Helen Mautner (foreword by A. Hyatt King) was published in London in 1956, from which the above extract (p. 69) was taken.

engravings and eighteen music 'Beylagen' – some really quite extensive. In the first *Jahrgang*, for example, readers were given the entire score of Mozart's Aria 'Io ti lascio, o cara, addio' (K.621a), engraved from the autograph manuscript, a Duet from Haydn's as yet unpublished *The Creation* (taken down by ear, as we shall see, and simply pirated), a movement in score from a String Quartet by Andreas Romberg, and so forth. The quality of the reviewing was, for the times, of a very high standard, though somewhat pedantic in tone; among the regular contributors were the editor, Friedrich Johann Rochlitz (who continued in that position until 1818), and Carl Friedrich Zelter (who wrote the famous review of *The Creation* which will be quoted *in extenso* – *vide infra*, p. 592). *AMZ* later numbered among its distinguished contributors E. T. A. Hoffmann, who wrote appreciatively of Beethoven's Fifth Symphony. It enjoyed a long existence and continued until December 1848.

In the Summer of 1798, Breitkopf & Härtel wrote to Haydn, asking him to contribute to the new journal; perhaps the letter never arrived, but in any case there was no answer. The publishers then repeated their request in April 1799; but soon afterwards, they were able to establish a reliable contact with Haydn in the person of G. A. Griesinger. We shall follow Griesinger's correspondence in our forthcoming Chronicle.[1] Haydn did, however, subscribe to *AMZ* and was doubly pleased when the publishers sent the journal to him gratis.

Throughout this early period of the *AMZ*, we can sense the great veneration in which Haydn was held by the German musical public. But occasionally there was a very antagonistic criticism of what the Germans thought was Haydn's incorrect musical orthography (or grammar, if one will). One such criticism was the review of the late 'Salomon' Symphonies in 1799 (see *Haydn in England 1791–1795*, pp. 576–82, 605–9) which, as will be seen, annoyed Haydn considerably.

In 1798, the German public were discovering Mozart on a vast scale, and they were hungry for information about the composer. Accordingly, Friedrich Rochlitz, in the second number of *AMZ*, began a series about Mozart entitled 'Verbürgte Anekdoten aus Wolfgang Gottlieb Mozarts Leben, ein Beytrag zur richtigern Kenntnis dieses Mannes, als Mensch und Künstler' (Genuine anecdotes from M's life, a contribution to a better knowledge of him as person and artist). In these pages, Haydn's name appears, of course, many times. Speaking of the dedication to Haydn of the six String Quartets, Mozart is quoted (*AMZ* I, 53) as saying: 'That was an obligation, for it was from Haydn that I first learned how to write quartets.' 'Never', continues the *AMZ*, 'did Mozart speak without the greatest [*lebhafteste*] respect for that composer, despite the fact that they both lived in the same place and neither lacked opportunities for jealousy of the other.' There then follows the story of a composer who regularly scored up Haydn's symphonies and quartets and showed them in triumph to Mozart, pointing out every defect in style. 'Mozart changed or broke off the conversation. Finally, however, it was too much for him. "Sir", he said very energetically, "if both of us were melted down, it would still be a long way from Haydn."' In a later issue (I, 116) we read: 'But there is no one,' Mozart added, 'who can do everything – to joke and to terrify, to evoke laughter and profound sentiment – and all equally well: except Joseph Haydn.' Perhaps the best-known anecdote is about Haydn and *Don Giovanni*. After the Viennese première, Prince Razumovsky (who in November 1788 married Elisabeth, Countess Thun; the Viennese première of *Don Giovanni* occurred in May of that year) gave a large party.

1 Hase, 8f.

> Most of the musical connoisseurs of Vienna were present, also Joseph Haydn. Mozart was not there. There was much talk about the new work. After the fine ladies and gentlemen had talked themselves out, some of the connoisseurs took up the work. They all admitted that it was the valuable work of a versatile genius and was of an endless imagination; but for one it was too full, for another too chaotic, for a third too unmelodic, for a fourth it was uneven, etc. In general one cannot but admit that there is something true in all these opinions. Everyone had spoken by now, only – not Father Haydn. At last they asked the modest artist for his opinion. He said with his usual fastidiousness: 'I cannot settle the argument. But one thing I know' – he added very energetically – 'and that is that Mozart is the greatest composer that the world now has.' The ladies and gentlemen were silent after that. [I, 52]

In the fourth number of *AMZ* there was a letter from Vienna, signed 'C. —' (the initial cannot now be identified), in which the writer complains of the low standard of choral singing 'in almost all the German cities through which my travels have taken me'. The correspondent then continues:

> Altogether I cannot impress upon you how low is the level, all things being considered, of the taste and love for music in this I. R. city. One hears a great deal of music here, a great deal, but it is of no account *which* music. To have music belongs to the *chose-à-faire* of fine society, just like drinking chocolate in the morning; and the one interests the *bon vivant* just as little as the other. Some single exceptions you will no doubt make without my reminding you. Therefore no one asks any longer: is the composition good? But only: is it new? If you ask the majority of our elegant patrons of art and so-called musical connoisseurs, for instance, about our old, worthy Albrechtsberger: no one even knows of his existence. Even the great Joseph Haydn is less known here in his own town than in any other town of respectable size in Germany, England or France. Of Mozart there has not for a long time been a single opera except *Die Zauberflöte* . . . [I, 62f.]

Perhaps a few words of explanation are required to account for this latest outburst against musical taste in Vienna. For one thing it is very doubtful if Herr C entered the salons of the high aristocracy such as Princes Lobkowitz, Esterházy, Liechtenstein or Lichnowsky. Their soirées were socially very exclusive affairs, at which Haydn and Beethoven participated regularly. It is even doubtful if Herr C will have gained access to the recitals at Baron van Swieten's, Count Fries's or Count Erdödy's. Thus the real arbiters of taste must have escaped his notice – as well as the salons where Haydn quartets and Beethoven sonatas were assiduously cultivated and appreciated. On the other hand, for the vast bourgeois public, Beethoven sonatas and Haydn quartets were difficult, intellectual music; for the average Fräulein's hand or the young dandy's bow, Gyrowetz's quartets and Steibelt's 'Storm Rondo' (from his popular piano Concerto No. 3 in E) would have been considered more modern and easier. As for the vast opera-going public, a part went to hear Wenzel Müller at the Leopoldstadt Theatre, a part went to Schikaneder's slapstick-cum-magic dramas and operas at the Theater auf der Wieden, and the better society went to the Court Theatres to hear Paer, Fioravanti and Cimarosa; for these opera-going persons, then as now, no other music existed, certainly not the uncompromising music by Haydn and Beethoven.

Restricting our view more or less to Haydn, we might remember that the Pleyels, Gyrowetzes and Witts were all pupils of Haydn, whether at first hand (Pleyel) or afar; that these *Kleinmeister* usurped their master's style to a point where the original often seemed slightly tame, or tarnished. On this subject, a correspondent of the *AMZ* (I, 152ff.) who signed himself 'Z. . . .' and was patently Zelter, had some pertinent remarks to make:

Modest Questions put to modern Composers and Virtuosi
[continuation]

My third question[1] only applies to composers – especially the young ones and imitators, and is more a request than a question. It has many subdivisions, for it concerns their blind imitations. This time I shall list only one subdivision. Everyone knows that Joseph Haydn built up the true great orchestral symphony:

The lion went ahead,
The tail dragged on behind.

And not only on the whole but also – and how poorly, how miserably – in the smallest detail. Haydn often, for example, employed the following device in the second part of his movements: a transition from the dominant, in which the first parts close, to a major third below. I mean, if the music was, say, in C major, the first part closed in G, the second part then went quickly and unexpectedly into E flat. – Now the tail dragged on behind, and we have heard it all so many countless times, and are still hearing it, to the point of nausea; the gentlemen should really find another way out, especially since they creep home exactly in the same way with the chord of VII♯. Haydn composed little original *bizarreries* in his symphonies and called them minuets: all the gentlemen ditto: originally these were a great success, but these flashes of genius and certain burlesque tricks in them have been hunted to death by the imitators; now they have become everyday occurrences and no longer have any effect. Haydn and Mozart were the first to dare to place the pedal point in the top at exceptionally passionate places: the tail dragged on behind and this, too, is now an everyday occurrence. Haydn, in some stately passages in his G or F major adagios, had the trumpets and drums in D or C enter with great surprise and noble effect; he did this discreetly and with care: but now the tail comes – and nowadays there is hardly a symphony, the andante of which does not have trumpets and timpani; we are used to them, they make no more effect. I could go on almost to make a whole list, but who is served by it? It is too late and these things have been spoiled by the imitators. But let us have a word about something that is not yet entirely spoiled, but which seems to have gained the attention of our Bright Stars so that they can ruin this too. Haydn, in one of his newest and finest symphonies in C [No. 95], had a fugue as a final movement; Mozart did this too in his tremendous [*furchtbaren*] Symphony in C [K. 551] in which, as we all know, he pushed things a little far: but *how* did those masters proceed? Haydn wrote a splendid whole that follows on a short and noble beginning: first, a serious but yet not too dark opening Allegro, a quiet Andante, a so-called Minuet which despite all its peculiarities is in this case not at all comic, and now he chooses for the last movement a theme which has something light and *galant* about it, but for all its simplicity has much dignity about it and is especially suitable for the strongest and most varied development. This theme was chosen as

1 The first question has to do with the flute and its use in the high register which, the writer believes, was first introduced by Mozart, 'as, for example, in the Overture to *Don Giovanni*'. The second question reads in part: '. . . Why do most of the modern composers write for the horn, clearly against its nature and intrinsic beauty, like the trumpet; and the trumpets, not seldom, and also against their nature, like horns? Why do they, for example, give to the former sharply formed, blaring, trumpet-like entrances? And to the latter, long-held notes in *piano*, even in adagio . . . I know full well that as far as composers are concerned, the *Duces gregis*, Mozart often, Haydn less so, are precedents; but does one have to copy *everything* blindly and slavishly? And then – when did those men do it? Where it should and must excite special attention! Does one have to do it *all* the time? [etc.]' (I, 141–4)

> being light and gentle, like the theme of a typical rondo: the public was fooled, having expected the usual rondo. But all at once the principal theme's main thought is taken up, played with strength and fullness, and even out of this thought he works out a fine fugue. Dear People, who wish to imitate him in all things – consider the matter once again! I can well believe that you like it, but you don't have to copy it. Look at it once again: there is nothing of sound and fury in it! Look again: it's not really for you. If it will not annoy you, I would like to say a few words to you. If I think about your so-called fugues, I cannot escape thinking that you are quite honest and mean it all well; but most of you don't really know what a fugue is. And quite frankly, you won't learn it from the above-mentioned example by Haydn – at least you won't learn how to write fugues. For consider: who would want to learn the first rules of the theory of poetry from Klopstock's Odes or Latin grammar from Persius or Greek from Aeschylus? And simple inspirations of genius don't make fugues – let's hope you realize that . . . [Otherwise] you will produce something like the brand new work by the young A— [Johann Anton André (1775–1842)], which I received recently, and which would seem to be a *pendant* to that Haydn Symphony. Here we find a forthright rondo theme, very common, which is broken off; now there is a kind of fugal section which is in no way connected to the rondo movement. . . . Herr A— is certainly not without talent, otherwise I would not have taken the trouble to mention him here. But as I have said, something like this doesn't write itself in a lazy hour and, like an ode, it must be made either excellently or not at all. . . .

All the above articles appeared in the *AMZ* between October and December 1798. *Inter alia*, Haydn will have also read with interest a long letter, published in instalments, by his old friend Carl Ditters von Dittersdorf, on the subject of taste in vocal music ('One complains about church music in comic operas and comic operatic music in the church . . .'),[1] and also on the problem of accents in Italian recitatives, etc. We shall continue to follow *AMZ* in our forthcoming Chronicle, and we shall note that the famous letter by Baron van Swieten on the text of *The Creation* (quoted *supra*, p. 116), together with the Duet (Adam-Eve) in piano score, appeared in a January issue, followed a week later by the entire libretto. It must have been quite clear to Haydn that the new journal immediately set a new and serious tone to German-language music reviewing. Consequently it was doubly hard when even Haydn's great London Symphonies were attacked, as we have recalled that they were in 1799. Even Beethoven was not immune to the criticism of his muse in the *AMZ*. On 22 April 1801 he writes to Breitkopf & Härtel:

> . . . Advise your reviewers to be more circumspect and intelligent, particularly in regard to the productions of young composers. For many a one, who perhaps might go far, may take fright. As for myself, far be it from me to think that I have achieved a perfection which suffers no adverse criticism. But your reviewer's outcry against me was at first very mortifying . . .[2]

1 I, 138 *et seq.*

2 *Selected Letters of Beethoven*, trans. Emily Anderson, ed. Alan Tyson, London 1967, p. 30. In the complete edition of the Anderson translation (London 1961), this letter may be found in vol. I, no. 48.

Long extracts of these early criticisms of Beethoven's music and piano playing published in the *AMZ* may be found in *Beethoven as I knew him* (Schindler, ed. MacArdle), 76ff. One particular passage in the *AMZ* review of 'XII Variations sur le Thème: Ein Mädchen oder Weibchen, pour le Pianoforte, avec un Violoncelle obligé . . . No. 6. à Vienne chez F. Traeg', and 'VIII Variations sur le Thème: Mich brennt' ein heisses Fieber, pour le Pianoforte . . . No. 7. à Vienne chez F. Traeg' (*AMZ* I, 366f.), after criticizing the piece in general – 'Whether he is equally successful as a composer is . . . a question that it would be difficult to answer in the affirmative, judging from these samples of his work' – and in particular – 'see especially Var. XII, where in broken chords he modulated from F major to D major. [various musical examples] . . .' – continues: 'Whichever way I look at and judge such modulations, they remain trivial [*platt*], the more so as they become more pretentious and rhetorical. Altogether – though I do not intend this strictly for this composer alone – an enormous number of variations are produced and unfortunately also printed, without many of their composers really knowing what it means to vary a theme properly. May I give you all a good piece of advice, as far as one can do so in two words? To the front, those who have wit and taste enough to write good music – for without those properties one remains sounding brass and tinkling cymbal – and you should learn (1) to choose a good theme from Jos. Haydn. The subjects of this master are generally *a*) simple and easily understood, *b*) highly rhythmical and *c*) not common, and capable of further extension in melody and harmony. If one would then like hints on how to work out a well chosen theme . . . one should study . . . Vogler's criticism of the Forkel Variations on the English Hymn 'God save the King"'. The review is signed 'M. . . .'. This is one of the first times Haydn was used as a (largely unapproachable) model on which Beethoven would have done well to pattern his music. It did not contribute to Beethoven's appreciation of Haydn.

Slightly later in the 1799 season, the *AMZ* printed another review of a Beethoven set of 'X Variations pout le Clavecin sur le Duo: la stessa, la stess[iss]ima, par L. van Beethoven. No. 8. à Vienne chez Artaria, which reads as follows:

'With these [Variations] one cannot be at all satisfied. How stiff they are and contrived, and how many unpleasant passages therein, where hard tirades in continuous half notes clash against the bass in hateful relationship. No, it may be true that Hr. v. B. can improvise, but he does not understand how to write good variations.'

The review, also in 1799, of the Op. 12 violin Sonatas dedicated to Salieri is hardly an inprovement ('It is clear that Herr van Beethoven is going his own way: but what a bizarre and difficult way! Learned, learned and always learned, and no nature, no melody! Well, if one examines it carefully, it is only *learned raw-materials* that we are given, *without a proper method* . . .', etc., etc.).

See *AMZ* I: 366f., 370f., 607.

CHAPTER TEN

Works of 1798

Die Schöpfung / The Creation
(XXI: 2)

I. GOTTFRIED VAN SWIETEN'S LIBRETTO

Survey of the Material: (1) quality and criticism; (2) the Germanic tradition – its presumed theological and literary background; (3) its English origins; (4) the Masonic elements; (5) the Swieten autograph.

(1) Quality and Criticism

When the Viennese first heard *The Creation*, Gottfried van Swieten's share in the proceedings – both as the 'author' (or at least translator) of the libretto and as the *spiritus rector* of the Gesellschaft der Associirten – was known and appreciated. From all the available Viennese criticisms, including foreign correspondents such as Carpani and Silverstolpe, it would indeed seem that the libretto was as much liked as was the music; or at least, the libretto's excellence was taken for granted. Within a few years, however, criticism of the libretto began to grow and has ceased only within the last few years. An explanation for the libretto's initial success in Vienna, and its subsequent fall from grace, may be seen in the following circumstance.

Haydn's literary taste was undoubtedly old-fashioned. He loved the poetry of his youthful years, the writers of Theresian logic and Josephinian Enlightenment such as J. W. L. Gleim, C. F. Weisse, G. E. Lessing and especially Haydn's favourite, Christian Fürchtegott Gellert, whose poetry he often set to music. But if Haydn's literary horizon was not large, the fault was only partly his; for the whole of Vienna was, compared to northern Germany, semi-literate at best. After the golden journalistic and literary freedom permitted by Joseph II, the censors under Emperor Franz had gradually forced out any literature which smacked even faintly of what was considerd republican or revolutionary; which meant that most of Schiller's plays were quite simply banned in Vienna. Being effectively cut off from German literary sources after *c.* 1795, the Viennese soon became very backward in their literary and poetic education. We all recall that it took the Empress's personal intervention to enable Beethoven's *Fidelio* to be staged at all, the censor (not without some justification from his standpoint) considering the libretto as rather revolutionary and anti-Establishment. The Viennese were, and are, by nature conservative; and they found the Baroque elements of *The Creation*'s libretto to their liking and the religious aspects overwhelming. It was, in short, a libretto not only to Swieten's and Haydn's taste but also to that of the whole of educated Vienna. Mozart's work with the most symbolism, *Die Zauberflöte*, was the composer's most popular work; and Haydn's symbolism (and not only the 'Thonmahlerey', or evocation of tigers, lions etc., through the music) appealed at once to Viennese sensibilities. No one considered the libretto undramatic (on the contrary!) or prosaic.

When the Oratorio began to circulate in Germany at the beginning of the new century, however, criticism of the libretto soon began and grew steadily. Schiller's works may have been anathema to the Viennese censors, but *The Creation* was also anathema to Schiller, who in a letter to Christian Gottfried Körner of 5 January 1801[1] describes the work as a 'charakterloser Mischmasch'. He writes: 'On New Year's evening [1801] *The Creation* by Haydn was performed, but I had little pleasure in it for it is a characterless potpourri . . . Haydn is a skilful artist who, however, lacks inspiration . . .'. Here we see that Schiller condemns not only the libretto but even more the music itself. That which particularly incensed the critics was the 'Thonmahlerey', depicting in the music 'the tawny lion', 'the flexible tyger', 'the nimble stag', 'the sprightly steed with flying mane and fiery look' and, in the quaint phrase, '. . . o'er the ground, as plants, are spread the fleecy, meek and bleating flock'. This last piece of Baroque delight brings us to still another reason for the steadily increasing criticism of the libretto: the English version which appeared simultaneously with the German in the authentic first edition of the full score (1800). Like the Viennese, the English were overwhelmed by the music, and especially by 'The Heavens are telling'; but the old-fashioned and occasionally rather odd English –

O happy pair, and always happy yet,
if not, [*sic*] misled by false conceit,
ye strive at more, as granted is,
and more to know, as know ye should!

– soon excited the anger and later derision of British critics. Writing to Haydn's English librettist, Mrs Anne Hunter, at the end of 1804, the Scottish publisher George Thomson wrote:

> It is not the first time that your muse and Haydn's have met, as we see from the beautiful canzonets. Would he had been directed by you about the words to *The Creation*! It is lamentable to see such divine music joined with such miserable broken English. . . .[2]

In the course of the nineteenth century, not only the libretto but also the music of the Oratorio went totally out of fashion. By the beginning of the present century, critical opinion of *The Creation* reached perhaps its lowest point. We do not wish to discuss this point at length (which will form part of the material of chapter 13, *infra*), but we may quote briefly from a standard Haydn biography of 1902.[3] The libretto, says Hadden,

> stands to the present day as an example of all that is jejune and incongruous in words for music . . . It is a matter for wonder how . . . English-speaking audiences have listened to the arrant nonsense with which Haydn's music is associated. . . . The suburban love-making of our first parents, and the lengthy references to the habits of the worm and the leviathan are almost more than modern flesh and blood can bear. [Another critic is quoted as saying that the libretto] 'seems only fit for the nursery, to use in connection with Noah's ark'. . . . There is in *The Creation* a good deal of music which is finicking and something

1 *Schillers Briefwechsel mit Ch. G. Körner* (herausgegeben von K. Goedeke), 2nd ed., Leipzig 1878, II, 363. See also Pohl III, 369.
2 Hadden, *Thomson*, 288.
3 Hadden, 131ff.

which is trumpery . . . In another fifty years, perhaps, the critic will be able to say that its main interest is largely historic and literary.

Contrary to the placid expectations of Mr Hadden, however, the Oratorio has quietly returned to its eighteenth-century position of eminence. It has again become one of Haydn's most admired works, and curiously enough, not only has criticism of the libretto almost entirely ceased but van Swieten's unique position as Haydn's collaborator has come to be appreciated more than at any time since the beginning of the nineteenth century. In fact van Swieten's role has of late been compared to those of da Ponte and in particular Hugo von Hofmannsthal. As early as 1909, the great German scholar Max Friedländer[1] wrote that the Baron was among 'the most discerning advisors and cleverest librettists . . . that a composer ever found'. Perhaps the most generous appreciation of Swieten comes from the pen of a brilliant Swiss scholar, Professor Martin Stern, who writes in a recent study (with which we shall be directly concerned later in this analysis):[2]

> *The Creation* brought in the biggest box-office returns in the history of Vienna; it conquered, in one fell swoop, about the turn of the century, a Europe divided by war; it reunited all classes – Catholic Austria, Anglican England, Evangelical Berlin and even a laicized Paris – in admiration, and repeatedly moved thousands and thousands of listeners to tears of devotion and emotion. It brought, with the approval of the First Consul, to the composer the highest musical order that the French republic could confer, and remained the most frequently performed choral composition in Prussia for decades. To all this van Swieten's text contributed its part, though that part is difficult to measure precisely. If one reads the letters of gratitude and the reports of those performances which were sent to Haydn, or circulated and/or published by listeners and critics, one begins to get the impression that in this libretto the wishes and dreams of a whole generation were realized artistically; for otherwise such an echo cannot be explained. To have realized these needs shows that van Swieten, even if not primarily creative, must have had astounding powers of perception amounting almost to seismographic sensitivity. For not only Haydn, who since the deaths of Gluck and Mozart was unquestionably the leading composer of his age, but also van Swieten might have said that his language was understood by the whole world.[3]

Criticism of *The Creation* was never so strong in German-speaking as in Anglo-Saxon countries. An annual performance of the Oratorio continued in Vienna almost without a break from 1798 to the present day; in this respect it occupied the position of *Messiah* in England and America. Thus Haydn's Oratorio, at least in Austria, and probably in Germany, became a tradition almost sacred, and certainly such as to put the work in a category of its own, 'beyond criticism'. In England, on the other hand, not only was the libretto a subject of vexation but equally the fact that it was considered a presumption for Haydn to have entered a field in which Handel was considered to be unique. We shall see that very soon after the first performance of the

1 'Van Swieten und das Textbuch zu Haydn's "Jahreszeiten" ', in *Peters-Jahrbuch 1909*, pp. 47ff.

2 'Haydns "Schöpfung": Geist und Herkunft des van Swietenschen Librettos. Ein Beitrag zum Thema "Säkularisation" in Zeitalter der Aufklärung', in *Haydn-Studien* I/3 (1966), pp. 121–98, esp. 129.

3 A reference to Haydn's famous *bon mot* of 1790. Before he left for London, Haydn had a 'merry meal' with Mozart and Salomon (Griesinger 22), at which Mozart said, 'You won't stand it for long and you will soon be back, for you're not young' ('But I am cheerful and in a good state' said Haydn) (Griesinger 22). Then Mozart said (Dies 78): 'Papa! You don't have the education for the great world and you speak too few languages.' 'Oh,' said Haydn, 'my language is understood by the whole world'.

work in London, voices were raised criticizing Haydn for having written an Oratorio at all and angrily protesting the work's inferiority to Handel's masterpieces. As the Handelian tradition dies, this aspect of *The Creation*'s unpopularity in England and America ceases to be valid. And the language of Swieten's text has now gathered a patina which renders even the gaucheries charming rather than quaint. And finally, no one objects to the 'Thonmahlerey' any longer. Beethoven was particularly severe in his criticism of this aspect of Haydn's work, and when the 'Pastoral' Symphony was first given in 1808, Beethoven was careful to state in the programme that his work was 'more an expression of feeling than painting'.[1] Yet not only does the 'Pastoral' Symphony contain a generous portion of 'Thonmahlerey' – its composer's protestations to the contrary notwithstanding – but no one objects to its use by Handel (*Israel in Egypt* is the supreme example) or Bach (the veil of the temple being rent in twain in the *Passion according to St Matthew*) or Wagner (storm at the beginning of *Die Walküre*); and thus the old objection to Haydn's score and Swieten's libretto has also quietly disappeared. The case of *The Creation* as a *Gesamtkunstwerk* (music and libretto considered together, that is) is almost classical in its 'curve of popularity'. From its explosive success in Vienna, the work became – as will be seen – an instant success all over Europe, including Russia; its popularity then waned, especially in Anglo-Saxon countries, reaching a low point about 1900; and after its first recording[2] in 1949, the Oratorio has very quickly become a standard choral work and one of its composer's most admired and most loved compositions.

(2) The Germanic Tradition: its presumed theological and literary background

In 1966, the Swiss *Germanist*, Professor Martin Stern, published a large monograph on *The Creation*, the title of which has been cited *supra*. It was the first serious literary study ever devoted to the background of the libretto and as such it was clearly of epochal importance to Haydn scholars. A brief outline of its contents will show the monograph's breadth of conception:

I. On the history of research into the work.
II. Matters of principle.
III. Composer and Librettist.
IV. Lidley, Milton, and the Bible as sources for *The Creation*.
V. The figurative Adam tradition before the Enlightenment up to the Cantatas of J. S. Bach.
VI. The crisis of the Dogma of Original Sin in the Eighteenth Century.
VII. The Enlightenment's 'Creation' homages before Haydn's Oratorio.
VIII. Van Swieten's text.
IX. Trends of the Secular and the Sacred.

In a survey of this kind, we cannot provide more than a brief outline of this fascinating, intelligent and cultivated monograph. But one of its principal theses is the

1 Landon, *Beethoven*, 241.

2 Made by the Haydn Society (HSLP 2005) with Trude Eipperle, Julius Patzak and Georg Hann, the Chorus of the Vienna State Opera and the Vienna Philharmonic Orchestra conducted by Clemens Krauss. A parallel recording of *The Seasons* with the same artists was issued in 1951 (HSLP 2027). The late Clemens Krauss told the present writer that these recordings, which were made for the Austrian radio (or rather *Reichsrundfunk*, Vienna station) shortly before the end of the war, were to be the beginning of a series which was to include all the late Haydn masses with the same artists. The extant recordings of the Oratorios were milestones in recording history and it may be said that their appearance, and that of the 'Nelson Mass' (also in the autumn of 1949), caused a sensation the echoes of which may still be felt. Overnight Haydn's music was placed in an entirely new and different category for many Anglo-Saxons. *The Creation* won the Grand Prix du Disque in 1950.

supposition – carefully put forward by the author – that Swieten's work on the libretto was much more than he or anyone else has ever admitted. Professor Stern writes (133f.):

> On all this information [about the English original], which must be described as uncertain, we may counterclaim that this *Ur*-librettist Lidley or Linley seems not to be identifiable with any living person, that his manuscript has not survived, and that van Swieten only mentions this middleman anonymously. Thus one can understand that one has doubted, even refused to admit, his existence. And the result of Paula Baumgärtner's work [a dissertation, *Gottfried van Swieten als Textdichter von Haydns Oratorien*, Vienna 1930] makes it even possible that van Swieten, using Protestant models of religious poetry from the period of the Enlightenment – which we will discuss in detail – himself put together his text from the Bible and Milton's epic poem . . . Van Swieten, with his many literary contacts made during his career as a diplomat in Berlin (1770–7) or as Librarian in Vienna, could very well have come across Milton all by himself. If he nevertheless chose to insert between himself and Milton an 'anonymous' as the actual designer of the libretto, the explanation may be that the musically enthusiastic Baron wished to credit himself not as a poet but as a composer; and also another wish to preserve discretion. . . .

If we accept this new theory that Swieten and Haydn invented the English libretto, then Swieten's wish for discretion is easily understood: firstly for reasons of dogma – Swieten was right about this, too, because the Church immediately objected to the work and banned it from ecclesiastical edifices – and secondly for the strong Masonic tendencies (which Professor Stern overlooks except for a brief mention); we must remember that Freemasonry was already forbidden in Austria.

Having cast serious doubts on the English original, Professor Stern proceeds to show all the possible historical influences on the libretto: Miltonian, Biblical and from the rich legacy of German-language religious publications of various kinds. Naturally the latter presupposes that in fact most of the libretto was van Swieten's original creation. But after the publication of this monograph, Edward Olleson in 1968 published an article entitled 'The Origin and Libretto of Haydn's *Creation*'[1] which necessitates a thorough re-examination of the libretto, van Swieten's part in it, and the English original.

(3) Its English Origins

Olleson begins with a survey of the authentic sources about the work, its first performance and the libretto, of which we have quoted all the relevant documents *supra*. We have seen the question of Linley and Lidley and the authorship of the English original. But how does all this fit into the new theory that the English libretto was a convenient invention? The first piece of evidence is the fact that Salomon wanted to sue Haydn for misuse of the English libretto. Promising though this appears at first, it actually adds nothing to what we know already. It does not prove conclusively that Haydn's text followed the English model closely, since Salomon would have recognized the origins of the oratorio if van Swieten had adopted the title and nothing else. Conversely, Haydn's defence – that he had only used Lidley's idea, and not his actual words – is no more decisive in proving that the libretto was largely the original work of van Swieten. . . . As for the man who might have told – 'Lidley was already dead' (p. 155).

1 *Haydn Yearbook* IV, 148–66.

Olleson then proceeds to examine the plan of the Oratorio and to compare it with the Bible and Milton, which 'can reveal much about the nature of the English model and how closely it was followed by van Swieten' (156). The first two parts cover the first six days of Creation. 'Each day has its own internal organization, whereby it opens with a biblical narration, has a middle section of descriptive or lyrical commentary, and closes with a song of praise' (156). Of course this was not a rigid plan and van Swieten broke it whenever he felt it necessary to do so. In Part III, 'there is no biblical narrative, and the mood is entirely lyrical and idyllic'. The narrative is taken from Genesis, chapters 1 and 2. *Paradise Lost* is the chief source for the descriptive and lyrical passages, and the 'hymns' at the end of the Day are often paraphrases of Psalms (e.g. 'The Heavens are telling the glory of God', Psalm 19, 1 and 2). The sunrise (fourth Day) 'owes its verbal imagery to the fifth verse of [Psalm 19]; the moralising trio "Zu dir, o Herr, blickt alles auf" ("On thee each living soul awaits") is derived from four verses of Psalm 104' (156).

Olleson then demonstrates that the biblical passages

> show their English derivation most clearly, being an almost syllabic translation from the English of the Authorised Version of the Bible.
>
> This is immediately recognizable to an English reader, but when Paula Baumgärtner admitted that an extensive search through German translations of the Bible had failed to reveal the source of van Swieten's narrative, she unwittingly raised an important point. It is usually reasonable to assume, as she did, that a translator will not prepare his own version of biblical prose, but will draw on whatever vernacular translation of the Bible is most commonly in use at the time. In the case of *The Creation*, however, van Swieten did not do this. Furthermore, the indebtedness of the narrative to the English Bible is not only seen through the German translation; the actual words of the Authorised Version are found in the English text to the oratorio, as printed in the first edition of Haydn's score. [156f.]

The indebtedness of the libretto to Milton's *Paradise Lost* is then brilliantly demonstrated by Olleson. The 'animal' recitative begins in German:

> Gleich öffnet sich der Erde Schoß,
> Und sie gebiert auf Gottes Wort
> Geschöpfe jeder Art,
> In vollem Wuchs' und ohne Zahl.

This comes from *Paradise Lost* (VII, 453–6):

> . . . The Earth obeyed, and strait
> Op'ning her fertil Woomb teemd at a Birth
> Innumerous living Creatures, perfect formes,
> Limbd and full grown . . .

which the English librettist, as revealed in the full score, wrote as follows:

> Straight opening her fertile womb,
> The earth obey'd the word, and teem'd
> Creatures numberless,
> In perfect forms and fully grown.

It is only by examining the English that we can discover other derivations. The river, 'in mancher Krümme' would hardly remind us of *Paradise Lost*'s 'with Serpent errour wandering' (VII, 302) if it were not for the full score's English 'In serpent error rivers flow'. Olleson then quotes 'Ihr, deren Flug die Luft durchschneidt', which is, in *Paradise Lost*, '. . . ye Birds, / That singing up to Heaven Gate ascend' (V, 197–8) – recognizable only if we look at the score's English 'Ye birds that sing at heaven's gate'. All this gives us reason to doubt that the English is a retranslation from the German. Even the lines quoted above

> And o'er the ground, as plants, are spread
> The fleecy, meek and bleating flock

may be traced to *Paradise Lost*, '. . . Fleec't and bleating rose, / As Plants' (VII, 472–3), and similarly lines such as

> In long dimensions creeps
> With sinuous trace the worm

come from Milton (VII, 480–1):

> These as a line their long dimension drew,
> Streaking the ground with sinuous trace . . .

Where the English version paraphrased the Psalms, Swieten often seems to have retained the original verbatim. 'A giant proud and glad / To run his measured course' obviously derives from the Book of Common Prayer, '. . . and rejoiceth as a giant to run his course' (Psalm 19, 5). 'Once one is rid of the preconception that the English text to *The Creation* is a "retranslation by a German from the German" [Tovey], it becomes clear that much of it cannot be van Swieten's own work, simply because – of all the unlikely reasons – the English is too good,' writes Olleson (159). He produces genuine English translations by Swieten used in *The Seasons*—here, too, the librettist thought to market a simultaneous English (and also French) translation – which by comparison make the language of *The Creation* a paragon of English prose. Here, for example, is Swieten's translation of Bürger, 'Spinning Song' in *The Seasons*:

> Blank without, and pure within
> Ought the maiden's breast to be;
> Well fits it the veiling.

Since Swieten intended to deliver Haydn a text which would fit the music in both languages, he retained as much of the original English as he could; sometimes there had to be differences, and Haydn made the necessary musical changes when publishing the full score in 1800. *The Seasons* shows us that Swieten's English was *not* fluent, and that he tried to keep to a minimum those passages where he felt obliged to change the original English text. One has been cited above in another connection ('O happy pair', *supra*, p. 343). Another is the Trio 'In holder Anmuth steh'n' / 'Most beautyfull appear, with verdure young adorn'd, the gently sloping hills'.

> . . . For a start, the English words are grotesquely stilted, even by the standards of *The Creation*. In addition, there are two pieces of corroborating evidence: the material derives from neither Milton nor any other known English source; and the metrical scheme – a succession of short lines – is not typical of the oratorio as a whole. The actual verse-form can give further hints of van Swieten's activity. Like most English libretti of the time, *The Creation* shows a preference for iambic verse. Where changes in metre occur, it is often for the sake of special effect, as in the dramatic accelerando of:
>
> Vor Freude brüllend steht der Löwe da;
> Hier schießt der gelenkige Tyger empor.

Van Swieten is known to have held strong views on the importance of rhythm in musical verse. Can we then assume that these lines are his own?

In view of the strong evidence produced by Olleson for this English original, we must take Swieten's own evidence (in the article for the *AMZ* quoted *supra*, p. 116) more at face value. The essence of the libretto is Miltonic and Biblical, and above all English in origin. This being the case, we may now examine in the light of what has been said up to now the next problematical point, namely:

(4) The Masonic Elements

In Masonic circles, *The Creation* was long ago held to contain strongly Masonic elements.[1] It is known that the great physician, Gerhard van Swieten (the Empress Maria Theresa's personal doctor), was an ardent Freemason, and it is always asserted – though on no written evidence that this writer has ever been able to discover[2] – that his son Gottfried was also a Mason; it is not unlikely but the matter cannot be established from available records. The Masonic message of *The Creation* may be established at several levels. On the most general, its appeal to the Brotherhood of Man, its 'Verkündigung gottebenbildlicher Humanität' (Stern's admirable phrase, which might be freely translated as the 'propagation of a humanity in God's image'), are clearly designed, in the words of the old Masonic character, to 'unite in true friendship men who otherwise would have remained strangers.' *The Creation*, both its music and its libretto, are of the same stuff as *Die Zauberflöte* and *Fidelio* (both by Masonic composers): representatives of a great humanitarian era in Central Europe, a golden age of freedom, cultivation of intellect and true sophistication which were soon to disappear for ever.

In a more detailed examination, we may notice that the Oratorio is in three parts, rather than the traditional two of Italian oratorios; and that there are three main soloists. The stress of three (an old Masonic symbol) is obvious. But did this glorification of humanitarian principles (in the general sense) and this involvement of the 'Three-Symbolism' derive from the original English libretto, or are they Swieten's additions? It is difficult to answer. Freemasonry, in the stricter sense, was an English institution and all the Austrian Lodges were 'daughter' (or 'sister') Lodges of the British Parent Lodge (the Grand Lodge of Great Britain). The Masonic aspects of the text could certainly have been present in the British *Ur*-libretto. The organization of the work into three (rather than two) parts is typical of many Handelian oratorio libretti. Yet there are some curious details. The English *Ur*-libretto reads:

The Marv'lous work behold amaz'd
The glorious hierarchy of Heaven.

What Swieten wrote is much more Masonic and even Republican:

Mit Staunen sieht das Wunderwerk
der frohen Himmelsbürger Schar.

1 Jacques Chailley, noting in a recent study ('Joseph Haydn and the Freemasons', *Studies in Eighteenth-Century Music* [Geiringer Tribute], op. cit., p. 123) that *The Creation* 'always enjoyed [great favour] among high-class Masons of the nineteenth century', has devoted several specialized papers to the subject: *L'Education Musicale* (May 1963) and an extract of a longer paper in *Revue de Musicologie*, December 1964, pp. 290f.

2 Only one protocol of a Viennese Lodge ('Zur Wahren Eintracht') has survived, for the years 1781–5 (Haus-, Hof- und Staatsarchiv, Vienna). Haydn was a member of that Lodge, and Mozart was frequently a visitor. Van Swieten was not a member of that Lodge, and although there were many other Lodges in Vienna, we have no exact records of their members.

'Citoyens du ciel' is a rather compromising expression. The whole attitude which presents God the 'Workman', the 'Engineer' who created the world, is very Masonic. But it is not necessarily anti-Catholic, as some critics have implied; on the contrary, it is very unlikely that Haydn would have set a note of music to paper if he thought that any aspect of his work would be considered anti-Catholic. He was a good son of the Mother Church, and the combination of God the Creator (in the Catholic sense) with God the Grand Architect of the Universe (in the Masonic sense) presented no sense of incongruousness either to Haydn or to van Swieten, both true sons of the Enlightenment. The glorification of man in Part Three may be Masonic but it is also a profoundly eighteenth-century attitude altogether. Perhaps one of the many strengths of *The Creation* is its capacity to appeal to Mason and Christian alike; or to use a Masonic *Kettenlied* of 1782 from the lodge 'Zur Wahren Eintracht',

> O messet die Kette, ihr findet
> kein Ende daran, sie umwindet
> die Erde von Osten bis West,
> die Erde von Osten bis West.
>
> (O measure the chain: you shall find
> no end to it ever; it encompasses
> earth from the East to the West,
> earth from the East to the West.)

(5) The Swieten Autograph

The autograph of *The Creation*'s libretto is a precious part of Haydn's legacy and is now in the Esterházy Archives of the National Library in Budapest (Ha. I. 12), from which institution we received a photograph – one of the innumerable kindnesses shown to us by that generous and helpful Library. A few years ago, Horst Walter published both the late Oratorios' textbooks from the Swieten autographs; particularly important in the case of *The Seasons*, since the original has disappeared and we have its contents only from some notes and five pages in photograph from the library of the late E. F. Schmid (acquired by the Haydn Institut, Cologne).[1] From this publication we may see concrete evidence of Swieten's participation in the musical side of the two works. His advice was in good taste, sensible and to the point; Haydn followed it gratefully but not, of course, slavishly. There are a few small textual differences between Swieten's autograph and the final printed score (and printed libretto) of *The Creation*, the texts of both having been scrupulously revised for the printer and corrected by the Baron. One notes, interestingly, that the angels are at first anonymous: 'Mehrere Engel' says the autograph's list of persons, and the earliest scores and parts entitle the various arias as sung by 'Ein Engel'; the names were added shortly before the first performance, for they appear in the earliest libretto (29/30 April 1798): Gabriel (soprano), Uriel (tenor), Raphael (bass) are the names, probably taken from Milton's *Paradise Lost* (Books IV, V and VII).

We follow the plan here of citing Swieten's advice to Haydn on the music. The numbers and page references are to the score by Edition Eulenburg (E.E. 3250, 1925; textually based on the critical score edited by Eusebius von Mandyczewski for Breitkopf & Härtel, *Haydns Werke*, Ser. XVI, Band 5, 1924) but the actual German text is taken from Swieten's autograph and the English text from the authentic first

1 Horst Walter, 'Gottfried van Swietens Handschriftliche Textbücher zu "Schöpfung" und "Jahreszeiten"', *Haydn-Studien* 1/4 (1967), pp. 241ff.

edition of the score (1800). The Baron's comments are underlined throughout in the original.

No. 1 (p. 11) 'Im Anfange schuf Gott' / 'In the beginning God created'. [Swieten's comment:] The descriptive [*mahlerischen*] passages of the Overture could serve as the accompaniment to this Recitative.

No. 1 (p. 12) 'Und der Geist Gottes' / 'And the Spirit of God'. [Swieten's comment:] In the Chorus, the darkness could gradually disappear; but enough of the darkness should remain to make the momentary transition to light very effective. 'Es werde Licht &c.' ['and there was Light'] must only be said once.

No. 2 (p. 23): end of the Tenor Aria 'zur ewigen Nacht' / 'to endless night'. [Swieten's comment:] It would be a good idea if the final ritornello of the Aria announced the Chorus and the latter then began immediately to express the feelings of the fleeing spirits of hell. [Haydn did not have a final ritornello but made the chorus break into the final notes of the tenor. He also 'manipulated' the text in his old Italian operatic manner, that is to say, he goes back to the tenor's earlier words.

No. 12 (p. 106). Swieten wrote the following instructions in his autograph: the passage 'Mit leisem Gang und sanftem Schimmer schleicht der Mond die stille Nacht hindurch' / 'With softer beams and milder light steps on the silver moon thro' silent night' is bracketed and marked 'in tempo'; the succeeding two lines 'Den ausgedehnten Himmelsraum ziert ohne Zahl der hellen Sterne Gold' / 'The space immense of th'azur sky innumrous host of radiant orbs adorns' (p. 107) are bracketed and marked 'ad libitum'; while the last lines before the Chorus No. 13 'und die Söhne Gottes' / 'and the sons of God' are marked 'ohne Begleitung' (without accompaniment). Haydn in the event wrote 'a tempo' at 'With softer beams', changed the tempo to allegro at 'The space immense', but did not follow the Baron's suggestion about having no accompaniment for the end of the section.

No. 13 Chorus (p. 108). The entrance of the solo voices (p. 111) is marked 'Einzelne Stimme oder auch zwey' (a single voice or rather two); the next entrance of the soli (p. 116) is marked 'Eine, zwey, oder auch drey Stimmen'. Haydn used his three vocal soloists for all these sections.

No. 15 Aria (p. 152), at the words 'Noch drückte Gram' / 'No grief affected' [Swieten writes:] NB. Because of the last three lines only the joyful twittering, not the long held tones, of the nightingale can be imitated here. [The (in)famous 'Thonmahlerey' was, as we see, planned not only by the composer but by the librettist as well; Haydn imitated the twittering but he also found a clever way to introduce a 'long held' note in the solo soprano part; see pp. 154, 156.]

No. 16 (p. 159), 'Seyd fruchtbar alle' / 'Be fruitful all'. [Swieten writes:] Here it seems that the bare accompaniment of the bass moving solemnly [*feyerlich*] in a straight rhythm would create a good effect. [This was Haydn's first idea of the final, finished version – an earlier sketch will be discussed *infra* – and it would seem that it was performed that way on the first evening; then he added two violoncelli and still later the divided violas.]

No. 18 Terzetto (p. 162). [Swieten writes:] For these strophes, a quite simple and syllabic melody would probably be the best thing to have, so that the words can be understood clearly; but the accompaniment could paint [*mahlen*] the course of the brook, the flight of the bird and the quick movement of the fishes. [Haydn in the middle and sometimes also upper strings gives a convincing feeling of flowing water, and he also imitates the birds (p. 166), the bottom of the ocean (p. 170) and, delightfully, 'th'immense Leviathan'.]

No. 19 (p. 174). [Swieten's comments:] This Chorus should only reinforce that which the three voices sang previously and thus it should not be long. [Haydn wrote a chorus of sixty-five bars.]

No. 28 (p. 250). [Swieten's comment:] To 'alles lobe' ['Glory to his name'] a fugue if one wants to. [Haydn wrote a fugue.]

Third Part No. 29 (p. 269). [Swieten's comments:] Here a rather lengthy introduction, which expressed the sweet sound and the pure harmony, could serve to introduce the Recitative, and thereafter could be used as the accompaniment for the first six lines [from 'Aus Rosenwolken' / 'In rosy mantle' to 'zur Erde hinab' / 'on ravished earth' (pp. 271f.)]. Also it seems that more attention should be given to harmony rather than melody, and the latter would have to be at most only floating or stretched out [*gedehnt*]. [Haydn wrote a long introduction, of which the orchestration will be discussed *infra*, and used the material for it in the course of the ensuing Recitative, in the manner of an Italian *scena*; but contrary to Swieten's idea, Haydn's melody, while perhaps 'stretched out', is more essential to the passage than the 'harmony'.]

No. 30 is entitled on Swieten's autograph 'Lobgesang / mit abwechselndem Chore der Engel / Basso. Adam und Eva'; Haydn did not, however, set the piece for several choruses, but for one. [Swieten's comments:] Since here the first, as yet inexperienced and innocent human couple expresses its innermost feelings, it goes without saying that the song must be simple and the melody syllabic; but there could be a more solid rhythm for Adam than for Eve, and the difference in emotion caused by the difference in their sex could be suggested by alternating major and minor keys. [Haydn took great pains in this particular case *not* to follow the Baron's advice: the lovers are treated as one entity and their song interspersed and woven into the Chorus of the Angels (= the Swieten autograph; the score simply calls for 'Chor'), nor at any point is the difference in their sex emphasized. However, in the section (p. 285), when Adam sings 'Der Sterne hellster' / 'Of stars the fairest', Haydn uses a tune so simple as to be almost a folk-song, and also a syllabic treatment. Swieten then adds when the Angels' Choir enters the first time (p. 277):] The inserted Choir of Angels should break the monotony of the strophes and should stand out particularly from their melodic pattern, which would probably be best expressed through harmony. [Haydn obviously treated the whole section in a different way.]

No. 34 (p. 358). [Swieten's suggestion:] The last verse ['Des Herr(e)n Ruhm' / 'The Lord is great'] and the Amen could be treated as a fugue in a singing match [*Wettgesang*]. [Haydn wrote a double fugue at this point in the score.]

II. THE SKETCHES

There is a curious story about the collaboration between Haydn and van Swieten which is related by the great Austrian poet and playwright, Franz Grillparzer,[1]

1 From the complete 20-volume edition of Grillparzer's works herausgegeben und mit Einleitungen versehen von August Sauer, Vol. XV (Aesthetic Studies), 4 ('Zur Musik'), Stuttgart 1893, p. 124. Horst Walter (*Haydn-Studien* 1/4 (1967), p. 242), from whose study of the Swieten autographs of the libretti this quotation was taken, thinks that Raphael Kiesewetter (1773–1850) would have been the 'well-informed contemporary'. In the excellent monograph about Kiesewetter by Herfried Kier (*Raphael Georg Kiesewetter [1773–1850], Wegbereiter des musikalischen Historismus,* Band 13 of 'Studien zur Musikgeschichte des 19. Jahrhunderts', Regensburg 1968, p. 58), we read: 'there are no indications of a personal acquaintanceship between Kiesewetter and van Swieten, but it is not out of the question that the young Kiesewetter established personal contact with van Swieten or with his concerts. Grillparzer's man can, of course, have been one of many people who were still living in the 1820s and 1830s.

according to which the Baron 'had each piece, as soon as it was ready, copied and pre-rehearsed with a small orchestra. Much he discarded as too trivial [*kleinlich*] for the grand subject. Haydn gladly submitted [*fügte sich*], and thus that astonishing work came into being which would be admired by coming generations. I have all this from the lips of a well-informed contemporary who himself took part in these pre-rehearsals.'

On the face of it, the story sounds rather improbable; yet upon due consideration, it would seem a sensible way to try out the effect of a huge oratorio with many different and strongly contrasting sections. The story would perhaps explain something quite unique in Haydn's *œuvre*, namely the existence of so many discarded versions of single numbers. Of course, we have relatively few sketches by Haydn, who probably threw them away as soon as the final score was completed, and there is no way of knowing if there were as many discarded arias and choruses for (say) *Il ritorno di Tobia* or one of the big operas such as *La fedeltà premiata*. But one is inclined to doubt it. All the known evidence suggests that Haydn (as he himself said) did not begin to write something until he was sure of what he wanted to say. One is therefore justified in viewing not only the discarded versions for various numbers of *The Creation* as unique but also the very number of extant sketches altogether – and that which has survived is obviously only a fraction, which has come down to us by a happy accident (perhaps through Elssler, perhaps through Baron van Swieten). Consider that there are three extant sketches *in score* for 'Chaos'. If we compare the sketches for Symphony No. 99's Finale (reproduced in Volume XII of the Philharmonia's edition of Haydn's Complete Symphonies, also in *Haydn-Studien* II/3 [1970]), we can see graphically the difference between even a great, mature symphonic Finale and the orchestral introduction to *The Creation*. The symphonic Finale gives the impression of being *the* sketch: it was from this draft that Haydn wrote out the full score of the autograph manuscript. With the Oratorio sketches, Haydn was not only more circumspect but also much more hesitant. Perhaps, then, the story of the Baron's 'pre-rehearsals' has something to it.

The first major article in which Haydn's sketches to *The Creation* were discussed was that by Karl Geiringer,[1] who drew the attention of the scholarly world to the two codices of sketches, which include many to the Oratorio, in the Österreichische Nationalbibliothek. Since Professor Geiringer's article could not, for reasons of space, 'mention . . . all the plans projected in the pages of *The Creation* sketches' (p. 308), we include here a complete list of all these sketches, and also those from other libraries, with several transcriptions which will show how this work evolved and developed in Haydn's and, one presumes, van Swieten's critical hands.

1 'Haydn's Sketches for "The Creation"', *Musical Quarterly* XVIII/2 (1932), pp. 299–308; reprinted in the Haydn Society's booklet to the above-mentioned first integral recording of the Oratorio in 1949. The only drawback to Professor Geiringer's transcriptions is that they are given with English words, whereas Haydn wrote them in German; as van Swieten planned a word-for-word and syllable-for-syllable translation from the English, this substitution of English for Haydn's original German could proceed without changing any notes.

LIST OF KNOWN SKETCHES TO 'THE CREATION'

(numbers refer to the Eulenburg score)

THE MANUSCRIPTS

(1) A collection of sketches consisting of forty pages of sixteen-stave Italian paper in oblong format, with some blank pages and also including the autograph part of the contrabassoon ('Doppelfagott'), Österreichische Nationalbibliothek, Vienna, Codex 16835 fol. I-XX. Facsimile of fol. XVIIv. in *Musikerhandschriften von Palestrina bis Beethoven*, eingeleitet und kommentiert von Walter Gerstenberg, Zürich 1960, p. 97. Facsimile of XIXv. in Geiringer 1932, facing p. 114, of fol. VIv. facing p. 145. Part of XIXv. in Somfai, p. 168.

Concordance of Codex 16835

(a) according to pages

Fol. Ir. No. 30.
Fol. Iv. No. 27.
Fol. IIr. No. 27.
Fol. IIv. blank.
Fol. IIIr. No. 34.
Fol. IIIv. blank.
Fol. IVr. blank.
Fol. IVv. No. 13.
Fol. Vr. blank.
Fol. Vv. No. 24.
Fol. VIr. Nos. 24, 26 (28).
Fol. VIv. No. 30.
Fol. VIIr. No. 30, No. 29.
Fol. VIIv. No. 30.
Fol. VIIIr. Nos. 29, 30.
Fol. VIIIv.–XIIIr. Haydn's autograph part for the double bassoon; four written pages, four blank.
Fol. XIIIv. Nos. 34, 32, 31.
Fol. XIVr. No. 31.
Fol. XIVv. blank.
Fol. XVr. No. 16.
Fol. XVv. No. 10.
Fol. XVIr. No. 10.
Fol. XVIv. No. 18.
Fol. XVIIr. Nos. 18, 17, 19.
Fol. XVIIv. Nos. 14, 15.
Fol. XVIIIr. No. 15.
Fol. XVIIIv. No. 15.
Fol. XIXr. blank
Fol. XIXv. No. 1 (score).
Fol. XXr. No. 1 (score).
Fol. XXv. No. 2.

(b) according to numbers

No. 1 (Einleitung) XIXv., XXr.
No. 2 XXv.
No. 10 XVv., XVIr.
No. 13 IVr.
No. 14 XVIIv.
No. 15 XVIIv., XVIIIr., XVIIIv.
No. 16 XVr.
No. 17 XVIIr.
No. 18 XVIv., XVIIr.
No. 19 XVIIr.
No. 24 Vv., VIr.
No. 26 (28): VIr.
No. 27 Iv., IIr.
No. 28: *vide* No. 26.
No. 29: VIIr., VIIIr.
No. 30: Ir., VIv., VIIr., VIIv., VIIIr.
No. 31 XIIIv., XIVr.
No. 32 XIIIv.
No. 34 IIIr., XIIIv.

(2) Sketch to No. 1 'Chaos' in full score on eight pages of sixteen-stave Italian paper in 4° format (a page left blank), Österreichische Nationalbibliothek, Codex 18987, fol. I–IV.

(3) Sketches to Nos. 10 and 13 on four pages of sixteen-stave Italian paper in oblong format, British Museum (*ex. coll.* Mme Emilie von Wölfül; see Larsen, *HÜB*, 39, and Hoboken II, 33). Add. 28613 f. 1–11.

(4) Sketch for fourteen bars of 'Chaos' in score, one page of ten-stave Italian paper in oblong format. New York Public Library, *ex. coll.* Anton Schmid and Alexander Posonyi, Vienna). Reproduced in Emanuel Winternitz: *Musical Autographs*, plate 57.

THE TOTAL SKETCHES ACCORDING TO NUMBERS

No. 1 'CHAOS'.

(a) Presumed earliest sketch; No. (4) *supra*, transcribed below as Sketch I.
(b) Draft in score of bars 1–23; No. (1) fol. XIXv. & XXr. *supra*, transcribed as Sketch II.
(c) Sketch in score of bars 1–5 in the final form; No. (1) *supra*, transcribed as Sketch III.
(d) Draft in score of 'Chaos' up to the recapitulation in the final form; No. (2) *supra*, transcribed as Sketch IV.
(e) Sketch of bars 61–3 in score from No. (1) *supra*, transcribed as Sketch V.
(f) Sketch for one of the transition bars (perhaps 55?) from No. (1) *supra*; (e) and (f) are to be found on fol. XXr. Transcribed as Sketch VI.
(g) Sketch for bars 50–62 in short score from No. (2) *supra*, fol. IVr., transcribed as Sketch VII.

No. 2 Aria & Chorus

Sketches in Codex 16835 (ÖNB), fol. XXv.

No. 10 Chorus
(a) Sketch in D major (beginning etc.), British Museum, Add. 28613, f.2.
(b) Sketches for the fugue, Codex 16835, fol. XVv., XVIr.
No. 13 Chorus with Soli
(a) Sketch in D major (beginning etc.), British Museum, Add. 28613, f.2.
(b) Sketches in C major, Codex 16835, fol. IVv.
No. 14 Recitative
Sketches in Codex 16835, fol. XVIIr.
No. 15 Aria
Sketches in Codex 16835, fol. XVIIv., XVIIIr., XVIIIv.
No. 16 Recitative
Sketches in Codex 16835, fol. XVr.
No. 17 Recitative
Sketches in Codex 16835, fol. XVIIr.
No. 18 Terzet
Sketches in Codex 16835, fol. XVIv., XVIIr.
No. 19 Chorus with Soli
Sketches in Codex 16385, fol. XVIIr.
No. 24 Aria
Sketches in Codex 16835, fol. Vv., VIr.
No. 26 (28) Chorus
Sketches in Codex 16835, fol. VIr.
No. 27 Terzet
Sketches in Codex 16835, fol. Iv., IIr.
No. 29 Recitative
Sketches in Codex 16835, fol. VIIr., VIIIr.
No. 30 Duet & Chorus
Sketches in Codex 16835, fol. Ir., VIv., VIIr., VIIv., VIIIr.
No. 31 Recitative
Sketches in Codex 16835, fol. XIIIv., XIVr.
No. 32 Duet
Sketches in Codex 16835, fol. XIIIv.
No. 34 Chorus
Sketches in Codex 16835, fol. IIIr., XIIIv.

The presence of the part for double bassoon among the sketches and the fact that some of it was not included in the main body of the authentic printed score of 1800 but was placed in an appendix, suggest that it may have been a later addition. Just when Haydn decided to add it is impossible to say; the evidence only permits us to observe that it was included in the original set of parts and thus was played as early as the performance of 22 December 1799, for one of the violoncello parts has this date noted by the player. Probably, however, it was added shortly after the first performance in 1798. It seems that the third trombone was also a later addition: the sketches to 'Chaos' never list more than two trombones, the alto and the tenor in one sketch, and two alto trombones in the other; the third, or bass, trombone figures in the original performance material but contains additions in Haydn's own hand – the most important and effective being in 'Chaos' when the words 'And there was light' appear. Perhaps the original lack of a third trombone part may be part of the explanation for a copy of the three trombone parts, in 'score', for Parts II and III, written by Haydn and now in the Bibliothèque du Conservatoire, Paris. The three trombone players may have practised from such a score.

The original performance material, largely copied by Johann Elssler, was discovered in 1950 – together with that to *The Seasons*, the Madrigal 'The Storm', and the Oratorio *Il ritorno di Tobia* – by the present writer in the Vienna City Hall (Rathaus). It indicates the forces used for the very large public performance in 1799, which a Swedish eye-witness lists as some 400 people. There are triple wind and brass (as well as timpani) parts in this fascinating material, though it is hard to say if they all played at one performance or if this was a 'collection' of Haydn's authentic MS.

orchestral parts. Probably they were at least doubled and possibly really tripled in the Burgtheater performance of 1799. The parts were probably also used for the very first performance in 1798 and added to as the size of the chorus and orchestra grew. We discuss this problem briefly at this point because in effect Haydn's changes are sometimes as drastic as between sketch and final draft. The two most important changes which were obviously made *after* the first performance (otherwise they would not have been copied by Elssler in the 'old' versions) are (1) in the recitative 'Seyd fruchtbar' / 'Be fruitful', where as we have pointed out *passim* the work was conceived and performed as a *secco* recitative; then the string parts were added, little by little; and (2) the beginning of Part Three, where the three flutes were at first unaccompanied, Haydn himself adding the *pizzicato* sections to principal copies of the string parts.

The 'Chaos' music is so original that Haydn's sketches deserve to be reproduced here in their entirety. It will be observed that the lonely violin figure of bars 3/4 of the final product –

p

– does not appear at first, nor does what Geiringer calls 'the impetuous thud of the orchestra' in bar 5. Note, too, how Haydn dematerialized the overall sound as the sketches progress. The triplet figure appears in the second sketch in the first violins (bar 5), the horns (bar 6), the clarinets (bar 11). Later two things happen to this triplet figure: the number of times it appears is reduced from nine in Sketch II to seven in the final version, and secondly the instrumentation is changed so that the figure only appears in less 'substantial' sounding instruments: bassoon, viola, violoncello and second violin. The parts for the trombones are reduced, too; the part of the second sketch at bars 10/11 is changed to avoid the prominent drop of a fourth. Conversely, the trumpets and timpani are more often used in the final version. In the fourth sketch it will be noticed that Haydn has already closely approached the final version, but in the D flat major section, 'which brings the idea of life into Chaos' (Geiringer p. 307), the bassoon figure (final version: 21ff.) is still lacking and at bar 49 (= 29) of the fourth sketch there is a clarinet flourish and a timpani roll instead of the austere bassoon *arpeggio* of the finished score.

In Sketch I – probably Haydn's first idea – the only concept that was transmitted to the final version is the use of suspensions and something of the fundamental harmonies. In Sketch III Haydn has worked out the beginning, but he later cancelled the trumpet and bassoons at bars 4/5. In Sketch IV, we note that Haydn originally proceeded very quickly to the recapitulation, which would have occurred at bar 30 of the sketch; the enlarged middle section was then conceived on the following sheet.

Towards the end of Sketch II we find an earlier (later discarded) version of bars 61–3 of the final score; the clarinet figure at bar 61 was discarded as being too obtrusive, yet another example of Haydn's attempt to dematerialize the sound; we refer to this draft as Sketch V. Sketch VI, perhaps intended for one of the transition bars (such as bar 35) towards the recapitulation, was later discarded, despite a large 'NB' that Haydn placed beside it. Both Sketches occur in fol. XXr. of codex 16835 listed above. On the final page of codex 18987 (fol. IVr.), there are further sketches to the last bars of 'Chaos' which in the event were much more simple; Haydn retained the interplay between oboe and clarinet and the first violin line is already firmly established. The flute passage (final score: bar 55) is much more elaborate here. Note that the characteristic clarinet phrase in the second half of (final) bar 57 is already placed in the violin stave.

['Chaos' – Sketch I (New York Public Library)]

['Chaos' – Sketch II (Österreichische Nationalbibliothek, Codex 16835, fol. XIXv. and XXr.)]

(1) ? Fag. II

(1) ? (?)

['Chaos' – Sketch II, *cont.*]

(1) [sic] (2) erased, perhaps to

['Chaos' – Sketch III (Österreichische Nationalbibliothek, Codex 16835, fol. XXr.)]

['Chaos' – Sketch IV (Österreichische Nationalbibliothek, Codex 18987, fol. I–IV)]

(1) Almost all the notes of the woodwind and the first half of the bars in the strings have been heavily revised.
(2) At first *f*: or *fz*:
(3) At first *p*

['Chaos' – Sketch IV, *cont.*]

(1) At first <>

15
[erased]
[erased]
f
p
p
3
[3]
p
fz
fz
p
p

['Chaos' – Sketch IV, *cont.*]

(1) Originally Haydn had a crotchet at the beginning of each bar instead of the rest.

['Chaos' – Sketch IV, *cont.*]

(1) Autograph has 𝅘𝅥𝅯 instead of 𝅘𝅥𝅯

(1) Autograph has 𝅘𝅥𝅮 instead of 𝅘𝅥𝅯
(2) At first *ff*, the *f-ff* added in another ink.

['Chaos' – Sketch IV, *cont.*]

(1) This clarinet run is spaced across two bars (for lack of space)
(2) Haydn's reminder to himself to add another bar here. The ⊖ insert was added to the far right-hand side of this page.

(1) For insert *(vide infra)*.

['Chaos' – Sketch IV, *cont.*]

['Chaos' – Sketch V (ÖNB, Codex 16835, fol. XXr.)]

['Chaos' – Sketch VI (ÖNB, Codex 16835, fol. XXr.)]

['Chaos' – Sketch VII (ÖNB, Codex 18987, fol. IVr.)]

The sketch to No. 10 in the British Museum consists of an otherwise blank title page with the words 'Heilige Reliquie / erhaltend einige Eigenhändige Skizzen J. Haydn's / aus diesen / unsterblichen Werke / Die Schöpfung' (f. 1r.), while f. 2v. contains a page of sketches to the fugue. The most interesting part of this manuscript is, however, the following two pages (f. 2, r. & v.), which contain sketches for No. 13 but in D major rather than C major. We see that Haydn arrived at the final tonal scheme of the Oratorio's first part only *after* the great chorus had been drafted in D major. On f. 2v. (No. 13 – Sketch I) we find the beginning of the chorus:

The variant violin part, written above the vocal parts as indicated (we have omitted the blank part of the stave up to that point), was used in the final version at bars 12ff. On the previous sheet we find a sketch to bars 38 (with upbeat) ff. of the final version, but still in D major. The sketch is surprisingly close to the final version, including the upward scales at bars 38ff. in the strings and flute. The trumpet, however, originally had at bars 42ff.

rather than the majestic and slower *cantabile* line of the final version:

In the other sketch for No. 13, from the Vienna codex, we find Haydn already writing in C major, drafting the great sequence towards the end of the work (bars 176ff.). It will be seen that there are skeletal outlines for violin I, the chorus and the basso continuo (see Sketch II), as there are in the next extract, bars 159ff. (Sketch III). It is clear that the main outlines of the piece, and in C major, were by this time clearly in Haydn's head. This is perhaps the place to say that the extant sketches can only represent a fragment of the total sketches and first drafts in score that Haydn made of the Oratorio; we are fortunate in having any at all, for as we have seen, most of Haydn's sketches were destroyed as soon as the final copy was prepared.

[No. 13 – Sketch II]

[No. 13 – Sketch II (*cont.*)]

[No. 13 – Sketch III]

If the sketch to the Recitative No. 14 is relatively clear and unproblematical, the sketch to No. 15 is interesting in that Haydn originally cast the Aria in three-four time, as follows (codex 16835, fol. XVIIv.):

This coloratura writing is, as Geiringer says (p. 304), reminiscent of *Il ritorno di Tobia* twenty years earlier, and 'only the strictest self-discipline could ever have led the composer to the vigorous, native simplicity of *The Creation*'. In the midst of this sketch in three-four time, however, we already find a draft for bars 80–85 of the final version in four-four *alla breve*:

(The vocal part is aligned under the violin only in bars 81–3.) A further sketch for the four-four version reads:

This was not used. It is continued for some bars.

The Viennese codex, on fol. XVIIIr., then gives us further sketches: for bars 25ff. (with upbeat), also for bars 54ff. (again with upbeat). At bar 57 Haydn planned the following violin part:

– later replaced by the decorous clarinet solo we hear today. The sketches also include drafts for the *gruppetto* figure (bars 150ff., flute); for the opening tutti (violin I, bars 8ff., with a different beginning to bar 8); and for other sections such as the "Liebe girrt das zarte Taubenpaar' (bars 67ff.). On fol. XVIIIv. there are still more sketches: bars 119ff., in which the three little notes of the final version are abbreviated in the sketch by the crossed turn, and leading to the flute solo at bars 133ff. and the passage 'ihr reizender Gesang'. Here Haydn had at first an elaborate kind of cadenza for the voice

which was not used (see bars 148–50). The final sketches on this page are for the soprano at bars 170f., with a cadenza at bars 174ff. as follows:

The sketch for No. 16 ('Seyd fruchtbar' / 'Be fruitful'; fol. XVr.) is for a *secco* recitative. Baron van Swieten's suggestion for a 'walking bass' (*vide supra*) has been adhered to.

[sic]
woh - ner der Luft, ver - meh - ret euch und singt auf je - dem A - ste!]
[ossia]

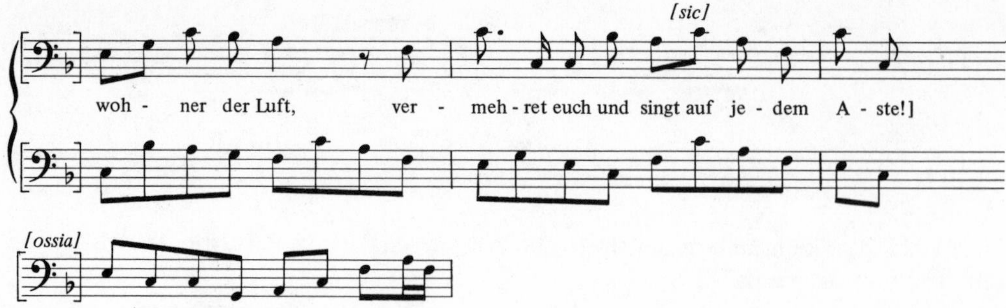

Interesting though this stately and deliberately conservative 'walking bass' is, the whole conception pales beside Haydn's later version, with the divided sets of lower strings.

The melodic line of the sketches to No. 18 ('In holder Anmuth' / 'Most beautyfull appear') is similar to the final version but lacks the latter's sophisticated line. We give both the violin's line and the entrance of the soprano.

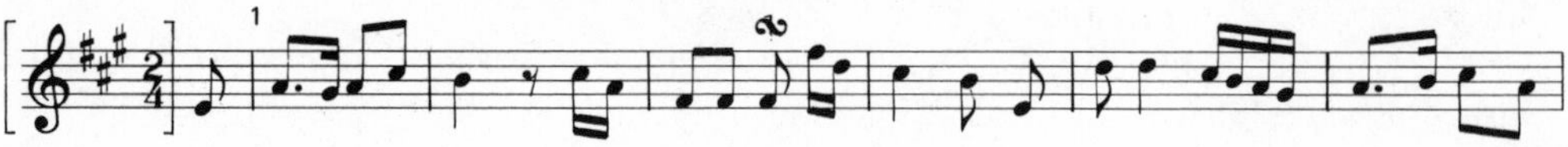

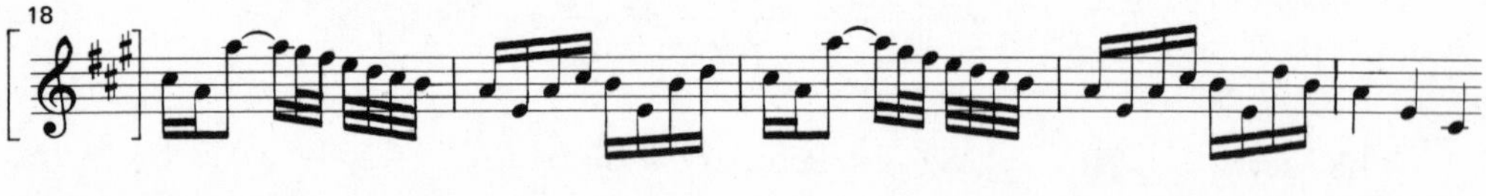

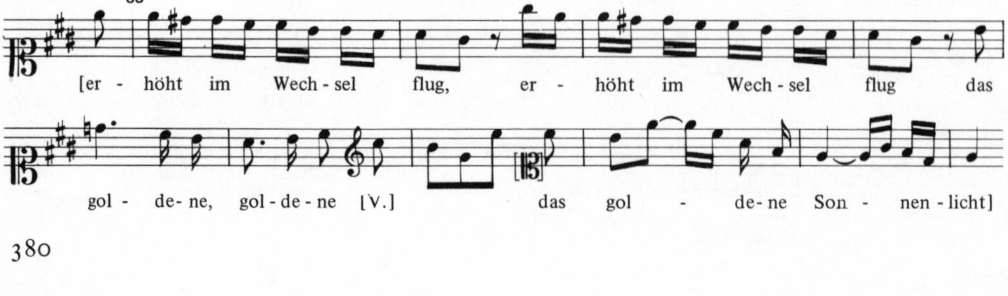

1

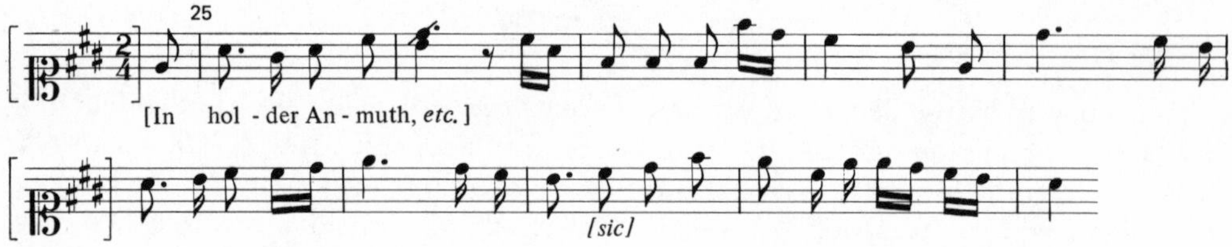

25
[In hol - der An - muth, etc.]
[sic]

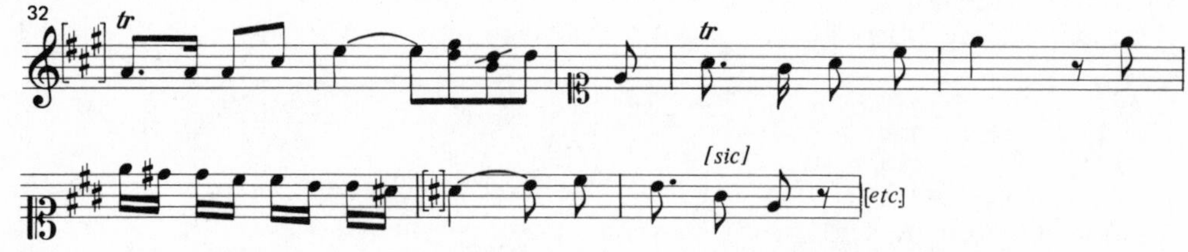

32
tr
tr
[sic]
[etc]

18

63
[er - höht im Wech - sel flug, er - höht im Wech - sel flug das
gol - de - ne, gol - de - ne [V.] das gol - de - ne Son - nen - licht]

Note in the second quotation (bars 32ff.) that the soprano repeats the *tr* of the violins (bars 32, 34), a feature that ought to be included in modern scores (where the soprano's trill is wanting). Later we find the slightly more conventional first draft for the violin figure at bars 18ff., and for the soprano's 'sighing' figure of bars 63ff. In all these drafts, it is striking how much more poised the final version will turn out to be. On the other hand, Raphael's entrance at bar 76 is the same in the sketch as in the final version, except that bars 85–7 were differently conceived.

In No. 24, Uriel's famous Aria, 'Mit Würd' und Hoheit' / 'In native worth', the sketch shows that the polished beauty and elegance of the final score was once again achieved by self-discipline. In the opening ritornello, the ending (bars 8f.) was different, and more like an operatic aria of the Eszterháza years:

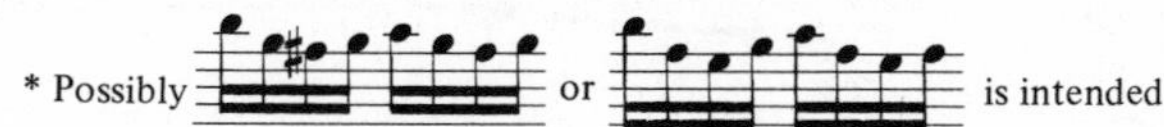

On this page (fol. Vv.) the final version of the passage in question is noted above the other one in short score (violin I and bass). There are also sketches for bars 40ff. Fol. VIr. continues the sketches for the Aria: bars 48ff. in violin I and bass. but bar 51 is different (and longer):

Immediately following, on the same sheet, is a sketch to No. 26 (or 28) – in No. 26 the passage in question is at bars 6ff. (with upbeat). At bar 13 (No. 26) there is a violin figure, later discarded:

The passage is a kind of half-cadence.

Fol. Iv. of the Viennese codex 16835 contains sketches for No. 27 in its final form, with the solo wind instruments, up to and including bar 26. Fol. IIr. has a continuation of the clarinet solo, together with a vocal passage in canon and the basso continuo – a flute solo is also briefly noted – which Haydn decided not to use. It is not entirely easy to fit the words to the (wordless) voices here, but the following bracketed text would seem to have been Haydn's intentions.

Clar. Solo [Sib]
Fl.
[Sop.] [Du wen - dest ab dein
[Tenore] [ge - sät - tigt wer - den sie, ge -
[Basso continuo]

[sic]
An - ge - sicht, du wen - dest ab dein An - ge -
sät - tigt wer - den sie] da be [bet]

Instead, the music of the final version remains in B flat and then starts to modulate with the entry of Raphael ('Du wendest ab dein Angesicht'), a passage that turned out to be one of the most striking moments in the work.

The first violin part of the ritornello in No. 29 appears in our Viennese codex (fol. VIIr.), at what would later be bars 16ff., in the following guise:

This is an interesting and characteristic example of how much of such a sketch was accepted and how much rejected: the ending was taken over verbatim (but with added phrasing: phrasing and dynamic marks are usually missing entirely from these sketches), but the earlier part was made more refined and also shorter ('sighing' figure removed, and so on).

On fol. VIIIr. we have more sketches for No. 29, the most ingenious of which is the elaborate horn solo, possibly Haydn's first idea of what would later become bars 39–40:

This reminds us of earlier horn soli in Haydn: Symphony No. 51's second movement, but perhaps even more the great muted horn solo in Celia's Aria in Act II of *La fedeltà premiata*, 'Deh, soccorri un'infelice'. In the end, Haydn allowed his horns only two bars of solo: the time for such moments of instrumental virtuosity, he obviously felt, was not in such a recitative.

Bars 41ff. are also sketches (without words), prefaced with Haydn's word, 'gilt' (valid). Towards the bottom of the page we find a sketch for bars 1ff. (3 flutes on 2 staves); at bar 8, instead of the repeat being written out, Haydn writes 'l'istesso' (the same). At the very bottom of the page we find sketches for the vocal part at bars 23ff.

(at the beginning even with the words 'Aus Rosenwolken') extending to bar 38. Here, interestingly, the finished vocal line contains more ornaments than the sketch: the little notes of bar 26 and the figure in the middle of bar 35 are missing (bars 34–5, for example, read:

without any bar-lines).

We have many sketches for No. 30, one of the longest and most involved numbers in *The Creation*. Here, we reproduce the sketch on fol. Ir. of codex 16835, using modern clefs; as it happens the entire movement was sketched out for the four voices and basso continuo:

Sop.
Alto
Ten.
Basso
B. C.

ge - seg - net sey des
ge - seg - net sey des [Her - ren Macht, sein
ge - seg [- net sey des Her - ren Macht, ~~sein~~ des

Her - ren Macht sein [Lob er - schallt in E - wig keit, sein
Macht, sein
~~Lob er - schallt~~
Her - ren Macht [sein Lob er - schallt in E - wig - keit, sein

Lob er - schallt in E - wig- keit sein
E - wig- keit sein Lob er - schallt
E - wig-keit,] ge - seg- net sey des Her - [ren
Lob er - schallt in E - wig- keit sein

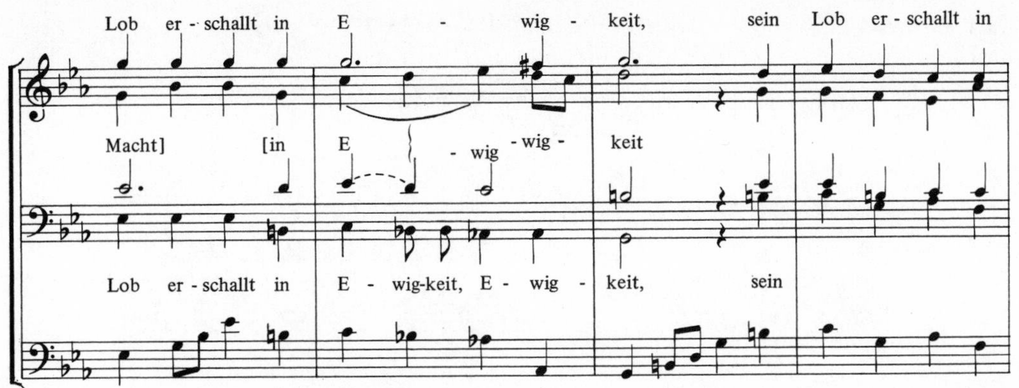

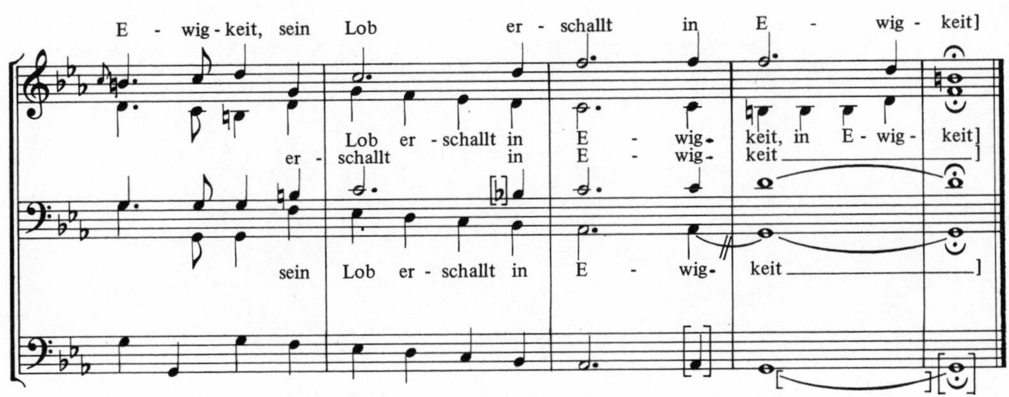

From this sketch we can see that Haydn originally intended to break the text into two parts: to start with 'Von deiner Güt' / 'By thee with bliss', and then to create a new choral number with the entrance of the words 'Gesegnet sey des Herren Macht!' / 'For ever blessed be his pow'r!'.

On fol. VIv. we find a sketch for the final version. The part for the bass solo (Adam) is left blank and the chorus laid out differently; note the curious double stems in bar two of the chorus part's soprano; we have transposed this sketch into modern notation (see overleaf). The sketch continues for some bars along these lines. At the bottom of the page (which contains various words, phrases, places where Haydn tests his quill pen, etc.) is a long passage of the final version's first violin part with its characteristic rhythm [rhythm figure].

Even before this rather complete draft, we can find, on fol. Ir., the bass entrance at bar 5 and with the chorus murmuring the words

[No. 30 – sketch for final version (ÖNB, Codex 16835, fol. VIv.)]

Sop. Solo: Von dei - ner Güt, O
Sop.: ge - seg - net sey des Her - ren
Alto
Ten.
Basso
B. C.

Herr - und Gott, die Erd'
sey Macht ge- [seg - net sey des Her - ren Macht]

but with the harmony shifted slightly. There are also sketches for the figure

(bar 18, etc.). In this same series of sketches, we find an interesting proof of Haydn's old method of writing appoggiature. In the famous 'Applausus' letter of 1768 Haydn asks that the following section

(see CCLN, 9–11). In our sketch at bar 20 we find the following

which in the final version is written out as

This particular example answers the many queries that have been made, as to whether the same kind of appoggiatura notation prevailed in 1798 as it had thirty years before. Max Friedländer was, therefore, quite correct in applying this 'Applausus' example to Schubert *Lieder* (see his standard edition for Edition Peters, Leipzig).

On fol. VIv. there is another sketch (quoted above), which is also continued on VIIr. – all to the first part. We also possess sketches to the Allegretto (bars 48ff.), on fol. VIIv. Once again, the turn at bar 62 is a crossed turn in the sketch. The choral entry at bars 83ff. (with upbeat) is also present in short score, also the soprano passage at bars 158–61 ('Groß sey sein Nahm') and several other sections (soprano solo, bars 148–51, with text). Fol. VIIIr. has more sketches to the Allegretto but written in four-four time, e.g. at bars 195ff. the sketch reads:

– basically the same except for the notation.

There are brief sketches for No. 31 (hardly anything was changed) and No. 32 (fol. XIIIv. and XIVr.), including the entrance of Adam in No. 32 at bars 9ff. (up to bar 30, with the whole text), and also for the part at bars 51–8. Of the final fugue in No. 34 we have a draft of the fugal subject which is slightly different to the one Haydn finally chose:

[Des Her-ren Ruhm, er bleibt in E - wig - keit]

And on fol. IIIr. we have sketches for No. 34, including the stretto at bars 27–31, in its definitive form.

Throughout these sketches and drafts, we have the powerful feeling of looking over Papa Haydn's shoulder and watching the care with which he revised this long masterpiece – one of the few times that we are able to do so. The result bears eloquent testimony to Haydn's self-criticism, industry and innate sense of taste, for almost every single change is one for the better, sometimes significantly so.

III. THE MUSIC

Survey of the Material: (1) List of the Numbers and their orchestration; (2) the authentic sources – (a) the libretto, (b) the music; (3) problems of notation; (4) the general form; (5) the general key structure and problems of tonality; (6) symbolism in the music; (7) the orchestration; (8) analytical notes.

(1) List of the Numbers and their orchestration – based on the Eulenburg miniature score (No. 955), 1925

The principal Soloists are: Gabriel (soprano); Uriel (tenor); Raphael (bass); Adam (bass; = Raphael); Eva (soprano; = Gabriel). [A nameless alto soloist appears in the final chorus, No. 34, only.]

PART ONE

No. 1 Einleitung: Die Vorstellung des Chaos, C minor, *Largo alla breve*→C major. Soloists: Uriel, Raphael. Chorus (SATB). 2 fl., 2 ob., 2 clar. in B, 2 fag., contrafag., 2 cor. in E, 2 *clarini* (trpts.) in C, alto, tenor and bass trbns. (3), timpani, strings. At bar 60 *Recitativo* 'Im Anfange schuf Gott' / 'In the beginning God created'.

No. 2 Aria (Uriel), A major, *Andante alle breve*. With chorus (SATB). 2 fl., 2 ob., 2 fag., contrafag., 2 cor. in A, 3 trbns., strings. 'Nun schwanden vor dem heiligen Strahle' / 'Now vanish before the holy beams'.

No. 3 *Recitativo* (*secco* and *acc.*) Raphael [No tempo, then:]*Allegro assai*. 2 fl., 2 ob., 2 clar. in C, 2 fag., timp., strings [cembalo].

Progressive tonality: six of E minor to V of C. 'Und Gott machte das Firmament' / 'And God made the firmament'.

No. 4 *Chor* [with soprano solo: Gabriel] (SATB). C major, 4/4. 2 fl., 2 ob., 2 clar. in C, 2 fag., contrafag., 2 cor. in C, 2 *clarini* (trpts.) in C, 3 trbns., timp., strings. 'Mit Staunen sieht das Wunderwerk' / 'The marv'lous work beholds amaz'd'.

No. 5 *Recitativo* (*secco*) Raphael. [Progressive tonality: six of D minor to B flat.] 'Und Gott sprach' / 'And God said'.

No. 6 Aria (Raphael), D minor→major, *Allegro assai*, 4/4. 2 fl., [the first edition specifies clearly 'Flauti', not 'Flauto I' as in Eulenburg], 2 ob., 2 fag., 2 cor. in D, str. 'Rollend in schäumenden Wellen' / 'Rolling in foaming billows'.

No. 7 *Recitativo* (*secco*) Gabriel. [Progressive tonality: six of G to B flat.] 'Und Gott sprach: Es bringe die Erde' / 'And God said: Let the earth'.

No. 8 Aria (Gabriel), B flat major, *Andante*, 6/8. 2 fl., clar. solo in B♭, 2 fag., 2 cor. in B♭ [*alto*], str. 'Nun beut die Flur' / 'With verdure clad.'

No. 9 *Recitativo* (*secco*) Uriel. [Progressive tonality: six of G to V of D.] 'Und die himmlischen Heerscharen' / 'And the heavenly host', leading to:

No. 10 *Chor* (SATB), D major, *Vivace*, 4/4. 2 fl., 2 ob., 2 fag., contrafag., 2 cor. in D, 2 *clarini* (trpts.) in D; alto, tenor and bass trbns. (3), timpani, str. 'Stimmt an die Saiten' / 'Awake the harp'.

No. 11 *Recitativo* (*secco*) Uriel. [Progressive tonality: six of C to D.] 'Und Gott sprach: Es seyn Lichter' / 'And God said: Let there be light'.

No. 12 *Recitativo* (*accompagnato*) Uriel. *Andante alla breve*, D major→C major. 2 fl., 2 ob., 2 fag., 2 cor. in D, 2 *clarini* (trpts.) in D, timp., str., cembalo. 'In vollem Glanze' / 'In splendour bright'.

No. 13 *Chor* [with the three soloists] (SATB), C major, *Allegro alla breve* [later 'più allegro']. 2 fl., 2 ob., 2 clar. in C, 2 fag., contrafag., 2 cor. in C [*basso*], 2 *clarini* (trpts.) in C; alto, tenor and bass trbns. (3), timp. 'Die Himmel erzählen' / 'The heavens are telling'.

PART TWO

No. 14 *Recitativo* (*accompagnato*) Gabriel. [Progressive tonality: six of C to F.] *Allegro*, 4/4, str. 'Und Gott sprach: Es bringe das Wasser' / 'And God said: Let the waters bring forth'.

No. 15 Aria (Gabriel), F major, *Moderato alla breve*. 2 fl., 2 clar. in B♭ [not in 'F' as in first edition – merely a misprint of nomenclature because the notation shows that the parts are in B♭], 2 fag., 2 cor. in F, str. 'Auf starkem Fittige' / 'On mighty pens'.

No. 16 *Recitativo* (*secco* and *acc.*) Raphael, D minor. [At first no tempo, then *Poco adagio*.] The *accompagnato* section for 2 violas, 2 'cellos and basso continuo. 'Und Gott schuf große Wallfische' / 'And God created great whales'. Acc. section begins: 'Seyd fruchtbar alle' / 'Be fruitful all'.

No. 17 [*Recitativo secco*, marked in first edition: 'Ad libitum', i.e. Haydn may have omitted it in performance, going straight from 'Seyd fruchtbar' to the *Terzetto*.] Progressive tonality within A minor. Raphael. 'Und die Engel' / 'And the angels.'

No. 18 *Terzetto* (Gabriel, Uriel, Raphael), A major, *Moderato* 2/4. 2 fl., 2 ob., 2 fag., 2 cor. in A, str. 'In holder Anmuth' / 'Most beautyfull appear', leading to:

No. 19 *Chor* (with the three soloists) (SATB), A major, *Vivace*, 4/4. 2 fl., 2 ob., 2 fag., contrafag., 2 cor. in A, 2 *clarini* (trpts.) in D; alto, tenor and bass trbns. (3), timp., str. 'Derr Herr ist groß' / 'The Lord is great'.

No. 20 *Recitativo* (*secco*) Raphael. [Progressive tonality: six of A major to D major.] 'Und Gott sprach: Es bringe die Erde' / 'And God said: Let the earth'.

No. 21 *Recitativo* (*accompagnato*) Raphael. [Progressive tonality: B flat→A flat→A major→D major.] *Presto – Presto – Andante – Adagio*. 1 f., 2 fag., contrafag., alto and tenor trbns., str. 'Gleich öffnet sich der Erd Schoß' / 'Strait opening her fertile womb'.

No. 22 Aria (Raphael), D major, *Maestoso*, 3/4, 2 fl., 2 ob., 2 fag., contrafag., 2 cor. in D, 2 *clarini* (trpts.) in D, timp., str. 'Nun scheint in vollem Glanze der Himmel' / 'Now heav'n in fullest glory shone'.

No. 23 *Recitativo (secco)* Uriel. [Progressive tonality within C major.] 'Und Gott schuf den Menschen' / 'And God created man'.

No. 24 Aria (Uriel), C major, *Andante alla breve*. 2 fl., 2 ob., 2 fag., 2 cor. in C [*basso*], 2 *clarini* (trpts.) in C, timp., str. 'Mit Würd' und Hoheit angetan' / 'In native worth and honour clad'.

No. 25 *Recitativo (secco)* Raphael. [Progressive tonality: six of F to B flat.]'Und Gott sah jedes Ding' / 'And God saw ev'ry thing'.

No. 26 *Chor* (SATB), B flat major, *Vivace*, 4/4. 2 fl., 2 ob., 2 fag., contrafag., 2 cor. in B♭ [*basso*], 2 *clarini* (trpts.) in B♭; alto, tenor and bass trbns. (3), timp., str. 'Vollendet ist das große Werk' / 'Achieved is the glorious work'. Leads without pause to:

No. 27 [*Terzetto*: Gabriel, Uriel, Raphael], E flat, *Poco Adagio*, 3/4. 1 fl., 1 ob, 2 clar. in B♭, 2 fag., 2 cor. in E♭, str. 'Zu dir, o Herr' / 'To thee each living soul'. Modulates to and leads into:

No. 28 *Chor* (SATB), B flat major, *Vivace*, 4/4. Instr. and text – No. 26.

PART THREE

NO. 29 *Recitativo (accompagnato)* Uriel. E major, *Largo*, 3/4. 3 fl., 2 ob., 2 fag., 2 cor. in E, str. 'Aus Rosenwolken bricht' / 'In rosy mantle'. Towards the end the tempo changes to 'Più moto' and the music modulates to G major.

No. 30 [*Duetto* with chorus: SATB; Eva and Adam]. C major (*Adagio*)→F major (*Allegretto*)→C major; *alla breve*→2/4. 2 fl., 2 ob., 2 fag., contrafag., 2 cor. in C [*basso*], 2 *clarini* (trpts.) in C, timp., str. 'Von deiner Güt' / 'By thee with bliss'.

No. 31 *Recitativo (secco)*. Adam [Progressive tonality: six of B flat to E flat with two tempo changes: *Allegro*, then *Andante*.] 'Nun ist die erste Pflicht erfüllt' / 'Our duty we performed now'.

No. 32 *Duetto* (Eva, Adam), E flat, *Adagio* 3/4→*Allegro* 2/4. 2 fl., 2 ob., 2 clar. in B♭, 2 fag., 2 cor. in E♭, str. 'Holde Gattin' / 'Graceful consort'.

No. 33 *Recitativo (secco)* Uriel. [Progressive tonality: six of C minor to B flat.] 'O glücklich Paar' / 'O happy pair'.

No. 34 *Chor* (SATB) [with four solo voices (SATB)]. 2 fl., 2 ob., 2 clar. in B♭, 2 fag., contrafag., 2 cor. in B♭ [*basso*], 2 *clarini* (trpts.) pn B♭; alto, tenor and bass trbns. (3), timp., str. 'Singt dem Herren alle Stimmen!' / 'Sing the Lord, ye voices all!'.

(2) The Authentic Sources

(a) The sources of the libretto are:

A. Autograph by Baron Gottfried van Swieten, Országos Széchényi Könyvtár (*ex coll.* Esterházy Archives and Haydn's library), Ha. I. 12. *Vide supra.*

B. Original Libretto: 'Die Schöpfung. / In Musik gesetzt / von / Herrn Joseph Haydn / Doktor der Tonkunst / und / Kapellmeister in wirklichen Diensten / Sr. Durchl. des Hrn. Fürsten von Esterházy. / Wien, / gedruckt bey Matthias Andreas Schmidt, / k. k. Hofbuchdrucker. / 1798'. Copies: Gesellschaft der Musikfreunde (Vienna), Österreichische Nationalbibliothek, Vienna. In this form, with slight variations, the libretto was printed in the *AMZ* I, Beilage VII (30 Jan. 1799), pp. xxi-xxiv.

(b) The sources of the musical score are:

A. Copy of the lost autograph by Johann Elssler and assistants, in three volumes in oblong format from the Tonkünstler-Societät; now Stadtbibliothek, Vienna. The score has no room for the wind instruments (cf. Mozart's *Don Giovanni* autograph, K. 527, also the autograph of Mozart's Mass in C minor, K. 427, and the late Haydn Masses of 1801 and 1802, for similar procedures).

A¹. The original performance material, also from the Tonkünstler-Societät Archives and now in the Stadtbibliothek. Both A and A¹ have many holograph additions and corrections by Haydn. A¹ was prepared by Johann Elssler and assistants. This original performance material shows the large forces which Haydn used at the public performances of 1799: one of the violoncello parts is dated 22/23 Dec. 1799: *vide infra* for this performance of the Tonkünstler-Societät. Both A and A¹ were discovered in 1952 by the present writer. In A and A¹ the angels do not yet have names, which appear for the first time in the original libretto for the first performance.

B. MS. score by Johann Elssler and an assistant (the so-called 'Anonymous 63'), with many holograph corrections and additions by Haydn and from his library, in the Stiftung Preußischer Kulturbesitz (formerly Preußische Staatsbibliothek), Berlin,

The opening of the Introduction to *The Creation* – 'Chaos' – in the first violin part from the original performance material copied by Johann Elssler in 1798. The '*f*' at the beginning of line 2 and some other small additions are in Haydn's own hand.

Mus. ms. 9851. Here, too, the angels were at first anonymous, their names being added, as was the English text, apparently by van Swieten himself. Several textual details show that B represents a 'middle source' between the A group and the definitive version.

B[1]. The orchestral material that originally belonged to B, prepared by Johann Elssler and assistants, now in the Esterházy Archives of the National Széchényi Library, Budapest, Ms. mus. o, 15. In the Haydn *Verzeichniss musicalischer Werke*, No. 219 lists 'Die Schöpfung ausgeschrieben samt der / Partitur nach dem Original', which in the final inventory of Haydn's effects was listed as 'ausgeschrieben mit doppelten Stimmen für ein/stark besetztes Orchester' (item 350). The score 'copied from the original' ended up, as we have seen, in the Berlin Library, while the parts 'with doubles for a large orchestra' were acquired by Prince Esterházy, who also received the authentic parts for *The Seasons* (see Source A[1]).

C (1–4). Authentic MS. scores by Johann Elssler and assistants in: (1) Lobkowitz Archives, now Prague; (2) Landeskonservatorium Graz (a Vienna copy but probably based on, or prepared under the supervision of, the Elssler copyist group); (3) Gesellschaft der Musikfreunde; and (4) also Gesellschaft der Musikfreunde with the same particularities as to its origin as in source (2) *supra*. No doubt there are more of these scores, which were probably prepared in the Summer of 1798 and the Spring of 1799, in other libraries in Europe.

D. The engraver's MS. for E. D is in tall folio score, with all the instruments, written by Johann Elssler, Gesellschaft der Musikfreunde, Vienna, III 7938. It also contains the English text and also the 'Appendix' just as it is found in:

E. The authentic first edition, with German and English text, of the work issued by subscription in 1800 and printed for Haydn himself (distribution by Artaria & Co.). Later Breitkopf took over the plates and reissued the score. 'DIE SCHOEPFUNG / Ein Oratorium / In Musik gesetzt / von / JOSEPH HAYDN / Doctor der Tonkunst, der köngl. Schwedischen Academie der / Musik Mitglied, und Kapellmeister in wirklichen Diensten / seiner Durchlaucht des Herrn Fürsten von Esterhazy. / THE CREATION / An / Oratorio / Composed / by / JOSEPH HAYDN / Doctor of Musik [*sic*], and Member of the Royal Society of Musik in Sweden, in actuel [*sic*] Service of his Highness / the Prince of Esterhazy. / Vienna / 1800.' With a list of subscribers. (Concerning this list, *vide infra*, pp. 619ff.) Some copies were printed on Japan paper ('Büttenpapier') and signed personally by Haydn. The original edition consisted of some 550 or 600 copies (507 copies are given in the subscribers' list, but this list was not quite complete; *inter alia* Breitkopf & Härtel and at least two names from England, the Duke of Leeds and Sir William Pearson, are wanting from it). Apart from the title page, subscription list, etc., the score consists of 303 engraved pages of music. Copies are in most of the major libraries; we used the one in our own library.

Modern critical edition: as Series 16, Band V of *Joseph Haydns Werke*, Breitkopf & Härtel 1924, edited by Eusebius von Mandyczewski from source E. From this the above-mentioned Eulenburg edition was taken in 1925. Although E undoubtedly represents the musical text Haydn chose to send into the world, certain details of the earliest authentic manuscripts were *not* incorporated into it: for a striking example, *vide infra*, p. 395, under 'Problems of Notation' (the 'stopping point' for a 'hairpin' *crescendo-decrescendo* in the violins of 'Chaos'). Although these are details that Haydn considered not sufficiently important (or too complicated for the engraver) to include in the final score, it would be useful to have a new critical score of *The Creation* which showed all the earlier readings as well as such matters as the 'stopping point' mentioned above. But on the whole, Haydn's Oratorio, having been issued by subscription in an authentic score, has always been one of the composer's works with the least textual problems; compared to it, earlier works such as *Il ritorno di Tobia* (1775) contain textual problems of monumental size.

(3) Problems of Notation

The Creation would seem to be an obvious choice among Haydn's late works to discuss briefly some problems of notation which had arisen since Haydn had abandoned his own band in 1790 to write for the public orchestras of London. Since 1761, Haydn had been with the Esterházys, and before that he had composed orchestral works for his own band at Count Morzin's (*c.* 1759–61). This means that most of Haydn's ensemble music between 1759 and 1790 had been composed for his own musicians. Naturally within a short period they must have become used to Haydn's notation, his curious 'shorthand' phrasing, his idiosyncratic ornaments, whereby ♩♫♩ ♩♫♩ | ♩♫♩ was the kind of pattern usually phrased ♫ throughout and the performance of ∾ was known as an abbreviation for a 'crossed turn' ♬♩. The slipshod and internally chaotic and often self-contradictory phrasing marks of his autographs must be largely the result of knowing that the work in question would shortly after its completion be rehearsed under the composer's supervision and such notational problems solved on the spot. Nevertheless there are problems which not even Haydn's own musicians could have solved easily. One of these concerns the discrepancies that often occur between nearly identical material in the exposition and recapitulation of a given work. In a previous book we have discussed this and other problems,[1] some of which arose because Haydn wrote out his recapitulations from memory – a phenomenal feat in itself which however also repeats itself in Mozart's and Beethoven's scores. Mozart was accustomed to write for 'pick-up' orchestras and was thus very careful about phrasing marks; and Beethoven's apparently chaotic scores show, upon careful examination, an admirably precise notation which is finely organized and belies the rather wild appearance of the handwriting. Nevertheless their expositions and recapitulations show clear evidence that the latter were composed (or rather put down on paper) from memory: otherwise how is one to account for the extraordinary differences between the phrasing of the main subject in Mozart's Symphony in E flat, K. 543, as it appears first in the exposition and then in the recapitulation? Or the almost equally inexplicable differences between the second violins' phrasing (a) the first time the second subject of the 'Jupiter' Symphony's (K. 551) Finale appears at bars 74ff. and (b) when that passage reappears in the recapitulation (bars 272ff.)? In our edition for the *Neue Ausgabe sämtlicher Werke* of these last three Mozart Symphonies, we have occasionally attempted to show these differences by putting the reading of Mozart's autograph in bold-type phrasing marks and placing Mozart's own phrasing marks in the other context underneath in dotted lines.[2] Similar problems may be observed in

1 Landon, *SYM*, 74ff.

2 *Serie IV, Werkgruppe 11: Sinfonien, Band 9*, Kassel 1957, pp. 4f., 15f., 240f., 255f.; the discrepancies in K. 543's opening movement were so profound that the parallel system of bold-face slurs and dotted lines could not be carried out without introducing an element of total chaos into the finished score. The conductor's problems, even in this late-eighteenth-century music, are graver than some of them realize; for it is, in the last analysis, they and not the musicologists who must make the ultimate decisions in such cases. The student unaware of these problems should perhaps be warned that these notational problems in Mozart cannot be seen in the average practical score, where the editors have had to make a decision and 'adjusted' the Mozartian discrepancies as best they could.

Beethoven's works, especially those of the so-called first period, when his musical language was most closely allied to those of his illustrious predecessors.

When Haydn went to England in 1791, he found, of course, orchestras which were not only unknown to him but with which he could not rehearse properly since, at the beginning of his stay in London, his English was practically non-existent. We note that the autograph manuscripts of Symphonies Nos. 96 and 95 – the first two 'Salomon' Symphonies to be composed (and in that order: *vide Haydn in England 1791–1795*) – are hardly different from those works written shortly before for Eszterháza, e.g. the 'Oxford' Symphony of 1789. But as Haydn's London sojourn continued, the phrasing, dynamic marks and the notation altogether become more precise; marks like 'vicino al ponticello' (such as we find in Symphony No. 97's autograph of 1792) or the delicately accented phrasing in Symphony No. 99, first movement, second subject (autograph of 1793) are things that hardly appear in Haydn's works composed for the Esterházy band.

When Haydn returned to Austria in 1795, he continued to compose for a 'house orchestra' at the Esterházy Castle in Eisenstadt; but as readers of the Chronicle will have observed, only the nucleus of that orchestra remained constant. The wind instruments varied widely between one year and the next; the soloists changed, too; and besides, Haydn sometimes conducted early (or indeed even first) performances of some of his Esterházy works with pick-up orchestras, such as the Piaristenkirche performance in December 1796 of the *Missa in tempore belli* which has been discussed *supra*. Apart from the Masses of 1796–1802, and the occasional theatrical music (such as that to *Alfred* of 1796), Haydn's works were now largely for the general public and for unknown groups: unknown in the sense that he could hardly foresee, when he began such a work as *The Creation*, the exact disposition and constitution of his vocal and instrumental forces – e.g. who would be first clarinet or second trombone, or who would be his choral singers. Thus we note that from 1795 to 1803, Haydn's scores continue to be more precise than his pre-1790 scores had been, and that he was, in Austria, continuing the new tradition established in his later English works. But enough problems remain. There are still curious and largely inexplicable differences between exposition and recapitulation, especially as regards phrasing. The Trio of the last completed Quartet (Op. 77, No. 2; 1799) poses as many problems as did the first movement of Mozart's K. 543. Did Haydn really intend these differences? The phrasing of the recapitulation is dotted.

There are many problems of this kind in *The Creation*, and the few we mention are typical. In bar 7 of 'Chaos', the viola has the famous triplet figure . All the other instruments have this figure with staccato dots only. Does the viola's slur and '3' mean that Haydn wanted a portato phrasing, e.g. all three notes staccato but under one bow, or does it mean simply the old Baroque notation for triplets, which was automatically rather than our simple '3'? Haydn obviously expected his conductors to 'adjust' the occasional slur missing in the woodwind which is doubling, say, the first violin. But how far was the conductor to 'adjust'? In No. 2, the melody begins:

At bar 2, the flute (doubling) has an added slur . Is the violin supposed to have that slur, too? The very opening dotted figure, on the other hand, is not slurred in the flute but presumably should be. When the voice enters, it and the flute have the melody; both the dotted upbeat and the bar corresponding to bar 3 are without slurs in the flute. Perhaps he would have remembered his phrasing from before, or perhaps the conductor would adjust it to correspond with the opening. But what happened in the following situation? In bar 3, the second violin had

When the voice enters the first violin takes over this line and is phrased as follows: . We wonder if the players and the conductor really took the trouble, in performances where there was no Haydn to supervise matters, to iron out these small creases in the otherwise smooth musical fabric. Nowadays, of course, our editions try to solve all these problems before the music ever reaches the players' stands or the conductor's desk.

Another point in the notation proved so problematic that Haydn simply dropped it before the first edition was engraved. It concerns a new experiment on the composer's part to fix the exact middle point of that which is commonly termed, in musicians' language, a 'hairpin' – a combination of *crescendo* and *decrescendo* signs such as are found in great abundance throughout 'Chaos'. The original performance material (sources A–A[1]) show clearly what Haydn wrote, which was as follows (bars 4–7):

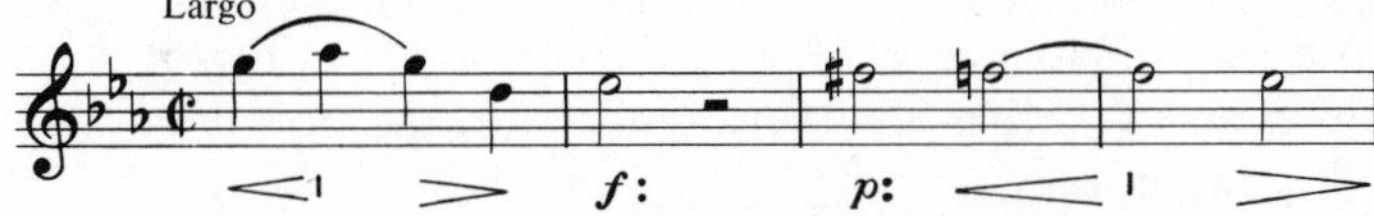

These vertical slashes, which look like Haydn's tall staccato marks, seem to serve two purposes: to 'fix' the middle point of the 'hairpin' but also to provide an accent so that the 'fixing' is aurally noticeable. It was a bold innovation and would have been useful; but Haydn obviously thought it would be misunderstood and so the marking is not included in the first edition, and thus (not being circulated outside Vienna or at most Pest or Eisenstadt, where Haydn may be presumed to have taken the orchestral material with him when he conducted *The Creation* at those places) it was never adopted into general musical language.

A final point may be mentioned as typical of Haydn's musical language. When he was a young man, the kettledrums played scarcely any rolls in Austrian music of the period. Later, when rolls became increasingly fashionable, the notation remained imprecise: or (cf. Symphony No. 103/I, bars 1f.) were often synonymous with rolls, particularly in slow movements. Haydn knew the wavy line, and even the trill and the wavy line; he used them together in bar one of 'Chaos', where he needed the timpani to play

tr

f

Here, he could hardly use or a variant. On the other hand, the tremendous timpani part at the words 'Let there be Light' is written *ff*. In Vienna, this is always played as a trill, as is a similar passage in the introduction to the *Missa in tempore belli*, where at bar 5 Haydn writes (in Largo context)

ff

In our edition of the 'Salomon' Symphonies we have added in brackets our interpretation of [*tr*] or a wavy line when the music is written in the old-fashioned way. The late choral works contain several passages of this nature.

We have said that 'in Vienna, this is always played as a trill'. With that statement we are in the middle of the question of notation and tradition. The former director of the Music Division of the Library of Congress, Harold Spivacke, tells an amusing story. In 1945, the American authorities in occupied Japan asked the late Richard Franko Goldman to go there to conduct some of the highly skilled Japanese orchestras. Having arrived in Tokyo, Goldman started to conduct Beethoven's *Egmont* Overture. After five minutes he put down his baton, horrified. 'What was the matter?' asked Spivacke. 'They were just playing the notes,' explained Goldman.[1] The tradition was missing.

'Just playing the notes' is an unheard-of idea to us, of course, and it is astonishing how much we take for granted in questions of notation. The rolls of the timpani, which the Viennese kettledrummers take to mean, are a case in point. As a matter of fact, the Viennese kettledrummers, who have been playing *The Creation* in an unbroken tradition from 1798 to the present day (not a single year has passed in Vienna without a performance), are quite correct. For this assertion we have, most fortunately, autograph evidence in Haydn's own hand. Just before the recapitulation in 'Chaos' (which occurs at bar 40) there is a bar on the dominant with the timpani playing the following notes

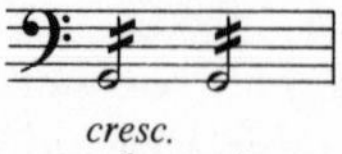

cresc.

Nowadays this is laboriously performed as sixteen semiquavers – except in Vienna. But in the 'final' sketch of 'Chaos' (Codex 18987, fol. 2r., Österreichische Nationalbibliothek) Haydn tells us unmistakably that what he wanted was a long roll.

1 As told to us in January 1973 by Dr Spivacke.

Unfortunately this explanation never reached the first edition, probably because the notation was quite clear to everyone. The sketch is written:

and thus we have first-hand evidence that in slow movements the notation for the drums means, simply, a roll.

(4) The General Form

The Creation is in three rather than the then customary two parts. Although the third part, with its humanistic emphasis on man, was particularly relished by eighteenth-century audiences in Vienna, where the Josephinian heritage was still strong, it later caused problems for audiences. It was felt in some way to be an anticlimax, and in England it was soon omitted entirely. Recently the problem of Part Three has been examined by Siegmund Levarie in a brilliant essay.[1] He writes:

> To Haydn, man was the crown of all creation. Man, therefore, has to be shown in both his aspects as partaking of divinity and succumbing to worldly pleasures. God has touched him, but the snake will get him. He is heroic but also pathetic. He is the protagonist but also his parody.

The higher and lower elements of man's constitution are, continues Levarie, portrayed often in the *commedia dell'arte* and, we might add, are an interesting aspect of Haydn's own marionette opera, *Das abgebrannte Haus* (*Die Feuersbrunst*), wherein the higher people speak and sing in *Hochdeutsch,* the lower in Austrian dialect. In *Le pescatrici* there is the same division of *parte serie* and *parte buffe,* as we might expect from its librettist, Carlo Goldoni, the greatest protagonist of the *commedia dell'arte* and, characteristically, the poet Haydn chose for no less than three of his operas. In Mozart's *Zauberflöte*, the division between the higher and lower elements is well known; in *The Creation,* Haydn's Adam and Eve correspond to Mozart's Papageno and Papagena.

The key structure bears this out, too. In No. 30 we have a complicated pattern in contrast to the simple No. 34 (the love duet), which hardly leaves the tonic and uses the rhythm of the Viennese popular song: Levarie notes (318) that the 'opening horn duo [in the Duet's *allegro*] above a harmonic bass provides the atmosphere of a country dance, which becomes intensified by the fiddling response eight [bars] later. The rhythm ♫ | ♫ ♩ is that of an écossaise, which enjoyed its greatest popularity in Vienna precisely around 1800.'

The fall from grace is spectacularly illustrated in Haydn's choice of keys for Part Three. The basic key of *The Creation* is C, as we shall observe in section (5) (p. 400). But the Oratorio ends in B flat: literally a fall from grace, preceded by a still further fall, the E flat Duet between Adam and Eve. Naturally, the language of the first couple cannot be the same as that of the Divine Spirit.

Having illustrated this point – which is, too, the essence of *Don Giovanni*'s conclusion, also regarded as an anticlimax by the unwary – we may discuss briefly the overall structure of *The Creation*. By the time Haydn began writing the work, in 1796, he had heard and studied the major works of Handel; thus he was in a far better position to provide a balanced oratorio than he had been in 1774–5, when he began to

1 'The closing numbers of *Die Schöpfung*', in *Studies in Eighteenth-Century Music* (Geiringer Tribute), op. cit., pp. 315–22.

write *Il ritorno di Tobia.* At that time, there was no van Swieten (he was in Berlin in Austrian diplomatic service), and Haydn had only his Italian originals (and the Viennese copies thereof): the Metastasian oratorio in two parts which had, in turn, grown out of a long Italian tradition during the century before. The ties between the musical Italian prototypes and the Viennese counterpart were made closer by the fact that Metastasio had settled in Vienna as Court Poet and had even lived in the house on the Michaelerplatz where Haydn had a garret in the early 1750s, and that many Italian composers such as Antonio Caldara had lived in Vienna or parts of the Austrian monarchy (e.g. Prague) and had written oratorios there.

Gottfried van Swieten was a connoisseur of Handel and had indeed instigated a highly successful revival of that composer in Vienna. Swieten's and Haydn's idea was obviously to create a modern Handelian oratorio, using the basic structure of the Baroque era but clothing it in the rich orchestration and harmonic structure of the Viennese classical style. It will be noted that Swieten was very careful to avoid the magnificent pitfall of *Israel in Egypt* – that gigantic masterpiece which is 'like a vast series of frescoes painted by a giant on the walls of some primaeval temple' (Streatfield): possibly Handel's greatest *tour-de-force* but a work rendered difficult by the simple fact of having too many choruses and practically no arias. Haydn was very much aware of the importance of the aria in such a structure. He said to Griesinger (61):

> Handel is great in his choruses but indifferent [*mittelmäßig*] in arias; Gluck is to be praised for his correct intentions and strength, Piccin[n]i because of his grace and his delightful arias. In church music the work of his brother Michael deserves one of the first places, but it is too bad that this genre is so badly paid; for one could earn more money with bagpipes than with Offertories and Masses.

The division between Overture (this was the original title, also in the parts of A[1]), arias, *recitativo secco* and *accompagnato*, and chorus is very delicately balanced. The only duet is between Adam and Eve in Part Three, but the soloists are often used with the chorus (e.g. Duet and Chorus No. 30, also Part Three; the beautiful Terzetto No. 27, which is really part of a larger structure; and of course the famous conclusion to Part One, the Chorus No. 13 'The heavens are telling'). Haydn and Swieten achieved diversity of structure and unity of spirit in their *Gesamtplan*. Here was a real innovation in the oratorio. We may observe the subtlety with which they worked in one aspect of their collaboration, the recitative. The authors seem to have felt that the straight, old-fashioned *secco* would be only of limited use, and we find much of Haydn's finest musical thoughts in the accompanied recitative, of which the sunrise in Part One is perhaps the most spectacular example. Otherwise the *secco* recitatives are kept very short: none at all appears until No. 5, and it is twelve bars long. Nos. 7, 9, and 11 are all less than ten bars long. By the time Part I ends, we see that the *secco* has become a foil, a method of relaxing the ear after the heavily orchestrated choruses, the rich arias and the colourful *accompagnati*. The recitatives in Part Two are equally short: only one (No. 23) is longer than ten bars, and it is only eleven. When we reach Part Three, we realize that the *secco* has become primarily modulatory, colouristic and structural; for here we are suddenly confronted with the only long *secco* in the whole Oratorio: No. 31. Bearing in mind Haydn's and Swieten's determination to reduce the tension after the stupendous No. 30, to prepare the *Singspiel*-like, *commedia dell'arte* atmosphere of our first parents, Adam and Eve, the ensuing *secco* assumes quite a different meaning. What better way to reduce poetry to prose (*secco* declamation being the next thing to real prose), to introduce the richly orchestrated but nonetheless 'conventional' Duet No. 32? After Adam and Eve have sung with the angels and partaken of the Divine Hand – rather like Michelangelo's awe-inspiring fresco in the Sistine Chapel of Adam receiving Life – they now sing with each other. And to lower the musical and spiritual plateau to earthly size, we have the least dramatic musical form of the Oratorio: the *recitativo secco*. The angels are fled: we are among mortals. And that is why it is not the three Archangels who sing in the final chorus but four mortals (including, to make the point even clearer, an alto solo who has never appeared before). The great final chorus is in Haydn's most splendid B flat – but sung by mortals and therefore a whole note below the raptures of the Archangels where 'no tongue was foreign'.

Baron van Swieten was a great admirer of contrapuntal forms, as one might expect from a man of his taste and musical convictions. Haydn, too, was one of the last composers to whom fugal writing was as natural as putting pen to paper. Thus we should not be surprised at the large-scale and magnificent fugues with which the two collaborators provided their Oratorio at crucial points: Nos. 10, 13, 28 and 34 all contain splendid, large fugues or double fugues and there is *fugato* writing in other choruses such as Nos. 19 and 26. Of course, these fugues are not simply neo-Baroque but are rather modern, that is, not only with modern orchestration but in free form. The stupendous modulation towards the end of No. 13 ('The heavens are telling') up to the supertonic is typical of the 1798-ish twist which Haydn constantly manages to give this old-fashioned form. It may be said that Haydn and Mozart kept the fugue not only alive but gave it a new direction; from Haydn's Op. 20 fugal finales in the 'Sun' Quartets, through Mozart's fantastic fugues in the Mass in C minor (K. 427) – known to the Viennese at that time only in its slightly later adaptation as *Davidde penitente* (K. 469) – and the C minor fugue for two pianos (later the end of the stunning Adagio & Fugue for strings, K. 546), to the late choral fugues of Haydn – all formed part of what we might call the Second Viennese Contrapuntal School. Nor were these fugues without a persuasive literary and scholastic advocate in Johann Georg Albrechtsberger, whose theoretical works were widely known and respected, and who himself was a composer of no mean abilities. But if, with the exception of such works as Mozart's Mass in C minor and Haydn's *Missa Cellensis* ('Mariazellermesse'), both composed in 1782 (Mozart's possibly also in 1783 as well), the Viennese tradition in fugues had lately tended to be instrumental rather than vocal, largely because of the Josephinian reforms in church music forbidding 'figuraliter' Masses, after Mozart's *Requiem* (1791), the use of large masses revived, and with it choral fugues. Haydn's late choral music, which only occupied six or seven brief years of his life (1796–1802), created such a profound impression that it completely revived not only the oratorio as a form but also the choral fugue as an integral part. Without it, we can hardly imagine Beethoven's *Missa solemnis* and the whole revival of Austrian church music (Schubert, Diabelli, Bruckner, etc.), or the reinvigorated oratorio form which gave us Mendelssohn, Elgar and even Franz Schmidt and Benjamin Britten.

(5) The Key Structure

As readers have gathered, *The Creation* is in progressive tonality. The reasons for this procedure have been explained above and concern the introduction of Adam and Eve into the world of the angels, of God and Satan, the fallen angel. Interestingly, man's fall, in Haydn's and Swieten's scheme, is in some ways greater than Satan's, who falls in C minor, the key of 'Chaos' – *vide infra* – and still the main key; in the Miltonian scheme, and thus in Haydn's and Swieten's, Satan was still, after all, an ex-angel and nearer the central scheme of the universe than man after the Fall. Man starts in C but, having fallen, can never regain that heavenly key.

The overall tonal scheme of *The Creation* is as follows:

Part One

No. 1	*No. 2*			*No. 3*
C minor→C major	A major→	C minor→ (hell's spirits and the endless night of 'Chaos')	A major→ ('Und eine neue Welt' / 'A new created world')	F major→

No. 3 (cont.)		*No. 4*	*No. 5*	*No. 6*	
D minor→ ('storms now dreadful' show us 'as chaff by the wind are impelled the clouds')	C major	C major	→	D minor→	D major

No. 7	*No. 8*	*No. 9*	*No. 10*	*No. 11*	*No. 12*	*No. 13*
→	B flat	→	D major	→	D major→	C major

Part Two

No. 14	*No. 15*	*No. 16*	*No. 17*	*Nos. 18–19*	*No. 20*	*No. 21*
[C→]	F major	D minor	→	A major	→	B flat→A flat→

No. 21 (cont.)	*No. 22*	*No. 23*	*No. 24*	*No. 25*
D flat→A major→D major [= C sharp]	D major	→	C major	→

Nos. 26	*27*	*28*
B flat	E flat→	B flat

Part Three

No. 29	*No. 30*	
E major→G major	C major→F major → [F→B♭→A♭→G♭→[E♭ minor→F minor→ G minor→G major→]	C major

No. 31	*No. 32*	*No. 33*	*No. 34*
→	E flat	→	B flat

First, a few words about Haydn's association of keys. Anyone who has studied the music by the Viennese classical masters knows that they – consciously or unconsciously – associated certain ideas with certain keys. A great deal has been written about Mozart's use of G minor and Beethoven's of C minor, to choose two obvious cases. With Haydn, we remember that C major always meant the key of pomp, princes and emperors (or rather empresses): his symphonies show a small but characteristic line of such C major symphonies, which at the beginning graced the splendid baroque halls of monastery and castle and later the concert halls of Paris and London. But for the average Austrian, C major also meant something quite specific: it was *the* key of the *Missa solemnis figuraliter*, with trumpets and kettledrums. If we examine the thematic catalogues of Austrian monasteries at the time when Haydn's name emerged from the *Kleinmeister* to become Austria's leading composer, we may note that for Göttweig, Melk, Herzogenburg, Kremsmünster or Stams, C major was the predominant key of solemn Masses. Over half of the instrumental Masses from 1750 to 1800 in Austria are in C major. Consequently it was clear to Haydn's audience at the end of the century that the heavens told the glory of God in C major, as countless Masses and Oratorios and cantatas had done before – including Haydn's own Masses for Mariazell (the first of 1766, the second of 1782) and the Cantata *Applausus* for Zwettl Abbey in 1768, not to speak of most Mozart Masses, just then becoming famous. The progress from darkness and chaos to light, or from C minor to C major, was equally obvious, given the fact of Heaven being in C major.

Other keys represented other things. D minor was one of Haydn's old *Sturm und Drang* keys – the key of the *Sinfonia lamentatione*, the first great String Quartet from Op. 9 (No. 4) – and it also represented *Sturm* in a more direct sense. In *Le pescatrici* of 1769, Haydn had written a 'storm' aria in that key:

Varca il mar di sponda in sponda
Quel nocchier ne si sgomenta,
Ed allor, che meno il teme
Sorger vede il vento e l'onda
Le sue vele a lacerar.

Haydn's Madrigal 'The Storm' (London, 1792) is in D minor. And in *L'anima del filosofo* (1791), the opera closes with a ferocious D minor chorus in which the lascivious *baccanti* are drowned and the stage left empty – in D minor. In No. 3 of *The Creation*, we have noted above a description of a storm, and as we might expect it is in D minor. Not only that: when Haydn returns to D minor in No. 6, not only does the text describe waves rolling and crashing but Haydn actually quotes from the storm words in No. 3. The figure

f (No. 3, bar 13)

becomes (No. 6, bars 32/24)

and

If C major is the heavenly key, D major – from Baroque times and even earlier, perhaps – meant rejoicing, brilliance and (in north Germany) the key of trumpets and kettledrums. This was not so much true of Austria, as we have seen, but D always sounds brilliant because of the open strings available. It is therefore no accident that 'Nun scheint in vollem Glanze der Himmel' / 'Now heav'n in fullest glory shone' (No. 22) is in D major. And once we associate it with 'fullest glory', it is clear that the first sun must rise over the darkened earth in D major, as it does in that miraculous passage so admired by Haydn's old English friend, William Shield (who quoted it in his book on harmony[1]). Haydn had once composed a Mass in D minor (the lost *Missa 'Sunt*

1 *Rudiments of Thorough Bass for Young Harmonists . . . being an Appendix to An Introduction to Harmony*, London, n.d. [watermark date of our copy: 1802], p. 21, 'the Diatonic scale in the treble most ingeniously accompanied'.

bona mixta malis') but it was not until the 'Creation' year, 1798, that he composed a late Mass in D; the 'Nelson' Mass is certainly the most martial and brilliant of all Haydn's extant works in the form.

It will be noted that Haydn, in Part Two, breaks away from C and does not return to it until No. 24. Here we have an aria of central importance to composer and librettist, 'In native worth', the music that celebrates the humanistic (also Masonic) concept of man. Untainted as yet, the first human is still in God's image, and therefore in C major. In the triple number that follows shortly (Nos. 26–28), however, the key already sinks to B flat with a long and beautiful Terzetto in E flat placed in the middle. Although sung by the angels – Adam and Eve have yet to appear on the scene – Haydn and Swieten tell us that the celestial key of C must give way to B flat and man must fall from grace. Yet the middle section introduces a new key to us: E flat major, the humanistic, Masonic key *par excellence*: it is, symbolically, related both to C major and to B flat. Its appearance at this critical juncture cannot have escaped the Viennese, steeped as they were in Mozart's *Zauberflöte* and its symbolic portrayal of the two sides of the universe and the two aspects of man. In this third-related key, the angels still sing, and man could become a Sarastro; but he could also, if the key were subdominant, fall from grace and end, as it were, in B flat. At the end of the sixth day, there is, *pace* Haydn and Swieten, still hope – but once we close in B flat (No. 28), the move to lower regions, tonally and morally, is clear. Similarly, Adam and Eve start their song of praise in C major (No. 30), and their fall is made into one of the most complex tonal structures of the whole work: the fall is at first catastrophic and takes us from F major through B flat, A flat, G flat(!) to E flat minor, then raises us through F minor, G minor, G major to the last pages of C major in the Oratorio. And so we take leave of 'this world, so great, so wonderful' which 'Thy mighty Hand has fram'd': no wonder that Sir Donald Tovey advocated bringing the work to a close with this number.[1] Yet the story is not yet over, and we cannot end here. If Adam and Eve are not so fascinating as the Archangels and the heavenly host, we deserve to hear their song nonetheless.

Those who have perused the scheme above will have noted that third-related keys play an important role, and not only between numbers but also within some of them. Two of the most spectacular uses within a single number are the fall in No. 2 discussed above and the modulation in No. 24 from the dominant (G) to A flat, the flattened submediant of C: and once again we note the inherent warning, for the 'breath and image of his God', while couched in C major, 'falls' into the *flattened* submediant (not to the real submediant, which would have been A major). This is perhaps the most famous piece of *Terzverwandschaft* in the work, but there are others equally interesting. One is the fact that immediately after light has been given to earth (C major) we plunge without warning into A major, the real submediant (naturally the real and not the flattened: this is still the heavens), and then return to C minor for the description of hell's spirits. Another is the interesting enharmonic and third-related modulation in No. 21, where D flat must be considered also as C sharp and in this way the link to the A major that follows without transition. As a final example we might mention the beginning of Part Three. Here in No. 29 the music begins in the radiant key of E major (the mediant major of C); Haydn uses the real mediant rather than the flattened mediant (which would be E flat major) because, at the dawn of life ('the morning young and fair') the 'blissful pair, where hand in hand they go' is still innocent; when

1 *Essays in Musical Analysis*, V, 145 (London 1937), hereinafter '*Essays*'.

they have partaken of the apple we find them in E flat (Duetto No. 32). But at this stage they still reflect heavenly grace, and at the end of the E major introduction the music modulates to G (the mediant of E) which in turn is the dominant of C major, the key of the next number (No. 30). C major is the home key and, as we have said above, the submediant of E.

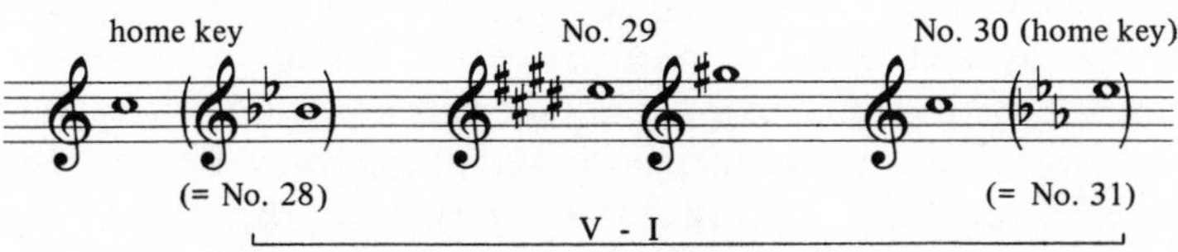

From this very brief survey it will be seen that the tonal construction of *The Creation* is of great intricacy, and is inextricably connected with the symbolic nature of Swieten's text and, even more, Haydn's music. It therefore seems natural to discuss, also briefly, the Oratorio's symbolism.

(6) Symbolism

The Creation's text is, of course, full of symbolism; it is also full of descriptions which automatically suggest *Thonmahlerey*, or the musical realization of these descriptions. We have seen in the section above how Haydn was able to use tonality in a symbolic fashion and at a very subtle level – sometimes, indeed, almost unconsciously. In the present section we propose to deal with the symbolism of the Oratorio on two levels: (1) *Thonmahlerey* (to use the eighteenth-century spelling), and (2) word-symbolism in the larger sense.[1]

Gottfried van Swieten in the libretti to *The Creation* and *The Seasons* shows that he was much attracted to 'word pictures', and from what we know of Haydn's music before 1796, it is clear that the composer – like most eighteenth-century artists – allowed himself to be inspired by the word. The earlier operas are full of 'word pictures', many of great sensitivity and beauty, as are the *Lieder*, the English Canzonettas and other vocal works, secular and sacred. Examples are almost too numerous to require quotation, and we will limit ourselves to mentioning: (a) the 'word painting' in such an opera as *L'infedeltà delusa*, which ranges from 'vices and sins' (No. 10,[2] bars 48ff.) to a laughing fit (No. 12, bars 64ff.), a limping old woman (No. 9, bars 1ff.) and a man who looked for a dowry and found only woe ('guai') instead (this is especially striking: No. 7, cf. in particular 'guai' at bars 113ff.); (b) the 'word painting' in Haydn's Masses – 'descendit', 'ascendit', 'judicare', 'vivos et mortuos', etc., all call forth musical descriptions of the word or phrase in question.

1 One of the first to study this aspect of Haydn's Oratorio was the Mozart scholar, Otto Jahn; cf. his *Gesammelte Aufsätze über Musik*, 2nd ed., Leipzig 1867, pp. 168 (on 'hier sproßt den Wunden Heil' / 'here shoots the healing plant'), noting that in No. 8, bar 86, 'Haydn has given the word 'Wunden' a strongly accentuated expression of pain through the use of G flat in the bass, while the comforting resolution in the major triad is enough for him to paint the word 'Heil [healing]'. This is also possible because the passage in question comes at the end of the Aria, after we have heard the words many times; following the word 'Heil', there are only three concluding bars of orchestral ritornello. There is a large literature on the subject of Haydn's *Thonmahlerey*. The most recent and detailed examination of the subject is perhaps Anke Riedel-Martiny's penetrating *Die Oratorien Joseph Haydns. Ein Beitrag zum Problem der Textvertonung*, Dissertation, Göttingen 1965 (typewritten); using it, the author compiled an article entitled 'Das Verhältnis von Text und Musik in Haydns Oratorien' (*Haydn-Studien* 1/4, 205–39) from which we have greatly profited. We owe our knowledge of the Jahn quotation also to the Riedel-Martiny article.

2 Numbering of the Philharmonia miniature score (No. 450) and the piano-vocal score of the Haydn-Mozart Presse, edited by the present writer (1960).

Objections by theorists such as Johann Georg Sulzer[1] and others seem to have had very little effect on composers, who went on with their *Thonmahlerey* despite critical objections. Actually, Swieten goes further than most librettists: he obviously expected his composer to set to music dogs barking (*Seasons*), thunder and lightning (both Oratorios), crickets chirping (*Seasons* – we shall see that Haydn objected to that idea), lions roaring (*Creation*), and so on. Except for some of the more extravagant ideas in *The Seasons*' libretto, such as the (in)famous 'Praise of Industry', Haydn seems to have gone about his task with relish and great good humour. The German theorists, literary people (and also Beethoven) may have objected to the contrabassoon describing giant animal footsteps, or Haydn's musical description of the loathsome worm; but audiences loved it as much as they loved Papageno's antics with a padlock on his mouth and have been amused by such *Thonmahlerey* ever since – all except the Victorians who, as we have seen and will see in more detail *infra*, were not amused.

In *The Creation*, these descriptive sections are mainly set by Haydn as accompanied recitatives. Aware that such descriptions might cause a loose musical structure, the composer had recourse to rather devious methods to cement such loose musical forms, *inter alia* by thematic similarities in the vocal line. Riedel-Martiny (215) shows a group of patterns used in the *Recitativo* No. 21:

Another form of symbolism is the use of instruments to express a concept. Like the use of keys, this is a very personal attitude and has no more scientific validity than the supposition (say) that E minor is more poignant than D minor. One example will suffice to show that Haydn remained true to such an instrumental symbolism all his life. The Finale of Symphony No. 8 (*Le Soir*) of the year 1761 is subtitled *La tempesta*, and in it the flute makes a zig-zag pattern down the scale in arpeggios which is obviously supposed to depict lightning. A generation later, in *The Creation*, we find the same thing: No. 3, bars 19ff. ('Die Luft durchschnitten feurige Blitze' / 'By heaven's fire the sky is enflamed') where the lightning is portrayed by the flute doubled by the clarinet. And at the beginning of the great storm scene in *The Seasons* (No. 17 in the numbering of the Philharmonia miniature score), the vivid flash of lightning is once again depicted by the flute.

1 *Allgemeine Theorie der schönen Künste*, 2 vols., Leipzig 1771, 1774 (see 'Malerey').

In the second part of the Aria No. 6 it is the violins' legato triplets that describe the brook meandering through the valley – another facet of water as a force, for the beginning of the Aria describes a storm wherein the waves are again described by the violins. It will be recalled that the Swedish diplomat Silverstolpe was particularly enchanted by the second part of this Aria when Haydn played and sang it to him at the pianoforte in his house at Gumpendorf.

On a more subtle level, we may note in 'Chaos' that the slow, swirling mass of void is broken by the first sign of life in the triplet figure ♩♩♩ ♩♩♩ (3 3) and that the void is interpreted for us by Haydn in that there is hardly a single 'complete' resolution of any harmonic progression: at bar 5, when the orchestra comes in with what Karl Geiringer calls an 'impetuous thud', it is neither a C unison chord (as at the beginning) nor a C minor chord, but a mixed chord which sounds like the first inversion of A flat major. We will return to 'Chaos' in section (8) *infra*; suffice it to say here that this 'Overture' or 'Einleitung' is a whole work of symbolism without words: it is, in a sense, up to the listener to make up his own 'programme' when he listens to what is officially called 'Die Vorstellung des Chaos'.

A striking projection of word to music occurs in No. 27, 'Du wendest ab dein Angesicht; da bebet alles und erstarrt. Du nimmst den Odem weg; in Staub zerfallen sie.' / 'But as to them thy face is hid, with sudden terror they are struck. Thou tak'st their breath away; they vanish into dust'. This was one of the passages that impressed Count Zinzendorf. Here Haydn uses several methods to treat the words symbolically: (a) he breaks the flow of the music by suddenly switching to triplets; (b) he leads the bass solo (Raphael) to the bottom register; (c) he takes us to G flat major (home key: E flat). In the English version the low G flat of the Archangel coincides with the word 'dust'; in German it is equally effective, coming earlier but on the note C flat. Notice, too, how Haydn prepares the words 'Du wendest' ('you turn', not quite the same in the English original). Up to this point the orchestra has consisted of wind instruments only (flute, oboe, clarinets, bassoons and horns) with Gabriel and Uriel. They finish their cadence at bars 33f., then the music 'turns away' (a) from the wind band, (b) from the major and (c) from the soprano and tenor soli. All this is 'tone symbolism' of the highest and most effective order.

When Haydn's friend Shield selected the sunrise an an 'ingenious' harmonic example for his textbook, the symbolism will not have escaped him: the music begins *pp* and the inner voices with their chromatic passing notes are indeed like the last shadows of night slowly fading away before the sun's first rays; and when the sun has climbed over the horizon, these passing dissonances disappear and the music resolves the huge *crescendo* on a consonant, blazing D major cadence.

The opposite effect is most beautifully drawn, in black and white, when God exhorts His creatures to be fruitful and multiply (No. 16): here the divided violas and divided 'cellos with the double bass in its lowest register,[1] together with the key of D minor, create a mysterious, veiled sound – as mysterious as the secret of life itself. The whole passage remains *piano* and the complexities of the divine spark of life are mirrored in the intricate, almost Bachian lines of the stringed instruments. Another opposite effect to the sunrise is, of course, the appearance of the first moon

1 The double bass must have a contra-C string: the authentic parts (A^1) and the first edition are clear about this. Eulenburg (pp. 160f.) and other modern editions put the contrabasso part up an octave whenever it goes for longer periods below the present bottom E; but throughout late Haydn, the double bass was expected to have contra C (not E) as its lowest string.

33
tacet
Ob.
Clar. Sib
Fag.
V. I
V. II
Va.
G.
wer - den sie
U.
wer - den sie
R.
Du wen - dest ab dein An - ge-sicht,
B.
Vc., B.
p senza Cembalo Vc.
39
V. I
V. II
Va.
R.
da be - bet al - les und er - starrt.
Vc., B.

---

immediately after the sun's first rays: to greet the moon, the heavy scale is used once again, but softly and at first unharmonized. The moon also rises, but its arrival is 'schleichend' ('slipping' would perhaps be the word, but the English is different here) and also slower (più adagio). The slower tempo is an artifice, of course, designed to aid Haydn's purposes. The 'schleichend' is expressed not only by the slow-moving orchestra (strings only) but also by the two violins' line: the first in a huge legato arc, the second 'slipping' down in suspensions:

The symbolism in *The Creation* is in fact manifest at many different levels – from 'word painting' to the mysticism of 'Chaos' and the identification of keys, especially third-related keys, with philosophic concepts. We can do no more, in a survey of this kind, than hint at the enormous range of this symbolism; but it is there for the student to pursue at far greater length than is possible here.

(7) The Orchestration

'Chaos' gives us a hint – despite its being a kind of programme music – of what the slow movements of Haydn's symphonies might have been like if he had written any after London. The fact is that Haydn evolved a new kind of orchestration with this astounding introduction – the kind of work which must be studied on several levels and from several viewpoints if one is to understand all its ramifications. The score is 'decompacted'. If we examine any late Haydn symphony, the difference will be obvious at first glance. It is not only that 'Chaos' uses more instruments (e.g. trombones) but that they are used throughout in a kind of gigantic obbligato. In particular, we notice the new position given to the wind instruments. Haydn always had a particular affection not only for woodwind but also for brass and timpani, all of which he had used during his career with varying degrees of panache; he had used them, however, according to a well-laid scheme. Melodies were doubled by the flute, the oboe, the bassoon; or by flute and bassoon, flute and oboe, oboe and bassoon. The 'filling in' by wind instruments also proceeded according to a set plan, as did the use of the horns, trumpets, and timpani. Of course, *nulla regola senza eccezione*, and we can easily recall sensational exceptions to all this: horn soli that reach the heights and depths, muted drums and trumpets, and so forth. But there was a definite pattern in Haydn's orchestral scores up to Symphony No. 104; yet a year later (for 'Chaos' was on the whole composed by the end of 1796, as the sketches inform us) we have an entirely new kind of instrumentation: the sort of score in which the strings accompany in quavers (*f* on first beat, *p* on fifth), the second oboe, clarinets, second bassoon, horns (and at the beginning also the trombones) accentuate the first beat but otherwise hold semibreves or breves, while the flutes and first oboe play a melodic fragment and the first bassoon has a semiquaver figure derived from the triplet 'life' figure of the first few bars (see the musical example overleaf).

This is distinctly 'nineteenth-century' music. A few bars later we notice the figure in the strings: that 'throwing off' the bow connected with a sharp *crescendo* which we noticed in connection with the String Quartet in D minor (Op. 76, No. 2). At the end, this curiously unsettling orchestral effect is connected with great *ff* hammer-like chords in the wind instruments and drums, out of which (bar 49) the bassoon emerges alone in an arpeggio figure of repellent force. Just from the standpoint of orchestration, 'Chaos' is the most modern, forward-looking work of Haydn's whole career.

Unfortunately Haydn was adamant in refusing to compose any more symphonies, and one of the reasons was undoubtedly his fascination with combining voices and instruments. Basically almost all eighteenth- and early nineteenth-century composers regarded the combination of voice and instrument as the highest one could offer to the muse: certainly this is the case with Mozart and the old Beethoven ('old' in the relative sense, of course: he was in his fifties . . .), and it is clear that once Haydn began to compose Masses for Esterházy in 1796 and Oratorios for van Swieten and his group, the composer became spellbound by the powerful vehicle he suddenly found himself guiding. Here was a form, in the Mass, that went further than the symphony; and here, in the Oratorio, was something fit to close the career of music's greatest craftsman.

Yet, although he no longer intended to write symphonies – or indeed after the great Trumpet Concerto any purely orchestral works (if we except the mysterious Violin Concerto of 1799: see *Haydn in England 1791–1795*, pp. 168f.) – 'Chaos' shows us the agility of his nearly septuagenarian mind in creating new orchestral sounds. One of the interesting things that strikes us in this introduction is the new and vigorous clarinet writing. Thereby hangs a tale.

In 1761, Haydn wrote a tiny *Divertimento* for two clarinets and two horns (II: 14), the autograph of which, formerly in Riga, is now in Leningrad. About the same year he also used clarinets (always in C, incidentally) in a much larger work, the *Cassatio* in

[Largo]
22
Fl.
Ob.
Clar.
Fag.
Cor.
(Es)
Trbn.
V. I
V. II
Va.
Vc.
B.

C for two clarinets, two horns and strings (II: 17). Haydn was always eager to experiment, but his confrontation with the clarinet in 1760 seems to have been unsatisfactory. Probably the instruments were primitive and lacked completely that 'clarinet sound' which we associate with the instrument. In the 1780s and 1790 we also find the occasional work for clarinet, e.g. the March in *Armida* (1784) or the *Notturni* for the King of Naples (1790) – always with instruments in C. When he went to London in 1791, there were no clarinets in the Salomon orchestra but clarinets in the Gallini Opera. We find, therefore, Haydn's first really characteristic clarinet writing in *L'anima del filosofo*, especially in the mourning chorus of Act III (see *Haydn in England 1791–1795*). In 1794 and 1795 Haydn's orchestras in London all had clarinets, but once again the instruments seem to have been well behind the technical and musical level of Mozart's players in Vienna. Haydn's clarinet writing in Symphonies Nos. 100, 101 and 104 is very cautious; only in Nos. 99 and 103 do we find B flat clarinet parts and 'characteristic' writing for the instrument – though the parts for Clarinets in No. 100 are delightfully written for those military-like instruments in C (alas no longer used).

When Haydn returned to Austria in 1795, he found that the Esterházy musicians in Eisenstadt included a *Feldharmonie*, or *Harmonie-Musique*, consisting of clarinets, oboes, bassoons and horns. The clarinet parts of the two Masses of 1796 (*vide supra*) were composed with these players in mind. They were obviously superior to most of the players Haydn had known hitherto, and the great clarinet solo in the 'Et incarnatus est' of the *Missa in tempore belli* shows that they were capable of a fine tone. But Haydn was still cautious, and there are in fact two sets of clarinet parts for both Masses, the second ones seemingly afterthoughts (this problem has been discussed in some detail, *supra*).

Once Haydn's activities shifted to Vienna, however, things were quite different. We do not know the constitution of the orchestras that played in *The Creation* and *The Seasons*; but from the eye-witness report by Berwald, quoted *infra* (p. 455), on the first public performance of *The Creation* in 1799, we note that both Wranizky brothers led their respective sections of the violins and that therefore the Court Opera Orchestra participated. According to the *Hof- und Staats-Schematismus* for the year 1801 (when Haydn conducted *The Seasons* for the first time), the clarinet players of the K. K. Hofmusik still included 'Klarinetisten. / Hr. Johann Stadler, woh[nhaft] auf der Wien 45. / Hr. Georg Klein, woh. auf der Wieden 167.' Johann was the younger brother of Anton Stadler, for whom Mozart wrote the Clarinet Concerto (K. 622) and the solo clarinet parts of *La clemenza di Tito*, and who was responsible for the basset horn and clarinet with the enlarged bass range. Anton Stadler was prematurely pensioned from the Court Orchestra[1] but lived in Vienna. It is likely that Haydn would have engaged him as first clarinet, or if not Anton, certainly his brother, Johann, the 'official' first clarinettist of the Court Opera. Actually the point is immaterial. What is significant is that Haydn now had the first opportunity of his life to write for clarinet players trained in the Mozartian school (or, if one prefers, in the Stadler brothers' technique and using their newly perfected instruments). We are just beginning to appreciate the close inter-relationship of Mozart and the Stadler brothers, especially Anton, for the development of the clarinet and basset horn between the years *c.* 1782 (when, on 8 February, an imperial *Reskript* suggested that they be

1 For new documentary evidence about the Stadler family, see the article by K. M. Pisarowitz, 'Beitragsversuche zu einer Gebrüder-Stadler-Biographie', in *Mitteilungen der Internationalen Stiftung Mozarteum* XIX 1/2 (1971), pp. 29ff.

engaged in the Court Orchestra) and 1791, when Mozart completed the clarinet Concerto in A (following a draft for basset horn in G, K. 584b) with the extended compass.[1] The characteristic writing for the *chalumeau* register seems to have been a speciality of the Stadler brothers (and, obviously, their instruments). The idiomatic and beautiful clarinet writing in *The Creation* is one of the few instances in Haydn's late works when we may really speak of a Mozartian influence. But without the Stadler brothers and their *buona scuola* neither Mozart's great clarinet 'school' nor Haydn's clarinet writing in the late Oratorios would have come to pass. Examples of the Mozart-Stadler clarinet writing in Haydn's late works are plentiful; we have drawn attention to a fine detail in the *Twenty-Four Minuets* for orchestra (*supra,* p. 85), and if we had to select one completely 'Stadler-ish' passage in *The Creation*, our choice would certainly be the beginning of the Terzetto (No. 27): a long wind-band solo which combines in a fascinating way Mozartian colour and Haydn's language (e.g. the high horn passage in bar 4; the vocal entrance, at bar 4, has been omitted).

Another passage in the finest Stadler tradition is in 'Chaos', where the B♭ clarinets, totally exposed some of the time, have the following figure (bars 27ff.):

(etc. for two more bars).

1 This is obviously not the place to enter into a discussion of the extended compass, but we would point out that, lacking any musical (manuscript) sources of the *Urfassung*, our knowledge that the Breitkopf & Härtel first edition of the clarinet Concerto K. 622 was a falsification of the solo part comes from a detailed review in the *AMZ* IV (1802), 408ff. In various musical examples the reviewer shows that the solo part was altered to be playable by an A clarinet of normal range. Extended basset horns of this type were also produced by Stadler, whose gifts extended to instrumental manufacture as well. In 1801 Anton Stadler left his wife and children to live with his assistant in the clarinet (basset horn) shop, Friederika Kabel. Pisarowitz, 31f.

This whole footnote in Haydn's biography illustrates once again the dependence of the eighteenth-century composer upon local conditions; if Haydn had written *The Creation* in London or Paris at that same time, it is very unlikely that he would have dared to write for the clarinet in this fashion, because it is very unlikely that there were any clarinet players in those capitals trained in the Stadler technique. Once *The Creation* arrived in Paris and London – well ahead of Mozart's solo clarinet music, incidentally, which was not yet printed – the players found a way to perform the music, as indeed they did Mozart's clarinet parts. But it is doubtful if Haydn would have taken the risk *a priori* in Paris or London (or St Petersburg or Rome).

In this survey we have concentrated on essentials, and to close this section on orchestration there is one important innovation to discuss that occurs at the very beginning of the Oratorio. There, we notice in the first edition that there is a bracket across the whole string section, from 'Violino I' to 'Basso', reading 'Con Sordini'. At first we were inclined to believe this must be a mistake. In his symphonies of the early 1770s, where that effect is very prevalent, Haydn *never* marks more than the violins 'con sordino'. Perhaps, we considered, even sources A and A[1] had misread the violins' mutes for the whole string section. But happily, this astounding breakthrough is confirmed by Haydn's autograph sketches in the Österreichische Nationalbibliothek: Codex 18987 (reproduced *supra*); the 'final' sketch for 'Chaos' has at the top of fol. 1, 'Tutti con Sordini'. Since this instruction is written on the top of the score, we wonder in fact if it does not mean that Haydn originally intended also the horns and trumpets to be 'con sordini'. Lacking the autograph itself, we cannot tell whether this was an idea Haydn later abandoned.

We have otherwise taken Haydn's brilliant orchestration for granted. Those who have studied the Masses of 1796 will realize that from the choral-cum-orchestral standpoint, they are the proving grounds for the orchestration of *The Creation*. This is not to overlook such works as *Il ritorno di Tobia* (especially the choruses added for the 1784 revival, 'Ah gran Dio' and 'Svanisce in un momento'), the Madrigal 'The Storm', *L'anima del filosofo* and even Haydn's earlier Masses. But *The Creation* uses trombones, for example, frequently, not just in isolated choruses (as in Act IV of *L'anima del filosofo*). And for the first time Haydn employs the double bassoon, an idea he certainly imported from England. (Were there double bassoons in Vienna, or did they have to be specially constructed? There is hardly any evidence of a double bassoon in Austrian music of the period.) The fabulously professional use of this enormous band in *The Creation* puts the work in a special class of its own.

(8) Analytical notes

We now proceed to analyze the constituent parts of the Oratorio, number by number:[1]

1 The literature on Haydn's late Oratorios is very large, as may be seen even from the articles and books quoted so far. Notes on the music of *The Creation* are even more plentiful. We must restrict ourselves to the essential writings. A penetrating analysis of 'Chaos' was made by Heinrich Schenker, *Das Meisterwerk in der Musik*, Band 2, Munich 1926, pp. 159ff. The most extensive and serious analysis of the music as a whole in English is D. F. Tovey's *Essays in Musical Analysis*, London 1937, V, 114–46. Some useful background material, including some pretty engravings (Haydn's house in Vienna, his birthplace in Rohrau, etc., often detached and sold separately), in the *Denkschrift zur 25jährigen Jubelfeier der Gesellschaft der Musikfreunde des österreichischen Kaiserstaates durch Aufführung der Schöpfung am 5. November 1837*, Vienna 1840. R. von Perger, 'Haydn und das Oratorium', in *Musikalisches Wochenblatt* XL (1909), Leipzig, Heft 9. M. Chop, *Haydns Schöpfung*, Leipzig 1912. E. Schandorfer, 'Die drei Erzengel in Goethe's "Faust" und in Haydn's "Schöpfung" '; in *Musica Divina* XXV (1937), pp. 91ff. All these are useful background articles and booklets.

Part One
No. 1: *Einleitung*

When Raphael enters as the first human voice after the description of 'chaos', he describes the beginning of the world as we know it from Genesis 1, 1–2: 'In the beginning God created the heaven and the earth. And the earth was without form, and void: and darkness *was* upon the face of the deep.' At bars 69f., after Raphael has described an earth 'without form, and void', Haydn writes

We suddenly remember that this double dotted figure was the 'theme' or motif – whatever we wish to call it – that suddenly appeared in D flat major shortly after the opening of 'Chaos': the passage is quoted *supra* (p. 410). In other words, Haydn is telling us that part of his 'Chaos' is 'without form, and void'. This double dotted figure, however, is the *second* sign of life, or organized motion, in 'Chaos'; and it follows us to the end, joining the very opening bars of 'Chaos' to make a vision of unutterable sadness and loneliness such as music would not see again before *Tristan*:

In its inverted motion, we encounter it at bar 31 in the first violins:

where it has a strangely healing effect, as if Haydn himself were bringing order out of chaos. Its appearance thus seems to signify the solidification of matter, perhaps even the forming of the earth, because in the afore-mentioned first recitative, just after Raphael's first words, '. . . created heaven and earth', the orchestra (strings and clarinets) has

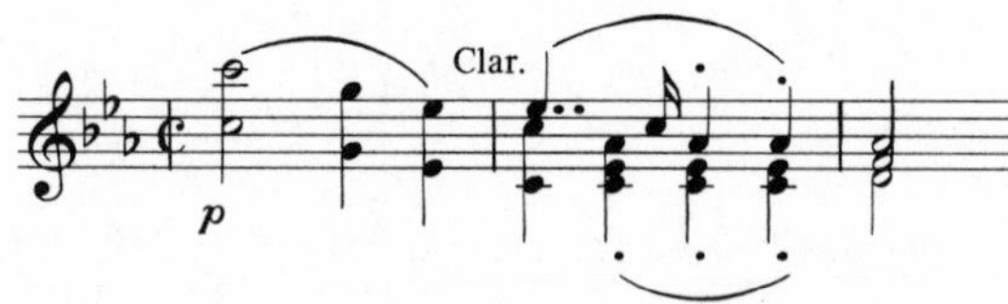

And to make the matter even clearer, the beginning of the No. 2 is based on the same motif:

allied to the arpeggio pattern of the first part in the previous example.

The first sign of life in the total darkness comes in the bassoon figure at bar 6 which may be seen in the sketches. As 'Chaos' continues, this figure gradually becomes more organized: instead of triplets, it becomes semiquavers in the first bassoon (see the quotation, *supra,* p. 410) and then sextuplets in the clarinet (also quoted above). If the development of these two motifs, and the later use of the double dotted one, show a clear progression towards order, many other aspects of the music paint the disorder. It is true that 'Chaos' is in a vague tripartite form, yet the tonal arrangements, as said many times, are so vague and elusive as to mock the basic A-B-A[1] pattern, For one thing, the modulation towards the relative major, E flat, is rudely thrust aside by the D flat passage which introduces the double dotted figure. For another, the ebb and flow of dynamic marks, the characteristic 'hairpin' *crescendo-decrescendo,* is not only what Heinrich Schenker calls 'chaotisches Wogen' but also, of course, the movement of the great oceans with their tides – the first giver of life on this planet. Two instrumental sweeps, one in the clarinet (illustrating 'boundless loneliness' in Geiringer's words) at bar 31 and one in the flute leading to the recapitulation must have sounded as startlingly original in 1798 as did the clarinet glissando in Gershwin's *Rhapsody in Blue* a century-and-a-quarter later. The recapitulation, introduced by a huge crescendo, is like a thunderclap (six staccato sextuplet semiquavers), out of which the horns long-held minim emerges like some frightening formless horror: we are instantly reminded of a similar long-held minim for muted trumpets towards the end of Symphony No. 102's Adagio.

In short, 'Chaos' is the most modern piece of music of its time. Not even Mozart's hair-raising chromatic patterns (as at the beginning of the String Quartet in C, K. 465 – characteristically, one of those dedicated to Haydn – or the Adagio, K. 546, or even the twelve-note flirtations of the Gigue, K. 574), nor Beethoven's bold first and second-period works approach the unorthodox harmonic, structural and instrumental depths of 'Chaos'.

What is really astonishing is that Haydn could compose music that would even outdo the gigantic effects of his introduction; but he did. Miraculous as is the *sotto voce* entrance of the chorus describing the arrival of light ('And the Spirit of God moved upon the face of the waters'), in a burst of choral and orchestral splendour (the mutes having been removed during the previous bar) and introducing C major for the first time, is in the words of Rosemary Hughes (*Haydn*, 134) a stroke of genius at its 'simplest, most inevitable and most elementally moving'. It has never lost its gripping effect on any person of taste and sensitivity.

No. 2: Aria with Chorus

We have spoken of the complex and symbolic key relationships in this A major-C minor-A major piece. The shadows of night flee to 'the deep of abyss, to endless night', and when A major reappears 'A new created world springs up at God's command'. It was the eighteenth-century concept of order restored, it was Masonic symbolism (even to the tripartite form) and man's longing for symmetry; it was Josephinian Enlightenment and the negation of darkness and violence, the banishment

1 In referring to the text without the music, we have given the words in their English original, with Swieten's German adaptation, but when quoting musical examples we have given only the German text. The sketches show that Haydn set to music the German and added the English afterwards. This was not difficult because Swieten had taken immense trouble to see that they were almost identical, and Haydn hardly had to change a note in the concerted numbers (as opposed to the recitatives, where more, albeit small, changes were sometimes necessary). Nevertheless it was the German text that Haydn set to music.

of 'Unordnung und frühes Leid'. Haydn's radiant music – the choice of A with its bright horns is characteristic, and was also dictated by the fact that the trumpets and timpani were silent in this key – is a masterpiece of understatement: the 'new' is treated in such a fashion that each time the musical phrase of eight (typical!) bars is repeated, it is given a slightly 'new' harmonic twist, the final time even to introducing G major (bar 141) as a passing chord. We may single out one detail. When the chorus enters to describe the abyss, the basses begin as follows:

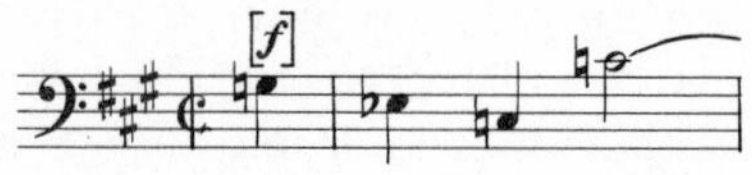

when in the end order has been restored, the chorus sings in unison:

Order has been restored, also motivically.

No. 3: Recitative

We now arrive at the first recitative in which there is only a bass line at first, mostly unfigured; later this number changes into an accompagnato. The Swedish report on the first public performance of 1799 informs us that Haydn's continuo consisted of a fortepiano – not a harpsichord, *nota bene* – with one violoncello and one double bass. Even ten years ago, the presence of a fortepiano would have caused great difficulty even in many major Western cities. Nowadays, restored instruments or modern reproductions are plentiful and this is the instrument that should be used in the secco recitatives of *The Creation* and *The Seasons*.

This is the first of the famous descriptive recitatives in which the music describes some aspect of the universe; these sections are so constructed that the music comes first, the words afterwards. Here we have (1) 'outrageous storms'; (2) 'as chaff by the winds are impelled the clouds'; (3) lightning; (4) thunder; (5) 'showers of rain'; (6) 'wasteful hail'; (7) 'the light and flaky snow' – all portrayed with relish and a great sense of instrumental colour. No. 3 leads directly to

No. 4: Chorus with Soprano Solo

In No. 4 the Archangel Gabriel appears for the first time in a stunning Allegro with oboe obbligato the main subject of which, as we have seen, is taken from the great violoncello solo of the Qui tollis in the *Missa in tempore belli* (*supra*, p. 169). The chorus comes in at bar 16 with as Baroque a conceit as was ever found even in the *Missa Cellensis in honorem B.V.M.* of 1766: the violin's rhythm is doubled by the kettledrums ***f*** and by an oboe arpeggio. (In fact, the *Missa* has just such a drum solo, at bars 29f. of the Credo. It is one more instance of *The Creation* summing up Haydn's whole career.) Formally, the layout seems to be one huge ritornello: solo oboe, soprano, then chorus, then chorus and soprano. There are rudiments of three-part form (with a modulation to the dominant) but all *en miniature*. At the end there is a stupendous passage where the soprano soars above the chorus and orchestra to high *c'''* – only the first flute is in that range, otherwise. No. 4 rounds out the first C major cycle of the Oratorio; the key will not return until the end of the Part One.

No. 5 (Recitative), and No. 6: Aria (Raphael)

A *secco* recitative leads to the first Aria in *The Creation*. Mozart's *Don Giovanni* contained nothing but 'hit' numbers, it was said. The same is true of *The Creation*, and especially its arias, all of which became drawing-room favourites and have remained so ever since. At a time, in the 1920s and 1930s, when *The Creation* was seldom performed in England and almost never performed in the United States, the arias were sung in recitals. There was no complete recording, but the arias were popular on single records, and even an operetta singer like Nelson Eddy turned his hand to 'Rolling in foaming billows'. *The Creation* contains a total of five arias, two in Part One and three in Part Two; the soprano and bass have two each, the tenor one. It is hard to say which of these five is the most popular.

Haydn's bass arias were always said to 'sing themselves', and in his earlier years, his bass soli were indeed of a singular force (e.g. *Stabat Mater*, *Applausus*, *L'infedeltà delusa*, etc.). It is, therefore, with a certain sense of nostalgia that we examine the two magnificent bass arias in *The Creation*. No. 6 even has some technical devices from the music of the late 1760s, for example the violins' repeated semiquavers doubling the voice (bars 42f.) just before the cadence, followed by the ritornello, in the relative major:

Similarly, the series of coloratura quavers in the vocal part at bars 63–5 recalls such passages in the D minor Aria 'Si obstrudat ultimam sors calamitatem' from *Applausus* (1768). But in both instances of *The Creation*, the musical line has to do with the text. In the above example, the top of the mountain coincides with the top of the bass line. In the following

(No. 6, 63ff.) the running quavers literally describe 'runs' in German and the delightful 'in serpent error' of Miltonian English; whereas the equally stunning bass coloratura of the *Applausus* Aria

is simply a technically brilliant method of introducing the conventional bravura runs of the period. We can see in these two instances how Haydn takes technical devices from his earlier works and uses them practically unchanged but in an entirely different concept for *The Creation*.

Formally, too, the Aria has now become the handmaiden of the word and its changing expression. Instead of the A section of the recapitulation (three-part form, A-B-A, with modulation to the relative major), the music stops on a half-cadence and changes to D major, introducing the 'softly purling . . . limpid brook'. To all practical intents, this Aria is *durchkomponiert*: the old form has been totally discarded. We would draw attention to one attractive detail. The horns figure largely in this second section, conjuring up (as they did to the *settecento* gentleman) visions of fields and green countryside. When the oboe solo enters with its bucolic phrase

the second horn, both times (bars 82, 102), has a stopped note which (like the famous 'dying fall' stopped note in the second horn part seventeen bars before the end of the Funeral March in Beethoven's 'Eroica' Symphony) ought to be produced by hand-stopping, not by mechanical means (valves):

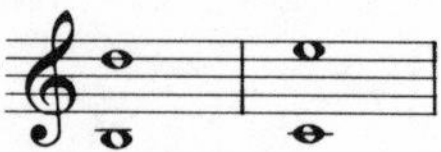

Here again, this stopped note comes from another D major Aria in Haydn's past, also for bass: Melibeo's 'Mi dica il mio signore' from Act I of *La fedeltà premiata*. There it signified the devious character of Melibeo: when the note *c′* is stopped to become *b*, the tone becomes 'cramped'. In *The Creation* it describes 'leise rauschend' / 'softly purling'. The stormy waters of D minor (beginning) are 'cramped' to become a small brook – if the devious metaphor be excused.

No. 7 (Recitative), and No. 8: Aria (Gabriel)

Probably this B flat Aria, 'With verdure clad' is the most famous single Aria in *The Creation*. In its classic simplicity of melody, its elegant off-the-beat phrasing (♪ | ♪ 𝄾 ♪ ♪ 𝄾 ♪ | ♪) and its limpid orchestration (no oboes: only flutes, solo clarinet, bassoons, and B flat *alto* horns), it has become a touchstone for the Viennese classical style in vocal writing – and rightly so. There is just enough coloratura to enable the soprano soloist to display her agility, but never too much. We note the very short ritornello: four bars. This extreme brevity is a far cry from the introductions of Hadyn's operas – often six times that length (e.g. *Le pescatrici,* 'Tra tuoni, lampi e fulmini' [No. 2][1], 'Già si vede i vezzi, e vanti' [No. 18]) – or *Il ritorno di Tobia* (e.g. the slow [Andante] Aria of Tobia, 'Non parmi esser fra gl'uomini', with thirty-seven bars of instrumental introduction). Somewhat the same change took place in Mozart's German operas: compare 'Martern aller Arten' from *Entführung* with 'O Isis und Osiris' or 'In diesen heil'gen Hallen' from *Zauberflöte*. It was part of the trend towards simplicity of expression that is especially apparent in German-language vocal works.

No. 8 is perhaps the end of the great eighteenth-century pastoral tradition. But it shows a real love for the fields 'in verdure clad', not the Petit Trianon pretence of the false farmyard. Haydn's late pastoral style is the logical result of Rousseau's call, 'Back to nature!' It is a cry to which Mozart was, because of upbringing and inclination, largely insensitive. But Haydn, always closely attached to the soil, and now with

1 The numbering from our edition for the Haydn-Mozart-Presse, No. 204, Salzburg 1971.

immense sophistication of musical language, was able to sum up eighteenth-century man's longing for real nature. In a civilization with so much magnificent artifice, the 'Back-to-nature' movement was vitally important, indeed life-saving (or at least, in Haydn's case, life-enhancing). The horn calls (bars 16, 18 and of course later) are all part of Haydn's bag-of-tricks to conjure up the field and hedge: *La chasse* was never far from man's concept of nature in those days, and certainly not from Haydn's. Yet his references to it are oblique: the Aria is in the 'hunting' metre of six-eight, yet we are never given the direct horn calls *à La Chasse* (= Symphony No. 73). The horn and the metre are there, but the 'calls' are nostalgic rather than martial – once again the 'tendre et peut-être un peu berger' of Watteau's art.

No. 9 (Recitative), and No. 10: Chorus

Familiar as we are with the whole of Haydn's *œuvre*, we cannot but be struck with the similarity between this brilliant, energetic chorus No. 10 and the Gloria or Credo of the 'Nelson' Mass; though of course the Mass was composed after *The Creation*. If there is any part of the Oratorio which suggests a direct comparison with Handel, this Chorus is surely it: partly because it is in Handel's characteristic trumpet key of D, partly because we have a fugue in the middle. But we must recall that this is modernized Handel, with the orchestration of the Mozart-ized *Messiah* and with the trumpets restricted (as they were in Mozart's much criticized adaptation). One wonders if Haydn would not have reorchestrated Handel more fittingly than Mozart, to whom this style was basically foreign: we mean not, of course, the Baroque but rather the Oratorio. Mozart was certainly the most universal genius in the history of music, but Oratorio writing did not suit him at all, and Vincent Novello's pious thought that Mozart would have excelled in the 'epic style' (i.e. in the style of Haydn's last Oratorios) can only be excused by the common British attitude towards Handel as the pinnacle of greatness.

Yet if the structure is vaguely Handelian the economy of means is typically Haydnesque. In the fugal middle section, Haydn drops the trumpets and timpani, thus giving more prominence to the trombones, which approximately double the lower vocal lines but never slavishly: note that they do not, for example, follow the opening fugal entries at bars 11ff. (bass, tenor) but join in with the alto entry at bar 15; while the bass trombone enters at bar 19, doubling the *second* vocal bass entry of the fugal subject. By not having the trombones double the vocal lines slavishly, Haydn gives us the aural impression that these ancient brass instruments have obbligato parts of their own. At bar 37 they drop away from the chorus, leaving only the strings in the field for the next few bars. This is to clear the way for the reintroduction of the trumpets, timpani, and indeed all the other wind instruments as well at bar 42. By economy of means, we refer *inter alia* to this famous trumpet- and drum-less gap in the middle of the work. By performing only in the first ten, and the last fifteen, bars Haydn much increases their effect. It is in details such as this that one sees the guiding master-hand. Another detail of typical contrapuntal experience is the pseudo-augmentation of the main theme:

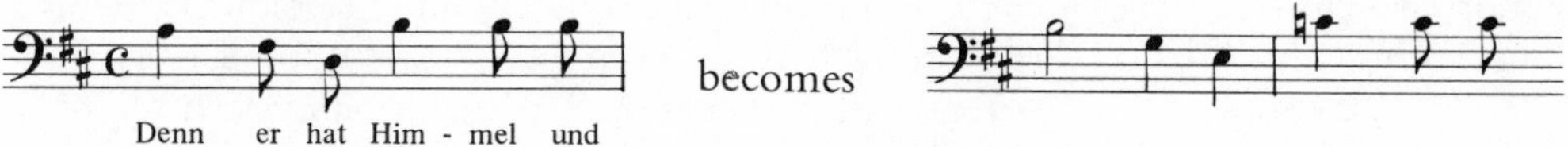

(but the listener has the clear feeling that he is hearing the theme in augmentation which, as Sir Donald Tovey points out, would 'make the theme spread over four bars and a half' [op. cit., 130]).

No. 11 (Recitative), and No. 12 (*Recitativo accompagnato*)

A *secco* leads into the justly celebrated first sunrise, the first moonrise, and the sons of God, gathering together and shouting for joy – and leading without pause or even cadential resolution into

No. 13 Chorus (with the Three Archangels Soli)

The most famous chorus in *The Creation* and for many years Haydn's most played choral piece altogether, 'The heavens are telling' sums up the first part in a glorious outpouring of C major. The entire material is found in the opening bars:

The three Angels sing of the day, and then of the night; and once again the music drops to a *sotto voce* (the score's marking) C minor. And then comes the central part of Swieten's text and Haydn's music:

> In all the lands resounds the word,
> Never unperceivèd, ever understood,

which in the German ends 'jedem Ohre klingend, keiner Zunge fremd' (literally: 'sounding in every ear, foreign to no tongue', not quite the same thing; but so cleverly reworded and re-scanned by the Baron that the two collaborators only had to put the English original on top and it worked perfectly). The bracketed portion (a) from the main subject is now transformed to

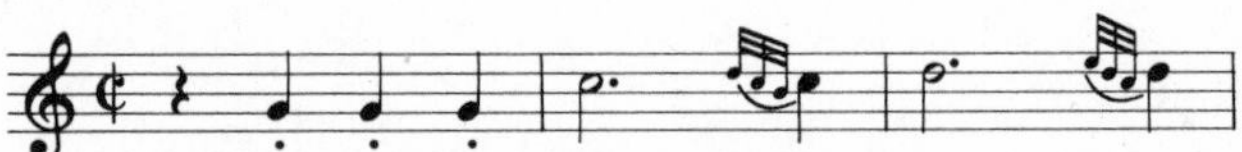

and at rapturous length Haydn develops and extends this part, even adding the dove of peace (= the flute) warbling above the soloists at bars 31ff.: the dove is, of course, the ancient symbol for 'Et incarnatus est' and we find it, most charmingly, in Haydn's penultimate Mass of 1801 (*Schöpfungsmesse*, its name coming from this Oratorio). Here 'das Wort' was made incarnate, and the symbol of peace flutters above it all. After a series of pauses, the tempo suddenly accelerates to 'più allegro' and a mighty fugue develops. Once again the horns, trumpets and timpani drop out, to rejoin the music after some forty bars. By the time we get to the pedal point, thundered out by the timpani across eight bars, we realize an astonishing thing, namely, that the whole of this extraordinary and heart-lifting piece has been in the tonic, if we except a few short excursions in the fugue. Hardly in Haydn's whole life had he stayed so close to the home key for so long as in 'The heavens are telling'; bar after bar of the section with the soloists remains firmly in C major. But now we gather forces for still another mighty cadence, in the course of which we learn the *raison d'être* for this insistence of C major (which, of course, is the symbol for order). In a wild excursion, beginning innocently with a *b* flat marked *fz* in the bass, we soon find ourselves lifted away from C major and propelled away in a thrilling sequence. The first violins are at their top register and the whole orchestra stamps out the beginning of each bar with *fz*, leading us in solemn splendour to the six-four of E minor, then to the supertonic and gradually back to the tonic. The excitement generated in this passage is produced by various components, not least the long-held trombone and tenor notes at a high tessitura and the rhythmic acceleration of the bass line 𝅗𝅥. ♫ to ♩ ♫ ♩ ♫ to 𝅗𝅥. ♫(3) to 𝅗𝅥. ♬. When the horns, trumpets and kettledrums come crashing in with their ♩ ♫ ♩ ♩ – a pattern which has previously appeared no less than twenty times in one form or another (sometimes ♩ ♫ ♩) – the vastness of Haydn's design, in which the tonic predominated for almost the whole of the number, is made thrillingly clear. The triumph of order has been accomplished, and 'Their line is gone out through all the earth, and their words to the end of the world.'

Part Two

No. 14 (Recitative), and No. 15: Aria (Gabriel)

Haydn always intended this to be a bravura piece, as the sketches show. Although the accompanied recitative starts on the six chord of C major, 'as if to continue a narrative that has been punctuated rather than interrupted' (Tovey, 134), the ritornello of the Aria is so long – 34 bars – that it was obviously made to serve as the introduction to Part Two. As in the previous soprano aria, the oboes are dropped and the clarinets have a prominent part.

This is the section in which 'God said, Let the waters bring forth abundantly the moving creature that hath life, and fowl *that* may fly above the earth in the open firmament of heaven' (Genesis I:20). Remembering the firmament displayed so dramatically in the previous chorus, Haydn links them together with his favourite ornament and the progression up one third:

The music describes the proud eagle, then the lark, then, with obvious affection, the billing and cooing of doves – Michael Haydn thought this part particularly effective (see H. Jancik, op. cit., p. 256) – and, lastly, the nightingale's 'delightful notes'.

No. 16: Recitative (Raphael)

This is the great description of life multiplying with the divided lower strings.

No. 17: Recitative (Raphael), and No. 18: *Terzetto*, leading to No. 19: Chorus

A very short *secco* leads to the A major *Terzetto*, scored with the characteristic delicacy that Haydn always reserves for this key (flutes, oboes, bassoons, horns, strings). The words are first given to Gabriel, who sings of the 'sloping hills' and the 'crystall drops' of the fountains. Uriel then describes the 'chearfull host of birds' with their wings shining in the sun, and Raphael follows with the fish in the ocean and 'th'immense leviathan [who] sports on the foaming wave'. The separate entries give Haydn the opportunity for a large-scale presentation; we appear to be in the midst of a huge ritornello form, but in fact we have just concluded what might be termed the 'exposition' of the material when Haydn breaks off and the Chorus takes over (with the three soloists participating). The use of the soloists in conjunction with the chorus is probably the most original concept of *The Creation*. Here we note Gabriel's difficult fioritura, while Uriel's imitation is hardly less exacting. The symbolic use of the word 'ewig' (forever) is particularly noteworthy, the upper voices holding the note '*e*' across four and one-half bars, while the bass moves in slow patterns beneath. Trumpets, trombones, double bassoon and timpani join the orchestra for this Chorus.

No. 20: Recitative (Raphael), and No. 21: Recitative (Raphael)

A short *secco* leads to what is probably the most famous of the descriptive accompanied recitatives. The 'tawny lion' is portrayed, 'chearful roaring' with *ff* trombones and double bassoon, followed by the 'flexible tyger' and the 'nimble stag'. For the stag's music, we move to the 'hunting' metre of six-eight but, more surprising, the music is a quotation from the recapitulation of the 'Surprise' Symphony's first movement, bars 207ff. There then follows the horse 'with flying mane and fiery look' and the bucolic scene with the 'fleecy, meek and bleating flock', and finally the famous imitation of the worm creeping 'in long dimensions'. The final bass note of the recitative, '*d*', is usually put down an octave here, a liberty of which Haydn would certainly have approved.

No. 22: Aria (Raphael)

Here is another of the Oratorio's famous arias; Raphael sings of heaven's glory, with stiff horns, trumpet and timpani fanfares the basic rhythm of which – ♩ 𝄾 ♬ ♫ – colours much of this music. There is a famous bassoon and double bassoon passage that suddenly growls out from beneath the bass solo's words, 'By heavy beats the ground is trod.' The principal message of the Aria comes in the middle:

> But all the work was not complete.
> There wanted yet that wond'rous being . . .

The centre of God's Creation was, in the minds of Swieten and Haydn, man, and in the next recitative

No. 23: Recitative (Uriel), and No. 24: Aria (Uriel)

'God created man in his own image . . . He breathed into his nostrils the breath of life, and man became a living soul.'

If one had to choose the greatest single aria in *The Creation*, it would probably fall on this majestic, poetic and original piece. Its freedom of form is extraordinary and has been much admired: 'Here', writes Tovey (140), 'we have not only the quintessence of Haydn but the perfection of *bel canto*.'

> In native worth and honour clad,
> With beauty, courage, strength adorn'd,
> To heav'n erect and tall, he stands a man,
> The Lord and King of nature all.
> The large and archèd front sublime
> Of wisdom deep declares the rest,
> And in his eyes with brightness shines
> The breath and image of his God.
> With fondness leans upon his breast
> The partner for him form'd,
> A woman fair and graceful spouse
> Her softly smiling virgin looks,
> Of flow'ry spring the mirror,
> Bespeak him love and joy and bliss.

We have quoted the text in full because it is the reason for the formal shape of the Aria, which falls into two distinct sections. As soon as Haydn has described man, the trumpets and timpani leave the orchestra and a beautiful obbligato violoncello part emerges and dominates the texture to the very end. To illustrate 'the breath and image' Haydn introduces a fantastic modulation to the flattened submediant (A flat). The second part of the Aria is a song to 'love and joy and bliss' which dies away *pianissimo*. The story of a French officer coming to see Haydn in 1809 and singing this Aria to the old man, the tears streaming down his cheeks, is well known. It is less well known that Michael Haydn used to sign his letters, 'Think of me in love from *The Creation* with the ob[bligato] violoncello'.[1]

No. 25: Recitative (Raphael), No. 26 (Chorus), No. 27 (*Terzetto*), and No. 28: Chorus

After an eight-bar *secco*, we begin the mighty 'Finale' with which Haydn concludes the Second Part of *The Creation*. No. 26 is a shortened version, with a different *fugato*, of No. 28; but the final ritornello of No. 26 cleverly introduces material from which the great double fugue in No. 28 will be formed. We have spoken of the remarkable orchestration of No. 27 *supra* and also the passage when the strings are introduced,

> But as to them thy face is hid,
> With sudden terror they are struck.
> Thou tak'st their breath away;
> They vanish into dust.

In the final part of this solemnly beautiful trio, Haydn creates a recapitulation with the words

> Thou lett'st thy breath go forth again,
> And life with vigour fresh returns.
> Revived earth unfolds new force and new delights.

Haydn depicts 'new force and new delights' with a new motif which rises up an octave in all three voices, starting with Archangel Raphael. The *Terzetto* leads into the much enlarged version of the preceding chorus, of which the magnificent double fugue is one of Haydn's most inspired. Sir Donald Tovey draws our attention to the 'almost completely modern treatment of the brass', with the stunning trombone writing (op. cit., 141); but perhaps the most spectacular innovation is the timpani solo at the end, which thunders across the short orchestral chords and would inspire dozens upon dozens of nineteenth-century kettledrum finishes, from Beethoven's 'Leonore' Overture No. 3 to Tchaikovsky.

Part Three

No. 29: Recitative (Uriel)

The three flutes used here symbolize 'the morning young and fair' and the still innocent Adam and Eve. Constructed like a large-scale Italian *scena*, we note that in the first section, or until the recapitulation of the opening material, only flutes, horns and strings are used. Bars 29–32 present us with the repetition of the beginning but *in its original state*, i.e. just the three flutes unaccompanied. As we have noted above, these unaccompanied flutes were to open No. 29, but Haydn later added the pizzicato strings. In working out this little tableau, the orchestral plan is very carefully matched to the progress of the words. After the flutes have repeated the opening material, they are silent. Similarly, the horns have a short solo section and are then removed, making way for bassoons and oboes. By the time we have modulated from E to G, we can see No. 29 for that which it really is, namely a vast slow introduction to No. 30, the central part of this section of the Oratorio and of a vast design such as we previously knew

1 Neukomm, *Bemerkungen*, 30.

only in the finales of Haydn's (and of course Mozart's) operas. But though the Finales to Acts I and II of *La fedeltà premiata* – they both represent the most extended treatment of third-related keys in Haydn – are miracles of complicated construction made to sound easy, this finale-like

No. 30: Duet and Chorus (Adam and Eve)

represents an even more complex structure. For one thing, the structure is adorned by a huge orchestra (but, interestingly, without clarinets) and chorus, as well as the soloists, whereas Haydn's operatic productions at Eszterháza, at their most elaborate, could mount some eight soloists but only the modest orchestra (which even in the Finales mentioned above consisted merely of a flute, two oboes, two bassoons, two horns and strings). One of the secrets of Mozart's new operatic style is the lavish orchestration with which he provided all his stage works from *Entführung* to *Zauberflöte*. This secret was certainly not lost on Haydn.

In the very slow build-up, we note at first a fine oboe cantilena emerging from the strings' triplets; then Adam and Eve begin their song of thanksgiving. It is not until bar 24 that Haydn adds more woodwind (flutes, oboes, bassoons); at the end of that bar the chorus comes in, almost chanting. At bar 31 the extraordinary timpani solo begins and continues all through this Adagio: its effect is better understood with the German text, 'Sein Lob erschall' in Ewigkeit'. Haydn had, of course, used such a kettledrum effect in the *Missa in tempore belli* (Agnus Dei), and the effect here in the Oratorio was clearly borrowed from the Mass of 1796–7. (Note that the last two bars of the drum part are written | which is, once again, an abbreviation for a sustained roll, not semiquavers.)

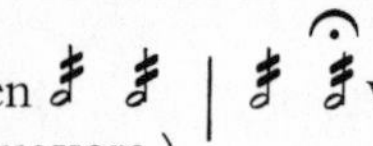

The Adagio now changes to Allegretto and the key to F. The entire texture of the music is lightened as Adam describes

> Of stars the fairest,
> O, how sweet they smile at dawning morn!

In this very large form, Haydn must plan over long periods. Adam yields place to the chorus, then to Eve, who sings

> And thou, that rules the silent night,
> And all ye starry host.

In slow sections, Haydn modulates to B flat and Adam's words

> Ye strong and combrous elements,
> Who ceas'less changes make.

We modulate to A flat, then to E flat, where Eve and Adam unite in resounding 'the praise of God our Lord', to which the chorus then joins together with the double bassoon. As a sustained effort of large form, this entire No. 30 is unique in late-period Haydn. The care with which he adds instrument to instrument, the architectural mastery with which the key structure is planned, are as admirable as the invention and inspiration with which the whole piece is informed. Another large section in A flat with Eve begins

> Ye purling fountains tune his praise.

As is often the case with Haydn's largest vocal forms, this one is formed from a gigantic ritornello (or rondo) form, of which the main subject, as it were, is the melody

By bar 200 of this gigantic structure we are modulating towards G flat. The time between the modulations now grows shorter as Haydn slowly prepares us for G major and a return to 'A' melody. At bar 263 the flat in the signature is cancelled – it was placed in jeopardy long before – and the music moves in a *crescendo* to a climax in C major, where for the first time in this section the orchestra is reinforced by horns, trumpets, trombones and timpani as the chorus shouts, 'Hail, bounteous Lord! Almighty, hail!' With this mighty affirmation of the tonic we begin the third section of this number. It is organized as a kind of introduction to a *fugato* sung to the words 'wir preisen dich in Ewigkeit' / 'we praise thee now and ever more'. The various methods by which Haydn lengthens the music to the word 'Ewigkeit' excited the admiration of his brother Michael, who regarded the passage as 'something exceptional' (Jancik, op. cit., p. 256). Indeed, the whole number is magnificently organized, and Tovey (145) thought it 'the greatest movement, or pair of movements, that [Haydn] ever wrote, whether vocal or instrumental'. It must have been very tempting to end the work with this great achievement, but that was not Swieten's or Haydn's intention.

No. 31: Recitative (Adam–Eve), and No. 32: Duetto (Eve–Adam)

After nearly four hundred bars of No. 30, we need the widest possible contrast, and Baron van Swieten provided Haydn with the simplest method – a long *secco* recitative. In our discussion of key relationships *supra*, it was noted that the B flat chorus ending Part Two could also be regarded as the dominant of the forthcoming E flat Duet. To underline this relationship, Haydn has recourse to a clever device. Adam sings 'Our duty we performed now in off'ring up to God our thanks', immediately followed by a clear reference to the B flat theme that begins Nos. 26 and 28:

The first part of the Duet's main theme is a quotation from Euridice's dying *Cavatina* in Haydn's *L'anima del filosofo* (1791), Act II, also in E flat and a slow tempo. Clarinets, silent in No. 30, now rejoin the woodwind section. Adam had sung, in the foregoing *secco*, 'Now follow me, dear partner of my life', and this is what Haydn has Eve do in the *Duetto*. Only the form is not altered and Eve's music is in the dominant. When the tempo shifts to allegro, the horns have the following dance-like melody which Haydn later incorporated bodily into the *Schöpfungsmesse* of 1801 – hence the name:

After the heavenly hosts, and even Adam and Eve singing, as it were, with the angels in No. 30, this introduction of the tavern into the proceedings must come as a shock. This could be a love duet from a German *Singspiel*, and even the words are *gemütlich*. 'With thee,' sing the happy pair, 'is ev'ry joy enhanced,' and the band thumps out

Even the accompaniment, with its oom-pah-pah-oom rhythm, is like a piece from a Hanswurst comedy. Adam and Eve have become Papageno and Papagena.

No. 33 Recitative (Uriel) and No. 34 Chorus with Soli

The final chorus from *The Creation* is like a movement from a late Haydn Mass. There is a kind of slow introduction (andante) which leads to a double fugue in the course of which the four soloists enter with the word 'Amen'. The main motif of the fugal subject detaches itself and becomes a powerful leading rhythm of its own, hammered out by the whole orchestra (the trumpets and horns *ff*)

There is a magnificent digression once more on the word 'Ewigkeit' which leads us to the supertonic and another *ff* outburst as we swing round majestically to the tonic in a series of timpani fanfares. At the very end, there are choral *staccati* at the second syllables of the words 'A-men'. There is no lingering, however, and the actual conclusion is almost abrupt, as it often is in Haydn's choral music.

The Creation was unquestionably Haydn's greatest achievement. On completing his Oratorio at Eisenstadt in 1797, Haydn must have experienced some of Gibbon's emotions on having finished his *History of the Decline and Fall of the Roman Empire*:

> After laying down my pen, I took several turns in a berceau, or covered walk of acacias, which commands a prospect of the country, the lake, and the mountains. The air was temperate, the sky was serene, the silver orb of the moon was reflected from the waters, and all nature was silent. I will not dissemble the first emotions of joy on the recovery of my freedom, and, perhaps, the establishment of my fame. But my pride was soon humbled, and a sober melancholy was spread over my mind, by the idea that I had taken an everlasting leave of an old and agreeable companion. . . .[1]

Considerable, if small, revisions were made to *The Creation* between its first performance in April 1798 and its first public performance at Vienna in 1799. In the Chronicle we shall follow the preparations for the first edition – and in particular the subscription list – which then followed in 1800, and the performances in the major European capitals which rapidly spread *The Creation*'s fame. As our analysis has attempted to show, the Oratorio is in the great liberal, humanitarian tradition which brought forth *Die Zauberflöte* and would shortly give *Fidelio* to the world. To this tradition *The Creation* was one of the fundamental and lasting contributions.

1 *The Miscellaneous Works of Edward Gibbon, Esq., with Memoirs of His Life and Writings, composed by Himself*, ed. by John, Lord Sheffield, London 1837, pp. 107f.

Missa in Angustiis ('Nelson' Mass) in D minor (XXII: 11)

Basic scoring: 3 trumpets in D, timpani in D – A, strings, organ (used as a solo intrument in many places), soli (maximum: SSATB; usually SATB), choir (SATB); presumably a bassoon or bassoons doubled the basso continuo.

I Kyrie (*Allegro moderato*): full scoring.
II Gloria –
 (a) Gloria in excelsis Deo (*Allegro*): full scoring.
 (b) Qui tollis (*Adagio*): strings, organ, soprano solo, bass solo, choir.
 (c) Quoniam (*Allegro*): full scoring.
III Credo –
 (a) Credo in unum Deum (*Allegro con spirito*): full scoring without soli.
 (b) Et incarnatus est (*Largo*): full scoring.
 (c) Et resurrexit (*Vivace*): full scoring.
IV Sanctus (*Adagio–Allegro*): full scoring without soli.
V Benedictus (*Allegretto–Allegro*): full scoring.
VI Agnus Dei (*Adagio*): strings, organ, soli (SATB).
 Dona nobis pacem (*Vivace*): full scoring.

Martin Chusid's proposed scheme[1] for dividing the 'Nelson' Mass into three vocal symphonies is as follows (op. cit., 132):

Vocal Symphony No. 1.

MVT.	TEXT	TEMPO AND NO. OF BARS	METRE	KEY
I	Kyrie	as *supra* = 160 bars	3/4	D minor
II	Gloria	as *supra* = 105 bars	4/4	D major
III	Qui tollis	as *supra* = 65 bars	3/4	B flat → V of D minor
IV	Quoniam incl. material from Gloria	as *supra* = 82 bars	4/4	D major

Vocal Symphony No. 2

MVT.	TEXT	TEMPO AND NO. OF BARS	METRE	KEY
I	Credo	as *supra* = 83 bars	*alla breve*	D major
II	Et incarnatus	as *supra* = 54 bars	3/4	G major
III	Et resurrexit	as *supra* = 108 bars	4/4	D major (during the opening bars, 1–6, there is a modulation from B minor to the tonic, D major)

Vocal Symphony No. 3

MVT.	TEXT	TEMPO AND NO. OF BARS	METRE	KEY
I	Sanctus	as *supra* = 10 bars	4/4	D major→V of D minor
	Pleni	as *supra* = 44 bars	3/4	D major
II	Benedictus	as *supra* = 135 bars	2/4	D minor → V
	Osanna (= previous Osanna concluding Pleni)	as *supra* = 26 bars	3/4	D major
III	Agnus Dei	as *supra* = 21 bars	3/4	G major → V of B minor
	Dona	as *supra* = 77 bars	4/4	D major

1 Reprinted by permission of George Allen & Unwin Ltd.

The Sources

The autograph is in the Musiksammlung of the Österreichische Nationalbibliothek and is entitled, on an otherwise blank first page, 'Missa'. At the top of the first page of music, the work is signed and the beginning dated: 'In Nomine Domini di me giuseppe Haydn mpria $\overline{798}$ 10ten Julj Eisenstadt'; at the end of the work it is signed 'Fine Laus Deo 31 August'. The entry in the *Entwurf-Katalog* is without *incipit* but gives us the name 'Missa in Angustiis' (literally 'narrow' or 'constricted'). The original performance material, by Johann Elssler and his assistants, is in the Archives of Schloss Esterházy, Eisenstadt. It contains some holograph corrections by Haydn on the original parts, which corrections were generally incorporated in the duplicate parts. The trumpet parts are by another hand. A third authentic source is the set of parts by Elssler and his assistants in the Augustinian Monastery of Klosterneuburg (Lower Austria) which the present writer discovered there some twenty-five years ago. The trumpet parts are in the same hand as the Eisenstadt MS. Thus we have three early and authentic MSS. on which to base a critical edition.[1]

In this reduced version, the Mass also circulated to Oradea Mare (Grosswardein) and the Benedictine Monastery of St Paul in Lavanttal (Carinthia), also in a few other places such as the Emperor's private chapel in Vienna (Hofmusikkapelle) and the Lobkowitz Archives: Haydn was probably responsible for many of these copies, since we find Elssler parts in the MSS. of Oradea Mare, the Hofmusikkapelle and the Lobkowitz Archives (now in the Prague National Museum). An accurate copy of the autograph, supposedly by Johann Elssler (but if it is by him, it must have been made long after Haydn's death, for the handwriting is quite different from the Elssler copies we know of the period 1794–1809), is in the British Museum (*ex coll.* Julian Marshall, Add. MS 31711). It contains a false Haydn signature and other curious details but it is unquestionably a copy of the autograph made after the widespread changes Haydn introduced into the soprano part.

And here we come to the first in a series of changes which were made partly by Haydn and later by others. At some time after September 1798, Haydn found himself with a soprano for whom the tessitura of her taxing solo part lay too high, and he lowered her part several times. He also changed two high parts in the solo tenor (Gloria, bars 28f., 33f.). These alterations undoubtedly represent compromises. At the beginning of the Gloria, when soprano solo and choir answer each other, it is much more effective to hear

1 The first critical edition of this 'original version' was edited by us and published in 1963: score by Eulenburg (no. 995) and performance material by Schott & Co., London (piano score 10808). In this edition, only Haydn's original score was published. In the Henle edition of *Joseph Haydn Werke* (Reihe XXIII, Band 3, edited by Günter Thomas, 1965), the non-authentic supplementary wind parts of the Eisenstadt material are also included, so that the student may examine these additions. *Vide infra.* The first recording of the Mass was made by the Haydn Society in 1949 and included Lisa della Casa, Elisabeth Höngen, Horst Taubmann, George London, the Akademie Kammerchor, the Vienna Symphony with Josef Nebois (organ), conducted by Jonathan Sternberg (HSLP 2004). The first recording of the original version (then in MS.) was made in 1952 for the Club Français du Disque and included Theresa Stich-Randall, Mona Paulee, Rudolf Schock, Gottlob Frick, the Akademie Kammerchor, the Orchestra of the Vienna State Opera with Anton Heiller (organ, playing from the Elssler MS. part of the Klosterneuburg MS.), conducted by Jonathan Sternberg. Both these recordings were supervised by the present writer. The first stereo recording of the Schott-Eulenburg original version was made in 1962 by Argo (Decca) RG 35 and included Sylvia Stahlman, Helen Watts, Wilfred Brown, Tom Krause, the Choir of King's College, Cambridge, and the London Symphony Orchestra (Simon Preston, organ), conducted by David Willcocks; it was recorded in the Chapel of King's College, Cambridge.

than the later version of the solo which reads

Almost every change is for the worse, also those for the tenor, in which the original versions exploit the tense high range of the voice which Haydn understood so well. On the other hand, it is not that the later soprano was incapable of singing high notes, for Haydn left unaltered the magnificent recapitulation of the Kyrie in which she soars over the choir to high *b* flat (bars 99ff.). Yet Haydn took the trouble to incorporate these later changes into the autograph, literally erasing the original versions. We cannot establish (a) when he made this change or (b) for whom. We might suggest that he adapted the soprano part for the Empress Marie Therese with her 'weak voice': that would explain why Haydn was courteous enough to eradicate his own earlier versions on the autograph. We know that Haydn and the royal family were much together at the turn of the century, and that he conducted performances in the Burg; perhaps the adaptations were for this high personage, made about 1800. Although we have dutifully incorporated these readings in the main text of our new edition, we can see no particular reason for condoning them. Haydn sent out several sets of parts, such as those at Klosterneuburg and Oradea Mare, and they do not contain these changes.

Another difference between autograph and the other parts is even more spectacular and cannot at present be explained satisfactorily. When the music changes to B flat, at the end of the Benedictus (bars 122ff.), and the trumpet signals come in, the autograph has a timpani part which supports the strings' chords at intervals. This reading is found in the British Museum copy as well. The autograph shows no signs of being tampered with here. But the authentic parts at Eisenstadt, Klosterneuburg, etc. have an entirely different part which doubles the trumpets throughout the passage. The two authentic parts may be examined on pp. 145f. of the Eulenburg score (and its enlargement for conductors in the Schott material). Where did the copyist at Eisenstadt get his reading from? Perhaps it is a change that Haydn dictated orally to the copyist; it would then have been passed on because Elssler and his team distributed parts made from the master copy (Eisenstadt), not from Haydn's autograph.

The next change concerns the whole orchestration. Haydn took into brilliant account the lack of wind instruments at Eisenstadt in 1798. The use of the solo organ and the trumpets with kettledrums is a stroke of genius, and Haydn was – as we have seen – quite content to deliver authentic MSS. with this restricted orchestration. Nor did he feel impelled to rewrite the work for a later performance (e.g. in 1800, when he composed no new Mass for Eisenstadt and could perfectly well have rewritten the work with the new increased wind band ('Harmonisten') that Esterházy had engaged in November 1799. But Haydn left the orchestration as he had written it. However, when Breitkopf & Härtel were planning the publication of Haydn's Masses, the composer thought that something ought to be done about the lacking winds. In a letter to Leipzig on 4 December 1802, G. A. Griesinger writes to Breitkopf & Härtel: 'Haydn told me that in the Mass you wrote about he put the wind instruments in the organ part, because at that time Prince Esterházy had dismissed the wind players. But he advises you to put everything that is obbligato in the organ part into the wind instruments and to print it that way.' We must not forget that Haydn was also displaying the new (1797) organ in the Bergkirche (though in fact the première was in the Stadtpfarrkirche, where the organ was by the same builder; *supra*, p. 327).

Now there exists one version of such an enlarged orchestration in the parts at Eisenstadt. The added wind parts were simply copied out and could be played with all the original parts except, presumably, the organ, where the player would have omitted all the solo passages. A new title page was also made, retaining the original historic date – we note, at Eisenstadt, an increased awareness that the chronology of Haydn's late Masses was of public interest and considered worth preserving on the title pages – but noting the enlarged instrumentation, 'Flauto / 2. Obois / 2. Clarinetti / Fagotto / 2. Corni / 3. Clarini / Tympano' etc. Previously it was thought that the later *Kapellmeister* Hummel might have done this rather competent reorchestration, but the *AMZ*[1] tells us of the true author. 'The present head [of the Esterházy music operations] is Herr *Kapellmeister* [Johann Nepomuk] Fuchs, formerly Haydn's colleague, to whom we are indebted for the enlarged wind instruments in Haydn's printed masses.' This remark refers, of course, to the 'Nelson' Mass (No. 3 of Breitkopf's Mass series), but probably includes the *Theresienmesse* which, though not printed by Breitkopf, had received an enlarged wind band for a later performance at Eisenstadt (*infra,* p. 477).

Breitkopf & Härtel followed Griesinger's instructions; but they did not print the Fuchs version of which they (and presumably Griesinger) apparently knew nothing; instead, they commissioned some local Leipzig composer or *Kapellmeister* to do the job. Unfortunately the copy of the Mass that they had pirated was full of mistakes quite apart from the question of added instrumentation, so that textually this first edition – which had the great merit of making the work popular throughout Europe – was something of a disaster. Not only did they transform the organ part into a wind group of one flute, two oboes and two bassoons but they also rewrote the trumpet parts. First they removed many of the *clarino* passages (such as the magnificent solo in the Credo), either omitting them entirely or putting them down in a lower register; thus they had to rewrite the timpani part as well. Then they went to work on the third trumpet, which puzzled them, as indeed it might have. Haydn wrote on his autograph '2 Clarini/in D' at the beginning of the Mass, but over the top of the first notes 'a Tre'; at bar 123 of the Benedictus he again wrote 'a Tre unisono'. But otherwise there is no separate part for the third trumpet, which was expected to double the menacing parts for *Clarini* I & II in the Kyrie and in the fanfare passage of the Benedictus. This fastidious use of the third trumpet was not to Breitkopf & Härtel's taste, and they commissioned their hack to rewrite that part, too. The finished product was a curious third trumpet part, which cluttered up the musical text with useless fanfare figures in the lowest register which can hardly be heard in performance and are best forgotten as quickly as the whole Breitkopf & Härtel score of 1803.[2] The part was entitled 'Clarino Principale' (the adjective deriving from the old division of the trumpets into various registers, of which the 'Principale' was in the low register).

1 XXIX, No. 49, column 818, in a report from their Vienna correspondent.

2 The new edition for Peters, edited in 1931 by Wilhelm Weismann (score, piano score, material), is based on the Breitkopf score; it is thus rather quixotic of Peters to include this publication under their list of *Urtext* editions.

Analytical notes

The 'Nelson' Mass has always been one of Haydn's most popular Masses. It has been performed regularly in churches throughout Austria and southern Germany since Haydn's own lifetime.[1] Written in fifty-three days, there is no doubt that the work has a startling unity of inspiration – startling because it must have been a considerable feat to follow *The Creation* with a work of such intensity, nervous vigour and emotional stress. The *Entwurf-Katalog*'s description, 'Missa in Angustijs',[2] tells us much more about the work's character than the popular designation 'Nelson'. It is a Mass written in time of fear, in time of the 'narrow'. More prosaically, 'Angustijs' can also mean 'composed in a short time'. Whatever the exact meaning of 'Angustijs', the opening of the Mass, with its menacing trumpets in their lowest register, is one of Haydn's most striking innovations. The rather acid colour is also the result of the long held organ chords. Everything is worked out instrumentally to produce the final result, even the viola part with its characteristic octave jump which prepares us for the entry of the vocal parts a few bars later (see musical example overleaf). The viola's *Urlinie* then becomes

when the voices enter (bar 16), and when the soprano solo enters at bar 29. This motivic concentration may be seen in most of the Mass, and its presence accounts for the extraordinary intensity of expression that prevails throughout the work. In form, we proceed in one of Haydn's most brilliant adaptations of sonata allegro to a vocal work. Being a work in the minor, the modulation is to the relative major, in which key the soprano solo sings her 'Christe eleison', later supported by four other solo voices. The rhythm of the trumpets appears in many other voices to remind us of the menacing background: in the basses at bar 32, in the first violins at bars 43 and 45. An accompanimental figure in the viola at bars 28f.

becomes the cadence for the solo soprano:

What appears to be a minor figure in the chorus just after their entrance

suddenly turns out to be the whole fabric of the music after the cadence of the solo soprano ('Christe eleison') in F. Used to progress a note downwards

1 It was the first mass to be recorded in extract: the Austrian firm Christschall issued the 'Qui tollis' between the World Wars.

2 The double 'i' was often written 'ij'. 'J' was also used as a substitute for a single 'i' as in the 'Julj' date at the beginning of the autograph.

[*Missa in angustiis*: opening]

this fragment is the basis for a large-scale *fugato* which takes us to A minor and, after a short orchestral interlude, proceeds with enormous vigour like a big symphonic development to the recapitulation, which is led in by a stupendous entrance of the trumpets and timpani. The recapitulation is enhanced by the tremendous solo soprano part which floats over the chorus in a magnificent passage which cannot fail to thrill any listener. Note the subtly different orchestration. The viola, not having to play the octave passage as at the beginning, doubles the organ's line, while the violins now assist the trumpets and drums in the ominous war-rhythm. For sheer motivic concentration, this Kyrie is one of Haydn's mightiest achievements, and it produces a D minor movement of unparalleled power and splendour. We show the end of the development and the beginning of the recapitulation in full score as evidence of the new language so magnificently formed in this Kyrie (see musical example, pp. 434–5). One question remains: for whom did Haydn invent this fabulous soprano solo part? Was it perhaps the Pressburg girl, Barbara Pilhofer, who had now studied at Eisenstadt (and possibly Vienna) for a year? She had, it will be recalled, made her début in the *Missa in tempore belli* at Eisenstadt in the Autumn of 1797. If so, she had indeed made fantastic progress, for the soprano solo part in the 'Nelson' Mass is worthy of Therese Gassmann.

If one influential aspect of this Mass was its D minor sections, another – equally influential – was those parts in D major. For some curious reason Haydn had never written a D major Mass, and the impact of the *Missa in angustiis* was therefore all the greater. Such sections as the Gloria, Credo and Sanctus had repercussions even in the swift sections of Beethoven's Mass in D (e.g. the very Haydnish Pleni in the Sanctus) or Cherubini's Mass in D minor (e.g. the Gloria), not to speak of numerous works by early nineteenth-century *Kleinmeister*.

In the first part of the Gloria Haydn continues the antiphonal responses between soprano solo and choir that we noted in the Kyrie. The menacing mood of the beginning now changes to one of great brilliance and joy. The words 'Et in terra pax' are set over a pedal on the note D (of course the contrabassi must have contra C as their lowest string, not E) in a very effective passage for the soloists. The 'Laudamus' introduces a series of syncopations which remind us once again that this particular aspect of Haydn's art was perhaps that which had the most profound influence on Beethoven. Not only do the strings have but against that pattern the chorus was creating a double syncopation which was so unusual that this entire section was bowdlerized in the Breitkopf & Härtel first edition. The 'glorificamus' is announced with one of those characteristic *ff* interjections of which the Mass has several of breathtaking power; it is in this section, too, that the sopranos rise to *b''*. The forward-driving character of this section is produced *inter alia* by a typical rhythmic acceleration in the kettledrums .

Formally, this part of the Gloria is in A-B-A form but using the one opening theme only. B is in the dominant but is merely the 'Gloria in excelsis' tune given to the alto solo with the words 'Gratias agimus tibi'. Another way of looking at the form would be to say that it is in Haydn's favourite ritornello pattern; in that case A simply appears, Vivaldi-like, first in the tonic, then in the dominant, then in VI ('Domine

95
[Allegro moderato]
I, II
Trbe
III
Timp.
V. I
V. II
Va.
Sop. solo
e -
CORO
S.
- - - - son, e - lei - son, e - lei - son, Ky - ri-e
A.
-son, e - lei - son, e - lei - son, Ky - ri-e
T.
- - - - son, e - lei - son, e - lei - son, Ky - ri-e
B.
- - - - son, e - lei - son, e - lei - son, Ky - ri-e
Org.
B. C.

100
-lei - - - - - - son, e - lei - son, e - - - - -
Ky - ri-e e - lei - son Ky - ri-e e-
Ky - ri-e e - lei - son Ky - ri-e e-
Ky - ri-e e - lei - son Ky - ri-e e-
Ky - ri-e e - lei - son Ky - ri-e e-

Deus', bars 62ff.), then back in I. Yet the fact that the famous D pedal point also returns at the end, now to the words 'Domine Deus' and introducing, suddenly, a whole section in D minor (with a solo organ part in slow chords), gives the whole a tripartite feeling which is stronger than the ritornello aspects of the piece. The above-mentioned D minor section is so long (from bars 81 to 96) and so striking that we soon realize that its appearance is to remind us of the work's principal tonality; another, even more startling, reminder occurs in the middle of the Et incarnatus est (*vide infra*). The close of this initial Gloria section is a brief and exultant passage in D major with virtuoso timpani writing in rhythmic acceleration similar to that noted above; the similarity also extends to the violin writing (broken chords in repeated semiquaver patterns). Just as in the Kyrie, Haydn uses motivic patterns to cement together what would otherwise be a loose construction; as it turns out, it is one of Haydn's tightest.

The Qui tollis introduces a magnificent bass solo for Christian Specht, the veteran member of the Esterházy troupe for whom Haydn had created, twenty-five years earlier, the part of Nanni in *L'infedeltà delusa* and, three years before that, the part of Lindoro in *Le pescatrici*. In 1775 Specht had created the role of Calandro in *L'incontro improvviso*, and that same year Haydn had taken him to Vienna to participate in the first performance of *Il ritorno di Tobia*. Specht had been a viola player in the orchestra at Eszterháza, and had also repaired the clocks and the keyboard instruments, for which he received an extra payment in the form of a roasting pig. It was for this many-sided musician – certainly now with only traces of his former vocal glory – that Haydn composed a last tribute in this Qui tollis.[1]

We have seen in *The Creation* how Haydn changed the old forms to suit his new purposes. In this Qui tollis we may observe something similar. First, we note the progressive tonality. Starting with B flat major (the flattened submediant in relation to D), we proceed to the dominant, back to the tonic (thus far in a kind of A-B-A form), then to the relative minor (VI) and then, all very smoothly, to – D minor. Again we are reminded forcibly of the work's principal key, and in another passage of sufficient length (bars 49 to 65, the end of the section) to drive the point securely home. It is interesting to observe how Haydn manages to create a tight unity of this progressive key scheme. He does it primarily by motivic allusion. Thus when we arrive in the relative minor, the main theme is introduced – also showing off what was once Specht's famous low register. Similarly, other parts of the opening thematic group are used throughout the piece. But the most striking effect is that of the chorus, which is used in a semi-chant such as we remember in 'By Thee with bliss' from *The Creation*, and which appears throughout the Qui tollis like a group of monks quietly chanting behind the screen of some great Gothic cathedral. 'Miserere nobis' chants the choir, then 'deprecationem nostram', the latter after another stroke of colour in which the soprano solo suddenly joins the proceedings (see example opposite). The characteristic use of the solo organ may be noted. It, too, appears in three crucial places with the *gruppetto* (as in the example opposite, bar 30) followed by a short melodic fragment: (1) at the end of the lead-back to the restatement of the main theme; (2) in the passage quoted above; (3) at the end of the movement. It is with such devices that Haydn creates a musical whole out of this Qui tollis; but above all, it is the murmuring chorus – which occasionally raises its collective voice to a *forte* (again at crucial places: bars 36f., 49f., 62ff.) – that gives the movement its devotional spirit and its musical as well as formal unity.

1 Concerning Specht, see Janos Harich's article in *Haydn Yearbook VII* (1970), pp. 30f.

[Gloria: Qui tollis]

By the time the Quoniam starts, using the identical music of the Gloria's beginning, we realize that the Gloria as a whole is in three-part form: a large-scale A-B-A-Coda, the coda in this case being a magnificent double fugue on the words 'in gloria Dei Patris, amen'. And again Haydn discards all the old rules. The fugue concludes at bar 61 and we suddenly find ourselves in the pedal point on D which Haydn took great care *not* to introduce in the Quoniam hitherto. Once more the solo voices rise up in imitation, but instead of modulating away from the tonic (as the music had done in the Gloria at this point) the whole pedal point is repeated, still with the soloists[1] but now with a six-bar timpani roll (notated, incidentally, [timpani notation]). This time the chorus breaks into the pedal point, and with a trumpet part of ascending Handelian grandeur, the movement comes to an end with another vigorous timpani solo.

The autograph manuscript contains the subtitle 'In Canone' for the Credo: and in fact the first movement is a strict canon between soprano and tenor on the one hand and alto and bass on the other, at the time interval of one bar and the musical interval of a fifth. This interweaving of the two sets of octaves:

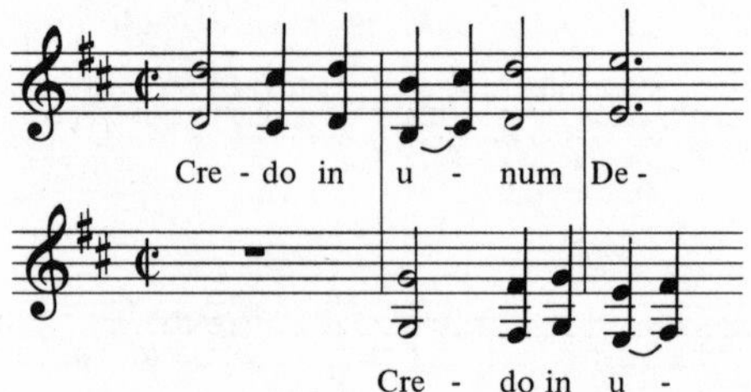

makes the canon's layout much more original and interesting than if it had been scored in the more conventional way SA against TB; as it is Haydn's music has a S–A / T–B plan which gives the vocal writing an innate richness. Here we have another example of an old Baroque contrapuntal form awakened to new life in Haydn's well-trained hands. It will also be noted that the melodic curve in the example quoted has something strongly Gregorian about it. The same, incidentally, applied to the melody of the Gloria itself which bears a close resemblance to a Gloria intonation in the Brixen *Gesangbuch*.[2] At the end of his life, Haydn even introduced a Gregorian melody into the late Te Deum, as we shall see. The fascinating thing about Haydn's late choral music altogether is its smooth fusion of older traditions with newer musical ideas – Baroque canons and fugues and Gregorian chant, and the tradition of chanting altogether, with the orchestral methods of the turn of the century and the symphonic forms perfected by the Viennese classical masters. In this opening Credo of the *Missa in angustiis* Haydn even revives the lost art of *clarino* playing, for the trumpets, unsupported by any other instrument, sound forth the following at bars 41ff.:

1 This whole passage has been hopelessly corrupted in the Breitkopf & Härtel print. The chorus is introduced long before Haydn intended that it should, the trumpets and timpani are likewise falsified.
2 On this general subject, see our article, 'Die Verwendung gregorianischer Melodien in Haydns Frühsymphonien', in *Österreichische Musikzeitschrift*, Jg IX (Vienna 1954), and esp. p. 121.

Altogether the taxing trumpet writing in this Mass suggests that the Eisenstadt trio of Sebastian Binder, Michael Altmann and Johann Pfann were technically first-rate.

The Et incarnatus is one of the most beautiful slow movements Haydn ever wrote. It begins with a soprano solo of melting beauty in the great *bel canto* tradition, and the music is then taken over by the choir, the violins contributing beautiful arabesques that float over and round the choir like the angels in some Giottoesque fresco. After this ravishing hymn of praise to the Virgin – to Whom Haydn was especially devoted and to Whom he dedicated innumerable works – the words 'Crucifixus etiam pro nobis' introduce one of the most striking pages in the Mass: the return to the fanfares of the Kyrie. Since the 'Et incarnatus est' is in G major, Haydn produces the stalking D minor by shifting the music into G minor and having the trumpets and timpani play the notes D as a V pedal point. But the reminiscence is perfectly clear (see example overleaf). At the end the choir sings 'et sepultus est' with choral *staccati*, another new invention of the old composer's; and beneath it growl the lower strings in the lowest register – another place where five-string double basses with the contra C are absolutely essential to the spirit (and of course letter) of the music.

The 'Et resurrexit' begins in B minor so that Haydn can save D major, and his trumpets with the kettledrums, to introduce the words 'judicare' with pomp and ceremony: this is always a great moment in a Haydn Mass. In the long dogmatic sections, the music is again written like a chant, the whole choir singing in octaves ('Et unam sanctam Catholicam et Apostolicam ecclesiam'). Haydn was a faithful Catholic and he thought he knew his Mass text by heart, which, on the whole, he did; but now and then a part of the long dogma would escape him, and here in the *Missa in angustiis* it is the words 'qui ex Patre Filioque procedit', which someone[1] noted as missing on the appropriate page of the autograph. With one final 'Et' from the chorus the music comes to a half cadence and one of Haydn's most ravishing soprano solos announces life eternal, 'et vitam venturi', with a rich bass (or rather tenor) undertone consisting of violoncello and organ left-hand. The soprano's subsequent triplet coloraturas have the grace and innocence of the ornaments that adorn the pillars in Vézelay; and in fact the soprano singing her mightiest (or, *pace* W. H. Auden, the juggler dancing for the Almighty) is in the great medieval tradition of which Haydn's art is the direct descendant (see example, p. 441). This, too, (without the coloratura, of course) the choir takes up, ornamented by a jubilant series of semiquavers in the violins and joyous fanfares from the trumpets with the kettledrums.

sound the trumpets, and the choir answers

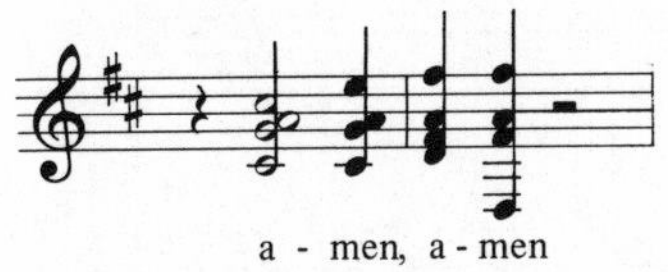

The whole choral section is presented twice, as if the composer were reluctant to tear himself away from the visionary view of everlasting life. At the very end there is a

1 Not, as Alfred Schnerich maintained, Haydn who noted the *lacuna*. See Brand *Messen*, 343. In the first part of the Credo, the words 'Et in unum Dominum Jesum Christum filium Dei unigenitum' are also missing.

[Et incarnatus]

[Et resurrexit]

---

stunning and sudden *ff* which raises the level of the last three bars to the very loudest; the cadence is very abrupt. This Gloria in its totality represents an entirely new tonal concept. It is not like the solemn C major Glorias of Haydn's Masses in that key, nor like the subdued rejoicing of the B flat Masses; here, in the Gloria of the 'Nelson' Mass, we have the same kind of festive sense of *Pracht* with which D major in *The Creation* is so closely associated. It is *par excellence* the key of jubilant rejoicing, in short the natural key for a Gloria. Its tonal and psychological lesson was not lost on Haydn's contemporaries and especially not on Beethoven.

The Sanctus has yet one further innovation which must have astonished the Princess Marie Hermenegild when she first heard the whole choir and string orchestra singing and playing:

p < *f* > < *f* >

Sanc - tus, sanc - tus

In the middle of this authentic 'hairpin' – a legacy of 'Chaos', of course – the trumpets and timpani come in with a single thud marked with a tall staccato; while the organ has an extraordinary 'rolled' chord across both staves. The whole is a very strange sound and full of mystery, as is appropriate to a Sanctus. Haydn treats the movement in two parts: a slow introduction that ends on V with a long roll on the kettledrums (*pp*), then a dashing *Allegro* at the words 'Pleni sunt coeli'. What starts out as a unison passage for the chorus turns into a majestic passage with slow-moving choral words – the Latin text, so carefully set by Haydn, is badly distorted in Breitkopf & Härtel's first edition – against fast moving strings: 'gloria tua'. The 'Osanna in excelsis' is set as a little *fugato*. Just before the end of this enormously energetic section the second trumpet has the following 'stopped' note

(this, too, was changed by the Leipzig hacks), which the trumpeter produced by some trick (either hand stopping – difficult with long D trumpets – or by a slide in the manner of the British trumpeter Hyde (*vide supra*, p. 227).

Now we come to the central movement of the Mass's second part: the famous Benedictus. Once again we are in D minor, and we return to the atmosphere of the Kyrie, to the 'angustiis'. A long ritornello includes a very curious trumpet solo

which sounds strangely uneasy. Altogether the marching rhythm is given a sense of uneasiness by having rests between the notes. As in the Kyrie and Gloria, the soprano solo intones the words, the chorus follow her. And we follow the Kyrie in that the music modulates to the relative major, as we would expect, where the soprano has a long solo passage with ornaments, the closing section given to the choir. There is, as in the Kyrie, a kind of development, the solo voices entering one after the other in imitation and in most beautiful part writing; and there is a recapitulation. But suddenly there is a rest of half a bar and the music plunges into B flat for what must be called the boldest and most powerful music in the whole of Haydn. The trumpets hammer out a fanfare on unison *d′* and the chorus also sings its text on the note *d*, its message interrupted by the 'clash of arms and the horrid sublimity' that is war. It is a passage from the Old Testament and unique in eighteenth-century music: only Don Giovanni's meeting with the Commendatore (also D minor) can be compared to it. The Benedictus closes with a *da capo* of the *fugato* in the Sanctus, on the words 'Osanna in excelsis'. Coming after the horrifying passage in B flat, they sound, inevitably, anti-climactic.

The Agnus Dei starts with a richly accompanied (harmonically, that is: only the strings play) solo for the alto. Her long, cantabile line is broken off by the soprano, who enters in a kind of recitative complete with rhetorical flourishes from the strings ***f*** . Coming to a close on the words 'Dona nobis pacem', and with the music ending expectantly on the dominant of B minor, this first section serves as a slow introduction to the powerful fugue with which the work closes (vivace). Its sense of power is generated by its syncopated entry on the second beat. When we arrive at the dominant the strings have a highly flippant passage in *piano* which sounds wildly secular even in a secular age like ours:

This passage reappears in the recapitulation – for although a fugue, there is a strong tripartite feeling to this movement – and once again over a particularly lovely vocal passage (bars 62ff.). The conclusion to this majestic *Missa in tempore belli* is as exuberantly secular as many of the details in Melk or Wilhering or Schlierbach. Against cascades of scales in the strings, the trumpets have repeated fanfares, the chorus sings its off-beat principal fugal theme in unison, and at the end the kettledrums have an extravagant Baroque conceit

which reminds one of those kettledrumming angel-figures that lean precipitously over the organ lofts of the great Austrian monastery churches, flanked by the angelic trumpeters with their rosy cheeks puffed out and their golden or silver instruments jutting upwards towards heaven.

Breitkopf & Härtel's first edition of the Mass was reviewed together with the *Missa in tempore belli* in the *Allgemeine Musikalische Zeitung* Vol. VI (5 October 1803; pp. 8–10); we have quoted Rochlitz's review of 'Messe No. 2'; we may now include his notes on 'Messe No. 3'.

> We now come to the second Mass, No. 3. It is in D major [*sic*] for a large and complete orchestra but without horns. A *Clarino principale* is specially included beside the two usual trumpets. Division and treatment of the text are like that of the preceding Mass, *viz.* the Qui tollis, Et incarnatus and Agnus Dei are big pieces for the solo voices with some tutti passages woven in; the others are large choruses.
>
> It is, as we have already noted, in a fiery, bold style and is a work that brings great honour to the high artistic principles of its composer. One only need see with what insight the Gloria has been written, with what art the solo and tutti movements are apportioned, which sense of order, which warmth, and how the artist always remains so constant and never leaves his inspired course! – The fugue 'in Gloria Dei' is a masterpiece of the art, though it is only developed for some 40 bars and closes with other imitations and thoughts. The true admirer of music will surely thank the good Haydn, for he is almost alone in undertaking to write large fugues for the public. How little has been done recently in this respect, how bald and meagre are the Oratorios, church pieces and so forth even of German masters, who once so distinguished themselves in this field. Of course it is not so easy to write a good fugue. To drag a theme in a schoolmasterish way through a few related keys and to paste together some poor imitations does not mean writing a fugue. Heaven preserve us from that: for it is precisely those witless potpourris that have for many persons put the fugue, that crown of harmony, in discredit. Fugues such as Handel once used to compose, and as Haydn writes them now, so well founded and yet so clear and at the same time expressive, will be applauded by any public. But one must study one's art as these two above-mentioned men did, and must not allow oneself to be carried along by a certain frivolous *Zeitgeist*.
>
> The first part of the Credo is a two-part canon at the fifth: the one voice (discant and tenor, and alto and bass, are coupled together) starts the theme, which

is then imitated note for note by the second a bar later, and this goes on here for no less than 70 bars. How difficult are such tasks, and how little they frequently deserve the effort, need hardly be said. It is true that one finds in some of the newer theatrical pieces, for example in *Lilla* by Martini, three-part canons that create a fine effect. But such a large and extensive chorus as the present canon has not come to our attention in recent times. In every respect it is remarkable and worthy of study, especially because of the original way in which the orchestra is treated.

But the most learned [*studirteste*] piece in the whole Mass seems to us to be the Et resurrexit. It is composed with such insight; without being based severely on one principal subject, it is only the harmonic changes, the out-of-the-way modulations and really massive rhythmic effects that combine to make this piece such a beautiful whole. How hard it is, without middle movements, without interspersing solos, to keep such a piece from being boring only through harmony. Certainly, in gentle melodic movements there are those who equal Haydn, nay even surpass him: but in the true holy-of-holies of the art there is not one among our contemporaries who has penetrated deeper than he.

We would still like to comment on the beautiful *tutti* of the Benedictus, where especially the unexpected passages with the trumpets and drums on page 96 [the B flat section discussed *supra*] must make a noble effect; and on the Dona nobis, full of fugal imitations and beautiful harmonic passages and inversions; but we fear that we have told the reader enough for him to have formed – from what we have said so far – an opinion of the character of this musical work. We imagine, however, that this Mass will present more difficulties in performance than the previous one [*Missa in tempore belli*]. The soli, though short, of the soprano in the Kyrie pages 5 to 7 [bars 39ff.], pages 12 [bars 99ff.] and 15 to 17 [bars 130ff.]; then the passage on p. 74 [Quoniam, bars 65ff.] – these are hard to produce well. The violins, required in all the brilliant movements, need trained and experienced players. It might be possible that the effect of this music in a large temple would perhaps for this reason not always approach that of the first one in C [*Missa in tempore belli*], something one would not dare to assert, however, from just looking at the score. But he who appreciates richness of harmony and fugue, a learned development, a proper sense of proportion and the finest rhythmic effects will give this work a first place among the masterpieces of, say, a Handel or Durante.

Aria da 'Il Canzoniere' di Francesco Petrarca

(Sonetto XXVIII)

(XXIVb: 20)

Scoring: 2 clarinets in B♭, 2 bassoons, 2 horns, strings. *Adagio*, B flat, 3/4 – *Allegretto*, F→B flat, 2/4.

Critical edition from the only source, the autograph (Conservatoire de Musique, Paris, *ex. coll.* Charles Malherbe; title: 'Aria dal Haydn mpria le parole del gran Prencipe di Russia' signed at the top of the music 'In N. D. – Joseph Haydn mpria 798'), issued in 1961 in score, orchestral material and piano score, edited by the present writer, Haydn-Mozart Presse (Salzburg) with *Revisionsbericht* (HMP 192).

Solo e pensoso i più deserti campi
Vo misurando a passi tardi e lenti
E gli occhi porto, per fuggir, intenti,
Dove vestigio uman l'arena stampi.
Altro scherno non trovo che mi scampi
Dal manifesto accorger delle genti;

Perchè negli atti d'allegrezza spenti
Di fuor si legge com'io dentro avvampi:
Sì ch'io mi credo omai che monti e piagge,
E fiumi e selve sappian di che tempre
Sia la mia vita, ch'è celata altrui.
Ma pur sì aspre vie nè sì selvagge
Cercar non so, ch'Amor non venga sempre,
Ragionando con meco ed io con lui.

[Haydn's modernized Italian version]

Petrarch's stately and evocative Sonnet XXVIII was suggested to Haydn by a Russian Grand Prince, as the autograph informs us, and it turns out to be Haydn's rather nostalgic and wistful farewell to the Italian aria – a form which he had cultivated so long and so well for half a century. His first German opera, *Der neue krumme Teufel* (1753?), had contained a series of Italian arias, and he had composed them for his own and other people's operas from 1762 (*Acide*) to the present work of 1798. We have discussed the work's probable first performance at the Tonkünstler-Societät in the Chronicle, *supra*.

Anno 1798 is *The Creation* year, and as we would expect, this Aria reflects the great Oratorio as well as the style of the late Masses. The orchestration, without any oboes, shows once again its composer's devotion to the clarinet in later years. The opening theme itself has a rather religious feeling: are we reminded of the Agnus Dei from the *Missa in angustiis*? Both pieces start with a ritornello, the theme of which is then given to the solo voice:

The beginning of the Allegretto section starts out like Nos. 26 and 28 of *The Creation*; and the basic figure is strongly reminiscent of many parts in the late Masses, especially those in B flat (e.g. the beginning of the Credo, and the beginning of the Et resurrexit, from the *Harmoniemesse* of 1802). It is the kind of *incipit* that is very typical of late Haydn, and even more *Spätstil* is the extraordinary swerve into D flat (a characteristic third-related key: B flat – F major – D flat: D flat being the flattened mediant of the tonic and the flattened submediant of F), in which key the music remains until bar 96. This *outré* harmonic excursion describes, of course, the 'mettle' (*tempre*) of the poet's life, the 'aspre' and 'selvagge' ways of which are known to the whole of nature. The acts of joy are spent and Haydn chooses this subtle way to underline the poem's quiet slide into pessimism (lines 9ff.; see musical example overleaf).

The long return to the tonic is signified by this characteristic phrase

which returns just before the final section. The short coda has some very modest *fioritura* passages: this is definitely an aria of expression, of content. And on this subdued note, Haydn ends his career as a composer of Italian operas (for this Aria may be considered at least a derivative of the Italian aria or *scena*). His mind was now fully occupied with other things, and the spirit of the Masses and late Oratorios is in this Aria.

It is odd that not only was this Aria never published until 1961 but, like the Trumpet Concerto, it survived in one single source: the composer's holograph manuscript. One of the most curious and inexplicable facts of Haydn's final years is the withholding of so many eminently marketable works from publication. On the one hand he sells Breitkopf & Härtel 'Dr. Harington's Compliment' (see *Haydn in England 1791–1795*) – which is really a *Gelegenheitswerk* if there ever was one – while on the other hand, this Aria, the Music from *Alfred*, the Trumpet Concerto, the Concerto for two horns and the *Theresienmesse* all remained unpublished in Haydn's lifetime.

CHAPTER ELEVEN

Chronicle 1799

THE FIRST PERFORMANCE OF *Le tre burle* (otherwise known as *Falstaff*) by Antonio Salieri was given on 3 January at the Kärntnerthor-Theater. It was very well received. Rosenbaum (57f.) wrote in his Diary, 'Many numbers were repeated, one duet ['La stessa, la stessissima'] three times over. After the opera Salieri had to appear twice before the public, and the whole cast was called out. . . .' On the 6th there was already an 'opposing party' which, Rosenbaum noted, 'prevented Salieri's being called out after. . . .' Count Zinzendorf thought, with his customary brevity, 'that it was a bore' (7 April 1799: '. . . falstaff qui ennuyit'). But the opera was sufficiently popular for Beethoven to compose piano Variations on one of the numbers ('La stessa, la stessissima', WoO 73) which Artaria issued.

On 7 January Rosenbaum informs us that the harp virtuoso Josepha Müller or Müllner, 'who has just returned from a tour' lunched with the Gassmanns. 'Afterwards they drove out to see Haydn; I remained at home.'

On 6 February Silverstolpe reported to his father a huge *souper* and ball at Prince Esterházy's, where there were 400 people present, including the Duke and Duchess of Södermanland (as 'Count and Countess von Vasa') and other Swedes (Mörner, 337). It may be for just such an occasion that Haydn performed his Twenty-Four Minuets which have been discussed *supra* (pp. 84f).

Haydn should have attended a session of the Tonkünstler-Societät on 12 February, but in the protocol we read: 'Herr J. Haydn, Assessor Senior, excuses himself through the Hon. Secretary that he is unable to come and proposes to the session that at the next Academy the 7 Words be given, which he would conduct.' The protocol notes, 'The Society accepts with very best thanks and with profound delight the most generous proposal of Herr Haydn.' The concerts in question were scheduled for 17 and 18 March in the Burgtheater.

On 14 February Michael Haydn wrote a letter to Sigismund Neukomm, Haydn's star pupil (and the ex-pupil of Michael).[1] It reads:

Salzburg, 14 February 1799.

Dearest Cousin,

I have finally found enough time to write you a little note and to thank you heartily for all the many thoughtfulnesses you showed me during my stay in Vienna; late, it is true, but nonetheless with all my heart. Every note that you wrote in my honour, except for the 'Willkomm' (which I've meanwhile left at Herr v. Reich's) will be carefully kept and viewed with delight. Just for this reason it gives me much pleasure that you can continue your musical studies with my dear brother. (Recommend me to him and his wife in the warmest manner.) It

1 Burgenländisches Landesmuseum, Eisenstadt (*ex coll.* Landon).

pleases me no less that you have so many lessons and are altogether so well. Continue to stay on in Vienna, for then I will certainly hope that in time you will make your fortune there. If I had only not made such extraordinary haste to leave Vienna entirely, perhaps (as Friend Hummel once wrote to me) I might have become a big animal (an ass or an ox). On my death bed it will pain me still that I could not die in Austria [Salzburg being 'extra-territorial' and an Archbishopric]. But so long as I live I will continue to delight in my life and my friends, and I will think of the many thousand steps we trotted together in Vienna. The fact that I didn't send you a personal greeting in my letter to H[err] v. Eybler, you must put down to my distractedness at that time. Ungratefulness isn't my mistake, otherwise: but I was too late, and thought of it only as I was taking the letter to mail. Then what could be done? Now fare thee well, my dear; think of me kindly in the future, too. I embrace you and remain with gentlest affection, my dear cousin, Your sincerest friend and cousin and father, or whatever you want. Johañ Michael Haydn mpria.

P.S. All kind things to Mons. Keller and Sauter. I will write Herr v. Reich in the next day or two. PPS. My best compliments to H[err] v. Eybler, his *Fr[au] Mutter* and his reverend brother. Nothing for Mlle Lisette the sister? O yes, a great deal! Kiss her hand for me and tell her that I said she should remain my dearest friend for ever; that I will soon write her a long, long letter so she can have lots and lots of wise and foolish things one after another to read; tell her all sorts of pleasant things she wants to hear. A Dieu Lisi! If I just think of you, I can't go on!

[Address] à Monsieur / Monsieur Sigismond Neu-/kom̄, Maitre du Clavecin, / mon tres- cher Ami / à Vienna. [Neukomm's hand: Rec'd 17[t] Horng [March] / Ans'd. – 18[t] April – .'

The letter shows that Johann Michael had a great deal of Joseph's famous charm, and also his affection for children ('Lisi' is obviously Eybler's youngest sister). Apart from the information it gives us about the writer, Neukomm and Joseph Haydn, the letter is significant in its reference to Vienna. This was always Mozart's idea, too – one need only read the first letters to his father Leopold in 1781. Whether a Viennese position would have made Michael Haydn as famous as his brother is, however, a matter of some doubt. (After all, Joseph's career was mainly in Lukavec, Eisenstadt, Eszterháza and London.)

On 15 February Haydn was conducting once again at the Lobkowitz Palace; this time it was one of the new Masses. Zinzendorf (Olleson, 55) writes: '. . . au Concert de Lobkowitz. Musique de Hayd'n et ennui. Messe bruyante . . .'. Both the *Mass in Time of War* and the 'Nelson' Mass are very 'bruyantes'. This was the time for another official announcement, and perhaps the most significant one in Haydn's life hitherto: the first public performance of *The Creation* was set for 19 March at the Burgtheater. The *AMZ* carried a letter in its issue of 20 February from a Viennese correspondent.

13 February 1799.

Another piece of news which will not be uninteresting to you. It is believed here, as far as I know, quite generally that Jos. Haydn actually wrote his *Creation* for England, that he is not allowed to give it here, at least not for the present. Probably you make reference to this situation in the remarks in the 16th number of your journal, p. 255. But – the circumstances or the composer's plans having apparently been changed – in short, we shall get this masterpiece performed here in public and at a ceremonious occasion. On 19 March it will be given in our Court Theatre. The orchestra will consist of 180 persons. The aristocracy pays for the costs of the performance, so that the whole income goes to the composer. And that this will be respectable you can see from the fact that now, at present writing, not a box more is to be had. We are just now beginning to know and appreciate our Father Haydn; and it is good that Heaven permitted him a ripe old age, so that he can enjoy his deeds and does not receive after his death something like a magnificent – stone.

The reference to the *AMZ* p. 255 was a *Nachricht* (piece of news) at the end of the issue of 16 January, which said a few words about the *Beylage*. That supplement was a version of the Duet beginning with the quick section, 'Der thauende Morgen', taken down by ear and consequently with some curious mistakes, from Part Three of *The Creation*. It was obviously the first (and not entirely representative) foretaste of the work that many German musicians had. The absence of copyright laws prevented even Haydn from prohibiting such a procedure. The *AMZ* added a few words which we may include here:

> . . . About the work itself we have nothing to add [to the long letter by Baron van Swieten, *vide supra*, p. 116] except that all the opinions of connoisseurs and amateurs that have arrived here bear out [Swieten's] opinion; they describe the work as Haydn's greatest, most sublime [*erhabenstes*] and most perfect – that means, surely, the greatest, most sublime and most perfect of the newest period of music? The enclosed song cannot of course give any idea of the whole, not even a foretaste – it is a single little page from the wreath of immortality which Haydn, the old man, created for himself. But it can satisfy the wish of those who wanted to have at least something of the piece; and finally it can suggest once more that Germany still leaves the most perfect works of its greatest artists to the foreigners and at best can receive such works from them *ex gratia*. And to give an idea of the plan of the whole, we include as a supplement to the next issue the German text by Freyherr van Swieten.

In fact it seems that Breitkopf & Härtel secured Haydn's permission to print an extract of the Oratorio. At this point, Haydn was not yet in regular correspondence with the firm, and perhaps all this was done by van Swieten, who was. Later the *AMZ* rather sheepishly explained that the Duet 'was only a part of a whole movement, was from a musician who had attended several performances, listened, remembered it and wrote it down from memory and, without telling us of the circumstances, sent it to us' (II, 441). It was all not quite correct even *de jure*, and possibly the above explanation was requested by the Baron and Haydn when they saw the mangled remains of their Duet thus printed. Interesting, however, that the correspondent chose just this particular piece as representative of the whole; it bears out the discussion of this whole section with Adam and Eve which has concerned us *supra* (p. 424).

Breitkopf & Härtel tried to persuade Constanze Mozart, who was on friendly terms with Haydn, to buy *The Creation* for the Leipzig firm, but Constanze firmly declined:

> Vienna, 25 February 1799 . . . As far as the score of *The Creation* is concerned, I am not able to be of service to you. I could hardly offer Haydn 100, much less 20, ducats . . .

Shortly thereafter, we have another extract from Constanze on the same subject. She writes:

> Vienna, 2 March 1799 . . . I hear from Herrn Baron [van] S[wieten] that you have received the Duet from *The Creation*. Now they are going to play it on the 19th [*sic*] in the theatre at Schwarzenberg's with 181 instruments . . .

It almost sounds as if Constanze had something to do with the sending of that Duet. Interesting, otherwise, is the fact that even in the relatively cramped quarters at Prince Schwarzenberg's winter palace, Haydn was now using his 'monster' orchestra, of which several reports quote the figure '180'.[1]

Rosenbaum was, of course, hoping that Therese Gassmann would be chosen to sing the soprano part since it was known that Christine Gerardi had retired. On 20 February we read in Rosenbaum's Diary (58f.)

> Elsler [*sic*] promised to fetch me, but . . . left without waiting for me. I would so much have liked to visit Haydn today, in order to know who is to sing in his *Erschaffung* [*sic* for *Schöpfung*]. . . . Thursday, 21st: . . . [after lunch] I drove out to see Haydn, talked with him about *The Creation* and learned that [Therese] Saal will sing instead of Gerardi, which will offend Therese [Gassmann] greatly. I told Haydn so in the driest possible words; he apologized by saying that the cavaliers had so ordered it against his will, because they are paying all expenses. . . . Saturday, 23rd: . . . After lunch I wrote, in Mama [Gassmann's] name, a letter to Haydn about Therese being slighted, and about the vocal part being given to Saal. . . .

We now come to the arrival of the extremely pretty and, from all accounts, talented soprano, Therese Saal upon the Viennese stage. She was seventeen years old when she made her début in *The Creation* and became so famous in the role that the great Füger even painted her as Eve in the Oratorio, holding a page of the soprano part in her hand. In one of the destroyed letters from Griesinger to Breitkopf & Härtel there seems to have been a reference suggesting that Therese Saal became Prince Kaunitz's mistress, in which case he may have manoeuvred for her to appear in *The Creation* as early as 1799 (the letter in question is dated 18 March 1801). It is clear that Swieten's Gesellschaft der Associirten was behind Therese Saal. Although Haydn was later to speak rather negatively of her abilities, she certainly captivated the public at first. 'The Eve in Haydn's *Creation* will hardly be sung with such spiritual depth, delicacy and a holy innocence', wrote the Viennese correspondent of the *AMZ* in 1805, when Therese Saal married a rich merchant and left the stage. Joseph Sonnleithner said of her:

> Mlle Saal, who sang soprano, was soon thereafter the darling of the Court Theatre. Her talent, her youth, her pretty face made her an irresistible drawing-card; everybody was in love with her, I too. Unfortunately this flowering of the pretty blonde did not last long; she was already half wilted when she married. . . .[2]

On 24 February an enormous ice-floe on the Danube broke up. In this exceptionally cold winter, the Danube itself continued to freeze over in places; the ice-floe jammed against bridges and other obstacles and flooding began. Rosenbaum writes in his Diary (59):

> Tonerl and I drove to the Augarten Bridge, where the ice-floe had halted and had caused the river to overflow both banks. It froze last night and so the flooded area looked like a mirror. [Later they] went to the Rothen Thurm Bastion . . . and about 4 o'clock the ice-floe, driven by the surge of the water, rose with

1 Arthur Schurig, *Konstanze Mozart*, Dresden 1922, pp. 13f.

2 *AMZ* VII, 593; for Sonnleithner, see Pohl III, 143; for Kaunitz, see Günter Thomas, *Haydn-Studien* 1/2 (1966), p. 68. The Füger portrait reproduced in Somfai, 172; also in the present volume, pl. V, in colour.

considerable noise. It was an awesome, grandiose spectacle at the moment when the water rose by 4 feet, overflowed its banks on the Leopoldstadt side where the boats are anchored, and monstrous blocks of ice, boats and wreckage were swept downstream.

On 28 February there was a soirée at Prince Georg Adam Starhemberg's, at which Zinzendorf found 'Swieten qui y est a tout moment. Il parla de sa musique de la création', a remark which we have quoted above but which even Zinzendorf found a little strong (Olleson, 55).

A few days later there was another pair of *Creation* performances at Prince Schwarzenberg's palace on the Neuer Markt. On 2 March was the first of these performances, and Silverstolpe on that day wrote a *dépêche* to King Gustav IV in which we learn: 'This evening the *Herr Graf and Frau Gräfin* Vasa [Södermanland] are invited by the *Kaiserlichen Kammerherren* Prince Schwarzenberg to a grand concert under Haydn's direction, at which . . . *The Creation* . . . will be performed.' The Duchess of Södermanland wrote in her Diary:

> . . . Lapredinée je fut à un concert ches le Prince Svartzenberg [*sic*], ou j'entendris la fameuse musique de Haydn intitule la creation, qui et bien le morceaux le plus superbe qu'on puisse entendre, il est imposible de pouvoir exprimer qu'il efet fait l'instance ou il est dit – Das verde [*sic*] Licht, c'est sublime. . . . [Mörner, 337]

On 2 March Zinzendorf could not obtain a ticket, but he was there on the 4th, noting in his Diary all the things he particularly liked:

> . . . chez le P^ce^ Schwarzenberg au Concert de Haydn die Schöpfung. J'ai trouvois une petite place entre les Dames au premier rang, d'abord entre Me de Hardeg Ctesse Chanoinesse et Melle de Hadik, puis entre la dernière et Lisette Schoenborn, puis voit un V^au^ de guerre, Me de Hazfeld qui me deplaça et ensuite pensa m'etoufer. Mes Mailath, Wallis et Melle Hadik moi donnent leur places dans les entr'actes, cet P^ce^ K[aunitz]. et a moi. Und es ward licht – – leise rauschend gleitet fort im stillen Thal der helle Bach – Nun beut die Flur das frische Grün – Mit leisem Gang – – der Mond die stille Nacht hindurch. L'air de la création de l'homme et de la femme, celui qui le precede – – du nimmst den Odem weg; in Staub zerfallen sie. Den Odem hauchst du wieder aus und neues Leben sprost hervor. Ces mots surtout si bien accompagnés penetrent l'ame d'une sainte veneration. Puis le Duo d'Adam et d'Eve . . . Tems triste et doux.
> [Olleson, 55, and Zinzendorf MS.]

Zinzendorf seems to have put down half the Oratorio – including the Duet between Adam and Eve which has been discussed so much – and like the rest of the audience the music obviously went straight to his heart. Unfortunately no one has recorded the participants; the obvious open question was the soprano part: was it still sung by Christine Gerardi (already married) or was this the début of the pretty blonde, Therese Saal? We note that Kaunitz, *vrai expert de la défloration Viennoise*, was in the audience (*vide supra*) . . .

That morning ('cold and bright') Rosenbaum had gone into town to the Prince [Esterházy] and Count [Carl Esterházy]:

> the latter asked me to drive immediately to Haydn and to order two boxes for him for the [forthcoming public] performance of *The Creation*. Haydn promised me them. . . . Tuesday, 5th: . . . throughout the entire night and day it snowed an unbelievable amount, blew as well, and gave rise to the most dreadful weather . . . Wednesday, 6th: . . . At about 6:30 Tonerl and I drove to Galliani's academy at

> Jahn's [rooms]. Therese and Pasqua sang. . . . I talked very little to Therese, but when we drove home Therese waited at the steps and we dallied and chatted with one another for half an hour. God! Those were blissful moments. . . . I love Therese inexpressibly! – She is such a rare, sweet girl, worthy of the love of the best of men! . . .' [*Rosenbaum*, 59f.]

On the 8th was a grand concert, with chorus and orchestra, at Prince Lobkowitz's; the entrance was guarded with 'barrières' to prevent hopeless congestion. Zinzendorf noted 'Il y avoit des barrières, ce qui vaut mieux qu'autrefois. On chante un choeur d'un Oratoire, on joua des Symphonies, je partis avant le tempête [Madrigal, 'The Storm'] de Haydn. . . .'

The Lenten concerts of the Tonkünstler-Societät, at the Burgtheater on 17 and 18 March, were devoted to *The Seven Words* in the vocal version, conducted of course by Haydn himself. For a man of nearly seventy, his activity would have broken many a younger artist: *The Creation* on 2 and 4 March, a Lobkowitz concert on the 8th, *The Seven Words* on the 17th and 18th and the first public performance of *The Creation* on the 19th. In *The Seven Words* the soloists were Therese Gassmann, Antonie Flamm, Carl Weinmüller and Sigismund Hüller. At the beginning was a 'Große Sinfonie v. Ritter v. Gluck' (probably the Overture to *Iphigénie en Aulide* with the so-called Mozart ending); in the interval of 17 March, the Court oboist Georg Triebensee played a concerto of his own composition, while on 18 March Peter Fuchs played his own violin concerto. The *Wiener Zeitung* (No. 24, March 23) simply reported the programme and noted the 'general success' of the Oratorio, while Zinzendorf, who went on the 17th, also did no more than note the fact in his Diary (Olleson, 56), adding 'Très belle journée'.[1]

According to Rosenbaum's Diary (61), Fuchs played his concerto on the 17th rather than the 18th; perhaps the oboe and violin concertos were reversed.

> Sunday, 17th, Palm Sunday . . . I read Haydn's announcement of *The Creation* to the Prince [Nicolaus] and the benefactor [Carl Esterházy], both of whom disliked it, the latter considering it beggary . . . and [later I] went with Tonerl to the academy of the Society. Fux played a violin concerto, then Haydn's *Words of the Saviour* was performed. The two Umlauf sisters [daughters of the composer Ignaz Umlauf, who had died in 1796] came over to us and I gave them sweets . . . went to Therese in her box and could notice her childish jealousy of the Umlauf girls. After the academy I saw the Umlaufs home, then Ninna [Gassmann] went to Scheidemayer, gave him the tickets to the rehearsal [of *The Creation*], because Haydn had sent me three, one of which I had given to Ninna . . .

The announcement to which Rosenbaum refers is in fact the poster for *The Creation*, of which the Österreichische Nationalbibliothek (Theatersammlung) owns a copy.[2] Actually it is Haydn's rather wordy request for the audience not to applaud between numbers of the first public performance of the Oratorio. The wording suggests that the Baron van Swieten may have had a hand in the formulation. The poster reads:

1 The report of a concert at the Schwarzenberg Palace on 17 March (with part of *The Seasons*) as reported in Mörner (337f.) is a mistake for the Tonkünstler-Societät performance on that evening. Apparently the Duchess of Södermanland attended the concert on the 17th. Pohl, *Denkschrift*, 66.

2 Facsimiles in Hadden's *Haydn*, p. 137, also Rosemary Hughes's *Haydn*, facing p. 112.

Today Tuesday the 19th of March 1799
Will be performed in the K. K. Hoftheater next to the Burg
THE CREATION
An Oratorio
set to music by
Herr Joseph Haydn, Doctor of Music and Kapellmeister
to His Serene Highness Prince Esterházy

Nothing can be more flattering to Haydn than the public's approval. To earn that has been his most earnest wish, and he has had the fortune to win it often – more, indeed, than he would have believed his due. Now he hopes, it is true, for the work here announced that same attitude which he has to his inner peace and thankfulness observed to prevail hitherto; but he would furthermore like to observe that if in case there arises the opportunity for applause, it will be permitted him to receive it as a much appreciated mark of satisfaction, but not as a request for the repetition of one or the other individual piece; for otherwise the true connection between the various single parts, from the uninterrupted succession of which should proceed the effect of the whole, would be necessarily disturbed, and therefore the pleasure, the expectance of which a perhaps too favourable reception on the public's part has awakened, would of nature be markedly reduced.

The beginning is at 7 o'clock.

The prices of admission are as usual.

The words will be given out gratis at the box-office.

On Monday Haydn had not only the Tonkünstler-Societät concert in the evening but the general rehearsal of *The Creation* at noon. Rosenbaum was there and wrote (61): 'Monday, 18th: A lovely, bright day . . . [I] worked very diligently and went at about 12 o'clock to the rehearsal of *The Creation*, and at 1 o'clock to the Bastion . . . I was cut to the heart to know I would not see or hear my sweet Therese in Saal's place. At table we were cordial but downcast . . .'.

We now arrive at Tuesday, 19 March, the first public performance of the Oratorio at the Burgtheater. Since there are many authentic documents concerning this famous event, we may quote them one after another. It will be noted that although the concert began at seven o'clock in the evening, there was utter chaos in the Burgtheater by four in the afternoon.

(1) [Rosenbaum, Diary (61):] . . . At about 7 o'clock [a.m.] I went into town . . . and saw the march through of the Russians in Schönbrunn. The benefactor [Carl Esterházy] was not in a good humour today. . . . At about 4 o'clock Agnes and Tonerl and I went to Haydn's concert at the Burg Theater. Never since the theatre was built has there been such a fearful and dangerous press. Pfersman let us through the office and gallery to the box-office, and we were thus able to get good seats. – Casanova [brother of the famous libertine] was also there and, as it happened, sat next to me; we conversed together. Before *The Creation* began there were . . . incidents [as the crowd battled for seats]; the time passed unnoticed. I was very attentive and enjoyed it greatly. Haydn was greatly applauded, but by no means so greatly as I had expected. – After the concert Haydn was called forward, and only long afterwards the three vocal soloists, Saal, his daughter and Rathmayer. . . .

(2) [Zinzendorf's Diary (Olleson, 56):] . . . a 7^{h} au Concert de Haydn la Création au Theatre de la Cour. Dans ma loge, la P^{csse} Auersb[erg], ma belle-soeur, el la P^{cse}

Lobk[owitz]. . . . On entendit plus commodêment et il fesoit plus d'effet que chez Schwarzenb . . . Belle journee. Vent aigre. boutons des arbres.

(3) [Report to the *Allgemeine Musikalische Zeitung*, dated 24 March 1799, unsigned; I: 446ff.] Now I have been six weeks here and have still not found time to write to you about the present condition of music here, nor to give you even the slightest news of interesting events. I hope to be that much more diligent hereafter. I shall begin my news with an event which is a good omen for you.

On the 19th inst. I heard Haydn's *Creation*. Not to report immediately on this happy occasion (for I feel it was such) were to display too little feeling for the Art, or too little for Friendship. This masterpiece of the new musical age was given in the National Theatre next to the Burg. The audience was exceptionally large and the receipts amounted to 4088 Fl. 30 Kr., because the price of a box was 6 ducats and a *Sperrsitz* [a seat the owner of which could lock with his key] raised to 2 Fl.: – a sum that has never been taken in by any Viennese theatre. Even Marches[i], Crescentini and Mde. Vigano, who have had the biggest successes here in Vienna up to now, did not have receipts like that. Apart from this, the aristocracy paid for all the by-no-means inconsiderable costs (the singers and orchestra consisted of more than 180 persons). One can hardly imagine the silence and the attention with which the whole Oratorio was heard, gently broken only by soft exclamations at the most remarkable passages; at the end of each piece and each section there was enthusiastic applause. Herr Saal and his daughter much distinguished themselves. Now Haydn is working on a new great work, which the worthy *Herr Geheimrath Freyherr* van Swieten has arranged metrically from Thomson's 'Seasons', and of which he has already completed the first part, 'Spring'. The curiosity of all music lovers is already stretched to the breaking-point. Haydn is also at present working – as he himself informed me – on six new quartets for the Hungarian Count K. –. . . .

(4) [*Eipeldauer-Briefe 1799* (Pohl III, 144f.), in Viennese dialect:] This day, dear cousin, we've had a different spectacle in Vienna, and for this spectacle our fine society even forgot the march through the city by the Russian [troops under Marshal Suvorof]. For the famous Hayden performed *The Creation of the World* set to music, and I can't tell you, cousin, how full it was. As long as the theatre has stood, it hasn't been so full. I was standing at the door by 1 o'clock, and only at the risk of life and limb did I get a little seat in the last row of the 4th floor: Eipeldauer didn't find the right entrance, otherwise he would have snapped up a better seat. My wife reserved 2 seats – she likes things comfortable – and so she got to the theatre about 6 o'clock, and she couldn't get to her seats any more, so the usher was kind enough to let her sit on his seat by the door, otherwise she'd have had to stand on her fine old feet. . . .

[Our friend] The Merchant would have gladly paid for it if he could have got a box or a couple of *Sperrsitze*; but they were all sold long ago. Since the income belongs to the famous composer, and 'cause everybody is so fond of him, the fine ladies and gentlemen auctioned off their boxes and *Sperrsitze* among themselves just like an auctioneer at a death-duty sale.

So that everyone could understand what the music wanted to say, they handed out libretti of the Cantata *gratis*, and it's beautiful to read: what I liked about it specially was that it's written in *hoch* [*deutsch*] but you can understand it.

Since all our best poets are dead, a poetess appeared and distributed quite a nice poem gratis [Gabriela von Baumberg, *vide infra*]; and she compared the music to a good wine, and just by reading the comparison I could tell she was a real poet, 'cause it has to be a bad poet, dear cousin, who doesn't appreciate wine.

Before the Cantata started, there was a noise and a yelling so that you couldn't hear yourself think. They yelled: Ow! My arm! My foot! My hat! And ladies were calling for the servants they'd sent to keep the places for them, and the servants were calling for their mistresses, and people were almost climbing over each other so that *fichus* and shawls and skirts were crack-cracking all over the place. A small child was almost crushed if it had not been for a fine Reverend Sir who lifted it up into his box. . . .

Finally the music began, and all at once it became so quiet that you, cousin, could have heard a mouse running, and if they hadn't often applauded, you would have thought that there weren't any people in the theatre. But cousin, in my whole life I won't hear such a beautiful piece of music; and even if it had lasted three hours longer, and even if the stink- and sweat-bath had been much worse, I wouldn't have minded.

For the life of me I wouldn't have believed that human lungs and sheep gut and calf's skin could create such miracles. The music all by itself described thunder and lightning and then, cousin, you'd have heard the rain falling and the water rushing and even the worms crawling on the ground. In short, cousin, I never left a theatre more contented and all night I dreamed of the Creation of the World.

(5) [In 1799, Georg Johann Berwald and his *Wunderkind* son, Johan Fredrik, travelled through Europe on a concert tour and stayed in Vienna from March to 10 May; these Berwalds were cousins of the later famous composer Franz; Johan Fredrik, violinist and composer, was born in 1787 and later wrote his memoirs under the title, *Anteckningar utur mitt lif*, from which the following notes are taken:[1]]

Here in Vienna I became acquainted with Mozart's widow and her two sons. It is perhaps worth mentioning that we heard *The Creation*, which was at that time, in 1799, performed for the first time [in public] at the Imperial Burgtheater. Paul Wranitzky arranged to get us tickets for this musical celebration. As early as 4 o'clock in the afternoon, our temporary servant came and said we should hasten to the theatre, because it was besieged by a large number of people although the concert was not to start until 7 o'clock. When we entered, we saw that the stage proper was set up in the form of an amphitheatre. Down below at the fortepiano sat *Kapellmeister* Weigl, surrounded by the vocal soloists, the chorus, a violoncello and a double bass [as continuo]. At one level higher stood Haydn himself with his conductor's baton. Still a level higher on one side were the first violins, led by Paul Wranitzky and on the other the second violins, led by his brother Anton Wranitzky. In the centre: violas and double basses. In the wings, more double basses; on higher levels the wind instruments, and at the very top: trumpets, kettledrums and trombones. That was the disposition of the orchestra which, together with the chorus, consisted of some 400 persons. The whole went off wonderfully. Between the sections of the work, tumultuous applause; during each section, however, it was as still as the grave. When it was over, there were calls, 'Father Haydn to the front! Father Haydn to the front!' Finally the old man came forward and was greeted with a tumultuous *Applaudissement* and with cries, 'Long live Father Haydn! Long live music!' Their imperial majesties were all present and joined in the 'bravo' calls. Among the persons of rank I noticed several princely persons driven out by the French, also the Grand Duke of Tuscany and his wife, the Duke of Parma with the daughter of Louis XVI, and so on. After the end of the concert, my father and I were introduced to Haydn by Paul Wranitzky. He [Haydn] was very polite and said we should call on him; a mark of favour which, as Wranitzky said, he doesn't confer on everyone; for he is plagued by travellers who all want to see and speak to him.

1 C.-G. Stellan Mörner, 'Haydniana aus Schweden um 1800', in *Haydn-Studien* II/1 (1969), pp. 5ff.

On the morning of the next day, we drove to him in the suburbs, where he has a fine house with a garden. When we asked if Doctor Haydn was at home, a servant said he was not but that Frau Doctor was in the garden, and showed us there. On a bench sat an old woman, surrounded by some dogs and cats, and when my father said he had learned that the Doctor was not at home, she answered in Viennese dialect, 'He ain't in but he'll be back soon'. As to my father's question, if Frau Doctor had been on the trip to England from which he [Haydn] had recently returned, she said: 'No, my husband had enough to do to persuade me to go to the suburbs. I'll never leave my dear Vienna.' When the conversation fell on that excellent work, *The Creation*, which we had heard yesterday, she said: 'People say it's supposed to be good, I wouldn't know.' – We gathered from the old lady's words that she was neither educated nor musical. They say in Vienna that Haydn's rather unhappy and childless marriage is the reason why he composed so much.

Haydn came, and his wife trotted off with her dogs and cats. The old man was very cheerful and invited us into his study, spoke a great deal about music, especially about it in Sweden, and finally asked if his symphonies were played there. My father said yes, and added that they were much loved. Haydn wanted to know how quickly they took his so-called minuets. My father sung one in the tempo that they were taken at Stockholm. He [Haydn] said it was not his intention to have them played so quickly, for the double basses would not be able to play at such a tempo unless the gentlemen in Sweden were virtuosi of the first order. My father said, that was by no means the case. 'Then they will ruin my minuets, of which I flatter myself to be the inventor as far as this style is concerned', answered Haydn, 'for these minuets are a cross between minuets for dancing and prestos'. (Scherzos [adds Berwald by way of explanation], which generally go very quickly, are the invention of a later era.) After [fulfilling] his wish to hear me play, we made our adieux.

Next Sunday at Wranitzky's I played him [Haydn] some quartets, and he seemed to be satisfied.

(6) [A poem written for the occasion (and perhaps distributed in the Theatre?) by 'I. B. R . . . t' (broadsheet owned by the Wiener Stadtbibliothek);]

Verstummt Kalender und Autoren,
Und bringt die Leute nicht um's Geld.
Das größte Labsal unsrer Ohren,
Die Schöpfung – kam erst jetzt zur Welt.

Vertilge, blutendes Jahrhundert!
Nur Deutschlands Größe, Deutschlands Ruhm.
Was Welt und Nachwelt noch bewundert,
Bleibt demnoch – deutsches Eigenthum.

Mit allen ihren Herrlichkeiten,
Mit Himmels Reitzen ausgeziert,
Vom größten Autor aller Zeiten,
Groß und erhaben aufgeführt.

Vom größten Autor aller Zeiten –
Und jeder stimmt frohlockend ein:
Der Schöpfer solcher Herrlichkeinten,
Kann nur der große Haydn seyn.

I. B. R . . . t.

Auf Haydns Schöpfung, am 19. März im K. K. Hoftheater aufgeführt. Wien, 1799.

(7) [Letter from G. A. Griesinger to Breitkopf & Härtel, 9 November 1799, concerning the rental of the Burgtheater for *The Creation* (Pohl III, 146):] . . . It is in fact difficult to organize a financially profitable concert. The Court-(Burg) and Kärntnerthor-Theatres are let to a Baron Braun, who has many friends at Court. He doesn't easily lend his orchestra for accompanying, or on the day when the concert is supposed to take place, he announces a new or very popular piece and ballet, and thereby deprives the poor musician of his numerous public. Would you believe it, but even Haydn, when he performed his *Creation* for the first [time] in public, had to get the Empress to put in a special word for him in order to get a satisfactory day for the performance of his masterpiece.

(8) [A poem by Gabriela von Baumberg, distributed at the concert in the Burgtheater:[1]]

An den grossen
unsterblichen Hayden.

Erquickend – sanft – wie alles Schöne
Und feurig – wie gerechter Wein,
Ströhmt oft der Zauber *Deiner* Töne
Durch's Ohr, in unser Herz hinein.

Jüngst schuf *Dein* Schöpferisches WERDE!
Den Donner, durch den Paukenschall;
Und Himmel – Sonne – Mond – und Erde,
Die Schöpfung ganz – zum Zweitenmal.

Gefühlvoll – staunend – wonnetrunken!
Wie Adam einst im Paradies,
Am Arm der Eva hingesunken
Zwar sprachlos den Erschaffer pries:

So huld'gen wir im Aug die Thräne
Dem Kunstwerk deiner Phantasie –
Der Allmacht deiner Zaubertöne
Und *Dir*, dem Gott der Harmonie!

[device]

Von
Gabriela von Baumberg,
bey Gelegenheit als die *Schöpfung*,
dieß Meisterstück der Tonkunst, im k. k. Nationaltheater aufgeführt wurde
Am 19. März 1799.

[Somfai, 173]

1 There are several contemporary sources for this poem, *inter alia AMZ* I, 416 (1799) and Dies (174). In these sources, the last stanza is different:

So hören wir enzückt die Töne
Des Kunstwerks Deiner Phantasie –
Und huldigen, im Aug' die Thräne,
Dir, Schöpfer hoher Harmonie!

We follow the broadsheet distributed on the evening, of which a copy was in Haydn's library and is now in the Esterházy Archives, Budapest, Ha. I. 21. Gabriela von Baumberg also wrote verses for the monument erected to Haydn by Count Harrach in Rohrau: see *Haydn in England 1791–1795*. In 1805 she married Johann (János) Bacsányi, a Hungarian poet. See also Pohl III, 395.

The size of Haydn's forces seems to have been about 400, as the reliable Swedish witness informs us; the figure of 180 for the orchestra quoted in earlier documents (or 180 for chorus and orchestra) may have been based on the usual size of the Tonkünstler-Societät academies, or on a previous statement by Haydn and/or the Theatre. It will have been observed that Haydn followed his favourite amphitheatrical seating-plan for the orchestra and chorus, which he had used in the very first Salomon concert in 1791 (see *Haydn in England 1791–1795*). The brass instruments (in this case horns, trumpets and trombones) were placed at the very top with the kettledrums and were thus, for one last brief instant in history, restored to their former place of honour in Baroque orchestras. Those slashes of *ff* colour from brass and timpani in Haydn's Oratorio literally 'came down from on high' in these first Viennese performances. Although the English adopted this pyramidal shape for Handel's oratorios in the early 1790s – apparently following Haydn's scheme of 1791 – it seems not to have been accepted by posterity except in the occasional concert.

The concert, which took place on Haydn's name day (St Joseph), was such a success that the repercussions – which must have continued for weeks – may have induced Haydn to publish the score himself. No doubt many enthusiastic members of the Austro-Hungarian aristocracy encouraged him in this undertaking and promised to become subscribers; one of those who certainly approved the plan was Gottfried van Swieten. In fact Haydn himself, in his subscription announcement (15 June 1799; *vide infra*), gives two principal reasons for issuing the score himself: (1) the success of the work in Vienna and (2) the hope, expressed in the *AMZ* (*infra*, p. 471), that its publication would not be left to foreign music-publishing institutions.

All things considered, Haydn had entered the hearts of his countrymen in a way that no composer had ever done to that extent previously. It is really almost as if *The Creation* was man's hope for a peaceful future (uncertain, at best, in 1799) and man's consolation for a clouded present. That it brought real comfort, consolation and joy to thousands of Viennese and, very soon, other Europeans, is clear from every document quoted above. Never in the history of music, not even Handel with his *Messiah* (hardly known, for example, in France, Spain, Italy, or Russia), had a composer judged the temper of his time with such smashing success.

The time was indeed clouded, for although Haydn may have won the Viennese away from the spectacle of 'barbarian' Russian troops marching through Vienna on their way to Italy, the troops were there nonetheless and everyone knew that the theatre of the war had considerably broadened. Napoleon was still in Egypt and no one knew his plans, but against France there had been formed a new coalition including England, Austria, Russia, Turkey, Portugal and such Italian States as were not occupied by France. As usual, matters looked more optimistic at first, and the French were soon pushed back to the Rhine, while from the Tyrol another offensive was successfully launched against Switzerland. The Russian army joined Austrian forces and marched to Italy, where they had great initial successes; but later a French offensive under Masséna would be crucial and the Russian army would at the end of September be forced to retreat with grave losses; and this in turn forced the Tsar to sign a separate peace treaty with France. To continue our brief preview of events in Europe, Napoleon then returned to the Continent, landing on 9 October in Fréjus and taking command of the Italian army shortly thereafter, with results that we shall examine in the Chronicle of 1800.

The Viennese, meanwhile, had a good look at their new allies. Rosenbaum, on Maundy Thursday (21 March), went to Schönbrunn where the Russians were stationed (61f.):

> Cold windy and dull . . . The . . . grenadiers made a good impression, but I can't bring myself to like the officers – there is so little about them that is promising. One cannot admire their artillery at all. Their Cossacks are crude barbarians. I liked their hospital coaches the best of all; they have a great similarity to our *deligence* [*sic*] coaches.

On 23 March, the day before Easter, *Messiah* was given at Prince Schwarzenberg's in the Mehlmarkt (Neuer Markt). The Duchess of Södermanland found it less exciting than *The Creation* but her fellow Swede, Silverstolpe, thought 'it excels everything'.[1] A week later, on the 30th, a new production of Cimarosa's *Il matrimonio segreto*, including Therese Gassmann and Irene Dutillieu (*née* Tomeoni), was given at the Burgtheater. Rosenbaum (62) 'liked very much' a trio (in which Therese participated); 'otherwise I was bored at the theatre. . . .' Had closer knowledge of Mozart's late operas and Haydn's late choral music made Cimarosa slightly less intoxicating for the Viennese?

Readers will recall *Herr Z* (Zelter?) and his criticism in the *AMZ* of the lion's tail quoted above. The composer 'A——' whom Zelter criticizes for having copied Haydn turns out to be Johann Anton André Jr. (he signs himself 'Ant. André') who wrote a trenchant 'Anti-Kritik' which the *AMZ* published in its *Intelligenz-Blatt No. X* (March 1799); this 'Anti-Kritik' was read by 'Z' who added some rough footnotes of his own. The whole is then capped by an open letter to André by the well-known Leipzig organist, *Thomaskantor* and *Kapellmeister*, August Eberhard Müller. The whole contretemps is very amusing and shows a new spirit among German musical criticism which must have astonished many people. We cannot quote more than extracts, and of course those pertaining to Haydn. In order to simplify the typographical layout, we place the footnotes to the right of the original 'Anti-Kritik':

Anti-Kritik	['Z' 's footnotes]
. . . Without precisely wishing to call myself a *modern composer*, much less a *virtuoso*, I must answer the above-listed questions [in Z's article] because I am personally quoted in the third section. . . .	Hr. André Junior of Offenbach, who as his notes will show absolutely refuses to be called 'Junior' – took it upon himself to send in this article, which bears witness to the writer's impudence, and only shows up his own ignorance and uncertainty. . . .
. . . As far as the second question goes, I am quite of the opinion that the horn and trumpet are often used wrongly, but that doesn't mean that the horn should sound only soft and the trumpet only blare: both *can* and *each must* be able to do so as the effect requires; but that the newer composers only *copy* Haydn and Mozart and that *only they* use the trumpet and horn properly is, with your permission, *not true*. Both men often paid no attention whatever to the effect of the wind instruments. . . .	. . . Hr. A, think a little – who said *that*? I said (clearly for everybody except, as I see, for you): Haydn and Mozart were the first to have the trumpet play sustained *piano* notes and the horn blare – *sometimes*, to achieve a *special* effect. . . . But that some modern composers make this *special* effect of the trumpets and horns a *regular* feature seems to me wrong. That is what *I* said, what are *you* trying to prove? . . .
. . . Haydn as well as Mozart are, neither of them, the *first* in many cases of that which we call original in their scores; whoever had studied the older composers can see that for himself.	

1 Mörner, 338f.; Zinzendorf MS. Diary.

[Anti-Kritik, *continued*]

But it is true that they used in the newest style of composition much that was already said long ago. . . . The Haydn Symphony mentioned [No. 95] is op. 70 Liv. 1 in my father's publishing house and much though I like it as a whole, I cannot possibly agree with Hr. Z what he says about the final allegro; the cited Mozart Symphony ['Jupiter'] op. 38 is quite another affair, wherein the last allegro is a real final fugue, from the analysis of which Hr. Z should teach himself what one *may* or *may not* call a fugue. But back to the Haydn allegro. H. takes, after he has let us hear the pleasant theme, the first two bars of the theme in the second violins, repeats it twice a third lower and after an episodic passage closes on the third of the tonic. The first violin then answers this section one third higher [= V] and after that the bass enters also on the lower sixth [= V] and carries on the passage for five bars, all of which is quite contrary to the rules of fugues at the fifth. The following 29 bars are without any reference to the theme, [etc, etc.] From all this one sees that H. did not *want* to make a fugue, and indeed it takes quite a different pair of ears to hear a fugue *here*; moreover a large portion of *immodesty* is required if, as Hr. Z. does, the public is to be misled in this fashion and is expected to believe what he says blindly only on the *strength of his word*. Before Hr. Z dares to let the *word* fugue even cross his lips, let him read first what Bach, Bononcini, Matheson, Werkmeister, Prinz, Stuse, Spies, Marpurg, Kirnberger, Albrechtsberger and many others have said about the theory of the fugue and also in part delivered the practical results thereto. . . .

. . . Flattering though it would be for me to have my Symphony considered a clear *pendant* to the cited Haydn work in Hr. Z's essay, even if I could accept such a position, alas, my Symphony was already written in the Summer of 1794 and Haydn's did not become known to me until one year thereafter [as Op. 77 (*recte*) Liv. 1, André, announced on 14 Feb. 1795]. So I don't dare even do that. To remain for a final moment with Hr. Z's parallel:

The lion went ahead,
The tail dragged on behind –

I must assert that, far from having the slightest resemblance to a lion, Hr. Z. may be followed by a long tail of yapping mongrels; and it is to show them and their master the whip in good time that I have written this defence.

Offenbach am M[ain] in February.

Ant. André.

['Z''s footnotes]

Read 'possibly agree with that which Hr Z.' etc. [Z had many occasions to correct *Herr* Andrés angry grammar.] The following, truly not short, musical list, which is supposed to be learned and is constantly getting tripped up in its author's grammar, would require printing the score of both movements in question if one is to refute his thesis (which *is* certainly learned) point for point . . . I shall have to leave it as undecided if the reader trust me to know what a fugue is, and what is not; to know, more precisely, if that Haydn movement is a fugue; if that André movement is a *good* one, is a fugue, and makes a *unity* with his rondo, etc. The reader can hear both movements and form his opinion. But that Hr. A. quite certainly knows nothing of the matter in question is shown clearly by his dismissing the Haydn movement as a fugue because it goes against the *fugue of fifths*. So that's it: whatever is not according to the *fugue of fifths*, is no fugue! . . . Who can, without the gorge rising, instruct such an arrogant and prejudiced man in such common things? The public shall judge between us. . . . How decisive this taste [for the noisy] is for Hr. A. may be seen in one of his newest symphonies, in which he has (forgive the comparison – like Mozart in his *Magic Flute* Overture) used trombones but in such a fashion as if this work of art were to create a headache. The so-called *flauto piccolo* helps to create this unfortunate state. Not to speak of the endlessly drawn out, indescribably larmoyant andante. . . . Hr. A wanted to 'remain . . . with my parallel' and even that he's not understood. The talk was about the 'tail of a *lion*' and he speaks about dogs! Pfuy!

. . . He who speaks of dogs and whips must be flogged; and all sensible educators suggest that if the cat *must* be used once, it should be well laid on. As far as I'm concerned, however, one should not have frequent resort to this kind of nausea; but that I promise, and I warn all dabblers here and how, that I will not compromise in any respect the truth as I see it.

Z. . . .

[*AMZ* I: Int.-Blatt. X, 45–54]

Count Fries gave a grand concert in his palace on the present Josephsplatz on 5 April. Zinzendorf writes:

> ... A 6h½ passé dans la maison de Fries ... Le Concert dans un beau salon tres sonore. Toute la ville y etoit ... Symphonie de Haydn. Saal et sa fille, Vogl et Melle [left blank] chanterent trois couplets du jeune Doppelhof assez joliment ecrits, mais la musique peu de chose. Un Suedois, enfant de dix ans, joua du Violon comme un Ange un Concert de Jiornowich [Giornovichj]. Il a des medailles au cou de l'academie de musique de Stockholm et du roi de Pol[ogne]. Ses cheveux, que ce feu Exroi lui a arrangé paroissoit l'incommoder ... Me de Schoenfeld chanta un Duo de l'opera seria de Paisiello Elfrida avec M. Paer qui s'accompagnoit de Clavessin ... [Olleson, 57]

The young Swede (aged eleven, not ten) was, of course, J. F. Berwald, whose own report follows. The exiled Polish king was Stanislaus II Poniatowski; Johann Michael Vogl was later Schubert's friend; the composer was the dilettante Carl von Doblhof-Dier. Berwald writes:

> ... we were invited to a grand musical soirée at Count Fries's, where there was a large number of persons of rank, and artists. Among the former we noticed the Duke of Södermanland (later Carl XIII) and his wife. From the Duchess, I received a present of a golden watch. Among the artists may be mentioned: Josef Haydn, Beethoven (who gave his excellent Quintet for piano and wind instruments [Op. 16, already played in public in 1797] for the first time), Weigl, Süßmayer, the two Wranitzkys, Vanhall, Kozeluck, Gyrovetz, Salieri, Abbé Stadler, Seifrid, Cartelieri, Krommer etc., all more or less famous men. I played and was applauded, especially for my Adagio; also from the old man Haydn. He asked my father if he might keep me with him for a time, for he had no children, he added sighing; but my father said he only had one son, even though that son would of course be better off with Doctor Haydn than he was now. ... I must mention, too, that the Royal Swedish Musical Academy at this time made Haydn an honorary member. The old man came up to see us and asked my father to translate the diploma which was, as usual in such cases, in Swedish. He seemed to be very flattered. [Mörner in *Haydn-Studien* II/1 (1969), 7]

On 1 May the Vienna correspondent of the *AMZ* reported *inter alia* about Haydn conducting at Count Fries's *soirée* with a description of one Finale which enables us to identify the work as Symphony No. 102 (Finale, bar 8 is in A major)[1].

> ... A friend has just come to me and tells me another story about our Father Haydn which I must pass on to you. Haydn introduced once again two brand new symphonies at Count F. ... that are most remarkable, but they are so atypical that one is completely astonished at the extraordinary powers of invention of their composer. A particular stroke of genius is the following. The rondo theme of the one begins in B flat, modulates in the most natural way to A major within a few bars, and concludes right afterwards just as naturally in B flat again. I tell you this in detail – not just because it is new and curious but because, for all its newness and curiosity, it is so delicate, so appropriate and so marvellously accomplished – Go on living for a good long time, dear old Father Haydn! [I, 544]

1 'A dur', not 'As dur' as in Pohl III, 148. Olleson (57), who commenting on this concert, notes that 'it seems far from certain that Zinzendorf and the correspondent [of the *AMZ*] are discussing the same concert.'

Of course Symphony No. 102 was neither a 'brand new' work nor was it unknown to the Viennese, but it may well have been unknown to a visitor from Germany, where the work (like several of the later Salomon Symphonies) was not yet printed.

From Silverstolpe we learn that the young Berwald, '. . . who really plays excellently', gave his own concert during these days; but 'he hasn't made much money from his stay in Vienna. The Duchess [of Södermanland] had him once [at a tea party], on which occasion there were more than 60 persons' (Mörner, 339). We shall note another concert given by young Berwald on 3 May.

On 1 April 1799 ('Cold and exceedingly snowy') Prince Nicolaus Esterházy had left for Russia; Rosenbaum notes 'We ate sausage, drank beer and made merry until the Prince drove off, which was after midnight' (63). Six days later 'at 10:30 our beloved Princess was delivered of a boy' who was christened Nicolaus Carolus the next day (Sunday, 7 April). On the 9th, the Empress Marie Therese gave birth to a prince and the day following there was free admission to the theatres. On 10 April Rosenbaum went to the Burgtheater: 'the exceedingly large crowd, the heat, the smell and vapours beggar all description' (63).

On 13 April the *Wiener Zeitung* carried an official announcement about those Viennese composers who had received honorary membership in the Royal Swedish Music Academy:

> The Royal Swedish Musical Academy, whose purpose it is to treat with distinction those who have with success cultivated the art of music or have accomplished some signal service therein, and which considers itself fortunate to number such men among them, have as a mark of their esteem made the following men members: *Herr* Joseph Haydn, Doctor of Music and *Kapellmeister* to Prince Esterhazi [*sic*], and Johann Georg Albrechtsberger, *Kapellmeister* at the Cathedral of St Stephen in Vienna; their diplomas were prepared by the Academy's President, *Herr* v. Fredenheim, *Oberintendant* of the Royal Buildings and Knight of the Order of the Northern Star. Under date 30 January 1799, the above-mentioned Academy also created *Herr* Antonio Salieri . . . a member in the same fashion. These three artists are the first foreign members of the Royal Swedish Musical Academy, which since its formation 28 years ago has limited itself to national artists and friends of the art.

On the 10th Silverstolpe had written to Stockholm that he had received the four membership diplomas. 'The one for me made me blush. The others, for Haydn, Albrechtsberger and Salieri, I will deliver this week, after I have seen to their translation and also for an announcement in the Vienna Court newspaper' (Mörner, 339). Haydn thanked the Academy in the following letter:

> [To C. F. Fredenheim, President of the Royal Swedish Academy of Music in Stockholm. *German*] [End of April 1799]
>
> Nobly born,
> Most highly respected Sir!
>
> I cannot express adequately in words the surprise and delight which I felt, and will always feel, upon receiving, through the Councillor of Legation Herr von Silverstolpe, the diploma wherein I am graciously nominated a member of your worthy Royal Swedish Academy of Music. I only regret that at present my advanced age and weakened powers do not permit me to repay this great honour. If, however, PROVIDENCE should grant me a few more years of the necessary musical strength, I shall try to compose a small remembrance for your worthy

Society; meanwhile I take the liberty of conveying my respectful thanks to the President C. F. von Fredenheim, and to the whole worthy Society, and am, Sir, most respectfully,

Your obedient servant,
J:H: [CCLN, 152]

On 19 April *The Times* carried an announcement from Longman, Clementi & Co. (formerly Longman & Broderip): 'Shortly will be published, Three Grand Quartetts, by Haydn.' Haydn had sent these first three Quartets from Op. 76 to London on 27 March; he sent the second three on 15 June. Artaria was to publish them in Vienna: the first set in July, the second in December. We shall return to the Artaria print later.

On 24 April 1799, the Stadttheater in Linz put on the first of two performances of Haydn's opera, *La fedeltà premiata*. The composer will certainly have heard of the event and no doubt will have pondered the curious life-of-their-own that his operas now had; for it is very unlikely that Haydn at this period even owned a complete copy of the score to *La fedeltà premiata*, one of his most brilliant and forward-looking stage pieces. It had caused a furore when it was given (in German) at the Kärntnerthortheater in December 1784 by the Kumpf-Schikaneder Company. The tradition of Haydn's operas was now (in 1799) gradually dying out. They had never had a large public career, and many of them (like *L'infedeltà delusa*) had never been performed outside Eszterháza; but for a while, several of the later ones, such as *La fedeltà premiata*, *Orlando Paladino* and *Armida* had enjoyed a certain amount of success in German translations. The Linz production was in the Kumpf-Schikaneder translation as *Belohnte Treue*.[1]

This was also the time when Rellstab brought out a selection of *Orlando Paladino* in piano reduction; Rellstab also offered the whole score for sale in MS. Three of the pieces were warmly praised in a 'Kurze Anzeige' of the *AMZ* in its issue of 17 April (I, 464), for example 'Ah se dirvi io potessi' (Aria of Eurilda in Act I, with the authentic text, 'Ah se dire io vi potesse') is reviewed with the note: '. . . is a very charming and melting Aria that one cannot sing often enough'.[2]

Orlando Paladino was popular enough to warrant Simrock issuing a fairly complete piano score, which came out in German translation as *Ritter Roland* during the year 1799. Naturally Haydn was not informed or consulted about such a publication, but Simrock, who was a personal acquaintance of Haydn's, might have sent him a copy. All this last flurry of activity round Haydn's beloved stepchildren will have filled him with nostalgia.

The prodigy Berwald gave what appears to have been his final concert at Jahn's rooms on 3 May. Rosenbaum was there and noted 'Therese [Gassmann] sang an aria and a rondeau, both of them timidly and not to my satisfaction. After the concert I saw her to the coach and gave her a tiny reproof . . . The evening was very pleasant' (64).

We now learn of Haydn in an entirely new role: as one of the principal editors in a series of historical *Denkmäler* which would trace music from its earliest beginnings to the end of the eighteenth century. A long announcement of the series, and an

1 For a listing of some of these post-Eszterháza performances of Haydn's operas, see *Haydn in England 1791–1795*, p. 320 and *passim*.
2 Miss Cari Johannson was kind enough, many years ago, to point out a copy of this print, which consists of the Overture and six numbers. Mr Hermann Baron graciously allowed me to study his copy of the Simrock piano score.

invitation to subscription, signed by Joseph Sonnleithner, was published in the *Intelligenz-Blatt* No. XVIII (September 1799) of the *AMZ* which began:

Announcement

History of Music in Denkmählern from the oldest to the newest times. With the portraits of the most famous composers, according to an historical plan of Herr Doktor Forkel, Music Director at Göttingen under direction of the Herren, Georg Albrechtsberger, Kapellmeister at the Cathedral Church of Saint Stephan in Vienna, Joseph Haydn, Doctor of Music and Kapellmeister to Prince Esterházy, and Anton Salieri, I. R. First Court Kapellmeister; edited by Joseph Sonnleithner.

Joseph Sonnleithner was the son of the lawyer and composer Dr Christoph Sonnleithner, who was Prince Nicolaus I Esterházy's legal advisor and whose compositions were often distributed under Haydn's name; the Wurzbach *Lexikon* informs us that at the auction of Christoph's effects after his death on Christmas Day 1786, Haydn bought up much of the music. Christoph's daughter was the mother of Grillparzer, the poet and playwright. His eldest son, Ignaz, was Doctor of Laws and a good amateur musician (bass voice). His second son, Joseph (1766–1835), became secretary to the Court Theatre in 1804 (succeeding Kotzebue) and wrote or rather translated from the French the libretto for Beethoven's *Leonore*. In 1799, Emperor Francis sent Sonnleithner abroad to collect material for the Imperial Library, and it appears he intended to visit London, to which purpose Haydn gave him the following letter of introduction to his old friend Salomon:

[To Johann Peter Salomon, London. *German*]

Vienna, 18th May 1799.

Dearest Friend!

The bearer of this letter is Herr von Sonleithner, a distinguished young man of great wit, whose character you, with your great insight, will be able to judge far better and more accurately than I am able to do. His musical project is one of the most interesting, but I fear that without the help and counsel of many people he will not be able to realize it. He has asked me to recommend someone in London who was honest and well-informed, and I therefore took the liberty of suggesting you, my dear friend. If you are able to assist him in his project, you will be of great service to the world. Apart from this I am, with every esteem, dearest friend,

Your sincere friend and servant,
Jos: Haydn [m.p] ria.

[Address:]

M^r. Salomon.
N^ro 34,
Clipstone Street, London,
Fitzroy Squarre [*sic*]

[CCLN, 153]

Sonnleithner later became one of Schubert's admirers and friends. Haydn was in fact rather sceptical about the *Denkmäler* project and as we shall see (*vide infra*, 25 May) he doubted if anything would come of it. But as matters turned out, Sonnleithner actually engraved a volume, the plates of which were destroyed during the French invasion of Vienna in 1805.[1]

In the year 1799, a young German arrived at Vienna. He was Georg August Griesinger, who had studied theology and came to the Austrian capital to be tutor to

1 Concerning the Sonnleithner family see C. F. Pohl's useful article in *Grove I* (iii, 632ff.), Frimmel's *Beethoven-Handbuch* II, 219ff., O. E. Deutsch, *Schubert: Die Erinnerungen seiner Freunde*, Leipzig 1957, pp. 3 *passim* and Herfrid Kier, *Raphael Georg Kiesewetter*, Regensburg 1968, esp. pp. 240ff.

the son of the Saxon Ambassador, Count von Schönfeld. Griesinger later became Secretary, then Councillor, to the Legation. To musicians he is well known for his Haydn biography, but also for his interesting comments on Beethoven[1] and Viennese society in general. Griesinger was known to Gottfried Christoph Härtel who, as the editor of the Griesinger-Härtel correspondence, Edward Olleson[2] notes, 'was to raise the publishing house to a position of such eminence'. Härtel, having had no response from Haydn himself, asked Griesinger to act as go-between, and the result was eminently profitable both for Härtel as well as Haydn. Just to mention one result of this operation, Breitkopf & Härtel acquired *The Seasons* and later the plates of *The Creation*. The first letter on the subject reads as follows:

18 May 1799.

Dearest Friend:

I have just received your letter of 4th May and hasten to assure you by the next outgoing mail that I will do everything in my power to fulfil your request to your satisfaction. By this you have given me the pleasant task of making the acquaintance of one of the greatest composers, as well as enabling me to do a small favour to you at no great difficulty to myself. I will look up Haydn tomorrow and let you know in detail the result of our conversation.

I have enquired about the five composers whose names you gave me before my departure [from Saxony]. Kozeluch has been described to me as the *purus-putus musicus*, who is incapable of writing a proper article [for the *AMZ*], the others are partly not known, partly too busy through lessons (which are well paid here) to be able to accept more work. One of my compatriots, [the piano builder Johann Andreas] Streicher, whose wife is the daughter of the famous instrument maker Stein from Augsburg, and is in good credit here, promised me material for the *Musicalische Zeitung*, which I should edit. The good man is also so busy with lessons, however, that up to now he couldn't keep his word. Altogether I arrived at a time here when most rich people go to their country houses and not many concerts are given; that's why I haven't yet seen a group of musicians all at once. They tell me that Mozart's widow refuses to confirm the anecdotes which were published in the *Music-Zeitung*.[3] – The orchestras in the main theatres are excellent, but hardly better than in Prague. Church music doesn't exist since Emperor Joseph.

Keep your word and come, if you can this summer. You will find in this town, which is entirely given up to sensuality, much to amuse and distract you.

The sight of such a mass of people and stones is still new to me and in some respects very attractive. I am on the whole pleased with my domestic position; my pupil is but a nine-year-old child, whom I must start from the ground up, and who

1 Landon, *Beethoven*, 156f., 159, etc. Some of the hitherto unpublished letters from Griesinger to Court Councillor Böttiger in Dresden are included (complete photographs of the originals, in the Sächsische Landesbibliothek, Dresden, are owned by the present writer).

2 'Georg August Griesinger's Correspondence with Breitkopf & Härtel' in *Haydn Yearbook* III (1965), hereinafter 'Olleson, *Griesinger*'. The correspondence was destroyed during air raids on Leipzig during World War II and survives only in some printed extracts and, mainly, in copies made by the late Dr Carl Maria Brand, who made them available to Olleson. The correspondence has also been published by Günter Thomas in *Haydn-Studien* 1/2 (1966).

3 After having published the Rochlitz 'Anecdotes' which have been mentioned above, the *AMZ* in No. 19 (6 February 1799) published 'Einige Anekdoten aus Mozarts Leben, von seiner hinterlassenen Gattin uns mitgetheilt' – probably stories that Constanze told Rochlitz on her concert tour to Dresden and Leipzig in 1796 and of which she was now perhaps embarrassed ('. . . Guten Morgen, liebes Weibchen, ich wünsche, daß du gut geschlafen habest, daß dich nichts gestöhrt habe, daß du nicht zu jäh aufstehst, daß du dich nicht erkältest, nicht bückst, nicht streckst, dich mit deinen Dienstbothen nicht erzürnst, im nächsten Zimmer nicht über die Schwelle fällst', etc.).

is round me the whole day. How many hours disappear in childish occupations! But these objections are inseparable from my position, and I support them with patience. . . .

Once again: Whatever I can do with Haydn, I shall certainly do. More shortly, and meanwhile I remain &c. . . .

Your most obedient
Griesinger.

The next event of note in Vienna was a Cantata by Salieri, 'to benefit the Imperial and Royal subjects in Tyrol and Vorarlberg who have suffered devastation by the enemy', entitled *Der Tyroler Landsturm*. Therese Gassmann sang. The general rehearsal was on 21 May ('cold and rainy . . . Therese sang quite prettily . . . I enjoyed the cantata . . .' [Rosenbaum, 65]), and the concert itself on Corpus Christi, Thursday, 23 May. Although there was an 'admission price one gulden, gallery 2 gulden, but no limitation is placed on charitableness', Rosenbaum notes that the Redoutensaal 'was not very well attended, and very few of the nobility were there. The Court gave 500 gulden and together with these the receipts were 2590 gulden' (65). The *Wiener Zeitung* (No. 42), of 25 May) tells us: 'The beginning consisted of a grand and excellent Symphony by Herr J. Haiden [*sic*], princely Esterhazi [*sic*] Kapellmeister, who himself took over the leadership of it'. Where charity concerts were concerned, Haydn was hardly ever missing. We may assume, too, that for this reason he was so often away when Griesinger went to call on him. Rosenbaum's Diary (65) of 23 May notes, too, that Therese Gassmann's singing was 'faint-hearted' and that Prince Esterházy had arrived back from his grand tour, which had taken him to the Austrian troops in Italy, where 'the Grand Duke had given him a very lovely box set with diamonds, with his portrait on it.'

On 22 May Silverstolpe had collected three letters (from Haydn, Albrechtsberger and Salieri), thanking the Swedish Academy for their membership (Haydn's was quoted *supra*). 'Together with this letter the Academy will receive three others, from the noblest disciples of music, whom [the Academy] honoured' (Mörner, 341).

Meanwhile Griesinger had been trying to see Haydn, and on the 25th he finally succeeded:

25 May 1799.

Dearest Friend:

After having vainly called several times on Haydn in one of the outer suburbs, I finally found him in this morning. I made your suggestion to him and to strengthen it I read him most of your letter. He was ashamed, he said, that he hadn't yet answered you; but he hoped that you will forgive a man of 67 to whom every moment is precious. The proposed edition of his piano works you intend to issue [*Oeuvres Complettes*] has his undivided approval, and I have the firm message to assure his complete agreement. Since much has been issued under his name which is not his, he asks you to send him a catalogue of the compositions which you intend to print. He doesn't own the originals any more, for in his youth he gave away most of his scores. It's not possible for him to promise three new sonatas, for he is swamped with business, and has to take care of old orders for the Empress [*Te Deum*], for Prince Esterhasy [*sic*] [*Theresienmesse*] and many other wealthy Viennese. For the last five years [i.e. since 1794] he has a contract with English publishers,[1] who pay him seventy-five pounds Sterling for three sonatas [trios]; altogether he owes the English a great deal, for it was only after he

1 See the contract with Hyde, *supra*, p. 101.

returned from England that they began to appreciate him a little in Germany. Perhaps some of the private persons to whom he has promised new works will allow him to let you have them for publication; he wants to have a try and it would be pleasant for him if he could do you a service in this way. Your editions of Mozart's works pleased him a great deal, and I should thank you for the volumes you sent him. Recently a certain Sonnleitner (or Sonnleiter) had left here and will certainly turn up in Leipzig to seek subscriptions for a History of Music, in which his works (I mean Haydn's) are also supposed to appear. He considers this plan to be a swindle [*Beutelschneiderey*] and is sure that nothing will come of it; he couldn't refuse in order not to offend some good friends. But you shouldn't be alarmed about this form of competition.

That, my respected friend, is the contents of my conversation with Haydn; he is a cheerful, still well preserved man and is for all his colleagues a model of modesty and simplicity. – If you have some points to clarify with him, write me. . . . [In another letter Haydn showed signs of weakening about the sonatas; he said] . . . he wouldn't be bound to them in any way, but it would give him pleasure to be able to do a favour for Breitkopf & Härtel and that if he finds time, he will give you preference about all others . . . [Olleson, *Griesinger*, 9f.]

A young German artist, J. C. Rössler (1775–1845), had arrived in Vienna. On 29 May Rosenbaum went to see him where he was staying in the Plankengasse and 'requested him to paint me'. On 3 June he went to Mother Gassmann and 'showed her my portrait; she did not find it a good likeness', but on the 15th we read nevertheless that Rössler 'began to paint Therese' (66). Rössler was later in Eisenstadt (*vide* 21 September *infra*), and some time between May and perhaps October he painted Haydn's portrait in oils which now hangs in the Faculty of Music, Oxford University, and is signed 'Wien/1799'. On the reverse side of the painting is the following note by Rochlitz: '. . . painted from life and in a series of sessions that the master gave to Rössler, in the year 1799, shortly after Haydn's 2nd visit to London and so like him that I, who had spoken to him shortly before on his way through Leipzig, recognized him at the first glance, before I knew whom the portrait was supposed to represent'. We are now inclined to be less enthusiastic, particularly since we have much better Haydn portraits of this period. We may therefore interrupt our Chronicle and list these portraits of the year 1799:

(1) The Rössler portrait (*vide supra*). Reproduced in colour in the Haydn article in *Musik in Geschichte und Gegenwart* (V, 1956), in black-and-white *inter alia* in Somfai, 167. Detail in colour on the cover of Decca's *Haydn: The Symphonies* (Nos. 82–92).

(2) Sepia drawing by Vincenz Georg Kininger (*recte*), one of three done by that artist, one *c.* 1784 and two in 1799. Discovered by Hans Swarowsky in the antiquarian shop of Gilhofer in Vienna in 1964 (subsequently sold). In the subsequent Chronicle, we shall hear how this portrait came into being. The first of the Kininger studies turned out 'to no-one's satisfaction'; we cannot see that the third, which Somfai calls the 'most successful', is any better. It is one of the worst portraits of the period. Reproduced *inter alia* in Somfai, p. 172.

(3) Bust in plaster-of-Paris, without wig, life-size (lost; according to Pohl III, 401, it was in the Gesellschaft der Musikfreunde), with the motto 'Tu potes tigres comitesque sylvas ducere et currentes rivis morari'. The dating comes from Griesinger's letters of 1799. It is believed that this bust by Anton Grassi, Haydn's sculptor friend, may have served as the basis for the Artaria engraving of 1808 engraved by David Weiss which shows the composer without a wig 'en antique'.

(4) Unsigned lead bust, *c.* 1799, life-size attributed by Dies and others to Grassi but by Somfai to Thaller. It was owned by Haydn, is listed among his effects, 'aus Bleÿ auf Postament' (lead, on a base), was left by him to Count Harrach, in whose possession it still remains (Schloss Harrach, Rohrau). It is one of the greatest of all Haydn portraits, showing the man 'warts and all' (in this case, pock-marks and all). It is reproduced *inter alia* as the frontispiece (and dust jacket) of Landon, *The Symphonies* . . ., also Somfai, 180 (another view).

(5) Three wax busts by Franz Christian Thaller, *c.* 1799. One was under a glass dome in Haydn's own flat and is described as '. . . wax bust under glass dome'. It was, fortunately, photographed before its destruction in 1945, in the Museum der Stadt Wien, during World War II (see pl. 1). A second version, identified in 1932 by Dr Jean Paul de Courade, Trieste, was then owned by his mother's family, Meynier, in Fiume. Haydn gave it to the Trieste composer, Count Ruggiero Manna, an ancestor of Mme Meynier.[1] A third version has survived and is in the Kunsthistorisches Museum, Vienna (see pls. I and 2; also reproduced in black-and-white in Somfai, 180 and XI, and as a postcard at the museum in Vienna). The lost Vienna bust by Thaller is illustrated in Schnerich's *Haydn*, facing pp. 26–7 (front and profile); it was 29 cm. high (with stand). The busts by Thaller are, with the lead bust (Grassi?), the greatest and most realistic three-dimensional portraits of Haydn that we have. Technically the later Grassi busts (1801–2) are more perfect, but this group of *c.* 1799 has a particularly striking quality which comes through even in photographs. This, we feel, is the real Haydn.

(6) Bust in marble, life-size, without wig, signed by August Robatz ('von Au. Robatz verf. nach der Natur'), *c.* 1799–1800? Technically well executed, this bust is slightly flattering and altogether somewhat idealized: the mouth is good. Reproduced in plate 5. Owned by the Gesellschaft der Musikfreunde, Vienna.

The first fruits of Griesinger's toil were apparent in a rather long letter that Haydn sent to Breitkopf & Härtel on 12 June, together with a letter from Griesinger to Härtel of the same date.

[To Christoph Gottlob Breitkopf, Leipzig. *German*]

Vienna, 12th June 1799.

Dearest Friend!

I am really very much ashamed to have to offend a man who has written so often and honoured me with so many marks of esteem (which I do not deserve), by answering him at this late date; it is not negligence on my part but the vast amount of BUSINESS which is responsible, and the older I get, the more business I have to transact daily. I only regret that on account of growing age and (unfortunately) the decrease of my mental powers, I am able to dispatch but the smallest part of it. Every day the world pays me compliments on the fire of my recent works, but no one will believe the strain and effort it costs me to produce them: there are some days in which my enfeebled memory and the unstrung state of my nerves crush me to the earth to such an extent that I fall prey to the worst sort of depression, and thus am quite incapable of finding even a single idea for many days thereafter; until at last Providence revives me, and I can again sit down at the pianoforte and begin to scratch away again. Enough of this!

Yesterday Herr Griesinger brought me the 2nd, 3rd and 4th volumes of our immortal Mozart, together with the musical periodical. Please let me know how

1 Letter from Ernst Buschbeck to Otto Erich Deutsch of 6 March 1933. We have attempted to trace this bust, but to no avail.

much I owe you for them, and to whom I should give the money here in Vienna.

The publication of both these things does you great credit. I WOULD ONLY WISH, AND HOPE, THAT THE CRITICS DO NOT DEAL TOO SEVERELY WITH MY CREATION: THEY MIGHT PERHAPS OBJECT A LITTLE TO THE MUSICAL ORTHOGRAPHY OF CERTAIN PASSAGES, AND POSSIBLY SOME OTHER MINOR POINTS ELSEWHERE; BUT THE TRUE CONNOISSEUR WILL SEE THE REASONS FOR THEM AS READILY AS I DO, AND WILL PUSH ASIDE THIS STUMBLING-BLOCK. NULLA REGOLA S[ENZA] E[CCEZIONE]. N.B.: AS FOR THE TATTERED SECTION IN THE DUET OF THE 'CREATION', YOU WILL FIND IT ENTIRELY DIFFERENT IN THE EDITION FROM THAT WHICH HERR TRAEG HAD THE TWOPENNY KRAMER[1] PREPARE FOR HIM: but all this UNDERLINED INTER NOS.

Apart from all this, I shall be very happy to serve you in any possible way. Meanwhile, my dear friend, I remain, with every esteem,

Your obliging and obedient servant,
Joseph Haydn [m.p.] ria.

[Letter enclosed a full score of *The Creation* and also a letter from Griesinger to Breitkopf & Härtel; therefore no address; Breitkopf's clerk notes: 'V 99/ 12 Juny/ (rec'd) 3 July / Wien / J. Haydn'.]

[CCLN, 154f.]

12 June 1799.

Most excellent Friend,

I have just come from H[err]. Haydn and hasten to tell you the results of my visit. He is entirely satisfied with the announcement [of the *Oeuvres complettes*] of which I gave him the written text. . . .

His publisher in England is a Mr. Bay,[2] a rather unimportant man as Haydn said, but associated with Clementi and Broderip. His agreement is for five years, of which three are now finished, and Bay has agreed to take everything he composes, and the price for every psalm, sonata, etc. has been established beforehand. But because of the great amount of work on his shoulders, he has only delivered some quartets in these three years, and these were sent to England quite recently. Bay is pushing him especially hard for piano sonatas, but up to now he hasn't been able to fulfil his wish. . . .

Haydn is not satisfied with the portraits that are being sold to the public; he was engraved three times in England, one of them was even corrected by Bartolozzi,[3] but none of them turned out very well. The painting by Gut[t]enbronn is better, and he's given it to an acquaintance to be copied. The best is a profile by an Englishman, Danz [Dance] (at least that's how Haydn pronounced it), a very good head, which he's expecting every day from England and which he will gladly give you to be re-engraved for your edition of his piano compositions.

1 The *Allgemeine Musikalische Zeitung* had printed the Duet, 'Der thauende Morgen', as a 'Beilage' to the periodical: they had used the text printed by the Viennese publisher Johann Traeg, which was, however, very faulty. This '10-Kreutzer' Kramer, as it turned out, had copied the Duet from memory, after having heard a few performances of the work. Traeg issued the Duet, separately, in March 1799. See Alexander Weinmann, 'Verzeichnis der Musikalien des Verlages Johann Traeg in Wien' [*Studien zur Musikwissenschaft* XXIII, 1956, p. 147) and Hase, p. 10. 'Tattered section' (Ger.: 'zerrissene Stück') may mean 'torn out of the main body'; the Duet was only a fragment and a badly distorted one at that.

2 After Longman & Broderip went bankrupt, various new partners were added, among them a Mr Banger and a Mr Hyde; it was with Hyde that Haydn drew up the contract of 1796 (*vide supra*, p. 101).

3 In England, there appeared during Haydn's stay the following engravings: (1) Francesco Bartolozzi from a miniature by M. A. Ott in 1791; (2) Thomas Hardy after his own portrait in oils in 1792; (3) L. Schiavonetti from the portrait in oils by Guttenbrunn (*recte*) in 1792. The great Dance drawing exists in two authentic versions; both are reproduced in Somfai (148f.), as are all the other engravings here listed. Together with the Grassi busts and the Thaller wax busts, the Dance is the greatest portrait of Haydn we have – an opinion obviously shared by the composer himself.

Please don't print his biography before he has gone through it; things in his life occurred of which very few know. By the way, the idea did not seem to displease him.[1] Haydn will write a *pendant* to his *Creation*, called the *Four Seasons*; v. Swieten is doing the libretto. For Count Fries he has promised some quintets. . . . [About three further volumes of the Breitkopf Mozart edition that the publishers had sent Haydn,] he looked through the volumes several times and said: really fine, really fine; Mozart and I appreciated each other very much, he too used to call me his Papa . . . [As far as the publication of *The Seasons* was concerned, Haydn was uncertain whether to publish it himself; but] if I give it to a publisher, it will be to no one except Härtel, for with the local people here it's all a mess! [*ist alles Lumperey*].[2] . . .

[Olleson, *Griesinger*, 10f.]

The announcement of Haydn's *Oeuvres Complettes* in the *AMZ* appeared in the *Intelligenz-Blatt* No. XIV (June 1799) and read as follows:

Complete Edition
of
J. HAYDN'S WORKS

We believe that we shall fulfil the wish of all lovers of excellent and especially Haydn's music in announcing a complete, tasteful and exceptionally inexpensive edition of all the works of this great man, and starting with his piano compositions – in our publishing house, with the approval and by the authority of the composer. The public, so often disappointed, has nothing to fear in this case that anything whatever in this collection will be included which Haydn himself does not now recognize as worthy of him and authentic.

Our edition of Mozart's works is well known; – the same system will apply to Haydn's works, the same print, the same elegance and correctness, the same ornaments, the same price, the volume consisting of from 25 to 30 gatherings [Bogen] at 1 Laubthaler or 1 Saxon Thlr. 12 Gr., prepaid, and the fifth number gratis, for which price the volumes will be delivered in tasteful paper wrappers. After expiration of the subscription period, the volume will, also in this case, cost 3 Thlr. – The first volume is in the press and will be delivered in the course of this summer. To this will be added at least four volumes annually,

1 This is the first mention that Griesinger should do a biographical sketch of Haydn; the idea was not put into practice for ten years.

2 The last two extracts exist only in the Hase booklet, as extracts, and cannot be dated. Since the letter itself contains several omissions we assume that at least the first and possibly the second extract may have belonged to it. In any case, they cannot be chronologically far removed from June 1799.

This is perhaps the place to mention a strange fact, namely that the Haydn letter seems to have existed in two versions. We print from Haydn's autograph in the Stadtbibliothek, of course; but Griesinger quoted parts of this letter in his biography (p. 122 of the original 1810 edition), and it first appeared in the biography as it was published in instalments by the *AMZ* (XI, 747). The extraordinary differences between the autograph version and that of Griesinger-*AMZ* are, we believe, explained rather simply: two letters are put together. We have the complete letter of 12 June 1799; the other one, containing the remarks not in that of 12 June 1799, is lost. The missing parts read in translation (we used *AMZ* XI, 747 as our source):

'Unfortunately my business affairs multiply like my years; but it would almost appear as if my pleasure and drive to compose increase as my mental powers decrease. My God, how much still remains to be done in this wonderful art, and even by such a man as myself! Every day, the world pays [etc.] . . . and I can again sit down at the pianoforte and begin to hammer away. Then everything begins to work again, thank God! [After a shortened version of *The Creation* and the critics, the extract concludes:] But all that is entirely *inter nos*: otherwise one will construe what I said as self-satisfaction and pride, from which my Heavenly Father has preserved me all my life.' The last thought is one that we find often in Haydn's letters and in descriptions of him by reliable witnesses.

and if the public wishes it, more. The catalogue of the subscribers will be printed in one of the following volumes. For subscription, one may use the nearest book or musical shop.

We trust, moreover, that this our edition of Haydn's works will not be confused with another, recently advertised by Herr Lehmann in Leipzig.[1]

Leipzig, in May 1799. BREITKOPF und HÄRTEL.

Haydn now announced the subscription to the score of *The Creation*. He sent the letter to several publications, *inter alia* the *Wiener Zeitung* and the *AMZ*; the latter printed it at the beginning of the *Intelligenz-Blatt* No. XV (June 1799). The *AMZ* announcement reads:

[*German*]

The success which my Oratorio, *The Creation*, has been fortunate enough to enjoy here, and the wish expressed in the 16th number of the [*Allgemeine*] *Musikalische Zeitung* that its dissemination would not, as was often the case previously, be left to those abroad, have moved me to arrange for its distribution myself.

Thus the work is to appear in three or four months, neatly and correctly engraved and printed on good paper, with German and English texts; and in full score, so that, on the one hand, the public may have the work in its entirety, and so that the connoisseur may see it *in toto* and thus better judge it; while on the other, it will be easier to prepare the parts, should one wish to perform the work anywhere.

The price of the Oratorio, which will consist of some 300 pages, is to be 3 ducats, or 13 Fl. 30 Kr. in Viennese currency; and although payment does not need to be made until delivery, I wish nevertheless that those who contemplate its purchase would inform me provisionally thereof, and give me their names, in order that they may appear in the subscription list at the front of the score.

The actual appearance of the Oratorio in print – every copy will be signed – will be announced by a special notice, when the time comes.

Vienna, 15th June 1799.

Joseph Haydn,
Doctor of Music, *Kapellmeister* in the Service of His Highness the Prince Esterházy, and Member of the Royal Swedish Musical Academy.

In Vienna, Vorstadt Gumpendorf, untere Steingasse, Nr. 73.

[CCLN, 155f.]

Haydn's experiences with music publishers had not been encouraging. His principal publisher in the 1780s had been Artaria, whose editions were notorious for their carelessness and misprints. Haydn's English publishers had been – as far as their textual accuracy was concerned – the best he had ever enjoyed; but they were far away

1 L. F. Lehmann's pirated edition of Haydn's 'Complete Works' for piano was, of course, inspired by Breitkopf & Härtel's Mozart edition. Lehmann announced it all over the German-speaking world. In Vienna, the *Wiener Zeitung* printed his announcement in French, a snobbish gambit that earned the scorn of the dialect-writing Eipeldauer, whose letters we have often quoted. Immediately thereafter Haydn's pupil Ignaz Pleyel, now an eminently successful publisher in Paris, announced *his* edition of 'Oeuvres complettes' of Haydn, which he published in the *Journal générale de la Littérature de France* (April 1799, p. 94). Neither of these rival editions achieved the broad distribution and public support of the Breitkopf edition, nor was either Lehmann's or Pleyel's as complete as the other's. Pleyel soon began to concentrate on other facets of Haydn's work, viz. all the quartets, then a selection of symphonies and quartets in a kind of pocket score which was charmingly produced. Pohl III, 136.

and the war rendered communications hazardous. All in all, Haydn considered *The Creation* his masterpiece and he was going to supervise the score himself, note for note. Baron van Swieten probably corrected the German and English texts, which are really very accurate indeed. Haydn may have felt like the British poet William Cowper, who wrote on 23 May 1781 to the Rev. William Unwin:

> . . . I shall now have, what I should not otherwise have had, an opportunity to correct the press myself; no small advantage upon any occasion, but especially important where poetry is concerned! A single erratum may knock the brains of a whole passage, and that perhaps which, of all others, the unfortunate poet is the most proud of. Add to this, that now and then there is to be found in a printing house a presumptuous intermeddler, who will fancy himself a poet too, and what is still worse a better than he that employs him. The consequence is, that with cobbling, and tinkering, and patching on here and there a shred of his own, he makes such a difference between the original and the copy, that an author cannot know his own work again. Now, as I choose to be responsible for nobody's dullness but my own, I am a little comforted when I reflect that it will be in my power to prevent all such impertinence . . .
> [*English Letters of the XVIII Century* (ed. James Aitken), London 1946, pp. 120f.]

On 16 June Haydn conducted two of his Salomon Symphonies at another charity concert, which had been postponed from the 9th because of 'an unforeseeable circumstance'. The original announcement in the *Wiener Zeitung* No. 44 of 1 June had read:

> Musical Academy. On the 9th of June there will be a grand musical academy in two parts given by local musicians and dilettantes in the great hall of the I. R. Augarten, for the benefit of a distressed family. . . . It is to be added that on this occasion there will also be given two brand new Symphonies by the worthy *Herr* Haydn, Doctor of Music, which he only recently produced at London in England, where they were received with great esteem, but which have never been produced here in Vienna. [The postponement in *WZ* 47, 12 June.]

As we have noted before, with reference to the Fries concert, Haydn had produced all his Salomon Symphonies in Vienna, but probably these were two of the lesser-known ones.

Haydn had an idea that he could find many subscribers for *The Creation* in England, but he was not quite sure how to go about it. The following letter is perhaps his first attempt along those lines.

> [To a friend in England, possibly Christoph Papendiek.[1] *German*]
> Nobly born,
> Most esteemed Friend!
> You will certainly be surprised to receive this letter, after we have been separated for so long, but since I was convinced of your cordial friendship for me from the very first moment of our acquaintance, and since I know you are a truly good and generous man, I now take the liberty of asking you to read the following; you will then be able to decide whether you are in a position to help me.

1 Christoph Papendiek, a flautist, taught music to the Royal Family. His wife, Charlotte, was Assistant Keeper of the Wardrobe to Queen Charlotte, and wrote some delightful memoirs (see *Haydn in England 1791–1795*, pp. 51ff., for her description of the first Salomon concert). Of all Haydn's English friends, none stood closer to the Royal Family, and it is quite likely that this letter was addressed to Papendiek. At any rate, almost the whole Royal Family subscribed, including the King.

Last year I composed a German Oratorio called *The Creation*, which has met with exceptional approval by everyone. This approval moved me to publish this Oratorio in full score, with German and English text; the score, which should be ready in 4 or at the most 5 months, will be correctly engraved, and printed on the finest paper, at a subscription price of £1 10 shillings, which sum, however, does not need to be paid until delivery. The subscription offer is made in advance so that the subscribers' names can be included in the score. The publication will be so arranged that those living abroad will be sent their copies 3 or 4 weeks earlier; I shall pay the consignment charges myself. Now my most ardent wish is to enjoy the royal favour of having Her gracious Majesty the Queen of England condescend to subscribe to this work (N.B. without making a deposit): the presence of her name in the printed list of subscribers will convince the world that during my sojourn in London I enjoyed the royal favour of having displayed my small talents to the royal court by playing there. In the hope that you will heed my request, and at the proper moment yourself persuade Her Majesty the Queen (before whom I prostrate myself), I am, my most esteemed friend, most respectfully,

Your most obedient friend and servant,
Joseph Haydn [m.p] ria.

Vienna, 25th June 1799.

If I should be fortunate enough to receive an answer, please address the letter to me in Vienna.
P. S. My respectful compliments to your wife. [CCLN, 156f.]

Griesinger was meanwhile trying to organize the Haydn engraving for Breitkopf to use as the frontispiece of their *Oeuvres Complettes*:

3 July 1799.

Most excellent Friend,

H. Kinninger agrees to copy the portrait, as you requested. With [the engraver] H. Kohl I've not yet been able to speak; he's in the country.

H. Hayden will send me the Gut[t]enbrunn portrait in three days; he is afraid that it will make a poor effect as an engraving since it shows him in a position where he is working on a composition. I suppose that the gentlemen Kinninger and Kohl will have to decide about that. In case the Gut[t]enbrunn portrait is not found suitable, and if the Danz [Dance] one does not come soon from England, Haydn suggests getting hold of the one Artaria[1] issued, which many of his friends find not unlike him. I will get the opinion of Messrs. Kinninger [*sic*] and Kohl on this point and let you know.... [Olleson, *Griesinger*, 11]

On 5 July Haydn sent one of his *Regens chori* friends[2] a copy of a Mass:

1 Somfai (222) suggests that the Artaria portrait referred to is the one engraved by J. Neidl from the Zitterer painting; but this engraving was issued in 1800 (Pohl III, 406) and it is unlikely, therefore, that 'many of his friends' can have studied it in 1799. Olleson (*Griesinger*, 12) thinks it was the portrait on the title page of Artaria's edition of Op. 76; but that, too, was announced on 15 July 1799. Besides, it is a small portrait, only part of the title page (by Sebastian Mansfeld from the Hardy engraving). We consider that Haydn meant the old (1781) Mansfeld engraving, which Artaria was still selling.

2 There are several possibilities: the first choice would be perhaps Anton Stoll, the *Regens chori* at Baden, who was Mozart's friend, and at whose house Frau Haydn later boarded. As music director of the Stadtfarrkirche, Stoll often performed Haydn's late masses. If the 'Nelson' mass (1798) is the work referred to, the letter may be addressed to the *Regens chori* of Klosterneuburg Monastery near Vienna, where we discovered an authentic set of parts of the 'Nelson' Mass, copied by Johann Elssler (Haydn's copyist). Klosterneuburg also owns a very early and important set of parts of the *Missa in tempore belli* (1796) which Haydn may have sent them.

[To an unknown friend. *German*]

Vienna, 5th July 1799.

Dearest Friend!

I sent you the Mass with today's mail-coach. The costs for copying it were 11 f. 46 xr. and the carrying charges 1 f. 34 xr. If you should ever have a similar wish in the future, you have only to command your servant,

Joseph Haydn.

[CCLN, 157]

Haydn now had another idea about collecting English subscriptions, and he wrote to his German friend Theodor Küffner (the spelling of the MS. *Creation* subscription list, with the address N$^{ro.}$ 35 great Winchester Street, Broad Street) or Kuffner, a music teacher in London:

[Haydn to Theodor Küffner (Kuffner). *German.*]

Dearest Friend!

Perhaps you will have heard that last year I had to compose an Oratorio entitled the Creation for our high nobility, which because of its undeserved but exceptional and general success will appear in score with German and English text, cleanly and correctly engraved and 300 pages in length with the subscription price of £1 10s., within 3 or at the most 4 months; the money will be paid only upon the work's delivery, however, and the subscribers are invited beforehand so that their names can be included in a subscription list attached to the work; the postage is at my expense: Now, dearest friend! You will certainly remember that I had the honour to instruct your then pupil, Lady Elisabeth Greville. I would like to have the permission of her father, the Earl of Warwik [*sic*],[1] to send the Lady a copy with her name printed in [the list of subscribers], without the slightest obligation to her, just to show the occasionally sceptical world that I had the fortune to be received kindly also in England: Since I am convinced of your friendship for me, I hope that you won't refuse to do this favour for me, and I would be still more in your debt if through your good word I might receive some further subscribers; I will not fail to show my appreciation. In the hope of receiving an answer soon, I am, with every mark of respect,

My dearest friend's

Obedient friend and servt.
Joseph Haydn mpria.

P. S. My respectful compliments to the worthy *H*[*err*] Doctor von Mayer, his goodhearted wife and his *H*[*err*] brother.

Vienna, 9th July 1799.

[On the reverse side, MS. notice by Küffner: 'Dr. J. Haydn's first letter'.]

[Not in CCLN]

Haydn left for Eisenstadt on the 10th or 11th (we have a letter from him dated 12 July from Eisenstadt), and before doing so he prudently turned over the collection of Austrian subscribers to Artaria, who inserted the following notice in the *Wiener Zeitung* (No. 56, 13 July):

1 This letter, discovered after CCLN had been printed, was first published by Hubert Unverricht (*Musikforschung* XVIII [1965] Heft 1, 40f. The autograph is in the Stadt- und Universitätsbibliothek, Frankfurt. Lady Elizabeth (born 1784) was the third child of George Greville, Earl of Warwick, and his second wife, Henrietta, daughter of Richard Vernon. None of the family subscribed to *The Creation*. See Edmund Lodge, *The Peerage of the British Empire*, London 1834, pp. 462f. In Unverricht's transcription 'Marwil' instead of 'Warwik'.

Notice. *Herr Kapellmeister* Joseph Haydn, who will be away from town for several weeks and will be departing in the near future, has transferred the collection of subscriptions for the complete score of his Oratorio *The Creation*, as announced in the *Wiener Zeitung*, to us. In order that those who are thinking of acquiring this work do not seek for *Herr* Haydn in vain at the quarters indicated by him for collecting the subscriptions, we do not hesitate to put this notice before the public.

The 10th of July 1799. Artaria and Comp.

Haydn found Eisenstadt, in Rosenbaum's words (66), 'as cold as November'. The cold and rain continued until the end of the month. Meanwhile Artaria's handsome edition of the first three Quartets of what we call Op. 76 had appeared and they had hastened to send Haydn a pre-publication copy. Haydn wrote to them:

[To Artaria & Co., Vienna. *German*]

Messieurs!

I am most grateful to you for the copies of the Quartets you sent me, which are a great credit to me and – because of the legible engraving and the neat title page – to you.

Herr Count Joseph Erdödy wrote me many kind things, and thanked me for having made them available to the world at last. I hope that His Excellency will have received his copy by now. In a little while I will send the 5th Quartet in D major, and then the last in E flat.[1]

Meanwhile I remain, with respects to the whole firm,

Your most obedient servant,
Joseph Haydn [m.p.] ria.

Eisenstadt, 12th July 1799.

[Address:] Monsieur
Monsieur Artaria et Compag:
a
Vienne.

[Artaria's clerk notes: 'Haydn / Eisenstadt 12th July 1799./ rec'd 16th ditto/ ans'd 16th ditto'.]

Haydn was finishing his so-called *Theresienmesse* for the name-day celebrations of Princess Marie Hermenegild. It was once believed that this Mass was composed for the Empress Marie Therese; and while we now know (from the authentic performance material of the Mass in the Eisenstadt Archives, where it is entitled 'Anno 1799', and contains many corrections and additions in Haydn's hand) that the first performance probably took place at Eisenstadt, there is no reason why Haydn cannot have rededicated the work, as it were, to his Empress. That he actually gave her a copy is now certain: some years ago the writer of these notes examined the Archives of the *Hofburgkapelle* and found authentic parts to the *Theresienmesse* there – including some parts by Johann Elssler and a score which is obviously a copy of the autograph, though perhaps made about 1820. It seems likely that the Empress had the autograph manuscript for a time (it is now owned by the Austrian National Library).

During this visit we notice that the relationship between Haydn and Prince Nicolaus has changed considerably. We hear of the Prince toasting Haydn's health in the great hall, and altogether Nicolaus shows himself in an expansive mood: all of a

1 The MSS. of Op. 76, Nos. 5 and 6. Artaria issued the works in two sets: Op. 75 (= Op. 76, Nos. 1–3) and Op. 76 (= Op. 76, Nos. 4–6).

sudden he granted poor Rosenbaum permission to marry (25 July: 'I kissed his [Esterházy's] hand . . . the Prince had said she [Therese Gassmann] is a good girl, the whole family are fine people; this pleased me no end' [67]). Part of the reason for Nicolaus's changed attitude towards his *Kapellmeister* was undoubtedly the resounding success of *The Creation*, to which even a cynical *roué* could not be indifferent (after all, even the greatest lecher of them all, Prince Kaunitz, had attended the Oratorio, if only to ogle his latest potential mistress, Fräulein Saal). And we must recall that Prince Nicolaus was a genuine admirer of church music, and the latest productions of his eminent *Kapellmeister* in this field were already famous in Viennese church circles. Haydn was now a jewel in Esterházy's crown, and the Prince realized that he was the temporal owner, as it were, of Europe's greatest composer: all these things no doubt contributed to a new relationship between the two men.

On 17 July 1799, the *Wiener Zeitung* published Artaria's announcement of the first three Quartets from Op. 76 (or Op. 75 in Artaria's numbering):

> Notice. The undersigned Art and Musical Establishment announce herewith the publication of the latest 6 Quartets for 2 violins, viola and violoncello by *Hrn. Kapellmeister* Joseph Haydn. This opus has not yet been heard by the public, but may be recommended, if by nothing else than by the variations on that same 'Gott erhalte unsern Kaiser' which has been so successful; our edition appears in 2 sets. The first, of 3 Quartets, may be had from today and costs 3 fl., the second will follow shortly. We may allow ourselves, in recommending our edition of this work, to remark that nothing has ever appeared in our publishing house which – with the exception of the ornamented title page containing a portrait of the composer – can be compared to it in all the diligence and great expense lavished on it.
>
> The 15th of July 1799. Artaria and Comp.

We now arrive at the first hint of the vexing problem of the available instruments at Eisenstadt. It is contained in the following letter from Prince Esterházy:

> [To Haydn from Prince Nicolaus II Esterházy. *German*]
>
> *Herr Kapellmeister* Haydn:
>
> I expect your written opinion concerning the enclosed petition[1] of the trumpeters Sebastian Bindter [*sic*][2], Michael Altmann, and Johann Pfann, who ask that an annual salary be granted them for their services in the choir loft and in other musical performances here; in particular, what kind of yearly contract could be established, taking into account the number of services in which they perform? And what would be the best wages they would otherwise get for each single performance?
>
> By the way, I have instructed that their bill for 50 Fl. 15 xr. be paid to them.
>
> Eisenstadt, 18th July 1799.
>
> Exp. Esterházy. [CCLN, 158]

1 The three trumpeters began this particular period of their service, according to an attached bill, on 30 September 1798: thus, they had played the three trumpet parts in Haydn's 'Nelson' Mass, which had been first performed in honour of the Princess Marie's Name Day that autumn. The petition (Esterházy Archives, Acta Musicalia, Fasc. XXVI, 1855) is dated July 1799 and reads: 'Last year, the undersigned made bold most humbly to ask Your Highness if, in your graciousness, you would grant us an annual salary; the suppliants, however, have not hitherto received any decision regarding their humble petition, and thus take the liberty of presenting Your Highness the enclosed bill for 50 Fl. 15 xr. with the most humble request that Your Highness have the grace to instruct payment therefor to be made . . .'

2 Bindter's name is usually spelled 'Binder'.

[To Prince Nicolaus II Esterházy. *German*]

[Eisenstadt, between the middle of July and September 1799][1]

Inasmuch as, for some years now, the 3 trumpeters have been paid per performance, which amounted to an annual sum of 111 Fl., in my humble opinion it would be something of a saving to pay each of them a cash annual salary of 25 Fl. and two measures [*Metzen* = 6.88 litres] of corn: they, for their part, should be obliged to attend all the performances which are scheduled, in the church and otherwise.[2]

Joseph Haydn [m.p]ria,
Capell Meister.

[CCLN, 159]

The trumpeters' petition of July 1799 is headed 'Eisenstadt'; hence we know that Haydn had at his disposal apart from the usual voices, strings and organ – three trumpets and kettledrums. The *Theresienmesse*'s autograph is scored, as far as the wind instruments and percussion are concerned, only for two clarinets, two trumpets and drums. But the original performance probably included bassoon parts (one or more), doubling the basso continuo, for authentic bassoon parts to the Mass exist, and have been published in the excellent new critical edition by the Haydn Institut (*Joseph Haydn Werke*, Reihe XXIII, Band 3, ed. Günter Thomas); in fact the bassoon part(s) are included in all the authentic sets of parts, including Eisenstadt and the Lobkowitz MS. (now Prague), as well as the copy for the Empress. Haydn could have found a bassoon or two among local Eisenstadt players; possibly, on the other hand, the clarinet players had to be imported from Vienna.

Meanwhile the *hohe Herrschaften* were amused by a French comedy and shadow pantomime, rehearsed (at least) on 17 July and produced on the 20th in cold and rainy weather. Rosenbaum was in bed with a cold, but his mother went and reported 'both were bad'. On Sunday 21 July Rosenbaum (67) informs us, after 'Damn this weather!', that '... There was a ball [at the Castle] in the evening; 80 persons from the town were invited in addition to the castle personnel. The ball was said to be most entertaining and splendid in every respect. ...' Here is still another – if in view of the restricted orchestra in 1799 remote – possibility for the first production of those elusive *Twenty-Four Minuets* for grand orchestra by Haydn which have seen so often the subject of our speculations in these pages.

It is enticing to think of Haydn writing music for the 'French comedy', perhaps even the 'Fatal amour' musique discussed above in the 1796 season; but with its substantial orchestra of a flute, two oboes, two bassoons, two horns (with the usual strings), it hardly fits into a season during which there were, officially, only trumpets, kettledrums and (for the Mass in September) two clarinets. Yet one wonders what Haydn was conducting in the way of music at Eisenstadt Castle in July, considering the limited orchestra available; there may not even have been clarinets at this time, since they are not known to have been needed before the first week of September. Possibly

1 The date is uncertain. Its earliest date is 19 July (see above) and its latest 14 September, when the Prince decided to accept Haydn's proposal: Esterházy's letter to the Economic Administration, written in Eisenstadt, is preserved in the Esterházy Archives (Acta Musicalia, Fasc. XXVI, 1854). The letter ends with the request that the '*Kappelmeister* Haydn is to be reminded ...' of the acceptance.

2 German: 'in der Kammer' ('and otherwise'), which of course means not only 'in the chamber', i.e. for chamber music (wherein trumpets do not ordinarily play) but in symphonies, operas, etc. This fine distinction cannot, unfortunately, be rendered literally into English.

there was chamber music (piano trios, string quartets, and the like). On 20 July Haydn was still in Eisenstadt, attending to the final Quartets of Op. 76 for Artaria:

[To Artaria & Co., Vienna. *German*]
Messieurs!

I send you herewith the 5th Quartet, which you should arrange to have copied at the earliest opportunity; and as soon as you send it back to me, you shall have the last one. Please send me at the same time the names of the subscribers to date, so that I can enter them in my book.[1]

Meanwhile I am, most respectfully,

Your most obedient servant,
Jos: Haydn.

Eisenstadt, 20th July 1799.

[Address:] Monsieur
Monsieur Artaria et Compag:
a
Vienne.

[Artaria's clerk notes: 'Haydn/Eisenstadt 20th July 1799/ received 23rd ditto/ answered 24th ditto.'] [CCLN, 159f.]

That same day in Vienna, Griesinger reported to Leipzig about his progress with the Haydn portrait:

20 July 1799.

Most excellent Friend,

You will have wondered why I haven't sent you news about the Haydn portrait. This delay has occurred through no fault of my own. H. Haydn has gone to Prince Esterházy at Eisenstadt in Hungary, and his wife, a good old matron, made me wait until she got hold of the Gut[t]enbrunn portrait from one of her friends and had it delivered to me. It seems to me to be very similar, Haydn's wife thinks it is the best, and H. Kinninger [*sic*], to whom I consigned it immediately, is also satisfied with it. He will be ready with the drawing in fourteen days at the latest and then will give it to H. John to be engraved, because he thinks that John's manner is more elegant and nicer than that of Kohl. Since in your letters you have not shown a preference for either artist, and H. Kinninger's opinion deserves all due consideration, I made no objections whatever to his choice. No doubt you know Alxinger's[2] portrait in the Göschen edition. This is the way Haydn's portrait should be done. H. Kinninger will write directly to you about the price John asks and will send the design for the Mozart *Requiem* [which Breitkopf & Härtel were about to issue]. [Olleson, *Griesinger*, 12]

On 24 July Haydn was back in Vienna, answering the first subscribers from out of town, among them Franz Xaver Glöggl in Linz:[3]

1 Haydn's booklet, listing the subscribers to *The Creation*, is preserved in the Vienna Stadtbibliothek (cat. 99280) and is entitled: *Verzeichnüß der Praenumeranten über die Schöpfung*. It is important source of addresses and names of Haydn's friends. *Vide* Appendix, pp. 622ff.

2 Johann Baptist von Alxinger, poet and fellow-Mason of Haydn's at the Viennese lodge 'Zur wahren Eintracht'. See also *Haydn in England 1791–1795*, p. 216. The portrait was engraved by Friedrich John after Kininger. Olleson, *Griesinger*, 12.

3 Glöggl's father, Johann Joseph, was one of Haydn's ardent admirers; the Monastery of St Florian owns Glöggl's copies of four Haydn Symphonies. Franz Xaver (1764–1839) was City and Cathedral Chapel-Master at Linz and, like his father, *Thurnermeister* there. He later gained a certain reputation as the author of various musical treatises. See *Musik in Geschichte und Gegenwart*, V, 296–8.

[To Franz Xaver Glöggl, Linz. *German*]
Well born,
Most highly respected Sir!

You have done me an inestimable honour, Sir, by subscribing to *The Creation*, and it will be a pleasure to include your name in the subscribers' list; I am still more indebted to you for the important recommendation to my old and clever friend, the *Herr Abbé* von Stadler;[1] all this inspires an old man to further energies. Thus as soon as the work is printed, I shall not fail to send you a copy by the diligence. Meanwhile I am, Sir, with my compliments to the *Herr Abbé*, most respectfully,

Your most obedient servant,
Joseph Haydn.

Vienna, 24th July 1799.

[Address:] An den Wohlgebohrn Herrn Franz Xaver Glöggl
Stadt und Dom Capell Meister in Linz
in Oberoesterreich. [CCLN, 160]

It was at this time that the Vienna correspondent of the *AMZ* sent off a report, some parts of which may find a place in our Chronicle here:

Vienna, End of July 1799.

Some time ago I promised to write about the newest operas which have been successful here recently. . . . A new opera, *Der Marktschreyer*, with music by Süssmayr will begin on 1 August; then a new opera by Paul Wranitzky, the composer of *Oberon*, is to be given with the title *Der Schreiner*, and then another one by Süssmayr, *Die Liebe im Serail*. Herr Süssmayr has already given us, in his *Spiegel von Arkadien*, proof that he has studied operatic composition, and if in his following operettas he did not obtain the success that one had hoped for him, I doubt not that we shall hear something quite fine from him. – A new arrangement of *Jagd* by Weisse with Hrn. Schenk's music was recently given but enjoyed no success. In the Italian field, *La Principessa d'Amalfi*, a work that we have long appreciated by Hrn. Joseph Weigl,[2] was revived and listened to with the greatest pleasure. We are assured, too, that Hr. Gyrowetz is working on a German opera. . . . In the suburbs . . . *Der rothe Geist im Donnergebirge*, given at Schikaneder's, has very pretty music by Hrn. Ritter von Seyfried and Hrn. Trübensee [Triebensee]. It seems to me altogether that the public here is at last tiring of seeing the silliness of all these ghosts and magic Harlequin twaddle in the theatre, and wishes to have food which is heartier and more suitable for people with normal understanding.

It's now high time to consign these stupidities to oblivion; for it would be a pity if the public were deluded into this kind of thing by gorgeous costumes, stage sets and good (but more often bad) music, and were to be seduced away from real beauty by this marionette playing. A few waltzes, a single change of scene, a good stage set were until recently enough to place in a good light the worst poetry and music of an opera. One goes to look, for example, at *Der Alte überall und nirgends* [by Wenzel Müller, 1796] or the *Tyroler Wastel* [by J. J. Haibel, 1796] and thanks God that one survived them the first time. It would be very unfair, however, to use the above-mentioned circumstances in order to accuse the *whole* public of lacking good taste. When *Crescentini* sang at the time Haydn's *Creation* was being

1 Also a friend of the Mozart family, Stadler bought Haydn's Longman & Broderip piano after the composer's death in 1809.

2 When it was first performed, a few days before Haydn left for England, Haydn wrote a warm letter of congratulation to his godson Weigl about it: see *Haydn in England 1791–1795*, p. 230, and CCLN, 143f.

given, one saw clearly that there was as much sympathy for a great singer as for a great composer. . . . Schikaneder has more music in the grand style [than at the Court theatres]. Take *Zauberflöte*, the *Labyrinth* [Winter, 1798], *Babylons Pyramiden* [Gallus and Winter, 1797], etc. [Good voices, even with a bad opera and the grand style] gradually contribute sufficiently to make this category of opera (which offers much variety and is very well produced) such a habit that one quite overlooks the gigantic silliness. In this case and for this reason I can forgive the public. But when operas like *Die Ostinder vom Spittelberg* [Seyfried and Stegmayer, 1799], *Der Sturm* [Winter, 1798], *Das Donauweibchen* [F. Kauer, 1798] and many others just as revolting are applauded and well visited: what should one say? Just what the entrepreneurs of such opera theatre think: *Mundus vult*. . . .

[*AMZ* I, 814f.]

We now begin to see a sudden flowering of Haydn's correspondence. The astute student will have noted that during the period of composition and first production of *The Creation*, we have hardly a letter from Haydn's pen. We have seen that he simply did not answer correspondents, even Breitkopf & Härtel. From the beginning of 1797 to April 1799 we have only two or three extant Haydn letters (one of uncertain date, possibly written at the end of 1796). *The Creation*'s subscription involved its composer in an enormous amount of correspondence, most of which he had to answer personally (since he was the publisher). Haydn liked writing letters hardly more than Beethoven, and this flood of letter-writing which the older man was now obliged to undertake will have made him have careful second thoughts about issuing the scores of *The Seven Words* or *The Seasons* by subscription; and in fact both works were in the end given to Breitkopf & Härtel.

[To Karl Friedrich Moritz Paul, Count von Brühl,[1] Weimar. *German*]
Excellence!

Your Excellency has done me an inestimable honour and favour by subscribing to *The Creation*, and inspired an old man to further energies. Thus as soon as the work is printed, I shall not fail to send a copy, and also one to the most charming Baroness von Loewenstern, by the diligence. Meanwhile I am, in profound submission,

Your Excellency's
obedient servant,
Joseph Haydn [m.p.] ria.

Vienna, 10th August 1799.
[No name or address extant] [CCLN, 160f.]

1 The mention of the Baroness Loewenstern helps us to identify the Count von Brühl to whom this letter is supposedly written. Haydn's list of subscribers to *The Creation*, mentioned above, includes 'Baronesse Loewenstern von Weimar in Sachsen'; the young Count Brühl (1772–1837), nephew of the infamous Saxon Minister under August III, Heinrich (1700–63), was in Weimar during the year 1799. (The next year he moved to Berlin, as *Kammerherr* of Prince Heinrich of Prussia.) But despite the mention of the Baroness von Loewenstern, it is just possible that Haydn wrote the letter to another member of the family. The son of the Saxon Minister had been in Vienna and Burney had heard him play the viola in a Haydn quartet. See also Meyer's *Konversations-Lexikon*, 6th ed. (1908), III, p. 492f. To complete this picture of confusing Counts Brühl, one should add that Haydn had written his canons. 'The Ten Commandments', in London for Count Hans Moritz von Brühl, Saxon Minister to the Court of St James. Hans Moritz died in London in 1809, and it seems doubtful if he would have ordered *The Creation* for Baroness Loewenstern in Weimar. Haydn's invaluable subscription list does not help us in this case, for it says only: 'Graf Brühl königl. preussische Jagd Junker.'

[To P. Cornelius Knoblich, Grissau Monastery near Landeshut in Silesia. *German*]
Most worthy and Reverend Sir!

Your most worthy Abbot[1] has done me an inestimable honour by subscribing to *The Creation*, and thus as soon as the work is printed, I shall not fail to send a copy to Your Reverence by the diligence.

Inasmuch as my present young Prince issued the moderate command four years ago that in my old age I must compose a new Mass once a year, it will be indeed a pleasure to be able to send you one of them; but you must only write me if, apart from trumpets and kettledrums, you also have 2 oboes or clarinets, so that I can make the proper choice – that is, if you do not find 12 fl. too expensive for the copying charges.[2]

Your Reverence has only half enjoyed *The Seven Words of Our Saviour*, because 3 years ago I added a new 4-part vocal music (without changing the instrumental parts). The text was written by a well-versed and musicianly canon at the Passau Cathedral, and our great Baron von Swieten corrected it; the effect of this work surpassed all expectation, and if I should ever travel to your part of the world before I die, I would take the liberty of performing it before your Abbot. But at present no one possesses it except in our Monarchy. Perhaps —— ——.

Write me (BETWEEN OURSELVES) the day and the month of your Abbot's birthday and name-day. Hoping to receive an answer, I am, most respectfully,

Your Reverence's
most obedient servant,
Joseph Haydn.

Vienna, 10th August 1799.
[Address: To the Worthy and Reverend Herr Cornelius Knoblich
Music Director and Member of the Cistercian Monastery of Grissau bey Landeshutt [*sic*] in Silesia. [CCLN, 161f.]

Shortly after 10 August Haydn left again for Eisenstadt, to prepare for the first – or so we believe – performance of the *Theresienmesse* as part of the honours for Princess Marie Hermenegild Esterházy's name-day. On the 15th he had occasion to write Artaria once again about the Op. 76 Quartets:

[To Artaria & Co., Vienna. *German*]
Messieurs!

I take the liberty of sending you the enclosed letter from Frankfurt, and would ask you to inform me how and in what way I should react to the request of these two gentlemen, Gayl and Hedler, since I have never engaged in transactions of this kind. I realize that every publisher looks to his own interests in these matters, but I would like you to write me your frank opinion whether they ought to pay cash for every copy, or whether one pays the bill for each dozen sold with the 13th copy. I think, however, that neither the one nor the other applies here, because the application comes directly to me from abroad. I am convinced of this as a result of orders I have already received from Berlin, Danzig, Leipzig, Regenspurg [*sic*], and so forth. Nevertheless I should be glad of your opinion, and shall certainly be most grateful to you for all your trouble.

I should have delivered the Third Quartet[3] to you, but certain doubts hold me back from doing so: I have not yet received an answer as to the last three Quartets

1 Johannes Langer (note in Haydn's *The Creation* subscription book).
2 The invaluable subscription book (see note 1) tells us which Mass Haydn sent them. His entry reads: 'Knoblich from Grissau in Upper Silesia paid for a copy of *The Creation* and the Mass in C' (i.e. the *Missa in tempore belli* (1796)).
3 Op. 76, No. 6 (Artaria's Op. 76, No. 3).

which I sent to London,[1] and I fear that if the gentlemen issue all 6 Quartets together and not divided – i.e., if they have not yet announced them – your edition and announcement could appear earlier than that in London; though that is difficult to believe, for I sent the first 3 Quartets as early as 27th March and the last 3 on 15th June. If the publication in Vienna should be earlier than that in London (which I hope will not be the case), and if the gentlemen were to discover that you at once received the same 3 Quartets from me, I should lose £75 Sterling, which would be a serious matter. You must therefore take immediate action, *sub rosa*, to ascertain positively whether the first 3 are out, and likewise approximately when the last 3 will appear, so that I won't have a double fine imposed on me. I shall send you the Third Quartet shortly, but you must wait with the publication until we know that the 2nd set has been published in London. I rely on your integrity in this matter, and for my part I shall always be,

Messieurs,

Your most obedient servant,

[signature omitted].

I would ask you to answer by return of mail; if at the same time you can let me have some of the names of the subscribers [to *The Creation*], I should be grateful. Eisenstadt, 15th August 1799.

[Artaria's clerk notes: 'Haydn/ Eisenstadt 15th August 1799/ received 16th ditto/ answered 16th ditto'.] [CCLN, 162f.]

Haydn later entered into direct negotiations with Messrs. Gayl and Hedler (see letter of 21 September 1799, *infra*), but the correspondence has not survived. Now Haydn heard from another old English friend. He had written to Dr Burney on 15 July to enlist his help about getting British subscribers. With characteristic generosity, Burney promised to help and in the end he did more than any single man – the composer himself excepted – to gather subscriptions to Haydn's score.

[To Haydn from Charles Burney. *English*]

Chelsea College, August 19, 1799.

My dear and much-honoured Friend!

The reverence with which I have always been impressed for your great talents, and respectable and amiable character, renders your remembrance of me extremely flattering. And I am the more pleased with the letter which you have honoured me, of July 15th as it has pointed out to me the means by which I may manifest my zeal in your service, as far as my small influence can extend. I shall, with great pleasure, mention your intention of publishing your oratorio *della Creazione del Mondo*; by subscription, to all my friends; but you alarm me very much by the short time you allow for solicitation. In winter it would be sufficient, but now (in Aug.) there is not a single patron of music in town. I have been in Hampshire myself for three weeks, and am now at home for two or three days only, on my way to Dover, where I shall remain for a month or six weeks, and where I shall see few of the persons whom I mean to stimulate to do themselves the honour of subscribing to your work. I wish it were possible to postpone the delivery of the book in England till next winter. The operas, oratorios, and concerts, public, and private, seldom begin in London till after Christmas, nor do the nobility and gentry return thither from the country till the meeting of Parliament about that time. Now, three months from the date of your letter, my dear Sir, will only throw your publication to the middle of October, the very time

1 To Messrs. Longman, Clementi & Co., who issued them as Op. 76, Books 1 and 2. The first book, though announced as early as April, did not appear till June; the second book appeared nearly a year later.

in the whole year when London is the most uninhabited by the lovers of field sports, as well as music.

I had the great pleasure of hearing your new *quartetti* (*opera* 76) well performed before I went out of town, and never received more pleasure from instrumental music: they are full of invention, fire, good taste, and new effects, and seem the production, not of a sublime genius who has written so much and so well already, but of one of highly-cultivated talents, who had expended none of his fire before. The Divine Hymne, written for your imperial master, in imitation of our loyal song, 'God save great George our King', and set so admirably to music by yourself, I have translated and adapted to your melody, which is simple, grave, applicating, and pleasing. *La cadenza particolarmente mi pare nuova e squisitissima.* I have given our friend, Mr. Barthelemon,[1] a copy of my English translation to transmit to you, with my affectionate and best respects. It was from seeing in your letter to him, how well you wrote English, that I ventured to address you in my own language, for which my translation of your hymn will perhaps serve as an exercise; in comparing my version with the original, you will perceive that it is rather a paraphrase than a close translation; but the liberties I have taken were in consequence of the supposed treachery of some of his Imperial Majesty's generals and subjects, during the unfortunate campaign of Italy, of 1797, which the English all thought was the consequence, not of Bounaparte's [*sic*] heroism, but of Austrian and Italian treachery.

Let me intreat you, my dear Sir, to favour me with your opinion of my proposition for postponing the publication of your oratorio, at least in England, till March, or April, 1800. But whatever you determine, be assured of my zeal and ardent wishes for your success, being, with the highest respect and regard,

Dear Sir
your enthusiastic admirer and
affectionate Servant
Charles Burney.

[Address:]
Al Celeberrimo
Signore Giuseppe Haydn, in Vienna. [CCLN, 164f.]

In this Chronicle, Haydn's wife, Maria Anna, remains a rather shadowy figure. One of the few concrete documents about her is her last will and testament, which she drew up in Vienna on 9 September, when her husband was still at Eisenstadt. The document is not without interest, particularly since she made Haydn her residuary legatee. Far be it from us to attempt an analysis of the ills of the Haydns' marriage, but as Robert Franz Müller suggests,[2] Maria Anna may have been something less of an ogre than she is made to appear in the Haydn literature. That she was uneducated may be seen from the incredible spelling and grammar of her last will, alas untranslatable in this respect. And on the other hand, Haydn was well known (also to his biographer Dies) as having been a notorious womanizer in his youth. Frau Haydn had, no doubt, many Luigia Polzellis and Catherine Csechs with whom to contend. If anything, her last will and testament is rather a sympathetic document.

1 F. H. Barthélémon, the violinist, to whom Haydn was very attached. The letter Burney saw was probably about the violin Concerto that Haydn had promised to compose for Barthélémon, who had announced it in April 1799 (see *Haydn in England 1791–1795*, p. 169).

2 'Heiratsbrief, Testament und Hinterlassenschaft der Gattin Joseph Haydns, zum erstenmal veröffentlicht', in *Die Musik* XXII/2 (November 1929), pp. 93ff.

In the name of the most holy Trinity, to avoid any arguments that might arise after my death, I, being of sound mind, do hereby set forth my last Will which, being written entirely in my own hand, is to dispose of my few earthly goods, consisting of my few articles of clothing, jewels, the house which is situated in the Untere Steingasse No. 73 in Gumpendorf, and of which I own half. According to the terms of my marriage contract drawn up between me and my dear husband Joseph Haydn, I herewith append my last Will, to wit:

Firstly: my body shall be buried according to the wishes of my husband.

Secondly: 3 Holy Masses.

Thirdly: for the primary school [*Normahl schuel*] – 10 f.

Fourthly: for the Institute for the Poor – 10 f.

Fiftly: for my brother [Joseph] Keller, two hundred gulden.

Sixthly: for [the family of] my late sister, Barbara Scheiger, two hundred gulden.

Seventhly: for [the family of] my late sister, Elisabeth Bi[e]derman[n], two hundred gulden.

Eighthly: for my sister, Josepha Keller, two hundred gulden.

Ninthly: for [the family of] my late sister, Alosia Lindner, two hundred gulden.

Tenthly: for Herr v. Pinziger, my cousin, as a keepsake my gold repeating watch, for his wife my splinter of the True Cross which is in a crucifix, together with the three embroidered pictures as a keepsake; for her sister Elenora a lozenge-shaped ring fashioned like a heart, as a keepsake.

Eleventhly: for my sister Josepha Keller's poor maid, Magdalena Braun Miller [Braunmüller], one hundred gulden.

Twelfthly: for my washing lady Elisabeth Asmos, one hundred gulden.

Thirteenthly: for my sister Josepha Keller, 20 gulden to be distributed to the poor.

Fourteenthly: for Joseph Scheiger [son of the late sister Barbara Scheiger], a silly lad [may mean idiot], one hundred gulden.

Fifteenthly: for my foster-child, Ladislav Bidermann [Biedermann, son of the late sister Elisabeth Biedermann], one hundred gulden.

Sixteenthly: for my foster-child, Karl Keller [son of the late brother Karl], one hundred gulden.

Since I own fine linen and clothing, also silver, my husband, as residuary legatee, is asked to sell some of it, to give to the poor people that little which I have indicated should go to my principal legatees, which sum I am able to dispose of according to the contract between me and my dear husband of 9 November 1760, and in so far as it is not so specified, I hereby deem my dear husband Joseph Haydn as my residuary legatee, upon whose express authority and permission I have distributed the above monies, and I would ask the worthy authorities to regard this my last Will, if not as a proper testament, at least as a codicil or whatever is necessary to treat it as a legal and binding document, to the true expedition of which I have written this last Will and signed it in my own hand.

Vienna, 9 September 799. Maria Anna Haydn.

[The envelope was sealed three times and has the following note:] Here is included the autograph last will and marriage-letter of Maria Anna Haydn, [Official remark:] Opened the 22nd March 800 in the presence of the residuary legatee and H. Stohl [Anton Stoll] for the purpose of making copies.

Town Registry of Baaden [*sic*]
Grundtgeiger
[Synd(icatus)]

Eight days before her death – which was due, according to the authorities, to arthritis – Maria Anna added the following codicil to her will:

Codicil to my completed testament.

Inasmuch as I, the undersigned Anna v. Haydn, have found it meet to add something to my completed testament, I have appended the present codicil to my testament:

Firstly: I leave to my brother's son Karl Keller my gold watch and a silver spoon. If he should die before coming of age, the gold watch should go to Josepha Bi[e]dermann.

Secondly: I give to Ladislaus Bi[e]dermann a gold ring fashioned like a fly and also my own silver table service.

Thirdly: I leave to H. Ant. Stoll Regenschori my golden snuff-box and to his wife, Anna Stoll, my golden ear-rings with the two diamonds and also 2 silver salt-cellars.

Fourthly: I leave to Antonia Stoll [Anton Stoll's daughter by a previous marriage] my East Indian muslin dress and to my still-living sister the ex-nun my satin dress with the yellow stripes

I have sealed this codicil with my seal in the presence of the witnesses requested for the purpose.

Baaden, the 12th of March 1800.

[seal] Anna Haydn.

Bernath Severien
as witness
Johann Stürzl
as witness

Maria Anna left 2,746 fl. 50 kr., the list having been drawn up by Haydn himself. Fifteen hundred gulden were her part of the marriage contract of 9 November 1760, and she had 'free disposition' over that sun. Her share of the house was (very conservatively, for tax reasons) estimated at 1,000 Gulden, the rest was clothes, linen, furniture, silver and jewellery. The costs of her illness and burial were 209 fl. 49 kr.; the legacies amounted to 1,540 fl.; the fees were 16 fl. 56¼ kr.

Total	2,746 fl. 50 kr.
Minus expenses	1,760 fl. 45¼ kr.
Haydn's inheritance as residuary legatee	980 fl. 04¾ kr.

This sum was already invested in Haydn's house, of which he now inherited his wife's half. In due course Haydn had, moreover, to pay 59 fl. 06 kr. and 9 fl. as inheritance tax (7 July 1800).

It was still cold at Eisenstadt. Rosenbaum tells us that on 1 September 1799 there was 'a Te Deum in the parish church on the hill' (Bergkirche): we have no evidence which work was performed – not Haydn's *Te Deum for the Empress*, because (1) it required a very large orchestra (flute, oboes, bassoons, horns, three trumpets, timpani, etc.) which Haydn obviously did not have in 1799 at Eisenstadt, and (2) Haydn did not have the parts copied for Eisenstadt until October 1800 (*vide infra,* 28 Oct. 1800). On the eve of the Princess's name-day, Saturday 7 September, Rosenbaum further reports:[1] 'Cold and dull . . . At about 6 in the evening there was Turkish music on the

1 P. 68. The entry about the *Te Deum* not in Radant, *Rosenbaum*, but kindly supplied by her from her MS. notes.

square, then a French play. At the end there was a decoration with the Princess's portrait.' The name-day itself fell, in 1799, on Sunday the 8th. We assume that in the morning there was High Mass at the Bergkirche, and the first performance of the new *Missa* in B flat. This would also explain the toast proposed to Haydn later. We read in Rosenbaum:

> Sunday, 8th, name-day of the Princess: . . . At about 3 o'clock we looked in on the banquet in the grand hall, 54 persons strong. There were many healths drunk, each announced by trumpets and drums in the gallery and by the thunder of cannon in front of the castle. The Prince also drank Haydn's health, to general concurrence. . . . They were at table until 5 o'clock, but real merriment was lacking despite 80 items to eat and all sorts of wines . . .
>
> [Rosenbaum, 68; Brand, 359]

Haydn left Eisenstadt afterwards, for we find him in Vienna on the 14th. Thus he missed the arrival of Baron Braun at Eisenstadt, 'with a new-fangled char-à-banc for 22 persons', who left on 20 September to visit Eszterháza. Haydn also missed the arrival of a group of French prisoners at Gscheiß on the 26th:

> They looked miserable and fatigued, but the spirit of the nation and that certain revolutionary character are unmistakably distinguishable in each one of them. – We took up a small collection, and the noble pride with which they accepted our gift can only be admired. [Rosenbaum, 68]

Haydn meanwhile had received Dr Burney's letter and answered it:

[To Charles Burney, Chelsea. *Italian*]
Most esteemed and dearest *Sigr Dottore!*

I regret extremely, my dear Sir, that you did not receive my letter dated 21st September [*sic*],[1] in which I had said that I could not wait too long with the subscription, as you, my dear Sir, were thinking of doing, in view of the fact that I have promised publicly to issue my *Creation* towards the end of September, or at the latest in the month of January 1800. Meanwhile I am very happy to be able to include in my list of subscribers all the names which you, my dear Sir, indicated in your kind letter, and to these I shall now add the name of Sir William Parson, and also the name of the Duke of Leeds' son (I regret extremely the death of his amiable father). As soon as the printing of the *opus* is finished, I shall not fail to send all the copies immediately, and also a few extra ones besides.

It makes me very happy to be able to show to the world how I was, and still am, esteemed in England; I really don't deserve such a fine list of subscribers, but I hope that this work will meet with everyone's satisfaction, particularly when it is performed.

My dear and much-honoured Doctor! I cannot sufficiently express to you how very grateful I am for all your efforts on my behalf. God bless you for them! I shall always remember your good heart, and I only regret that I cannot be there personally to show you my gratitude: I do not find the words; but enough! He who knows YOUR GREAT TALENT also knows YOUR KIND NATURE: happy he who can

1 Obviously Haydn wrote the wrong date: we suggest that he meant '2' instead of '21'. Meanwhile Burney had written again, and had apparently rounded up a goodly number of subscribers; he then followed it up with a second letter, adding the names of Sir William Parsons (*recte*), the conductor and specialist in old music who is also mentioned in the London Notebooks (see *Haydn in England 1791–1795*, p. 273), and the son of the Duke of Leeds (op. cit., p. 106).

boast of enjoying your dear friendship! As for myself, there remains only to say that I am, and shall always remain, with every regard and the highest respect,

my dearest *Sig^r Dottore*,
your most humble and devoted servant,
Giuseppe Haydn [m.p] ria.

Vienna, 14th September 1799. [CCLN, 165]

While Haydn was away in Vienna, attending to his diverse activities (Op. 76 Quartets for Artaria, *The Creation* subscribers), entertainments continued in Eisenstadt. Rosenbaum records at least one play given in the princely theatre: Schikaneder's *Die Fiaker in Wien*, performed ('wretchedly') on 27 September; presumably there were other plays as well.

Haydn's correspondence continued:

[To M. B. Veltmann, Osnabrück (Westphalia). *German*]

Vienna, 21st September 1799.

Nobly born,
Most highly respected Sir!

I am most obliged to you for the honour you have shown me in subscribing to my *Creation*, and in your satisfaction of my poor talents; as soon as the work is printed, I shall send it to you through the music dealers Gayl and Hedler[1] in Frankfurt, and would ask you to inform them of this. Should you not find any banker in Osnabrick [*sic*] who is in correspondence with ours, please send me the money through the gentlemen I mentioned above. I should so much like to be able to admire not only the 4 great organs, but also you, who, I am told, are one of the greatest living players.

The best Roman gut strings are to be had of Herr Artaria here. Meanwhile I am, most respectfully,

Your most obedient servant,
Joseph Haydn.

[Address:] Sr Wohlgebohrn
Dem Herrn M. B. Veltmann Organist zu St. Marien und
Musikhändler
in
Osnabrick [*sic*]
in Westphalen.

[CCLN, 166]

[To E. L. Gerber,[2] (Sondershausen?). *German*. Only extracts preserved]

Vienna 23rd September 1799.

. . . [Speaks of his new Oratorio, *The Seasons*.] Since this subject cannot be as sublime as that of *The Creation*, comparison between the two will show a distinct difference. Despite this, and with the help of Providence, I shall press on, and when this new work is completed I shall retire, because of the weakened state of my nerves, in order to be able to complete my last work. This will consist of vocal

1 See also *supra*, p. 482. Haydn delivered the work about October 1800. One of Artaria's receipts to Haydn for copies sold – the receipt is undated but must have been written sometime in October 1800 – mentions '1 Es. spedito a Weltmann [*sic*] d'Osnabruck . . . . fl. 13.30' See F. Artaria and H. Botstiber, *Joseph Haydn und das Verlagshaus Artaria*, p. 83.

2 Ernst Ludwig Gerber (1746–1819), the famous German musical lexicographer, whose *Historisch-biographisches Lexikon der Tonkünstler* (Leipzig, 1790–2) and *Neues historisch-biographisches Lexikon der Tonkünstler* (Leipzig, 1812–4) are among the most important musico-biographical *lexica* ever written. The extract from this letter is taken from the second volume of this latter publication.

quartets,[1] with accompaniment only of the pianoforte, based on German texts of our greatest poets; I have already composed thirteen such pieces, but have not yet performed any of them. . . .' [CCLN, 166f.]

[To Haydn from Nicolaus Simrock,[2] Bonn. *German*]

Bonn, 30th September 1799.

To Herr *Kapellmeister* Haydn
in Vienna.

It was not until today that I discovered you are publishing the score of your *Creation*. I herewith subscribe to 2 copies, which I would ask you to send to me at the following address: Herr Halm, postmaster in Sieburg, for Herr Simrock *via Frankfort am Mayn*. When the time comes I shall arrange payment through the music dealer Träg [Traeg].[3] I wish I could have engraved the work myself, for I would have made every effort to do justice to it. [CCLN, 167]

Rosenbaum also made a quick trip to Vienna, where he arrived on 2 October and then

went to Therese who received me on the steps with a loving heart . . . [She] then told me a lot of gossip which was circulating about our wedding, and that the wedding must be postponed until after Easter according to Mama [Gassmann]'s wishes . . . In the evening I went to the K[ärntnerthor] Theater for the first performance of the *3 Sultaninnen* [*Die drei Sultaninnen*], an opera by [F. X.] Huber, the music by Süssmayer. Quite pleasing music, with lovely stage-settings by Platzer. – The music, the opera as a whole, was not received well.' [68f.]

Therese sang, and the opera was sufficiently popular for Beethoven to choose a theme from it for one of his Variations (WoO 76) on the melody 'Tändeln und scherzen', which he dedicated to Anna Margarete, Countess von Browne.

Haydn was now required in Eisenstadt again; exactly when he arrived cannot be determined. Before he left, he bade farewell to one of his pupils, Paul Struck. Silverstolpe reports to Duke Carl in Stockholm on 2 October:

A few days ago a German subject of Your Royal Majesty by the name of Struck, born in Stralsund, left Vienna to travel to his fatherland. For something more than four years he has studied composition with the famous Haydn and has made such progress that the master calls him one of his cleverest pupils that he ever taught. With those works he has published the young Struck has been eminently successful. His later works, which are not yet generally known, show real genius and a genuine, profound discernment; they have won him the respect of the greatest masters here, who see him leave this seat of music with regret. He has left behind the reputation of an artist and a young man of reliable conduct . . .

[Mörner, 343]

Haydn gave Struck the autograph manuscript of Symphony No. 49 ('La Passione') which eventually found a resting place in the Royal Swedish Musical

1 These choruses, of which Haydn was very proud, were later published by Breitkopf & Härtel (*vide supra*, p. 189).

2 Haydn had visited the famous German music publisher on his way back from London in 1792. Simrock published the first edition of Symphonies Nos. 99, 102 and 104 as Op. 98, possibly under Salomon's licence. (When Simrock published the pianoforte trio arrangement of the last six London Symphonies, he announced them as the property of Mr. Salomon, 'who has given me full rights to engrave, print and publish them.' See Hoboken, 204.)

3 The Viennese music dealer: *vide supra*, p. 469; also letter of 8 March 1789 (CCLN 80f.).

Academy. Struck's travels took him to Sweden and Italy, and he returned to Vienna from Florence in 1802, at which point we will meet him (and his correspondence) again in the Chronicle for that year (*Haydn: the Late Years 1801–1809*).

On 6 October Haydn was still in Vienna, for on that day he wrote another letter to his friend Theodor Küffner (Kuffner) in London:

[Haydn to Theodor Küffner (Kuffner). *German.*]

Most excellent Friend!

The honour that not only you but also the two excellent and worthy [brothers] *Herrn* v. Mayers[1] have shown me by subscribing to my *Creation* is not only invaluable to me but also urges my old head to further diligence, should I (when the time comes) be capable of completing another such work; about which I have my doubts, however, for I shall hardly again find such an interesting book.

Your noble letter, of which I am proud, and which was read with amazement by many of our savants, will be kept by me as a keepsake so long as I live; I only regret that perhaps I won't have the pleasure any more of being able to embrace you in London, because finally, at long last, the local *noblesse* does not want me to leave their circle, and to keep me firmly here, they've given me once again an oratorio with the title 'The Four Seasons' to compose, of which Baron Swieten is the writer of the text.

Now, my dear friend, fare thee well; when I send off *The Creation* I shall take the liberty of writing to you, and meanwhile I am with the greatest respect,

Your
most sincere friend and servant
Joseph Haydn mpria.

Vienna, 6th October 1799.
Please convey my compl. to the H. v. Mayer
and to his wife

[On the reverse side of the sheet, a note in Küffner's hand: 'meine Correspondenz / mit / Dr. Haydn'.]
[Not in CCLN; from H. Unverricht, *Die Musikforschung* XVIII (1965), Heft 1, 4]

[Draft of Küffner's answer to Haydn. *German.*]

Answer to Dr. Haydn's 2nd letter

My letter, for the answer to which I thank you kindly, contained nothing noble except the name of the subject to whom it was addressed; a name, which for anyone with a disposition and task for music calls up the most magical remembrance for everything that is great and beautiful in this Art; a truth that every artist can see for himself from your scores.

Not the praise of contemporaries (whatever it may be) can urge you to further diligence; such motivations can only influence artists of the second rank: a genius such as yours follows its own irresistible drive; self-reliance is its reward, the admiration of future generations its destiny. – Only small minds work for their contemporaries, and for them the reward of a limited approval by the small circle that surrounds them. Homer was poor and misunderstood; and nevertheless he created a model of excellence for all future generations. You are more fortunate: born in a period of enlightenment, you enjoy the general applause of your contemporaries and have justified expectation – I should say the greatest certainty – of becoming an object of veneration for posterity: for your poetry is for anyone and everyone, and your works a veritable musical encyclopaedia. To hear that we shall probably not have the pleasure of embracing you in London, because the

1 For Dr Mayer (Meyer), his brother and wife, see also Haydn's letter of 9 July 1799 *supra*.

Viennese aristocracy does not want to let you out of their circle, was as unexpected as it was unpleasant; but it pleases us that this class of your fellow citizens has also awoken to your value. Formerly everyone admired your genius; now they seem to want to reward it. Il vaut mieux fort que jamais. What your friends here will lose by your intentions will, I hope, be the world's gain; for active as your spirit is, your body needs rest, and such a long and arduous trip as that from Vienna to London would diminish your strength.

You see how impartial I am, for your most admired company would always be very delightful for me and everyone. – I await not only your *Creation* but every new chef d'oeuvre of your fruitful genius; and in this, Dr. Meyer, his dear wife, and his excellent brother completely concur. Although many hundred miles removed from us, you are yet always present among your most sincere admirers and friends, among which one of your most fervent is

Your devoted
Th. Kuffner.

[Not in CCLN; H. Unverricht, op. cit., 41f.]

Although Haydn's arrival in Eisenstadt cannot be precisely determined, we read in Rosenbaum (69) of an event which assures us that he was there on Sunday, October 13. 'In the evening Roesler arrived from Vienna; we went to the castle to hear the quartets, then to the ghetto to see the Feast of the Tabernacles. . . .' We may assume that the quartets were the first performances of Haydn's new pair for Prince Lobkowitz; the parts for this occasion, by Johann Elssler, are still preserved in the Esterházy Archives in Budapest.[1] On Wednesday, 16 October, we hear of Haydn participating in a concert at Andreas Seitz's, Provost in Eisenstadt. Rosenbaum (69) reports:

> . . . In the evening Therese [Gassmann] came to me gaily, and we went to the Provost's to hear the academy. There were several pieces from [Peter von Winter's] *Das unterbrochene Opfer Fest*, Pölt played a piano sonata by Haydn, [the young] Tomasini played variations by his father on the violin, and Haydn, at popular request, did 7 new German Songs [*Mehrstimmige Lieder*], which are unusually lovely. – The young Prince and Princess [Esterházy] were there with several of the Court and a few of the clergy.

This is the first reference to any public performance of the part-songs, of which Haydn had now completed at least seven since he began them in 1796. A hint as to what was actually performed may be a fragmentary manuscript from the Esterházy Archives[2] consisting of the tenor part only of '9 / Gesänge / von / Joseph Haydn'. The other parts have long since disappeared. The extant tenor part, in Johann Elssler's hand, consists of the nine four-part songs (XXVc: 1–9), of which Haydn seems to have selected seven for performance at Seitz's 'academy' in October 1799. Probably the composer performed these works frequently at intimate concerts. The Lobkowitz Archives (formerly Raudnitz Castle, now Prague) own a manuscript of the four-part songs in a slightly different, and perhaps earlier, order than that of the authentic first edition (Breitkopf & Härtel). The Lobkowitz order is closer to that in which the works were put into the Elssler Catalogue (HV) of 1805.

1 Each is entitled 'Quartetto / â / Violino Primo / Violino Secondo / Viola / e / Violoncello / Del Sig^{re} Giuseppe Haydn' and have the catalogue numbers Ms. mus. I. 125 and 124 respectively. See the new edition, by the present writer, for Doblinger, prepared in 1973.

2 Ms. mus. I. 171 now in the National Széchényi Library, Budapest.

On 24 (not 31) October 1799, Haydn's old friend, Carl Ditters von Dittersdorf died on the estate of Ignaz Freiherr von Stillfried in Rothlhotta (Bohemia). The news was made doubly grim by the fact that this famous composer, whose operas were still being staged all over Germany, died in complete poverty and obscurity. Two days before, he had completed the dictation of his autobiography to his son. In the final pages we read, heartbreakingly, that no one would buy his latest compositions:

> During the last five years I have strained my spiritual and mental faculties (which are, thank God, still in a relatively good state) and have completed a considerable collection of brand new works, viz. operas, symphonies, and a large number of pieces for the fortepiano. All these things were announced a quarter of a year ago in the new musical paper of Leipzig;[1] but – good God! – up to the present there has not been a buyer for one single piece; and alas, I can find no support for the undertaking, though I should certainly give good value for the money. . . .[2]

The autobiography appeared in 1801, printed by Breitkopf & Härtel. He was the first in a series of eighteenth-century musicians who were immensely popular during their lifetimes but of whom it could be said that by the time they died, their works were as good as forgotten. Although Dittersdorf cannot be called, strictly speaking, part of the Haydn school, there were others, pupils (directly or indirectly) of Haydn who would soon share the same fate: Ignaz Pleyel (who died in 1831) and Adalbert Gyrowetz (who died in 1850). In fact, taste was changing rapidly at the turn of the century, and we can follow what the average German musician was thinking in the columns of the *AMZ*. Old-fashioned works were disdained, even by such a popular idol as Mozart. A Hamburg publisher named Günther & Böhme brought out an edition of 'Quatres Simphonies pour l'Orchestre' by Mozart (K. 162, 183, 199, 202) which the *AMZ* reviewed in May 1799 (I, 484ff.). After starting out with the usual eulogies ('There is no one among our German composers of the recent era, except Haydn, from whom one may deduce the superiority of a musical genius through his instrumental works as clearly as is the case with Mozart...'), the reviewer rather testily complains:

> Without exaggeration, there is nothing more to be said about these symphonies except that they – although not without good value and content – are really just quite ordinary orchestral symphonies, without any conspicuous traits of originality or novelty, and without any special diligence to the Art . . . They are on the whole rather flat [*plan*] . . . [I, 494f.]

If we consider that one of these Symphonies was K. 183, about the *Sturm und Drang* characteristics of which so many pages have since been written, it is interesting to observe that it made no impact on the reviewer except for its being 'quite clearly [one of these] youthful works'. And not only were old-fashioned works scarcely tolerated, even by Haydn and Mozart – Gerber notes (*NTL* II, 573) that the nowadays much-admired Haydn Symphony No. 44 in E minor 'seems to show its age' – but the prolific members of the Haydn *scuola* now began distinctly to get on everybody's

1 They were announced, with a charming introduction, in the *Intelligenz-Blatt* No. V (December 1798) of the *AMZ*. The list included two Italian operas (1798), six German operas (1796–8) including *Die lustigen Weiber von Windsor* and *Die Opera Buffa*, six symphonies and an enormous quantity of piano pieces including *72 Vorspiele oder Präludien* in all the black and white keys. Breitkopf & Härtel agreed to distribute the works in MS.

2 *Lebensbeschreibung* (new edition by Norbert Miller, Munich 1967, pp. 275f.)

nerves. Reviewing a set of piano trios by Ignaz Pleyel (*44me Partie de Clavecin*, Artaria & Co., Vienna), the critic of the *AMZ* (I, 572f.) writes:

> These *largè* Sonatas – they are all of that, for they go on indefinitely – are really only for the large houses of poorer dilettantes; and they distinguish themselves neither by anything new nor by containing any other excellence. A reviewer sometimes has the very difficult task (and the present reviewer includes himself in that category) of looking in detail at something like this, and *horribile dictu*, for instance, to play through 366 bars (two short repeats included) – I repeat, three-hundred-sixty-six bars – on a bouncy theme such as this
>
> 
>
> which flutters through the rondo like a sylphide.
>
> If the reviewer errs not, *Herr* Pleyel has already made his début with this jingle theme elsewhere; but also this first Sonata, perhaps even all three, are also among Pleyel's own publishing articles. The one and the other would not be good manners. [After another musical example, the reviewer adds] If that is not musical poverty, then that doesn't exist. Pity, a great pity, that Hr. Pleyel seems to reach his goal by playing the polygraph. What can possibly come out of that?

Later in 1799, we find the following review of a then-famous Haydn *seguacio*, Adalbert Gyrowetz, about whose 'Divertimento per il Clavecin o Pianoforte con un Violino e Violoncello . . . Op. 25. Artaria' the *AMZ* (I, 652) writes:

> If amateurs find this interesting, more power to them, and let the fortepiano sound right merrily. There is not much to it: modish, a thousand times churned-out dingle-dangle. It is really a miracle that composers themselves don't go to sleep over such smeary objects of nausea and boredom. But we are glad to think that Hr. Gyrowetz tossed off this Divertimento to order for the common market. Buyers can probably be found, at that, at least on the Danube.

We shall see that Baron van Swieten found such criticism tasteless. However, the review reflects the public's gradual fury with all this second-rate pseudo-Haydn which, as Pohl[1] said, 'misled the public into neglecting the works of both master and scholar'. When Gyrowetz fell to copying whole movements of Haydn, he was soundly rapped on the knuckles, *inter alia* by Gerber (*NTL* II, 569) who, reviewing Haydn's 'Paris' Symphonies, notes that 'Haydn in these works seem to have outdone himself, and this applies especially to No. [85] in B flat with its heavenly Adagio and No. [86] in D with the unexcelled [final] Presto. This seems to have been noted also by Hr. Gyrowetz, since he used from this Finale not only the theme but the whole development in his [Symphony published by André] Offenbach Op. 13, Liv. 1, and more than copied it.' We have seen Zelter's strong objection to Anton André's Symphony which, if not literally modelled on Haydn's No. 95, has strong Haydnesque traits. We believe that this antipathy to the *scuola* of Haydn contains in it the seeds of the anti-Haydn wave which was to sweep Europe in the years after the composer's death. But at the moment, Haydn's reputation was never higher, and

1 Pleyel article in Grove I, vol. iii, 3.

many people all over Europe must have felt the veneration and affection of his English friend, Theodor Küffner (Kuffner), whose letter to the composer we have quoted above.

There now enters on the Haydn scene a Scotsman, George Thomson, who was to play a role in Beethoven's life, too. Thomson ran a publishing house in Edinburgh and became interested in the fashionable practice of issuing Scottish (and Welsh and Irish) 'national melodies' for which purpose he engaged popular Continental composers to write the accompaniments and the ritornellos in a 'modern style'. We have seen in *Haydn in England 1791–1795* that Haydn had arranged a large number of these Scottish airs while in London. It was, no doubt, the success of these airs which induced Thomson to try his hand at such publications. Shortly after Ignaz Pleyel left London in 1792, Thomson approached him for some 'symphonies and accompaniments' to thirty-two songs. In the course of the year 1793, Thomson's books show that he paid Pleyel £131 5*s*. for these songs and for six sonatas. Thomson had some kind of financial trouble with Pleyel for when he came to negotiations with Koželuch, he was insistent about having a stamped agreement. In a letter to an intermediary about this subject, under date 6 February 1797, he writes:[1]

> The reason of my wishing particularly that a formal written agreement should be entered into immediately after the terms are settled, is that I have been juggled, disappointed, and grossly deceived by an eminent musical composer with whom I entered into an agreement some years ago, which he has only fulfilled in part, after putting me to a world of trouble and expense. As he is a resident in France, I have no means at present of procuring any redress or satisfaction from him. The musicians are generally very incorrect in business and eccentric in their conduct, so that it is the more necessary to be on one's guard in a transaction of this kind.

Thomson found Koželuch's terms rather high: twelve sonatas for piano with accompaniment of a violin and 'cello = 400 ducats, and seventy Scottish songs = 100 ducats; but after pointing out the high expense, the publisher accepted. In fact Thomson purchased only six sonatas from Koželuch, and when the composer informed him that he had another three almost ready, Thomson wrote in 1801 to say that 'the six already published have had a very limited circulation'. The time for Gyrowetzes, Pleyels, Andrés and Koželuchs was running out.

In 1797, however, Koželuch was still a very desirable object to the Scottish publisher, who tried to get a formal agreement drawn up by Mr Straton of the British Embassy in Vienna, but the wily Koželuch – Beethoven called him a *miserabilis* – would have none of it. On 1 June 1797 Straton writes:

> I have had several conversations with M. Kozeluch, in the course of which I am sorry to say that I perceived an extreme reluctance on his part to enter into any legal agreement whatsoever. This he manifested by starting a variety of objections to a contract in any form, save that of a promissory letter to you, which were – or at least appeared to me to be – equally ill-founded and devoid of candour. To bring the matter to an issue, there therefore remained no other method of proceeding than to draw up and send to M. Kozeluch a sketch of what I thought consistent with your wishes, and calculated to meet his. The annexed paper is that

1 All this information about Thomson comes from an excellent book by J. Cuthbert Hadden, *George Thomson, the Friend of Burns: His Life and Correspondence*, London 1898, pp. 292ff. Koželuch's correspondence is quoted in *Studien zur Musikwissenschaft* (Beethoven-Kongress presentation), Vienna-Graz 1970.

which I sent to him, with a request that he would have it copied and executed in a proper manner. But, instead of complying with this request, he sent back the paper to me this morning in its present state, with a verbal message purporting that he had nothing more to add. [Hadden, *Thomson*, p. 297]

This paper had, according to Straton, 'extraordinary marginal annotations'. On 29 July 1797, Straton writes that Koželuch had still not signed the agreement in spite of repeated promises. The composer then said, according to a letter from Straton on 16 August 1797, that he could not go on 'owing to the very faulty manner in which the music [of the Scottish airs] has been copied'. The poor Embassy Secretary then started to argue, whereupon Koželuch floored him by 'entering into a discussion of so scientific a nature as far to outstrip my musical knowledge'. On 18 September Thomson informed Straton that he had spent a fortnight making new copies of the sixty-four songs. 'I have bestowed such particular care and attention on every one of this number as to be certain they are perfectly what they ought to be. If Mr. Kozeluch should still find any little defects in some of the modulations he must impute such to the peculiar nature of the compositions and make of them as he can.' On 28 October 1797 the desperate Straton wrote to Thomson as follows (pp. 298f.):

I am apt to imagine that the copy of those which you first sent was perfectly accurate, for Kozeluch called on me yesterday to mention that on perusing the airs lately put into his hands, he had found most of them *une musique barbare*, which set at defiance all the rules of art that he professed, and that therefore he did not think it worth while to add symphonies, &c., to them. In reply to this, I read to him your letter of the 18th September again, and being entirely of Arbuthnot's opinion in regard to M. Kozeluch's intellect, instead of standing up for our national music thus wantonly attacked, I left it burthened with the epithet of 'barbarous', and, courtier-like, told M. Kozeluch that you relied on his knowledge and genius for the civilisation of the part of it which you had transmitted hither. I added that you would naturally be desirous of seeing a specimen of it in its new garb; and M. Kozeluch having, by an extraordinary exertion of his mental faculties, fathomed the meaning of my observation, sent me this morning the enclosed paper [not extant].

On 15 November 1797 Thomson had, with his customary diplomacy, written to acknowledge the safe arrival of Koželuch's six sonatas:

They are most admirably composed. The fancy, the spirit, the taste which you have displayed throughout the whole, and particularly in working upon the Scottish subjects, entitle you to the highest praise. I never heard any music more brilliant in the *allegros*, or more charmingly expressive in the cantabile parts. [p. 300]

Thomson, alas, was a fatal dabbler, always trying to make the piano parts of his various continental composers suitable for the dainty amateur hands that he fondly hoped would purchase his editions. 'I have taken the liberty in a very few instances to simplify your pianoforte accompaniment,' writes Thomson (pp. 300f.) and asks Koželuch to simplify the piano writing of the works now in progress. (We will hear the same *ostinato* lamentation in Thomson's correspondence with Beethoven.) Thomson now suggested bribing Koželuch:

'Perhaps [the banker] Fries' arguments may be more prevailing than either yours or mine; if so, they must, no doubt, be employed, though I really think they

> have said enough already. Kozeluch should consider it his duty to do at last what I represented to be an essential requisite at the first. Had he attended to my original representation in regard to the songs, I would not only have saved a very considerable expense, but what I have felt much more, the loss of much precious time and indescribable trouble. [Letter of 10 January 1801 to Straton.]

Straton, on 3 February 1801, sends 'a rude epistle' of Koželuch's (no longer extant) and adds the following:

> I fancy that it will not be requisite to trouble you with a repetition of the arguments which the nature of the subject could not but suggest to me, in opposition to his penning so extraordinary an epistle. Suffice it to say that they, however pointed in themselves and forcibly directed, were not tantamount to force a passage through the fated armour which encompasses our friend's intellect. To my representations I received answers of gigantic absurdity, and had the mortification to perceive that the more I endeavoured to fight the battle on the principles and within the sphere of common sense, the greater did he extend the line of tangent at which he had quitted it. In short, *c'est une mauvaise tête*. [p. 301]

The argument went on, and Thomson writes on 21 February 1801 that he was 'never more surprised nor more hurt than by reading the very extraordinary letter', that 'people in this country will not look at any other but a simple and easy accompaniment to their national songs'. But Koželuch was stubborn. Straton tried to explain to Thomson:

> He strenuously maintained that they were perfect, and that those who advised you to require of him to alter them were evil counsellors, who wished to spoil your work, and to detract from his reputation. I argued the point with him for some time, then opened a battery on his vanity, but to no purpose. The thickness of his skull baffled the efforts of reason to make an impression on his brain, nor would his tympanum resound to its proper place the appeal which I made to his *amour propre*.

Such, then, was some of the background to Thomson's attempts, in October 1799, to open negotiations with Haydn. The publisher himself has set down a short history of his relationship to the famous composer:

> My first application to Haydn was upon the 30th October 1799, when I sent him part of the Scottish melodies, which in the following summer he returned united to his admirable symphonies and accompaniments. And from that time we continued in correspondence till the year 1804, when I received the last of his many precious compositions. I wrote him in 1805 with more national airs. My letter, perhaps, was miscarried, for I received no answer, and therefore in June 1806 I despatched a duplicate of it which was returned to me by my banker in London in consequence of information from his correspondent at Vienna that Haydn could not compose any more owing to illness. In 1808, having heard that he was restored to health, I wrote him once more with part of my Irish melodies, in the hope of his composing ritornelles and accompaniments to them, but I received no answer; and therefore sometime after I sent those melodies to Beethoven, worthy in all respects to be the successor of Haydn. [p. 304]

Thomson wrote a letter to Straton as well, who was to deliver the letter personally to Haydn and 'say whatever you conceive is likely to produce compliance' and if necessary to offer a few more ducats for each air. But Haydn 'must not speak of what he gets'. Thomson does not expect that Haydn will do the accompaniments better than Koželuch: 'that is scarcely possible'(!); but in the symphonies (ritornellos) he will be 'great and original'. Thomson had offered two ducats for each air; Mr Straton wrote to say that Haydn 'seemed desirous of having rather more than two ducats, but did not precisely insist upon this point'. Straton, as a result of the interview, adds that 'Upon the whole he appears to be a rational animal, whereas all that can be said of the other, I mean Koz[eluch] is, that he is a Biped without feathers' (p. 305).[1] The idea obviously occurred at once to Haydn that he could give some of this work to his pupils and then 'look over' the result; and we shall see (in *Haydn: the Late Years 1801–1809*) that some, if indeed not a great deal, of the arrangements for Thomson were done by Haydn's pupil Sigismund Neukomm. But the old composer clearly sensed that this would be an easy way to collect a substantial amount of pounds, as indeed did Beethoven afterwards (Hadden, *Thomson*, p. 305).

At the end of October Haydn returned to Vienna for the winter. He attended the comic opera, *Der Wundermann am Rheinfalle* (text by Schikaneder, music by Seyfried) at the Freyhaustheater auf der Wieden. The next day he wrote a letter to Seyfried in which 'he thanked me for the pleasure my work had given him and wished me hearty congratulations, in his charming, good-natured way, on my success.'[2]

On 1 November Haydn wrote to Breitkopf & Härtel:

[To Christoph Gottlob Breitkopf, Leipzig. *German*]
Well born,
Most highly respected Sir!

The score of *The Creation* will not appear until the end of December, and so if you will let me have the names of your subscribers by January, I shall be able to include them in the printed subscription list at the front of the score; perhaps no work has ever been published with as many different subscribers as this one.

You do me great honour by supporting my undertaking with such assiduity, and I shall be pleased to send you the copies you asked for: the subscription price will not be raised by a single farthing [*Heller*] after publication.

You shall receive one copy for the use of your concerts for the widows' benefit, and I shall send it to you by mail as soon as it comes off the press; I would like to be able to conduct it myself.

Since *The Creation* will be engraved and printed here in Vienna, I was obliged to give Herr Artaria the principal commission. But as far as the pianoforte arrangement is concerned, lack of time prevents me from doing this myself. Anyone is free to do it.

Apart from all this, I am much obliged to you for all your kind wishes and remain, as always, Sir, most respectfully,

Your most obedient servant,
Joseph Haydn.

Vienna, 1st November 1799. [CCLN, 167f.]

On 4 and 18 November Haydn attended meetings of the Tonkünstler-Societät, and also one on 9 December, no doubt preparatory to the second public performance of *The Creation* which Haydn had decided generously to donate to the widows' and orphans' pension fund (*vide infra*, 22 and 23 December).[3]

1 *Vide* Straton's letter of 16 February 1800, p. 541.
2 The letter has not survived. Seyfried reported on it in the *Wiener Allgemeine Musikalische Zeitung* No. 112, 1841. See Deutsch, *Freihaustheater*, p. 27; Pohl III, 153. In the *AMZ* IV (1801), p. 605 Haydn is quoted as having said: 'I wish you luck; you've given us a really fine work' (*Wundermann*).
3 Pohl III, 123.

Griesinger now had occasion to write to Breitkopf & Härtel about various matters:

6 November 1799.

Most excellent Friend,

. . . Haydn is not inexperienced in the book-trade business. . . . He has three or four unprinted Masses in his drawer, and suggested that I ask you if they would sell and whether you would like to take them for your house. They have the advantage that they can be easily performed by not very full orchestras and they are certainly good; 'I'm rather proud of my Masses'.

. . . People were very well satisfied with [Wenzel] Pichl's work [a Mass]. . . . Haydn wasn't in Vienna, but he thinks well of Pichl and said he had once heard a good Mass by Pichl in the Augustiner Kirche [next to the Albertina] . . .

. . . It is in fact difficult to organize a financially profitable concert [etc.: *vide supra*, p. 469, where this part of the letter has been quoted.]

[Olleson, *Griesinger*, 12]

Breitkopf & Härtel decided not to publish Haydn's earlier Masses and on 7 December Griesinger reported that he would 'try to refuse H. Haydn with his Masses as politely as possible' (12). The Pichl *Missa solemnis* in question was performed on St Cecilia's Day (22 November) to commemorate the relief of Mantua in 1796 (Olleson, *Griesinger*, 13), and Breitkopf & Härtel were apparently wondering if they should publish it. (They did not.)

On 9 November the *Wiener Zeitung* carried the announcement of the *Oeuvres Complettes*, such as we have already seen in the *AMZ*, but with the additional final sentence: 'The first volume has already been sent to press, and will, graced by Haydn's portrait by Kininger and Bolt, appear shortly. . . .' But on 13 November Griesinger had to report to Leipzig that 'Kinninger's copy is a total failure'. Kininger was ready to attempt the portrait again but Haydn had sent his wife to Baden, 'where she intends to spend the winter because of the baths' and she took the Guttenbrunn portrait with her. '. . . Gut[t]enbrunn was, said Haydn, formerly her lover, and for that reason she lets it out of her possession as infrequently as possible' – an astonishing statement which throws much light on the Haydns' marital life during the Eszterháza years. It also suggests that which the experts have long believed: that the Guttenbrunn portrait was first made during the Eszterháza years when the painter was working for Prince Esterházy (about 1770), and then brought up to date in London in 1792, when both Haydn and Guttenbrunn were in the British capital; for the clothing of the two extant Guttenbrunn portraits is definitely of the period 1792, not 1770.[1] Various schemes were proposed: Griesinger thought an engraving could be made from the Grassi bust, and sent a medallion which Grassi had copied from it – alas, that too has not survived.

. . . As far as the resemblance is concerned, it is certainly present in this cast, especially the under lip, fleshy and massive, is characteristic. The good-humoured expression that appears in Haydn's face as soon as he speaks; his brown, pock-marked skin; his full eye; the wig – all that couldn't be included in this head *à l'antique*; but it's only that which is missing and you'd know him at once. . . .

[Olleson, *Griesinger*, 13]

1 One version, in a deplorable state, was owned by Wolfgang von Karajan in Salzburg (now in the Eisenstadt Museum) and was first reproduced in colour as the frontispiece to Landon, *Essays*. The other is owned by Mrs Eva Alberman in London and may be seen, in black-and-white, on p. 125 of Somfai. The Alberman version is in better condition and is in some respects more delicate. We imagine that it was the latter copy that was used for the 1792 engraving by Schiavonetti. The 1770 version no longer exists.

'Haydn is sturdy, short and broad-shouldered', added Griesinger, and the composer was living 'in two very modest rooms in town', probably to avoid the snow and ice of his house in the suburbs. As we read in every contemporary diary, the winter of 1799–1800 was exceptionally cold and snowy.

On Sunday, 24 November 1799, the Pensionsgesellschaft bildender Künstler gave their annual ball, to the rehearsal of which, in the Redoutensaal, Rosenbaum (70) went. The dances were by Joseph Lipavsky (minuets) and Franz Teyber (German dances). Haydn did not attend but in the Archives of the Society we read 'Beethowen der Ältere 4 [free tickets] / Beethowen der jüngere 4 [free tickets]', as well as tickets for Anton and Franz Teyber, Lipavsky, Maschek, Henneberg, Eybler, Süssmayer and Kozeluh [*sic*].

On 5 December there was a performance of Mozart's *Figaro* at the Kärntnerthortheater, with Therese Gassmann as the Countess and Therese Saal as Cherubino. Rosenbaum (71) tells us that 'Saal was called out by her group of dilettantes'; she already had an unpaid *claque*. A little more than a week later, on the 13th, we note 'extreme cold and wind', and on the day of the general rehearsal for Haydn's Oratorio at the Burgtheater, Saturday 21 December, we read (71): 'Constant extreme cold. . . . At about 10 o'clock I went . . . to the B.Th. for the rehearsal . . .'

The second public performance – or rather pair of performances – of *The Creation* was a great event. There was a rather lengthy announcement in the *Wiener Zeitung* (No. 100, 14 December); it read:

> Musical Academy. On 22 and 23 December 1799 there will be given in the I. R. Court Theatre next to the Burg a performance by the Musical Society for the Benefit of Widows and Orphans of the laudable and well known Oratorio, already received with decided and general applause,
>
> *The Creation*
>
> set to music by *Herr* Joseph Haydn, Doctor of Music and *Kapellmeister* in the actual service of His Highness the Hrn. Prince of Eßterhazy, and performed by an orchestra consisting of 200 musicians. Persuaded through long experience of the active participation which Vienna's noble population gives to every charitable organization and particularly the Widows and Orphans Society, it hopes that it will not be taken amiss if once again the public is encouraged to appear in greatest numbers for the Widows and Orphans, considering the pleasure which this concert will certainly give to the admirable members of that public. In the expectancy of which the otherwise customary entrance prices, for all seats whatsoever, have been doubled. . . . The printed text will be given by the box-office gratis to everyone.

The same newspaper later printed a short account of the concerts and in it (22 January 1800) we read that the Emperor, the Archdukes, the Grand Duke, the Duke Albert of Sachsen-Teschen, etc. were members of the audience. The soloists were Therese Saal, Rathmayer and Saal *père*. It snowed the whole day of 22 December. Zinzendorf tells us: '. . . Au Concert de la Création. J'arrivois pour la seconde partie assez avancée, des morceaux de musique qui me plûrent beaucoup . . . Il a neigé a fine toute la journée' (Olleson, 57; Zinzendorf MS.). Silverstolpe was also present and reported to Stockholm in a letter written on Christmas Day: 'Haydn's *Creation* was once again performed, and I listened to it with the same delight as before. In a little while I shall own this work printed in score. I do wish that [Kraus's] *Aneas in Carthago* could be so published . . . [In a letter of 18 December he had written about that opera:]

... If it were translated and played in other countries, it would make *époque* in the musical world ...' (Mörner, 345f.)[1]

We learn from Pohl-Botstiber (III, 155)[2] that the Tonkünstler-Societät had financial difficulties in the Autumn of 1799, and that this series of performances of *The Creation* were, in a way, Haydn's gift to the Society to help it out of its financial problems. He only asked as conditions, first, that Wranizky lead the first violins; secondly, that the chorus and orchestra contain the same members and be placed exactly as they were on 19 March; and thirdly, that textbooks be printed and distributed gratis – a point which Haydn obviously regarded as essential. Naturally all these conditions were accepted and the protocol notes: 'Tausend Dank dem Wohlthäter!'

Two visits may be recorded. The first did not directly concern Haydn but was of immense importance to the history of Mozart and his music: the arrival in Vienna of Johann Anton André, whose acrimonious dispute with Zelter has been recorded in this Chronicle. André acquired from Mozart's widow the entire musical remains, 'an act', as C. F. Pohl says[3] 'which spread a veritable halo round the establishment of which he was the head', his father having died in 1799. André became the principal publisher of Mozart, giving us work after work, often engraved from autograph manuscripts which have since completely disappeared (e.g. the Benedictus of the great Mass in C minor, K. 427).

The second important visit was that of the young soprano, Anna Milder, who was later to become Beethoven's first Leonore in *Fidelio*. She came to Vienna aged fourteen and sang for Haydn. 'My dear child,' said Haydn, 'you've got a voice like a house.' He entrusted her to his pupil Sigismund Neukomm, with whom she studied the 'Haydn manner of singing' for three years. She made her début on 9 April 1803 as Juno in Süssmayer's opera, *Der Spiegel von Arkadien*, and was an instantaneous success. In that year Griesinger tells us that 'her voice sounds – and that's rarely the case – like the purest metal and she gives us, since she's studied with Neukomm from the Haydn school, long, powerful notes without arabesques and exaggerated ornaments'. Apart from our interest in Beethoven's first Leonore, Anna Milder's career tells us the kind of singer of which Haydn approved and the *scuola* he had established for training such voices.[4]

And while on the subject of Beethoven, we should mention two publications of great importance: on 21 December the *Wiener Zeitung* carried an announcement by T. Mollo & Comp., who offered for sale the piano Sonatas, Op. 14. Earlier in the autumn, Beethoven had published his epochal *Sonate pathétique*, Op. 13. We will not enter into a discussion of these famous pieces except to say that in Op. 13 Beethoven

1 About this remarkable opera, Gluck said to Salieri (Mörner, 346): 'der Mann hat einen grossen Stil, wie ich ihn noch nie bei jemand gefunden habe'. Mr Newell Jenkins informs us that he is preparing a performance of it at the Drottningholm Theatre in Stockholm which is to be recorded. Like everything else of Kraus, this opera is of a very high standard and full of originality and genius.

2 In Pohl *Denkschrift*, 51, we read that protocol of 4 November *verbatim*: '*Herr* Josef Haydn, our worthy Assessor, is good enough to let the Society have an oratorio for performance.' When the doubled prices were proposed (as was done in opera performances with singers like Crescentini or Marchesi), Haydn insisted that all the performers received two Gulden each, which however had to be paid in his name 'because of further consequences'. The Society took in a net total of 4162 fl. 1 kr. (after expenses) for the two performances. *The Creation* netted more than 65,000 fl. up to and including the year 1868.

3 His article on the André family in Grove I, i, 66f.

4 Pohl III, 155f.; Frimmel *Beethoven-Handbuch* I, 412ff.

continued a great Viennese tradition in which both Haydn (Symphony No. 52) and Mozart (piano Concerto in C minor, K. 491) had excelled: the *Sturm und Drang* of C minor, a key which obviously awoke in their hearts the strongest emotions of power, grandeur and tragedy. If the Haydn Symphony had been a milestone in the early 1770s, Mozart's Concerto must have a shattering effect on the Viennese audiences of the mid 1780s, followed by the equally stunning force of Beethoven's piano Sonata. And can it be an accident that the most powerful piece of late eighteenth-century music, 'Chaos' from *The Creation*, is in C minor?

It was the end of the eighteenth century – an artificial division, man-made, to be sure, but one that is always of profound effect on anyone with a sense of destiny. On the last day of December 1799, the snow lay deep, even in the streets of Vienna, and the cold was intense. In front of their stoves, men celebrated, rejoiced, or were silent. It was a time for dreams. And the great war with France was seldom absent from men's minds.[1] Much of all this sense of time passing, of a new age beginning, is in the great entry in Zinzendorf's Diary, the spirit of which might be Haydn's, if he were addicted (which he was not) to writing down his innermost thoughts.

> . . . Une neige profonde dans les rues. Le froid ne pas diminué. . . . Rapeler de mon education religieux, l'espoir d'une autre vie et d'une société meilleure dans l'autre monde que dans celui ci, celui d'une assimilation a la morale sainte et bienfesant de J. C. Rendre des humbles actions de genres a Dieu, de toutes les bontés que j'ai epruvé dans l'annee qui finit, le suplier de couvrir mes fautes, mon rôle [?] de ma destination dans ce monde, et ma petitesse, de sa misericorde, et de me rendre plus sage, plus humain, plus bien fesant, plus indifférent sur les miseres de l'ambition. Voila mon devoir a la fin de l'année!

In the silent, snowbound city of Vienna, the eighteenth century – a hundred years that may be numbered among man's greatest achievements in literature, art and music – thus drew to a close.

1 Napoleon wrote on Christmas Day to the King of England and to the Emperor. To the former he asked, 'Is the war that for eight years has devastated the four quarters of the world to be eternal? Is there no possibility of coming to an agreement? How can the two most enlightened nations of Europe, both more powerful than is needed to secure their safety and independence, sacrifice to some vague notion of superiority the interest of commerce, internal prosperity, and the happiness of families? How can they fail to see that peace is the first of necessities and the greatest of glories? Your Majesty must see in this overture nothing but my sincere desire by prompt action to contribute efficaciously for the second time to a general pacification.' To the Emperor he wrote: 'Once more in Europe after an absence of eighteen months, I find war raging between the French Republic and Your Majesty. The French nation has summoned me to its chief magistracy. Far as I am from any sentiments of vainglory, my greatest desire is to prevent the effusion of the blood that is about to flow. Your Majesty's reputation leaves me no doubt as to your most heartfelt desire. If that sentiment is given its course, I do not doubt that we can conciliate the interests of the two countries.' *The Corsican: A Diary of Napoleon's Life in His own Words*, ed. R. M. Johnston, Boston 1910, pp. 116f.

CHAPTER TWELVE

Works of 1799

The two String Quartets (Op. 77)
dedicated to Prince Franz Joseph Maximilian Lobkowitz
(III: 81, 82)

These Quartets, entitled on the autographs 'Quartetto',[1] for two violins, viola, and violoncello, were composed in 1799 (dated autograph) for Prince Franz Joseph 'Max' Lobkowitz. They were published in an authentic edition by Artaria & Co., Vienna, in or before September 1802 (announced in the *Intelligenz-Blatt* II of *AMZ*, Vol. V, 6 October 1802) with the dedication to Lobkowitz; also published about the same time by Clementi, Banger, Hyde, Collard & Davis (the successors of Longman & Broderip)[2] in a textually independent edition for which Haydn obviously furnished the engraver's copy. The Breitkopf & Härtel edition, announced in the *AMZ* together with Artaria's, is a direct reprint of Artaria's edition, as Hase (46) informs us. Possibly therefore we may be able to back-date Artaria's edition; if it was for sale at Leipzig on 6 October 1802, it must have been on hand at least a month to enable Breitkopf & Härtel to re-engrave their edition from it. Perhaps Artaria issued it some time in the summer of 1802.

Apart from these three authentic sources (autograph, Artaria, Clementi), we also have the original parts, copied by Elssler, which were part of Haydn's own library and later passed to the Esterházy Archives and are incorporated in the National Széchényi Library, Budapest, MS. mus. I. 125 and 124 respectively. These were no doubt the very parts from which the works were first played at Eisenstadt in the autumn of 1799 (*supra*, p. 490). They are interesting because they show that Haydn made some changes *vis-à-vis* the autographs, and many of these changes also appear in the authentic prints.

1 National Széchényi Library, Budapest, from the Esterházy Collection, Ms. mus. I. 46 A and B. Recently (1972) they have been published in facsimile by the National Széchényi Library, edited by László Somfai; we recommend these handsomely produced volumes to every student of Haydn, for they show graphically the problems facing the scholar when transcribing such matters as Haydn's tall staccato markings or his *fz* (which often turn out to be *f:* and *vice versa*). Similarly, there are beautiful phrasing marks which seem to be of an optical design rather than a literal indication of bowing; one typical example, the Trio of Op. 77, No. 2, was quoted *supra* (p. 394).

2 There is no support to Larsen's assertion (*HÜB*, 136) that Haydn must have sent the Quartets to London at such a date as to enable Clementi & Co. to issue their edition before that of Artaria: 'vielleicht kurz nach der Ausgabe Clementis' is Larsen's suggestion for the dating of the Artaria and (*vide infra*) Breitkopf editions. We can see no evidence for this: the new combination of partners can only be dated approximately. On 3 September 1801, *The Times* carried an announcement that Longman no longer has 'any share whatever in the business'. On 6 November 1801, *The Times* carries the first announcement of the new constellation of 'Clementi, Banger, Hyde, Collard & Davis', and that group of men remained together at least until 26 July 1805, when *The Times* announces a new Haydn Sonata for pianoforte, Op. 94 (4*s*.) [apparently XVI: 51]. The last Quartet, Op. 103, was also printed by these men about 1807. In view of Haydn's operations with regard to Op. 76, it would seem clear that he also went to the same pains to ensure that Clementi's edition of Op. 77 did *not* appear before that of Artaria.

For details the interested student may consult the new edition published by Messrs Doblinger.

Quartetto I in G ('Op. 77, No. 1'). I *Allegro moderato*. II *Adagio*. III *Menuet Presto* & Trio. IV *Finale Presto*.

Quartetto II in F ('Op. 77. No. 2'). I *Allegro moderato*. II Menuet *Presto* (later changed, probably by Haydn, to *Presto, ma non troppo* in the Artaria edition; similar changes may be noted in the Corri & Dussek authentic print of Opp. 71/74 – *vide* Op. 74, No. 3, first movement – and the Longman, Clementi authentic edition of Op. 76 – *vide* Op. 76, No. 5, third and fourth movements: in all cases we have an addition of 'non troppo' or 'ma non troppo'). Tempo change of Menuet also in Clementi edition. III *Andante*. IV *Finale. Vivace assai*.

Critical edition: part of the Complete String Quartets published by Doblinger: Op. 77 edited by the present writer (1973).

In the *AMZ*'s review of the first public performance of *The Creation* (*supra*, p. 454), we have noted a reference to 'six new quartets for the Hungarian Count K—' which, as the composer himself said, he was in the process of writing. Probably these are the six String Quartets for Prince Lobkowitz of which Haydn finished only Op. 77, Nos. 1 and 2, in the year 1799. There is in fact something very odd indeed about the composer's indecision to complete the other four.[1] It is said that the composition of *The Seasons* took up all his time. Yet this is only partially true. In the first place, Haydn was already composing the Oratorio in 1799, when he also managed to complete the *Theresienmesse* as well as the Quartets in G and F. And in the years 1800 and 1801 he also wrote, apart from *The Seasons*, the great *Te Deum* and the *Schöpfungsmesse*. It was not, in fact, until 1803 that he began to work on the third Quartet, which would have been in D minor and of which Haydn completed the two inner movements, later published as Op. 103.

We believe that Haydn's refusal to go on with the quartet series stems from quite a different reason – his first direct confrontation with Beethoven as a composer. We have noted many times in our Chronicle that Beethoven, in the first Viennese years, was very careful to avoid writing music in genres wherein his muse would be in direct confrontation with that of the older man. Thus we find Beethoven composing string trios rather than quartets, a string quintet, a quintet for piano and wind instruments, wind-band music, piano sonatas, piano trios, piano concertos, etc. – all categories of works in which Haydn had hardly written, or had stopped composing some years earlier (e.g. piano sonatas, the last of which he composed in 1794). Even the piano trio was obviously chosen by Beethoven because Haydn had written none to the younger composer's knowledge since 1790 (and Beethoven, in 1795, could not know that Haydn had begun a whole series of piano trios during his second visit to England). Now, in 1799 a new situation arises. Haydn began to compose a series of string quartets for Prince Lobkowitz, to whom the two completed works were dedicated when published in 1802. Prince Lobkowitz also commissioned string quartets from Beethoven, who had previously refused to write any for Haydn's old patron, Count

1 That Haydn really intended to write six, and for Lobkowitz, is supported by the following letter from Griesinger to Breitkopf dated 4 (not 24) July 1801 (Olleson, *Griesinger*, 25): '. . . The six Quartets which Haydn has composed for Lobkowitz are the private property of that gentleman, and Haydn is paid well for them. Now there are only four finished [!]; perhaps in the future Haydn will be able to dispose of them. I believe it would be much more fruitful to leave this negotiation and your wish about the Mass until you can talk tête-à-tête to Haydn.' Horrible thought that Haydn actually finished four of the works and destroyed two . . . The agreement with Lobkowitz seems to have been for three years, thus leaving Haydn free to 'dispose' of them in the autumn of 1802 – which he did, but to Artaria.

Apponyi, but who now weakened and decided that he could afford to meet Haydn on his own ground. In 1799, Beethoven wrote at least two of the Quartets – those in D and F – from Opus 18;[1] and thus Lobkowitz was host to the latest quartets by both composers at the same time.

The relationship between Haydn and Beethoven had meanwhile deteriorated considerably. Beethoven was quite obviously jealous of the deep and widespread success of *The Creation* and later never lost an opportunity to take one of his famous 'sideswipes' at it. Moscheles, who arrived in Vienna before Haydn's death, relates an anecdote which is typical. Haydn had been told that Beethoven was speaking depreciatingly of *The Creation*. 'That is wrong of him,' said Haydn. 'What has *he* written, then? His Septet? Certainly that is beautiful; nay, splendid.' In the Wegeler-Ries *Notizen* we learn (from Ries) that 'Beethoven when composing often thought of a particular object, although he often laughed at, and dealt hard with, musical painting, especially the smaller varieties. In this respect *The Creation* and *The Seasons* by Haydn were sometimes placed under close scrutiny; not that Beethoven did not perceive Haydn's deeper services, for he used to praise, and rightly, many choruses and other things of Haydn's,' etc. We shall quote a particularly ambivalent remark of Beethoven's to Haydn's face about *The Creation* in 1801; and Haydn himself was gradually losing patience with the unruly younger man. The great innovator of the 1760s and 1770s, found, perhaps, Beethoven moving too fast into realms in which Haydn felt unfamiliar. At least some of the anecdotes told about this situation must be true, or contain (as we have often asserted in different contexts) a grain of truth. Speaking of Beethoven, Koželuch said to Haydn, 'We would have done that differently, wouldn't we, Papa?', to which Haydn answered, smilingly, 'Yes, we would have done that differently.' Doležalek, to whom we owe this story, adds 'Auch Haydn konnte sich nicht recht in Beethoven finden' (Haydn, too, couldn't rightly find his way about in Beethoven). Haydn's biographer Carpani, who also knew Beethoven, wrote in the second edition of *Le Haydine*: 'Haydn was asked once by one of my friends what he thought of that young composer. The old man replied with all sincerity: 'His first works pleased me considerably, but I must admit that I don't understand the later ones. It seems to me that he [now] continually improvises".' Of course it is difficult to place all these anecdotes in their proper chronological context, and certainly many of them took place about 1805 and not in 1799. But for our purposes the chronological order is immaterial. The point we are establishing is a gradual deterioration of the relationships between the two men.[2]

Apart from a letter to Hoffmeister of 15 December 1800, mentioned above, we have authentic information that Beethoven had not only completed the Op. 18 Quartets by December 1800 but was also playing them in Viennese salons. On 10 December 1800 Countess Josephine von Deym writes to her sister:

1 For a recent study of the Op. 18 Quartets, see Joseph Kerman, *The Beethoven Quartets*, New York and London 1967, pp. 3–86. The slightly earlier study by Philip Radcliffe, *Beethoven's String Quartets*, London 1965, is also very useful; there is also much to recommend in Daniel Gregory Mason's *The Quartets of Beethoven*, New York 1947. For the dating of the Op. 18 set see also Thayer-Forbes I, 261. The F major (now No. 1, earlier No. 2) was given to Amenda on 25 June 1799 (facsimile in Landon, *Beethoven*, 127). The earlier works of this set were heavily revised before publication, which was in two instalments (June and October, 1801), by Tranquillo Mollo & Co., Vienna (a former partner of Artaria); but by 15 December 1800 it would seem that the composer had finished the set (see his letter of that date to Hoffmeister (Anderson, *Letters*, No. 41). See also *infra*.

2 Moscheles: see Hadden, 113. Wegeler-Ries *Notizen*, 77 (placed in the year 1803). Doležalek: see Kerst, *Die Erinnerungen an Beethoven*, Stuttgart 1913, II, 191. Thayer-Forbes I, 259. Carpani, *Le Haydine* (2nd ed., Padua 1823), 257. Deym: see Landon, *Beethoven*, 130.

> . . . Yesterday we had music to honour the Duchess [Julia von Giovane]. . . . I had to play and was, moreover, responsible for all the arrangements and supposed to see that everything went off well. We opened all the doors and everything was illuminated. I assure you, it was a splendid sight. Beethoven played the Sonata with violoncello. I played the last of the three violin Sonatas [Op. 12] accompanied by Schuppanzigh who, like all the others, played divinely. Then Beethoven, that real angel, let us hear his new Quartets [Op. 18], which have not been engraved yet, and are the greatest of their kind. The famous Kraft played cello, Schuppanzigh first violin. You can imagine what a treat it was for us! The Duchess was enchanted and everything went famously.

'The greatest of their kind . . .' is not a statement that is nowadays made about Op. 18 which, being compared to Beethoven's late quartets, have been thought of as 'early works' and wanting in some aspects. This is to do a grave disservice to these extraordinary first fruits of Beethoven's in the genre, and also to remove them from their highly important position in the history of music: for it is idle to pretend that they are not, with Haydn's Op. 20 and Op. 76 and Mozart's Six Quartets dedicated to Haydn, the greatest sextet of such works in the eighteenth century (if we allow for a few months 'into' the year 1800, when the works will have been finished). It may be, as Kerman (op. cit., p. 86) writes, 'though to be sure, our taste for them [Op. 18] can never be quite the same as the partaking of "masterpieces of Art"'; but the fault is ours, not that of Op. 18; and if it does nothing else, it obscures their tremendous importance at the turn of the century.

A year later (1 July 1801) we find Beethoven writing to Amenda and cautioning: 'Do not lend your Quartet to anybody, because I have greatly changed it [Op. 18, No. 1], having just learned how to write quartets properly.' Thayer (Forbes I, 262) asks: 'Had he learned from study with Förster?'

Emanuel Aloys Förster is a composer about whom the Beethoven literature has occupied itself for some time. An interesting, eccentric composer whose *Trois Quatuors*, Op. 16 Livre 2 – the second set of six published by Artaria in Vienna – were reviewed in the *AMZ* in March 1799, just at this crucial period in Beethoven's development as a quartet writer. The reviewer, who signed himself 'K.—', contrasts Förster's work with that of Pleyel, etc., and underlines the 'bizarre' qualities and the idiosyncratic sense of humour but rather objects to their artificiality and lack of charm; he presumes Förster has his public who appreciate him. Beethoven, of course, dragged in Förster so that he would not have to suggest that Op. 18 might owe anything to Haydn – God forbid! – from whom he had officially said that he 'never learned anything (*vide supra*, p. 63). Förster may have been Beethoven's 'old master', but it is really astonishing that it could be thought that Beethoven will have profited from Förster's Op. 16 rather than Haydn's Op. 76.

Nevertheless, we must imagine that Beethoven was now carrying Op. 18 about Vienna, played by Schuppanzigh and his friends, and saying that he had really learned how to write quartets from Förster (almost a paraphrase of Mozart's famous words about Haydn).[1] And Op. 18 was a formidable achievement, not alone for the

1 A selection of Förster's quartets and quintets are published in the *Denkmäler der Tonkunst in Österreich* XXXV, No. 67 (1928). For Förster and Beethoven, see Thayer-Forbes I, 261f., Frimmel, *Beethoven-Handbuch* I, 144. In Thayer-Forbes, we read: 'A criticism of three quartets [*AMZ*, 1799], which failed to *give the name of the composer* [Förster], had been applied erroneously by some writers to Beethoven's Op. 18' (I, 261); we fail to understand this reference. The criticism in the *AMZ* is clearly marked as being by Förster (I, 365f.) and the reviewer mentions Förster's name quite clearly, beginning 'Herr Förster muß ohne Zweifel sein eigenes Publikum haben . . .'.

'theatrical' depths of the D minor *Adagio affettuoso ed appassionato* from Op. 18, No. 1, but even more for the marvellously professional language of the whole set: a professionalism which would seem to suggest Haydn rather than Förster. And not only Haydn. The ghost of Mozart hangs heavy over much of this music, especially in the A major (we know that Beethoven greatly admired Mozart's K. 464, on which Op. 18, No. 5, is clearly modelled). If Beethoven used Förster as a red herring, the music of Op. 18, on the other hand, is quite clear about its spiritual heritage – embarrassingly so in Op. 18, No. 2, with its Haydnesque traits; or is the embarrassment perhaps intended? Knowing Beethoven's wildly ambivalent attitude towards his old teacher at this period, one wonders.

If Josephine Deym thought the Op. 18 quartets 'the greatest of their kind', we may be sure that this opinion was shared by Prince Lobkowitz, who later became one of Beethoven's greatest admirers and supporters. Op. 18 was the first major dedication to Lobkowitz, and Haydn will have heard the set and pondered its import – *per se* and to Viennese society *de anno 1799*. No doubt the younger generation much preferred Beethoven's language and considered Op. 18 the greatest achievement in the field of the quartet. Haydn's Op. 77 may even have seemed something of an anticlimax after the great spiritual heights of Op. 76. Op. 77, on the other hand, though it introduces all sorts of novel ideas, is perhaps 'understated'; its subtleties lie far under the surface (as we shall shortly see). Once, in connection with *The Seasons*, Haydn was very offended at what he believed to be a lack of reaction on the part of the Viennese public (*vide infra*). What would Haydn's reaction have been to this direct confrontation – Beethoven's Op. 18 and his own Op. 77 at the Palais Lobkowitz? What would, especially, have been his feelings as he noticed a certain condescension on the part of the younger 'pro-Beethoven' aristocracy? A certain arrogance on the part of Beethoven himself?

We have, very much *mutatis mutandis*, a precedent. When Haydn was indirectly confronted by Mozart's supreme achievements in the piano concerto and in the opera, the older composer simply withdrew: after *c.* 1782 he wrote no more piano concertos, after 1784 no more operas (before he went to London in 1791 and was commissioned to compose an *opera seria*); and we have noted (*Haydn in England 1791–1795*, p. 505) that Haydn never wanted to, and in fact never did, compose string quintets after he had heard Mozart's. Perhaps we must judge the non-composition of the intended Op. 77, Nos. 3–6, in this light; that is, of Haydn quietly withdrawing from the stage, leaving it to Beethoven and his Op. 18. One thing becomes increasingly clear: that Haydn soon became very much in awe of Beethoven, as a little publicized but authentic encounter, in which Griesinger rather extraordinarily played the go-between, would show (see *Haydn: the Late Years 1800–1809*). And so Haydn abandoned the quartet, and in fact instrumental music as a whole, with this fragment of six quartets Op. 77. About large-scale vocal music he clearly felt no hesitation at all (whereas, conversely, Beethoven was very worried – and rightly so, as matters turned out – about the effect his new Mass in C would have on Prince Esterházy in 1807).

There are even some curious sections in the music itself that suggest that on the stylistic level Haydn was preoccupied with Beethoven's language. In the following, extremely 'Beethovenian' passage, which is the Trio of Op. 77, No. 1, is Haydn experimenting in the *Großmogul*'s dialect? Is this a gigantic spoof (which Beethoven will not have thought amusing at all)? Or is it a very subtle piece of flattery for a young Viennese–Bohemian aristocrat with known sympathies for *Großmogul* and his ideas? Or is this pure Haydn, the new style which he, alas, abandoned after Op. 77? In many respects Haydn is as enigmatic as one of the ancient Greek play-masques. And although *we* may think the passage sounds like the *Großmogul*, one wonders whether the Viennese audience of 1799 thought so. And if it is Haydn's nod to the younger generation, on what particular piece or pieces by Beethoven is it based? None presents itself as an obvious candidate for consideration.

In an earlier analysis (*supra*, p. 286), we have suggested that Haydn may have taken the concept of the one-in-the-bar scherzo from Beethoven and applied it to the minuets (so-called) of Op. 76, especially such a movement as that in Op. 76, No. 1. With the two minuets in Op. 77 we reach a new level of one-in-the-bar sophistication, and this is peculiarly true of the Menuet in Op. 77, No. 2. It comes second, after the opening movement and before the slow movement – a reflection (a) of Haydn's Quartets, Op. 9 of *c.* 1768, and Op. 17, of 1771; and (b) of a more subtle juxtaposition necessary because of the greatly increased speed of the Menuet; sometimes this became so fast that it would have been quicker than the Finale. This would have obtained in Op. 77, No. 2, whose 'German dance' finale is in the same kind of tempo as we have seen in Haydn's piano trios of the period – marked 'Vivace assai' but nevertheless in a sturdy three beats rather than a flying one beat in the bar. For this reason the order was changed to have the not-so-slow Andante come third, the scherzo-like Minuet second. That which is wonderfully new is the rhythmic displacement that takes place in the actual music. Of course, we have had such displacements before, as in the famous case of Symphony No. 65's Minuet, where Haydn superimposes a four-four rhythm on the three-four beat (quoted in Landon, *SYM*, 330f.). But in the Menuet of Op. 77, No. 2, the whirling speed necessitates a displacement over a wider space (e.g. the superimposition of a rhythmic two-four over a metric three-four at bars 6ff.) and at a far quicker tempo. Here we have a stylistic test even more delicate than the Trio of Op. 77, No. 1, quoted above. Although rhythmic displacements of this kind are indelibly fixed in our mind as being a characteristic of Beethoven's style (e.g. the Scherzo of the Ninth Symphony, with the 'Ritmo di tre [quattro] battute'), in fact the origin is Haydnesque, as are the off-beat *fz* in the viola at bars 8ff.; in the latter passage, the viola has no *crescendo* in the autograph and the *fz* marks are thus presented in a different dynamic plane, spearing through the whole texture (see musical example overleaf).

If we think that this music is Beethovenian (and it is), we would do well to remember the long road in Haydn's music that led up to this particular passage. We have, nevertheless, reached a point in the older man's music where many stylistic elements fuse with those of Beethoven at this period; and curiously enough, as both men continue, Mozartian elements are further and further left behind. We are only on the threshold of the nineteenth century, not even a decade after Mozart's death; yet these two musical examples – and scores of similar ones in Beethoven – could not possibly be confused with Mozart. A new musical language is being created before our very eyes: the vocabulary will soon be vastly extended, but the basic language is that of Haydn's late style.

A great deal has been said about third-related keys in this biography. Hitherto it has been considered a typically Beethovenian trait, but its origins are all in Haydn's later style (from 1780). The Op. 77 Quartets have abundant displays of this device. In Op. 77, No. 1, the basic key scheme is G, but the slow movement and the Trio are in E flat. Op. 77, No. 2, has F major as the tonic, but the Trio is in D flat and the slow movement in D major. It is curious that Haydn's third-related keys are almost all downward rather than upward. This obtained even in his first large-scale experiment along those lines, the Act I Finale of *La fedeltà premiata*; there the basic key was B flat, and the key sequence begins B flat – G – G minor – E flat – C – A flat [etc.]. This curious tendency to downward third-related keys (a darkening rather than a lightening of mood) has its parallel in Haydn's equally strong tendency to enharmonic modulations into the flat (rather than sharp) range, i.e. −12 rather than +12 fifths. All this is in direct contradistinction to Haydn's outwardly jovial and optimistic nature; it reveals,

[Op. 77, No. 2—Menuet]

in fact, a composer with a distinctly depressive, if carefully hidden, side to his being which is so much at variance with the 'official' portrait he presented to society that one wonders if even his most astute contemporaries realized the profound dichotomy in Haydn's psychological make-up. Such a movement as the D minor Adagio from Beethoven's Op. 18, No. 1, is deliberately, indeed brilliantly, pathetic – a piece of rhetoric which is near to the declamatory world of *opera seria*. Next to it, Haydn's last Andante (in Op. 77, No. 2), with its fastidious two-part writing and its severely restrained, unpathetic, undemonstrative, undeclamatory style must have seemed pale beside Beethoven's growl of thunder on the dark horizon. From the rapier-swift lunge, the reserved old man quietly withdrew. And many hardly seemed to take note of his absence . . .

The two Quartets of Op. 77 have long been considered the *non plus ultra* of Haydn's quartet style. Sir Donald Tovey even went so far as to describe Op. 77, No. 2, as 'perhaps Haydn's greatest instrumental composition, with two of the last

The first page of music of the autograph manuscript (the preceding title page bears the title only) of the String Quartet, Op. 77, No. 1; it is inscribed by the composer 'In Nomine Domini' and at the right 'di me giuseppe Haydn mpria 799'.

symphonies [Nos. 102 and 104, as we learn in another context] to bracket it with'.[1] If both works lack the monumental quality of some of Op. 76 (and perhaps its intellectual experimentation at the level of, say, Op. 76, No. 6), they have a quiet self-assurance and a certain tinge of melancholy.

No. 1 is the more 'open' of the two. The first movement is built round a kind of march, not a Mozartian march of the ♩ ♫ ♩ ♩ sort but almost an operatic scene:

1 Article 'Haydn' in Cobbett's *Cyclopedic Survey of Chamber Music*, I, 545.

If Symphony No. 104 could be considered a work built upon the intervals of a second, a fourth and a fifth, Op. 77, No. 1, and especially its first movement, is a work almost exclusively constructed on *Urlinien* of thirds. The arch of the main theme is a third:

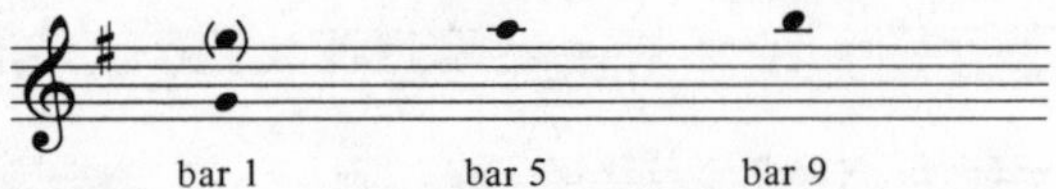

while all the component parts are based on the interval of a third:

Even the transition to the dominant has the same arch-like rise to the third that we saw in the first subject, viz.:

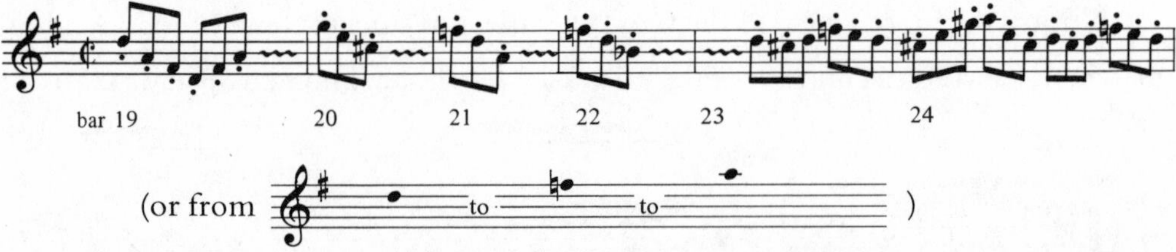

and it will have been noticed that the smaller intervallic relationships within bars 19–24 are also third-dominated. The second subject has as its melodic climax the fall of a third:

while the triplet accompaniment and also the viola part

are third-oriented, as is the following second violin part which occurs shortly before the double bar:

Even the cadential pattern is a sequence of thirds:

while the last interval of the fifth is an extension of earlier cadences, viz. bar 13

and at bars 39f.

(the beginning of the second subject, repeated at the upper octave). In the development we note a very curious use of the sham recapitulation (*fausse reprise*), which is so far along in the course of things that it really startles the listener when it becomes obvious, after a few bars, that we are still a long way from the real thing. Another interesting point is that, having relied so heavily on the second subject all through the development, Haydn simply drops it thereafter; it never reappears at all in the recapitulation. Throughout the movement, the music achieves a fine balance between the 'Napoleonic quick step' of the main theme and the triplets which are, of course, the strongest antipole of the dotted rhythm: or are they? In the recapitulation we suddenly find the viola singing through the score (and the first violin's triplets):

with a subtly transformed phrase from the main subject. The same happens once again shortly before the end (bar 181).

The second movement is Haydn's last sustained instrumental adagio (not counting, of course, the famous 'Winter' from *The Seasons*). The confrontation with the dense, dynamically much more 'loaded' slow movements of Beethoven's Op. 18 must have particularly struck contemporary listeners. Here was Haydn's transparent, rhythmically 'open', intensely lyrical music set against a much more difficult technical task. The form of the Op. 18 music is of a supreme technical mastery, but the string technique is not yet completely assured: many vexing passages, which do not lie well in the string players' hands, make Beethoven's difficult task complicated. With Haydn, this problem simply does not arise. Even the most involved modulatory and enharmonic problems are solved by tricking the players (through the easiest notation) into thinking they are playing aurally in a double sharp or double flattened key whereas literally they are playing in another. The most sensational example of this occurs in the opening movement of Op. 77, No. 2, but there is a fine example in the middle of this movement, too (bars 42ff., *vide infra*). Also in this detail, one can see the vast difference between Haydn – always the practical musician watching out for his players and their problems – and Beethoven, to whom the players' problems were of little interest. Beethoven no doubt thought Haydn's attitude a compromise, while Haydn no doubt considered Beethoven's attitude arrogant pigheadedness. *Vive la différence* . . .

Two technical-cum-musical points need to be made at the outset. The music, once it begins to move in even quaver accompaniment, looks back extraordinarily to similar movements in Haydn's *The Seven Words*:

Subconsciously, perhaps, we have music very similar to 'Pater, dimitte illis, quia nesciunt, quid faciunt'.

The second point is the way in which Haydn links this Adagio rhythmically and intervallically to the preceding movement. The principal subject of the slow movement is:

(Notice the new musical sign for a small accent, **v** , at bar two; it never reached Artaria's printed page, though Elssler copied it perfectly; similarly the big *portato* slur at bars 2–3 was simply omitted by Artaria – and thus both points were never incorporated into modern printed editions prior to the Doblinger critical edition. We mention only these two points, but there are many similar corruptions throughout even these great, famous and – one would have thought – textually well-studied Quartets. Not so . . .) Bar one is, of course, derived from the second subject of the preceding movement (bars 39ff., quoted *supra*), while the figure at the beginning of bar two is a literal transformation of the dotted figure of the main subject (bars 1–2 or rather the extension at bars 5–6 – *vide supra*). It is also quite clear that the marching crotchets of the Allegro moderato have become the sharply enunciated quavers of bar three in the Adagio. The cadential figure in the first movement

now becomes

And of course the series of thirds in chains in the main subject of the Adagio

as indeed the interval of the third plays a major role in the Trio (quoted *supra*) – while (to continue this motivic relationship between movements), the Menuet proper is linked to the first movement by its accompaniment, which we know both intervallically and from its across-the-bar phrasing, previously seen in the first subject of the opening movement.

The slow movement is in a free sonata form, with a modulation to the dominant, a middle section and a recapitulation, though without any second subject in the strict sense. The most stupendous effect is achieved in the middle of the development by a modulation that slides, Beethoven-like, up a half-note, as follows (previous modulation from B flat to D flat and the dominant of F minor):

The recapitulation begins not with a unison, as it was at the beginning, but with a new harmonization and a different dynamic scheme (no *decrescendo*, no little accents):

This has the effect of immensely widening the horizon. On the other hand, the ending, with its sorrowful pedal point and the diminished chords, appears almost like a slow curtain being drawn over what Rosemary Hughes, with her customary felicity, calls this 'fathomlessly profound Adagio'.

We have dealt with various aspects of the Menuet & Trio above. Formally it is interesting to see Haydn writing out the whole of the first section (in two groups of twelve bars). Having made the point with regard to the accompaniment and its relation to the first movement, the whole pattern is changed for the repetition and the across-the-bar slurs become six quavers and a bass line of a crotchet to begin each bar.

Another innovation is that the first violin is now taken up to the unprecedented altitude of *d''''* just before the end of the second section, where Haydn later has a new point in store for us, to wit:

which is the straight *Urlinie* (*vide supra*) of the first movement's main subject. Taking a leaf from the Trios of Symphonies Nos. 99 and 104, which were both in third-related keys, the Trio of this Quartet modulates gradually back to the da capo and to the rhythm of the Menuet. It is a very subtle piece of writing.

The main subject of the Finale is Haydn's farewell to the world of Eastern European folk music which he had done so much to cultivate and to introduce to 'art music'. As far as we can tell, no one has traced, or attempted to trace, this gypsy-type tune after Hadow and Kuhač, who quite rightly see (south)-Eastern melodic origins not only in the Finale but also in the Menuet. In this respect we would also point out a recent article by the late Bence Szabolcsi, who maintains that the opening 'march' theme of Op. 77, No. 1, comes from the old Hungarian recruiting music ('bokázó'). Of all these Hungarian-Gypsy-Croatian melodic prototypes, however, it is the Finale which is the most obviously 'eastern' in flavour. The first time it is announced unison, the second time with a ninth harmony at the second and sixth bars, which comes as a delicious surprise:

The rhythmic displacement caused by the *fz* accent at bars 3 and 7 gives the theme a great sophistication, and it is not till the second time round that the 'normal' stress (bars 2 and 6) is *also* added (even in the violin I part). Haydn now proceeds to show us, with fantastic virtuosity, what can be done, contrapuntally, with such a gypsy theme. To make his point even clearer, the movement is put into sonata form (not rondo, as Cecil Gray maintains). The string writing in this Finale is the nearest Haydn ever comes to showing off his players – the rushing semiquavers, the jumping from high to low strings (which we could hear, too, in the Minuet) and the dazzling arpeggios across the board

are all in the best *primas* tradition. 'The idiom,' writes Cecil Gray, 'is throughout pure string quartet writing of the most highly organized description . . . Altogether it ranks among the most attractive and exhilarating movements in the whole series of Haydn's string quartets.' Op. 77, No. 1, is in fact a summing-up of one whole side of Haydn's many-sided nature, not least his love for folk music and his brilliantly successful attempt to wed it to the great tradition of Western music. The Finale is the last and one of the finest examples of this fusion.[1]

Op. 77, No. 2

Cecil Gray first drew attention to the striking resemblance (indeed, note-for-note) between the 'Catalogue Aria' in Mozart's *Don Giovanni* and the first subject of Haydn's Op. 77, No. 2:

(Mozart:) 

(Nella bionda egli ha l'usanza)

(Haydn:)

Haydn was thinking more and more of his former friend and ally, and in 1799 he had received, as a present from Breitkopf & Härtel, the 'Oeuvres Complettes' of Mozart's

1 Sir W. H. Hadow, *A Croatian Composer* (etc.), London 1897, pp. 48, 51 (based on Kuhač: see details in *Haydn in England 1791–1795*, p. 598). Bence Szabolcsi, 'Haydn und die Ungarische Musik', in *Bericht über die Internationale Konferenz zum Andenken Joseph Haydns* (Budapest, 1959), printed Budapest 1961, pp. 172f. Cecil Gray, *Haydn String Quartet Society*, Vol. I (London 1932), pp. 17ff. Marion M. Scott, *The Complete Haydn Quartets* (Op. 42, 77): Analytical Notes, Haydn Society, Boston (Mass.) 1952. Rosemary Hughes, *Haydn*, pp. 167f.

piano music. We shall find, in *The Seasons*, another poignant reference to Mozart's music. But despite the clear thematic allusions in both cases, it is hard to agree with Cecil Gray when he writes:[1]

> The most striking stylistic feature of the present work consists in its strongly marked Mozartean character. The personalities and styles of the two masters are widely different when one looks on their work as a whole, but there are isolated examples which might conceivably have been written by either of them, and this is one of these works. . . . This Mozartean character comes out, firstly, in clarity, precision and classical symmetry of form, whereas Haydn . . . is frequently anything but classic and orthodox in this respect; secondly, in the prevalence of balanced eight-bar periods, whereas Haydn often shows a marked predilection for asymmetrical groupings of five, six, seven, nine, or ten bars; thirdly, in the cultivation of a vein of chromatic harmony which we associate far more readily with Mozart than with Haydn. . . . But it is not merely the chance resemblance of a single phrase – such reminiscences, whether conscious or unconscious, are common to all music great and small – that makes us instantly think of Mozart; it is the whole poise of the musical sentences.

If anything, the whole spirit of Beethoven is in this music. It is hard to associate Mozart either with the following passage (which is somewhat like a similar passage, at a similar place, in Op. 76, No. 4):

1 *Haydn String Quartet Society*, Vol. V (1936), p. 15.

or with the compression of the second violin part in bars 20/1 and 21/2:

The second subject is really a variant of the first; or rather the counter-melody in the second violin is an extension of the opening melody:

The development seizes on the fragment

and with it effects one of the most extraordinary modulations in the whole range of Haydn. It is one of the several occasions on which the music modulates into descending enharmonic flat keys from which Haydn has to extricate the players by skilful trickery. László Somfai[1] has subjected this particular passage to a brilliant analysis:

> . . . The development starting in C major modulates stepwise without enharmonic tricks to the key of E flat minor (bar 89). However, in bar 98 we are doubtlessly in the (written) key of E minor which logically should be F flat minor. (The remainder of the development recedes again stepwise to F major [written] which logically should be G double-flat major). What happened in these few bars? Bars 92–95 would have been more rational in a modulation from E flat minor to F

1 'A bold enharmonic modulatory model in Joseph Haydn's string quartets', in *Studies in Eighteenth Century Music* (Geiringer *Festschrift*), London 1970, pp. 377f. Reprinted by permission of George Allen & Unwin Ltd.

flat minor (−5 fifths) than in a modulation from E flat minor to E minor (+7 fifths). Without considering the point of view of logic or of musical orthography it seems truly remarkable that in an F major movement these two keys should appear next to each other. Let us see, however, how Haydn makes it appear plausible that a real E flat minor key may be followed by E minor. We are quoting the passage from the autograph score with Haydn's own annotations.

This is in fact a bolder, more modern, modulatory solution than Beethoven's well known 'quasi-modulation' with a stiff semi-tone direct jump which, incidentally, Haydn too liked to use (cf., e.g., the gliding modulation from F minor to G flat major in the second movement of the Quartet Op. 55, No. 2 in F minor). First (bars 81–93) the note E flat is the root of an E flat minor triad (reinforced by the 'Neapolitan leading note' F flat). However, the same E flat, spelled as D sharp (bars 93–94), is considered the leading note of the new key of E minor. A more extreme functional reinterpretation of the two neighbour notes half a note distant is inconceivable within the classical style. The fact that Haydn inscribed into the part of the cellist the remark 'l'istesso tuono' ('the same note') between the notes E flat and D sharp is to be interpreted as a forced confession of enharmonic thinking within the tempered tonal system. The remark 'das leere A' ('the open A string') is, as it were, an act of desperation; the motive A G G G favours playing on the D string (today the passage is usually performed on the D string by string quartet players). Haydn, however, in the interest of pure intonation, refers to the open A string as the only firm point. [This] 'irregular' type of modulation provides an excellent characterization of Haydn's art. His imagination draws him into unknown, almost unrealizable, experimental adventures; but with the realism of the practical musician he clings to a solution allowing for 'pure' intonation. Out of a synthesis of these tendencies results an exciting, fantastic and still flexible new idiom.

(We reproduce the extraordinary passage, also in Haydn's autograph manuscript, from the Esterházy Archives of the National Széchényi Library in Budapest: see below.)

This is the kind of movement in Haydn which is usually described as 'monothematic' (the most famous example being, perhaps, Symphony No. 103's Finale); but of course it is not monothematic at all in the strict sense. The second subject is, as we have seen, a derivative of the first, and it is true that Haydn makes much use out of the principal thematic material. But what is always interesting in such cases is to observe the wide diversity that he is able to give the music even while using, say, a small derivative of a passage, such as that which dominates the development. The unity is gained, as throughout music of the Vienna classical period, by diversity. One small point may illustrate Haydn's careful attention also to dynamic diversity within formal unity. The recapitulation is, like the beginning of the Quartet, marked *f*,

A page (fol. 3v.) from the autograph manuscript of the String Quartet, Op. 77, No. 2, including bars 74–95 of the first movement. In this section Haydn introduces the bold modulation in which the violoncello moves enharmonically on the pivotal note *e flat* = *d sharp*; the first violin is instructed to use 'das leere A O' (open A-string).

and originally Haydn led into it by a series of sharp *f* chords followed by a whole bar of rest, viz.:

At the first performance, or one of the early performances, Haydn changed this lead-back in the Elssler parts (Budapest) to read *p* at bar 113; and in the Artaria edition, this is changed (obviously on the basis of the manuscript parts Haydn delivered) to read *ff* at bar 112 and *pp* at bar 113 – so that the formal break of the recapitulation will be made still more dramatic. It is a typical gesture of Haydn at this period, and the kind of rhetorical gesture that will become part and parcel of Haydn's greatest pupil. . . .

Both the Menuet ('Presto' in the autograph, changed to 'Presto, ma non troppo' in the authentic editions) and the Trio in the flattened submediant have been quoted above in other contexts (*supra*, pp. 507–8 and 518). The most supple Minuet, rhythmically, of Haydn's whole career is followed by that nostalgic Trio, to be played as softly as possible (marked 'pianiß:' in the autograph, which corresponds to our *ppp*); to modulate back to the tonic there is a puckish Trio which is hair-raisingly Beethovenian; it, too, is marked *pp* and at the end Haydn cautions 'Menuet da capo e [or 'ma'] forte'.

If the Menuet & Trio were the most flagrantly modern-sounding section of the work, the third movement (Andante) looks back to an earlier age. Geiringer[1] notes that

> It is limited to two parts only [at the beginning: first violin and cello], thus recalling the distinctive 'thinness' of Philipp Emanuel Bach's piano compositions. In this period, when true expression seemed more important to Haydn than a perfect balance between form and content, the composer was getting closer to the style of Johann Sebastian Bach's eldest son, and at the same time to his own Storm and Stress period.

There is, in point of fact, a model in Haydn's own music for this beginning: the start of Symphony No. 74's slow movement (also an Andante – this kind of device would not work well in a slower tempo), where there is a similar dialogue between first violin and violoncello. In the Quartet, the mood is what the composer himself used to call 'innocentemente', a great understatement after the boisterous preceding scherzo. The form is a theme and variations, in which Haydn had written so much and so well. The music rises in one of the longest *crescendi* Haydn ever wrote to a *ff* six-four D major scale, after which the music subsides to the principal theme, *pp*, and with rich new harmonies. At the end there is what Cecil Gray calls 'a murmuring, undulating figure in semiquavers', which gives the music a lingering poignance; to contribute to this farewell atmosphere, Haydn provides one of his rare 'hairpin' *crescendo–decrescendo* marks which ease the music over a typically 'closing' pedal point, with shifting chromatic harmonies, to a very quiet closing *fermata*. Time seems to stand still. Never was a farewell movement concluded so undramatically. But it is clearly a farewell nonetheless.

The Finale is Haydn's last essay in the 'German dance' three-four closing movements which were so successfully used in the piano trios; and we are reminded of such a movement as the Finale of Piano Trio No. 32 (XV: 18) or the Finale 'in the German Style' of Piano Trio No. 45, analysed *supra* (pp. 224f.). The Hungarian exoticisms are stronger at the beginning of the A major Trio –

– but the second subject of our Quartet is definitely 'eastern European', too:

and particularly this Gypsy (Hungarian) figure

etc., which we have encountered in Haydn's music many times before in different, though similar, guises. As an exercise in closely worked canonic entries, the beginning

1 1947, p. 281.

of the development is as superb as the canon in the first movement of Symphony No. 102:

The same sort of motivic tension as in the Symphony is also generated in this fantastic development section of Op. 77, No. 2's Finale, which moves at the same level of tension right through to the recapitulation: that section arrives so suddenly that, as with a similar section in the Finale of Op. 76, No. 6 (*vide supra*, p. 310), Haydn has to throw in a *fz* in all the parts to remind players and listeners that the reprise has actually started:

In its effortless weaving-together of sonata form, German dance and Hungarian *primas*, this Finale is a brilliant conclusion to Haydn as an instrumental composer. Although he was nearly seventy, the music has the wit, brevity and energy of a thirty-year-old; but in formal mastery, it shows the uncanny stamp of authority and experience that is now on everything Haydn composed.

In the *AMZ* (V, 832f.) of September 1803, these works were reviewed, but not in the original form. Breitkopf & Härtel had made arrangements of the Quartets for flute and piano (No. 1) and violin with piano (No. 2). In ordinary circumstances, we would hardly pay any critical attention to such arrangements, of which there are several thousand in Haydn's *œuvre*; but in this case, we must do so to clear up a quite incredible misunderstanding. Until very recently, it was thought that these works were originally composed for flute (violin) and piano. Considering the fantastic string writing, commentators were much puzzled by the supposed 'original' for piano with 'accompaniment of' a flute or violin. 'Both of them [Op. 77],' writes Cecil Gray, 'are authoritatively stated to have been composed first as sonatas for violin and piano, but it is difficult to believe that this is possible, so perfectly conceived and realised are they in the medium of the quartet.' And even Tovey had written: '... There is a musically very great sonata with piano in G, which, with the addition of a minuet as large and powerful as a mid-Beethoven scherzo, was afterwards re-written as one of the last and greatest of the string quartets.'[1]

The *AMZ*, however, stated matters quite clearly. There the anonymous reviewer wrote:

> The title is not clear enough: these are two Sonatas for pianof[orte], the first with accompaniment of the flute, the second with accompaniment of the violin, both from the newest violin quartets arranged here for the indicated instruments. For this reason, the pieces cannot be discussed here at length, and one may assume that every lover of instrumental music already knows the originals, and knows, moreover, that here Haydn aims less for the simple and noble such as he did in his quartets of the middle period, but that with tireless industry and inexhaustible art he has woven together the small and often apparently heterogeneous elements into humoristic entities. The first movement of the first Sonata (in G) and the whole excellent Adagio (E flat) are, each in their way, quite masterly. The first and third [= fourth of the Quartets, since the minuets were left out of the arrangements] movements of the second Sonata displays much artistry. The arrangement for the instruments has been done with so much care that one really has the *whole* of the Quartets before one's eyes, and yet the Sonatas are really playable but – mainly because of the changing principal part, which is often in the middle or in the left hand – are not all as easy as they look. The *expression* demands, moreover, practice even at the hands of professional performers; but the marvellous Haydn rewards, and bountifully, for the care bestowed!

From Hase's essential book,[2] we learn not only that these sonatas are arrangements but also who made them. 'Breitkopf & Härtel published them in May 1803 . . ., and since then they have enjoyed the honour of being considered original compositions of Haydn, but the [arrangements] are not by Haydn; they are, rather, by the *Thomaskantor* A. E. Müller, who received a fee of twenty Rthlr. for the work . . .'.[3]

1 Gray, op. cit., p. 15. Tovey, Haydn article in *Cobbett's Cyclopedic Survey of Chamber Music*, p. 526.

2 *Joseph Haydn und Breitkopf & Härtel*, Leipzig 1909, pp. 46f.

3 Apart from the literature quoted in particular for Op. 77, see also László Somfai, 'A Klasszikus Quartetthangzás Kialakulása Haydn Vonósnégyeseiben' (*Zenetudományi Tanulmányok* VIII, pp. 295–420. Louise E. Cuyler, 'Tonal Exploitation in the Later Quartets of Haydn', in *Studies in Eighteenth-Century Music*, op cit., pp. 136–50. The dissertations are listed in the bibliography. At the time of our own writing, Reginald Barrett-Ayres' full-length book on the Haydn quartets (Barrie & Jenkins, London) had not appeared. (It has, meanwhile, appeared: 1975.) Robert Sondheimer's eccentric book, *Haydn: A historical and psychological study based on his quartets*, London 1951, has been mentioned earlier.

Missa ('Theresienmesse') **in B flat**
(XXII: 12)

Basic scoring: 2 clarinets in B flat, 2 bassoons as part of the continuo (not expressly required in the autograph but included by Elssler in all the authentic parts, including those of the first performance at Eisenstadt), 2 trumpets in B flat, timpani in B flat and low F, strings, organ (occasionally used as a solo instrument, as at the beginning of the Dona), soli (SATB) and choir (SATB).

I. Kyrie (*Adagio–Allegro–Adagio*): full scoring.
II. Gloria –
   (a) Gloria in excelsis Deo (*Allegro*): full scoring (no soli).
   (b) Gratias agimus tibi (*Moderato*): full scoring.
   (c) Quoniam (*Vivace*): full scoring.
III. Credo –
   (a) Credo in unum Deum [*Allegro*]: full scoring (no soli).
   (b) Et incarnatus est (*Adagio*]: full scoring without clarinets and without choir.
   (c) Et resurrexit (*Allegro*): full scoring.
IV. Sanctus (*Andante–Allegro*): full scoring.
V. Benedictus (*Moderato*): full scoring.
VI. Agnus Dei [*Adagio*]: full scoring without soli, trumpets and timpani.
   Dona nobis pacem (*Allegro*): full scoring.

Martin Chusid's proposal (op. cit., pp. 132f.) for dividing the *Theresienmesse* into three vocal symphonies is as follows:

Vocal Symphony No. 1

MVT.	TEXT	TEMPO AND NO. OF BARS	METRE	KEY
I	Kyrie	as *supra–Adagio I* = 28 bars; *Allegro–Adagio** = 76 bars (*same material as initial *Adagio*)	*alla breve*	B flat →V B flat
II	Gloria	as *supra* = 111 bars	3/4	B flat→V of C minor
III	Gratias	as *supra* = 137 bars	*alla breve*	C→G minor
IV	Quoniam	as *supra* = 90 bars	4/4	B flat

Vocal Symphony No. 2

MVT.	TEXT	TEMPO AND NO. OF BARS	METRE	KEY
I	Credo	as *supra* = 48 bars	4/4	B flat
II	Et incarnatus	as *supra* = 48 bars	3/4	B flat minor
III	Et resurrexit	as *supra* = 63 bars, overlapping at final cadence with Et vitam venturi	4/4	G→B flat minor
IV	Et vitam venturi	as *supra* = 62 bars	6/8	B flat

Vocal Symphony No. 3

MVT.	TEXT	TEMPO AND NO. OF BARS	METRE	KEY
I	Sanctus	as *supra* = 21 bars	3/4	B flat→F major
	Pleni	as *supra* = 41 bars	3/4	F major→B flat
II	Benedictus	as *supra* = 141 bars	*alla breve*	G major
III	Agnus Dei	as *supra* = 44 bars	*alla breve*	G minor→V
IV	Dona nobis pacem	*as supra* = 158 bars	3/4	B flat

1 Reprinted by permission of George Allen & Unwin Ltd.

THE SOURCES

The situation with regard to the sources has been discussed *supra*, in connection with the size of the orchestra at Eisenstadt in the Summer of 1799. The autograph is in the Musiksammlung of the Österreichische Nationalbibliothek and is entitled, on an otherwise blank piece of paper, 'Missa'. At the top of the first page of music, the work is signed and dated: 'In Nomine Domini di me giuseppe Haydn mpria $\overline{799}$'; at the end of the work it is signed 'Laus Deo'. The work was not entered in the *Entwurf-Katalog*. The original performance material is at the Esterházy Castle in Eisenstadt and is entitled *inter alia* 'Anno 1799'; it was prepared by Johann Elssler and his assistants but there are many small corrections and additions in Haydn's hand, e.g. even some actual notes towards the end of the final page of the 'Basso Rippieno' part: perhaps the copyists were getting tired at that particular juncture. The original 'Violoncello e Basso' part has the name of one of the original players, 'Manker', in red crayon on the outside page: Manker was the first 'cellist in the orchestra at this period (*supra*, p. 52). There are supplementary parts for two oboes and two horns for which probably Haydn's successor Fuchs was responsible. A third authentic source is the set of parts by Johann Elssler and others in the Archives of the Hofburgkapelle in Vienna; it was this set of parts that we have mentioned *supra* in connection with the name of the Mass (p. 475). A fourth authentic source is the set of parts by Elssler and his copyists in the Archives of the Princes Lobkowitz (now National Museum, Prague).

Curiously, Breitkopf & Härtel never printed this Mass, the only one of the last six not to appear in their series of Haydn's Masses in full score. Possibly someone sent in the *incipit* and the Leipzig editors glanced at it hastily and thought they had the *Schöpfungsmesse* (1801) in front of them: the first three notes are identical. Actually, the Theresa Mass was not published until the 1840s by Giuseppe Passerai in Florence – a copy is owned by Maestro Natale Gallini in Milan which we have been able to consult – and it is not known from which source this handsome full score was engraved; but it is textually interesting, because it includes the bassoon parts not found in the autograph.[1]

The *Theresienmesse* has been one of Haydn's most popular Masses in the last generation – especially in Austria and southern Germany. Part of this popularity may no doubt be laid to the rather mundane fact that this Mass was one of the first to be published in modern score (1924). If such a work as the *Missa Cellensis in honorem B. V. M.* (formerly known as the *Missa Sanctae Caeciliae*) was hardly known, it was principally because there was no edition of it whatsoever, except for the truncated old score of Breitkopf & Härtel. Yet the *Theresienmesse* has always raised a certain confusion in modern critics. On the one hand we read the devastating criticism of the Crucifixus by Ernst Bücken (1928), a 'failed' (*versagt*) piece, to which we may offer as a curious contrast the opinion of Charles Rosen (1971) who, while thoroughly

1 The first attempt at a critical edition was the pocket score by Philharmonia (No. 121), edited in 1924 by Alfred Schnerich and Carl Rouland. The first critical score using not only the autograph but also the other authentic sources was edited in 1965 by Günter Thomas in *Joseph Haydn Werke* (Henle), Reihe XXIII, Band 3, from which a miniature score was prepared by the Bärenreiter Verlag, Kassel. The *Theresienmesse* was the first Haydn mass to be recorded before World War II: it was made by R. C. A. Victor and was performed by the Swarthmore College Choir, Soli and Orchestra conducted by Alfred J. Swan in 1936. This private recording, pressed by Victor in a large album, was put on sale by the famous Gramophone Shop in New York in 1938. The first commercial recording was made in Vienna in 1950 by Clemens Krauss for the Vox Company. The first recording to use the new critical text (Henle) was made for Argo (Decca) in 1965 by soloists, the Choir of St John's College, Cambridge, and the Academy of St Martin-in-the-Fields, conducted by George Guest. It was recorded in the Chapel of St John's College, Cambridge.

disapproving of Haydn's (and Mozart's) Masses, manages to concede that 'The more dramatic sections also present no problems, and there are passages in Haydn's Masses, particularly the magnificent Kyrie of the [*Harmoniemesse*] and the Crucifixus of the [*Theresienmesse*], which are among the most affecting that Haydn ever wrote.'[1]

What seems to have disturbed the critics in the *Theresienmesse*, is an apparently reckless contrast between sacred and secular, or between severe and mild: *bel canto* lines, such as the slow section of the Kyrie, are next to fugues (quick section of the Kyrie), and aria-like movements (e.g. the Moderato section, 'Gratias agimus tibi') follow vigorous, aggressive quick movements (beginning of the Gloria); even the contrasts of keys in the latter example are violent: the Moderato is in the supertonic, C major.

Possibly this dichromatic side to the Mass has an explanation in the work's origin. (1) Whether it was composed for Marie Hermenegild Esterházy or Empress Marie Therese, it was certainly intended for one Mary (or perhaps two). (2) It is obviously Haydn's thank-offering for the gigantic success of the first public performance of *The Creation*, in April 1799. Knowing Haydn's strongly Marian leanings – the huge *Missa Cellensis in honorem B. V. M.* (1766) is the composer's thank-offering for becoming head *Capellmeister* to Prince Esterházy and (Haydn's predecessor Werner, who was in charge of the church music, having died) being allowed to compose church music – it is perhaps permissible to regard the *Theresienmesse* as a Marian work. For a good son of the Church, this meant that the music must, at least in part, be of a gentle, mild cast. At any rate, we put forward this tenatative explanation for the work's psychological dichotomy.

For the basic tripartite form of the Kyrie, Haydn returned to the French Overture of Symphony No. 15, composed forty years earlier: slow–fast–slow. In the Mass, the middle section begins with a fugue. The slow and solemn introduction is in the manner of the Salomon Symphonies, and like those works it provides the thematic basis for (a) the fugue subject and (b) for the subject of the 'Christe eleison':

This is interthematic connection of the most highly organized sort. The middle section, too, is in three parts. The fugue moves in stately contrapuntal fashion to the Christe, which is given out by the four soloists and acts as a kind of second subject. The fugue is then taken up again, to arrive slowly at a big fermata; whereupon a shortened

1 Bücken, *Die Musik des Rokokos und der Klassik* (a volume of the series *Handbuch der Musikwissenschaft*), Potsdam 1928, pp. 202f.: '. . . ihre Naivität ist freilich nicht zu verteidigen, wo in Fragen, bei denen es sich nicht um kirchlich oder weltlich, sondern schlechthin um richtig oder verkehrt handelt, wie in dem Crucifixus der Theresienmesse von 1799 der Komponist versagt. Hier liegt in einem Beispiel [quoted in score], das leider nicht vereinzelt dasteht, ein solches Mißverständnis zwischen der schneidenden Tragik der Worte und dem schwelgerischen[!] Ausdruck der Musik vor, daß nichts als die Jüngerschaft Hasses dem Komponisten als durchaus ungenügende Deckung dienen kann.' Rosen, *The Classical Style*, p. 369. On the next page of Rosen, we read: 'The setting of the first part of the Credo in the [*Theresienmesse*] . . . has vigour and some power, but one would have to look far in Haydn's music to find another rhythmic structure equally turgid and unimaginative.' The literature is full of similar contrasts.

version of the slow introduction concludes the Kyrie. Here, then, we have a fusion of the symphonic style, sonata form (the second subject in the dominant), fugue and overall tripartite form (the middle section, as we have said, is also in a kind of A–B–A).

Strikingly though the trumpets and kettledrums are used throughout the Mass – they enter with great effect at bar 17 of the Kyrie – the clarinets are used with almost suspicious caution. The explanation for this timidity is once again in the circumstances of the Eisenstadt first performance – and the reticent use of the clarinets also provides one more piece of evidence that Haydn's first thoughts about the Mass were directed to his own small forces and not to the splendid large orchestra of the Hofburgkapelle: while Haydn knew who his trumpeters and kettledrum player would be, he was not at all sure who would play the clarinet parts. The three trumpeters and drummer had been engaged permanently in 1798; in 1799 there were no regular clarinet players until the decree made at the end of 1800 (*infra*, pp. 565–6).

Critics have noticed that the fugue theme bears a certain resemblance not only to the 'Kyrie eleison' fugue in Mozart's *Requiem*

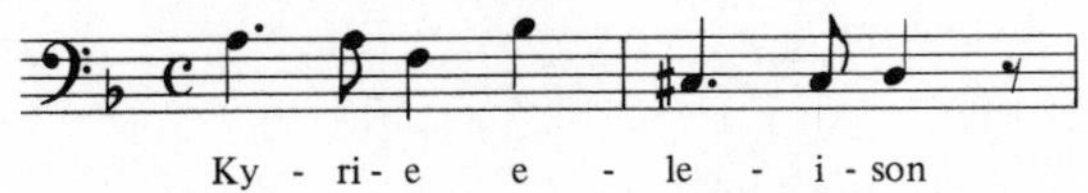

and to the traditional fugue theme that Haydn also used in his string Quartet, Op. 20, No. 5

The resemblance to the Mass fugue is perhaps most obvious when the subject comes in as follows

The juxtaposition of the musical examples by Haydn and Mozart reveals an interesting point: Mozart divides the word 'eleison' into its customary four syllables, whereas Haydn always writes 'e-lei-son' in the Austrian and southern German tradition whereby the word was probably pronounced in a Teutonic fashion, viz. 'e-*lye*-son'.

The Gloria is divided into the sections enumerated in the list above. The 'Gloria in excelsis Deo' has a stirring orchestral accompaniment, and the fanfares for clarinets, trumpets and drums after 'benedicimus te' and 'adoramus te' are in the great Baroque tradition. In the last section of this initial Allegro we have a kind of recapitulation in which the violins dance across the texture in semiquavers, while the clarinets, trumpets and timpani add tight rhythmic leads and stabs of orchestral colour. It is a typically Haydnesque sound (see example overleaf). A few bars before the final vocal cadence, the sopranos rise up to high *b* flat: Haydn is not shy of using the sopranos in this high tessitura but he takes great care to approach the range with a stepwise motion:

and, of course, using the most open vowel in the available text. This effortless technical mastery is an aspect of these late choral works which everyone takes for granted, but which is an essential element of the works' success and durability.

[*Theresienmesse*: Gloria]

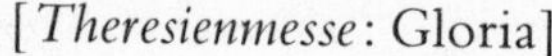

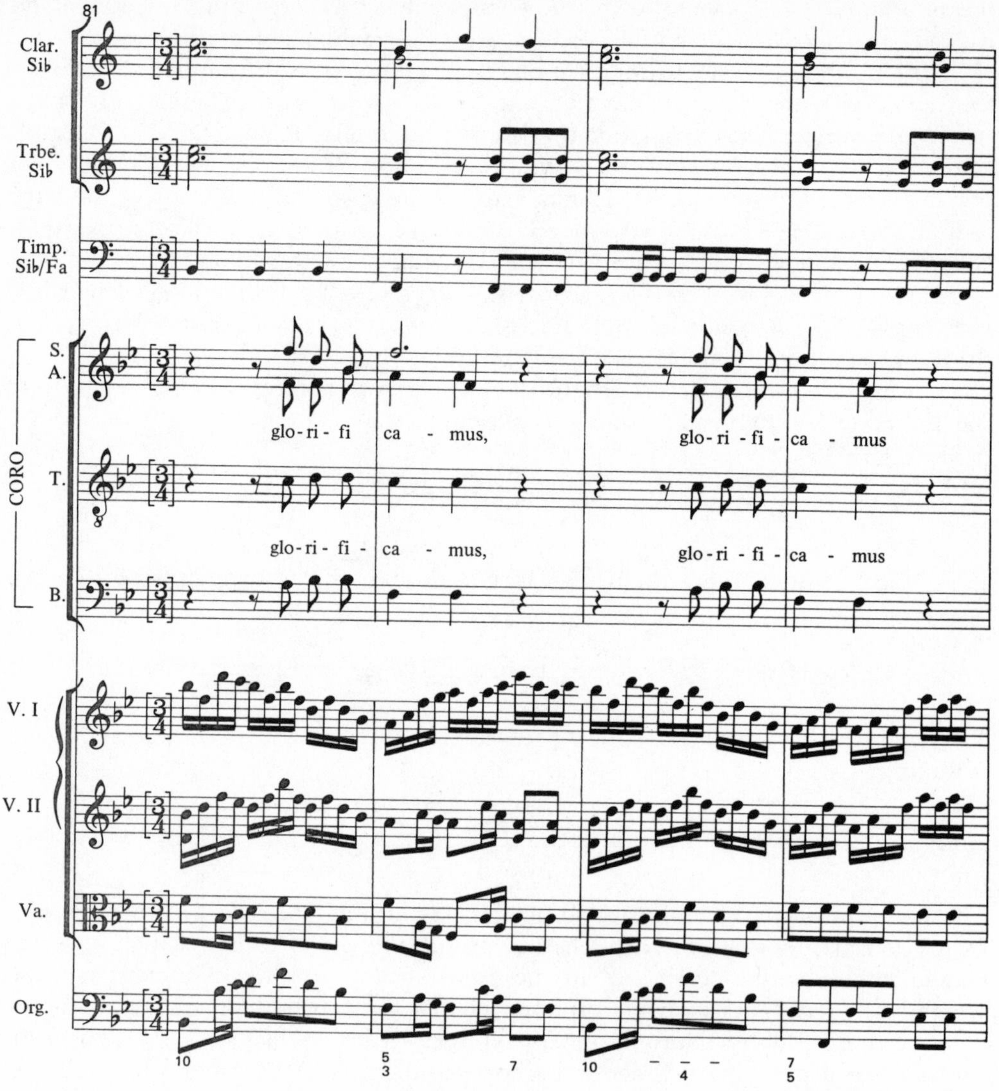

The 'Gratias agimus tibi', in C major (supertonic), is the first of the peculiarly 'Marian' sections of which we have spoken above. It begins with a famous alto solo, preceded by a ritornello of an astonishing irregularity (nine bars), no doubt to offset the rather lush melodic line:

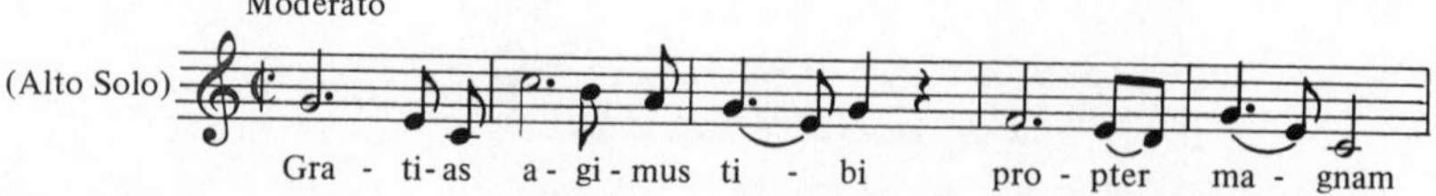

This opening irregularity turns out to be an essential part of this movement's structure. The ritornello is nine bars, the alto solo's opening phrase has twelve, the soprano, on the other hand, begins her version of the phrase with five plus six bars. Basically, this

five-bar opening is felt in almost all the entries, also in the tenor's solo at bars 159ff. The key scheme is also as intricate as the bar lengths: C major⟶D minor⟶F major⟶G minor and leading to the Qui tollis in C minor (new key signature but *not*, as in the Philharmonia score, 'Più animato'). At this point the music is dominated by a series of triplet quavers which persist to the end of this section. The chorus enters antiphonally and at bar 185 the trumpets and kettledrums enter for the first time in the Moderato. Since they are pitched in the tonic (B flat), Haydn very cleverly has them accompany an E flat section, where they ring out a series of dominant (B flat) pedal points. The 'Suscipe deprecationem nostram' drops to *pianissimo* and into A flat. Using (a) the 'Qui tollis' motif (antiphonal) and (b) the 'Suscipe' motif like component parts of a Vivaldian ritornello form, we find ourselves, after 'qui sedes' (= 'Qui tollis'), in a variant of 'Suscipe': G minor and 'miserere nobis', which leads us elegantly back to C minor and a really very striking *a cappella* passage ending on the V of C minor. On the whole, this movement presents a characteristically ambivalent mood of calculated irregularity beneath a 'Marian' song of deceptive simplicity.

The 'Quoniam tu solus sanctus' is another example of Haydn's persistence in using motivic interconnection to cement disparate pieces of music, especially in a long movement such as this one. The ritornello of the beginning

serves the solo quartet when it enters and also forms the extension (sop.)

It then appears as subject *and* countersubject of the concluding 'Amen' fugue, thus:

The opening ritornello even reappears in its entirety – a procedure which operates as no other device could to give a unity to the whole movement. There is a startling chromatic modulation which Haydn repeats. We show it the second time, leading into a brilliant *ff* with the trumpets actually doubling the sopranos and altos in the old *clarino* style:

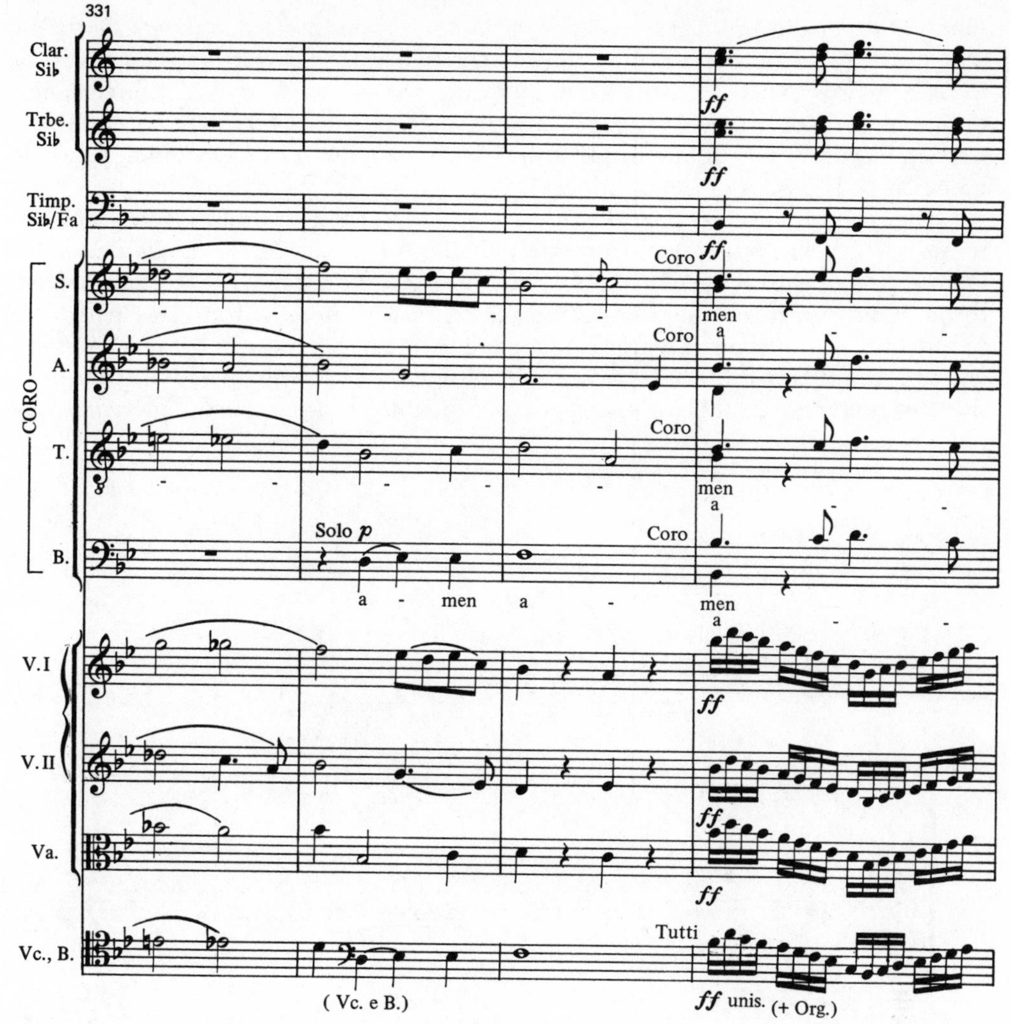

331
Clar. Sib
Trbe. Sib
Timp. Sib/Fa
CORO
S.
A.
T.
B.
Solo p
a - men a -
Coro
men a
V.I
V.II
Va.
Vc., B.
(Vc. e B.)
Tutti
ff unis. (+ Org.)

Brand (392) thought that the theme of the Credo might be an old chorale melody:

Cre - do in u - num De - um Pa - trem o-mni - po - ten - tem

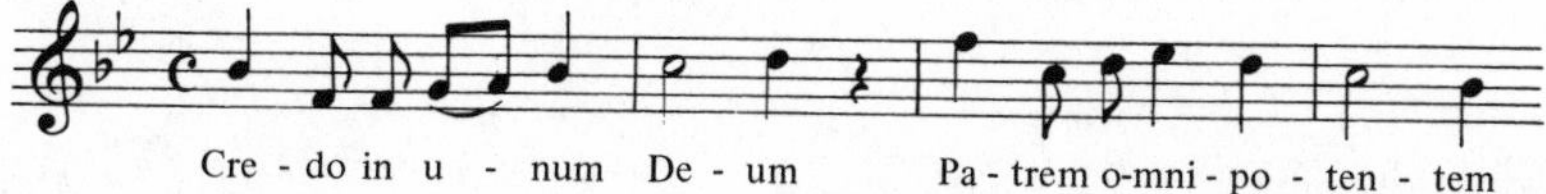

The 'antient' effect is heightened by the theme starting *unisono*. Like most of the first parts of Haydn's credos, this one begins *forte* in a very solid and almost four-square manner. The upper strings soon settle into semiquavers which carry the momentum from bar 3 to the end of the section. It is in its way a remarkable *tour-de-force*, for the intensity is maintained from first to last, and even the *piano* interjections only serve to heighten the swift, forward-moving music. There is a charming 'Baroque conceit' at the words 'visibilium omnium et invisibilium omnium', where the top (soprano) line slides under the alto and becomes 'invisible', as it were (bars 10–12, also in the succeeding *f* section). Haydn was still composing his Mass texts from memory, and this time he omitted the really vital words, 'et in unum Dominum Jesum Christum filium Dei unigenitum'. However, both Schnerich, in his preface to the Philharmonia miniature score, and Brand (393) have suggested rather clever ways to insert the missing words when Haydn, as it happens, repeats the words 'et invisibilium omnium'. In concert performances and altogether in non-Catholic countries, the missing words are nowadays simply omitted. (Haydn might have said, like Nelson on his death-bed, 'I was not a *great* sinner . . .'.)

The Et incarnatus is of great originality: first in the extraordinary key of B flat minor (which we remember from the Agnus Dei of the *Missa Sancti Bernardi de Offida*); second in the fact that only the vocal soloists are used; the choir is silent throughout, and so are the two clarinets. The music is in a kind of three-part form, modulating to the relative major (D flat) and then back again to B flat minor. At the end – to accompany the words 'passus et sepultus est' – the trumpets and timpani enter; the trumpets are in their lowest register and contribute a rather sinister, metallic sound to Christ's Death and Burial:

The Et resurrexit begins, surprisingly, in G minor – a procedure we have observed also in the 'Nelson' Mass (there in B minor, of course). Haydn saves B flat major (which he reaches *via* a long excursion to D minor) and his clarinets, trumpets and kettledrums for a violently dramatic entrance to the words 'judicare vivos' – always a passage which excited Haydn's imagination and usually ends with a *thonmahlerische* description of death ('et mortuos'). Here we have a *ff* section, laid out with Haydn's usual precision and economy but which nevertheless explodes out of the previous texture with elemental force:

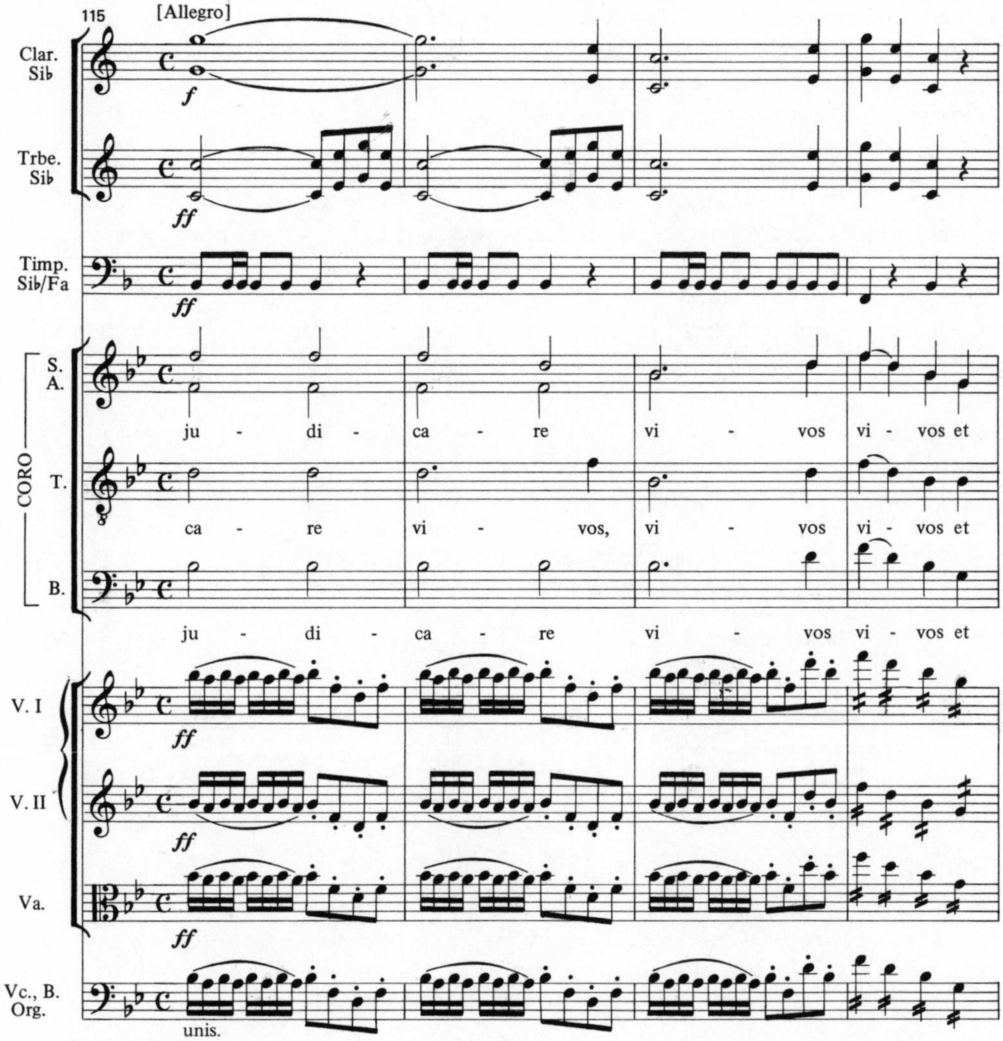

115
[Allegro]
Clar. Sib
Trbe. Sib
Timp. Sib/Fa
CORO
S. A.
ju - di - ca - re vi - vos vi - vos et
T.
ca - re vi - vos, vi - vos vi - vos et
B.
ju - di - ca - re vi - vos vi - vos et
V. I
V. II
Va.
Vc., B. Org.
unis.

The 'middle part' of this section carries us from the words 'et in Spiritum Sanctum Dominum' up to the fugue, 'Et vitam venturi'. It is in ritornello form, the characteristic theme coming first in the subdominant for tenor solo

et in Spi - ri - tum San - ctum Do - mi - num

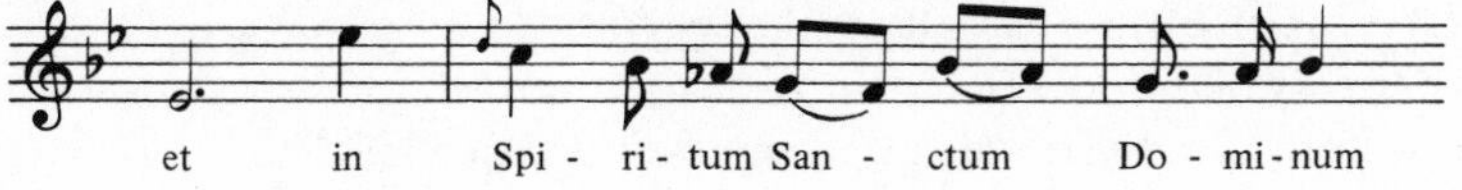

then for soprano solo (in F minor), bass solo (C minor), tenor solo (G minor), soprano solo (B flat), after which there follows the tightly unit fugue with the following subject (note the accent on bar two, which is always repeated with a thematic entry):

In this fugue the soloists also join in – *Creation*-like – to sing the Creator's praise; also to lower the pressure of the music so that Haydn's last effect may appear the more dramatic – an extraordinary entrance of the fugue subject for the basses alone (doubled by clarinets at the octave and lower strings) and with the upper strings holding what is known as an inverted pedal point, while the trumpets and timpani pound out an insistent rhythm:

The effect, culminating in that *ff* outburst as the music suddenly swerves into the six-chord of A flat major, is enormous, and worthy of a thank-offering to *The Creation*.

The Sanctus, with its subdued and chant-like beginning, leads to a swift section beginning at the words 'pleni sunt coeli et terra'. Like all Haydn's Sanctus movements (and because of the liturgical requirements of the Mass), this is the shortest of the six basic sections.

The Benedictus is another very 'Marian' movement, and certainly the most Austrian of the Mass. The highpoint of this pastoral music occurs in a very interesting way. Being in G major, Haydn modulates to the dominant (D) and then in the middle section he arrives at the central key of the Mass, namely B flat major. With enormous effect, the clarinets, trumpets and drums enter this movement for the first time and in a *ff* context (the trumpets and kettledrums remain in B flat throughout the Mass). This brilliant ray of light illuminates in a striking fashion the originality of the choice of key for the Benedictus – i.e. the submediant major – and draws our attention to the 'thirdness' of its position. To continue the 'third-related' pattern, Haydn starts the Agnus not in B flat but in G minor and treats the initial part as a huge slow introduction to the Dona; the trumpets and timpani are silent. The Dona itself, with its fanfares for brass and timpani, makes a martial and rather aggressive ending to the work and is in almost shocking contrast to the lyric, rather sentimental Benedictus. The use of the solo vocal quartet is remarkable here. After the fanfares have announced B flat and the promise of 'Ite missa est' (and a good Sunday lunch in the near future), Haydn has the text given out not by the chorus but only by the vocal quartet, which goes on in this fashion until bar 84, when the chorus finally enters. Another technical device executed with great smoothness is the little *fugato* which almost slips in (bars 101ff.), and which is of course based on the first vocal entrance of the movement:

The profusion of off-beat *forzato* accents is matched by the heavy, on-the-beat *fz* marks in the bass (organ) line: this is to become Beethoven's language, of course, and it is interesting to observe it fully fledged, if on a relatively small scale, in late Haydn. The proximity of accents (one-two-*three*-*one*-two-three) across the bar-line acts in a deliberately disruptive manner, to counterbalance which we find the series of heavily accented dotted minims in the bass instruments. At the end there is a long cadence, the outcome of which is protracted in a passage of great originality:

184 [Allegro]

Clar. Si♭

a2

Trbe. Si♭

CORO

S. cem, pa - - - - - - - - - - - - - - -

A. cem, pa - - - - - - - - - - - cem, pa -

T. cem, do - na no - bis pa - - - - - - cem, pa -

B. - cem,

V. I fz fz fz fz fz

V. II fz fz fz fz fz

Va. fz fz fz fz

Vc. e B. Org. fz fz fz fz ff

5 3 · 10 8 · · · · · · · · · · · · 6 4

Towards the very end we notice Haydn's newly acquired (as in the 'Nelson' Mass at the same place) alternating tonic-and-dominant kettledrums which once again suggest Beethoven:

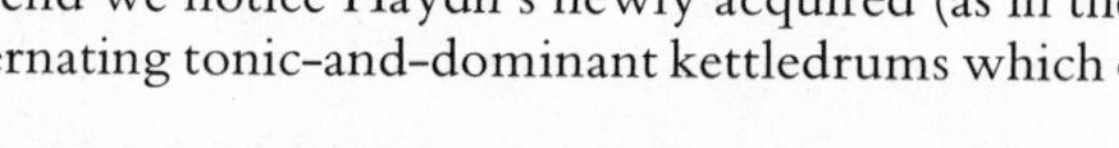

Haydn's treatment of the kettledrums is always vital to the ear and delightful for the player, much more so than Mozart's, whose timpani parts contain fascinating ideas in *piano* context but are less brilliantly original *per se* than many other features of his immaculate scores.

In the *Theresienmesse* we have music of the widest contrasts and the most varied emotions, ranging from what might be described as the most worldly movement in a late Haydn Mass (Benedictus) to moments of great religious intensity, even ecstasy (end of the Crucifixus section). If the Mass may be criticized – and being in chronological proximity to the other five late Masses and the great *Te Deum for the Empress* the *Theresienmesse* was bound to be compared to the others – one could perhaps say that it lacks the unity of spirit of the other works. The *Schöpfungsmesse*, though by no means a well-known work and certainly not rivalling the *Theresienmesse* in popularity, is in some respects a more perfect *whole* in the sense that it can be said to contain a spiritual line that runs through it from the beginning to the end; the same applies to the much more famous 'Nelson' Mass, or the *Missa Sancti Bernardi*, and of course especially to the *Missa in tempore belli*. It may be that just this dichotomy in the *Theresienmesse*, and also its 'Marian' spirit (which is very much of the Austrian kind), constitute its special appeal to Catholic congregations in Austria and southern Germany, and even to non-Catholics abroad.

The *AMZ* reviewed this Mass when it was played, apparently for the first time outside Austria, at Leipzig in the year 1805:

> *Herr Musikdirektor* [August Eberhard] Müller drew attention to a large and hitherto quite unknown Mass by Joseph Haydn in B flat with trumpets, drums and clarinets, which was played in our principal churches and has wonderful sections, e.g. Kyrie, Agnus Dei, Dona nobis pacem; we can only draw swift attention to it here. It will probably appear in print before too long a time.
>
> [*AMZ* VIII (1805), 12]

All the more curious that Breitkopf & Härtel never printed it, seeing that the work was circulating in Leipzig. But by 1805, Haydn was perhaps no longer the big business he had been . . .

CHAPTER THIRTEEN

Chronicle 1800

HAYDN'S PRINCIPAL PUBLISHER in Paris was Jean-Georges Sieber, and the composer had been in correspondence with him for over a decade. Possibly Haydn had been in contact with Sieber before 1789 (when the first extant letter is dated); certainly Sieber brought out a large number of Haydn's instrumental works, some of them in textually reliable copies. Now, at the beginning of 1800, we find a very odd document from Haydn to Sieber:

> [Page one: At the top of the page, there are three entries in an unknown hand (or hands): '26 juin 1799', 'oeuvre 90' and 'Haydn'; while under the 15 Kreutzer stamp is another note in an unknown hand, 'Haydn / 107'.]
>
> [15 Kreutzer stamp]

L'an mil-huit cent Indiction Romaine IIIe Jour de
Vendredi à Vienne en Autriche regnant Sa Majesté Fran =
çois Second Empereur des Romains Roi d'Hongrie & de
Bohème, Archiduc d'Austriche &c. &c. &c.

Constatué devant moi Notaire public Soussigné & te =
moins requis Mons. Joseph Haydn Docteur en Musique
Maitre de Chapelle au service de Prince Esterhazy &c. &c.
demeurant dans cette Capitale, a declaré de la manière
la plus solemnelle qui ni lui, ni les Sieurs Artaria & Comp.
Negocians d'estampes dans cette ville a jamais vendu Cin =
quante Copies des quatros ou quartettes Composés par M^{r}.
Haydn susdit à M^{r}. Sieber de Paris. En foi de quoi il
a signé cette declaration en presence de moi Notaire &
Temoins. ——.

Joseph Haydn mpria

Adalbert Nuss mpria

comme temoin requis.

Antoine Schulz mpria

comme Temoin requis

[Another hand:]
Moi Notaire Sussigné atteste & certifie a toux ceux qu'il
appartiendra que cette déclaration a été signé de propre
main
[lines to fill out rest of page:]

[Page two:]
de Mr. Joseph Haydn par dévant moi & temoins, que je connais très parfaitement. En foi de quoi ma signature & le sceau de mon Notarial. Fait & passé à Vienne jour mois & an comme ci-dessus.

[Sarchi's seal of office]

Francois Philippe Sarchi mpria
Docteur en Droit. Notaire
Imperial juré Admin in
fidem —

[not in CCLN][1]

Franz Philipp Sarchi was a notary public and lawyer who is listed in the *Hof- und Staats-Schematismus der röm. kaiserl. auch königl. und erzherzoglichen Haupt- und Residenz-Stadt Wien* (Vienna 1801, p. 159) as follows:

> Wechselgerichts-Advokaten und beeidigte Notarien.
> . . . Hr. Franz Phil. Sarchi, U. J. D. Hof- und Gerichts-advokat, und N. P. woh[nhaft] am Bauernmarkt 630.

Sarchi was also a member of the van Swieten circle and, as the above document shows, Haydn was known 'très parfaitement' to Sarchi. When Haydn's oratorio *Die sieben Worte* was published by Breitkopf & Härtel in 1801, it was decided to do an Italian translation of the vocal parts; van Swieten suggested Sarchi and *Legationssekretär* Griesinger – who was in close touch with Haydn in those days, acting as the go-between for Breitkopf & Härtel – went to see Sarchi, 'a fiery and jovial man', who agreed to do the Italian version. (See E. Olleson, 'Georg August Griesinger's Correspondence with Breitkopf & Härtel', *Haydn Yearbook* III, p. 22 *et passim*.)

The affidavit itself is curious enough. We have verified the rather odd indication of the date: the third of January – the month is not mentioned specifically – in the year 1800 was actually a Friday. Sieber obviously accused Haydn, or Artaria, or both of having sold fifty copies of some Haydn quartets which the composer had sold to Sieber. Apart from the strange idea of requiring an affidavit from Haydn, we may ask ourselves how such a sale could harm Sieber, and which were the quartets in question; for it is unlikely that Sieber could do much business in Vienna with Haydn quartets when there were so many copyists selling MS. parts (without Haydn's authorization, but there was nothing he could do about it), and so many publishers – not least among them Artaria – publishing every quartet by Haydn as it was released. Artaria reprinted Haydn's new works, e.g. the piano trios written for and in England from 1791 to 1797, even if Haydn had, as in the case of these trios, given the original publication rights to English publishers. All this must have been known to Sieber.

Which quartets was Sieber talking about? The top of the letter has a note which appears to read 'Oeuvre 90'; but Op. 90 in Sieber's list is an arrangement for string quartet of Symphonies Nos. 102, 104 and 103 (in that order) which appeared in 1799 (Hoboken, p. 461, with date 1798 – for revised dating, see *infra*). It appears very unlikely that the 'quatros ou quartettes' of the affidavit can have been arrangements of three London Symphonies. Nor is it probable that Haydn made quartet arrangements of his late symphonies: he had other and more important matters at hand, and left such

1 Autograph in the Mary Flagler Cary Music Collection of the Pierpont Morgan Library, New York. First published in the present writer's article 'Haydniana (II)' in *Haydn Yearbook* VII (1970), 317ff., from which the following notes are taken. For the earlier correspondence between Haydn and Sieber, see CCLN and 'Haydniana (II)', 308ff.

arranging to his impresario, J. P. Salomon. Sieber had, in 1789, brought out authentic prints of the 'Tost' Quartets Op. 54 and 55; but it had been Johann Tost, not Haydn, who had sold the works in question to Sieber; and anyway, it is very unlikely that Sieber would have objected to Haydn, or Artaria, selling copies of string quartets which had, so to speak, been in the public domain for eleven years. We must, obviously, find another explanation.

We believe that the entire document can only centre round the new string Quartets known today as Opus 76. They were composed in 1796 and 1797, and Haydn sold them to Artaria, who brought them out in two groups beginning in July 1799, and also to Clementi, whose firm also brought them out in two sets, the first of which came out a month earlier than Artaria's edition. It would seem entirely possible that Haydn also sold the new Quartets to Sieber, who in fact did issue all six works, once again in two sets. The first set, 'Trois Quatuors . . . Dediés à S. E. M. Joseph Erdödy' (see Hoboken, p. 433), has the plate number 1515, the second set 1525. Since the exact dating of 1515 is obviously of considerable importance to us, we may provide some collateral evidence (Cari Johansson's excellent monograph, *French Music Publishers' Catalogues of the Second Half of the Eighteenth Century*, Stockholm 1955, does not help us here, because too few of Sieber's late, i.e. turn-of-the-century, catalogues have been discovered).

On '25 germinal an VII' (14 April 1799) Sieber announced a new Haydn Symphony: 'La militaire ou turque. Cette Simphonie a été executée au Concert de Gara et Rode au théâtre du Grd. Opéra', i.e. No. 100 (see Hoboken, p. 208). His edition has the plate number 1508. If we examine some Haydn publications by Sieber immediately following Symphony No. 100, we see:

Sieber's plate number	*Work*	*Publication announcement*
1508	Symphony No. 100	16 April 1799 (in *Journal typografique et bibliografique*).
1509	Symphonies Nos. 100, 99, 101 arr. for quartet Oeuvre 89	none located
1512	Symphonies Nos. 102, 104, 103 arr. for quartet Oeuvre 90	none located
1515	Quartets III: 75–77 as Oeuvre 75	none located [Pleyel's reprint: 8 November 1799]
1525	Quartets III: 78–80 as Oeuvre 76	none located [Pleyel's reprint: 24 June 1800]

The close proximity of the 'Opus 76' (as we now call them) Quartets to a Haydn work brought out in the middle of April suggests that 1515 may be confidently assigned a publication date of June and 1525 a few months later at the latest. This means that Sieber must have received a manuscript from Vienna, because his edition appears either simultaneously or slightly before those of Artaria (July 1799) and Clementi (middle of June 1799). If we assume that he did not receive an 'illegal' or pirated copy from one of the Viennese copying establishments, why not take the affidavit as suggesting that Haydn himself supplied Opus 76? In that case, it is quite understandable that Sieber, imagining himself to be the sole owner of the works, was incensed to learn – no doubt from someone in Vienna – that many copies of Opus 76, manuscript and printed, were circulating in the Austrian capital. If this is the case – and it is difficult to find any other explanation – the document itself is rather equivocal; because Artaria was certainly selling printed copies of Opus 76, and Haydn himself may very well have sold the occasional Elssler copy to a princely court or monastery: Göttweig and Melk, for example, owned them all, and in the Gesellschaft der

Musikfreunde there are copies dated 1799 and 1800. The Sarchi document was probably intended to keep Sieber pacified. On the face of it, how extraordinary it is that there was regular postal traffic between two of the principal capitals in the Napoleonic wars!

The Viennese attitude towards the great Shakespeare tragedies is summed up in Rosenbaum's Diary for 31 January 1800. '*Othello*, by Shakespeare, was given again for the first time in ten years. . . . The play is too brutal and will not have a long run. – The acting was excellent' (74). It would be nearly half a century before the tragedies became really popular in Vienna. It was a great exception, too, for Prince Nicolaus Esterházy to have ordered translations of the historical plays and some of the tragedies in the 1770s for the theatre at Eszterháza Castle. No doubt the trip to England widened his horizon immensely, and we note that among his effects was a set of Shakespeare in English. But he continued to rely on Swieten in questions of literary taste.

The Seasons was occupying most of its composer's time. Griesinger reports that 'Haydn is quite far along with the [work]'. In this same letter (5 February) we hear of another project (Olleson, *Griesinger*, 14): '. . . Recently a Count Nostiz from Silesia sent him the text of an "Our Father" which pleases him so much that he intends to set it to music within the year.' Meanwhile Breitkopf & Härtel had published the first volume of the *Oeuvres Complettes* and sent Haydn a copy; Griesinger (ibid., 14) reports that the composer 'was very pleased with the edition; he will thank you himself and asks me to do so in the meantime'. Breitkopf & Härtel wanted to make a present to the composer for his assistance in preparing the edition, and the first suggested to Griesinger to send Haydn's wife some kind of gift. Griesinger reports Haydn's answer to this proposal verbatim: 'I must protest energetically against this; I love my wife and she has everything she needs, but she has done no services that earn her a reward. I don't ask for anything, and don't like to take on obligations, but if the gentlemen are in a situation where without difficulties they would like to repay my services (which have been up to now unimportant), of course I won't object' (ibid., 14). Breitkopf & Härtel were very noble and sent Haydn a diamond ring (*vide infra*, 6 April).

On 16 February, Alexander Straton of the British Embassy in Vienna wrote to Thomson:

> Dear Sir,
>
> Haydn called here yesterday and mentioned that he had already written to you and also begun the composition of the accompaniments to the scotch airs (15 in number) that you had sent him through me. He seemed desirous of having rather more than two ducats for each air, but did not precisely insist upon this point, which I therefore left undecided, exhorting him to proceed with his composition as speedily as its nature as well as that of his other occupations will admit of. This he solemnly promised but said he could not possibly determine a period for finishing the airs in question. Upon the whole he appears to be a rational animal, whereas all that can be said of the other, I mean Koz[eluch] is, that he is a Biped without feathers. [Pohl III, 159]

Haydn and Koželuch were not on intimate terms, and the latter seems to have been slightly jealous of *The Creation*'s success, for in a letter dated 7 January – well before the work was officially published – to the English publisher John Bland, he wrote: 'Vous m'obligerez aussi si Vous pouvez me faire savoir combien de prenumerents a eu Mr Haydn pour sa Cantate La Creation a Londres'.[1]

1 Christa Flamm, 'Ein Verlegerbriefwechsel zur Beethovenzeit', in *Beethoven-Studien*, Vienna 1970, p. 78.

Haydn kept his promise and delivered a whole collection of Scottish airs to Straton by the middle of June (*vide infra*, 19 June).

On the last day of February the printed score of *The Creation* appeared. Silverstolpe wrote to Stockholm on 1 March: 'Since yesterday one can get Haydn's *Creation* in score, and I am already the owner of this excellent work – as a subscriber' (Mörner, 349). On 1 March the *Wiener Zeitung* carried the following notice:

> The art shop of Artaria and Comp. on the Kohlmarkt has the honour of announcing to the worthy subscribers to the score, issued by *Herr* Joseph Haydn, of
>
> *The Creation*
>
> that this work may be now had in the above-mentioned art shop and can be collected whenever convenient upon the payment of the subscription price of 13 fl. 30 kr. [*WZ*, No. 18]

Copies were dispatched immediately to the principal capitals of Europe, and in a section which we have placed at the end of the Chronicle for the year 1800, we shall trace some of the more significant first performances of *The Creation* (London, Paris, etc.). The Oratorio was now public property. The first to capitalize on it were, as might be expected, Artaria & Co., who on 8 March issued the following announcement in the *Wiener Zeitung*:

> Musical Announcement. The general success with which the great musical work
>
> *The Creation*
>
> by Hrn. Joseph Haydn
>
> has unanimously met not only in England [where it had not yet arrived!] but also by its performance in our *Kaiserstadt*, has persuaded the art shop of Artaria and Comp., in this city, to issue this masterpiece also for amateurs of the violin and piano. We have the honour of announcing that *The Creation*, which was recently issued in score, may now be had not only in quintets for 2 violins, 2 violas and violoncello arranged by Hrn. Anton Wranizky, but also for the piano [*Klavier*] or forte piano [*sic*] with all vocal parts arranged by Hrn. Sigmund [*sic*] Neukomm with every precision, energy and great fidelity to the beauties and originality of the full score; both are for sale in this art shop. . . . The price of the Quintets is 6 fl. 40 kr., of the piano score 6 fl. 40 kr. [*WZ* No. 24]

On 8 March Haydn was in Ofen[1] to conduct *The Creation* for the Archduke Palatine, Joseph, with whom the composer was on particularly friendly terms (see also *infra*, 14 November), and for whose birthday celebrations at his palace in Ofen *The Creation* was intended as a surprise. For some reason this performance excited much interest. The *Wiener Zeitung* writes:

> On 9 March the birthday of H.R.H. the Archduke Palatine was celebrated at Ofen with every mark of joy. Among the many celebrations that of the birthday eve was particularly remarkable. Her Royal Highness the Archduchess, having specially called for Joseph Haydn, Doctor of Music, surprised H.R.H. in the most pleasant fashion with a performance in the rooms of the Royal Castle of that inimitable musical Oratorio of the famous master, entitled *The Creation*. . . . The Oratorio itself [was] performed to the complete satisfaction of Haydn by the musicians, singers and not least by the presence of many dilettantes. Both their

1 Ofen, the German name for Buda, the part of the city lying on the hill which is now known as Budapest.

Royal Highnesses and all those present gave this rare evening's entertainment their undivided applause. [*WZ*, No. 23, 19 March]

There was also a report on the forthcoming event by the Vienna correspondent of the St Petersburg newspaper, dated 5 March, in which we read: 'There is no other musical work which can please the public as much as this one.'[1] The report in the *Pressburger Zeitung* seems to be a shorter version of the *WZ* but in fact appeared a day earlier, on 18 March; it, too, stresses that the performance was a surprise. What astonishes us is to read a report of the event in the *Morning Herald* on 24 March:

> To celebrate the birth-day of the Archduke PALATINE, on the 9th ult. among other preparations, the ARCHDUCHESS desired the Master of the Imperial Orchestra, M. HAYDN, to proceed to Ofen, to give on that day his grand Oratorio, entitled 'the *Creation*'. The author of this piece has already gained 15,000 florins by it.

There was also a notice in the Hungarian newspaper *Magyar Hirmondó*. First we read, in their number of 4 March, that Haydn has left Padua on 17 February to go to Ofen. In fact Haydn was in Vienna on 15 February, as we have seen from Straton's letter to Thomson; but whether the composer actually went to Italy or not cannot now be determined. Pohl (III, 156f.) tends to regard the whole report as fictitious, and yet there is a rather strange gap in Haydn's life from 3 January to 15 February when we have no record of his being at Vienna. *Magyar Hirmondó* also reported on the success of the concert itself.

Haydn's name day, 19 March, was celebrated at the house of a medical friend in Baden, where Frau Haydn now lay dying. (Possibly the doctor in question, Karl von Schenk, was Frau Haydn's local physician in Baden.) There has survived, in the Esterházy Archives, the following manuscript[2] from Haydn's legacy: 'Worte / eines Freundes der Musen und der Musik / an / Herrn Joseph v: Hayden / Doktor der Tonkunst / gesprochen / als dieser das Haus des H: Karl v: Schenk / Medic: D^{or} mit seiner Gegenwart / beehrte / am 19ten März 1800.' ('Words of a friend of the muses and of music to Herr Joseph v: Hayden, Doctor of Music, spoken in his presence at the house of H: Karl v: Schenk, M. D. the 19th of March 1800.') All that has survived is the 'Epilogue', which reads:

> We are too incapable, too small, to praise and appreciate the greatness and eminence of a man who is the only doctor of music here; to see in our circle this most excellent of men, creator of the divine *Creation*, in which every sound is harmony and consonance, every phrase the expression of the creator's noble, sensitive soul: – to see HAYDEN, who has made himself immortal, in our circle must gladden our hearts and fill us with joy. Take, immortal mortal, this small offering by friends of your muse, not for what it could or might be, but only as a token of our joy and inner delight; and we shall ever remember that HAYDEN was the spirit of Austria's hymns and also Germany's German man.

The next day, 20 March, Haydn's wife died at the house of Haydn's old friend, the *Regens chori* Anton Stoll (for whom Mozart had composed the divine *Ave verum corpus* in 1791) in Baden. Frau Haydn was seventy years old and died 'of arthritis', as the

1 Boris Steinpress, op. cit., 86. *PZ*: *Haydn Yearbook* VIII (1971), 204.

2 Ha. I. 14. The Library kindly sent a microfilm of the document. Karl Schenk is listed twice in the *Schematismus*, once under the Lower Austrian *Landschafts Physici* as 'Hr. Karl Schenk, zu Baaden', and once under 'Doktoren der medizinischen Fakultät'.

Totenprotocoll informs us (Pohl III, 157), and was buried in the afternoon of 22 March. Haydn was too old to rejoice in his new-found freedom, but it was obviously a relief for him to be rid of his unmusical, bigoted, difficult wife, to whom he had been badly married for forty long years. A document in connection with the publication of her will (*vide supra*, pp. 483.) has survived:

> [To The Baden City Magistracy. *German*; only the signature autograph]
>
> [Baden, 24 March 1800]
>
> Worthy Magistracy,
>
> Inasmuch as my wife, the late Maria Anna Haydn, has deemed me residuary legatee under the terms of her last will and testament, dated 9th September 1799 and publ. on 22nd March 1800:
>
> I would ask to be declared legatee *cum Beneficio Legis et Inventarij* under the terms of said will, and request this my statement of legacy to be noted *prothocollando*.
>
> Joseph Haydn[m.] pria.
>
> [On reverse side of sheet the following remarks by the Baden *Syndicatus*: 'The original to be retained, and copies made upon request. Baaden [*sic*] 25th March 1800. In Baden City Mag. Joseph Grundtgeiger mp, *Synd*[*icatus*]. *Prato*: 24th March 1800. City Magistracy Baaden [*sic*] Joseph Hayden [*sic*] asks that this statement of legacy be accepted.'] [CCLN, 168]

At this period Silverstolpe was translating *The Creation* into Swedish. In a letter to Stockholm of 22 March we read:

> . . . For the last week I have had the pleasant task of translating *The Creation*, and I have already two acts in draft. . . . If I don't throw out the draft, I shall send it to you after it has been put aside for a few weeks. . . . When the time comes I want to make a small present to all my brothers, and I hope you will be pleased with it. It is *The Creation*, arranged by Wranitzky as sextets. It is quite effective in this version and much better than the quintets, in which form the work has already been printed, arranged by the same master. I would advise you not to buy the quintets if they come to Stockholm later, for the work loses too much if you hear it like that the first time. I have the sextets in my closet, but God knows when I will find a proper method of sending it to you, for the parcel is large. The work is only in MS. and won't be printed. The *flauto traverso* makes an effect that is indispensable to the whole. If my translation should turn out well, I'll put the Swedish words under the German in the sextets. Since it has no vocal parts, the words are to be declaimed between the music. . . . [Mörner, 350]

On 28 March was the concert of Haydn's trumpeter friend, Anton Weidinger, at which was given several Haydn symphonies (one 'brand new', i.e. one of the lesser-known ones composed in or for London) and the first public performance of the Trumpet Concerto in E flat. We have quoted Weidinger's announcement in the *Wiener Zeitung* (*supra*, pp. 227f.), and here we must record an astonishing fact. After the delirious success of *The Creation* in Vienna, one would have imagined that the Viennese would have flocked to a new Haydn première; but great is our amazement to read in Rosenbaum's Diary[1] that the concert, in which Therese Gassmann participated, was – empty.

1 This entry was not included in the printed extracts in Radant, *Haydn Yearbook* V, but were kindly put at our disposal by the editor.

28 March. Friday . . . I stayed there until 12 o'clock. Liesinger and Weinmüller came [to Therese's] to rehearse the duet for the academy today, but it won't be possible to do it, for the poor thing went hoarse while singing. . . . In the evening I was in the academy of the court trumpeter Weidinger in the Burgtheater. Therese sang after all, but was very hoarse. – It was empty.

It seems that Haydn did not actually conduct the concert. Can this be the explanation for the hall's being empty? The whole thing is almost inexplicable; yet we would do well to bear in mind that the second of Beethoven's two benefit concerts in 1824, when the Ninth Symphony was performed, was empty and even the first was not full,[1] as Rosenbaum informs us. But there is no doubt that the non-appearance of the Viennese at such a Haydn première constituted a straw in the wind. There were equally ominous signs at the next performance of *The Creation*. Is it an accident that between the empty Weidinger concert and *The Creation* on 6/7 April, there was another benefit concert at the Burgtheater, namely by Ludwig van Beethoven?

The programme reads as follows:[2]

To-day, Wednesday, 2 April 1800, Herr Ludwig van Beethoven will have the honour of giving a grand concert for his benefit in the R. I. Court Theatre beside the Burg. The pieces which will be performed are the following:

1. A grand symphony by the late *Herr Kapellmeister* Mozart.
2. An aria from Prince Esterhazi's *Herr Kapellmeister* **Hayden's Creation,** sung by Mlle. Saal.
3. A grand concerto for the piano-forte, played and composed by Hrn. Ludwig van Beethoven.
4. A septet, most humbly and obediently dedicated to Her Majesty The **Empress**, and composed by Herr Ludwig van Beethoven for four stringed and three wind instruments, played by *Herren* Schuppanzigh, Schreiber, Schindlecker, Bär, Nickel, Matauschek and Dietzel.
5. A duet from Hayden's *Creation*, sung by *Herr* and Mlle. Saal.
6. *Herr* Ludwig van Beethoven will improvise on the pianoforte.
7. A new grand symphony with full orchestra, composed by *Herr* Ludwig van Beethoven.

Tickets for boxes and stalls are to be had of *Herr* van Beethoven at his lodgings in the Tiefer Graben, No. 241, and of the box office.

Prices of admission are as usual.

The beginning is at half-past 6 o'clock.

We cannot, of course, identify the Mozart symphony, but it was presumably one of the late works, perhaps the 'Prague' (K. 504), which was still little known in those days, or the Symphony in G minor (K. 550) which Beethoven would have admired greatly. The 'grand concerto' was undoubtedly the piano Concerto No. 3 in C minor (Op. 37), of which the autograph is dated 1800; Beethoven later revised it when he received the Erard piano with the extended keyboard in 1803. The Septet is, of course, the famous Op. 20, which became an enormously successful work. When it was first performed at one of the concerts in the Palais Schwarzenberg, where it was highly

1 Landon *Beethoven*, 355, 357.

2 Thayer-Forbes I, 255. Facsimile of the original hand-bill in Landon, *Beethoven*, 107. *AMZ* criticism from the translation in Landon, *Beethoven*, 106f.

appreciated, Beethoven said, grimly, 'That is my *Creation*' ('Das ist meine "Schöpfung" '). At that point he obviously placed the Septet on the same level as Haydn's Oratorio. Later he was to rue the Septet's popularity ('He could not endure his Septet and grew angry because of the universal applause with which it was received', as Czerny observed to Mozart's biographer, Otto Jahn).[1] The dedication to the Empress was a strategical move; she was, as we have seen, very musical but very much in the Haydn camp. Beethoven was carefully laying siege to the Haydn bastions, and had already penetrated the Palais Schwarzenberg, the Burgtheater, and now even the Burg itself. But the Emperor Franz remained sceptical: 'There's something revolutionary about that music,' he said about Beethoven. The Symphony No. 1 in C, Op. 21, was dedicated to Gottfried van Swieten. Beethoven had laid his siege-train well. The *AMZ* contains the only known criticism of the concert:

> Finally, Herr Beethoven was able for once to obtain the use of the theatre, and this was the most interesting Academy held for a long time. He played a new concerto of his own composition which contains many beautiful things, namely the first two movements. Then a septet by him was performed; it is written with a great deal of taste and feeling. He then improvised with mastery, and at the close a symphony of his composition was performed, which revealed much art, novelty and wealth of ideas. But there was too much use of wind instruments, so that it sounded more like a wind-band than an orchestra. Perhaps we might do some good if we make the following observations on the subject of this Academy. The orchestra of the Italian Opera showed to very poor advantage. First: quarrels regarding the conductors. Beethoven believed, and rightly, that rather than Herr Conti no one could be better trusted to conduct than Herr Wranitzky. The gentlemen did not want to play under him. The shortcomings of this orchestra, already denounced above, were therefore even more evident, especially since B.'s composition is hard to play. In the accompaniments they did not take the trouble to consider the soloist. Of delicacy in accompanying, of following the sequence of the feelings of the solo player and so forth, not the slightest trace. In the second part of the symphony they were so condescending that they did not even follow the beat, so that it was impossible to get any life into their playing, especially in the woodwinds. In such cases, of what avail is their skill? – which one does not in the least wish to deny to the majority of the members of this Association. What significant effect can even the most excellent composition achieve?

Two days afterwards, on 4 April, Count Fries gave a performance of *The Creation* in one of the Wranizky arrangements, i.e. for string quintet or sextet, the former with piano and the latter with flute; but there were all the vocal parts, too. Pohl (III, 160) maintains that Haydn conducted, but there is no evidence for that in the diary notice of Zinzendorf and indeed it appears most unlikely:

> . . . Au Concert chez Fries. Jamais la musique de la Création ne m'a plû autant quoiqu'il n'y avoit que neuf instrumens, et surtout point d'instrumens a vent. Me de Schoenfeld chanta comme un Ange, Reitmeyer [Rathmayer] très bien, et le P^{ce} Lobkowitz malgré son peu de timbre avec expression . . . [Olleson, 58]

Countess Schönfeld was Count Fries's sister, while Lobkowitz is the famous Prince Franz Joseph Maximilian, whose *Kapellmeister* was the arranger of the quintets and sextets from *The Creation*, Anton Wranizky. On 7 and 8 April (Palm Sunday and the day thereafter) the Tonkünstler-Societät gave a performance of the Oratorio. On

1 Septet: Kerst, *Die Erinnerungen an Beethoven*, Stuttgart 1913, II, 193 (Dolezalek to Otto Jahn, 1852). Thayer-Forbes I, 256n.

the 5th was the rehearsal at the Burgtheater, which Rosenbaum (79) heard, and on that day Silverstolpe reported to Stockholm that Haydn was working on *The Seasons*:

> . . . The 'Spring' is already ready and Haydn is now writing with new zeal, since he has recently had the fortune to lose his evil [*böse*] wife. She followed Frau Gluck, who has also died recently. But they had quite different characters. . . .
>
> [Mörner, 351]

Originally, the Society intended to charge double prices, as they had in 1799. In their session of 15 March, the protocol notes; 'since the last academy turned out so well and brilliantly [from the financial standpoint], the same Oratorio will be given again, and also with double entrance prices.' But Haydn seems to have thought this slightly risky, for after the concerts were over, in the session of 12 May, the Society's protocol records: 'In the last session, it was decided to put double prices for the performance of *The Creation*. But at the express wishes of H. Haydn and on the advice of our Principal Director H. Count v. Kueffstein, only normal prices were asked for' (Pohl III, 160). Yet there seems to have been some confusion, for the dialect-speaking 'wiederaufgelebte Eipeldauer' ('Eipeldauer, awoken to new life') gives us an interesting picture of what went wrong, confirming Haydn's worst fears: for the first time, *The Creation* was not full!

The performance had the same soloists as on 22 and 23 December 1799: Therese Saal, Mathias Rathmayer and Ignaz Saal, and Haydn himself conducted. The *Wiener Zeitung* gives us some details: in its issue No. 26 of 29 March 1800 we read that 'the orchestra will consist of 200 musicians', and a short report, listing the soloists, was printed in *WZ* No. 32 (19 April). Count Zinzendorf was at the concert on Palm Sunday and wrote in his Diary:

> . . . A 7[h.] au théatre de la Cour entendre die Schöpfung von Haydn . . . Je me sentis l'ame elever par ces beaux morceaux dans le choeur du 1er Acte. Und eine neue Welt entspringt auf Gottes Wort – et a la fin jedem Ohre klingend, keiner Zunge fremd. 11[d] Acte. Le trio. Wie viel sind deiner Werke, Gott! Wer?? [*sic*] faßet ihre Zahl – l'air – doch war noch alles nicht vollbracht, dem Ganzen fehlt das Geschöpf – et celui de la création de l'Hom̄e et de la femme, Mit Würd' und Hoheit angethan – le Choeur Zu dir, o Herr, blikt alles auf – du nimmst den Odem weg, in Staub zerfallen sie – IIIe acte Le chant des Anges, et celui des Hommes. – Dich beten Erd und Himmel an – le Duo d'Adam et Eve et la fin. Cependant l'impression du 1er et second Acte fut pour moi tout aussi vive chez Fries, qu'ici avec les 200. musiciens. . . . [Olleson, 58]

Eipeldauer writes:

> In the Theatre this time they gave the famous *Creation* for the benefit of the widows of musicians, and the entrance price was doubled; but it wasn't so full as I would have thought: there must be quite a lot of folk who aren't lovers of double coffee.[1]
>
> [Later he continues in another volume:] On the last Palm Sunday she [my wife] took me with her to *The Creation*, and she did me a great favour thereby, for I could hear that beautiful music another twenty times. But that night in the taproom I met a couple of overseers with their worthy [*gestrengen*] wives from the country; and they didn't seem to like the beautiful *cantati* [*sic*] as much as I had. 'Leave me alone with your *Creation*,' said one of the men to me. 'If I'd known, I'd

1 Coffee-sellers sold 'simple' and 'double' coffee, the double being of a better quality. Pohl III, 161. Eipeldauer, Heft 13 [1800], p. 10; Heft 16, 4th letter, p. 25.

> have stayed home and paid gladly for her [ticket] [*und hätt brandelt dafür*].' 'Oh, you won't get *me* in there again,' said the other. 'That Uriel sticks in my stomach. Hey, Waiter! Give me a quart [*Maßl*] of Erlauer, so I can unstick meself.'
>
> The worthy ladies started to laugh at this conceit, and laughed until their sides shook [*d' Wampen gewackelt hat*]. Finally one of them asked who the gentleman was who wrote the *Cantati*. 'Don't rightly know,' said the other lady, 'but as far as I remember he had something of a Turk or a heathen [Haiden] in his name.'[1]

Eipeldauer is registering two significant facts about this performance (or rather double performance) of the Oratorio: (1) it was not full; (2) people were beginning to speak out against the work. In a word, the Viennese were losing interest in their darling. In the light of Eipeldauer's criticism (which must, in Vienna, take the place of daily criticism such as we know from London), the empty hall for the first performance of the Trumpet Concerto a few days earlier begins to form part of a pattern. Yet in the *Pressburger Zeitung* (No. 32, 22 April) we read a long notice of the pair of concerts, which concludes, 'His Majesty not only favoured the academy with his All Highest Presence, but he also presented the Society a substantial sum of grace-and-favour. Also H.R.H. Duke Albert [of Sachsen-Teschen], although His Highness was absent, gave generously to the Society.' Haydn's fears that the doubled price would keep people away were more than founded; with his uncanny instinct for the *vox populi*, Haydn was the first to register the beginning of his own decline in popularity.

On 6 April Griesinger wrote to Breitkopf & Härtel about the reception of the diamond ring that the Leipzig firm had sent Haydn:

> The venerable Father Haydn will not admit that he has earned anything from you, and he was delighted and embarrassed about your courteous and generous present. 'Tell the gentlemen, Breitkopf & Härtel, that they've touched my weak spot; I'm like a child; presents of this sort are much more pleasant for me than great sums of money. I shall make it my duty to show myself grateful and as soon as I find the time, I shall send them some music [for the *Oeuvres Complettes*]. . . .
>
> [Olleson, *Griesinger*, 14]

Haydn kept his promise: *vide infra*, 1 July. Meanwhile all this activity once again took its toll, and as in the Summer of 1798, Haydn fell ill, this time of a 'rheumatic fever of the head', and was forced to cancel his conducting of the next performances of *The Creation* at the Palais Schwarzenberg on 12 and 13 April; Weigl, who had played the fortepiano at the first public performance (and was patently a kind of 'assistant conductor'), led these two instead of the composer. Zinzendorf was there for the performance on Easter Sunday, the 13th.: '. . . <u>Passe toute la soirée a entendre la musique de la</u> Création chez P^ce^ Schwarzenb. . . . Ces foules ne m'egayent jamais . . .' (Olleson, 58). Griesinger was also there, and wrote to Leipzig on the 16th, 'I have already heard it [*The Creation*] five times, and could hear it ten times more with pleasure.' (Pohl III, 161.)

Haydn's 'rheumatic fever of the head' turned out to be more serious than at first appeared, and on the 26th Griesinger writes to Breitkopf & Härtel: 'He [Haydn] promises me his composition whenever I see him, but he's not yet ready with it. Don't be annoyed at him, he is not allowed to work much yet, and he can't produce even

1 This pun on Haydn's name is not readily understandable to English-speaking readers. 'Haydn' is pronounced in German just like the word for heathen ('Heiden' or, as Eipeldauer writes in dialect, 'Haiden'); the word 'Turk' was then synonymous for a barbarian (similarly, we used to say, 'a wild Indian').

his genius out of a hat' (Olleson, *Griesinger*, 15). Later Straton wrote to Thomson, apropos Haydn's illness, that 'we were not altogether devoid of alarm in regard to his recovery'. This is the first sign that not only was Haydn doing far too much conducting, but that *The Seasons* was proving very exhausting. His constitution was simply not up to such a pace.

The composer therefore missed the arrival of the great horn virtuoso, Giovanni Punto (Johann Wenzel Stich), for whom Mozart had composed, and who now made great friends with Beethoven. It was for Punto that Beethoven composed the Sonata for horn and fortepiano, Op. 17 (1800). Punto first appears in a soirée given by Prince Lobkowitz on 16 April. Zinzendorf writes: 'De la chez les Lobkowitz d'ou je ne sortis que sur les 1^{hr} après minuit passes . . . Me Frank chanta comme un ange. Punto fit entendre un Solo de cor de chasse. Steubel [Steibelt] traite le clavescin avec une volubilite peu interessante. . . . Apres le souper Mr Steubel joua un jeu d'enfant avec une espece de tambourin . . .' (Zinzendorf *Diary* MS.) Two days later there was a concert at the Kärntnerthortheater, which opened with a 'Große neue Sinfonie von Hr. Haydn, Dr. der Tonkunst', and included the first public performance of Beethoven's Sonata for horn and piano in F with Punto and the composer at the piano; the Sonata was greeted with 'very loud applause'. The two artists then followed Haydn's footsteps to what is now Budapest, where on 7 May they gave an academy as part of the birthday celebrations for Alexandra Pavlovna, wife of the Archduke Palatine Joseph.[1]

On 26 April, Griesinger offered Haydn's Oratorio *The Seven Words* in the choral version for publication to Breitkopf & Härtel, but the firm was not initially interested and at first flatly refused. Three weeks later Griesinger reports: '. . . Haydn was in the best of humour, still convalescent, apologized a thousand times to you and asks for your patience once again; but he assures me that he will certainly not prove unthankful' (Olleson, *Griesinger*, 15).

On 30 April, there was the Viennese première of Cimarosa's *I tracci amanti* (1793) at the Kärntnerthortheater. 'It was not well received,' writes Rosenbaum (81). The taste of the Viennese had now changed away from Italian opera – not permanently, for it was to swing back, much to Beethoven's and his followers' disgust, to Rossini in less than twenty years. But even the professionally secure Italian operas by a Cimarosa or a Paisiello could not disguise their thin and primitive orchestration and their threadbare forms compared to the glories of late Mozart, late Haydn and early Beethoven.

On 3 May, Artaria brought out the first three String Quartets of Haydn's famous Op. 20, dedicated to Nicolaus Zmeskall von Domanowecz. The announcement in the *Weiner Zeitung* of this revised edition ('Édition révue corrigée' on title page) reads:

> We believe that we perform no mean service to friends and connoisseurs of the Art, when we announce this valuable product of Haydn's earlier muse in the present edition. By its coming from the hand of, and under the direction of, the composer, it is not only freed from the many copyists' errors which made it almost useless, but also corrected by the addition of such marks as are necessary to its correct execution and concern the dynamic gradations of strong and weak, bowing marks, etc. Thus it would be hard to find such correctness in any other work.

1 On Punto see the sensitive writing of Horace Fitzpatrick: *The Horn & Horn-Playing and the Austro-Bohemian tradition 1680–1830*, London 1970, especially pp. 168ff. On Punto and Beethoven, see Landon *Beethoven*, 132ff. Punto's portrait, engraved by Miger from a drawing by Cochin the Younger, is reproduced both in Landon (p. 162) as well as Fitzpatrick, facing p. 139.

When the next three Quartets of Op. 20 appeared in April 1801, they were announced in *WZ* on 8 April, with the note: '. . . This edition is now the one and only which in its whole authenticity can be said to exist (since the work comes directly from its composer).'

The publishing history of Op. 20 is typical of many works by Haydn of the early 1770s, especially symphonies. The Quartets were composed in 1772, and were printed about two years later by Chevardière in Paris from a copy which they probably obtained from Vienna (but not from the composer). The Chevardière print is full of mistakes, and many of these mistakes continued right down to Pleyel's reprint of the complete Haydn quartets which he began at the end of the century. The autographs survived, and are now in the Gesellschaft der Musikfreunde, Vienna, from Johannes Brahms' legacy; but it is quite clear that when Haydn was preparing the new corrected Artaria edition, he did not own these autographs any longer and was forced to correct whatever kind of texts were circulating round Vienna at the turn of the century. Thus Haydn's revisions, while well meant, lack the one crucial textual factor which even his memory could not supplant after an interval of nearly thirty years – the autograph. As a result, the Artaria editions, although better than most others of the period, and certainly 'passed through the press' by Haydn, are not really authentic. Another problem also arises: in 1772 Haydn had a different style and a totally different attitude towards music, and when he came to revise this music in 1799 and 1800, he simply changed much of the phrasing and dynamic marks to conform with the vastly changed taste of the incoming nineteenth century. Nowadays we prefer to have Haydn's works of 1772 phrased, etc., as they were composed, not with the early Empire polish that Haydn gave the music twenty-seven and twenty-eight years later (allowing, in our time schedule, for several months' gap between Haydn's submission of the MSS. and Artaria's publication thereof).[1]

On 11 May, Ascension Day, there was a large church service at Eisenstadt. *Klaviermeister* Fuchs later (24 May) submitted a bill for the musicians' 'Kost-Dieten und Quartiergelder' (their *per diem* and lodging expenses) and travelling expenses from Vienna to Eisenstadt and back for 117 fl 30 × [Kreutzer]. The musicians included two horn players, a flautist, a bassoon player and a 'Violonist' (double bass player). As we happen to know, Haydn was still not well enough to go to Eisenstadt, and that is probably why the bill was submitted by Fuchs.[2]

We have no idea what kind of work was played on that Thursday, but possibly it was not even by Haydn. The Eisenstadt Archives own copies of a large Mass by Antonio Salieri, composed in 1799 'a doppio coro in ripieno' with an orchestra the wind part of which included two oboes, two bassoons, four trumpets, three trombones, timpani. To this Mass in C belong, apparently, a Graduale in D major 'Liberasti nos, Domine' (1799) for the same orchestration, another Graduale in C, 'Venite gentes' (1799), and/or an Offertorium in C, 'Cantate Domino omnis terra' (1799), of which Eisenstadt owns copies. The Offertorium 'a 4 in coro doppio' has only oboes, bassoons, two trumpets and timpani, while the Graduale 'Venite gentes', 'a 4 in coro doppio', has the scoring of the mass without trombones. The D major Graduale was intended for a specific purpose, 'pro Domenica 23 et ult. post Pentecostem'. It is

1 We remember László Somfai's brilliant lecture about Op. 20 at Duke University in 1969, where this problem of autograph *versus* Artaria was discussed and illustrated. For further textual points, see the new critical edition of Op. 20 prepared by Reginald Barrett-Ayres for Doblinger Verlag, as part of the series of the complete Haydn string quartets, issued for the first time from authentic sources.

2 Pohl III, 166; and further information from Dr Janos Harich, Vienna.

obviously no accident that all these works by Salieri, composed at Vienna in 1799, found their way to the *Schloßchor* at Eisenstadt.[1] It is natural to expect that Prince Nicolaus Esterházy was anxious to hear the latest church music. Now that he had his own regular band of strings, voices, organ and six 'Harmonie Individuen' (wind players), with the three trumpets and drums, and could recruit players not only from Vienna but also – and this is suspicious in view of the heavy trumpet-scoring of the Salieri Mass and other works – four trumpets and drums from the Eisenstadt *Thurnermeister* with his apprentices, he could mount quite large-scale pieces of church music. Later in the year we shall note that on St Mary's Day these four trumpeters and a kettledrummer came and played twice.

As we said, Haydn was still convalescing in Vienna. On Ascension Day he wrote to a friend in Berlin:[2]

> [*German*]
> My most esteemed Friend!
>
> I am most obliged to you for the 9 gold ducats you sent me (it is A RARITY for us Viennese to see gold coins) – I probably can't expect such from the Count von Brühl,[3] but meanwhile you might remind His Excellency, so that by degrees I can retrieve my large expenses.
>
> The 3 copies of the piano score you asked for will be sent from here on this coming Wednesday. It's true about the 4 *Seasons*; just now I am working on the 'Summer' and hope, despite the fact that I was very ill recently, that I can finish it by the end of the coming Winter. But if such a difficult task should not prove successful, every connoisseur of music will understand the reason why.
>
> The retail price of the score of *The Creation* is the same as the subscription price. As often as you speak our Naumann,[4] I envy you his friendship; perhaps I shall be able to see him before I die. Meanwhile I am, most respectfully,
>
> Dearest Friend,
> Your most sincere servant,
> Jos. Haydn.
>
> Vienna, 11th May 1800.
>
> [No address; on the cover someone has written the date of receipt: 'Praessent. Berlin/ den 23sten Mai'.] [CCLN, 169]

Silverstolpe had meanwhile secured a collaborator for the Swedish translation of *The Creation*: Count De la Gardie, who translated the first part and some of the rest, and even paid for the printing of the libretto in Vienna by the well-known Mathias Andreas Schmidt (copy at Näs Castle among Silverstolpe's effects). Silverstolpe sent the Swedish and the German original to his father and asked his family to be gentle with him since no Viennese printer had ever tackled a Swedish book before.

1 Rudolph Angermüller and Rudolf Ofner, 'Aspekte Salierischer Kirchenmusik', in *Mitteilungen der Internationalen Stiftung Mozarteum*, 21. Jhrg., Heft 1/2 (February 1973), pp. 1–18.
2 Perhaps the music publisher J. J. Hummel, with whom Haydn had been in contact often before, and who probably ordered the work to which Haydn refers after it had been printed (therefore his name is absent from the subscribers' list); at any rate, the recipient seems to have been a music publisher.
3 See *supra*, 10 August 1799.
4 Johann Gottlieb Naumann (1741–1801). Haydn went all the way to Dresden on his return from England in 1795, to see Naumann, but found him away. See also letter to Naumann's widow of 22 September 1802. Dies (159) notes: '. . . In Dresden he visited Naumann, but found he was not at home. A chamber maid was in the process of dusting the room. Haydn asked if there were not a portrait of Naumann, and upon hearing the affirmative, he had himself taken there so that he could make Naumann's acquaintance at least *via* a picture.'

23 May 1800. . . . I forgot to inform you that the recitatives in the Swedish translation are somewhat changed, but Haydn himself looked them through carefully and approved of them. Such changes have to be undertaken in each and every language, and in the English text Haydn did them himself, but such a procedure does not introduce any change into the modulations or the harmony. . . . [Mörner, 354]

Luigia Polzelli, Haydn's ex-mistress, had at one time extracted a promise from Haydn to marry her as soon as he and she were free (see *Haydn in England 1791–1795*, pp. 95f.). Now that Frau Haydn had died, Luigia actually managed to extract the following promise in writing from the good-natured Haydn:

[Statement to Luigia Polzelli. *Italian*]

I, the undersigned, promise to *Signora* Loisa Polzelli (in case I should consider marrying again) to take no wife other than said Loisa Polzelli, and should I remain a widower, I promise said Polzelli to leave her, after my death, a pension for life of three hundred gulden (in figures, 300 fl.) in Viennese currency. Valid before any judge, I herewith set my hand and seal,

Joseph Haydn
Maestro di Capella di S. Alt. il Principe Esterhazy.
[Haydn's seal]

Vienna, 23rd May 1800. [CCLN, 169]

Haydn was no longer in the least interested in marrying the olive-skinned Italian soubrette whom he had loved in the decade 1780–90 at Eszterháza. He was quite content to remain single, and with a few more letters to *la* Polzelli sending her money (see *infra*, 2 August), she fades quietly out of Haydn's life: for having extracted this promise, she was still free to marry, which she proceeded to do, leaving for Italy with her new husband, Luigi Franchi, a singer.[1] Haydn who always expected Luigia to remarry – he had written from London to ask her to tell him the name of the one 'who is fortunate enough to have you' (CCLN, 126) – was probably not sorry to see the last of her. He did not forget her in his will, but reduced the amount of money.

On 11 June Joseph Carl Rosenbaum finally married his girl, Therese Gassmann. The saga of that marriage is closely connected with Prince Esterházy who, as will be remembered (*supra*, 29 July 1799) finally gave his permission for Rosenbaum to marry. Rosenbaum's shock and surprise on 30 January 1800 can be imagined: '. . . went to the Prince and spoke about my marriage; the Prince was furious at reading in the petition that he had given me his promise, denied it and set up a violent hue and cry' (73). Rosenbaum, very dejected, returned to the princely house after lunch and found the following letter with the princely seal on it, which he quotes verbatim:

'189. The supplicant's petition to marry is hereby dropped; he is free, however, to conclude the preparations already made by proceeding directly to marry, which step will have as a consequence his immediate dismissal from service. Ex Secretariate . . . Principatus Esterhazyani. Vienna 30 Jannuai 1800. Ad Mandatum luce Celsitudinis Joannes Burgerth mp Secretarius.'. . . . I so little suspected such a thing: I so much deserved better treatment. . . .

[Radant *Rosenbaum*, 73]

1 Pohl II, 93.

Rosenbaum set every wheel in motion: counts, countesses, Princess Marie Hermenegild, even the Empress were 'laid under his siege'. The Prince then became even more intolerable and accused Rosenbaum of mismanaging the stable accounts. 'I . . . hurried home . . . to examine my accounts to see what there might be suspicious about them, and found nothing.' To add to his indignation, arrogant under-officials came and made the investigation. 'I was treated in an extremely insulting manner, which drove me into a fury' (pp. 73–5). Rosenbaum was a proud man, too, and he decided to take the consequences and resign; he was sure that Therese's mother was intriguing against him with Prince Nicolaus, and he managed to get a position with Count Carl Esterházy. As late as May 1800, we find Rosenbaum still begging for Prince Esterházy's letter of recommendation which was essential if Rosenbaum were to enter official service. On 5 May 'In the afternoon . . . I went to the princely house, spoke a full hour with the Prince and begged him for a written recommendation. – He was most gracious . . . and offered me a post in Eisenstadt again, which I cannot accept for love of Therese. "Do you still have that juvenile notion in your mind? – What sensible man will run after a woman?"' (81). The whole episode has something so Kafka-like about it that one would be tempted to imagine Esterházy having designs upon Therese Gassmann who, however, married Rosenbaum as a virgin, as he informs us in his Diary (83). On the wedding day, Rosenbaum took his beautiful presents – two diamond earrings and a diamond clip – 'to my darling Therese', and at six o'clock in the evening they were married at the Cathedral of St Stephen; among the witnesses was Antonio Salieri (Radant, *Rosenbaum*, 82f.).

The following letter to Haydn is self-explanatory.

[To Haydn from Joseph Michael Böheim,[1] Berlin. *German*]

Berlin, 16th June 1800.

. . . The writer, despite his profession as an actor, has run a music shop for the past 12 years; the only things missing in his stock are the articles from the Viennese publishers. Haydn should suggest someone with whom he could procure Viennese music. Böheim asks for 12 copies of *The Creation* in pianoforte arrangement, all his newest Quartets, etc. Mentions the first performance of *The Creation* in Berlin, which took place on 7th May 1800. The King had ordered it to be performed for the benefit of Weber,[2] music director at the *Schauspielhaus*; it was then performed twice again upon special request, each time to a full house, and with enormous applause. Böheim also wants good wind-band pieces and small symphonies, for these are in great demand by amateur orchestras, whose forces are suited for works of this kind. . . . [CCLN, 170]

About the middle of June, Haydn delivered thirty-two Scottish airs, harmonized, and with introductory and closing 'symphonies' (ritornelli), to Straton of the British Embassy for shipment to Thomson. Straton sent them on 19 June and adds that they would have been done sooner but 'poor Haydn laboured under so severe an illness during the course of this spring that we were not altogether devoid of alarm in regard to his recovery'.[3]

1 An actor at the Royal National Theatre in Berlin. Haydn turned the letter over to Artaria, which is why it was (is?) still preserved.
2 Bernhard Anselm Weber (1766–1821).
3 See also *supra*, p. 495. Hadden, *Thomson*, 305.

On 1 July Haydn sent a long letter to Gottfried Christoph Härtel in Leipzig, of which a substantial part has fortunately survived:

[To Gottfried Christoph Härtel, Leipzig. *German*]

Vienna, 1st July 1800.

. . . Please forgive an old and busy man who, instead of having written the late-lamented Herr Breitkopf,[1] writes to you, his successor, at this late date to thank you for the precious ring.[2] Dearest Friend! I shall never be unthankful, but I regret that at present I am not capable of serving you with new pianoforte Sonatas. The difficult task which I now have, to compose *The Seasons*, and my weakened physical state do not permit me to work on two things at once; but to show my gratitude, at least in some measure, I will, if it is agreeable to you, send you the full score of *The Seven Words* in the vocal version as soon as possible. You could then publish the work with the vocal parts by Michaelmas, either in piano score, which is already printed without the vocal parts, or in full score, as you see fit. I do not doubt that it will have a good sale, for it is undoubtedly one of my best works, and is not difficult to perform.[3] Meanwhile I send you two little Duets,[4] of which one is especially esteemed by the connoisseurs. As soon as *The Seasons* are finished, I shall serve you before everyone else, by writing a pianoforte Sonata. . . .

Between ourselves, I am really to be pitied that I entrusted my costly *Creation* to the sleepy Herr Artaria, the more so since I let them have the piano score, and some other small things, at no cost. Therefore I should be happy to come to some sort of an arrangement with you in the future, and meanwhile I should like to know, at your convenience, and after you have duly considered the matter, what you think about the entire production of *The Seasons*. . . . [CCLN, 170f.]

The death of Frau Haydn in Baden was still causing the usual legal complications, as the following letter to Haydn's friend, Anton Stoll in Baden, shows:

[To Anton Stoll,[5] Baden. *German*]

Dearest Friend!

Frau von Keller, my sister-in-law, has asked me to send her kind regards to both of you, and to send you the 30 fl. which she has long owed you for the board of her little son;[6] I would only ask you to send a receipt for it at your convenience. I would also ask you to give the enclosed receipt for 59 fl. 6 kr., which I paid to the Lower Austrian Receiver-General's Office,[7] and also the 9 Gulden which I am supposed to pay to the Baden Town Mortuary, to the City Receiver's Office, and to present my respectful compliments to that gentleman. Moreover, I shall not fail to send all the other receipts of the heirs, as soon as they have been paid out in full. Meanwhile I hope that everyone is well, and am,

Dearest Friend,

Your most sincere servant,

Joseph Haydn.

Vienna, 7th July 1800. [CCLN, 171f.]

1 Christoph Gottlob Breitkopf had died on 7 April 1800.

2 The ring that had been sent to Haydn; *vide supra*, p. 548.

3 Breitkopf & Härtel were not at first very anxious to publish the work, but then changed their minds. See Härtel's letter of 18 July, *infra*.

4 The Italian Duets, for soprano, tenor and piano (1796) on words by Badini: 'Guarda qui, che lo vedrai' and 'Saper vorrei se m'ami'. Breitkopf printed them in *Cahier* 8 of the *Oeuvres Complettes*.

5 See *supra*, p. 543.

6 His father was Joseph Keller.

7 Bills connected with Frau Haydn's death.

Härtel now wrote a very courteous letter to Haydn, accepting *The Seven Words* for publication:

[To Haydn from Gottfried Christoph Härtel, Leipzig. *German*]

Leipzig, 18th July 1800.

To Herr J. Haydn, Vienna.

Concerning your admirable music to *The Seven Words*, which every connoisseur considers a masterpiece, it is true that the instrumental version is already generally known, but my firm would nevertheless consider it an honour to publish this work in a correct score; for with the added vocal parts it will appear like a new work to its admirers, and will thus be the more interesting for them.

I presume that you would rather see it appear in score, and am therefore prepared to print it in its entirety, just as I receive it from you; I await only the manuscript so that I may begin with the publication. As far as my part of the transaction is concerned, this remains to be fulfilled, and I shall expect your terms. If, on the other hand, you should want me to make a proposal, I should have to admit, with a certain embarrassment, that my offer would by no means approximate to the high value of this work; but perhaps I may ask if – in view of the fact that I cannot set too high a price on this work if it is to achieve the proper distribution and recognition – you would be willing to accept 50 ducats as a token of our good will in this matter.[1] [Gottfried Christoph Härtel]

[CCLN, 172]

Härtel also wrote to Griesinger, who answered on 30 July:

. . . Haydn is now in Eisenstadt and won't be back here for two months. . . . The news that you will put *The Seven Words* into your catalogue will please him. As I wrote you already, you could have satisfied him with a smaller fee, and he hardly will expect that much. Since the work is supposed to appear before the Michaelis Fair, and Haydn certainly won't have it with him in Eisenstadt, I will write him a letter in order that he will make haste to let you have it . . .

[Olleson, *Griesinger*, 15]

The following three letters are self-explanatory:

[To Luigia Polzelli, Vienna (?). *Italian, 'Tu' form*]

Eisenstadt, 2nd August 1800.

. . . Up to now I have felt ill the whole time, and today is the first day that I am better; but in a little while I hope to be cured completely. . . . I shall answer your letter in a few days, and meanwhile I send you 15 fl. to pay the rent of your house. . . .

Your sincere and faithful friend,
Giuseppe Haydn. [CCLN, 172]

[To Georg Helbig,[2] Vienna. *German*]

Eisenstadt, 3rd August 1800.

Well born and respected Sir!

Since at present my many affairs of business do not permit my going to Vienna myself, I would ask you to pay out to the bearer of this letter, my copyist,

1 Haydn accepted the sum because, as Griesinger reported, 'he wants to return the many favours with at least one of his own.' (Hase, pp. 42f.) Haydn later signed the foreword which Griesinger, using information which the composer had given him, drafted (March 1801).

2 Georg Helbig a manufacturer of musical instruments. Almost nothing is known about him. On this day, Haydn wrote a receipt 'Eisenstadt den 3ten August 1800' signed 'Joseph Haydn. Fürst. Esterhazischer Capell Meister', which was sold by Henrici and Liepmannsohn at Berlin (Auk.-Kat. LXXVI, Berlin 1922, item 282) and probably has to do with Helbig.

this small bill in the amount of 37 fl. 30 × [Kreuzer] which is made out to you. He will give you a receipt for it at once. I hope to have the opportunity of making your personal acquaintance and remain, meanwhile, with every esteem, Sir,

Your most obedient servant,
Jos: Haydn.

[Address:] An den Wohl Edlen Herrn
Georg Helbig bürgerlichen Instrumenten Macher
in
Wienn. [CCLN, 173]

[To Artaria & Co., Vienna. *German*]

Eisenstadt, 11th August 1800.

Messieurs!

I would ask you please to read through the enclosed letter from Herr Lehritter[1] in Würzburg, and to send him the missing pages[2] as soon as possible. By the way, I would like to know the address of Herr Georg Helbig, *bürgerlicher*[3] instrument-maker, and if possible to deliver to him the enclosed letter[4] and a receipt for monies received in the amount of 37fl. 30 kr., and to send the receipt down to me through our Princely porter, Mayer. As always I remain

Your most indebted servant
Joseph Haydn. [CCLN, 173]

Haydn was now dealing directly with Muzio Clementi, who was one of the partners in the former firm of Longman & Broderip. We read:

[To Artaria & Co., Vienna. *German*]

Eisenstadt, 22nd August 1800.

Messieurs!

Yesterday I received a letter of 16th July from Herr Clementi in London, in which I read to my surprise that the copies of my *Creation* had not arrived there. I would ask you urgently to ascertain the reason for the delay, for they were dispatched more than 3 months ago. Because of this delay, I am in danger of losing two thousand Gulden, because Herr Clementi has already published the work himself.

Please write if you really have not received any confirmation of its arrival there. Meanwhile I remain, *Messieurs*,

Your most obedient servant,
Jos. Haydn.

[Pohl notes on his MS. copy – the earliest preserved source – 'Address as usual'.]
[CCLN, 173f.]

A few days later Haydn sent another pupil, Johann Spech,[5] into the world:

1 Or Leshritter, as in Haydn's MS. subscription list to *The Creation*.

2 An imperfect copy of *The Creation*.

3 Literally: 'bourgeois', i.e. not an 'Imperial and Royal' instrument-maker.

4 See the previous letter. Obviously Haydn's copyist, Johann Elssler, could not go to Vienna, and Haydn therefore asked Artaria to get the money instead.

5 Johann Spech was born in Pressburg about 1768, studied law and then, following the advice of his friend Count Leopold Nadasdy (with whom he is buried in the family vault at Oberlimbach [Felsö-Lerdya]), devoted himself entirely to music. After leaving Haydn, he went to Paris and studied for four years at the Conservatoire there. Upon his return to Hungary, he devoted himself to the reform of church music; he died in 1836. His great-great-grandson, *Studienprofessor* F. Boccali of Kempten in the Allgäu, owned this testimonial in 1958, when we photographed it for CCLN; the original is now owned by the Professor's son, M. F. J. Boccali, Jr., St. Hilaire Station, Quebec. See also *MGG* article on Spech (Erwin Major) and Renate Federhofer-Königs, 'Neues zur Lebensgeschichte von Johann Spech', *Musikforschung* XVIII (1965), Heft 4, pp. 414f.

[Certificate for Johann Spech. *German*]
I, the undersigned, acknowledge and certify that my pupil Herr Johan [*sic*] Spech, under my direction and supervision, has mastered advanced composition, and consequently everything which concerns the vocal and instrumental branches; I further certify that he has made sufficient progress therein to enable him to preside over any music school, not only as director but also as a teacher of pianoforte and organ. I herewith testify to this.

Eisenstadt, 28th August 1800

Joseph Haydn [m.p] ria,
Capell Meister to Prince Esterházy.
[CCLN, 174]

On 1 September, while Haydn was still at Eisenstadt, we find his name as a witness to the marriage in Vienna of his niece, Barbara Scheiger, and the *Magistratsdiener* (city government official) Franz Xaver Disenni; from the wording of the document,[1] Haydn must clearly have signed it *in absentia* or in anticipation before he left the city. In a letter to Artaria, we learn several interesting new facts about Haydn's life:

[To Artaria & Co., Vienna. *German*]

Eisenstadt, 3rd September 1800.

Messieurs!

Forgive me for bothering you once again. From the enclosed letter of my pupil Pleyel,[2] you will see that I cannot, in such critical times, procure for him the passport he requires from the Foreign Office [*Stadts Canzley*] – especially now, when the name-day of my Princess renders it impossible for me to go to Vienna, not to speak of Dresden. But I want to oblige him about my portrait, and so I would ask you, gentlemen, to send to Dresden, in my name, a pull of the very good portrait[3] which I saw at your office last time, and which is perhaps published by now. He will copy and publish it in a reduced size with the Quartets.[4] I shall pay the costs at the earliest opportunity. In the hope of your complying with this request, I am, *Messieurs*, most respectfully,

Your most obedient servant,
Joseph Haydn.

P.S. Two days after I received your last letter, I heard from Herr Clementi that the first hundred copies had arrived in London at last. N. B. If you are able and willing, Gentlemen, to go to the trouble of procuring that passport for Herr Pleyel from the Foreign Office, you will greatly oblige us both. I hope for a few lines about this. One more thing. My Princess, who has just arrived from Vienna, tells me that Mylady Hammelton [*sic*] is coming to Eisenstadt on the 6th of this month, when she wishes to sing my Cantata *Arianna a Naxos*; but I don't own it, and would therefore ask you to procure it as soon as possible and send it here to me.

[Address:] Monsieur
Monsieur Artaria et Compag a VIENNE.

1 The signature reads: 'Joseph Haydn fürstl. Esterhazischer Capell Meister als Beystand'. The document was sold by V. A. Heck's (cat. 42, April 1928, item 57). Haydn left his niece 300 gulden in his first Will.

2 Pleyel had meanwhile become a successful Parisian publisher and a French citizen. The Parisians intended to perform *The Creation* in the Grand Opéra, and Pleyel was supposed to persuade Haydn to go to Paris and conduct the performance personally. From Hamburg he wrote to Artaria on 19th August (in French!), asking them to forward letters for Haydn and Pichl, and announcing his arrival in Vienna. He must have asked Haydn to get him a passport. But neither Haydn nor Artaria could procure it, and Pleyel only got as far as Dresden. (Artaria-Botstiber, pp. 81f.)

3 Probably that engraved by J. Neidl after the Zitterer portrait: it is certainly not a 'very good portrait'.

4 Pleyel was preparing a collected edition of Haydn's quartets in parts.

[Artaria's clerk notes: 'Haydn / Eisenstadt 3rd Sept. 1800 / received 5th ditto / answered 5th ditto'.] [CCLN, 174f.]

On the same day, Haydn also wrote to his leader of *The Creation* band:

[To Paul Wranizky, Vienna. *German*]

Eisenstadt, 3rd September 1800.

Dearest and most highly-honoured Friend!

Much as I have tried to help everyone all my life long, I can only very unwillingly give my consent to this performance, for a work of this kind is not at all suitable for the place.[1] With your own profound insight you will surely understand my refusal; nevertheless, one could surely help poor Neuherz[2] a little if all the musicians in Vienna were to combine forces to assist him. But since I cannot be present at this proposed benefit concert, I take the liberty of sending him the enclosed bank-note for ten f. [Gulden]. I kiss your wife's hands, and remain, my high-honoured Friend, most respectfully,

Your most obedient servant,
Joseph Haydn [m.p] ria.

[Address:] Monsieur
Monsieur Paul Wranitzky
Maitre de la Musique très celèbre
a
Vienne

Enclosing 10 f. [CCLN, 176]

Admiral Nelson, Sir William Hamilton and the famous Emma, Lady Hamilton, arrived in Vienna on their way from Naples to England. Since the trip has been described in some detail in the principal Nelson and Hamilton literature,[3] we have drawn largely on local Viennese sources, most of which will be unknown to Nelson scholars. The trio arrived in the Austrian capital on 18 August; on the 19th they were in the Burgtheater and were greeted enthusiastically by the Viennese (Rosenbaum, 83). On the 23rd Lady Hamilton was given the score of *The Creation* (her copy is in the British Museum).

The Austrians badly needed a war hero. They had been decisively defeated at the historic battle of Marengo on 14 June, while on the German front, General Moreau had advanced along the south bank of the Danube in May and after a series of defeats the French reached Munich at the end of June. On 15 July was signed the armistice of Parsdorf. The Germans and Austrians were distinctly war-weary and many of them sympathized secretly with Napoleon and his new ideas, particularly the younger generation. When Napoleon entered Milan on 17 June, 'some Hungarian grenadiers and German prisoners passing by, who had already been prisoners in the campaigns of

1 Apparently Wranizky suggested that one of Haydn's operas or oratorios be performed.

2 Possibly Naucharz (Nohl's reading). In Rosenbaum's Diary (28 August 1800 – Radant, p. 84), a musician 'Neunherz' is mentioned.

3 *Inter alia* in Carola Oman's standard biography, *Nelson* (London 1947), especially pp. 394–6; in Walter Sichel's brilliant biography, *Emma Lady Hamilton* (London 1905, revised and corrected in 1905 and 1907 [Third Edition, here used]); and in the unsatisfactory biography, *Sir William Hamilton*, by Brian Fothergill (London 1969). The English publisher Robert Birchall had a go-between in Vienna named F. Oliver, who helped Leopold Koželuch sell his compositions in England. On 25 August we find Oliver telling Birchall that he had 'the pleasure to introduce Mr. Kozeluck [*sic*] to teach Lady Hamilton, who sings like an Angel & is a Queen in every respect.' (Christa Flamm, op. cit., p. 80). See also O. E. Deutsch, 'Haydn und Nelson', in *Die Musik* XXIV/6 (March 1932), 436–40.

1796 and 1797, recognized the First Consul. Many began to shout, with apparent enthusiasm, "Vive Bonaparte" '[1]. Anonymous pamphlets were printed, encouraging the German-speaking people to fight. One of them, entitled *Was ist besser, Krieg oder Frieden mit den Franzosen?* (dated 1800, no *impressum*), suggests that total war was the only possibility. 'I call you with a loud voice, boldly and with the utmost conviction: *war, forceful, decisive war* is and remains our only way of salvation' (p. 51). But the Germans, and even more the Austrians, remained apathetic at best to a war which Napoleon seemed constantly to win.

Thus Nelson was greeted with a frenzy amounting almost to hysteria on his trip through Austria, Bohemia and Germany in the autumn of 1800. They called him 'the Saviour and Deliverer of Europe'[2] and in the *Pressburger Zeitung* of 25 February 1800 – months before Nelson set off on his return trip – we read: 'Vienna, 22 February. Our ladies appear most frequently this winter in a kind of black cape [*Überschlag*], which however only reaches the calf and is adorned with gay borders or edges. They are called Nelsons.' People may not have felt, as did one of Osbert Sitwell's ancestors, that Napoleon was a 'modern Attila':

> Then Europe's sun is set in endless night –
> Then Faith, then Honour, wing their hasty flight –
> Then all the Ties of social life are o'er,
> From Moscow's snows, to fair Ausonias shore –
> Then Gothic Darkness spreads its baleful shade –
> Then Art, then Learning, Laws and Freedom fade![3]

But they were all in general agreement that Horatio Nelson was the Allies' best piece of propaganda.

They were less enthusiastic about Lady Hamilton, especially British citizens. Lord Minto, the British Ambassador to the Court of Vienna, wrote to his wife:

> [Nelson] does not seem at all conscious of the sort of discredit he has fallen into, or the cause of it, for he writes still, not wisely, about Lady Hamilton and all that. But it is hard to condemn and use ill a hero, as he is in his own element, for being foolish about a woman who has art enough to make fools of many wiser than an admiral. . . . He is devoted [writes Minto in a later letter] to Emma; he thinks her quite an angel, and talks of her as such to her face and behind her back, and she leads him about like a keeper with a bear . . . he is a gig from ribands, orders, and stars.[4]

Zinzendorf was introduced to Nelson on 24 August: 'Après 11^h. au Cercle pour la reine de Naples. J'y fit la conoissance de Nelson, dont la figure n'est pas si mal.' He noted that Sir William 'tient son chapeau' and added, with unusual nastiness, 'Lady Minto, horrible figure de femme, vielle laide . . .' (Zinzendorf *Diary*, MS.). About Emma Hamilton, the British have frequently been unable to preserve any sense of proportion, but that she was a fascinating woman even her enemies have sometimes been forced to admit. When she returned to England, Farington noted: 'She is bold & unguarded in her manner, is grown fat, & drinks freely.' Later he wrote: 'Lady

1 *The Corsican,* op. cit., p. 140.
2 Letter of Levett Hanson to Nelson, Hamburg, 29 September 1802, sold by Sotheby's on 6 February 1973 (Catalogue, p. 55, item 276, with extensive quotations).
3 *Address to the People of Great Britain*, by W. J. Denison, Esq., London 1803, quoted in Osbert Sitwell, *Left Hand, Right Hand*, London 1945, p. 57.
4 *Life and Letters of* [Lord Minto], *Sir Gilbert Elliot, 1st Earl of Minto, from 1751 to 1806.*, edited by the Countess of Minto, 3 vols., London 1874, III, 114, 117.

Hamilton is grown prodigiously large & exposed her fat shoulders & breast manifestly having the appearance of one of the Bacchantes of Rubens.'[1]

Silverstolpe, in a letter of 20 September 1800, gives us an interesting description not only of Nelson but also of Emma:

> [Nelson] is thin, without fire in his glance, speaks seldom or not at all, and is considered a complete *Rustre* in company. But I also find that he looks like an intellectual, which he never was. He knows no other language but his own . . . [Lady Hamilton] has *facons* with him as if he were her first *domestique* . . . At the theatre he turns his back to the stage to look into the eyes of his lady-love. . . .
>
> Míladi [*sic*] Hammilton [*sic*], once considered the most beautiful woman in Europe . . . wears the Maltese Cross so that she now has all the titles that can impress people. . . . She is now forty-six and the fattest woman I've ever laid eyes on, but with the most beautiful head. A voice such as hers excelled all my expectations and I don't think I shall ever again hear anything so heavenly. In her are combined voice as well as method, sensitivity and musical knowledge, so as to bewitch the listener. [Mörner, 359]

Nelson and his party (which apart from the Hamiltons also included Cornelia Knight and Emma Hamilton's mother, Mrs Cadogan) arrived at Eisenstadt on 6 September and stayed four days. All the reports mention that four concerts were given, and that the grenadiers were six feet high, but no details are given. Robert Southey tells us:[2] 'Public honours, and yet more gratifying testimonials of public admiration awaited Nelson wherever he went. The Prince of Esterházy entertained him in a style of Hungarian magnificence, a hundred grenadiers, each six feet in height, constantly waiting at table.' J. C. Jeaffreson writes:[3]

> . . . During the four days of their splendid entertainment at Eisenstadt by the Prince and Princess Esterhazy, the triumphal tourists feasted daily at a table where a hundred grenadiers, the shortest of whom was six feet high, acted as servitors. The concerts and balls equalled the cost and effectiveness. One of the four concerts was directed by Haydn, and at another of them the Prince's famous maestro di Capella is said to have produced his oratorio of 'The Creation'.

One of the British guests at Eisenstadt was Lord Fitzharris, who provides the only authentic, first-hand account of the festivities.

> Sunday [7 September], grand fireworks. Monday (the *jour de fête* [Princess Marie's name-day]), a very good ball. And yesterday, the *chasse*. Nelson and the Hamiltons were there. We never sat down to supper or dinner less than sixty or seventy persons, in a fine hall superbly illuminated; in short, the whole in a most princely style. Nelson's health was drunk with flourish of trumpets and firing of cannon. Lady Hamilton is, without exception, the most coarse, ill-mannered, disagreeable woman we met with. The Princess with great kindness had got a number of musicians, and the famous Haydn, who is in their service, to play, knowing Lady H. was fond of music. Instead of attending tc them, she sat down to the faro table, played Nelson's cards for him, and won between £300 and £400. . . .

Walter Sichel, from whose book *Emma Lady Hamilton* (op. cit., 332f.) this quotation is taken, wonders if Emma Hamilton won the vast sum of money from Fitzharris

1 Farington I, 307; II, 275.
2 Robert Southey, *Life of Nelson*, London 1813, II, 87.
3 J. C. Jeaffreson, *Lady Hamilton and Lord Nelson*, 2 vols., London 1888, II, 172.

himself: 'he may have lost his money in this encounter and, possibly, his temper.' The quotation is typical of the rage with which Emma has inspired the English; it is also typical, alas, of a dubious sense of justice and regard for truth. For in this particular case, we have a much more reliable witness, namely Haydn, who told Griesinger all about the Nelson-Hamilton visit to Eisenstadt:

> 21 January 1801 . . . H. found a great admirer in Milady Hamilton. She paid a visit, with Nelson, to the Esterházy estates in Hungary but paid little attention to their highnesses and never left H's side for two whole days. H. at that time composed an English song of praise to Nelson and his victory [at Aboukir]. Milady Knight, the Hamilton's companion, wrote the text. Artaria, who heard of it, asked H. to let them have it . . . [Olleson, *Griesinger*, 17]

On 15 September 1798, Miss Knight had written: 'The Battle of the Nile, a Pindarick Ode'; when she arrived in Vienna, she had it printed by Alberti's Widow with a dedication to Sir William Hamilton. Nelson gave a copy to the National Library and signed it. Haydn did not set the whole poem but only parts of it, and with the order changed (Verses 3–5, 8–9, 14, 11, 15, 16, 11), which is why the finished result was entitled 'Lines from the Battle of the Nile' (on the authentic MS., the whole text in Haydn's own hand, in the National Széchényi Library, MS. mus. I. 17[b]). Haydn must have given the autograph to Lady Hamilton, who had it with her after she left Vienna and went to Prague. The Irish widow, Mrs Melesina St. George, 'herself an authoress, musician and beauty' (Oman, 401), accompanied Lady Hamilton (more 'stamped with the manners of her first situation than one would suppose, after having represented Majesty, and lived in good company, for fifteen years', she wrote viciously in her memoirs, which were published by her son in 1862). Mrs St. George heard Emma Hamilton sing the Haydn piece – which the Irish lady only identifies by the author of the libretto, Mrs Knight – at Prague on 8 October, and found Emma's voice good and strong but often out of tune. It is not clear whether Lady Hamilton or Haydn sold the work to Clementi, Banger, Hyde, Collard & Davis, which firm issued it about 1801; the title page notes 'The Music Composed & Dedicated to / *Lady Hamilton* . . .'. The print is an exceptionally fine piece of music publishing, by the way.

Miss Knight's memoirs have this to say about her stay with Nelson and the Hamiltons in Vienna:[1]

> We had often music, as the best composers and performers were happy to be introduced to Sir William and Lady Hamilton. I was much pleased with Haydn. He dined with us, and his conversation was modest and sensible. He set to music some English verses, and, amongst others, part of an ode I had composed after the battle of the Nile, and which was descriptive of the blowing up of L'Orient:
>
> Britannia's leader gives the dread command;
>
> . . .
>
> And their firm bases to their centre rock.
>
> Haydn accompanied Lady Hamilton on the piano when she sang this piece, and the effect was grand. He was staying at that time with Prince Esterhazy, and presided over the famous concerts given by that nobleman at his magnificent palace in Hungary. . . .
>
> . . . it did not appear to me that the English nation was at all popular at Vienna. The people generally were opposed to the war with France, which had proved so unfortunate to them. . . .

1 *The Autobiography of Miss Knight*, ed. Roger Fulford, London 1960, p. 73.

There is, however, even more evidence of Lady Hamilton's visit at Eisenstadt. In British private possession there is a handsome MS. copy by Johann Elssler of Haydn's 'The Spirit's Song'; the owner, William Reeves, kindly sent us a photograph many years ago; on the title page is the following note in Lady Hamilton's bold handwriting: 'given to Lady Hamilton by the most / excellent Haydn at eisenstadt at the / princip Esterházy sept 9th 1800' – the day the British party left Eisenstadt. The song was not yet printed at that time; Haydn must have thought the piece well suited for Emma's voice.

Another striking piece of evidence as to what was performed at Eisenstadt comes from the Esterházy Archives. There are two documents: (1) a receipt, dated Eisenstadt, 28 October 1800, repaying Haydn 12 gulden which he had given to the *Thurnermeister* and his apprentices from the town of Eisenstadt for Mary's Day; on which they performed 'two services consisting of 4 trumpets and a kettledrummer'. (2) Another receipt, written by Haydn, for 'the copying of my Te Deum 6 f 24, received 28 October 1800' (Pohl III, 163, 166). Here we have the first dated notice of Haydn's last *Te Deum* – he had composed an earlier setting in the 1760s – and there is little doubt that the first performance, at least at Eisenstadt, took place on Princess Marie's name-day, 8 September, which was of course the ecclesiastical festival of the Virgin Mary's Birth. St Mary's Sunday followed on the 14th: possibly the *Te Deum* was played on that day, but it seems far more likely that Haydn made this gesture when Nelson was at Eisenstadt. Indeed, he may have used this pretext to satisfy the Empress, who was long expecting the work, and to celebrate the English admiral and his victory at Aboukir. The Eisenstadt parts, with Haydn's corrections and additions, are still extant.

Presumably the 'Nelson' Mass was also played, perhaps on Sunday the 7th, but more likely on Monday the 8th (or the 14th, if the 'two services' refer to that day). It is, no doubt, from this occasion that the work became known under that title, and Brand (315) is quite right in asserting that 'it is all too tempting not to believe that at that time the name "Nelson Mass" appeared'.

From Griesinger we learn that Nelson 'asked for the worn-out pen with which Haydn had written his compositions and in return gave [Haydn] a watch'. It is not clear when Haydn had a chance to dine with the Hamiltons, at which the composer's conversation was reported to be 'modest and sensible'. But in Haydn's effects were found two portraits of Nelson, one by Carl Schütz which Artaria had issued in the autumn of 1798, and also a view of the Battle of Aboukir (P. Peckenham, the engraver, after a drawing by Schütz) which Artaria had published in the spring of 1799. From all the evidence, there can be little doubt that Haydn, too, was captivated by the 'Nelson touch'.

Whether *The Creation* was performed is a matter of debate. It would have been a very large-scale work to mount with Haydn's relatively modest forces at Eisenstadt. But certainly Haydn's music followed the Nelson entourage. When at Laibach, the Philharmonic Society, which was in the process of making Haydn a member (*vide infra*), gave a concert to honour the Admiral, who was on his way to Vienna; the programme opened with the 'Military' Symphony, and Nelson praised the execution (which was by dilettanti). Lady Hamilton included at least three Haydn compositions in her repertoire: the Cantata in her honour, *Arianna* (the Cantata of 1790) and 'The Spirit's Song'. The 'Lines from the "Battle of the Nile"' was Haydn's last composition with English words, a postscript to the English experience which had so changed his life.

Among the illustrious guests at Eisenstadt in September and October was the Emperor Francis himself. Unfortunately our entire knowledge of this visit is confined to the following notice in Zinzendorf's *Diary* (MS.) for 15 October: 'L'Empereur a dit a Eisenstadt les plus belles choses a la P[esse] Marie sur ce que son frère avoit sauvé l'archeduc Jean et l'armée.' It seems slightly odd that the Austrians should be having these elegant celebrations at a time of such military disaster for their armies, but lest it be thought that the festivities were limited to Eisenstadt and the Esterházys, consider the following report on the marriage celebration of Count Fries; it is an unpublished letter written by *Hofrat* Heinrich Gabriel Freiherr von Collenbach (1721–1805) to his niece:

Vienne le 17 Octobre 1800

Je défie toute la puissance magnificence, et galanterie de L'Empire Mahometan de produire des Festins pareils à ceux aux quels je viens d'assister. La visite que la cour d'Autriche et celle de Naple ont bien volu faire au Baron de Braun dans son chateau de Schönau, occasionna les uns, tandis que la célébration des noces du Comte de Fries avec une Princesse de Hohenlohe nos procura les autres. Cependant pour ne pas abuser de votre patience ni de la mienne par une déscription fastidieuse de toutes ces brillantes orgies, je me réstreins à vous dire en gros que ni mes oreilles, ni mes yeux, ni mes gambes, moins encore mon éstomac purent suffire à tout voir, à tout entendre, à tout parcourir et à tout digérer. Carousel, feu d'artifice, illumination, promenades à cheval, en phäeton, en gondole, balle, comédie, mascarade, ballet dance villageoise, serenade, concert instrumental et vocal, des trompétes et des timbales, tout partout et qui reveillerent les echos les plus endormis à dix heure à la ronde: et puis de la prose poetique et des vers prosaïques que nos pauvres d'esprit débiterent à la louages des illustres convives: Ajoutéz encore la réunion des artistes les plus famés de l'Allemagne et de l'Italie qui prodiguerent leurs plus aimables talens dans l'ordonnance de ces fêtes, et vous convienderez ma chere Nièce que pour moi gentil-homme trés rétiré du monde et qui par vocation préfere la moindre petite félicité de la Haut aux plus piquantes jouissances de la bas – un pareil train de vie ne saurait être de saisson; mais, à moins de passer parmit les mondains pour un bourru atrabilaire je me vois dans le cruelle nécessité de devoir suivre les divertissemens terréstres de la societé. Grace au Ciel! c'est fait; me voila de nouveau rentré dans mon hermitage . . . [Autograph, author's collection.]

If all these extravagant festivities in the middle of a disastrous European war on which the Austrians were distinctly on the losing side strikes us as slightly frivolous, it nevertheless illustrates a profoundly Austrian trait of character, reminding one indeed of the old joke about the difference between the Prussians and the Austrians: a disaster for the Prussian is serious but not hopeless, whereas for the Austrian it is hopeless but not serious.

Meanwhile Haydn remained in Eisenstadt and attended to the complicated business of sending copies of *The Creation* abroad; the whole operation of publishing the Oratorio, with which the composer dealt punctiliously, reveals a new side of his nature, or rather it throws into even sharper relief Haydn's sense of neatness and efficiency. His business methods were as precise as his neat scores.

[To Artaria & Co., Vienna. *German*]

Eisenstadt, 6th October 1800.

Messieur! [*sic*]

Please be good enough to send a copy of my *Creation* as soon as possible to M[r]. Silvester in London. The bearer of this letter, a servant [*Cammerdiener*] in the

Princely house, will give you the address. You make me more and more your debtor by your diligent attention, for which I shall always remain

Your most obedient servant,
Joseph Haydn.

[Underneath is the following address, written in pencil by another hand: 'adressate a Noveletti e Bombardoni / per spedirle a Londra: / a Mr. Charles Silvester / Messenger / at Lord Grinvills [*sic*] office / London'.]

[Address:] Monsieur
Monsieur Artaria et Compa[g]
à
Vienne.

[Artaria's clerk notes: 'Haydn/Eisenstadt 6th Oct. 1800/received 8th ditto/answered O'.] [CCLN, 176f.]

[To Artaria & Co., Vienna. *German*]

Eisenstadt, 16th October 1800.

Messieurs,

Yesterday I received the two enclosed letters, of which the small slip, presumably from the House of Arnstein, contains the instruction (as you will see for yourselves) to send a copy [of *The Creation*] to Danzig.[1] In case none has been sent there yet, please do send a copy, packed, with a statement of costs, to the specified office in the Herrngasse. At the same time I should like to know if in the meantime some more copies [of *The Creation*] have been printed or not, and if not, I would ask you once again to press the matter through Baron von Swieten, to whom I send my respects; for yesterday I received a letter from Dr. Burney in London, in which he asks for 40 copies more to be sent to him as soon as possible. In the hope that you will grant my request, I am, most respectfully,

Messieurs,
Your most obedient servant,
Jos: Haydn.

[Address:] Monsieur
Monsieur Artaria et Compag
à
Vienne.

[Artaria's copyist notes: 'Haydn/Eisenstadt 16th Oct. 1800 / received the 17th inst./ answered O'.] [CCLN, 177]

We next learn from the *Pressburger Zeitung* that Haydn went to Eszterháza Castle (which was still being used as a kind of hunting lodge and glorified hotel) at the end of October and the beginning of November, probably to see his protector, the Archduke Palatine Joseph, with whom, as this Chronicle informs us on countless occasions, Haydn was on the best of terms. We read:

Oedenburg, on 10th Nov.

In these days *Herr* Count Joseph von Károlyi, as leader of the Insurrection Troops of the Szathmar and two other districts [*Gespanschaften*], arrived here to wait upon H.R.H. the Archduke Palatine. Also the C.-in-C. of Hungary and General Ordnance Master, Freyherr von Alvinzi, Excellency, has been here for

1 The letters were from one Johann Friedrich Wagner and are dated 1st July and 30th September. The autographs were formerly in possession of Artaria and Co. The Arnsteins directed a famous banking house with branches throughout Europe.

some days. – On the 31st *ult.* there was a grand hare and pheasant hunt at Eszterház, during which H.R.H. the Archduke Palatine was much amused. Her Imperial Highness, the Archduchess Pawlowna amused herself during the hunt in the Princely Castle, where the Princess [Esterházy] knew how to entertain that All Highest with a select concert, which was led by the famous Princely *Kapellmeister* Haydn and rendered magnificent by his performance on the Forte-Piano. . . .

[*Pressburger Zeitung* No. 91, Friday 14 Nov. 1800, kindly photographed for us, from the Budapest copy, by Dr Janos Harich]

This is, possibly, the last time that Haydn and his musicians gave a concert at Eszterháza Castle, which must have been full of ghostly memories for the composer – of his dead Prince Nicolaus I; of his then pretty mistress, Luigia Polzelli; and of countless operas performed at the gaily lighted theatre; of marionette operas; of the Empress Maria Theresa, long dead. Perhaps it was even the last time that Haydn saw Eszterháza, which was soon to become a forgotten rococo castle in the wilderness of the bleak and lonely Hungarian plains on which it stands.

In November Haydn returned to Vienna, in time to take part in a meeting of the Tonkünstler-Societät – the last that the old man took part in, as matters turned out. The protocol informs us that at this meeting, on 14 November, Haydn complained 'that the draught at the performance of the academy is so strong that he catches cold every time'.

On the next day, as the *Wiener Zeitung* (No. 90, 18 November) informs us, *The Creation* was given as a benefit for all the orchestral members of the Marinelli Theater in the Leopoldstadt, and 'no effort or expenses will be spared'. Haydn was present, at least at the rehearsal, for in a letter written the same day (15 November) by Griesinger to Breitkopf & Härtel we learn that 'Haydn was only moderately satisfied with the rehearsal'.

. . . After four months [continues Griesinger] I saw Father Haydn once again yesterday. He is not satisfied with his sojourn in Hungary; the sharp air caused him disturbances and bad humour robbed him of the desire to work. . . .

. . . I am very surprised that he hasn't sent you *The Seven Words* yet, since the whole matter seemed to be close to his heart in the summer. He explained to me that he has in mind next year to travel to Dresden, Berlin, Hamburg and, if there is peace, to France; and in order to perform something that isn't everywhere known, he wants to take with him *The Seven Words* with the vocal parts and *The Four Seasons*. – Since you only undertook the publication of *The Seven Words* out of courtesy, perhaps you won't mind very much that Haydn has changed his mind again. . . . [Olleson, *Griesinger*, 16]

We interrupt Griesinger's long letter – of which we only have extracts, anyway – to insert an important notice regarding the orchestra at Eisenstadt.

At this period, Prince Esterházy found that engaging wind players from Vienna was a rather expensive necessity. He had, as we have seen, firmly engaged three trumpet players and a kettledrummer, who not only played in secular concerts and in the church but also assisted at banquets with fanfares, of which the foregoing Chronicle often told us. Now he re-engaged the Feldharmonie ('Harmonie Individuen') musicians whom he had dismissed after 1797; curiously he did not include bassoons, which meant that Haydn must have considered that he could recruit bassoon players from the local community; yet we find him having to import a bassoon player from Vienna for the music at the castle church on Ascension Day, 1800.

(He had to import a flute player as well.) The six wind players were:

Jakob Hyrtel (oboe)
Joseph Elssler (oboe)
Johann Michel Werlen (Verlen, Varlen, etc.) (clarinet)
Georg Werlen (clarinet)
Anton Prinster (horn)
Michael Prinster (horn)

They were engaged officially from 1 November 1800 and earned 300 gulden per annum each; on 4 December 1800, the 'neu aufgenommenen Chor Harmonie Individuen' each received four fathom-cords [*Klafter*] of wood.[1] Haydn's problems with the wind instruments at Eisenstadt were, from this point, finished. Within a short period, all the missing woodwind players would be firmly engaged.

The following extract from Griesinger's letter of 15 November 1800 suggests that Prince Esterházy did engage eight, not six, players, i.e. including two bassoon players. (Can the bassoonists have been listed, as they sometimes were, among the military units, the *Insurrections-Battalion* or the Company of Grenadiers?)

> Prince Esterh. has enlarged his band by 8 members, so that there is a complete wind band once again – a worthy sacrifice at a time when the war requires such large expenses. . . . [Olleson, *Griesinger*, 16]

On the 17th, Rosenbaum's *Diary* (84) has a curious passage:

> Dull and rainy . . . I went to the Dietrichstein office, I met Th[erese], we went together to the princely house, met Haydn there. He was embarrassed at seeing us but acted quite courteously. . . .

Rosenbaum never explains why Haydn should have been embarrassed, but the reason was probably the old one, namely that Therese Saal was now the regular soprano soloist of *The Creation* and no doubt Haydn and the members of Swieten

1 From the Castle Archives at Eisenstadt. This information was generously furnished by Dr Janos Harich in a letter of 16 October 1972. The dissolution of the 'Feld Harmonie' had meant financial disaster for the members who, being bound to Eisenstadt by various family ties, could not earn enough money in the little town to live properly and were, because of those same family ties, unable to go to Vienna to seek their fortune. On this subject we have the following pathetic letter from the oboist, Joseph Elssler (who always signed his name 'Elsler'), brother of Haydn's valet and copyist Johann and the son of the old copyist Joseph Sen. who had died in 1782. The letter is undated and might be from 1798–9.

> Most Serene Highness! Noble Prince of the Holy Roman Empire!
>
> In the service of Your Serene Highness, I supported my poor old mother, who from Your Highness's great grace and in view of the letter written by *Herr Kapelmeister* [*sic*] Haydn according to whom my father served true and faithfully for eighteen years as copyist, now receives four xr. pension daily, from which sum she can hardly pay for room and wood.
>
> Since the Grenadiers' wind band was dismissed I am without service, and must eke out a precarious existence, and must forgo the one consolation of being able to make the few remaining days of my poor, helpless mother's existence easier to bear because of my small assistance. I beg therefore Your Highness in deepest submission for grace and pity on my poor old mother, to help her small pension only so long until I am again taken into service, though I have no other wish – since according to his own explanation *Herr Kapelmeister* Haydn maintains that an oboist is absolutely necessary in the chapel music – than to enjoy once again the great grace of being in the service of Your Highness.
>
> With the repetition of mine and my old mother's wish I kneel in humble submission and remain in profound respect
>
> Your Highness's
> servant on bended knee
> Joseph Elsler
> Former Oboist. [Valkó II, 612]

Gesellschaft der Associirten had her in mind for the soprano part of *The Seasons*, which must have been three-quarters completed by this time.

Even while in Vienna, there were still routine business matters connected with the Esterházy band:

> [To Prince Nicolaus II Esterházy. *German*]
>
> [October or November 1800]
>
> Since the petition of Gabriel Lendway[1] contains nothing but the complete truth, I can equally truthfully make the obedient request to Your Serene Highness that, in connection with the present enlargement of the orchestra, and since he is a very useful individual, he be engaged in YOUR SERENE HIGHNESS' SERVICE, at a yearly salary of 200 Fl. and the assurance, WHEN THE TIME COMES, of a lodging and SOME firewood; this is in accordance with the two oral resolutions which Your Highness gave me on 1st October 1800.
>
> Joseph Haydn [m.p] ria,
> *Capell Meister* [CCLN, 178]

On 19 November Griesinger again wrote to Leipzig:

> . . . Haydn will not move into town this winter as he usually does but will remain in his house in one of the most remote suburbs. He lives more quietly there but every visit to him is a small journey in itself. 'Even if I have to spend 1 fl. every day for a *Fiaker*' [carriage], he said to me, 'it costs less than having a *pied-à-terre* in town.' Judge the domestic man from this statement. . . .

Haydn did not attend the masked ball at the Redoutensaal for the benefit of the Gesellschaft bildender Künstler at the end of November; but Beethoven did, and received four free tickets. In the large hall the music was by Wenzel Pichl, in the small hall by Ignaz von Seyfried.[2] From this point in our Chronicle, the Redoutensaal event is no longer mentioned; such activities now quietly fade out of Haydn's life.

The Philharmonic Society of Laibach (now Ljubljana, Jugoslavia) asked Haydn to be a member. In a letter, the date of which cannot now be ascertained, but which must have been written about this time, Herr Schmith Jun. wrote to the Society as follows:

> No doubt it will very much please the whole worthy Society to hear that our immortal Haydn so gladly accepted the membership; you will gain new honour from his joining. His words were: 'I acknowledge the honour that the Philharmonic Society in Laibach has bestowed on me by their invitation, and I appreciate it, but I only regret that through my joining it will not have much benefit.' He was very pleased that a native society had so flourished. How proud I was of my home city at this moment! At our request he gave us a new Mass of his composition, for which I paid the copying costs of 12 fl.; he played on the piano and sang most of the beginnings, so that the *Canonicus* could hear not only the various tempi but also on occasion the proper expression, and he in turn will then tell you, *via* the worthy music director, how Haydn wants it; you can teach this to the performing artists, singly and together, especially in all matters of unnecessary ornamentation, which is of no use except to damage such a most delicate composition, since the latter already contains in itself all sorts of expression; and

1 Gabriel Lendvay (or Lendway) had been engaged as a horn player in 1787. In the Esterházy band of 1800 he appears in the list as 'Supernumerarius Gabriel Lendvay'. See Brand, op. cit., p. 318.

2 *Wiener Zeitung* No. 92 of 15 November 1800 (pre-announcement). MS. protocol of the Society in the Archiv der Stadt Wien. The other musicians who received free tickets were Anton Teyber (6), Franz Teyber (2), Lipavsky (4), Henneberg (2), Eibler [Eybler] (3), Süssmayr (2), Koželuch (2), Pichl (18), Seyfried (12), Capoll (3), Hillmayer (3)

the greatest beauty, as you yourself know, only depends on the right tempo, proper shadow and light and exact performance.[1]

The letter is one more proof that Haydn strictly forbade the adding of vocal (and instrumental) ornaments in his late choral works. We do not refer to the obvious use of appoggiature (drops of a third changed into drops of a second, etc.), which Haydn naturally took for granted, but to additions in the 'numbers'. There is a great difference in tradition between early Bellini and Donizetti compared to late Haydn. The two traditions should never be confused, as they sometimes are nowadays.

The Mass that Haydn sent was the *Missa in tempore belli*, which the Laibach Society performed at the Jakobskirche on 28 December 1800. The copy of the Mass is still in the Society's Archives. The *Canonicus* mentioned is Joseph Pinhak; the Laibach conductor was probably Johann Baptist Novak.

The Esterházy band was gradually becoming as fixed an institution as it had been under Prince Nicolaus I. Students of Haydn's life at Eszterháza will remember that the composer often intervened in matters of discipline between the autocratic Prince and the musicians. Now, in 1800, we have another such case.

[To Haydn from Prince Nicolaus II Esterházy. *German*]

To *Herr Kapellmeister* Haidn:

Well born, Dear *Kapellmeister* von Haidn!

Inasmuch as frequent warnings to the violoncellist Mankert[2] have had so little effect that, against the standing orders, without my permission, and without informing you, he has ignored his duties and gone to Vienna, I wish you to remove him permanently from his post, and I also wish you to look for the best possible substitute for his job, concerning which I shall expect your proposal.

Eisenstadt, 10th December 1800.

Exp. Esterhazy. [CCLN, 178]

Haydn seems to have made the appropriate excuses for Manker, for on the 'Personal und Salarial Stand' of 14 July 1801 we find 'Ignatz Manka' listed with one of the highest salaries of all the musicians.[3]

The war with France now reached a point of catastrophe. Having reconquered most of Italy and having occupied Tuscany (against the terms of the armistice), the French drove the Austrians back against her old frontiers; and on 1 January 1801 the Adige was abandoned, followed by the Brenta ten days later. On 15 January 1801 the Austrians signed the armistice of Treviso. Meanwhile matters were even worse on the German front. The Austrians launched a counter-attack against Moreau on 27 November 1800 that culminated in the total disaster of the Battle of Hohenlinden on 3 December, in which the Austrians lost 14,000 men and 80 cannon. Later Moreau collected vast numbers of prisoners. On Christmas Day the Armistice of Steyr (Upper Austria) was signed, by the terms of which the Austrians agreed to sue for peace without Great Britain, who soon found herself totally alone against a hostile or

1 F. Keesbacher, *Die philharmonische Gesellschaft in Laibach seit den Jahre ihrer Gründung 1702 bis zu ihrer letzten Umgestaltung 1862. Eine geschichtliche Skizze*, Laibach 1862, p. 25.

2 Ignaz Manker (in most lists he appears as 'Manka' or 'Manker'), who had been in the band for several years.

3 From a document in the Esterházy Archives made available to us through the former Archivist, Dr Janos Harich.

indifferent Continent. The actual peace treaty was signed between Austria and France at Lunéville on 9 February 1801.

In the midst of these military defeats, French troops poured into the Archbishopric of Salzburg, where Johann Michael Haydn was leading a quiet and fruitful existence. The Archbishop fled the town on 10 December, but he ordered his disbursar to pay all the members of the court three months' salary – a kindly gesture which makes one wonder if Archbishop Colloredo may not have had better qualities than those he displayed *vis-à-vis* Mozart in 1781. On 14 December the French troops arrived at Salzburg, and the next day two French Hussars appeared at Michael Haydn's door, levelled pistols at him and demanded all the household's valuables. Michael lost almost everything of value, including his three months' salary.

Joseph Haydn heard of all this and to make up for the loss of a silver pocket watch he sent a gold watch and a gold snuff-box, and promised money as soon as the dividends on his invested capital came due.[1]

On 11 December 1800 the Viennese court paid a state visit to Eisenstadt. Haydn was on hand to conduct. The *Wiener Zeitung* (No. 103, 24 December) reports:

> December 12th and 13th were festive days for the Royal Hungarian Insurrection Army. On the 11th, Their Majesties the Emperor, the Empress and the Queen of Naples, Their Royal Highnesses the Grand Duke of Tuscany, the Archduke Anton, Prince Leopold and three Princesses of Naples and Duke Albert von Sachsen-Teschen arrived from Vienna in Eisenstadt with their entourage, and stopped at the castle of Prince Esterhazy, where Their Imperial and Royal Highnesses the Archduke Palatine and his Consort arrived that evening from Oedenburg. Moved at this display of favour, the Prince and Princess [Esterházy] mustered all at their command to make the sojourn of their Royal guests as pleasant as possible, and left nothing forgotten. . . . The princely *Kapellmeister*, Joseph Haydn, that artist famed throughout Europe, achieved with his two masterpieces given on that day and the following (the performances of which he himself conducted) the most flattering applause from Their Majesties.

Rosenbaum was in Vienna at the time but on Sunday the 14th we read:

> In the morning we let ourselves be invited to Brandl's, who brought us bacon and green beans from my mother. – He had gone to Eisenstadt on Thursday for the visit to the Prince of the Emperor [etc.] . . . They arrived on Thursday evening, inspected the troops after Mass on Friday, and had music by Haydn and Fuchs in the small hall that evening. . . .
>
> [Radant, *Rosenbaum*, 86]

Haydn received a gold and enamel snuff-box from the Emperor 'and the compliment that the Emperor and Empress take an active part in the applause which he receives from the whole of Europe'. The orchestra was given 100 ducats, the distribution of which was entrusted to Haydn (Pohl III, 167). We have no indication of the works played: possibly the new *Te Deum* for the Empress and, at Mass on Friday, perhaps the new Salieri pieces which we know were acquired by Prince Esterházy (*supra*, p. 550).

On 19 December Silverstolpe went to see Haydn with a proposal to dedicate to him some string quartets by the late Johan Wikmanson, a protégé of Silverstolpe's brother, Gustaf Abraham. He had written from Stockholm on 24 October, asking his

1 Hans Jancik, *Michael Haydn, Ein vergessener Meister*, Vienna 1952, p. 229.

brother to go and see Haydn about the matter and enclosing the scores 'as proof of the works' value'. On 20 December Frederik Samuel wrote to his brother:

> . . . I didn't meet Haydn till yesterday, because he's been in Hungary. Haydn is most flattered by the dedication of the Wikmansson [*sic*] quartets and most generously praised the piece, which I showed him on approval. . . .
>
> [Mörner, 362]

On 22 and 23 December the Tonkünstler-Societät gave their by now customary performances of *The Creation*. No doubt rather tired from the Eisenstadt festivities, Haydn asked Paul Wranizky to conduct, about which the regular conductor of the Society, Joseph Scheidl, was so annoyed that he refused to conduct the other concerts of the Society (Pohl III, 167). There was now a certain danger in the Oratorio's overexposure.[1] Familiarity breeds contempt, and we note even former enthusiasts such as Silverstolpe having second thoughts:

> I am very glad and flattered that you are satisfied with my translation of *The Creation*. I promise you will be delighted when you hear the music. I think a severe critic would object to various things. Aesthetics are not Haydn's strong point, and Kraus would certainly have entertained other views. But nonetheless the listener, if he has any feelings, feels that in this whole work the pure taste is predominant, and that the master often reaches up to Handelian strength. . . .
>
> [Letter of 8 October 1800; Mörner 361]

It must have been about this time that Silverstolpe purchased 'the whole *Seven Words* by Haydn, for piano, as a present for Frau Mozart'; Constanze had invited Silverstolpe to hear what appears to have been a performance of the Mozart Serenade in B flat (K. 361), given after supper at her house (22 January 1800).[2]

An undated letter by Haydn dealing with sending copies of *The Creation* to Braunschweig (Brunswick) has recently come to light. It reads:

> [To August Hartung, Braunschweig. *German*]
>
> Dearest Friend
>
> The most delayed sending of the subscribers' names from England was responsible for this delay. I sent herewith the 7 copies, for yourself, Mess. Aldafeld, Meinek, Schwanberg, Sießtorf, Veltheim, Bierey and am in the greatest haste,
>
> Your most obedient servant Dr. Jos. Haydn mp

1 Even Zinzendorf left after the interval. Part of the trouble was that the French were advancing rapidly towards Vienna. The Count writes:

'A 6h. ½ au théatre pour entendre un Concert de 200. instrumens die Schöpfung von Haydn. Le theatre etoit bien eclairé moyennant le grand lustre. Seul dans ma loge, l'Electeur de Cologne dans la loge de la cour a coté m'appella pour me dire que l'Emp. ait faire avetir toute la famille excepté lui de partir de Vienne. Apres le premier Acte je m'en allois.' [Olleson, 58, and Zinzendorf MS.]

In Rosenbaum's Diary (86f.) we read of the growing panic. On the 23rd, 'everywhere, people are busily packing . . . Moureau [*sic*] will not accept a cease-fire . . . [24th:] Today the proclamation was published, stating that the Emperor himself will lead the army to defend Vienna, to continue peace negotiations and thus bring about this beneficial deed. – Fiat! [25th:] . . . Police decree. All persons not born in Vienna, or who are needless here, must leave Vienna within 3 days . . . Earthworks are being thrown up in front of the Linie.' Theatrical life and concerts went on as usual. The news of the cease-fire signed at Steyr did not reach Vienna until Saturday, 27 December (Rosenbaum: '. . . At about 9 o'clock Archduke Carl arrived at the Imperial Palace. – Immediately afterwards, the news of a 30-day cease-fire began to spread').

2 Mörner, 363: 'Nach Tisch von meinem Manne eine Harmoni musique seyn wird, die Herr von Silberstolpe [*sic*] gewiss nie gehört haben, und die auch nicht länger, als höchstens eine Stunde dauern darf.'

[Address:] S[e] Wohlgeb
Herren August Hartung, Herzogl.
Braunschweigischen Kamer Musicus
in
Braunschweig
[across the page:]
7 Exempl.
Mess: Hartung, Aldafeld, Meinek
Schwanberg, Sießdorf, Veltheim
Bierey

[seal]

NB: they have been paid for.

[Not in CCLN; from the autograph, Lovejoy Library, Southern Illinois University, Edwardsville, Illinois, *ex coll.* Tollefson, Brooklyn, New York.]

We now have a new diarist on the Viennese scene. It was Beda Plank of the great Benedictine Monastery of Kremsmünster in Upper Austria, who with the Abbot Wolfgang II Leuthner and a servant fled from the advancing French troops and arrived in Vienna on 21 December 1800. Being a good musician, Plank's comments on the Viennese scene are invaluable. The Diary was first published in 1956 by the music archivist in Kremsmünster, P. Altman Kellner, O.S.B., in his excellent book, *Musikgeschichte des Stiftes Kremsmünster* (Kassel 1956), pp. 566ff. A week after Beda Plank arrived he met Haydn:

> [Christmas Day, 1800, Mass at 11 o'clock St Peter's] The music there was for singers and instruments *concertante*, I found it *per se* beautiful, but not suitable for the church. [In the evening at 7 o'clock he went to the Redoutensaal (large) to hear Süssymayer's *Der Kampf für den Frieden* . . .]The Music is particularly beautiful: too bad that it did not, in view of the present troubled times, make the expected effect. Here I had the fortune to meet the famous Doctor of Music Herr Joseph Haydn and to have a long talk with him.

From Rosenbaum's Diary (87) we learn that at the performance Therese Gassmann 'sang with rare art . . . during the cantata people were talking of a defeat [Hohenlinden]'. The Cantata was supposed to celebrate 'the observance of the millennium of the Empire'.

As we have observed, theatre and opera still went on in Vienna, but on the 26th, when Therese Gassmann sang at the Burgtheater, it 'was already perceptibly empty' (Radant, *Rosenbaum*, 87).

On Sunday the 28th Beda Plank went to hear a Haydn Mass at St Peter's and wrote in his Diary:

> On Sunday 28 December [1800] I heard High Mass at 10 o'clock . . . in the Michaelspfarrkirche. The well-known Mass by Joseph Haydn in G [*Missa Sancti Nicolai*] was sung in a very quick tempo. The music here, like that in St Peter's, is more comical than sacred. . . . [In the Hofburgkapelle he noted that the vocal parts were quadrupled, the violins six to each section,] but not too loud for this chapel, because the organ loft is low and the chairs for the court over the loft remove something of the free resonance. Here there are no vocal solos, but often instrumental solos, and the very fullness of the vocal section makes the music more festive and noble [*erhabner*].

The quick tempi in Haydn Masses seems to have been a Viennese tradition (but was it Haydn's? – note that Beda Plank, when hearing *The Creation* on 16 January 1801, was surprised to find the authentic tempi slower than those Plank had adopted in Kremsmünster). Sir George Smart, hearing the *Schöpfungsmesse* at St Michael's on Sunday, 11 September 1825, wrote: 'Haydn's Mass was played too fast; Mecchetti, who stood next to us in the church, gave as a reason that the singers would be more exposed if it were played slower – a curious reason enough – but why were not the band, that is the wind instruments, in better time together? The double-bass here had four strings and Mittag said some had five, but with three Dragonetti does more than I have heard' (Smart, 112).

Smart also reports on the Hofburgkapelle, and we learn that in 1825 the size of the orchestra seems to have been the same as that of a quarter of a century earlier:

> . . . Mass, which was a very fine one by Albrechtsberger in the good old style. . . . Mr. Eybler was director and stood at a desk facing the altar. On his right, in two rows, were twelve violins, two viole, two 'celli, and two basses. . . . On the left, close to Eybler, began the row of ten boys, dressed in plain court uniform with the master among them. Behind the boys, on the left, facing the violins, sat ten men in two rows. The boys were most excellent, and infinitely better than ours. The men were good and the performance here was the best I have heard without wind instruments. . . .
>
> [Smart, 113]

THE PROGRESS OF 'THE CREATION'

As soon as the score of *The Creation* appeared and was sent abroad, local first performances took place all over Europe. It is outside the scope of this biography to describe, or even to list, these many performances throughout Germany (in particular) but also in Scandinavia, the Low Countries, Bohemia, Russia, and so on; and we have selected three such premières of special interest: (1) the first series of performances in London, with which, of course, J. P. Salomon was intimately connected; (2) the première in Salzburg, which Michael Haydn conducted; and (3) the spectacular first performance in Paris, which was preceded by a nearly successful attempt on Napoleon's life as he was on his way to the Oratorio.

Salomon had meanwhile forgiven Haydn for having composed a libretto to which Salomon believed he had certain rights, and the two men were in correspondence. As soon as the work was published, Haydn sent off a score to England by normal mail, and being a very heavy score, its weight caused poor Salomon to pay £30 16*s.* postage; but the great impresario was even unluckier, for his rival, John Ashley, had already – one day earlier – received a copy which had been sent to him by the courier of the British Embassy in Vienna, for which, incidentally, he only had to pay £2 12*s.* 6*d.* postage.[1]

Great, therefore, was Salomon's chagrin when the London newspapers began to trumpet forth the first performance of Haydn's new Oratorio conducted by Ashley. Ashley started announcing on 24 March in *The Morning Chronicle*, and on the 25th and 26th (and also later) in *The Times* and *The Morning Herald*:

1 Pohl *H in L*, 315f. Ashley's copy arrived on Saturday, 22 March and was at once copied for 150 performers by Thomas Godwin. Hoboken II, 48.

ORATORIOS, at PLAY-HOUSE PRICES during LENT.
LAST WEEK BUT ONE.
THEATRE ROYAL, COVENT-GARDEN.

On Wednesday next, March 26, will be performed (for the last time this Season), the Sacred Oratorio of

The MESSIAH. [etc., with the performers]. . . .

The Public are respectfully informed that this is the last time the Messiah can possibly be performed this season, Mr. Ashley having obtained from Vienna a Copy of Dr. Haydn's celebrated Oratorio of The Creation, and which will be performed on Friday next. – Doors to be opened at 6, and the Performance to began at 7. . . .

The Morning Chronicle on 26 March also carried the following note:

Among the principal engagements which have given such considerable satisfaction this season, in the performance of the Oratorios, Mrs. Dussek has not only manifested great talents and taste as a singer, but also as a very powerful Performer on the Piano Forte and Pedal Harp; on the latter of which instruments she displays her eminent abilities, this evening, between the Acts of that divine Oratorio of Handel, the Messiah. – The commencement of Haydn's very celebrated Oratorio of the Creation for Friday next; and for which Performance we perceive a copy has been procured from Vienna, has excited much attention through the town.

Salomon had received his copy on 23 March, because the next day he inserted a statement which, in two newspapers, had the misfortune to be placed under Ashley's detailed announcement of the first performance (*The Times, The Morning Chronicle* for 27 March; *The Morning Herald* published Ashley's notice on 27 March and Salomon's on the 29th):

ORATORIOS, at PLAY-HOUSE PRICES during LENT.
LAST NIGHT BUT TWO.
THEATRE ROYAL, COVENT-GARDEN.

TO-MORROW, March 28, will be performed (for the first time), the Sacred Oratorio of

The CREATION. – Composed by Dr. HAYDN.

Principal Vocal Performers, Mrs. Second, Master Elliot, Miss Capper, Miss Tennant, Miss Crosby; Mr. Incledon, Mr. Dignum, Mr. Denman, and Mr. Sale.

Leader of the Band, Mr. G. Ashley, Organ, Mr. J. Ashley.

The whole under the Direction of Mr. Ashley, senr.

Doors to be opened at 6, and the Performance to begin at 7 o'clock precisely. . . .

HAYDN's Celebrated ORATORIO, the CREATION of the WORLD.

MR. SALOMON having received from Dr. Haydn a correct Copy of his New Oratorio, called The CREATION of the WORLD, and having been favoured by him, exclusively, with particular Directions on the Style and Manner in which it must be executed, in order to produce the Effects required by the Author, begs to acquaint the Nobility and Gentry, that he intends to perform it on Monday, the 21st of April next, at the King's Theatre, Haymarket. The Names of Performers, and other particulars, will be advertised in a few days.

A correspondent of *The Morning Herald* on 28 March wrote the following short piece on the Oratorio:

If ever HANDEL's Oratorio of the MESSIAH had a rival in grandeur and sublimity, it is that of HAYDN's oratorial composition, entitled the CREATION, and which, to the high expectation of every Musical Connoisseur in this city, is announced for the present evening, being its first performance in this kingdom. – Many persons now in London, who have heard this celebrated Oratorio at Vienna, assert, that it has repeatedly been known to attract an audience of upwards of six thousand persons.

The London première took place as expected on 28 March, and we have one contemporary newspaper criticism and reports by two eye-witnesses, William Parke, and Dr. Burney:

The *Oratorio* of CREATION, composed by HAYDN, was performed at Covent-garden last night with much deserved applause. It is certainly a fine composition, in every respect worthy of its great author. It combines with the happiest effect the agreeably simple with the most sublime strains; and although not equal in grandeur to the divine compositions of the immortal HANDEL, is, nevertheless, on the whole, a very charming production. [*Morning Herald*, 29 March 1800]

It was received with great applause, particularly the first act of it, in which the sublime chorus, 'The Heavens are telling', excited the admiration of the whole audience. [Parke I, 279]

Finding a blank leaf at the end of my reflections on the prelude or opening of the Creation, [I may] observe, that though the generality of the subscribers were unable to disentangle the studied confusion in delineating chaos, yet, when dissonance was tuned, when order was established, and God said,

'Let there be light! – and there was light.'. . . .

the composer's meaning was felt by the whole audience, who instantly broke in upon the performers with rapturous applause before the musical period was closed. [Lonsdale, 453]

From these reports we may note three facts: (1) that many listeners found 'Chaos' of a modernity and dissonance more than they could accept; (2) that the work was a success; but (3) a certain objection to Haydn putting himself in competition with Handel may be distinctly felt in the newspaper criticism. This was the small beginning of a British movement which was to end up piling scorn, ridicule and even hate on all or parts of Haydn's Oratorio: we shall, in this biography, watch this tendency develop to the point, at the end of the nineteenth century, when a British critic could call the work 'a third rate Oratorio', and his opinion be cited with approbation in a Haydn biography (Hadden) which is in itself one of the most incredible works ever written about Haydn.

Ashley meanwhile announced a repeat performance, and added an open letter which was directed at Salomon's statement:

ORATORIOS, at PLAYHOUSE PRICES during LENT.
LAST NIGHT BUT ONE.
THEATRE ROYAL, COVENT-GARDEN.

TO-MORROW EVENING, April 2, will be performed (for the 2d time), the Sacred Oratorio of

The CREATION. – Composed by Dr. HADYN [*sic*].
End of Part I. a Concerto on the Clarionet, by Mr. J. Mahon.
End of Part II. a Concerto on the Violin, by Mr. G. Ashley.
Principal Vocal Performers [as before].

Mr. Salomon having insinuated that he alone is in possession of a Correct Score of the celebrated Oratorio, I feel compelled in justice to myself, to state, that the Oratorio was published by Subscription at Vienna, and that the printed Copy from which I had the Parts transcribed, was delivered by Dr. HAYDN to a Subscriber in Vienna, and brought from thence expressly for me, and on which is the Doctor's initials. The accuracy with which it was performed, and the enthusiasm with which it was received, are, I hope, convincing proofs that no other directions are necessary to 'produce the effect required by the Author'.

I should not have thus obtruded myself, but I conceive it requisite to justify myself from the imputation of having attempted to impose a spurious production upon that Public to whom I am under so many obligations. I am, with the greatest respect, and gratitude,

Their most obedient Servant

March 29. JOHN ASHLEY.

[*The Times*, 1 April; *Morning Chronicle*, 31 March; *Morning Herald*, 2 April 1800.]

This elegant reply produced the following article in *The Morning Herald* on 3 April:

The *rencontre* between SALOMON, and ASHLEY, respecting the copy-right of HAYDN's Oratorio of *Creation*, has been a smart one. SALOMON had the advantage at first, from his drawing *so long a bow*, but young ASHLEY on this stepped forth, and *measured fiddlestick* with him, when his adversary soon cried out *peccavi*, and acknowledged himself to be out-*Generaled*, at least!

Salomon was not a man to give up so easily, and the next day, on 4 April, we find his open letter to *The Times*:

HAYDN's celebrated ORATORIO, The CREATION.

IN reply to Mr. ASHLEY's Advertisements, Mr. SALOMON thinks it incumbent upon him to state to the Public, that when he announced his intention of performing this celebrated ORATORIO on the 21st of April at the KING'S THEATRE, he did not assert to be alone in possession of a correct score of this excellent Work, but said, what he can prove by Dr. HAYDN's Letters, that he had been favoured, exclusively, by Dr. HAYDN with particular directions on the stile and manner in which it ought to be executed, to produce the effects required by the Author. Dr. HAYDN's wish having been that this Composition should be performed first in this country, under the direction of Mr. SALOMON, for which purpose he forwarded the first Printed Copy to him from Vienna, in the month of January, but which Copy, owing to the detention of the Mails, did not arrive in London until the 23rd ult.

That same day, 4 April, *The Morning Herald* wrote that

HAYDN's *Creation* has added greatly to his fame; indeed a more indifferent production might have become a favourite, from the exertions of the Covent-Garden performers.

If that statement is ambiguous, to say the least, the following is the first all-out attack on *The Creation*, printed once again in *The Morning Herald* (7 April):

As the *Profession* have enjoyed the full benefit of HAYDN's new *Oratorio*, we may now speak of this composition as it deserves: – it is correctly scientific, for all we know, and certainly not devoid of impressive harmonies; but it breathes no more the sacred inspiration of HANDEL, then KOTZEBUE does of that which immortalized our own SHAKESPEARE! It must afford surprize to the musical world, that even two Gentlemen of the *bow* should think it an object to measure *fiddlesticks* about it! If it be again performed in this country, we recommend at least that the misnomer of CREATION be erased, and that of CHAOS *come again*, be substituted in its stead.

Salomon's performance took place as announced, on 21 April; the detailed announcement reads as follows:

GREAT CONCERT ROOMS, KING'S THEATRE.

MR. SALOMON has the honour of acquainting the Nobility and Gentry, that finding the present Performances in the Opera House will not allow sufficient time and space to erect an Orchestra upon the Stage, he has determined, in compliance with the wishes of a number of the most distinguished Amateurs of the Art to perform HAYDN's celebrated Oratorio The CREATION at the above Rooms on MONDAY NEXT, the 21st instant. – Principal Vocal Performers: Madame Mara, and Madame Dussek; Mr. Small (being his first public performance since his return from Italy), Mr. Page, Mr. Denman, and Mr. Bartleman. – The Band will consist of the Opera Band, and other eminent Performers. The Chorusses [*sic*] will be complete, and supported by the young Gentlemen of his Majesty's Chapel, and St. Paul's and Westminster Abbey choirs. Doors to be opened at 7, and the Performance to begin at 8 o'clock. . . .

[*The Times*, 15 April; *Morning Chronicle*, 14 April]

[In subsequent announcements, the place was referred to as the Antient Music Room. 'End of Part II. a Concerto on the Organ by Mr. Samuel Wesley. . . . Organ and Piano-Forte, Mr. Samuel Wesley.' *The Times*, 17 and 18 April; *Morning Chronicle*, April 16, 17, 19, 21.]

For some strange reason, this performance was not very well attended; was the anti-*Creation* movement already making itself felt? The following announcements are self-explanatory:

Mr. SALOMON's band, on Monday night, performed HAYDN's Oratorio of *Creation*, at the Theatre, in the Haymarket. The company was more genteel and select than numerous. In the vocal band, Mr. SMALL, an Englishman, but lately returned from the Italian school, made his first appearance, and sung several airs in a capital tenor voice, and in a scientific and elegant style.

[*Morning Herald*, 23 April]

We are very happy to hear the Public will be a second time gratified with a perfect performance of the popular Oratorio of the Creation in a few days.

[*The Times*, 26 April]

The performance of the grand Oratorio of the Creation, given by Mr. SALOMON at his Benefit [on 21 April], justified the expectations that were formed of its success. The music is extremely grand, and the room was crouded [*sic*] by all the most refined *amateurs* in town. [*The Times*, 28 April]

GREAT ROOM, KING'S THEATRE.

AT the request of a number of the most distinguished Amateurs of MUSIC, who were prevented on the 21st last attending the Performance of the celebrated Oratorio, The CREATION, composed by Dr. HAYDN, the same will be repeated on MONDAY next, May 5, under the direction of Mr. SALOMON. . . .

[*The Times*, 29 April; *Morning Chronicle*, 28 and 29 April]

HAYDN's celebrated Sacred ORATORIO, the CREATION.

THE Performance of this Sublime Composition having given so much satisfaction, that unceasing applications are made for a Repetition of it, the same will be performed again, under the Direction of Mr. SALOMON, on MONDAY, the 9th of June next, at the PANTHEON in Oxford-street. Further particulars will be announced in a few days.

[*The Times*, 22 and 29 May; *Morning Chronicle*, 21 May]

[On 4 June *The Morning Chronicle*, and on 6 June *The Times*, announced that this performance was postponed till next season.]

Despite the controversy with which *The Creation* was now surrounded, it was very frequently performed, both in London and in the provinces (at Worcester in 1800, at Hereford with Madame Mara in 1801, and at Gloucester in 1802 with Mrs Billington). The following criticism from *The Morning Chronicle* of 18 February 1801 represents a moderate tone which would become increasingly more scarce as time went on:

A correspondent who was present at the first rehearsal of the selection from Creation, composed by Haydn, which is to be performed for the benefit of the New Musical Fund to-morrow, at the King's Theatre in the Hay Market, informs us, that from the precision, and correctness with which it went off, the public will have an opportunity of hearing that divine composition in a very superior stile. The amateur in particular will no doubt be highly gratified by perceiving from the public advertisements, that a selection from Handel's Messiah is also to form a part of the evening's treat; and when he reflects that it is thus in his power to compare the excellencies of those two great men upon a scale, in point of numbers unparalleled in this country since the Grand Commemoration at Westminster Abbey, it is to be presumed he will hardly suffer such an opportunity to pass by without seizing it with avidity.

The *amateurs* who have attended the rehearsal of *Mozart's Requiem*[1] declare it to be one of the most sublime compositions ever heard.

On Tuesday, 19 August 1800, Michael Haydn conducted his brother's Oratorio in the *aula magna* of Salzburg University. We have a first-hand report in the Diary of Dominikus, Abbot of St Peter's Benedictine Monastery, with which Michael Haydn was intimately connected:

A masterpiece of music, called *The Creation*, was performed by 95 musicians in the University hall; it is by the famous Joseph Haiden, esterhazi *Kapelmeister* [*sic*], a brother of our *Herr* Michael Haiden. The numerous audience applauded to such an extent that this music was repeated on the 22nd. I went the first time and allowed the young pupils [*Conventualen*], who showed a desire to hear this music, that they might go, and I even paid for their tickets, for the text is edifying and the music moving. The organizers twice collected more than 500 fl., with which they paid for the costs but gave the rest to the poor. This music was repeated four times.

One performance took place in the early period of the French occupation of Salzburg. The French listeners took a collection for the penniless Michael, who had just been plundered by French soldiers, which was very substantial but which, after subtracting the costs, only brought Haydn three kronen. Another performance took place on 2 April 1802.[2]

1 Performed at London for the first time on 20 February 1801.
2 Jancik, op. cit., 255.

We can see from the reaction to the Oratorio in the provincial Archbishopric of Salzburg how profoundly Haydn's music spoke to the hearts and minds of German-speaking peoples. A similar history could be found in hundreds of smaller towns and cities throughout the Austrian empire, Germany, Switzerland, and so forth. We have chosen Salzburg for the obvious reason that Michael Haydn is so closely associated with that city, and with the performances of his brother's masterpiece.

It had been Ignaz Pleyel's idea to come to Vienna and persuade his revered old teacher to go to Paris and conduct personally the first French performance of *The Creation*, but unfortunately, as we have seen, Pleyel could not organize the necessary papers and could get no farther than Germany.[1] A report in the *AMZ* from a Parisian correspondent, written in August 1800, informs us:

> The patriarch of new music, the famous Haydn, is expected in our capital city. *Herr* Pleyel, as one relates and hopes, will bring him here into our midst upon his [Pleyel's] return from Germany. The expectations of the connoisseurs are particularly concentrated on being able to hear Haydn personally conduct here his wonderful Oratorio, everywhere praised, *The Creation*. The pianist [Daniel] Steibelt brought back the first copy from his trip through Germany and is preparing the work for performance in the great opera house. . . . [*AMZ* III, 39]

By the autumn, it was quite clear that Haydn would have been very ill-advised to proceed to the French capital; besides his heart was really with his fatherland, and the dreadful defeats of Italy and Hohenlinden will not have encouraged him to conduct in Paris. But the French were, of course, disappointed; they entrusted the first performance to Steibelt, who scheduled it for Christmas Eve in the Théâtre des Arts. Steibelt had prepared what was considered a rather poor prose translation of the text, and M. de Ségur now put it into 'a miserable and often ridiculous' series of French verses. Steibelt, knowing the French taste, made considerable changes and, interestingly enough in view of that which we have heard, simply removed the Duet between Adam and Eve in Part III. Obviously this music was considered too Austrian, too Papageno-Papagena for the fastidious tastes of the French! The performance was launched with a wave of propaganda, and Steibelt, whose reputation was somewhat clouded because of dubious personal affairs and intrigues, hoped to rehabilitate his standing and increase his fortune by the performance on Christmas Eve. Steibelt also produced a piano score which was engraved by the Demoiselles Erard, but which had to fight the competition of other extracts which clever Parisian speculators had already issued in print.

The First Consul was very tired that day:

> I had been greatly occupied with business all day, and in the evening was sleepy and tired. I threw myself on a sofa in my wife's salon, and fell asleep. Josephine came down some time after, awoke me, and insisted that I should go to the theatre. You know that when women take a thing into their heads, they will go through with it, and you must gratify them. Well, I got up much against my inclination, and went in my carriage, accompanied by Lannes and Bessières. I was so drowsy that I fell asleep in the coach.

As they were passing through the Rue Niçaise, which is very narrow, the procession of carriages was halted by a cart blocking the street. In it, there was a huge

1 A report about Pleyel's trip appeared in the *AMZ* in October 1800 (III, 40).

bomb which exploded just after Napoleon's carriage had passed, illuminating the night with a flash of brilliant light and deafening the First Consul's ears with a terrific roar. There were some twenty dead and two hundred wounded.

> I was asleep [continues Napoleon] when the explosion took place; and I recollect when I woke experiencing a sensation as if the vehicle had been raised up, and was passing through a great body of water. The contrivers of this . . . [had] got a cart and barrel resembling that with which water is supplied through the streets of Paris, with this exception, that the barrel was put crossways. This [they] had filled with gunpowder, and placed it nearly in the turning of the street through which I was to pass. Possibly my coachman may have assisted by driving furiously round the corner, as he was drunk and not afraid of anything. He was so far gone that he thought the report of the explosion was that of a salute fired in honour of my visit to the theatre.

The Théâtre des Arts was filled with an elegant audience (1,417 persons who had brought in 23,975 francs) when Napoleon and his retinue arrived to hear *The Creation* only ten minutes late. Rumours of the attempt on the First Consul's life spread round the theatre and the audience could hardly concentrate on the music. In fact the large costs far exceeded the income, and the whole venture proved a financial disaster. When the work was repeated shortly thereafter, there were only 700 in the audience. But the musicians involved had been thrilled. At a dinner in the theatre, given by the Director of the Paris Opéra, Devismes – which lasted into the early hours of the morning – it was decided to strike a medal celebrating the occasion and send it to Haydn. But the First Consul, upon hearing of the dinner, forthwith dismissed Devismes from his post for breach of regulations governing illumination and curfew. Napoleon's rage indeed knew no bounds: freedom of assembly and freedom of the press were abolished, and forty-eight hours after the bomb attempt in the Rue Niçaise, sixty-three out of seventy Paris newspapers were suppressed.

A report in the *AMZ* reads as follows:

> Paris, 28th December 1800.
> (By a German art-lover living there)
>
> On the 24th inst. Haydn's *Creation* was given here for the first time in the great opera house. 250 artists, almost all enthusiastic for Haydn, executed the choruses in this Oratorio with rare perfection. Only now and then in the arias and recitatives did the listener miss something. Perhaps, however, the great beauty of the choruses and their marvellous effect were partly responsible. The worthy Music Director Rey conducted the music, and Steibelt sat at the piano – *there he sat*! Because he fitted the French text to the music and in the final section left out the Duet between Adam and Eve [Original footnote: 'On the programme was the note: *La musique est arrangée par le Cit. Steibelt.*'] he was paid 3,000 Liv. Even the announcement of the Oratorio, long before the actual performance, caused a real sensation here. Two weeks before the night there wasn't a box to be had. At 9 a.m. on the day of the performance the Opera House was surrounded by a crowd of people and in the evening the confusion was frightful. The public was exceptionally large and brilliant. Bonaparte and all the Government leaders were present. Another performance is announced for 1 January. A gold medal, worth 180 Liv., is to be struck in Haydn's honour and sent to him. The commotion which Haydn's *Creation* has created here is so great that the directors of a local *théâtre de vaudeville* have organized in a great hurry a parody which was performed here yesterday. It is entitled: *La récréation du monde, suite de l'oratorio: la création du monde, musique d'Haydn en vaudeville.* –

It is strange that despite all its devotion to music, Paris should now be so poor in public concerts. The reason is supposed to be that the singers are as exaggerated in their demands for fees as in their ornamentation [original footnote: 'Garat is paid 3,600 Liv. for singing the tenor solo in Haydn's *Creation* three times; but if one takes into consideration all the runs and trills that he introduces in the arias and even in the recitatives, his fee cannot be thought excessive']. At the moment there is only one concert series, called *Concert des Amateurs, Rue de Clary*. The orchestra is not very large there but consists of the choicest musicians. The Haydn symphonies are given there with a precision that surpasses *everything*. . . .

[*AMZ* III, 269f.]

The Creation in Paris continued to interest German and French correspondents of the *AMZ*[1] in Paris. Returning to Steibelt, we read in March 1801:

[translated from the French by *AMZ*]

Steibelt, who through his opera *Romeo und Julie* and his numerous compositions for piano has made himself known, is such a short time in Paris that one isn't quite sure what his plans are. He has just arranged, *in his own fashion*, Haydn's masterpiece, *The Creation*, with a French text by M. de Segur, and has published it in an *arrangement* for piano. Steibelt has now said that Haydn *requested* him to perform this work in the big opera house. If it is true that Haydn even requested Steibelt to make changes in this excellent work, to rewrite so many passages and transpose so many numbers into different keys – about that we are not so easily persuaded. This happened, for instance, in the part of Adam, which Garat was supposed to sing, who has only the low notes of a mezzo-tenore, whereas Haydn wrote the part for a rather solid bass voice. . . . [*AMZ* III, 415]

At the end of March 1801 the same correspondent sent off another in a series of Letters from Paris:

Translated from the French

Paris, End of March 1801.

. . . Since the sacrifice of the Arts in France, never was a more numerous and brilliant society gathered to do honour to music than at the first performance of this Oratorio, about which you are long informed. The great artists of *all* countries are no strangers to the French nation; we have had Piccini, Gluck and Sachini [*sic*] in our midst, have been enriched by the products of their muse and were proud of their talents. We have not had the fortune to welcome Haydn, but we honour him with the finest of his works; and also in the case of the masterpiece here under discussion, we have taken it to our hearts like a favourite child and in a sense made it our own. The performance of this noble Oratorio is as much a triumph for France as for the fatherland of this immortal artist. Great men belong to the nations who know how to appreciate them. . . .

The trace of that German way of thought, taste and manner may be found also in Haydn's Oratorio, admirable as it is. The choruses are noble, the orchestration

1 And not only *AMZ*; the *Zeitung für die elegante Welt* (No. 45, 14 April 1801) also carried an interesting article entitled 'Urtheil in Paris über Haydns Schöpfung', quoting from the *Mercure de France* and repeating many of the comments found in the *AMZ* letter. One new criticism, however, is that there was thought not to be enough disorder and confusion in 'Chaos' (which, the correspondent noted, Ovid described as 'rudis indigestaque moles'). Haydn was also accused of picking 'bizarre fragments' rather than a 'simple and noble' expression when describing the animals, or writing 'unimportant, cold and common details'. The correspondent also remarks that three hours of music 'without a plot' (i.e. opera) tended to bore the Parisians. The whole negative tone of the criticism in the *Mercure de France* is attributed to 'the hate on the part of French scholars for everything German', an attitude which, however, hardly ever applied to Haydn, who was immensely popular in France from 1764 onwards.

perfect, the effect of the harmony worthy of a great master, and nothing in the orchestra is wanting; but one sometimes looks in vain for the heavenly melody and the divine aria which the contents require and which only a genius can provide. Without any doubt the great importance of the subject raises one's expectations to the highest, as was the case, here, with all the amateurs and artists. Presumably one was expecting an aethereal, angelic melody and thought that Haydn's genius would provide us with concerts of heavenly hosts, such as Milton has given us in his *Paraside Lost*; but – *il est des efforts au dessus des mortels.* Haydn in his Oratorio has *painted* everything from Creation that mortal hand is capable of – and we are far from wishing to belittle the merits of this great man in our respectful estimation of his value; we wish it to be received and honoured in the proper light. From *that* standpoint, we unanimously agree that in our opinion one cannot hear a more perfect music than is found in several movements of that masterpiece, so long as we have not the fortune to hear the angels themselves. The whole of Paris recalls that at the first performance of Gluck's *Orpheus* one really expected to hear the magic songs of Orpheus; and what was the result? And yet we very much doubt that there is a single person in this wide world today who could improve on Gluck's *Orpheus* or Haydn's Oratorio.

The energy and efficiency of the opera administration, above all responsible for the happy success of this brilliant undertaking of *The Creation*'s performance, and who left no stone unturned to that end, cannot be praised highly enough.

The orchestra consisted of 250 players, and, as I have already reported, met of its own free will after the first part, and full of the greatest enthusiasm they agreed to raise a subscription to strike a medal in Haydn's honour. This is perhaps the first time that the great artist is so honoured. It is that much purer from being wholly untainted by any trace of money. This anecdote may serve instead of a description of the joy and respect with which this work of art was greeted and instead of praising the beauties with which it is filled – as much as we would have been glad to expand on some aspects of the latter.

He who has not attempted translation himself, a thankless task, can hardly appreciate in its true and complete value the insight and art with which M. de Segur prepared the translation of the German poem . . . [etc., etc.]

The singers earned their laurels: but Cheron's voice has something not at all attractive about it, even when it pleases. If now and then Garat's gentle and soft voice did not rise to the heights of musical dignity found in Haydn's work, the singer excelled in various numbers with all his magic tricks, especially in the Aria 'Brilliant de grace et de beauté' (Mit Würd' und Hoheit), which seemed to be much better suited to his peculiar talents than some of the other pieces. Mad. Walbone earned the approval of the connoisseurs through her exceptional taste and correct singing. But the instrumentalists were superior to the vocalists. We could not understand why *Herr* Steibelt permitted himself to change Haydn's sacred score, since everything he did in the way of changing or adding to the orchestration only resulted in the worst possible taste and a real *chiarivari*. We have the original score, signed by Haydn's own hand, before us and could not restrain ourselves from objecting to *Herr* Steibelt's sacrilege in touching such a sacred object . . . [*AMZ* III, 509–13; letterspaced names normalized]

As suggested elsewhere, it must be seriously doubted if the First Consul liked Haydn's music at all; he will have preferred Paisiello and the Italian operatic school of the period. We learn something of Napoleon's attitude towards music from the Cherubini literature. In his entertaining biography, Edward Bellasis[1] informs us that

1 Edward Bellasis, *Cherubini: Memorials illustrative of his life*, London 1874.

on Christmas Day of 1800, a delegation, composed of the various societies and corporations at Paris, including the Conservatoire de Musique, 'waited on the First Consul to offer their congratulations on his escape'.

> Cherubini [continues Bellasis] was among the deputation, but kept in the background, wishing to avoid any unpleasant meeting with Napoleon; who, however, ironically exclaimed: 'I do not see *Monsieur* Chérubin', pronouncing the name in this French way, in order to indicate, it is said, that Cherubini was not worthy of being deemed an Italian composer. When the composer came forward, ['croisant froidement et calmement son regard avec le regarde de Bonaparte',] neither said one word. Yet crowds were still rushing nightly to see and hear *Les Deux Journées*. Shortly after the above incident, Napoleon invited him to a banquet at the Tuileries, given to a number of distinguished men at Paris. After a frugal repast the company adjourned to the salon, where the First Consul entered into a conversation with Cherubini, both of them walking up and down the room. 'Well,' said Napoleon, 'The French are in Italy.' 'Where would they not go,' rejoined Cherubini, 'led by such a hero as you.' Napoleon seemed pleased, but talked now in Italian now in French, which so confused Cherubini that he could scarcely make out what the Consul was saying. At length the latter began on the old topic: 'I tell you,' he said, 'I like Paisiello's music immensely; it is soft and tranquil. You have much talent, but there is too much accompaniment,' and he instanced the celebrated air of Zingarelli, 'Ombra adorata', as being the sort of thing he liked. Cherubini quietly rejoined: 'Citizen Consul, I conform myself to French taste; "paese che vai, unsanze che trovi"'. 'Your music,' continued Napoleon, 'makes too much noise; speak to me in that of Paisiello, that is what lulls me gently.' 'Je comprends,' replied Cherubini, 'vous préférez une musique qui ne vous empêche pas de songer aux affaires de l'Etat'. At this witty answer, Napoleon frowned.... [op. cit., 131]

It is hardly likely that the First Consul will have approved music with as 'much accompaniment' as *The Creation* must have seemed to possess.

British newspapers were amused at the whole business. *The Morning Chronicle*, on 8 January 1801, tells us:

> HAYDN'S *Creation* of the world possesses great attraction at Paris. The *gun powder plot* on the first night of its representation, formed an *overture* which has given an extra *éclat*!

We shall, however, see in the Chronicle of the next few years (*Haydn: The Late Years, 1801–1809*) that the intellectual élite of Paris was unanimous in its devotion to Haydn, whose music had been adored in the French capital since the early 1760s.[1]

Hitherto most of the poetry addressed to Haydn and *The Creation* had appeared in Vienna, but now it began to appear elsewhere, especially in Germany. In October 1800, the *AMZ* printed an anonymous sonnet which reads as follows:

Haydn's Schöpfung

Holde, fremde Zaubertöne binden
unsern Sinn, daß ihm die Welt vergeht
und das alte Chaos neu entsteht,
neu dem Chaos Welten sich entwinden.

1 Pohl III, 168f. *The Corsican*, 146f. Charles Malherbe, 'Joseph Haydn und die Schöpfung', in *Musikalisches Wochenblatt* (1909), pp. 230, 251. G. Gathy, 'Haydns Schöpfung in Paris', in *Monatschrift für Theater und Musik*, Vienna 1853, pp. 412ff.

Schüchtern muß der niedre Sinn erblinden,
wenn hervor die neue *Schöpfung* geht.
Wo der Schöpfergeist harmonisch weht,
darf der höh're Sinn nur kühn empfinden.

Ist's ein fremder Geist? und streift im Schweben
sein vorüberrauschendes Gefieder
fremde Luft nur mit harmon' schem Beben?

Liebend läßt er sich zur Heimath nieder
in dir selbst, mein Geist! Harmonisch Leben
kommt vom Geiste, kehrt zum Geiste wieder.

The finest poem addressed to Haydn in connection with *The Creation* is surely that by the German poet, Christoph Martin Wieland, whose poetry Haydn much admired and to whom he wished to turn for a possible oratorio libretto after Swieten had died. The poem about *The Creation* was brought to Haydn at Eisenstadt in the autumn of 1800 by the famous German musicologist and Bach biographer, Johann Nikolaus Forkel, who came to visit the composer in company with Beethoven's friend, the piano-builder Johann Andreas Streicher. Griesinger later sent the Wieland poem to the *AMZ* in Leipzig, where it was published anonymously in September 1801.[1]

An Haydn.
Nach Aufführung seiner Cantate: die Erschaffung der Welt.

Wie strömt dein wogender Gesang
In unsere Herzen ein! – Wir sehen
Der Schöpfung mächt'gen Gang.
Den Hauch des Herrn auf dem Gewässer wehen,
Itzt durch ein blitzend Wort das erste Licht entstehen,
Und die Gestirne sich durch ihre Bahnen drehen:
Wie Baum und Pflanze wird: wie sich der Berg erhebt,
Und, froh des Lebens, sich die jungen Thiere regen:
Der Donner rollet uns entgegen:
Der Regen säuselt: jedes Wesen strebt
Ins Daseyn, und bestimmt, des Schöpfers Werk zu krönen,
Sehn wir das erste Paar, geführt von deinen Tönen.
O jedes Hochgefühl, das in den Herzen schlief,
Ist wach! Wer rufet nicht: wie schön ist diese Erde,
Und schöner, nun der Herr auch dich ins Daseyn rief,
Auf daß sein Werk vollendet werde!

In the *AMZ* for 6 July 1803 there appeared an extract from a longer poem entitled 'Das Reich der Töne':

1 Pohl III, 188. *AMZ* III, 852. Olleson, *Griesinger*, 37. Griesinger in his biography of Haydn (38) quotes the poem (as does Dies, by the way) and tells us that it 'gave the composer much pleasure'. The poem is quoted from an uncited source in Pohl III, 397, which is textually slightly different, and apparently more reliable, than the version of *AMZ*; can Pohl have had Wieland's autograph? The title, too, is also missing in *AMZ* ('Nach Aufführung', etc.).

Ueber Haydn's Schöpfung

Nicht die Empfindung allein wird Laut und Leben im Liede,
Auch die ew'ge Natur drückt ihren heiligen Stempel
Auf den bildsamen Ton, und aus der Wesen Verkettung
Geht sie schöner hervor in idealischen Formen.
Als der Meister der Kunst das Werk der unendlichen Schöpfung
Dem begeisterten Ohr in Harmonieen gezaubert,
Stand die reine Natur, im zarten Gewande der Jugend,
Ihm zur Seite, den Geist in ihre Tiefen entzückend,
Die sie dem Auge verschloss. – Denn farblos ist das Gewebe
Der chaotischen Nacht, verworrene Kräfte vermischen
Sich in wechselnder Form, und widerstrebende Stoffe
Reissen sich gährend los zu ordnungsleeren Gestalten.
Aber, was dem Begriff, dem Gedanken ewig geschlummert,
Stellen die Töne dar in ihrer unendlichen Fügung.
Denn in ihnen erscheint die regellose Verwirrung
Todter Kräfte; die Schwere liegt auf tiefen Akkorden;
Dissonirend entsteigt und sinkt der Kampf der Naturen,
Und durch chromatische Gänge wälzt sich die träge Bewegung.
Izt herrscht Ruhe; nur schwach ertönt in gezogenem Klange
Hohles Braussen, wie wenn in des Abgrunds Tiefen verschlossen
Glut sich den feindlichen Händen entrafft; und schwächer und leiser
Wird der Kampf, und es reicht das Eine die Fessel dem Andern.
Aber ein schneidender Hauch wogt enharmonisch hernieder,
Und von neuem beginnt das Gewühl. Bald ordnet der Zerfall
Ein melodisches Bild, bald reisst es der Strom von einander,
Der sich flutend verliert in schweren Gewühlen der Masse.
Izt auf dem Rauschen der Wasser erhebt sich die Stimme der Gottheit.
Alles verstummt, sie gebeut: es werde Licht in dem Raume,
Und im erschütternden Flug entweicht der Töne Verwirrung.
Strömend brausst der Gesang; die dunklen Akkorde verschweben
Und ätherisches Licht dringt in die Adern des Liedes.
Heilige Kunst der Musik, in deren weiten Gebieten
Krafft und Schönheit herrscht, und Sprache frommer Empfindung,
Wo ist irgend ein Herz, dem du nicht tröstend erschienen,
Wenn die Stürme des Lebens den Staubkelch seiner Entfaltung
Klagend verhüllt, und mit heissen erleuchteten Thränen begossen?
Dir verbündet sich gern die schöne liebliche Schwester,
Die den Herrschenden Zepter trägt im Kreise der Götter.
Denn sie wieget sich sanft auf deinen Harmonikatönen,
Oder brausset einher im Donner deiner Orkane.
Welcher die gnädigen Götter ins Reich der unendlichen Dichtkunst
Huldvoll entzückt, dem nahten sie sich in deinem Getöne,
Heiliges Saitenspiel, du riefst den trunkenen Sinnen
Liebliche Weisen zu, und Ahnung hoher Gedanken.
Du belebest das Wort, das, kalten Lippen entflossen,
Noch in deinem Getöne verweilt; dem schweigenden Schicksal
Leihst du die Zunge, das ewig still der Vergangenheit Spuren
Mit der Gegenwart Blumen bedeckt! – O könnt' ich in deinen
Heit'ren Gefilden vergehn, und auf dem sterbenden Odem
Des entfliehenden Tons in schönern Fluren entschweben,
Die ein strenges Geschick von unserm Hoffen geschieden.
Dürft' ich das bleiche Bild des kommenden Todes nicht sehen,

Und, ein reiner Akkord, im Ruhepunkte des Daseyns
Sanft verschwinden zu heiligen Schatten entfernterer Tage;
Nimmer schreckte sodann das kalte Gefühl der Vernichtung
Den versunkenen Geist; mit schöneren Harmonieen
Kehren die Töne zurück, die in die Nacht des Verstummens
Ihr begeisterter Schöpfer rief; vereinigt umfassen
Sich die Lebenden wieder mit frohen Accenten der Freude
Und ein schönes Erwachen folgt auf die Stunden der Trennung.

D. C. Schreiber.

[*AMZ* V, 685–8]

The author of these verses, Christian Schreiber, later submitted an oratorio text entitled *Polyhymnia, oder die Macht der Töne* (after Dryden) to Breitkopf & Härtel who hoped that Haydn would set it to music (see *Haydn: the Late Years, 1801–1809*, 14 December 1803).

SELECTED CONTEMPORARY REVIEWS OF 'THE CREATION' FROM 'AMZ'

The Creation was now the most discussed musical work in Europe, and not only the full score but the many other arrangements were reviewed and analyzed. It cannot be within the scope of this biography to reprint these reviews *in extenso*, and it may be doubted that such a review from (let us say) Paris or Danzig contributes to our present knowledge of the work any more than the endless notices of performance all over Europe with which, for example, the *AMZ* was quite rightly then concerned. But there are several reviews in the *AMZ* which Haydn himself read, and we have permitted ourselves to break our rule for presenting such matters chronologically and have placed them all here. Swieten actually read aloud to Griesinger the review of 'Chaos' (*infra*, pp. 594f.); the Baron thought Reichardt might have written it but in fact it was by Goethe's friend Zelter, who was also responsible for the major review of 1802, which is said to have touched and moved both Swieten and the composer.[1] This latter review was widely read and even translated, without indication of the source, into Italian by Giovanni Simone (Johann Simon) Mayr, the well-known composer whose monograph on Haydn's *Creation* (Bergamo 1809) included an interesting article on Haydn's life partly cribbed, as we say, from Zelter. (We have quoted, in the original Italian, some of this adaptation in *Haydn in England, 1791–1795*.) Finally (pp. 589ff.), we have included a report on Haydn's position in German music which an *AMZ* correspondent published in March 1801 which, while not concerning *The Creation* directly, is a valuable insight into Haydn's position in German circles of the period and also attempts to place the Oratorio in Haydn's total *œuvre*.

Joseph Haydn's Oratorium: die Schöpfung. Im Klavierauszug von August Eberhard Müller. Leipzig, bey Breitkopf und Härtel. (Preis 2 Thlr. 16 Gr.)

Although a proper criticism of this masterpiece should be entrusted not so much to the reviewer of the piano score as to the reviewer of the full score, yet we cannot refrain from a dry [*kahlen*] criticism of the piano score (since we have the full score in front of us).

1 Apart from the evidence of Griesinger in his letters to Breitkopf & Härtel, we also have the statement in Dies' biography (179), wherein we read that Haydn considered the big Zelter review of 1802 'an excellent job' and wondered how Zelter could have found the right approach so well.

It is, in the real sense of the word, a psychological phenomenon that just those strengths of the soul that in normal people become duller with old age become, in Father Haydn,[1] ever stronger. In none of his earlier vocal compositions, such as *Orlando Paladino, L'isola disabitata*, and so on, that are known to the reviewer, do we find such an exalted and widespread inventive faculty, so much warm and luxuriant fantasy, as in *The Creation*. Even the small spots which a fearful critic might castigate are the mistakes of an all too fiery young man rather than those of a careful old man. This extraordinary characteristic of the work before us may be, to some extent, the explanation for the general applause of the whole musical world and the warm participation which has been accorded it by professional and amateur alike. It combines the studies of an experienced composer who has become grey in the service of his Art with an irresistible, all-consuming fire of a youth. '*Heil* to our German fatherland that may count a Haydn among its sons!' – that is the only thing that this reviewer has left to say, after having the opportunity once more to study this masterpiece. – The piano part is playable and does all honour to the diligence of *Herr* Müller. But we would have wished, for the convenience of the amateur (for whom the piano score is in fact intended), that the tenor and the bass arias had been transposed into the soprano clef.

[*AMZ* III, 180f.]

CORRESPONDENCE

Letters to a Friend about Music in Berlin

Sixth Letter. Berlin, 8th January [1801].

On the 5th of January Haydn's *Creation* was given here in the Royal Opera House for the benefit of musicians' widows whose husbands died in royal service. The Royal *Kapellmeister* Himmel and the *Konzertmeister* Haake conducted the Oratorio. The size was 30 violins, 7 violas, 12 violoncellos, 6 double basses, 6 bassoons, 4 flutes, 4 horns, 4 oboes, 2 clarinets, trumpets and timpani, and from this mass of performers I may single out such names as Haake, Möser, Seidler, Carl Benda, Bachmann, Semler, Düport Senior, Düport Junior, Hausmann, Gross, Ritter, Schwarz, Bär, Tausch und Krause . . . The chorus was nearly seventy strong, and the soloists were Mlle Schmalz, Mad. Schick, *Herr* Hurka, *Herr* Fischer and *Herr* Franz . . . The King, the Queen, and the whole Court graced the performance with their presence; the orchestra and all the boxes were packed, so that there were not enough libretti to go round, though they had printed more than 600. The income was 1,220 Rthlr. without the King's present.

Among all the products of recent German art, Haydn's *Creation* is without doubt the most original and free. It can only be compared to itself and is therefore difficult to judge. From the praise and criticism which are known to me in writing and by word-of-mouth, I soon realized in judging this very special [*eignen*] work that one cannot start from the old theory of oratorio (if there exists such a thing); but that this Oratorio, as the master has now decided to entitle it, constitutes a new task for the musical aesthetician, who must work out for it a new theory as valuable as the old one, which neither cuts nor pricks. That object that was hitherto called an oratorio and was known as holy music was, at least, no church music; and all the oratorios of Metastasio, Coltellino [*sc.* Marco Coltellini], Zeno, Pasquini, Ramler, Niemeyer, &c. are nothing but sacred dramas and cantatas, which belong in the chapel at best to edify the household and which therefore must be excluded from the general religious service because they are not 'general', which latter characteristic alone determines public religious service. From this

1 The letter-spacing ('H a y d n') omitted; readers may see such a spacing in the review quoted *supra*, p. 579.

standpoint, for which, upon closer examination, the most weighty reasons can be found, it could be easy for the Catholic Mass, as it was arranged by Italian masters at the beginning of the previous century for public worship, to be considered the only true church music to contain this element of 'generality', then and now. The first and hitherto the only man who transferred this spirit of generality to Protestant church music was the immortal Handel in *Messiah*, which he also called an oratorio, though the generally understandable (and understood) text consisted of simple phrases from the bible that filled the heart, fortified the senses, strengthened love and nourished the spirit.

Of all this we find nothing in Haydn's *Creation*. It is a 'creation' of its own kind, a free play of the Art, which serves the master's hand in constructing a new garden, a new earth. The Overture describes chaos. A gigantic *unisono* of all instruments, at the same time a light-less and formless mass, are suggested to our imagination. From it single notes come forth, which in turn spawn others. There are spun forth forms and figures, without line and order, that disappear only to appear again in different guise. Movement begins. Huge forces grate against each other and begin to gestate, and occasionally, as if fortuitously, they dissolve harmonically and then sink back into darkness. A swirling and twisting of unknown forces, which gradually separate themselves and leave clear breaks, announce that order is near. Each flood gradually seeks its proper bed, not without forcing. Here a star moves in its path, there another one. The swimming forces approach land. Similar forms attract each other and embrace. It is night. And God spoke: Let there be light! And there was light![1]

That there really is light, and that someone who can create such a chaos can also create light when necessary, goes without saying; and you will know from the score that the Overture is in C minor and played with mutes which, when the light shines, are removed so that C major may shine with all the magnificence and clarity worthy of the mighty composer. There is an incalculable value in this tone poem, which can hardly be compared with the meagre brush strokes, lacking strength and thought, with which some fabulous folk ask the public to table, to serve him with deaf legiminous fare, warmed-over figures and old fugue-steaks. No! This is not the Historia of Susanna or Bathsheba that is being served up but the true imagination of a great soul which should, and does, describe to the inner mind gigantic forces which gradually give way to order. And in this spirit I see the whole work. Whoever accuses the composer of missed inspiration, expression or analogies of things, would be asking something that he never wanted to do. To confirm my opinion, take the very first Aria in A major.

The text tells us, unadorned, that the grey shadows of darkness have fled from the holy stream of light, and this is the first day. 'Disorder' [English original] has had to make way for order; 'Affrighted fled hell's spirits back in throngs; down they sink in the deep abyss to endless night.'[2] Desperation, fury and terror are their guides in flight, and a new world springs up at God's command. What should the composer have done here, if he were not a rich giver of unlimited resources? He took from his own sources that which an unadorned tale could not give and

1 In a letter from Zelter to Goethe written a quarter of a century later, we read the following interesting comment: '. . . In the review of *The Creation* and in particular about the Overture which is entitled "Chaos", I remarked that such a theme should not be permitted as an artistic exercise; but that genius has everywhere, and also here, performed the impossible and admirably, and I supported my claim with examples. The old Haydn let me know the following [orally, through a friend]: that in no way had he thought or attempted all that, but my analysis agreed with his imagination which he just now realized, and he had to admit the validity of the pictures I had drawn . . .'. *Briefwechsel zwischen Goethe und Zelter in den Jahren 1796 bis 1832*, ed. Friedrich Wilhelm Riemer, Berlin 1834, IV, 149 (Brief No. 491). The aesthetic questions are, however, raised in the full-scale review quoted below.

2 Zelter clearly thinks, and rightly, that the original text was English. (H. C. R. L.)

created the first cheerful day of creation, and the rest of his task was to drive out Night and Darkness (which still appeared, at times, on the earth) and out of this feeling there was created an agreeable, clear, intelligent and learned piece which has all the feelings of a spring day and which, though long, is not stretched out. It is, however, true that the whole interest of this Oratorio is concentrated on Ideals and on instrumental music; but that which is peculiar and original about it, is its complete independence of the language's effect; it moves at its own pace and regards the telling of the story only as something of secondary interest. That is what occurs in the recitative describing the creation of the firmament [quotation beginning 'Da tobten brausend', etc.].

Here one may see clearly that only a vivid imagination could create picture after picture, describing natural occurrences as easily and with a few strokes as they were easily created in the first place. The most important thing has occurred; light is there, and at the same time the artist playfully calls forth wind and weather, snow and hailstones, and the text says each time: this was the storm, these were strokes of lightning, this was the thunder, rain, snow. One is accustomed to see the passionate upheavals of an actual person when one thinks of such concepts; or a soul in turmoil; but these are matters that should not be sought here; rather everything that one finds here is just as accidental and necessary as Creation itself. I doubt not that the master could have found a better choice for his genius than just this subject; and if it is true that he has chosen Thomson's *Seasons* as the next subject for his muse, this strengthens my opinion that Haydn knows his genius and asks of it, that which it gladly does. It moves under its own power and creates the atmosphere in which it will exist, and whoever will coexist with it, must learn to know this atmosphere as if it were a new climate. Everything warm, moving, that comes from participation and sympathy, is purposely avoided, and the poem stops just where sorrows and passions begin, before the Fall, with only the significant warning to the first human couple not to crave for more than they know and have. With every right, one could call this work of art the Paradise of Music. It is a garden, full of the loveliest flowers, crops, herbs and trees, so that imitators of the great master may have a rich harvest for their operas and concertos; for the physical side of nature, with its expressions, so far as they concern tone and movement, is collected here as thoroughly as for an encyclopaedia; and he who does not want to go himself, needs only look here, and if he understands how to look, he will find.

As far as style and content are concerned, Haydn remains here that which he has long been: the finest model of his time. Apart from learned sections and the figured passages, in which one learns to recognize the experienced master, it is the free motion here, with which everything moves according to the beautiful rules, that is heavenly and unique in its fashion. The choruses in praise of the Creator of the world are a happy bustling of all Nature, in which sun, moon, stars, and everything round them, enjoy their existence, and each go their course without confusion. All is clear, plain, whole and tasteful. Cheerfulness and spirit, grace and humour, intelligence and wit and goodness nurture this new world, in which nothing tastes used or known and everything is like a fresh morning dew. Some potent passages of instrumental music, especially in the Overture, are wonderful beyond words and immortal: of this sort is the 8th and 9th bar of the Overture, which is truly new and grand. There would be a great deal to say about this wonderful work, if I knew how to make an article out of my letters. For the fugal sections deserve the greatest attention by contemporaries. The fugue 'Denn er hat Himmel und Erde bekleidet' is an artistic and elegant piece of work, in which the entrances are always clear and beautiful. The countersubject lies very advantageously in the accompanying parts, and although very freely conceived (as in bars 3 and 4) it is most powerful all the same: the theme in augmentation is comprehensible and the stretto at the end makes a better effect the freer it is. The final fugue 'Singt dem Herren, alle Stimmen!' which in the German translation has become rather too verbose, is of pleasant vigour, while the solo parts therein are very attractive; but the best is the end, with the words 'Er bleibt in Ewigkeit!'. And so closes the work as it began and was continued, with a stroke of genius, leaving in every heart the fervent wish that this excellent master should never grow old and tired, and that his divine light should shine for a very long while.

What I have said here can and must only serve to open the door to an ever vital criticism; or if possible to establish a criterion whereby the obviously lost observer may follow the path of a new comet on the horizon of Art, which rises to high places. There will surely not lack for persons who say to the masses, with cold reasoning: Look here! Where is the trace of passion? A feeling that speaks to the heart? Where is truth of expression? etc. But the genius will not turn away, and will continue to follow its path; to fly through that which is, and to seek its path where only its belief and the admiration of the finest may follow him.

And thus, God be praised! Marvellous spirit! Appear again in new clarity, and renew the offering of your spirit, for you are a law unto yourself and your works are as you. Amen! [*AMZ* III, 289–96]

ARTICLE

Remarks concerning the Development of Music in Germany during the Eighteenth Century

(Continuation)

But everyone who ever composed symphonies and quartets remains behind *the* man who for nearly half a century worked with new, inexhaustible and astonishing force and was the greatest benefactor of German instrumental music in the third period of the last century. The whole of Germany has long revered the extraordinary genius of our great J. Haydn;[1] and long ago the hoarse voices of pedantic mosquito-critics who felt inclined to take up the cudgels against a work distinguished by a thousand beauties as soon as they discovered in it a few forbidden, even concealed, fifths and octaves and proceeded to tease Haydn about them – have been reduced to silence[2] since one realized that Haydn, in his profound knowledge of musical grammar, was also superior to many a proud contrapuntist. And who was not delighted when at the end of the century the name Haydn was mentioned with awe abroad, that London and Paris vied with each other to praise his last works – something no longer necessary with us to place him at the top of musical fame. But why should I add a drop to the ocean by my statements about his immortal services (though one is so easily persuaded to do so)? I would rather attempt to clarify for myself (and perhaps for those who have not yet considered the matter) that which constitutes Haydn's real greatness.

Everything is combined in him to raise him up to being the greatest instrumental composer. In his youth he was (like Graun, Hasse, Schulz, &c.) a very

1 Spacing, which *AMZ* applied to all proper names, omitted. (H.C.R.L.)

2 [Original footnote:] Here is a small, in itself trivial, anecdote which is, however, perhaps not unimportant for the honour of two great composers. – The late *Kapellmeister* I. A. P. Schulz found himself, some two years ago, in a concert at which a new symphony by Haydn was given. Next to him stood a former chapel and theatre singer who, as they say, had enjoyed a bit of the (old) school and gladly criticized that which he considered was not formed according to the old patterns. This man, to make himself important and (as he thought) to do a favour to *Kapellm.* Schulz – of whom he knew that he had been a Kirnberger pupil –, said at the end of the symphony: 'What do you think of this joker?' (meaning H[aydn]). Schulz, full of astonishment and annoyance over such a frivolous remark concerning his darling, answered: 'Before this joker I fall down and worship.' How the face of the other ignoramus lengthened after being put in his place in such a fashion, can be imagined.

popular singer. He studied the great Italian masters, and who could now wonder that he gave us such wonderful melodies; or that everything in his works, even the most complicated movements, sings so beautifully; that his principal movements, in serious or in comic style, have such a remarkable strength full of simplicity, which grip the emotions of connoisseur and amateur alike. He combined with this the most intensive study (through Bach's and other men's works) of harmony, the fruits of which are the boldest, most surprising and no less than Baroque[1] modulations which so delight us. Now one must add to all this the knowledge of each instrument's special character and effect, and all this combined with the rarest originality of a brain which even in the enormous amount of its products does not copy itself, though it has an unmistakable style (which anyone who even knows something about Haydn can hear in an apocryphal piece) – and so you have our great master before you, to be admired, it is true, but not an incomprehensible phenomenon. But with these things the explanation of his greatness is not yet completed. The quintessence of it seems to me to be in the exceptionally easy treatment of the rhythm, in which no one approaches him, and in that which the English call 'humour' and for which the German word 'Laune' is not quite the same. From this latter characteristic may be explained his penchant for the comic turn and the fact that he is more successful therein than in a serious vein. If one would wish to draw a parallel with other famous men, J. Haydn, in the richness of his fantasy, might be compared to our Jean Paul – except for the latter's chaotic order, of course, for clear presentation (*lucidus ordo*) is one of Haydn's no small accomplishments – and as far as the humor is concerned, his original caprice (*vis comica*), with Lor. [Laurence] Sterne. If one wanted to describe the character of Haydn's compositions with two words, they would be, I think, *artful popularity* or *popular* (meaning easily understood, penetrating) *artistry*. But in which genre of music is Haydn at his greatest and most masterly? One must ask this question of almost any important composer of this third period [of the eighteenth century], for one requires of him not only that he writes much but is many-sided. Now it is obvious that a *true* artist arouses interest in every aspect of his muse to which he turns his attention, but it remains constant that even the greatest genius – especially at a time where the Art was growing from a small plant to a great tree of many branches – can work in only one, or in some sections, of his genre with really *excellent* results. And so I fear not, if I set up the following classification of Haydn's works against the opinion of the majority of connoisseurs and critics. – The first place must be accorded, without any doubt, to his *symphonies* and *quartets*, wherein no one has yet surpassed him. The second goes to his *piano* works, but only because of their expression, gentleness and (for all their artistry) easily understood mastery; for in *other* respects – apart from Mozart –, several of the newer piano composers, especially Muzio Clementi with his fiery spirit (and perhaps later a Beethoven, if he calms his wild imaginings [*das wild schwärmende*]), and others too, will usurp his [Haydn's] place. After that follows his *church music* and finally his *theatrical pieces*, so far as these latter are known. The proof for *that* remark may be found *inter alia* even in a work which has caused an exceptional sensation (almost as much as Mozart's *Magic Flute*), to wit, *The Creation*. Of this work I dare to assert that it will neither subtract from, nor add to, Haydn's *true* artistic reputation – that is to say, not that which is provided by a large audience.[2] Respect for the great man must not blind us to the extent that we overlook the aesthetic demands posed by *such* a work. And what can one really say to a history of nature or a geodesy, set to music, wherein the objects are paraded in front of us as in a magic lantern? To a

1 AMZ means 'grotesque, whimsical' (*OED*) rather than a term of musical history.

2 [Original footnote:] All respect to the public; but in *matters of art* I know of no worse judge than the public *en masse*.

succession of tone-paintings, to the mixture of church and theatrical styles (and that shows us how far we've come along *those* lines)? In a word, to the tendency of the whole thing? Must it not pain every admirer of Haydn's to see the great strength of this man, *to the detriment of his art* (for *such* cases are often dangerous), wasted on a text unworthy of him? Truly, the writer of the old Mosaic text could not possibly dream that his work, adored with all the trappings of modern music, would be such a success at the end of the eighteenth century! Enough, it is my conviction (which if necessary can be defended circumstantially) that this work, *as a whole*, cannot increase Haydn's celebrity. But – it can hardly, if at all, subtract from it. For the text was not of his doing, and it was therefore not his fault if he was forced to a continual description of objects rather than subjects. Moreover, and we must not forget to take this into consideration, when thinking of the man's great services, he actually composed this Oratorio for the *English*, who are accustomed to Handel's rain and snow pictures, and who, if they are to remain true to their taste, must find in *The Creation* one of the greatest masterpieces that they have ever heard. [There follows a long footnote in which the author announced another forthcoming article 'Attempt to draw the Boundaries of Music, in particular with musical Tone-Painting' which, he asserts, is not intended to make him 'a judge of a rightly most famous man' – i.e., Haydn.] – And so, no composer of the previous century did so much for the development of *instrumental music* as our Father J. Haydn. None had such outward and inward force; none but he was capable not only of placing it in proper perspective to vocal music but, towards the beginning of the new century, forced the latter category to display all its forces so as not to remain behind. [*AMZ* III, 405–10]

Trois Sonates pour le Pianoforte av. Accomp. d'un Violon, composées sur des Idées prises de l'Oratoire de J. Haydn: la Création, et ded. à Msr. Le Prince August de Hohenlohe Ingelfingen par Joseph Woelfl. Op. 14. Chez Breitkopf et Härtel, à Leipsic. (2 Rthlr.)

It is a very strange, and as far as we know hitherto unproduced, thought of a really humorous composer to produce such sonatas.[1] The title is to be understood very clearly. The Sonatas are not arranged movements from Haydn's *Creation* but are pieces freely composed round the principal musical ideas of the Oratorio, and in such a way that these thoughts are numbered and at the end these numbers are provided with the words which belong to them. These ideas are sometimes put together in a surprising way, and appear so Baroque and curious, that one is delighted with the cleverness and humour of the compiler; here and there one cannot avoid the impression of a rather cutting musical persiflage – but it is not ill intended. One has accused the Germans that in their hands a joke [*Scherz*] almost always ends up a guffaw [*Spaß*]: this is really not the case here; it would not occur to the great Haydn and his admirers. Paris, shortly after (one may say) the glorious performance of *The Creation*, gave a satirical potpourri called *La récréation du monde, musique d'Haydn en vaudeville*, laughed until they could laugh no more; and no sensible person found Haydn's Oratorio less valuable afterwards; why shouldn't a German composer write, for example, variations on 'Nun beut die Flur das frische Grün'? Why shouldn't the amateurs enjoy such a thing, without in the least harming the just respect for Haydn and his work?

The reviewer enjoyed the second of these Sonatas the most, partly because of its witty compilation and partly because . . . it makes a rather pretty whole. The first allegro movement is arranged from the music to 'Nun scheint in vollem

1 [Original footnote:] Sarti wrote something similar: 'Intreccio di diverse Idee d'Opere favorite ossia Sonata per il Clavicemb[alo] *c.* Violin[o] oblig.

Glanze', 'Das Wasser schwellt der Fische Gewimmel', 'Das Gotteswerke dankbar sehn'; the Andante is from the music to 'In holder Anmuth stehn', and the Finale from 'Dir sey es ganz geweiht', 'Der Morgenthau', 'Mit dir erhöht sich jede Freude', 'Der thauende Morgen', of which the two latter are really satirical. The introductory Largo of the 3rd Sonata (taken from 'Chaos' and the appearance of light) turns out to be too thin, however, and the satire sticks the arranger instead, whereas 'der Höllengeister Schaar', particularly where they are attacked by 'Verzweiflung, Wuth und Schrecken', turns out quite respectably.

Herr W's works in fact turn out to have exaggerated difficulties for those who perform them and are approached with a certain amount of circumspection, and thus we mention that these Sonatas are easily played by any pianist with at least some training. . . . [*AMZ* III, 448–50]

REVIEW

Die Schöpfung. Ein Oratorium, in Musik gesetzt von Joseph Haydn, Doktor der Tonkunst, der königl. Schwedischen Akademie der Musik Mitglied und Kapellmeister in wirklichen Diensten Sr. Durchl. des Fürsten v. Esterhazy. Partitur, Folio, mit deutschem und englischem Text. Wien, 1800.

The announcement or criticism of intellectual products, after they have appeared and begin to make their presence felt, has become a necessity in our times, with which even a part of the musical public, especially in the provinces, must be satisfied, without enjoying a more direct confrontation of the works concerned; in short, the public is now generally accustomed to take proper notice of a work only – after it has been criticized; and thus to undertake the criticism of such a work as that in front of us would be more than justified.

Haydn's *Creation* requires neither announcement nor criticism, since the public has known and become well acquainted with this work and its value for more than two years. But since the better message of a work of art passes over many all too quickly without leaving a trace, it is neither too late nor superfluous to talk about it; on the contrary, many will welcome the possibility of comparing a public criticism with many individual impressions of the work.

It is permissible and human to be prejudiced in favour of an artist who for more than thirty years has, through masterpieces of the most varied and peculiar kinds, made a great name; who quietly tills his field and harvests his crops, which many near to him sell and barter; it is permissible to expect the finest from such an artist, to be mistrustful of one's own personal opinion and to await, in distance, that which time itself will do. It must indeed be allowed even the critic publicly to admit his prejudice for an active, happy genius whom nature has most richly endowed, though it would be too easy to regard as definitive an opinion about someone so favoured; and naturally, personal relationship and financial profit cannot force their way into the world of art. But where would the reviewer be who had to swallow his conscience in order to offer his public opinion about such a powerful work as *The Creation*? We are therefore entirely persuaded that should our comments on the work ever come under the glance of the worthy composer, he cannot prefer even our admiration to his own approval, and even our objections will be neither new nor hidden from *him*, since he himself will be in the best position to know what is best.

Before we enter the depths of the work in front of us, a description of the genius of its creator may be useful, whose earlier works have been, for so many years, more heard than appreciated and understood. Those works in which Haydn distinguished himself above other composers consist mainly in symphonies and quartets, in the production of which he entered entirely *new* paths not found in any musical piece before him. These symphonies and quartets are a suite of pieces whose parts stand in no relationship to one another: first an *allegro*, then an *adagio*, then a minuet and finally a *rondeau* or some other lively movement. The allegros are powerful, lively, intellectual and very flowing; the second sections are treated in several ways, are learned and developed in the most original manner. There is no musical thought, no matter how limited or colourful, which could not be made interesting through inversions, divisions, transpositions, and similar things. The certainty and fluidity in the arts of counterpoint, supported by a never-ending source of ideas, lead the ear unexpectedly into wilds and depths, wherein it follows such a leader gladly and is so richly rewarded. This play of easy imagination, which knows how to use every device, lends to the smallest aspect of a genius a boldness and confidence which spread over all its parts and enlarge into the infinite the field of aesthetic art, without causing damages or arousing fear. As with nature itself, which must succeed in each new project, so it is with this genius. Everything is contained in it, and when it is set in motion, the results are obvious. Haydn's pieces sometimes have no theme and seem to begin in the middle, and yet with all their lightness they contain a sweep and an order which proclaim the sure hand of the master. The adagios or andantes have the most varied forms. Mostly they are broadly conceived and have the appearance of the grand style, but they require a brilliant, lively performance and are, on the whole, not of the sentimental or moving variety; rather they breathe a national spirit of cheerfulness and caprice, which could not survive in a meltingly beautiful or serious atmosphere. Even that which one might term passionate therein is more a kind of idealized energy [*Übermuth*] or healthy animal spirit, rather than the arrival of a decisive or calculated change of mood [*Gemüthslage*]. The minuets are so richly adorned with treasures of practical art and genius that frequently in a single Haydn minuet there is enough erudition and genius to fill out a whole large work of music. One would be wrong to try to criticize these pieces according to the theory of real dance movements: rather they are *sui generis*, smallish shining bodies in the firmament of Art, which belong to the order of things just as much as one of nature's appearances, the reasons for which are often enough unseen or overlooked. The last allegros or rondos, for which Haydn employs all forms and devices to preserve the rhythm, tempo and harmony, consist usually of short, light movements. Through a very serious and diligent development, they are often brought to the highest level of comedy, which concept can never be so perfectly expressed in words as is here delivered and received with the greatest speed. In the middle and towards the end they are full of life, intellect and spices, and possess a freedom, boldness and strength which enchant and uplift the most experienced ear. Every appearance of seriousness is only there to make the light-heartedness of this pleasant play of notes most surprising; and to tease us from all sides until we are tired of guessing what will come next, of hoping that what we want will come, of asking for what is obvious – so finally we submit to discretion and allow ourselves to be placed by the master in an intellectual mood of comfort and cheerful, beneficial spirit which could not be happier.

This basic spirit, here set forth, has informed almost all Haydn's works up to now; and the result is that all Haydn's instrumental compositions are a brand new kind, created by him alone, of Romantic pictures for the ear, which may not be translated into words or concepts, just as our intellect and sensitivity cannot withstand their pleasant impressions.

With *this* spirit our master has now cultivated and harvested another field, as a result of which another new genre, quite different from the previous ones, had to be created; and it is, in its construction, just as out-of-the-ordinary as the elements themselves out of which it is constructed; and so the Oratorio *The Creation* came into being.

The poem is a collection of pictures, taken from the works of nature, and is like a succession of paintings passing before us; by means of practical music, these things are described and developed. The subject is the biblical story of the creation of the world, upon the principal moments of which the poet lingers from time to time, adding his own comments. Thus we are dealing only with an historical-cum-poetical description, where movement and repose are made to come alive by a magical play of colour on the imagination and by the art of the music; and all this is paraded in front of the inner eye like a fine shadow-play, showing us the beauties of paradise, a wonderful garden, or a world newly born, in which we may shed our daily outworn personality for a time to steep ourselves in the enjoyment of fresh and unadulterated beams of young innocence. To establish the necessary contrast, the poet has delineated the absence of light and order as inimical forces, which are set against light and order as a more powerful force. Here, then, we find neither persons nor action, and it is not clear why the poet introduced the angels Raphael, Gabriel and Uriel to tell us the story of the Creation as if they had been present. The fact that these quite unimportant names probably serve to introduce a variety of voices is no excuse, for just as the poet represents the chorus, he could and should have represented the other voices; in brief, so long as there is no character revealed by action and motive, no person and no name can be considered. We do not know if the poet started with a theory for this Oratorio, but he must have had a reason and that cannot be discovered. This apparently minor circumstance renders most difficult a clear understanding of the nature of this excellent work, even for very eager and experienced amateurs, who in their open enjoyment of it are unable to explain the actual constitution [*Bestand*] of the work itself. So much for the poem, upon which we shall not dwell, for it is very deficient throughout.

As far as the music and its treatment by the composer are concerned, in view of the above observations we may permit outselves to be shorter. About the Overture, we may refer the readers of this Journal to an aesthetic analysis (11th Number, 3rd Year), to which we wish to add but little. It reveals a master of the highest rank, this Overture, and is in our opinion the greatest section of the work: the crown on a royal head. It is called The Representation of Chaos. Here there are almost all available instruments for the theme and substance [*Stoff und Materialen*], out of which a gigantic, limitless fabric of artistic splendour is woven and organized. The argument that it is impossible to depict chaos by harmonic, melodic and rhythmic means falls to pieces here in view of a subtle intellectual pretension [*Verstandesprätension*] with which any composer can if necessary excuse himself for not wanting to solve such a task if he were faced with it. Yet despite this appearance of impossibility, of contradiction, of (as it were) the fabulous – this is, at the same time, the most poetic and thus the best of the whole plan, and our master has presented it in a truly poetic, rich and original fashion. There reigns here the richest luxury of chords, figures and passages, presented in oriental splendour and revealing a treasure of genius and art, such as a musical prince might display for the ear and taste of his most noble guest, and which rises out of the vasty deep like the morning sun. We have purposely refrained from any musical examples, which in our opinion would serve no purpose here, and we would rather wish to draw the attention of artistic disciples to the work as a whole, from which much is to be learned and, even more, understood. Almost all accidental dissonances appear here purposely unprepared. The strange mixture of figuration and types of notes (which consist of semibreves, minims, crotchets, quavers and semiquavers; of triplets, roulades, trills and grace notes) gives the score a peculiar, secretive look. One is amazed about the number of small, playing figurations, which swarm next to enormous dark masses like clouds of insects against a great horizon; but all together the result, in its context and with the dark concept of chaos, is an endlessly satisfying harmonic texture, wherein the paths of modulations are beautiful beyond belief and in many places so sublime and lofty as to excite our admiration. It is against the order of things and impossible that such an excellent piece of work could be everywhere recognized for that which it is, and can only be, especially since certain deeply rooted theories, formed from works of an earlier epoch, remain at permanent odds with the spirit of progress, and from which there naturally derives a type of criticism that only knows how to take and not to give. Such criticism must at all costs be prevented from the dangerous business of confronting such a work as this Overture; that, too, is obvious.

After this Overture follows, in biblical order, the story of the Creation, divided into the customary succession of recitatives, arias and choruses. The recitatives, being straight narrative, allow of no lyrical treatment and therefore are treated freely by the composer and are mostly accompanied by instruments, not so much through the emotion and sense of the action as because of the actual sound of the words themselves. They deserve attention particularly in view of the masterly orchestration and the great variety of thought which seems to pour out limitlessly. The arias, on the other hand, are much more considered, though there is a running narrative in them, too. But here we find a contradictory relationship between the composer and the libretto. The first aria is as follows:

'Nun schwanden' [etc., quoted *in extenso*]
Chorus
'Verzweiflung, Wuth' [etc., *in extenso*]

If the poet wanted to turn these words into an aria, he missed the nature of the aria, in which the main point must be, as one would imagine both literally and figuratively, the present; and where it is permitted to refer to the past or future only in so far as it is possible to regard them from today's standpoint. But if the composer wanted to write an aria here, at least the words of this narrative ought never to be repeated, as happens here: for who could hear with pleasure a story-teller so often repeating his words and thus interrupting the flow of his narrative (only as a result of which is the story made interesting)? The delight which this aria awakens every time it is heard is exclusively the composer's merit, however, who quite apart from the narrative content of the text lays the whole action in the present. The aria may be well compared to the cheerful morning of the first day, on which night and confusion have been driven out by light and order – a new world which develops by itself. The chorus with its fugal treatment enters magnificently here, and the metrical treatment of the ensuing text, 'Und eine neue Welt', is of great beauty.

That which has been said about the organization of the recitatives and the first aria may be applied to most of the arias and recitatives in this Oratorio. They have, in our opinion, all the same mistake which is covered up by innumerable numbers of outstanding melodic and harmonic touches of genius on the part of the composer and which excite our admiration so long as we do not look at the libretto.

The passage in which the moon appears is of touching, yearning beauty and it is a pity that this gentle impression is immediately afterwards destroyed; for the poet had at this point the best possibility of developing the most beautiful thought, based on the general concept of the quiet moon, and he should have been more concise about things that are less important than light.

The first aria of Part II is in every respect the most beautiful of the work; the composer could do nothing but to 'paint' the words of the poet, and if perhaps the eagle's flight and the dove's cooing do not specially enthuse, nevertheless the composer of

> 'Aus jedem Busch und Hain
> [etc. in extenso, up to:]
> Ihr reizendes Gesang'

reveals a purity and innocence which are most praiseworthy and for which words fail us. The vocal line, apart from the whole instrumentation, at the words 'Noch drückte Gram nicht ihre Brust' reminds one painfully of a state of innocence and strength [*Ungebrechlichkeit*] the loss of which must depress a beautiful soul. One sees with the greatest pleasure how the composer loses no opportunity of expressing, through his art, everything that this art can and does express.

The aria

> 'Nun scheint in vollem Glanze' [etc., *in extenso*]

is a most melodious, grand and broad description of the newly created universe's magnificence; the orchestration is of exceptional power and splendour; especially the horns and trumpets are used with mastery.

The prayer

> 'Zu dir, O Herr! [etc. to:]
> Gesättigt werden sie'.

is partly accompanied only by the wind instruments, which have great fluidity throughout and in this respect are to be recommended as a paragon for talented young composers.

There now appears, towards the end of Part II, a human being who with his wife finally, in Part III, gush over God's work – but much too late and in such watery speeches that it is a pity for the beautiful music.

We proceed to the choruses. If our composer was hitherto in his element, he is now right at home. These choruses are almost without exception treated fugally. The subjects are comprehensible and the countersubjects and inversions [*Repercussionen*] enter freely and naturally. Never darkness or confusion, and even the augmentations are clear and strong, though nowhere 'severe'. The treatment of the words is truer and more daring than in the arias and recitatives, while the orchestration is excellent beyond description throughout. Of particular interest are the two choruses

> 'Denn er hat Himmel und Erde bekleidet' [etc.]

and

> 'Vollendet ist das grosse Werk.'

The theme of the first of these choruses, from the oratorio and technical standpoint, sets a real standard because of its nobility and clarity, despite the many words of a period. But if eager young harmonists will not have overlooked the fact that in all the fugal choruses of this Oratorio there is a certain lightness, suppleness or exaggerated freedom; and if they will have remarked that in this whole huge work there is not a single strict fugue, though opportunity for them was not lacking; nevertheless let it be said to them that he who works so easily, fully and fluently can only do so if he knows how to set up a strict fugue with all its attributes. Such examples of the great masters are so seductive for young artists that they judge the art of learning how to write fugues (which even with decided talent requires many years of long dedication) far too readily as a dull, schoolmasterish exercise. It does not require an exceptional degree of talent and artistry to bring forth a piece whereby a score with many lines of music is concocted so that the unwitting hold it to be a fugue, the more readily if the writing therein is less natural and casual. But the art of dealing with a musical subject, of developing it in an interesting way, so that it remains an important part of the whole (and the whole being something beautiful) – to do that requires training in fugal movements, and this field was neglected far too long. Among Haydn's unforgettable merits is also this: his excellent compositions, their fire, their truth and their spice, are largely due to the fine use of counterpoint and to his way of writing fugues. He, who with his genius, his eternally fresh and youthful richness of thought has left all his contemporaries behind him, is not ashamed to adorn his works with contrapuntal beauties, as a result of which, despite all the changing fates of time and mode, they will remain immortal as long as music is an art. [III, 385–96]

To continue this section on *The Creation*'s progress, we return to a figure who had entered Haydn's life, as it were, by the back door: the composer Roman Hoffstetter (1742–1815), a monk at the Monastery of Amorbach in Germany, who had composed diligently in Haydn's style and many of whose works had circulated under Haydn's name in manuscript. Recent research[1] indicates that he was probably the composer of Haydn's String Quartets, Op. 3, which first appeared in Paris and had been engraved as 'Quartetto per due Violini Alto e Basso del Signor Hofstetter / Violino Primo [etc.] / No. 1 [etc.], the title later erased (but not completely) and Haydn's name substituted.

In 1800, Silverstolpe, who was collecting material for a biography of J. M. Kraus, heard that Hoffstetter had been on friendly terms with Kraus, and a correspondence between Vienna and Odenwald began, in the course of which Haydn's name, and *The Creation*, figure prominently. Hoffstetter's letters are in the University of Uppsala and were first published by Georg Feder in *Haydn-Studien* (I[1966], Heft 3, 199ff.):

[4 September 1800:] . . . Often when he [Kraus] raised his dear Gluck up to the stars, I did the same for my dear Hajdn, for whom I am enthusiastically prejudiced; we got into an argument, a musical fight, which ended to my satisfaction, however, in that we agreed that Gluck was for all times in theatrical matters the greatest master, but Hajdn was that in all other musical affairs . . .

[3 November 1800:] Many beautiful things have been said to me about Haydn's wonderful *Creation*, and that caused me a thousand times to wish that I could at least see the score of it [Hoffstetter was almost totally deaf in 1800]. Since that is never going to be the case, however, I would have purchased the piano score, which was announced in the newspapers, except for the fact that the price of 11 fl. exceeded my available cash, and that was an unavoidable hindrance. The work must be very long if the piano score is so expensive! No doubt the new work, the *4 Seasons*, of which you, Sir, were kind enough to inform me, will turn out to be just as wonderful, for out of that pen nothing but good can come! This great master – musical creator, I should say – has already written so much, almost unbelievably much which is beautiful, that one could almost believe he is inexhaustible.

[8 May 1801:] You, Sir, through the sending of the Haydn masterpiece have shown so much favour and goodness to my undeserving self, and have given me such a surprise, and placed me so much under obligation, that I am unable, much as I would like to, to express myself properly. I could hardly believe my own eyes when the wonderful work, unique in its fashion, was in my hands, and you, Sir, even paid the postage costs; really, that was too kind of you! Please accept my most profound, respectful and dutiful thanks! May I be able to recompense you in

1 Alan Tyson and H. C. Robbins Landon, 'Who composed Haydn's Op. 3?', in *Musical Times*, July 1964, p. 506; also Hubert Unverricht, *Die beiden Hoffstetter*, Mainz 1968.

some way for it! In this respect I wish more than ever that I had not been so precipitous in getting rid of my musical collection some years ago, for it was quite large and besides a large quantity of various printed and manuscript works contained well over one hundred operas; at least I could have had the pleasure of repaying you, Sir, at least in some measure for the debt and thanks I owe you. . . . Among the things that I still have there are 'Ah come il core mi palpita' [from *La fedeltà premiata*]. Also his beautiful *Stabat mater*. . . . My own newer works, which are of little or no importance, can hardly be placed on the scales; there are only Masses, which round here have been rewarded with a certain amount of success – perhaps because these people don't know anything better – but there in Vienna, where there is a confluence of masters and masterpieces, it would be a mistake to let them show their faces.

I haven't yet begun to study Haydn's wonderful *Creation* with care; first I wanted to complete a Mass that I've started on, because if I look at it [*The Creation*] beforehand it might rob me of all my will to continue working; when I've finished [with the Mass] I will fall on it ravenously, Meanwhile even at the first glance, though only fleeting (I couldn't resist that), I found a thousand beauties. Also *The Storm* [Madrigal, 1792] is excellent, it contains everything that one can consider wild, terrible and rushing, but also pleasant and graceful, and to the highest degree. Both works will be returned to you in good condition, thankfully, and without even a scratch on their covers, though I won't be able to stop from copying them (with your kind permission, on which I take the liberty of counting); it would be a pity to send them back uncopied!

[25 July 1801:] You, Sir, receive herewith in return the wonderful Haydn *Creation*, and for kindly sending it to me I am most grateful; although I copied it from beginning to end, I would still have sent it back to you earlier if I had not been forced to get the necessary paper from Frankfurth, and had to wait for five or six weeks until they sent it. During the copying I had the first opportunity of seeing all the many beauties that the great Haydn has placed all through this masterpiece. It is really beautiful in the highest sense! But only at great courts, where there are the greatest and most complete orchestras, can and should a performance be contemplated, since so many instruments are necessary. The trombones, which I also found in Gluck's operas and in many other scores as well, are instruments I don't know, and I can't imagine what kind of an instrument it is. Also the double bassoon is unknown to me unless, as I gather, it is really the Sarabant – or how do you call that thing? [serpent]. The introduction to *The Creat*[*ion*] is very profound and dark; I had to study long to grasp the musical sense; but it went that much better with the arias, choruses and accompanied recitatives; all is magnificent, unique of its kind. It is astonishing how many beautiful things, and in all musical genres, that great man wrote! And now the papers say that his new work, the *4 Seasons*, is just as beautiful and magnificent – perhaps to an even greater extent, than *The Creation*. How is the text of this new work organized? I cannot imagine it.

Many, many times I had the desire to pluck up my courage and write to *H*[*err*] *Kapellm*. Haydn, and to send the one or the other of my Masses to him to examine, judge and if necessary correct but I haven't had the courage because it seemed not the right thing to do; for one thing this famous man certainly has enough to do without wanting to take time off for an everyday plodder like me; and then the distance is much too great, and would require more freight costs than the whole bunch of Masses is worth. . . .

The engraving of *The Creation* is very handsome, nice and correct; hardly in the whole thing is a tiny note misprinted; it will also be very expensive: certainly a good business for a publisher! The subscription list shows more than 400 copies!

[11 January 1802:] With pleasure I take the opportunity to fulfil your gracious wish to see something of my Odenwald, very unimportant, musical products, though I do so with fear and trembling; knowing my great weaknesses, I can do nothing but to await anxiously an opinion which is born in regions that are in musical matters brighter than anywhere else, Berlin not excluded. I am specially afraid of the great Haydn, from whose knowledgeable eye nothing can escape, but also of your profound understanding, Sir, of which I was persuaded from the first letter with which you honoured me. Therefore I must ask you to be generous, and would remind you that he who wrote it, never had the advantage of having any kind of instruction in composition; that moreover I must forego using the piano [being deaf] and also forego the advantage of hearing a piece with all its instruments. Because of my unfortunate defect I am not able to hear all (or any) voices, near and far, and thus the whole full harmony either.

The Mass would have been sent sooner, but I wanted to make a new copy of the score, which you don't need to return. If only my handwriting were better! With artificial light, which considering the short days I require for most of the work, and even with four eyes I wouldn't make much progress.

There is a mistake, made in hurrying, that is apparent in the unexpected [*wiedrige*] transition from C to B [B flat?] at the Credo and incarnatus . . . let us hope it is the only mistake! I would like to add a bold confession, that in some passages I have perhaps deserved to be rapped on the knuckles by my dear Haydn. I find everything that comes from the Haydnish pen so beautiful, it remains deep down inside me, that I can't resist now and then copying him; then there is another thing, that when I wrote the Mass I was entirely convinced that it would mould away in Odenwald, and I never imagined that in time it would be put under the eyes of the great man himself! . . .

Herr Kapellm. Haydn will presumably spend most of the winter in Vienna? May I ask you, Sir, to greet him in my undeserving name, and to assure him of my boundless, profound respect and admiration? What will this Grand Master of music, this inexhaustible cornu copiae, now be writing? – now that the *4 Seasons* are long since completed. He does go on writing, and it would be a pity for the whole musical world if he did not.

[23 January 1802:] Recently I was given an article from the *Zeitung für die elegante Welt* to read, which contained a bitter criticism of the Haydn *Creation* and annoyed me to the depths of my soul. The man seriously fears that Haydn might be putting back music to its state thirty or forty years ago! He, who has left everyone behind, who sees more profoundly than anyone else, and perhaps anyone ever will.

To conclude this brief survey, we present this famous antagonistic criticism from the *Zeitung für die elegante Welt*. Apart from being a curiosity in its own right, it was to prove grimly prophetic of the attitude towards Haydn the man, Haydn the artist, and *The Creation*. The writer was the composer and *Kapellmeister* F. L. A. Kunzen (1761–1817).

Haydn's *Creation*

(Copenhagen, 20 Oct. 1801.)

(Since reports of performances of Haydn's *Creation* have become a *regular modish feature* throughout this year in German papers, a powerfully phrased (if also retarded) word on the subject, by an artist who has preserved his genius and his pure taste sufficiently through large and real works of art, may bring the series to a close.)

Finally, my friend, we too have now performed *The Creation*. We should really have had to be ashamed of ourselves if we had not finally been able to insert an article in the newspapers, as has been the case in almost the whole of Europe, that we had at last performed the famous *Creation* with a chorus and orchestra of 200 persons. This has now really happened and as a benefit for the wounded of 2 April [Nelson's naval battle of Copenhagen] in one of our largest churches. Many amateurs took part in the performance and they surpassed the greatest expectations, though only the most necessary rehearsals could be held. The audience was exceptional, as could not have been otherwise in the case of such a much trumpeted [*ausgeschrienes*] masterpiece and *non plus ultra* of art. I think I may truthfully say that 6,000 listeners were assembled. The impression that the music made seems to be very diverse, although it could not fail that – since such a complete chorus and orchestra had never been heard here – many who were disappointed thought they had discovered the great effects in *Haydn*'s music. Let us leave them with their belief and put forward, instead, our individual opinion about this famous music.

First, a few words about the text, if it is not already lost effort to write anything at all about that potpourri [*Machwerk*]. If one had wanted to set a trap for a composer and to reveal him in all his nakedness, I cannot imagine anything more successful. One considers the biblical sayings chosen without selection, the detailed cataloguing of all living creatures and finally Adam and Eve, who act wise beyond the event on the earth and produce much loud chatter about their impressions – those are the poem's ingredients. If anyone could dare to set this to music, it naturally had to be such a man as *Haydn*, whose musical talent displays itself more in instrumental effects than in places where it would be necessary to portray feelings and passion.

What he does with this is not more and not less than a *never-ending symphony*, mixed with recitatives and sublime [*erhabnen*] choruses. – How the poet must have rejoiced as he put into the composer's hand the idea of setting chaos to music; can there be a more unfortunate idea? All music is in itself order, rhythm. Without them no music is conceivable. A chaos of notes is no music but noise, shouting, racket; and everything that lies beyond the sphere of the beautiful, the idealistic, is lost for art. Lessing has shown this clearly in his *Laokoon*. – That H. used all his art to bring forth this chaotic impression is clear; but what is the result? –

In the beginning &c. it was dark and empty; but empty the Overture is not, though dark enough; but I could nowhere discover the *Spirit of God* moving on the face of the waters. But since I do not wish to write a review, I must be more brief. Haydn's *Creation* cannot become an aesthetic work of art and will long be forgotten when one is forever and ever delighting in his unexcelled instrumental compositions. As well and diligently as the choruses are composed, and grand though he reveals himself therein as a harmonist, and much as he displays his art in the use of the orchestra: yet one cannot escape the impression that the music does not fit the words and the words do not fit the music; nor that the declamation is faulty and sloppy; that the persons are not characterized, that for example the archangels sing more badly than Adam and Eve; that the recitatives are dry and uneven, the vocal parts are treated like instruments and drowned by the noise of the instruments; that the vocal line is broken off and not prominent enough; that the middle registers, not the most favourable for the singers, are used too frequently; that the descriptions [*Mahlerein*] of the snowflakes (a visible object!), of the roaring lions, the twittering larks, the cooing doves, the *lamenting* nightingale (though the poet says that in those days they did not yet lament) and the constant painting put us back to the times of rainbow-maker *Telemann*; that the style is uneven, sometimes old-fashioned, sometimes religious, but often all too theatrical; that it does not lack for quotations, ductility and trivial movements, which stand out the more when compared to the sublime choruses. Who has not meanwhile realized that many of the mistakes enumerated above may be laid to the poet and that he is the real sinner here.

The Danish translator, *Herr* Suldbergh, made every effort to ennoble the diction, and he succeeded admirably in the duets between Adam and Eve, where he could, without prejudicing the music, completely escape from his predecessor; but this was not possible with the remainder.

Here you have the result of my impressions about this work of art. Should my remarks be considered without foundation, I will be glad to supply the necessary proofs. Much as I otherwise admire H's talent, I consider it my duty to point out the wrong path that this and similar works have taken. Already they are praising *The Seasons* and *The Last Judgment* in periodicals in a tone that – if it were not meant seriously – would be taken for persiflage.[1] May the croaking frogs, which are supposed to appear in *The Seasons*, please those who are not ashamed of childishness; for my part I see with sadness that [theorists] Sulzer, Engel and other famous men have been talking into the wind, and that music's enlightenment has not made much progress, inasmuch as the taste of such works may put us back for thirty or forty years.

[*Zeitung für die elegante Welt*, No. 153, 22 December 1801; 'spaced' words are given in italics.]

1 [Original footnote:] Of *The Seasons*, which will soon be in the public's hands and in a few days will be performed in the Leipzig playhouse by *Herr Musikdir. Müller*, there has appeared in this journal (No. 130) a review which is in all seriousness favourable, and we will soon see if rightly or wrongly. *The Last Judgment* is not to be considered at all since H. is not working on any such work. Red[aktion].

CHAPTER FOURTEEN

Works of 1800

Cantata ('Lines from the *Battle of the Nile*')
for Soprano and Pianoforte (XXVIb: 4)

Text by Ellis Cornelia Knight, 1798. Dedicated to Emma, Lady Hamilton.
Recitativo 'Ausania, trembling 'midst unnumber'd woes'. C minor, *Adagio*, 4/4→B flat.

Air 'Blest leader!'. B flat, *Allegretto*, *alla breve*.
Critical edition in preparation by the present writer. In 1932 Ludwig Landshoff orchestrated the work very cleverly (even using 'natural' horns and trumpets) and published his score, with the original English text and a German translation by Franz Hessel and Landshoff: Edition Adler, Berlin (later: Heinrichshofen's Verlag, Magdeburg). We own a copy of this edition through the kindness of the original publisher, the late F. Charles Adler.

The 'Nelson Aria', as it is sometimes called, is of course an 'occasional piece' and does not compare with the power and splendour of the *Scena di Berenice* (1795); but Haydn's last piece in this style contains, as one might expect of any work he composed in the year 1800, many interesting formal devices and some felicitous touches. Basically, the piece divides in two sections (*vide supra*) and thus is not in the more complicated *scena* form used by Haydn in 1795 and by Beethoven a year later in 'Ah! perfido'. Yet the Cantata of 1800 manages to incorporate some subtle features from the *scena* form. For example, the tune of the Aria itself

is already announced *verbatim* (and even at the later tempo, Allegretto) soon after the Recitative begins. It then appears a second time in the Recitative, following an Allegro which describes 'the gallic navy', in C major. On the other hand, the recitative quality that prevailed even when the Air was quoted previous to its appearance in the second part is maintained in the actual aria. Thus the voice enters with a quite different, declamatory style over the melody:

Admirers of Nelson will be interested to see that Miss Knight, the daughter of a British Admiral, has recorded the famous description of Nelson and his admirals: 'This band of brothers . . . a small, determin'd band, their Country's pride', which lines occur in the middle of the Recitative.

The Air itself contains two melodic lines of exceptional beauty. The first unfortunately never appears again:

but the second is expanded, and is in the grand *cantilena* style of late Haydn vocal

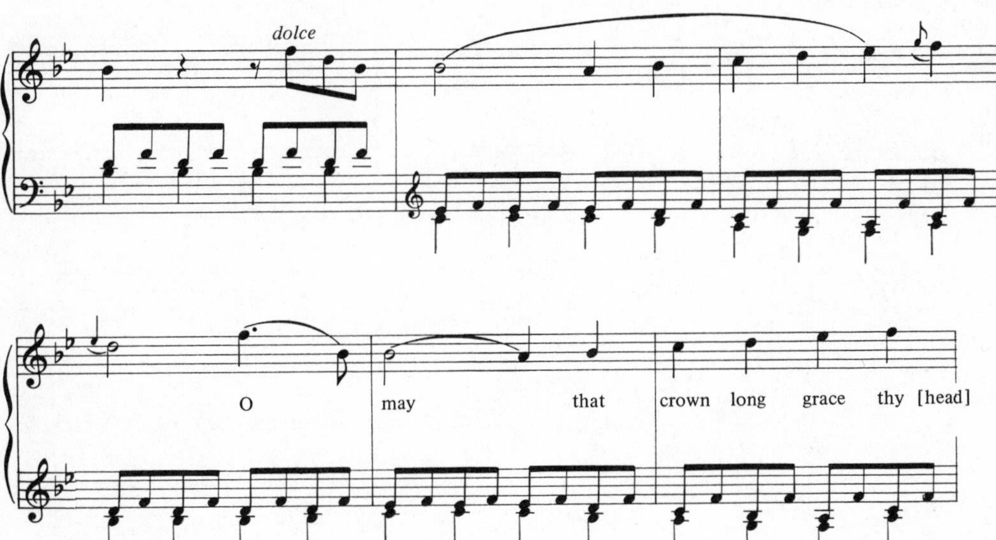

Another admirable point comes to illustrate the words 'Kingdoms to free from servile dread'. The first time, Haydn soars up to *f''* at the word 'free' and plunges down to *b natural* below middle *c* to illustrate the text, but the repetition introduced a magnificent modulation, from the bold harmony of which we see Haydn's concept of the famous British freedom (see example overleaf).

The work's most surprising and formally original part is its very end, which breaks into 'Recitativo' to introduce the words 'Eternal praise, great Nelson! to thy name and these immortal partners of thy fame'; after that, there are only four bars of concluding *ritornello*. It brings into dramatic spotlight the first introduction of Nelson's name in Haydn's version of the text and explains why the composer was at such pains to turn the text round and of course to shorten it as considerably as he did. This conclusion is a real stroke of dramatic insight.

It remains to observe that, like the final concert aria of 1798, 'Solo e pensoso', the main key of the Cantata is B flat, with which Haydn has a real obsession in his old age, particularly with vocal music (four of the last six Masses and crucial sections of both late Oratorios); it seems to draw him like a magnet.

King - doms to free from ser -
- vile dread, King - doms to free
from ser - vile dread
3
3
3
3

Te Deum in C (1800?) for the Empress Marie Therese (XXIIIc: 2)

'Te Deum laudamus' – *Allegro*, C major, 4/4 (later changed by Haydn to *Allegro con spirito*); 'Te ergo quaesumus' – *Adagio*, C minor, 4/4; 'Aeterna fac' – *Allegro moderato*, C major, 4/4 (later changed by Haydn to *Allegro con spirito*).

Scoring: fl., 2 ob., 2 fag., 2 cor. in C, 3 trpt. in C, (3 trbn.), timp., strings, organ, 4-part chorus (SATB).

Critical edition: score, piano score and parts (D. 10.000), also miniature score (Doblinger; also reprinted by Philharmonia, No. 454), Verlag Doblinger (1959), edited by the present writer.

THE PROBLEM OF THE WORK'S DATE

In her useful study of the sources to the *Te Deum*, Irmgard Becker-Glauch suggests[1] that the work was composed between 1798 and 1800, relying for this particular period on Griesinger's letter to Breitkopf & Härtel. Therein he mentions the work 'which he [Haydn] composed for the Empress two or three years ago', which would mean in 1798 or 1799. Haydn's 'vor 2. oder 3. Jahren' is, however, a typical Austrian expression and is perhaps to be meant no more literally than, for example, the Italian expression for cheap, 'costa tre soldi'. And in another letter to Breitkopf & Härtel of 25 May 1799, which we have quoted above (*supra*, p. 466), it is clearly to be understood that Haydn was making excuses to the Leipzig firm for not writing new works because he had a longstanding order from the Empress and also Prince Nicolaus Esterházy which he had not yet fulfilled, to wit the *Te Deum* and the *Theresienmesse*. Therefore, the tempting entry in Rosenbaum's *Diary* for 19 May 1799 – 'Sunday . . . A Te Deum Laudamus to bless our arms. The Court drove in gala to St Stephen's, the Hungarian and German Guard paraded . . .' (p. 65) – cannot refer to the Haydn *Te Deum* because it was not yet composed. The first authentic evidence of any performance is that at Eisenstadt at the beginning of September 1800, discussed above. There is a copy at the Cistercian Monastery of Heiligenkreuz in Lower Austria with the stamp 'I.D.' on the parts. These initials refer to Joseph Drasenberger, who died at Graz on 7 November 1800.[2] The interesting fact about this date is that the copy in Heiligenkreuz represents a revised version of the work which Frau Becker-Glauch discovered at Graz after our edition of the score had been published.

The Eisenstadt parts, discussed above, were copied in September 1800 and represent the authentic, original version. This was also the version of the Hofburgkapelle parts (Source C of our score) and the authentic score published in the autumn of 1802 by Breitkopf & Härtel. At some point, Haydn sent an authentic copy of the parts, written by Johann Elssler, to someone in Styria.[3] This source was discovered by Frau Becker-Glauch in the 1960s. Not only does the presence of Johann Elssler make the parts authentic, but Haydn also made some fascinating changes. These may be summed up here, and should be added to the Doblinger/Philharmonia edition. The most important is the change from Allegro to Allegro con spirito for the first section, and Allegro moderato to Allegro con spirito for the final section. The old tempo, Allegro moderato, is in fact a miscalculation, for Haydn certainly cannot have intended the final section to be *slower* than the opening. When the chorus enters at bar 9, Haydn originally left the voices without any dynamic marks, as was the custom: *forte* was intended and was regarded as self-evident. In the Graz copy, Haydn added *f*, but this obvious addition does not, as Frau Becker-Glauch writes, 'bring about that the chorus in bars 9 and 11, with their first cries to God ('Te'), raise the expression to one of majestic grandeur'. The majestic grandeur was there before; no one was going to sing the choral entrance 'Te Deum laudamus' *piano*. . . . What is far more interesting is that the timpani suddenly have a *ff* at this point (bar 9). Haydn also added the off-beat *fz* at bars 39, 41, 44, 46, 52 (these are also in our score, partly in brackets) as well as 53–55 (5th note) in the first and second violins.

1 'Joseph Haydns Te Deum für die Kaiserin – eine Quellenstudie', in *Colloquium Amicorum*, Joseph Schmidt-Görg zum 70. Geburtstag, Bonn 1967, pp. 1ff. See also her article 'Neue Forschungen zu Haydns Kirchenmusik', *Haydn-Studien* II (1970), Heft 3, pp. 167., esp. 236f.

2 Becker-Glauch in *Haydn-Studien* II/3, 236.

3 It is now owned by the Akademie für Musik und darstellende Kunst in Graz and bears the old stamp of the 'Musikverein in Gratz', also the initials 'F:B:D:' and 'Kargl mpria'.

The Heiligenkreuz source contains these changes, or most of them, and shows that this revised version of the *Te Deum* was sent away by the composer before November 1800. As we have seen so often, Haydn liked to look through a copied score before it was sent off – for example, the Op. 76 and 77 Quartets for Longman & Clementi – and frequently added changes that he did not bother to incorporate on the 'master score' or 'master parts' from which Elssler made his MS. copies. They were the kind of things, moreover, which he hardly bothered to add to the Eisenstadt parts because they were all matters that he could explain orally, and very quickly, too (the tempo changes, the *ff* in the drums, the accents in the violins could all be suggested by a wave of the baton in one form or another).

It is very curious that the autograph had disappeared. One would have expected that it would have ended in the Emperor's music collection in the Hofburgkapelle, along with the other authentic parts to the late Masses. Only this autograph would solve the exact dating, and also inform us about one final textual point which is worth mentioning. It seems that the very first score of this *Te Deum* started at what is now bar 9, i.e. without the eight bars of orchestral introduction; the Eisenstadt MS. seems to have started life in this fashion (but was immediately corrected), and there are two sources in the Hofburgkapelle in which these opening eight bars are not included. Perhaps the horns are also a later addition. They are wanting on the Hofburgkapelle set of parts, and also in an interesting MS. score in the Österreichische Nationalbibliothek, Musiksammlung. This leads us to

THE QUESTION OF THE BRASS SCORING

Except for the Hofburgkapelle, the early sources all lack trombone parts. In the Hofburgkapelle manuscript, the alto and tenor trombone parts are contemporary with the source itself (which is clearly a copy of a lost original of some kind), but the part for bass trombone is later. On the other hand, Haydn was now regularly using trombones in Vienna. If he actually omitted them from the original score – this means the Hofburgkapelle parts were added locally, which is entirely possible – one wonders if he was not thinking of the performance conditions at Eisenstadt as well as those of Vienna. And this raises one more curious point: Haydn had three trumpets and kettledrums in his band; they had been engaged permanently in the year 1799. Why then did Haydn have to engage four more trumpeters and a kettledrum player for St Mary's Day 1800? The staggering total would then be seven trumpeters and two drummers. And the obvious explanation, that two of them played horns, is unlikely (a) because the document in question specifically mentions trumpeters and (b) the Esterházy band had two horn players in the wind-band group ('Harmonie Musique Individuen'). At present we cannot even provide a remote theory to explain the presence of all these many trumpets during Nelson's and the Hamiltons' stay at Eisenstadt.

THE FIRST RECORDING

The first (semi-commercial) recording of Haydn's *Te Deum* was made by the British Broadcasting Corporation in 1958 as part of the series 'The Unknown Haydn' prepared by the present writer. At that time the performance, which like the whole series was released by BBC Transcription Records, was by the BBC Chorus, the BBC Symphony Orchestra with Charles Spinks (organ), conducted by Sir Adrian Boult.

ANALYTICAL NOTES

Throughout his life Haydn had grown up with the Gregorian plainchant, and he had lovingly used its agelessly beautiful melodies in earlier church music, in symphonies, even in wind-band *divertimenti* (II: 23, 'Incipit Lamentatio'). Now, at the close of his artistic life, he turns once more to the rich musical legacy of his Church, and incorporates the Eighth Psalm-Tone at the very beginning of the work. But though he does partly conceal the Psalm-Tone in a rich and jubilant texture of dancing violins and thundering kettledrums, his audience and the players would have discovered the melody at once as soon as the chorus enters, singing the melody in octaves. The concealment to which Haydn usually subjects such old tunes – we have seen another instance in the 'Heilig, heilig, heilig' in the Sanctus of the *Missa Sancti Bernardi de Offida* – operates in this case on several levels. When it appears at the beginning of the ritornello (see overleaf) the Psalm-Tone is given to the upper woodwind and the viola, a most unusual layout. Since the brass instruments cannot play the crucial note *a*, Haydn makes a virtue out of necessity and has the five brass players dissect part of the melody before, as it were, we have even heard it. Just as our ears have begun to discover that there is a very Gregorian-sounding background (or is it foreground?) to the orchestral beginning, the chorus enters and magnificently confirms the majestic presence of the Eighth Psalm-Tone. Notice that apart from the chorus, only the flute doubles the melody; not even the trombones, which more or less support the lower three voices, double in this case. Moreover, the brass instruments' 'dissection' is cancelled, so that the Psalm-Tone can stand out, ringing through the heavy orchestral texture – *ecclesia triumphans* (see p. 609).

Even in a work of this kind, the sonata-form principle of modulation to the dominant and, later, a kind of recapitulation must be adhered to; here we reach the dominant, and an extraordinary passage in which the timpani, viola and bass line punctuate the words 'Sanctus, Sanctus, Sanctus Dominus Deus Sabaoth', etc. with the following figure:

f p

At this point, Haydn's strong symbolic sense begins to operate: just like the word 'Sanctus', this figure appears three times. Similar *Thonmahlerey* may be observed at such a text as 'Patrem immensae majestatis', where the timpani unexpectedly enter, preceded and followed by many bars of rest. The 'symbolism of three' is altogether felt very strongly in the *Te Deum*: three large sections, to begin with, and even in a detail such as the fact that the above-mentioned timpani beats, to underline the 'immense majesty' of the Father, are three. And later, we find the Trinity concept appearing at such a phrase as

It goes without saying that Haydn's construction by motivic fragments obtains here in this work, and obtains brilliantly. The characteristic progression c–d–c in the Psalm-Tone becomes, later (67f.)

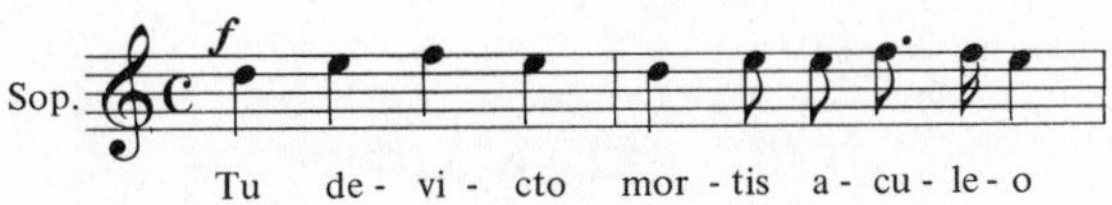

Allegro con spirito
Fl.
Ob.
[a2]
Fag.
Cor.
I/II
Trbe.
III
Trbn.
Timp.
V. I
V. II
S.
A.
CORO
T.
B.
Solo
Org. e B.

9
[Allegro con spirito]
Fl.
Ob.
Fag.
Cor.
I/II
Trbe.
III
Trbn.
Timp.
V. I
V. II
Va.
S.
A.
CORO
T.
B.
Org. e B.
Te, te De - um lau - da - mus: te, te Dominum confi - te - mur.

(progression up and down by the interval of a second), and in a burst of magnificent writing for the brass instruments and timpani,

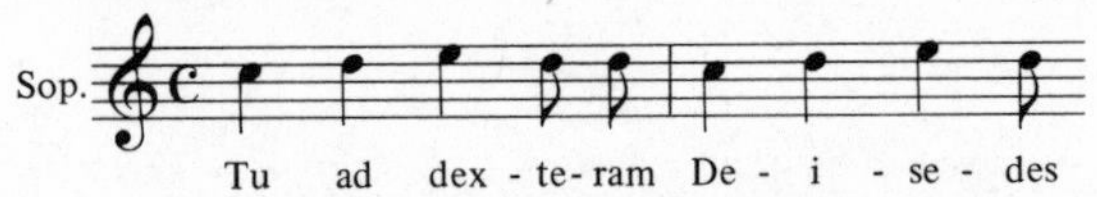

accompanied by massed crotchet chords of the horns, trumpets I and II, the three trombones and the timpani, which however soon (bar 77) break into fanfare rhythms of the old Baroque type:

The third trumpet holds a semibreve *g′* under and over all this brassy magnificence.

To hold together such a loosely constructed musical form required Haydn's greatest imagination, and that is why he not only had to work closely with such matters as symbolic numbers, motivic inter-relationships and the like, but also why he superimposed the A-B-A concept of sonata form not only, if one will, in the very largest sense (the overall three sections) but in particular within this first section. The 'recapitulation' comes, appropriately, at the words 'Tu Rex Gloriae, Christe' (bars 59ff.). With crashing brass fanfares we come to a gigantic pause on the dominant seventh, and the new section 'Te ergo quaesumus' begins, with vast echoes of the beginning of 'Chaos'. Here, in Catholic countries, the congregation kneels until the words 'Aeterna fac'. What simpler, more direct, more appropriate place for a division, and with what magnificent sense of drama and poetry the music floats over the kneeling faithful, after the gigantic 'empty' introductory chord (see example opposite). How beautifully the alto and tenor parts interchange at bars 85–6 (the final two bars of this example).

The congregation stands up, and the music changes to C major and *Allegro con spirito* for the third part. A long *pp* timpani roll starts to build up the tension ('Miserere nostri Domine'); the violins in the Eisenstadt MS. have a new accent mark which Haydn himself added to the parts:

(Nowadays we would write the accent turned round: >.)

'In te Domini speravi' are the inspiring words of the double fugue in which Haydn now reveals himself once again as the last great master to whom fugues were utterly second nature. It is one of his greatest and most exciting fugal movements, worthy to rank, for sheer physical excitement, with that incredible concluding fugue 'Et vitam venturi' of the Credo in the *Missa Cellensis in honorem B.V.M.* (1766). Towards the end come the bold syncopations to the words 'non confundar' which must have astonished the listeners at the dawn of the new century (see example, p. 612).

In these concluding bars we have *in nuce* Haydn's whole, positive philosophy. The break-down, as it were, reaches a point of total organized confusion shortly afterwards, when the orchestra *and* the chorus each have this series of syncopations: the forces of evil seem to be welling up (bars 177–9). But with a mighty shout of 'non', the three lower parts of the chorus thunder out the text 'non confundar in aeternam' *on* the beat, the soprano at first limping behind but then joining in this incredible affirmation of joy and goodness and God's Grace (see example, pp. 613–4, bars 178ff.).

Adagio
Fl.
Ob.
Fag.
Cor.
I/II
Trbe.
III
Trbn.
Timp.
Adagio
V. I
V. II
Va.
S.
Te er-go quaesumus, fa - mu-lis tu-is sub-ve-ni, fa-mu-lis tu-is sub-ve-ni,
A.
Te er-go quaesumus, fa-mulis tu - is sub-ve-ni, fa-mu-lis tu-is sub-ve-ni,
CORO
T.
Te er-go quaesumus, fa-mulis tu - is sub-ve-ni, fa-mu-lis tu-is sub-veni, quos
B.
Te er-go quaesumus, tu-is fa-mulis sub-ve-ni, quos
Solo unisono
Org. e B.

170
Fl.
Ob.
Fag.
Cor.
Trbe.
Trbn.
Timp.
V. I
V. II
Va.
CORO
S.
non con-fun - dar in ae-ter - num, non con-fun-dar in ae - ter - num,
A.
non con-fun - dar in ae-ter - num, non con-fun-dar in ae - ter - num,
T.
non con-fun - dar in ae-ter - num, non con-fun-dar in ae - ter - num,
B.
fun - dar in ae - ter - num, non con-fundar in ae-ter-num, in ae - ter - num, non con-
B. C.
unisono

178
Fl.
Ob.
Fag.
[Solo]
Cor.
I/II
Trbe.
III
Trbn.
Timp.
V. I
V. II
Va
CORO
S.
non confun-dar in ae-ter-num, non con-fun-dar in ae-ter-num,
A.
non confun-dar in ae-ter-num, non con-fun-dar in ae-ter-num,
T.
non confun-dar in ae-ter-num, non con-fun-dar in ae-ter-num,
B.
non confun-dar in ae-ter-num, non con-fun-dar in ae-ter-num,
B. C.
p senza organo

182
(f)
[a2]
f
non con-fun - dar, non, non con-fun-dar in ae - ter - num, non con - fun - dar
non con-fun - dar, non, non con-fun-dar in ae-ter-num,
non con-fun - dar, non, non con-fun-dar, non con-fun- dar in ae - ter - num,
non con-fun - dar, non, non con-fun-dar, non con-fun- dar in ae - ter - num,
8 76 7 65 10 10 10 76 76 76 76
f (Org.)

The last page (overleaf) seems to open the very gates of eternity. It is music that would inspire Austrian and German composers for generations; without it, the Bruckner *Te Deum*, to name just one offspring, would be unthinkable. Haydn's setting of the great Ambrosian Hymn is one of the crowning efforts of his old age, and it is gratifying to think that after the work's epochal re-launching by the British Broadcasting Corporation in 1958 and its publication the year thereafter (the Haydn Sesquicentenary), this sublime *Te Deum* has now uplifted thousands of hearts after being almost forgotten in the first part of the twentieth century.

Breitkopf & Härtel issued the *Te Deum* in a handsome full score (*Typendruck*) and included a German text by Professor C. A. H. Clodius; the score appeared in the autumn of 1802 and was reviewed by the *AMZ* in December 1803, as follows:

> *Te Deum a 4 voci coll'accompagnamento dell'Orchestra composta da J. Haydn; mit unterlegtem deutschen Texte vom Prof. C. A. H. Clodius. Partitur.* Leipzig bey Breitkopf und Härtel. (Pr. 1 Thlr. 8 Gr.)
>
> One knows the beautiful words of this song of praise, so suitable for musical composition. One also knows that which great masters such as Handel, Hasse etc. have made out of it. This composition of *Herr* Haydn is probably but an occasional work, where the composer could not work on a very large scale. The whole Te Deum is only a continuous Tutti of 183 bars in four-four, C major with the whole orchestra, in which only 9 bars of Adagio in C minor are inserted. But what could be done in such a piece is all done here. The harmonic progressions and the many modulations, necessary in such a long Tutti, follow very naturally and correctly. The words of the text are well expressed and nothing is omitted. The imitations at 'Tibi omnes angeli' are most beautiful, with the following 'Sanctus' and the unisono 'Majestatis' etc. on pages 6 to 9. The *piano* sections that are put in at 'sine peccato' on p. 27, but especially the beautiful section 'miserere nostri' on p. 29, spread over the whole that proper contrast between light and shadow. At the words 'In te Domini speravi' there appears a fugue with two subjects which continues for thirty bars (pages 31 to 37). The syncopations and augmentations, introduced with such consideration, at the words 'non confundar' (pp. 39 and 40) with the following fermata, prepare in a very artistic fashion for the noble [*erhabene*] cadenza with its long-held notes: 'in aeternum', with which the piece closes.
>
> Such a good note-for-note German text as that by *Herr* Professor Clodius is also a rare thing; it is very well fitted to the music, so that it can be sung in German as well as in Latin. Thus this work by Haydn may be recommended to every church- and chorus-director as useful and advantageous for his church; for because of its relative brevity, it can be used in almost any ecclesiastical ceremony. And on account of its easy style, in which it is written throughout, it can be easily performed by any choir. Moreover it lacks not in expression and in a magnificent orchestration, which greatly attracts the larger public, especially in Catholic churches.
>
> [*AMZ* VI, 191–3]

190
Fl.
[ff]
Ob.
[ff]
Fag
[ff]
Cor.
[ff]
I/II
Trbe.
III
[ff]
[ff]
Trbn.
[ff]
[ff]
[ff]
Timp.
tr
[ff]
V. I
[ff]
V. II
[ff]
Va.
[ff]
CORO
S.
[ff]
ter - - - num.
A.
[ff]
ter - - - num.
T.
[ff]
ter - - - num.
B.
[ff]
ter - - - num.
B. C.
8
3
[ff] [col pleno organo]

The title of this volume – *The Years of 'The Creation'* – is suggestive of its contents perhaps in a more literal way than might at first be expected: in the first place, Haydn's preoccupation with the actual composition and the series of semi-private and public performances of *The Creation*, and in addition the extraordinary influence of the Oratorio both on the world of the outgoing *settecento* in Europe and on Haydn's own works which immediately preceded and followed it. The various Masses of the years 1796 to 1799, the *Te Deum* and even the occasional works of the period – all of these (to paraphrase Boito apropos Verdi's old age) basked in the glory of its reflected rays. In the fifth and final volume – *The Late Years 1801–1809* (which might equally well be designated '*The Years of "The Seasons"*') – we shall follow the last great burst of Haydn's creative activity; the subsequent 'twilight and night' reveal to us something of a distilled Berensonian reflection and philosophy rare in any composer's life. The late years are, however, tinged with a sadness oddly at variance with the positive creative life that had preceded them over a period of half a century.

Appendix

Die Schöpfung (The Creation)

HAYDN'S MS. SUBSCRIPTION LIST (COMPILED IN 1799–1800) FOR THE FIRST EDITION

When Haydn printed his Oratorio in March 1800, there was a subscribers' list in the front. But there is an even better source for this subscription list than the first edition, namely Haydn's own autograph copy, which also includes details (such as addresses, and so forth) which were perforce omitted from the printed version. Since Haydn's MS. has never been printed, we herewith remedy this lacuna, thanks to the courtesy of the Historisches Museum der Stadt Wien, which institution owns the original – it is on exhibition in the Haydn Museum in Vienna – and kindly allowed us to examine it.

The imposing list is not only a tribute to Haydn's art but just as much a personal tribute as well. Quite obviously, many people subscribed not only to have the full score of the Oratorio in their possession but also to show their esteem and affection for its composer. It is touching to see, for example, colleagues in Vienna who were certainly not wealthy, such as *Kapellmeister* Joseph Preindl of St Peter's (later Cathedral Chapel Master) or Haydn's Viennese leader of the early performances, Paul Wranizky, ordering three copies. And, speaking of leaders, we are touched to see Johann Peter Salomon from London ordering twelve copies.

Of course the large English contingent is a reflection of the composer's popularity in that country. We meet again many old friends encountered in *Haydn in England 1791–1795*: 'nobility and gentry', and numerous 'simple citizens' who wanted to be remembered to Dr Haydn. The Royal family turned out in great numbers, and among Haydn's many English friends we find Mistress Schroeter, whose name must have caused Haydn a twinge of regret.

One of the most interesting aspects of this list is the presence of a large number of Russian subscribers. Haydn was well known in Russia. We have seen, in the correspondence between Count Razumovsky and Prince Subov (*supra*, p. 27), that the latter was interested in acquiring Haydn's latest 'Apponyi' Quartets, Opp. 71 and 74. Subov supported his own string quartet and was a favourite of the Empress Catherine II who, after the performance of a Haydn quartet at Court, called the Prince and said: 'If someone plays a solo, I know quite well that one applauds at the conclusion, but with a quartet I am embarrassed and am afraid to applaud at the wrong time – please, give me a look to show if the performance or the piece deserves to be praised.' Catherine also purchased a portrait 'du célèbre Haydn', as the Court bills for the year 1796 show. Haydn also had individual Russian friends and patrons who were outside the country. Once, when going to England for his second visit in January 1794, the composer even performed the duties of a secret messenger to the Russian Ambassador in London. The Russian Vice Chancellor, Prince W. P. Kotschubej, was in Vienna at the period and in a very confidential letter to Count S. R. Voronsov (Woronzow) of 18 January 1794, we read: 'Enfin, m^r le comte, après une vaine attente de plusieurs mois, je trouve une occasion sure pour vous parler à mon aise et à coeur ouvert. Mr Haydn, qui se rend à Londres, se charge de cette lettre.' Apart from showing the extraordinary reputation for diplomacy and discretion that Haydn enjoyed, it also suggests that Haydn's contact with the Russian colony outside that country was much wider than was hitherto suspected. No doubt one of Haydn's Russian friends suggested to the composer how he could organize a central post in Russia for gathering subscriptions to *The Creation*. Just at the period when the announcement appeared, Haydn's compositions were proving so popular in Russia that it paid local music publishers to start issuing their own editions, using a new opus series peculiar to Russia. Since information about these editions is totally wanting in Hoboken's *Verzeichnis*, and also partly missing in Boris Steinpress's excellent article[1] on Haydn's oratorios in Russia, we add a short list based on information sent to us by our British colleague, Cecil Hopkinson.[2]

The announcement in the *Moscow Journal* (1799, No. 72, 7 September, 1489f., also on 10 September) reads as follows:

> Mr Haydn, the famous music composer, has given the commission of asking the reverend public whether anyone would like to possess his latest musical composition entitled *Ssotworenije mira* [The Creation of the World] which has been acknowledged as the most outstanding of his works. It will consist of a volume of 300 pages with the words in German and English. The price will be 20 roubles a copy, and to please recipients, the name of each will be printed on the first page. Those wishing to own this composition may approach the music-seller Mr Dengler, to whom this commission was entrusted by Mr Haydn, and who lives near Rasguliai Street in the house of the merchant Goroshkoff, paying the stated sum of money at that time.

As the subscription list shows, the Russian response was generous. In fact, the principal number of Haydn's subscribers came from England, Austria-Germany and Russia. France, although eager to hear the new work, was prevented from

1 Boris Steinpress, 'Haydns Oratorien in Russland zu Lebzeiten des Komponisten', in *Haydn-Studien* II (1969), 2, pp. 77ff.

2 Mr Hopkinson kindly furnished this information in a letter of 19 March 1959:

Op. 1: Rondo. Pour le Clavecin ou Pianoforte composé par J. Haydn, op. 1. Au magazin de musique, chez [Johann Daniel] Gerstenberg et Comp., rue Grande Morskoi, maison de Charof, N 122 à St. Petersbourg', announced in August 1794. The slow movement of Symphony No. 94.

Op. 2: Adagio. Pour le Clavecin, Gerstenberg, 1794 [no copy located].

3 Sonates pour le Clavecin ou le Piano-forte avec accomp. d'une Violon & Violoncelle, a 4 R[ouble] . . ., Christian Kaestner & Co, Moscow, 1799 [no copy located].

3 Sonates. Pour le Clavecin ou piano-forte avec accomp. d'une Violon & Violoncelle. Reinsdorf et Lehnhold, Moscow 1799 [no copy located].

Maestro e Scolare. O Sonate con variazione a 4 mains. Reinsdorf et Lehnhold, Moscow 1799 [Hoboken XVIIa: 1.].

[In Russian:] The Newest Sonatas. Reinsdorf et Lehnhold, Moscow 1799.

[In Russian:] Once again have appeared the latest Sonatas by Mr Hayden [*sic*] for 89 K[opeks]. Christian Kaestner & Co. in Moscow 1799.

It seems likely that some of the later announcements in Moscow represent different advertisements of the same works, possibly imported piano trios.

participating in the subscription because of the war; while Spain was too far away and, despite Haydn's popularity, too isolated for the composer to be able to organize a centre on the lines of Dengler in Moscow. Italy, though geographically as near to Austria as Germany, was already in the state of apathy and (in part arrogant) cultural isolation from which it began to escape, musically, only with the arrival of Rossini. In 1800, moreover, it is doubtful if there was a single Italian city, even Rome, capable of executing *The Creation*: indeed, they were scarcely able to play it a quarter of a century later, as Mendelssohn was appalled to relate. The Italian attitude about 'questa roba tedesca' is summed up in Spontini's famous dictum: 'Les Allemands traitent la musique comme une affaire d'état.' In *The Creation*, they obviously envisaged a master-of-ceremonies at this 'affaire d'état', and they would have none of it. The entry in the subscription list of a priest ministering to the German community of Livorno is about the best Italy could offer Haydn.[1]

The printed list very often has a different spelling from Haydn's; but spelling was not his forte, and his rendering of several British noble families is, to say the least, confusing ('Earl of Inchinquin'). We have occasionally placed the version of the printed list in brackets after Haydn's own. A few points should be made: Haydn often writes 's' or 'sh' instead of 'sch' ('Braunsweig', for instance, instead of 'Braunschweig' = Brunswick), and he abbreviates Moscow as 'Mos' or 'Mosc', and London as 'lon' or even 'l'. 'Königlich' is often abbreviated 'Könl', the 'l' being a swish in the form of a circle which meant for Haydn an abbreviated ending: he uses a similar downward swish to abbreviated the 'en' endings of German words such as 'bringen', 'schücken', etc. Haydn's 'k' in German script is almost indistinguishable, at times, from 'ck' ('Franckfurt', 'Frankfurt'). The numbers added on the left-hand margin are apparently by Artaria, to whom the sending of the completed volumes was entrusted, and it was, it would seem, a clerk of Artaria's who added most of those entries in 'another hand' when Haydn turned over the little book to Artaria to have them check the subscribers' names and addresses for the final mailing. It is worth noting that some of the subscribers in the MS. list do not appear on the printed list, e.g. Mr. Daniel arrow Smith (*sic*) of London. We have left untranslated the recipe for making ink, at the end of the little book, which someone wrote down for Haydn. The most important amendments and cancellations made by Haydn are appended in the explanatory notes at the end of the list. The + signs and crosses appear to be Haydn's. One of the entries listed as in another hand – that for the two Schwarzenbergs and Countess Schönfeld – might be by Baron van Swieten, whose handwriting is similar in style. Explanatory notes are given on p. 632.

1 For a devastating account of musical life in Italy in the years 1830–1, see Mendelssohn's letters. In Milan, Dorothea von Ertmann played Beethoven sonatas to Felix, and General von Ertmann wept with joy, 'because his wife had not played for such a long time; in Milan there wasn't a single person who would listen to something like that'. In many respects, Italy has not yet recovered from her long period of isolation from the rest of musical Europe. See Mendelssohn's letter from Milan of 14 July 1831 (Ertmann). On 7 December 1830, he writes from Rome: '... and when recently they wished to perform Haydn's *Creation*, the instrumentalists declared it was impossible to play it.' Spontini: letter from Rome, 17 January 1831.

Verzeichnüß der Praenumeranten über die Schöpfung

Ihre Majestät die Kayserin ×
Ihre K:K:H.H. Großherzog und Großherzogin v Toscana.
S[e] Kurfürstl Durchlaucht zu Kölln.
Der Regierende Fürst v Thurn und Taxis ×
für den Erb Printzen ×
für die Frau des Erbrintzens [*sic*] ×
Die Herzogin Amalia aus Weimar ×
S: Königl Hoheit der Erzherzog Ferdinand v Mayland.
Frau Herzogin Francisca zu Wirtenberg in Stutgard. Durch den Hofrath Secretair v Mayer.
S[e] Königl Hochheit [*sic*] der Herzog Alberth × 2
Frau Fürstin Wilhelmine Friderike Caroline, Fürstin zu Schwarzburg Sondershausen. Die bezahlung geschieht durch den legations Rath v Dietrich. in Regensburger Hof 2ter Stock.
Herr Erb Prinz Emil August und dessen Bruder Friderich zu Sachsen Gotha . . . . × 2.
S[e] Königl Hochheit [*sic*] Palatinus . . . . . 2.
Printz v Hessen Darmstadt.
Kaysl Könl [*sic*] Bibliotek . . . . . . 2.
His Royal Highness Prince of Wales.
Her R: H: The Princess of Wales
Her R: H: The Dukchess [*sic*] of York.[1]
Her Majesty The Queen of England
Princess Augusta
Princess Elizabeth
Princess Mary
Princess Sophia
Princess Amalia
His Majesty The King of great Briton [*sic*].

A.

× Artaria . . . . 2 Expl.
× Herzog v Aremberg
× Apony graf . . . . 2 Ex:
i Herr Ph: Aldafeld. v Braunsweig Kaufmann und Director des Liebhabers Concert: ha pagato p Hartung ×
+ Atherton. Esqu: H[ny] Atherton Esqu: london[2]
× Fürst Carl Auersperg . . . . 2.
× graf Franz v Amade. abzugeben dem Kaufmann Meyer zur goldenen Tresborten am graben.
+ Mr Attwood. in Service at Prince of Wallis [*sic*]. london
+ Miss Abrams. london
+ Miss Teodosia Abrams. london
+ M:D: Albertazzi. durch Mosc: Maitre de Musique
+ Dr Arnold.
+ Dr Aylward.
+ Dr Ayston.
+ Miss Alderson. aston yorkshire[3]

——[4]
Anderson
J. B. Adams.
Mr T: Alsop

B.

\+ graf Blümingen. Reccours v Spangla
\+ Thadaeus Berger, Großhändler[5]
\+ Michael Bartenschlag. im Trattnerhof im 3ten St: Haupt Stiege ×
\+ graf Brühl Königl Preuß Jagd Junker. ×
\+ Joseph v Blank fürstl Taxischer Hofrath und Oberforstamts Verwalter in Nürnberg beÿ H Baamann unweit roth Thurm 695 1ten Stock.
——[6]
\+ John Henry Bluhm aus London.
\+ graf Braun . . . . × 3.
\+ Mr Bartolozzi Junr N: 30 Poland Street london
\+ Captain Blount. london.
——[7]
\+ Bundermann. K:K: Fiscal beamter.
× Conte Alessandro Brazzà di Udine.
× Graf Georg Berenyi. aus ofen.
\+ P. B. Bierey Music Director beim Secondaischen Theater ha pagato ×
le Prince Baratinsky. aus Moscau ×
P:P: de Babouschkin. aus Moscau
M. Odoardo Bianchi. Mait: de Musique Mos: ×
The R: Hon:ble lady Mary Benhinck. [*sic*]
lady Banks[8]
lady Burrat
Mr Barthelemon
Mr cha. R: Burney
Dr Burney
the R: Honbl lady Bruce
Mr Butt
Mris Broome.
Coundess [*sic*] of Berkley
Sr Patrick Blake Bt
W: Blake Esqu.
Mr Bridgeman organist at Hertford.
Mrs G: Baker
NB Johann August Böhne [*sic*]. aus Hamburg ist 6 Ex [*recte*: Böhme]
Miss Bellamy.
C. Bell Esqu.
Mr L: S. de Betay.
Baumberg. [Gabriela v]

Mr Banger
Mr Birchall. — 2
Miss Bonwick
Mr Betts. Junior

C.

[another hand:]

Calemberg gräfinn

[Haydn's hand:]

8 Johann Fürst v Clary. in der Herrn gasse.
graf Johann Chottek.

——[9]

8 Mr Cimador. No 8 Marylebone Street. golden Square L
10 Lady Cornewall. Stanhope Street Myfair.
12 Lady Clarges. Rudley Square
13 Mr Carreau. Nro 28 St: Martins Str: leicester Square
Conrad. Claviermeister.
——[10]
18 graf Cžernin 4
4 Cannabich. Music Director in franckfurt
11 Cobenzl Philipp.
6 Lord Chartley [Cartley] [*sic*]
Miss Creive [Crewe]
2 Mr Callcott B.M:
Mris NB oder Cosway[11]
18 Richd Cox Esqu:
9 Bethel Cox Esqu
——[12]
H: Compton Esqu.
Miss Collins.
Mr Cole.
Miss Chamberlayne. 5 [Chamberlaine]
Mr Clementi . . . . 7.
Mr Cloomenta. [?]
Mr Collard.

D.

× Frau v Dekret. v: der Frÿ v leithner
× Delorme. v Paul Wranizky
——[13]
× le Baron de Dürniz. p linz a Straubing. en Bavièrre
× general graf Dietrichstein. in der Johannesgasse N: 1031
× Peter Edler v Decret.
× H v Dier. K:K: Truchses.
× Diedon Baroness. v. Regensburg ×
i graf Johann Karl v Dietrichstein.[14] in eigenen Hauß Herrngasse
× Freÿherr v Douminik. [*sic*]
× Mr N: a: de Dourassoff. aus Moscau. ×
i J: Dengler. aus Moscau . . . . 3. ×
× Mris Davenport.
× Lady Mary Duncan
× The Revd John Dixin.
Mr Davis.
Mr Dester.

E.

Fürstin Esterhazÿ . . . . ×6
graf Johan Esterhazy. v Paul Wranizky
graf Joseph Erdödy 2
Anton Eberl Music Meister in Petersburg.
Ferdinand Elser. 3

F.

Herrn Hofrath Franck. in der Alstergasse Nro 130. im eigenen Hauß.
Herr Förster.
Se Excellenz Herr Fengler bischof v Raab. ha pagato.
graf Maurice Fries 4
Fries und Compa:
Joseph Fux. Pfarherr v Müllendorf in ungarn.
Johann gottfried Fischer aus Freyberg ha pagato
Frackmann Friderich aus Moscau.
Joseph Falk. aus Insbruck.
Mr Feray. Maitre de Musique. aus Mos: ×
Mr Joseph Fodor. professor de Violon. Mosc.
The Honble Mrs Fortescue lond.
Freÿherr v Ferber. finanz Rath in Dresden. ×
Miss Frye
Mr Ferrari
Mr Fisin

G.

H Franz Xav: Glöggl. Stadt. und Domkapelmeister in linz in oberösterreich. ×
Fürstin graschalkowiz . . . . × 6 14
graf Franz galantini.
Miss Griffith. N: 16 Portland Place. lond: 16
8 Goold Esqr N° 21 King Street gloucester Place L:
Gestewitz Music Meister beÿm Italienischen Theater in Dresden × 5
Mr Gostling. london
Mr Graeff. london
Peter Gstettenhofer v Tirnitz.
A: N: de Gantcheroff. Moscau. ×
S: Ex: le Prince A: N: Gallitzin aus Moscau. ×
Mr de Grizanovsky aus Moscau ×
N: P: de Glebnikoff. aus Moscau. ×
Mr grandmaison. Mos: 3
Mr granville.
Mr guise. B: M:
Andreas Gnart. in Wienn
Se Chevalier Gallini.
Mr G. Griesback.
Miss Grill.
Mris Graham.
Mr Griffin.
H v Gore. weimar v. Kranz

H.

Herr Holzer Chor Regent in lichtenthall.
20 Dr Hofmann aus Wetzlar. das Exemplar ist abzugeben an den H
Reichs Agenten v Pilgram in Wienn. à già pagato.
× Friedrich Franz Hurka. Königl Sänger in Berlin. 2
Joseph Henikstein. in der Karntnerstraß. N: 1001.
le Baron de Hayme Trefonçier 2
Hohenthal Gräfin v Regensburg. ×

Michael Höger oberösterreichisch Ständ Cassier in lintz
Jacob Heckel Concertmeister. 2
9 August Hartung. Herzogl Braunschweigl Kamer Musicus. × pagato.
Leopold Hildenmuth zum Heiligen Kreitz im Wald.
le Prince M: J: Hilkoff. aus Moscau. ×
Mr Ch. Höeke professeur du Violoncelle. aus Mos: × 19
Mr Haesler. Mos. ×
Hinry Hoare Esqu: mitcham.
The Revd Dr Hay.
Mris Ed: Henslow.
Mr Hobbes
graf Harrach Carl. mit 25 f.
Härtl Hof Agent.
Mrs Hunter.
William Hanbury Esqu.
Dr Herschel.
Thomas[15] Hammersley Esqu:
Mr Hempel.
J: Haering Esqu:
Mr C. F. Horn.
Miss Horn —— NB
Mris Hanbury.
Mr Hullmandel.
Richard Hare Esqu:
William Hunter. Senr } hanno pagato. e Sono mandati via.
Ditto John Hunter Junr }
Mr Hyde.
Mr Harrison.
Miss Heseltin.
Mr Havard
Mr Howell. Bristol
Hilsher. nach Dresden. ×[16]

I.

Earl of Inchinquin [*sic*]
Miss Caroline Jocelyn.
Mr John Immyns.

K.

Frÿle Madlaine v Kurzbeck.
Kraitschobitsch. Andreas. Succentor des Raaber Domstiftes.
Frau Rosa Fürstin v Kinsky. gebohrne gräfin v Harrach . . . . . 4 Exp:
Gräfin Antoinette von Kollowrat Stift Dame v Reichs Stift Buchau. in der Singerstraß in Bancohauß
Johann Kner oberöst. Stände Kassen Officiant v lintz. ×
Küffner aus London. Nro 35. great Winchester Street Broad Street. 11
Körner. Doctor, Appelations Rath un [*sic*] geheimer Referendair. aus Dresden × 7
le Prince B.A: de Kourakin. aus Moscau. ×
Madelle de Kiriloff. Mos: ×

Mr Chr: Kaestner . . . . . mosc: 2
E: C.Fr: Knorre. organist a Dorpat.
Mr Kollman. organist of h: Maj.
M^ris^ Knowlys.

[another hand:]

Kinski gräfinn, gebohrene Gräfin v Dietrichstein

[Haydn's hand:]

Mr Char: Kelly.
Mr Knapton. york
Kranz. weimar. NB: v H v Gore
Kahl. v Prag. hat beÿ mir bezahlt.
Knoblich aus grißau in oberschlesien hat bezahlt ein Ex^a^ und die Meß in C.

L.

Fürstin Isabella Lubomirska. 2 Ex.
Fürst Jos: Lobkowitz . . . . . 6.[17]
gräfin Landskoranska. v P: Wranizky.
lautenschlag.

[another hand:]

Fürstinn Lichnowski, geborne gräfinn Thun
———[18]

[Haydn's hand:]

Ignaz Baron v laÿkom. in der Johannesgasse N: 1031.
Joseph Lipawsky K:K: geheimer zahlamts officier.
Moritz graf lichnowsky } beide in Troppau in kaiserl oberschlesien
wilhelm graf lichnowsky }
Langer Joannes. regierender Abt des fürstl Cisterciener Stifts Grissau in Schlesien. Verlangt noch eine Meß. bey landshütt.
Baronesse Loewenstein. v Weimar. in sachsen. ×
Fürst Lichnowsky
Madem^le^ A: J: de Lavroff. aus Moscau ×

latus

M^r^ M: J: Lanz. aus Mosc: ×
Madame de Lapkoff. Mos: ×
Princess de Liechtenstein 2
The Countess of Leicester. Lond:
la Prencess [*sic*] Lubomirska née C^esse^ [Comtesse] Sconowska. ×
His grace The Duke of Leeds.

[another hand:]

Lyons. vide Brief v Atwood
Liechtenstein Fürst Louis . . . . 6 ex.

[Haydn's hand:]

Mr John Longman.
Friderick Leshritter [*sic*] Concertmeister v Würzburg
Mes^sr^ Linterns. Bath.

M.

Jacob Mendl. im Trattnerhof. 3ter Stock haupt Stiege.
H: Karl Marinelli[19]
Comtesse Auguste Marcolini
Paul Meinek Musicus in Braunsweig × ha pagato

Matheser. Könil Raitrath v ofen.
Doctor Meyer aus London . . . . 2.
Pietro Muschietti. di Moscau
The Right Hon[bl] Lady Malmesbury Spring Garden. lon
Joseph Mälzl. Kunst Mashinist [*sic*]
Franz v Mayersfeld Secretair beÿ dem Marisch-schlesischen gubernium. [*sic*]
Franz Maurer. Sänger beym Nazional Theater in Franckfurt
J: S: de Mossaloff. aus Moscau. ×
M[r] V: B: Mercoulovsky. aus Mosc: ×
Mr Ant: Fran: Millet. Mait: de Musique Mos: ×
Earl Macartney.
Countess Marcatney [*sic*]
——20

Dr Miller.
M[ris] Murray.
The Lady Mary Montgomery.
Madame Mara.
George Mostyn Esqu:
Mr Joseph Major
Mrs Montagne Burgogna [Montague Bourgoyne]
Mrs Mills.

N.

Viscountess Newark. Portman Square london
Franz Edler v Natorp. K:K: Großhändler.
Madame Anne de Nepluieff née de Teploff. mosc:
Mad:[le] Dorothée de Naoumoff. mosc. ×
M[r] N: de Nepluieff. mos: ×
M[r] J: P: Theodore Nehrlich. Mai[tre] de musique moscau
F. Nicolai Esqu:
The Rev[d] D[r] Nicholas.

O.

Johann Vincenz Oswald hochfürstl Passau. Hofkammerrath.
D: P: d'ouschakoff. aus Moscau. ×
Mrs Ord.

P.

Maria Theresia v Paradis.
Joseph Preindl [Preindl's hand:] [mp]ria Fischerstiege N[ro] 404.
Contessa Paar. Recc: v Mängle
Anton Phillebois. Actuar an der Universität im alten universitäts Hauß N[ro] 795.
gräfin Palffy gebohrne gräfin Hoyos.
gräfin Therese Pallfy.
——21

Freÿherr v Podmanizky. i ofen.
The Honble Miss Pierrepont. Portman Square. lond
M[ris] Peploe. Curzon Street myfair.
Miss Philott. lond:
gräfin Podstatsky. gebohrne gräfin v Kolowrat. in der Singerstrasse im Banco Hauß

le Prince de Paar.
de Potackoff. aus Moscau. ×
les demoi[lles] Petrof. aus Moscau ×
Mr Pozzi Mai: de Musique Mos: ×
M[r] le cons: du College de Pecken. Mos ×
——22
Honb[le] George Pomeroy
Miss Papendik.
Mr Robert Perry

R.

graf [at first: 'Fürst']Rosomovsky . . . . × 2
M[ris] Rigby. Upper Grosvenor Street Lon:
Reinsdorf. Heinrich aus Moscau. . . . . . 10.
Jos: v Reinlein.
georg v Reich. . . . . 3.
H v Robinig aus Salzburg.
M[r] J: de Rost. Mosc: ×
Angelique Princess de Radcziwil
Lady Rich.
Mr Rogers.
Rathmayer

[another hand:]

Mr Russel. Brief v Atwood.

[Haydn's hand:]

Mr Rolfa. Junior.

S.

Herr v Silverstolpe.
graf Sternberg. 3
le Comte de Schönborn.
Herr Referendaire Jean Schmidt zu Königsberg in Preußen. per Berlin in Hauß des Commerzien und Admiralitäts Rath. am schiefen Berge abzugeben. a gia pagato. NB: 2 Exp.
Frau v Spielman.
Fürstin Schwarzenberg 3

[another hand:]

Fürst Schwarzenberg. 6
Fürst Ernst Schwarzenberg. . . . .
gräfinn Schönfeld

[Haydn's hand:]

Abbé Stadler
Paul Stradtmann.[23] in der K: Hof Bibliotek.
Schacht Baron und geheimer Rath. Regensburg. NB die Bezahlung in Wienn ×
Schultz. 1ter Königl Preuß Ingenieurs Lieutenant von der Hauptfestung Glatz. hat bezahlt.
graf Stadion 2
Sigmund v Strobl Königl Rath v Fünfkürchen
Georg Schleifer. Regenschori v Stockerau. Franz Strauß in der Herrn gasse. Leopold Stadt.

graf Prosper v Sinzendorf beÿ der Grieß.
S: Excellenz Nicolaus Skorodynsky Lemberger Russischer unirter Bischof.
Die Fürstin Saalm Reifenscheid. [*sic*] aus Brün.
Johann Paul Schulthesius. Prediger beÿ der teutschen gemeinde in Livorno.
Herr Schwanberg. Capellmeister in Braunsweig × pagato.
Herr Schade Johann gottfried Herzogl Kammer Musicus und Music Händler in Sachsen Gotha. . . . . . × 2 pagato.
Sechehaye. Clavier Meister aus Dresden.
Anton Schmidt Hof Kamer Musicus in Dresden. ×
H. Strasser. Uhrmacher und Mechanicus. aus Petersburg.
Frau v Sierstorpf. aus Braunschweig.[24] ×
Baron v Swieten 4
Friderich Freyherr v Spiegelfeld K: K: landrechte Secretair zu Klagenfurt.
Ignazio Selmo.
Anton Schöckh. [Schick] aus London . . . . . 2 è pagato

Latus

latus S
N: Simrock aus Bonn. H Traeg bezahlt 2
A:g: de Savin, aus Mos:
de Salavovo. aus Mos:
Mr B. Schiroli. Mai. de Musi: Mosc: ×
Prince. D: M: Scherbatoff. aus Mosc: ×
Friderich Schmidt. 2
Ignatz Ritter v Seyfried.
Mris Schroeter.
Miss Stone.
Mr Smith. B: M:
Schoeps. Buchhändler in zittau. ×
Charles Sylvester. ha pagato. London.
W: Shukburgh. Esqu:
Edward Stephenson Esqu:
Mr J: P: Salomon. 12
Mris Th: Smith . . . . NB:
Mr Shield. | Schönfeld. Königsberg in Preussen. } erwarten noch andwort
Mr R: J: S: Stevens.
Mr Sanderson.
Mr Daniel arrow Smith Lond:
Schaufus v Petersburg. × und eine Russische Fürstin

T.

[another hand:]

Gräfinn Thun.

[Haydn's hand:]

Triebensee CapellMeister v S: D: Fürst Louis v Lichtenstein.
Madam de Tschirikoff. aus Moscau. ×
de Taticheff. aus Moscau. ×
S: Ex: Mr le consuler d'etat actual de Teploff. mosc:
graf Trautmannsdorf
. . . . 2
——[25]
The Revd Thomas Twining. Colchester

Miss Tate.
Mr Tomich.

[another hand:]

Gräfinn Truchseß- Zeil geb. Gräfinn Harrach

[Haydn's hand:]

Miss C: E: Todd.

U.

Herr v Van der Nül
Herr Veltheim oberkammerherr Braunshweig × pagato
M: B: Veltmann. organist zu St: Marien und Music Händler aus Osnabrik [*sic*]. in Westpfalen.
Ullmann. St: ord: Cister: in Neuzell.
graf Urbanowsky.
S: Ex: le general de Visotsky. aus Moscau. ×
Mr A: Vanicezéck. Maitre de Musique. Mosc: ×
Joseph v Ungar Kayl Königl Rath und Biblioteker auf der Hohen Schule zu Prag
le Baron Frederic de Venningen. ×
Udneÿ Esqu.

W.

——[26]

Wranizky 3
Herr Joseph Weigl, Großhändler.
geistl Herr Weghofer Stadtpfarher in Eisenstadt. pagato
Franz, Theodor, Wecús.[27] die bezahlung beÿ Fries u. Com zu schüken [?] – beÿ Siegburg Passau
Johann Friderich Wagner, aus Danzig.
Herr Hofrath Wagner. aus Wienn in kleinen Passauer Hof in der Canzley. 397.
Miss Wall- von Oxford.
graf v Wilhorsky ober Stallmeister v gallizien und Lodomerien
H: Wölfl. in Hamburg.
la Princesse Eugenie de Wiasemskoy moscau ×
The Reve^d John Wheler [Wheller]
giffin Wilson Esqu: lincoln Inn Fields.
Revd Osborn Wight.
J. Wilkinson. Esqu:
Wesley charles.
Mr Wilkins.
Fürst Wallerstein.

Ÿ.

les Dem:^lles de Yermolaieff. Moscau × . . . . .
Young. lady[28]

Z.

Baron Zinick. v Paul Wranizky
Niculaus [*sic*] Zmeskall v Domanovitz [Domanowetz]
gräfin Zinzendorf geb: Fürstin Schwarzenberg.
Herr Zosinger [Zösinger]. organist zu Nürnberg. von H Baaman in Wienn nächst rothen Thurm 695. 1ter St:

——[29]

Gräfinn Zichy geborne Gräfin Kollowrat[30]

[ink recipe, in another hand:]

Species zur Dinte
Grüner Gallus . . . . . 9 Loth.
Grünen Vitriol . . . . 6 ×
Gummi 4
Granatäpfel Schallen 2 Loth
Allaun 1/2
Ein Seitel guter Weineßig 8 Tag stehen lassen und öfters aufrühren. Dann 3 Seitl Fluswasser darauf gegoßen.

NOTES TO HAYDN'S LIST OF SUBSCRIBERS TO *THE CREATION*

1 Haydn wrote at first 'Princess of York' but changed it to 'Duchess of York'.
2 Haydn cancelled the title 'Master' for Atherton.
3 Haydn started to write 'Add' (misspelled) then crossed it out.
4 'Dr. Aylward', a duplicate entry which Haydn realized and then cancelled.
5 Haydn had put down the name of 'Herr Thadaeus Berger' as 'Sohn des H. Großhändlers v. Weigl', obviously a mistake which was corrected to 'Thadaeus Berger Großhändler'.
6 Haydn cancelled the entry 'P. B. Bierey Music Director beim Secondaisch Theater in Dresden'.
7 Haydn realized he had made a duplicate entry for the Palatin and crossed it out.
8 Haydn spelled the name first 'Banky' and cancelled it.
9 Haydn cancelled the entry for Prince Clari: 'Fürst Marie [?] Clari'.
10 Entry for 'Countesse de Cžichzi née Kolowrat' was crossed out.
11 Haydn first spelled the name Corway.
12 Three entries cancelled: 'Lady Mary Duncan, Mrs. Davenport and Reverend John Dixin, Taddington, Bedfordshire.'
13 The entry 'Dietrichstein, Frau gräfin' crossed out.
14 Haydn wrote at first 'Joseph' but changed it later to 'Johann Karl v. Dietrichstein'.
15 Haydn crossed out the letter 'F' and wrote Thomas.
16 Haydn started the entry with the words 'Mr. Knap' but changed it.
17 Haydn had put down Prince Lobkowitz for four subscriptions but crossed it out because the Prince bought two more.
18 Cancelled entries for 'Gräfin v. Podstasky-Lichtenstein, gebohrne gräfin von Kollowrat', 'gräfin Antoinette von Kollowrat' and 'Herr Joseph Weigl, Großhändler'.
19 Haydns pen seems to have slipped and he started again to write 'Marinelli'.
20 A duplicate entry, 'Hinry Hoare Esq: Mitcham' was cancelled and the words 'steht bei H' (listed under H) were added.
21 Haydn wrote 'Freule grafin v Paar, NB wie oben' and cancelled it.
22 A cancelled entry, barely readable: 'Partsch nach . . . London[?] . . . 2 ha pagato'.
23 Haydn crossed out 'Stadlmann' and wrote 'Stradtmann'.
24 The words 'ha pagato' were removed.
25 An entry which should have been and can be found under C, 'Cobenzl Philipp' was crossed out.
26 The Christian name 'Jos.' was cancelled.
27 An unreadable word after 'Wecús' cancelled.
28 Haydn cancelled 'Sr William' and wrote after the name 'Young lady'.
29 Haydn decided to list the Countess Truchsess under T and therefore crossed the entry out.
30 The printed list also includes: 'Zichy, Gräffinn [*sic*], geborne Fürstinn v. Schwarzenberg'.

Index

References to illustrations are shown in italics; references to artists, engravers etc., in captions to the plates are indicated parenthetically, e.g. (*pl. 2*). In documents cited in the text, variant forms (and misspellings) are frequently found; such variations are shown in parenthesis, e.g. 'Abukir (Aboukir)', 'Apponyi (Aponyi)' etc., as appropriate. For abbreviations of musical instruments, see p. 15.

INDEX OF COMPOSITIONS BY HAYDN

(HOBOKEN NUMBERS IN PARENTHESIS; PRINCIPAL REFERENCES IN THE TEXT APPEAR IN BOLD TYPE)

DOUBTFUL AND SPURIOUS WORKS ATTRIBUTED TO JOSEPH HAYDN